Canadian Readings in Personnel and Human Resource Management

Shimon L. Dolan
The University of Montréal

Randall S. Schuler
New York University

WEST PUBLISHING COMPANY
St. Paul   New York   Los Angeles   San Francisco   Toronto

Copyediting: Kimberly Bornhoft
Interior Art: Alice Thiede, Carto-Graphics
 (Exhibits 3–1, 15–1, 16–1, 17–1, 21–1, 21–2,
 29–1, 30–1, 30–2, 30–3, 34–1, 34–2b, 34–6)

COPYRIGHT © 1987 By WEST PUBLISHING COMPANY
50 W. Kellogg Boulevard
P.O. Box 64526
St. Paul, MN 55164–1003

All rights reserved

Printed in the United States of America

Library of Congress Cataloging-in-Publication Data

Canadian readings in personnel and human resource
 management.

  1. Personnel management—Canada.   2. Personnel
management.   I. Dolan, Shimon L.   II. Schuler, Randall S.
HF5549.2.C3C36 1987   658.3'00971   87–2211
ISBN 0-314-32487-9

Dedicated with sincere admiration to an outstanding humanitarian—the late Nissan Reich (S.L.D.)

To my brother Ed (R.S.S.)

Contents

Preface   ix

I. Overview of Personnel and Human Resource Management   1

1. Personnel and Human Resource Management/Choices and Organization Strategy   3
   R.S. Schuler, New York University

2. Labour Market Trends and Their Implications for PHRM Training in Canada   27
   J.M. Cousineau, The University of Montréal

II. Planning for Human Resource Management   39

3. Strategic Human Resource Planning: Why and How?   41
   D. Ulrich, University of Michigan

4. Human Resource Planning—A Federal Perspective   63
   A. Jacques, Labour Market Services, Canada Employment and Immigration Commission

5. Human Resource Information Systems: The Case of Provigo   69
   C. Marier, Corporate Director Human Resources, Provigo Inc.

6. Job Analysis   82
   C.P. Sparks, Serendipity Unlimited

III. Staffing   101

7. Forecasting The Costs and Benefits of Traditional Versus Scientific Employment Selection Methods in Canada to the Year 1990   103
   T. Janz, The University of Calgary

8. Employment Equity at Canadian National Railways: Initiatives and Proactive Measures   112
   L. Piché, Canadian National

9. Equality in Employment   127
   H.C. Jain, McMaster University

10. Equal Employment Opportunities—Challenges and Practices for Canadian Companies: The Royal Bank Experience   142
    L.J. White, The Royal Bank of Canada

11. The Selection Interview: The Received Wisdom Versus Recent Research   154
    T. Janz, The University of Calgary

12. Employee Selection and Placement: Practice, Problems, and Future Trends   162
    P. Broadhurst, Litton Systems Canada

13. Employment Testing in Canada: Strategies for Higher Organizational Productivity and Human Rights Compliance   176
    S.F. Cronshaw, The University of Guelph

14. The Assessment Center Revisited: Practical and Theoretical Considerations   186
    A. Tziner, Bernard M. Baruch College (CUNY) and Tel Aviv University

IV. Appraising and Compensating   195

15. Performance Appraisal: The State of the Art   197
    H. Schwind, Saint Mary's University

16. Some Neglected Variables in Research on Discrimination in Appraisals   211
    R.L. Dipboye, Rice University

17. Key Issues in Designing Compensation Systems   226
    R. Thériault, Université de Montréal

18. Obstacles to the Effective Use of Reward Systems   245
    P.M. Podsakoff, Indiana University

C.N. Greene, *University of Southern Maine*
J.M. McFillen, *Bowling Green State University*

19. Reward Management: A New Look   261
R.N. Kanungo, *McGill University*

V. Improving Employees Effectiveness and Motivation   277

20. An Overview of Training and Development in Canada   279
R.J. Adams, *McMaster University*

21. Improving Training Effectiveness Through the Use of Evaluation Research   289
R.R. Haccoun, *Université de Montréal*

22. Training and Development in High Technology Industry: Present and Future Trends   302
R.J. Szawlowski, *Pratt & Whitney Canada*

23. Canadian Experience in Innovative Approaches to High Commitment Work Systems   313
H.F. Kolodny, *University of Toronto*

24. Understanding and Managing Absence from Work   324
G. Johns, *Concordia University*

VI. Establishing and Maintaining Effective Working Relationships   337

25. The Canadian Industrial Relations System   339
A.W.J. Craig, *University of Ottawa*

26. The Shift in Labour-Management Relations as a Function of Changes in Social and Economic Conditions   353
S.L. Dolan, *The University of Montréal*

27. Employee Rights vs. Management Rights: Some Reflections Regarding Dismissals   367
G. Trudeau, *Université de Montréal*

28. New Structures and Techniques in Wage Determination: Final-Offer Selection—How Well Has It Worked?   379
J.M. Weiler, *Asia Pacific Business Institute*

VII. Improving Health and Safety at Work 389

29. Occupational Health and Safety: Acts, Actors, and Actions 391
    G. Atherley, Canadian Centre for Occupational Health and Safety

30. Stress and Burnout in Organizations: Implications for Personnel and Human Resource Management 400
    R.J. Burke, York University

31. Stress and Absenteeism at Work: Old Questions and New Research Avenues 418
    M.R. Van Ameringen, C. Léonard, S.L. Dolan, and A. Arsenault, The University of Montréal

VIII. Integrating, Trends, and Comparisons 429

32. Career Planning and Relocation Counselling: An Emerging Personnel Function 431
    M. Axmith, Axmith and Associates
    B. Mozes, BBM Human Resource Consultants

33. The Application of Theory Z in Canada: Implications for the Human Resource Function 438
    A.M. Jaeger, McGill University

34. Maximizing Use of Human Resource Information Systems (HRIS) 444
    E.B. Harvey, University of Toronto
    J.H. Blakely, Cornell University

35. Auditing the Effectiveness of Human Resources Management Functions 461
    G. Biles, American University

Preface

Personnel and human resource management functions are undoubtedly more vital to companies today than ever before. Stiff foreign competition and decline in productivity, the need to comply with vast and changing laws and regulations, and the increasing demands for a more skilled and better educated work force are just a few factors that have contributed to the importance of personnel and human resource management in modern organizations.

This book is designed for practitioners and academicians who wish to keep up to date with the changes and the contemporary challenges in the field. Three major personnel and human resource themes are addressed throughout the book: a) the strategic importance of personnel and human resource activities to overall organizational effectiveness; b) the legal environment that shapes the practice of personnel and human resource management in Canada; and c) the assessment of personnel and human resource activities as they contribute to organizational effectiveness.

Senior human resource managers from several Canadian corporations and some of the best known academic scholars in Canada, were invited to contribute to this volume. The aim was to capture the leading edge of theory and practice in the field. We feel this has been accomplished by not only balancing our coverage between theory and application, but also by stressing the eclectic and interdisciplinary nature of personnel and human resource management. Thus, topics draw on a number of disciplines, including: industrial and organizational psychology, labour law, industrial relations, operations research, management, labour economics, and industrial medicine.

The book is organized into seven major sections: overview, planning, staffing, appraising and compensating, improving employees effectiveness, establishing and maintaining effective working relationships, improving health and safety, and integrating. As an aid, we have prepared brief introductions to each section of the readings as a means of synthesizing the key ideas presented in the articles.

We hope that you will acquire a comprehensive understanding of the latest strategic, legal, and evaluative trends which are driving the practice of modern personnel and human resource management. If you are new to the field, we recommend that this book be used simultaneously with our text *Personnel and Human Resource Management in Canada* (St. Paul, Minn.: West Publishing Company, 1987). We hope all readers will find these selections as stimulating and intellectually intriguing as we found them during our editorial and review process.

Acknowledgments

First and most importantly we wish to thank the contributors to this volume for the time and effort they spent in preparation of the manuscripts. Most of them deserve special recognition for their patience with us and tolerance of numerous requests for revisions of the articles. Contributors include the following:

R. Adams, McMaster University
A. Arsenault, The University of Montréal
G. Atherley, Canadian Centre for Occupational Health and Safety
M. Axmith, M. Axmith and Associates
G. Biles, American University
J.H. Blakely, Cornell University
P. Broadhurst, Litton Systems Canada
R. Burke, York University
J.M. Cousineau, The University of Montréal
A.W.J. Craig, The University of Ottawa
S. Cronshaw, University of Guelph
R.L. Dipboye, Rice University
C.N. Greene, University of Southern Maine
R. Haccoun, The University of Montréal
E. Harvey, The University of Toronto
A. Jacques, Employment and Immigration Canada
A. Jaeger, McGill University
H. Jain, McMaster University
T. Janz, University of Calgary
G. Johns, Concordia University
R. Kanungo, McGill University
H. Kolodny, University of Toronto
C. Léonard, The University of Montréal
C. Marier, Provigo Inc.
J.M. McFillen, Bowling Green University
B. Mozes, BBM Human Resource Consultants
L. Piché, Canadian National
P.M. Podsakoff, Indiana University
H. Schwind, Saint Mary's University

C. Sparks, Serendipity Unlimited
R. Szawlowski, Pratt and Whitney Canada
R. Thériault, H.E.C.—The University of Montréal
G. Trudeau, The University of Montréal
A. Tziner, Bernard M. Baruch College (CUNY)
   and Tel Aviv University
D. Ulrich, University of Michigan
M.R. van Ameringen, The University of Montréal
J. Weiler, The University of British Columbia
L. White, The Royal Bank of Canada

We also wish to thank David Godden, West acquisition editor for his confidence, guidance, and support throughout this project.

Shimon L. Dolan
Randall S. Schuler
April 1987

Section I
Overview of Personnel and Human Resource Management

The two readings in section I are included to highlight the growing importance of personnel and human resource management (PHRM), the new strategic role it is playing in organization and the emerging trend towards professionalism amongst individuals who pursue careers in this field.

In the first article, Schuler presents a scenario which supports the utilization of human resources as partners in the strategic decision making process. The author explains how PHRM practices are related to the strategic effectiveness of organizations. He develops analytical frameworks which aid researchers and practitioners in comprehending the link between PHRM practices and strategy execution at the corporate and divisional levels.

In the second article, Cousineau analyzes the trends in the growth and evolution of employment, wages and socio-demographic characteristics and their impact on PHRM professionals in Canada. The first section of the article examines the growth of the demands for PHRM professionals from the 1970s to the 1980s. The author concludes that during this ten-year period, demand doubled. The second section of the article looks at the demographic distribution of PHRM practitioners for the same ten-year period. The findings reveal that the 1980s (compared to the 1970s) are characterized by: a significantly higher proportion of females; an accelerated increase in average wage compared to other categories of managers; and a relatively younger age group for the profession. The third section examines career possibilities for university graduates who specialize in PHRM. Finally, Cousineau draws some inferences with respect to future training needs of PHRM specialists. Especially, he claims that possession of a university degree, mastery of a second language, mathematics and computer training seem to be necessary in addition to traditional functional knowledge, for PHRM professionals to be successful in the future.

1. Personnel and Human Resource Management/ Choices and Organization Strategy

Randall S. Schuler, New York University

In two major studies recently conducted on companies' practices and policies regarding their utilization of human resources and the role of their personnel and human resource management function or department, significant results were reported. In one study done by the Conference Board of Canada, seven principles that facilitate effective human resource management were identified. These principles, to be read after the preamble "Effective human resource management is facilitated to the extent that . . ." include:

—there is an overall corporate purpose and that the human resource dimensions of that purpose are evident

—a process of developing strategy within the organization exists and is understood, and that there is explicit consideration of human resource dimensions

—effective linkages exist on a continuing basis to ensure the integration of human resource considerations with the organizations' decision-making processes

—the office of chief executive officer provides the climate for integrating human resource considerations to the needs of the business

—the organization at all levels establishes responsibility and accountability for human resource management

—initiatives in the management of human resources are relevant to the needs of the business

—it includes the responsibility to identify and interact in the social, political, technological and economic environments in which the organization is and will be doing business (Nininger 1982, x.)

In the second study, A. T. Kearney examined how corporations that lead America in productivity are run. In comparing well-run corporations with those

---

This article appears simultaneously in R. S. Schuler, S. A. Youngblood, and V. L. Huber (eds.) *Readings in Personnel and Human Resource Management*, 3e. (St. Paul: West Publishing Co., 1987). The author wishes to thank Susan E. Jackson, Stu Youngblood, Paul Shrivastava, Ian MacMillan, Anne Tsui, John Slocum, Mike Moore, Tom Kochan and Vandra Huber for their comments on earlier drafts of this chapter.

less well-run in the same industries, Kearney found that the leaders in productivity had a unique set of personnel and human resource management practices:

——Leaders define the human resource role in terms of the function's participation in the business decisions and in the implementation of business strategies
——Leaders focus the current resources devoted to the human resource function on important problems before they add new programs or seek additional resources
——Leader human resource staffs initiate programs and communication with line management
——Leaders' line management shares in the responsibility for human resource programs
——Leaders' corporate staffs share responsibility for human resource policy formation and program administration across organizational levels (Misa and Stein 1983, 28)

Together these seven principles and five practices suggest that effective human resource management is valuable to organizations; effectively utilizing human resources means viewing and treating them strategically as well as operationally, in the long run as well as in the short run; all functional areas in organizations have responsibility and accountability for human resource utilization; the personnel and human resource management department or function can take the lead in an organization's efforts to manage its human resources effectively; and when the personnel and human resource department takes this lead, it goes far beyond the role of administering traditional personnel activities and becomes involved in strategic human resource management and the strategy of the entire organization (Fombrun, Tichy and Devanna 1984; Foulkes 1986).

This reading is an attempt to provide an understanding of how PHRM practices are related to making organizations run strategically. Frameworks are presented in this reading that link PHRM practices with strategy execution at the corporate and divisional levels. These frameworks apply to those interested both in strategy and personnel and human resource management.

Parker and Ulrich (1983) suggested that PHRM practices can be used by companies in the formulation and implementation phases of strategic management both at the corporate and divisional levels. Opportunities for PHRM to participate in these two phases, and at these two levels, are illustrated in Exhibit 1-1.

Here part of their model is elaborated upon by suggesting that companies can use PHRM practices in two ways:

——To gain competitive advantage
——To foster and facilitate strategy execution

As shown in Exhibit 1-1, PHRM practices used in gaining a competitive advantage are focused on the formulation phase at the corporate level, while the practices used in fostering and facilitating strategy are focused on the execution stage at the corporate and divisional levels. In this chapter, only ways of fostering and facilitating strategy execution are described in detail.

Exhibit 1–1   Overview of PHRM Opportunities and Activities in Strategic Management

Strategic Management

Level of Analysis	Formulation	Implementation
Corporate	— Clarify culture and philosophy — Fit strategy with corporate culture — Assess and assure fit between strategy and management style and skills — Gain competitive advantage	— Assist in organization design — Work with senior and other line managers to overcome resistance to change — Work to gain commitment and mobilize resources to meet strategic objectives — Use PHRM systems to foster and facilitate strategy
Divisional	— Fit division strategy with corporate strategy and with divisional culture and management skills and style — Integrate PHRM functions (selection, appraisal, reward, development) into strategy — Create functional plan consistent with corporate and division strategy	— Use PHRM systems to foster and facilitate strategy — Fill jobs with the right people so that appropriate changes will be made — Prepare a clear and explicit plan of how change will occur

Adapted from D. F. Parker and D. O. Ulrich, "From Human Resource Strategies to Strategic Human Resources" (unpublished manuscript, 1983).

FOSTERING AND FACILITATING CORPORATE STRATEGY EXECUTION BY CHOOSING PHRM PRACTICES

PHRM practices enhance organizational effectiveness and profitability (Frohman and Frohman, 1984) by tailoring PHRM practices to a company's needs. This can be done by selecting PHRM practices that cue and reinforce or foster and facilitate the necessary employee characteristics. These necessary employee characteristics are determined by several company characteristics including product life cycle, goals, products, culture, technology, industry and strategy (Mirvis 1985).

Because the intent in this reading is to link PHRM practices with strategy execution, the focus here is only on the company characteristic of strategy as determinants of necessary employee characteristics. Although this is consistent with the strategy literature, much of what is discussed below is relatively new in the PHRM literature (Mirvis 1985; Fombrun et al. 1984; Hax 1985; Foulkes 1986; Schuler, MacMillan, and Martocchio 1985). Consequently, this is presented in a conceptual way. In addition, the major strategy-PHRM practice statements are made in testable proposition form.

PHRM and Strategy Execution

As stated by Reginald H. Jones, former chairman and CEO of the General Electric Company:

> When we classified ... [our] ... businesses, and when we realized that they were going to have quite different missions, we also realized we had to have quite different people running them. That was where we began to see the need to meld our human resources planning and management with the strategic planning we were doing (Fombrun 1982, 46).

> I believe the only game in town is the personnel game ... My theory is if you have the right person in the right place, you don't have to do anything else. If you have the wrong person in the job, there's no management system known to man that can save you. (Walter Wriston, former chairman and CEO of Citicorp)

Together these quotes typify what is beginning to appear in organizations: a growing awareness of the importance of and the need to link human resource management with business management. Most generally this awareness organizationally becomes articulated through efforts to link human resource planning to business planning as reflected in the quotes by both Jones and Wriston.

Within academia there is also a growing awareness for some sort of linkage between business management and human resource management. Although this awareness is being articulated in several ways, one of the most frequent is the investigation and/or conceptualization of the relationship between business strategy and top management characteristics (Song 1982; Snow and Hrebiniak 1980; Gupta 1984; Olian and Rynes 1984; Szilagyi and Schweiger 1984; Miller, Kets de Vries and Toulouse 1982; Hambrick and Mason 1984; Gupta and Govindarajan 1984a, 1984b; and Gerstein and Reisman 1983). Within this paradigm, particular management characteristics such as personality, skills, abilities, values and perspectives of top management are hypothesized to match particular types of business strategy. While some support has been found for the existence of top manager-strategy matches, only the Gupta and Govindarajan study (1984b) proposed several propositions using manager biographical background, personality orientation, organizational familiarity and industry experience.

In part, flowing from the manager-strategy match paradigm for studying business management and human resource management is a second and more recent paradigm. This paradigm is the strategy-personnel and human resource management practices match or fit. The issues that have been addressed in this paradigm include (1) identifying the major theme or thrust of the PHRM practices in different strategies (e.g., Miles and Snow's (1984) building, acquiring and allocating thrusts in defender, prospector and analyzer strategies, respectively); (2) describing how organizations can gain competitive advantage *a la* Porter (1980) through PHRM practices (Schuler and MacMillan 1984); (3) describing different PHRM issues within different strategy phases (Miles and Snow 1984; Hax 1985) and in different stages of a product life cycle (Ferris, Schallenberg, and Zammuto 1985); and (4) tailoring PHRM practices to specific strategies based on employee characteristics necessary to meet strategic demands (Kerr 1982, 1985; Slocum, Cron, Hansen, and Rawlings 1985; and Schuler, MacMillan, and Martocchio 1985). While all four of these issues are important, it is the last one that remains to be more fully articulated.

Matching PHRM Practices to Strategy

The notion of using PHRM practices with strategy is not novel. In fact it is a primary implication of the manager-strategy match paradigm (Gerstein and Reisman 1983). Gupta (1984), Miller (1984) and Olian and Rhynes (1984) present propositions relevant to this paradigm. Appropriately those propositions have the bulk of their implications for the staffing practise. Here in the strategy-PHRM practice paradigm all PHRM practises are addressed. Furthermore, the focus is on using PHRM practices to foster and facilitate necessary characteristics for all employees, not just top management or general managers. Accordingly propositions are presented that include all PHRM practices for employees, regardless of position in the organization.

The basic way of matching strategy with PHRM practices is by identifying needed employee characteristics. Once this is done the appropriate PHRM practices can be chosen. These in turn can be used to foster and facilitate the implementation of strategy because the employees are exhibiting the type of general characteristics really needed by the company for it to be effective. Two important premises are used in this discussion: (1) that needed employee characteristics vary by business strategy and (2) that there are a variety of ways PHRM practices can be done, some of which stimulate some employee characteristics better than others.

In presenting this strategy-PHRM practice paradigm, it is appropriate to begin by describing strategy types and necessary employee characteristics. Then the menus (or typology) of PHRM practices that can be used to match with strategy are described. This reading is concluded with several propositions relevant to strategy-PHRM practice matches.

Strategy Types and Employee Characteristics

There are well over a dozen frameworks for studying and understanding strategy types (Shrivastava and Peridis 1985). One that reflects and integrates features from several is that used by Gerstein and Reisman (1983). Based upon their empirical work, they developed the five strategy types shown in Exhibit 1-2.

These strategy types are consistent with several strategy writers including Hofer and Davoust (1977), Wissema, Van Der Pol and Messer (1980), Tichy, Fombrun and Devanna (1982), Wright (1974), Fombrun et al. (1984) and Hax (1985).

Critical to the strategy types shown in Exhibit 1-2 is the description of the business characteristics of each strategic type. These are critical because they suggest the employee characteristics necessary to meet strategic demands. It is on the basis of these business and employee characteristics that PHRM practices can be matched with strategy. While Gerstein and Reisman (1983) have identified necessary managerial characteristics, they have not systematically matched all the PHRM practices with each strategy type. Thus, here is presented a framework by which PHRM practices can be systematically chosen based upon strategy type. Instrumental to this objective is the identification of several general necessary employee characteristics from which choices can be made.

Necessary Employee Characteristics. Based upon an extensive review of the strategy literature and the personnel and the industrial, organizational psychology literature, several necessary employee characteristics are suggested. The

Exhibit 1-2 Corporate Strategy and Business Concerns

Entrepreneurial: In this strategy, projects with high financial risk are undertaken, minimal policies and procedures are in place, there are insufficient resources to satisfy all customer demands and there are multiple priorities to satisfy. The focus here is on the short run and getting the operation off the ground.

Dynamic Growth Strategy: Here risk taking on projects is more modest. There is a constant dilemma between doing current work and building support for the future. Policies and procedures are starting to be written, as there is a need for more control and structure for an ever expanding operation.

Extract Profit/Rationalization Strategy: The focus here is on maintaining existing profit levels. Modest cost-cutting efforts and employee terminations may be occurring. Control systems and structure are well developed, along with an extensive set of policies and procedures.

Liquidation/Divestiture Strategy: The focus of this strategy involves selling off assets, cutting further losses and reducing the workforce as much as possible. Little or no thought is given to trying to save the operation, as declining profits are likely to continue.

Turnaround Strategy: The focus of this strategy is to save the operation. Although cost-cutting efforts and employee reductions are made, they are short-term programs for long-run survival. Worker morale may be somewhat depressed.

strategy type dictates which employee characteristics are necessary. All of these characteristics are shown in Exhibit 1-3. Note that these characteristics are regarded as general ones, applicable in varying degrees across organizations. The challenge is to identify from these general characteristics the ones that are necessary across given types of organizations by strategy. Not addressed here are specific characteristics, especially employee skills, knowledges and abilities, (SKAs), necessitated by specific job demands. For a given organization, however, these need to be identified and matched with the appropriate PHRM practices similar to the way the PHRM practices are matched with the general necessary employee characteristics.

Based upon the characteristics of the five strategic situations shown in Exhibit 1-2, several necessary employee charac-

Exhibit 1-3 General Employee Characteristics to Complement an Organization's Strategy

Repetitive, Predictable Behaviour	Creative, Innovative Behaviour
Short-Term Focus	Long-Term Focus
Co-operative, Interdependent Behaviour	Independent, Autonomous Behaviour
Low Concern for High Quantity	High Concern for High Quantity
Low Concern for Quality	High Concern for Quality
Low-Risk Orientation	High-Risk Orientation
Concern for Process	Concern for Results
Preference to Avoid Responsibility	Preference to Assume Responsibility
Inflexible to Change	Flexible to Change
Low-Task Orientation	High-Task Orientation
Low-Organizational Identification	High-Organizational Identification
Focus on Efficiency	Focus on Effectiveness

teristics are proposed. These draw upon the organizational concerns for each strategy as described by Gerstein and Reisman (1983). The rationale for these characteristics is presented in detail after describing the menus of PHRM practices.

Menu of PHRM Practices. In this section, the menu of PHRM choices available to any company wishing to foster and facilitate necessary employee characteristics is described. The intent here is to communicate the variety of characteristics and methods that shape and give flavour to each PHRM function (i.e., planning, staffing, appraising, compensating, and training). The intent is also to provide a menu of choices for the PHRM practitioner to select after a determination is made of what employee characteristics are necessary based upon organizational strategy. Only those choices most relevant to each strategy type are described here.

Planning Menu. The following choices reflect those that many PHRM practitioners make, though perhaps not as explicitly as presented here:

Planning Choices

Informal .... Formal
Loose .... Tight
Short Term .... Long Term
Explicit Analysis ..... Implicit Analysis
Narrow Jobs............... Broad Jobs
Segmental   Integrative
Design .... Design
Low Employee   High Employee
Involvement .... Involvement

The first choice in the planning menu is the extent or degree of formalization. This ranges from informal to formal. The more formal the planning activity becomes, the more attention and concern shown to explicit planning procedures and activities for human resource management. One result of more formal planning is Hewlett-Packard's willingness and ability to state and support its human resource policy of "not to be a hire and fire company." An advantage of this type of formalized planning is that it enables a company to provide employees job security, a facet of human resource management critical to the success of such companies as IBM, Dana, and Delta, as well as to HP (Peters and Waterman 1982; Dyer and Heyer 1984; Mills 1985).

Other examples of more formal planning include designing jobs to attract and retain the best people and to maximize their performance contribution to the organization, designing organizational structures to match the product needs of the organization and developing organizational climates that cultivate trust and openness (Angle, Manz, and Van de Ven 1985).

A second choice in the planning menu is the degree of tightness. Almost necessary to the implementation and success of a more formal planning policy is the establishment of a tight rather than a loose link between the human resource planning and corporate planning. The articulation of this necessity is most evident in the recent discussions of corporate strategic management and human resource management (Milkovich, Dyer and Mahoney 1983). However, since organizations can choose not to have a tight link between corporate planning and human resource planning, the degree of tightness of this linkage is another critical choice in planning.

A third choice is the time horizon of the planning. As such, companies can choose to plan only for the very short-term human resource needs or extend themselves much farther into the future. It appears, however, that companies need to have a longer-term time horizon, since a company's human resource characteristics are so slow in changing (Skinner 1981). Nevertheless, since a company's environment may be volatile, short-term responses and adjustments by the company may be required. Thus, companies may benefit from some long-range planning considerations with shorter-range flexibility.

The next two choices relate more directly to job analysis and job design. A critical choice in job analysis is choosing the degree of explicitness. On the one hand, job dimensions and requisite skill and behaviour requirements can be detailed precisely and on the other hand, they can be described in general terms and with more emphasis on the results expected of the job incumbent. Another choice related to job analysis could also be offered here, and that is whether or not to do job analysis at all. However, because performing job analysis is more likely to result in getting the best people to do the jobs correctly and is essentially a legal necessity, job analysis should be done (Schuler 1987).

The choice in job design is the degree of breadth of the jobs. Ranging from very narrow to very broad, companies have a great deal of choice in designing their jobs. More broadly designed jobs provide for more employee autonomy, skill usage, and identification with the product itself. More narrowly designed jobs limit these employee/task attributes.

Organizations can be designed or structured in many ways. The recent attempts to rationalize organizations and eliminate middle management represent ways of restructuring. Another way is matching the structure to an organization's environment. Still another way that appears more relevant to human resource management is the degree of integration across the company. At the low end, companies can choose to be relatively segmented and at the high end they can choose to be highly integrated. The more integrated the company the more interaction, formal as well as informal, that employees have with their counterparts from other areas of the organization (Kanter 1983a).

Staffing Menu. The human resource manager needs to consider several staffing choices that reflect the recruitment and selection activity:

Staffing Choices

Internal Sources ...... External Sources
Narrow Paths .... Broad Paths
Single Ladder .... Multiple Ladders
Explicit Criteria .... Implicit Criteria
Limited   Extensive
Socialization .... Socialization
Closed Procedures .... Open Procedures

The first choice from the staffing menu is choosing the source from which to recruit applicants. At one extreme, for example, other departments in the company and other levels in the organizational hierarchy. At the other extreme, they can use external sources exclusively. Although this choice may be limited for entry level jobs, it is a very important one for most other jobs. Recruiting internally essentially means a policy of promotion from within. While this policy can serve as an effective reward, it commits a company to providing training and career development opportunities if the promoted employees are to perform well.

Associated with this first choice is the second choice of establishing broad or narrow career paths (London and Stumpf 1982). The broader paths that are established, the greater the opportunity for employees to acquire skills relevant to many functional areas and the greater the opportunity to gain more exposure and visibility in more parts of the organization. Both of these aspects resulting from broader career paths enhance an employee's skill acquisition and opportunities for promotion within the organization. The time frame for this process of the acquisition of many skills, however, is likely to be much longer than that required for the acquisition of a more limited skill base. Thus promotion may be quicker under a policy of narrow career paths, although an employee's career opportunities may be more limited over the long run.

Another staffing choice to be made is whether or not to establish one or several promotion ladders. The decision to establish several ladders enlarges the opportunities for employees to be promoted and yet stay within a given technical specialty without having to necessarily assume managerial responsibilities. Establishing just one promotion ladder enhances the relative value of a promotion and increases the competition in getting it.

Part and parcel of a promotion system are the criteria used in deciding who to promote. The choice here is in the degree to which the criteria for promotion are explicit. The criteria can vary from very explicit to very implicit (Cummings 1984). The more explicit the criteria, the less adaptable the promotion system is to exceptions and changing circumstances. What the company loses in flexibility, however, the individual may gain in clarity. This clarity, however, may only be beneficial for those who fulfill the criteria exactly. The more implicit the criteria, the greater the flexibility to move employees around and develop them more broadly (Cummings 1984).

Once initially employed or promoted, organizations can decide how extensively they wish to socialize the individuals. With minimal socialization, organizations convey few informal rules of games and establish few procedures to totally immerse the individuals into the culture and practices of the organization. Although it is probably easier and cheaper to do this than provide for maximum socialization, the result is more likely to be the establishment of a more restricted psychological attachment and commitment by the individual to the organization (Schein 1970).

A final choice is the degree of openness in the staffing procedures. The more open the procedures, the more likely there is to be job posting for internal recruitment, self-nomination for promotion and self-nomination and involvement in assessment centers for promotion. The less open and more secret the procedures, the more limited the involvement of employees in selection decisions, but the faster the decisions can be made. To facilitate a policy of openness, however, companies need to make the relevant information accessible and available to the employees. Such a policy, however, is worthwhile since it allows individuals to select themselves into entrepreneurial jobs, a critical aspect of successful entrepreneurship (Pinchot 1984).

Appraising Menu. The choices in the appraising menu include:

Appraising Choices

Loose, Incomplete   Tight, Complete
Integration .... Integration
Behavioural Criteria ... Results Criteria
Purposes: ....

DAP RAP MAP

Low Employee   High Employee
Participation .... Participation
Short-term   Long-term
Criteria .... Criteria
Individual Criteria ...... Group Criteria

Because performance appraisal is a system with many components, a first choice on the menu is deciding on the degree of integration of these components. This integration includes: (1) establishing the link between job analysis and the performance appraisal forms and criteria; (2) identifying who can provide relevant appraisal data on the criteria identified; (3) developing and connecting the types of appraisal forms that can be selected with the purpose to be served; (4) gathering and combining the various sources of performance data as expeditiously as feasible; (5) feeding back the results to the employees in a timely fashion and allowing for appeal; and (6) ensuring that the results are utilized for their intended purposes, such as compensation, and are still relevant (valid) for the employees and jobs. Point (6) brings the process of performance appraisal full circle and suggests that continual monitoring and potential adjustment of the process are necessary. Companies, however, may choose not to engage in this continual monitoring and adjustment. Similarly, they may choose not to conceive of performance appraisal in such a systematic manner, or if they do, they may choose not to establish a tight connection between the components. If these choices are made, the company establishes a loose integration. If the opposite choices are made, the integration becomes much tighter.

Another choice in appraising is whether the preference is to appraise and evaluate behaviours or results. Appraisal of behaviour focuses on *how* things are done, while appraisal of results focuses on *how many* things are done. Many appraisal forms that organizations can choose to use can be distinguished by their emphasis on behaviours or results. For example, behavioural anchored rating scales (BARS) focus on behaviours, and management by objectives (MBO) focuses on results. If a company chooses, both types of forms can be used together and equal emphasis can be given to behaviour and results (Carroll and Schneier 1982).

A third choice is selecting the general purpose to be served by appraisal. As identified by Cummings (1984), appraisal can be used to develop employee performance, to maintain it, or to improve it. He refers to these three purposes of appraisal as DAP, RAP, and MAP respectively. DAP is future-oriented and focuses heavily on spotting employees who are likely to do well on more challenging jobs and providing developmental opportunities to help ensure they will do well. In contrast, RAP is more present-oriented and seeks to spot current performance deficiencies, analyze the reasons for them and then design programs to remove them (Mager and Pipe 1970). MAP is concerned with maintaining current employee performance levels.

A fourth choice is the degree of employee participation in the entire performance appraisal system. Companies can choose to have employees involved in each of the components of the system, in only some of them, or in none. For example, human resource managers can involve employees in writing their own job descriptions, identifying critical job dimensions, and then identifying examples of effective and ineffective performance on those dimensions. In addition, the employees could be excluded from actively participating in any of these components.

Another choice for companies is whether to emphasize short-term criteria or long-term criteria in appraising and evaluating employees. While short-term criteria could be included in many performance dimensions, all have in common a twelve month or less time horizon within which employees demonstrate their ability to perform. Alternatively, there could be many long-term criteria, but all would share a time horizon of more than twelve months within which employee performance would be appraised.

A final choice in appraising is selecting whether more weight is to be given to individual determined criteria or more to group determined criteria. On one hand, employees may be appraised individually on criteria over which they collectively have a great deal of ability to influence. If collective action is required to get results, group criteria are more appropriate in appraising individual performance than when collective action is not required.

Compensation Menu. As with the preceding PHRM functions, this menu also offers many choices. They include:

Compensating Choices

Low Base Salaries	High Base Salaries
Internal Equity	External Equity
Few Perks	Many Perks
Standard, Fixed Package	Flexible Package
Low Participation	High Participation
No Incentives	Many Incentives
Short-term Incentives	Long-term Incentives
No Employment Security	High Employment Security

One of the first choices is determining the level of base pay. Base pay can range anywhere from low to high. As a part of this choice, companies can choose to pay this base pay on an hourly basis or on a salary basis. Implied in the use of any hourly basis is that employees are not paid for time missed as it is when employees are paid on a salary basis. Thus companies can choose to have base pay on an hourly or salary basis and range from low to high.

The determination of the level of base pay may be influenced in part by another choice for the company: whether to be more concerned with internal equity or external equity (Lawler 1984). That is, companies can choose to determine pay rates for jobs that better reflect their relative worth determined by a company's own internal job evaluation results or to determine these rates for jobs that better reflect what other companies pay.

Another critical choice is whether to provide few perquisites or many. Though often presented in the context of benefits, companies can also choose to offer varying degrees of flexibility in the total compensation package employees receive. Companies can choose to offer a standard package of direct and indirect compensation or they can offer a great deal of variety and flexibility in the mix and value of components in the total compensation package such as found in flexible pay programs.

In offering more flexibility in total compensation packages or in just the indirect component, companies are also in part making the choice of how much employee participation to have in compensation. Offering flexibility in compensation is often done in order for employees to get what they really value and thus for the company to get more bang for its buck. Since employees are the best judge of what they really value, having high employee participation along with offering flexibility makes a great deal of sense. There are also other aspects of compensation, however, in which employees can participate, for example, job or skill-based evaluations and salary increase decisions (Lawler 1984). Companies can choose, of course, not to allow any employee participation in compensation. To allow participation obliges the company to be ready to provide relevant pay information and abandon any attempts for pay secrecy.

Other compensation choices are whether or not to provide incentives, and if so, are they to be more short-term based or more long-term based. For example, companies can choose to offer either cash or stock to reward the achievement of short-term (less than twelve months) goals on criteria such as output, sales or return on capital, or offer rewards such as incentive stock options (ISOs) or stock appreciation rights (SARs) for longer-term goal attainment (Bentson and Schuster 1983).

A final choice in compensating employees is whether to offer extensive guarantees at all. This choice is perhaps one of the most critical, but one that excellent companies seem to make in favour of employment security (Peters and Waterman 1982). It appears as if employment security facilitates employee risk taking, longer-term orientations and greater loyalty and commitment to the company (Mills 1985).

Training and Development Menu. As with other PHRM functions, the training and development menu also consists of many choices:

Training and Development

Short Term.................Long Term
Narrow   Broad
Application................ Application
Productivity   Quality of Work
Emphasis ....Life Emphasis
Spontaneous, Unplanned,   Planned,
Unsystematic............... Systematic
Individual   Group
Orientation................ Orientation
Low   High
Participation .... Participation

The first choice in this menu is the extent to which focus on the short-term versus the long-term needs of the employees. To the extent emphasis is given to the short term, there will be more training programs and fewer development programs.

Even though training may be more short-run focused, it can still be offered so as to improve an employee's SKAs to do his/her present job or offered to enable an employee to learn SKAs more relevant for other jobs in the organization. A similar distinction can also be made with development programs. The choice here then is to provide training and development for a more narrow or a more broad application. This choice to some degree is also influenced by whether the utilization of human resources focuses primarily on a company's need for improved quality of work life or for productivity. Although those improvements are not mutually exclusive, the primary emphasis is and as such constitutes a training and development choice.

Another critical choice is the degree to which the training and development activities are planned, formalized, and systematically linked to the other PHRM activities. At issue here is how closely the training and development activities are delivered to individuals as individuals or as members of a cohort group. Being a member of a cohort-like group can facilitate the socialization process as well as the training and development activities. Group membership can also buffer its individual members against the stress and time pressures in the company.

A final choice in training and development is the extent of participation to allow employees. For example, companies can allow employees to identify preferred career paths and career goals. They can also allow employees to help identify their own training needs. This type of participation may better enable companies to spot training needs and performance deficiencies since employees may ordinarily attempt to hide this information from their supervisors. Nevertheless, companies may still choose to allow their employees a relatively limited amount of participation or implementation of their training and development activities.

It is suggested that the choice in this case as well as in the case of all the other PHRM practices can be made on the basis of the necessary employee characteristics needed by the organization based on its strategy.

Matching Strategy Types and PHRM Practices. In the discussion thus far, it has been suggested that there are several PHRM practices which practitioners and researchers may utilize. Also described have been several choices or ways in which to implement these practices. The selection of the right choice depends upon what a company needs from its employees. Necessary characteristics that a company needs from its employees are determined by strategy type. Thus, for companies to obtain the necessary characteristics from their employees, they need to systematically select the right choices from each menu of the PHRM practices and implement them together after determining this strategy type. The PHRM practices that may constitute the right choices for each strategy type are now proposed and summarized in Exhibit 1–4. Note that the rationale for these strategy-PHRM practice matches rests upon the necessary employee characteristics and the presumption that different PHRM practices stimulate and reinforce different employee characteristics.

Entrepreneurial Strategy. In this strategy, the organization needs employees to be innovative, risk taking, and willing to assume responsibility. In propositional form here are the PHRM practices likely to be appropriate for the entrepreneurial type of strategy:

Proposition 1a:

Planning. Entrepreneurial strategy is fostered and facilitated to the extent that planning practices are formal, tight, implicit, broad, integrative design, and encourage high employee participation.

These planning practices are hypothesized to stimulate innovation, willingness to work well, and cooperate with others and get employees to assume responsibility (Angle, Manz, and Van de Ven 1985; Burgelman 1983; Kanter 1983b; Milkovich, Dyer, and Mahoney 1983; Schuler 1986).

Proposition 1b:

Staffing. Entrepreneurial strategy is fostered and facilitated to the extent that staffing practices offer individuals broad paths and multiple ladders, have implicit criteria and open procedures, and allow extensive socialization.

These staffing practices are hypothesized to stimulate employee innovation, cooperation, and longer-term focus in the organization (Burgelman 1983; Cummings 1984; London and Stumpf 1982; Maidique and Hayes 1984; Peters and Waterman 1982).

Note that these in part are the same characteristics stimulated by the planning practices. Essential to the framework is that there be a consistency attained across PHRM practices within a strategy type. A result of this is that different PHRM practices will unavoidably stimulate some of the same characteristics. Consequently, it is critical that all the PHRM practices be selected to match with strategy to avoid fostering and facilitating incompatible behaviours.

Proposition 1c:

Appraising. Entrepreneurial strategy is fostered and facilitated to the extent that appraising practices are loosely and incompletely integrated, emphasize results criteria, are future-oriented, encourage high employee participation, and recognize the accomplishments of groups of individuals.

These appraising practices are hypothesized to stimulate risk taking, a willingness to assume responsibility and a longer-term orientation (Carroll and Schneier 1982; Cummings 1984; George and MacMillan 1984; Giles and Landauer 1984; Kanter 1983a; Roberts and Fusfeld 1981; Timmons 1979).

Exhibit 1–4   PHRM Practices-Corporate Strategy Matches and Needed Employee Characteristics

Corporate Strategy	Needed Employee Characteristics	PHRM Practice Choices
Entrepreneurial	To varying degrees, employees need to be innovative, cooperative, longer-term oriented, risk taking, and willing to assume responsibility. It is critical that key employees remain.	(1) Planning—formal, tight, implicit, broad, integrative, high participation. (2) Staffing—broad paths, multiple ladders, open, implicit criteria. (3) Appraising—loosely integrated, results; longer-term, high participation. (4) Compensation—external equity, flexible, high participation. (5) Training—broad application, informal and high participation.
Dynamic Growth	Employees need to have high organizational identification, be flexible to change, look short term for survival, have a high-task orientation, and work in close cooperation with others.	(1) Planning—broad, informal, integrative. (2) Staffing—broad, open, implicit. (3) Appraising—employee participation; combination of individual and group criteria and short-and long-term focus. (4) Compensation—employee participation, short- and long-term rewards; internal and external equity. (5) Training—broad application; productivity and QWL emphasis, some participation.
Extract Profit	The focus here is on quantity and efficiency, the short term and results with a relatively low level of risk and a minimal level of organizational identification.	(1) Planning—formal, narrow, explicit job descriptions, low involvement. (2) Staffing—narrow, closed, explicit criteria, little socialization. (3) Appraising—results criteria, maintenance purposes, individual evaluation. (4) Compensation—short term, internal equity, low participation. (5) Training—narrow application, low participation, productivity focus.

Continued on next page

Exhibit 1-4—Continued

Corporate Strategy	Needed Employee Characteristics	PHRM Practice Choices
Liquidation/ Divestiture	Employees need to be flexible to change, have a high-task orientation, have a longer-term focus, and engage in some nonrepetitive behavior.	(1) Planning—formal, segmental, narrow, explicit. (2) Staffing—narrow paths, explicit criteria, limited socialization, closed procedures. (3) Appraising—remedial purposes, behavioural criteria, low participation. (4) Compensation—low participation, few perks, fixed package, no incentives. (5) Training—unplanned, narrow application.
Turnaround	Employees need a short-term, narrow orientation, low organizational commitment, a low need to remain, and a limited focus on high quantity.	(1) Planning—informal, loose, high employee involvement. (2) Staffing—extensive socialization, openness, informal, implicit criteria. (3) Appraising—results criteria, group criteria, high participation. (4) Compensation—short- and long-term incentives, high participation. (5) Training—broad focus, high participation, productivity emphasis.

Proposition 1d:

Compensating. Entrepreneurial strategy is fostered and facilitated to the extent that compensating practices emphasize external equity, are flexible, contain many perks and long-term incentives, and encourage high employee participation.

The compensation practices are hypothesized to reinforce the appraising practices quite nicely. Accordingly, they should stimulate and reinforce risk taking, or willingness to assume responsibility and a longer-term orientation (Bentson and Schuster 1983; Hutton 1985; Lawler 1984; Lawler and Drexler 1984; Timmons 1979).

Proposition 1e:

Training and Development. Entrepreneurial strategy is fostered and facilitated to the extent that training and development practices are characterized by broad applications, emphasize quality of work life, are spontaneous, informal and unsystematic, and encourage high employee participation.

These training and development practices are hypothesized to stimulate a willingness to assume responsibility, innovation, and a willingness to work with others. These practices should also help retain key employees (Maidique and Hayes 1984; de Chambeau and Shays 1984).

Turnaround Strategy. In general, in this strategy the organization needs employees who have high organizational identification, will engage in rapidly paced short-term activities for the benefit of the longer term, are willing to change and adapt, and desire to work in close, teamwork-like cooperation. Thus, PHRM practices likely to be appropriate for this strategy include:

Proposition 2a:

Planning. Turnaround strategy is fostered and facilitated to the extent that planning practices are informal, flexible, and emphasize high employee involvement.

These planning practices are hypothesized to stimulate and reinforce high organizational identification and loyalty, flexibility and willingness to change, and a high level of short-term task orientation (Milkovich et al. 1983).

Proposition 2b:

Staffing. Turnaround strategy is fostered and facilitated to the extent that staffing practices reflect extensive socialization, openness, more informal implicit criteria, and broad career paths.

These staffing practices are hypothesized to be helpful in stimulating organizational identification, flexibility, a high-task orientation, and willingness to work in close cooperation with others (Cummings 1984).

Proposition 2c:

Appraising. Turnaround strategy is fostered and facilitated to the extent that appraising practices reflect results criteria, high employee participation, and a group basis of appraisal.

These appraising practices are hypothesized to be helpful in the turnaround strategy by stimulating and reinforcing cooperative behaviour, high organizational identification, and focus on the short-term tasks while keeping in mind the longer-term issues of the organization (Carroll and Schneier 1983; Schuler 1987).

Proposition 2d:

Compensating. Turnaround strategy is fostered and facilitated to the extent that compensation practices reflect a combination of short- and long-term incentives and high employee participation.

These compensation practices are hypothesized to stimulate and reinforce employee company identification and concern for the short-term as well as the long-term interests of the organization (Lawler 1984).

Proposition 2e:

Training and Development. Turnaround strategy is fostered and facilitated to the extent that training and development practices reflect a productivity emphasis, high employee participation, and broad rather than narrow focus.

These training and development practices are hypothesized to be helpful in a turnaround strategy because they should stimulate cooperative employee behaviour, a high task orientation and high organizational identification (London and Stumpf 1982).

Extract Profit/Rationalize Strategy. This strategy, which by the way, is consistent with an organization or product in a mature stage (Hax 1985), is facilitated by necessary employee behaviours that focus on high quantity of output, the short-term, low-risk and highly repetitive behaviours while requiring only a minimal level of employee identification with the organization.

Proposition 3a:

Planning. Extract profit/rationalize strategy is fostered and facilitated to the extent that planning practices focus on formality, a narrow focus, explicit job descriptions, narrow segmental design and low employee involvement.

These planning practices are hypothesized to be helpful for the extract profit/rationalize strategy because they stimulate low-risk, highly repetitive behaviours, an orientation to the short-term, and minimal organizational identification.

Proposition 3b:

Staffing. Extract profit/rationalize strategy is fostered and facilitated to the extent that staffing practices reflect narrow, single ladder promotion and career paths, explicit criteria, limited socialization, and relatively closed procedures.

These staffing practices are hypothesized to be helpful in an extract profit/rationale strategy because they stimulate and reinforce highly repetitive behaviour; a narrow, segmental, and short-term concern; and low organizational identification (London and Stumpf 1982; Burgelman 1983).

Proposition 3c:

Appraising. Extract profit/rationalize strategy is fostered and facilitated to the extent that appraising practices can be characterized by results criteria, maintenance purposes, low employee involvement, and an individual basis of evaluation.

These appraising practices are hypothesized to be effective in an extract profit/rationalize strategy because they stimulate and reinforce narrow, repetitive behaviour, low organizational identification, and a focus on quantity rather than quality (Carroll and Schneier 1983; Cummings 1984).

Proposition 3d:

Compensating. Extract profit/rationalize strategy is fostered and facilitated to the degree that compensation practices emphasize high perks, low employee participation, short-term criteria, and internal equity.

These compensation practices are hypothesized to be useful here because they can stimulate and reinforce a high-quantity, short-term orientation with emphasis on efficiency rather than effectiveness (Lawler 1984; Bentson and Schuster 1983).

Proposition 3e:

Training and Development. Extract profit/rationalize strategy is fostered and facilitated to the extent that training and development practices have a narrow application, a productivity emphasis, and relatively low employee participation.

These training and development practices are hypothesized to be effective because they can stimulate a high-quantity, high-efficiency orientation, and a short-term focus with minimal organizational identification (Peters and Waterman 1982; London and Stumpf 1982).

Dynamic Growth Strategy. This strategy is one that is particularly appropriate for a company or product in the growth stage. For this strategy, the necessary employee characteristics include a need for flexibility and adaptability, a high-task orientation, a longer-term focus, and some innovativeness.

Proposition 4a:

Planning. Dynamic growth strategy is fostered and facilitated to the extent planning practices are broad rather than narrow, somewhat informal, use an integrative design, and have some employee involvement.

These planning practices are hypothesized to be helpful for a dynamic growth strategy because they stimulate a longer-term focus, some innovativeness, and, some flexibility and adaptability (Milkovich et al. 1983; Fombrun et al. 1984).

Proposition 4b:

Staffing. Dynamic growth strategy is fostered and facilitated to the extent staffing practices are broad rather than narrow, are more open than closed, and utilize some implicit criteria.

These staffing practices are hypothesized to be effective for a dynamic growth strategy because they stimulate the needed flexibility in employee behaviours, a longer-term orientation, and an ability to be innovative (Miller 1984).

Proposition 4c:

Appraising. Dynamic growth strategy is fostered and facilitated to the degree that appraising practices serve development purposes, have employee participation, focus on behavioural as well as results criteria, and use individual and group bases for evaluation.

These appraising practices are hypothesized to be helpful for the dynamic growth strategy because they stimulate and reinforce cooperative, longer-term behaviour, and concern for product innovation and individual adaptability (Cummings 1984; Carroll and Schneier 1982).

Proposition 4d:

Compensating. Dynamic growth strategy is fostered and facilitated to the extent that compensation practices involve employee participation, reward short- and long-term behavioural results, and have concern for external as well as internal equity.

These compensation practices are hypothesized to be effective for the dynamic growth strategy because they stimulate and reinforce the same employee characteristics that the appraising practices do (Lawler 1984; McGill 1984).

Proposition 4e:

Training and Development. Dynamic growth strategy is fostered and facilitated to the degree training and development practices have broad application, emphasize both QWL and productivity, are well planned and integrated with the human resource and corporate planning activities, and allow employee participation.

These training and development practices are hypothesized to be effective for the dynamic growth strategy because they stimulate employee innovativeness, a longer-term orientation, and individual adaptability and cooperativeness (Pinchot 1984).

Liquidation/Divestiture Strategy. This strategy is quite appropriate for a business or product in the state of decline. Accordingly, the necessary employee characteristics are hypothesized to reflect a short-term orientation, a low company identification, a limited focus on quantity, and a low need to remain with the organization (Milkovich et al. 1983; Lorange and Murphy 1984).

Proposition 5a:

Planning. Liquidation/divestiture strategy is fostered and facilitated by planning practices that are described as having low employee involvement, segmental design, and relatively high fomality.

These planning practices are hypothesized to support a liquidation/divestiture strategy because they stimulate low company identification, a short-term and narrow orientation, and a low desire to stay with the organization.

Proposition 5b:

Staffing. Liquidation/divestiture strategy is fostered and facilitated by staffing practices that are characterized as reflecting narrow paths, explicit criteria, limited socialization, and closed procedures.

These staffing practices are hypothesized to support a liquidation/divestiture strategy because they stimulate low employee involvement with the company, a short-term focus, and a limited focus on high quality (Ferris et al. 1985).

Proposition 5c:

Appraising. Liquidation/divestiture strategy is fostered and facilitated by appraising practices best described as having behavioural criteria, for remedial purposes, individually based, and having low employee participation.

These appraising practices are hypothesized to be useful here because they should stimulate and reinforce a low-quantity emphasis, a short-term orientation, and a low desire to remain with the organization (Carroll and Schneier 1982).

Proposition 5d:

Compensating. Liquidation/divestiture strategy is fostered and facilitated by compensation practices that have low employee participation, few perks, a standard, fixed package, and no incentives.

These compensation practices are hypothesized to be useful for a liquidation/divestiture strategy because they should reinforce a short-term orientation, low involvement with the organization, and a narrow orientation (Ferris et al. 1985; McGill 1984).

Proposition 5e:

Training and Development. Liquidation/divestiture strategy is fostered and facilitated by training and development practices that have a narrow application, are rather unplanned if they exist at all, and have low employee participation.

These training and development practices are hypothesized to be useful because they should stimulate and reinforce short term behaviour and a low desire to remain with the organization (Hall 1984; London and Stumpf 1982; Stumpf and Hanrahan 1984).

SUMMARY

While the discussion here of strategy types and PHRM practices is meant to be as encompassing as possible, it is still filled with untested hypotheses and propositions. Consequently, these remain to be tested. Alternatively, a different strategy-PHRM practice paradigms could be offered and tested. If this were the result of this reading, the effort at constructing this paradigm would indeed have been worthwhile.

IMPLICATIONS AND CONCLUSIONS

As suggested in the beginning of this reading, the effective management of human resources for organizations is vital. Organizations can effectively manage their human resources by incorporating them into their overall strategies. But this incorporation alone is not sufficient for effective human resource management, although it is very necessary. What is also necessary is an integration of PHRM practices with strategy since PHRM practices really determine how an organization's employees are treated. This integration of PHRM practices with strategy, though complex, can be achieved by a systematic understanding and analysis of strategy and PHRM practices. While this analysis is critical to strategy formulation, it is also critical to strategy implementation as in the strategy-PHRM practices match.

Due in part to the strategy imperative, PHRM managers traditionally have not had a major role in strategy and the general operation of organizations (Nininger 1982; Misa and Stein 1983; Parker and Ulrich 1983; Hax 1985; Skinner 1981; Foulkes 1975, 1986). Rather, they have, as personnel managers, played more limited roles such as making sure that employees got paid and that the retirement checks went out (Foulkes 1975). Conditions are changing, however, and personnel managers are playing more important roles in organizations. The recognition by organizations and the personnel field of the importance of human resources and the options available in managing human resources have been significant in changing the title of the personnel area and manager to PHRM and the PHRM manager respectively. These changes have been supported by the increased recognition of the impact environmental changes have had on organizations, especially their human resources. For example, since the supply of human resources can no longer be taken as given, there is increased interest in human resource planning. There is also a growing interest in human resource programs to improve productivity and the quality of work life (QWL). In some organizations, PHRM has been involved in developing these programmes.

What these changes and events suggest is that PHRM and the PHRM manager have an excellent opportunity to become involved in strategy and the running of the organization (Fombrun et al. 1984; Foulkes 1986; Harris and Harris 1983; Skaggs 1984; Carroll and Schuler 1983). It has been suggested here that this opportunity can be seized by incorporating PHRM practices with strategy to foster and facilitate necessary employee characteristics as determined in part by company strategy type.

Selection of the most appropriate practices should be appropriate to the strategy and lead to behaviours that are supportive of the strategy. For example, if cooperative behaviours are needed among employees, then group- or organizational-level compensation incentives should be provided rather than an individual-level incentive system. If product quality is critical, quality circles and union-management cooperation should be developed. Thus, determination of the needed employee behaviours is critical. The suggested way to do that is through identifying the company-industry stage. In essence then, strategy implementation is fostered and facilitated with the needed employee behaviours as determined by company strategy type.

But, as companies begin to think in terms of matching PHRM practices to business strategy and using them for competitive advantage, employees will face ever changing employment relationships. A significant implication that follows from firms changing their practices is that employees of a single firm will be exposed to different sets of PHRM practices during the course of employment.

Consequently, workers will be asked to exhibit different characteristics and will be exposed to several different conditions of employment. Unclear at this time are answers to questions such as: How feasible or desirable is it for workers to continually change?; What can firms do to aid the adjustment to change?; What should firms do if workers fail to change?; and, Will the need to change PHRM practices with strategy be uniform across all levels of the firm? Equally important as these questions is: What will be the reactions of workers, unions, and government? While it is difficult to predict the exact answers to this question, it is unlikely that firms will be able to proactively and singly change PHRM practices unless they have a significant balance of power (Cooke 1985). The very act of changing PHRM practices may not only require a significant degree of power, but also cause a further shift of power (Cooke 1985). Given a relative balance of power, cooperation among the interested parties, such as between the United Auto Workers and the Saturn Division of General Motors, may be more typical. Government intervention is also a possibility when firms elect to move operations, if employees resist change of PHRM practices. State laws already exist in Wisconsin, Maine, and Massachusetts constraining certain forms of plant or office closings. Consequently, the attempts by firms to change their PHRM practices are likely to be done in a rather dynamic context (Osterman 1984).

Another implication of changing PHRM practices is that firms with more than one business are likely to have more than one set of PHRM practices. Thus, a single firm (with several businesses) may have different conditions of employment to the extent that it has businesses (divisions or plants) operating with different strategies or pursuing different competitive strategies. Attendant with the challenge of matching PHRM practices with different strategies then is the challenge of managing the interface of these different practices. Here enter the challenges of treating employees equitably across divisions regarding issues such as career development, equal opportunity, and compensation.

Thus the PHRM area is likely to be filled with challenges and opportunities for researcher and practitioner alike. Seizing these challenges and opportunities is apt to increase the strategic importance of PHRM as a discipline, as well as a function in organizations.

References

Angle, H. L., C. C. Manz, and A. H. Van de Ven. 1985. Integrating human resource management and corporate strategy: A preview of the 3M story. *Organizational Dynamics* (Winter): 25–33.

Bentson, M. A., and J. R. Schuster. 1983. Executive compensation and employee benefits. In *Human Resources Management in the 1980s*, edited by S. J. Carroll and R. S. Schuler, ch. 6, 1–31. Washington, D.C.: The Bureau of National Affairs.

Burgelman, R. A. 1983. Corporate entrepreneurship and strategic management: Insights from a process study. *Management Science* (December): 1349–1364.

Carroll, S. J., Jr. and C. E. Schneier. 1982. *Performance Appraisal and Review Systems.* Glenview, Ill.: Scott, Foresman and Company.

Carroll, S. J. and R. S. Schuler, eds. 1983. *Human resource management in the 1980s.* Washington, D.C.: The Bureau of National Affairs.

de Chambeau, F. and E. M. Shays. 1984. Harnessing entrepreneurial energy within the corporation. *Management Review* (September): 17–20.

Cooke, W. N. 1985. Toward a general theory of industrial relations. In *Advances in Industrial and Labor Relations*, edited by D. B. Lipsky and J. M. Douglas. Greenwich, CT: JAI Press.

Cummings, L. L. 1984. Compensation, culture, and motivation: A systems perspective. *Organizational Dynamics* (Winter): 33–43.

Dyer, L. and N. D. Heyer. 1984. Human resource planning at IBM. *Human Resource Planning* 7(3).

Ferris, G. R., D. A. Schallenberg, and R. F. Zammuto. 1985. Human resources management strategies in declining industries. *Human Resource Management* (Winter).

Fombrun, C. 1982. An interview with Reginald Jones. *Organizational Dynamics* (Winter).

Fombrun, C., N. M. Tichy, and M. A. Devanna. 1984. *Strategic human resource management.* New York: John Wiley & Sons, Inc.

Fossum, J. A. 1984. Strategy issues in labor relations. In *Strategic Human Resource Management*, edited by N. M. Tichy and M. A. Devanna, 343–60. New York: John Wiley & Sons, Inc.

Foulkes, F. K. 1975. The expanding role of the personnel function. *Harvard Business Review* (March/April): 145–56.

Foulkes, F. K. 1986. *Strategic human resource management: A guide for effective practice.* New York: Prentice Hall, Inc.

Frohman, M. and A. L. Frohman. 1984. Organization adaptation: A personnel responsibility. *Personnel Administrator* (January 29): 45–47; 88.

George, R. and I. C. MacMillan. 1984. Corporate venturing/senior management responsibilities. Working Paper, Center for Entrepreneurial Studies, New York University.

Gerstein, M. and H. Reisman. 1983. Strategic selection: Matching executives to business conditions. *Sloan Management Review.* (Winter): 33–49.

Giles, R. and C. Landauer. 1984. Setting specific standards for appraising creative staffs. *Personnel Administrator* 29: 35–47.

Gupta, A. K. 1984. Contingency linkages between strategy and general manager characteristics: A conceptual examination. *Academy of Management Review* 9: 399–412.

Gupta, A. K. and V. Govindarajan. 1984a. Build, hold, harvest: Converting strategic intentions into reality. *Journal of Business Strategy* 4: 34–47.

Gupta, A. K. and V. Govindarajan. 1984b. Business unit strategy, managerial characteristics, and business unit effectiveness at strategy implementation. *Academy of Management Journal* 9: 25–41.

Hall, D. T. 1984. "Human resource development and organizational effectivenes." In *Strategic human resource management*, edited by C. Fombrun, N. M. Tichy, and M. A. Devanna, 159–82. New York: John Wiley & Sons, Inc.

Hambrick, D. C. and P. A. Mason. 1984. Upper echelons: The organization as a reflection of its top managers. *Academy of Management Review* 9: 193–206.

Harris, P. R. and D. L. Harris. 1983. Human resources management: Charting a new course in a new organization, a new society, part 2. *Personnel* 39: 32–42.

Hax, A. C. 1985. A methodology for the development of a human resource strategy. MIT working paper, 1638–85.

Hofer, C. W. and M. J. Davoust. 1977. *Successful strategic management*. Chicago, Ill.: A. T. Kearney.

Hutton, T. J. 1985. Recruiting the entrepreneurial executive. *Personnel Administrator* (January): 35–36; 38; 40–41.

Kanter, R. M. 1983a. *The change masters*. New York: Simon and Schuster.

Kanter, R. M. 1983b. Frontiers for strategic human resource planning and management. *Human Resource Management* 22: 9–21.

Kanter, R. M. 1985. Supporting innovation and venture development in established companies. *Journal of Business Venturing* (Winter): 47–60.

Kerr, J. L. 1982. Assigning managers on the basis of the life cycle. *Journal of Business Strategy* 58–65.

Kerr, J. L. 1985. Diversification strategies and managerial rewards: An empirical study. *Academy of Management Journal* 28: 155–179.

Lawler III, E. E. 1984. "The strategic design of reward systems." In *Readings in personnel and human resource management*. 2d ed. edited by R. S. Schuler and S. A. Youngblood, 253–69. St. Paul: West Publishing.

Lawler III, E. E. and J. A. Drexler, Jr. 1984. The corporate entrepreneur. Working Paper, Center for Effective Organizations, University of Southern California.

London, M. and S. A. Stumpf. 1982. *Managing careers*. Reading, Mass.: Addison-Wesley.

Lorange, P. and D. Murphy. 1984. "Bringing human resources into strategic planning: Systems design considerations." In *Strategic Human Resource Management*, edited by C. Fombrun, N. M. Tichy, and M. A. Devanna, 275–96. New York: John Wiley & Sons, Inc.

MacMillan, I. C. 1983. Preemptive strategies. *Journal of Business Strategy* 4: 16–26.

Mager, R. F. and P. Pipe. 1970. *Analyzing performance problems or "You really oughta wanna"*. Belmont, Ca.: Fearon Pitman Publishers, Inc.

Maidique, M. A. and R. H. Hayes. 1984. The art of high technology management. *Sloan Management Review*. (Winter): 17–31.

McGill, A. R. 1984. "Practical considerations: A case study of general motors." In *Strategic Human Resource Management*, edited by C. Fombrun, N. M. Tichy and M. A. Devanna, 149–58. New York: John Wiley & Sons, Inc.

Miles, R. E. and C. C. Snow. 1984. Designing strategic human resource systems. *Organizational Dynamics* 36–52.

Milkovich, G. T., L. Dyer, and T. A. Mahoney. 1983. "HRM planning." In *Human resources management in the 1980s*, edited by S. J. Carroll and R. S. Schuler, ch. 2, 1–28. Washington, D.C.: The Bureau of National Affairs.

Miller, D., M. F. R. Kets de Vries, and J. M. Toulouse. 1982. Top executives locus of control and its relationship to strategy making, structure, and environment. *Academy of Management Journal* 25: 237–253.

Miller, E. 1984. "Strategic Staffing." In *Strategic human resource management*, edited by C. Fombrun, N. M. Tichy, and M. A. Devanna, 57–68. New York: John Wiley & Sons, Inc.

Mills, D. Q. 1985. *The new competitors.* New York: The Free Press.

Mirvis, P. H. 1985. Formulating and implementing human resource strategy: A model of how to do it, two examples of how it's done. *Human Resource Management* (Winter): 385–412.

Misa, K. F. and T. Stein. 1983. Strategic HRM and the bottom line. *Personnel Administrator* 39: 27–30.

Nininger, J. R. 1982. *Managing Human Resources.* Ottawa: The Conference Board of Canada.

Olian, J. D. and S. L. Rynes. 1984. Organizational staffing: Integrating practice with strategy. *Industrial Relations* 23: 170–83.

Osterman, P., ed. 1984. *Internal Labor Markets.* Cambridge, MA: London.

Parker, D. F. and D. O. Ulrich. 1983. Why and how to add human resources to the firm's strategic team. Working paper, University of Michigan.

Peters, T. A. and R. H. Waterman, Jr. 1982. *In search of excellence.* New York: Warner Books.

Pinchot, G., III. 1984. Intrapreneurship: how to top corporate creative energies. *The Mainstream* 1(2).

Porter, M. E. 1980. *Competitive Strategy.* New York: Free Press.

Roberts, E. B. and A. R. Fusfeld. 1981. Staffing the innovative technology-based organization. *Sloan Management Review* (Spring): 19–34.

Schein, E. H. 1970. *Organizational Psychology.* Englewood Cliffs, N.J.: Prentice-Hall.

Schuler, R. S. and I. C. MacMillan. 1984. Gaining competitive advantage through human resource management practices. *Human Resource Management* 23: 241–55.

Schuler, R. S., I. C. MacMillan, and J. J. Martocchio. 1985. "Key strategic questions for human resource management." In *Handbook of business strategy, 1985/1986 Yearbook*, edited by W. D. Guth. Boston: Warren, Gorham & Lamont.

Schuler, R. S. 1986. Fostering and facilitating entrepreneurship in organizations: Implications for organization structure and human resource management practices. Working paper, New York University.

Schuler, R. S. 1987. *Personnel and human resource management* 3d ed. St. Paul: West Publishing.

Shrivastava, P. and T. Peridis. 1985. Assessing the conceptual language of strategic management: An analysis of typologies. Paper presented at the National Academy of Management, San Diego.

Skaggs, J. H. 1984. ASPA will move strategically toward future challenges. *Personnel Administrator* 29: 48–54.

Skinner, W. 1981. Big hat, no Cattle: Managing human resources. *Harvard Business Review* (September/October): 106–14.

Slocum, J. W., W. L. Cron, R. W. Hansen, and S. Rawlings. 1985. Business strategy and the management of plateaued employees. *Academy of Management Journal* 28: 133–54.

Snow, C. C. and L. G. Hrebiniak. 1980. Strategy, distinctive competence, and organizational performance. *Administrative Science Quarterly* 25: 307–35.

Song, J. H. 1982. Diversification strategies and the experience of top executives of large firms. *Strategic Management Journal* 3: 377–80.

Stumpf, S. A. and N. M. Hanrahan. 1984. Designing organizational career management practices to fit strategic management objectives. In *Readings in Personnel and Human Resource Management* 2d ed., edited by R. S. Schuler and S. A. Youngblood, 326–48. St. Paul: West Publishing.

Szilagyi, A. D. and D. M. Schweiger. 1984. Matching managers to strategies: A review and suggested framework. *Academy of Management Review* 9: 626–37.

Tichy, N. M. 1982. Managing change strategically: The technical, political and cultural keys. *Organizational Dynamics* (Autumn): 59–80.

Tichy, N. M., C. J. Fombrun, and M. A. Devanna. 1982. Strategic human resource management. *Sloan Management Review* 23: 47–61.

Timmons, J. A. 1979. Careful self-analysis and team assessment can aid entrepreneurs. *Harvard Business Review* (November/December): 198–200; 202; 206.

Wissema, J. G., H. W. Van Der Pol, and H. M. Messer. 1980. Strategic management arechetypes. *Strategic Management Journal* 1: 37–47.

Wright, R. V. L. 1974. *A system for managing diversity*. Cambridge, MA: Arthur D. Little.

2. Labour Market Trends and Their Implications for PHRM Training in Canada

Jean-Michel Cousineau, The University of Montréal

INTRODUCTION

That the world of labour is in constant evolution has obvious repercussions for human resources and industrial relations management. In Canada, for the past decade, we have seen the development of a large, unionized public and parapublic (mainly education and health) sector, a growing importance of youth and women in the labour market and the growth of the overall level of education for the whole labour force. While some of these trends (women and education) will still be with us in the near future, other trends will emerge such as the development of new technologies, deregulation of the economy, free trade and a possible reduction in the growth of government and union activity. It can be expected that all those changes will have important impacts on the demand for personnel and human resource management (PHRM) professionals, the nature of their activity and the formation of new graduates in that field.[1]

In the United States, the status and growth of PHRM professionals has been largely documented. Strauss (1984, 2), for example, argues that "management is now the militant party" in the industrial relations field, and that "the new hard line has meant ... the wholesale replacement of old-time industrial relation experts who had been identified with the old policy of accommodation". More positively, Kochan (1985) stresses the numerous innovations introduced in the personnel and human resource management policies in the nonunionized plants. Such policies range from semi-autonomous groups to quality circles, grievance rights, employment security rules, flexible task and work classification, and pay on the basis of competence and qualifica-

The author wishes to thank Bernard Brody, Kathy Cannings, Shimon Dolan and Gilles Guérin, professors at the Ecole de relations industrielles Université de Montréal and professor François Vaillancourt, assistant director of the C.R.D.E., Université de Montréal and associate professor at its department of economics, for their valuable comments, and Yves Létourneau, M.Sc. student at the Ecole de relations industrielles, Université de Montréal, for his assistance in data gathering and processing. Our special thanks also to the research group on the small and medium size enterprises in Quebec (Université du Québec à Trois-Rivières, department of administration and economics) for having organized a special seminar on that question and commented my communication.

tions instead of a strict job task classification.

Megginson (1985) stresses the improving position of personnel management. The situation has moved from a low status and prestige occupation with inadequate funding of personnel department and a poorly qualified manpower in the late 1950s, to the exact opposite in the early 1980s.[2] He also points out that in the United States the field is expanding rapidly, "the number of personnel jobs has grown from 52,000 in 1950 to 450,000 in 1985.... This almost ninefold increase is expected to accelerate during the rest of this decade". Other changes have also been noticed in the United States. Such as the long-term decline of unionization, which now stands at approximatively eighteen percent of the total labour force. In addition, concession bargaining which appeared in the early 1980s, and the growing successful and sometimes illegal intervention of management in the NLRB elections process (Freeman and Medoff 1983; Weiler 1983).

In Canada, research on such questions has not been as much developed.[3] Does the growth of PHRM professionals in Canada compare to the growth in the United States? Has the profession followed the same upgrading process? Are the challenges for the future the same in Canada? This chapter attempts to answer these questions in part, given the data and information available for Canada. It also attempts to pinpoint some of their implications for appropriate training of new graduates. The first section looks into the growth of the demand for PHRM professionals in the 1970s and the evolution of their characteristics by age, sex, and educational level. The second section examines other characteristics of PHRM and industrial relations (I.R.) professionals such as their concentration in specific sectors of activity and the degree of competition between PHRM and I.R. specialists with other university graduates, that is the relative degree of exclusivity of the profession. Finally, the third section scrutinizes the more recent developments for the new PHRM and I.R. graduates in the early 1980s. The conclusion summarizes our observations and examines some of the implications for the training of personnel and future human resources managers.

LONG TERM GROWTH TRENDS

Employment

To analyse the evolution of the profession, Canadian Census data are presented in Table 2–1.

Table 2–1 shows that the growth of the PHRM profession has been quite significant (for the period 1971 to 1981, one hundred percent on the average): twenty-nine percent for personnel officers but more than five hundred percent for directors of personnel.[4] Comparatively, the overall growth of total employment for all occupations was thirty-nine percent over that same period (not shown in the table). On the whole, it thus appears that the profession is expanding and that many of the personnel officers were reclassified to directors: In 1971, there was one director for six officers. In 1981, there was approximately the same number of directors and officers (1 for 1.24). Obviously, many of the officers were promoted to the rank of director.

Sex, Age and Educational Level

Analysis by sex suggests also that the growth of female employment exceeded that for males.

Table 2-1   The Growth of Managerial Occupations in Personnel and Industrial Relations, 1971–1981

	1971	1981	% change
Directors	4 050	26 030	542.7
Officers	25 005	32 292	29.1
TOTAL	29 055	58 322	100.7

Source: *Census Data*, Statistics Canada, Cat. no. 92–220.

In fact, the number of female directors of personnel was multiplied by a factor of sixteen times. For personnel officers, their growth was also higher (175 percent) that for males. Moreover, male representation in that category of occupation decreased both in relative and absolute terms. In 1981, close to fifty percent of the personnel officers were females. For the group of directors, while only one out of ten directors were female in 1971, the ratio is now one to five.

Comparative census data also show that the profession is getting younger and more educated individuals.

While the median age was above forty years old in the early 1970s, it is clearly under this benchmark in the early 1980s. As for the educational level, we now approach one out of three directors of personnel that has a university degree or more. The proportion is close to fifty percent for personnel officers. Ten years before, the proportions were respectively twenty-eight percent and twenty-five percent.

Earnings. Finally, if we examine the earnings situation for the PHRM professionals, some interesting observations can be made. First, as shown in table 2–4,

Table 2-2   Growth of Managerial Occupations in PHRM and I.R., by Sex

	1971	1981	% change
Males: Directors of Personnel	3 610	18 820	421.3
Personnel Officers	19 490	17 125	−12.1
Females: Directors of Personnel	445	7 210	1 520.2
Personnel Officers	5 515	15 170	175.1
Males total	23 100	35 945	55.6
Females total	5 960	22 380	275.5
Females as a % of total	20.5	38.4	—
Directors	11.0	27.7	—
Officers	22.1	47.0	—

Source: *Census Data*, Statitstics Canada, Cat. no. 92–220.

Table 2-3   Age and Educational Level of PHRM Professionals, Canada, 1971–1981

	Age (Median) 1971	Age (Median) 1981	% University Graduates 1971	% University Graduates 1981
Directors	44	38	28	32
Agents	41	37	25	48

Source: *Census Data*, Statistics Canada, Cat. no. 92–220.

earnings levels for directors of personnel are slightly *above similar occupations*, especially for women. In 1980, the average earnings were $30,844 for men and $20,746 for women. In 1985 dollars, the average for both sexes correspond to an annual average of $40,916 and $33,211 for directors of personnel and personnel officers respectively.

Over time, the average wage *increased more rapidly* for PHRM professionals than for the other categories of managerial occupations. As shown in table 2–5, the average wage for directors of personnel increased by 116.6 percent, (that is close to the general consumer price index increase over that same period 116.8 percent). For other top managerial professionals, it only increased by 57.3 percent. Thus, the wage of male directors of personnel increased relative to other male managers. The same is true a fortiori for female directors of personnel. Their wage increases amount to 200 percent for the 1970–1980 period. Finally, personnel officers also benefited from generous wage increases: 138.5 percent for males and 158.9 percent for females.

More recently, the 1985 annual forecast of excess supply or demand by occupation in the Quebec labour market indicated expected shortages for top human resource and industrial relations managers. (Ministère de la Main-d'oeuvre et de la sécurité du revenu, 1984).[5]

In summary, the accumulated evidence for PHRM professionals shows that there were some excess demand for that profession in the 1970s up to the mid 1980s, that their wage is slightly above

Table 2-4   Wages of Personnel Managers and Officers, Canada, 1980, Males and Females

	Men	Women	Average	1985 $
Personnel Managers	30 844	20 746	28 417	40 916
Personnel Officers	26 075	18 942	23 066	33 211
Other Managers	30 044	17 358	—	—
Other Officers	27 121	17 822	—	—

Source: *Census Data*, 1981, Statistics Canada, Cat. no. 92–220.

Table 2-5 Wage Increases for Personnel Directors and Officers in Canada, 1970–1980, by Sex

	% Change	% Change
	Males	Females
Directors of Personnel	116.6	200.5
Other managers	57.3	109.4
Cost of living	116.8	116.8
Personnel Officers	138.5	158.9

Source: *Census Data*, Statistics Canada, Cat. no. 92–220.

other comparable occupations and that it grew faster than the one for those other occupations.

Employment also increased rapidly during the 1970s, especially for female directors of personnel. In fact, the profession is getting younger, more educated, feminine, and highly valued in the firm's hierarchy. For the future, it remains to be seen if such trends will go on. One way to approach the question is by looking at the distribution of the profession in the industrial structure of the economy and project the demand for such an occupation given the expected changes in that structure.

OTHER CHARACTERISTICS

The Demand for PHRM Professionals

Table 2-6 provides a distribution of PHRM professionals by sector of activity. The first and second sectors that come out of the list are the public administration and personal and commercial services. Those two single sectors absorb 59.7 percent of the total PHRM employment. The third sector of importance is the manufacturing sector with 15.1 percent of the PHRM employment. After this comes finance (8.1 percent), transportation (8.1 percent), and commerce (7.8 percent). The remaining sectors are rather marginal (mines, construction, forestry, trapping, and agriculture).

The incidence of PHRM professionals amongst the different industries also differs significantly from one industry to the other.

On average, the ratio of PHRM professionals to total employment is five to one thousand. For the public administration sector, however, it is as high as twenty to one thousand, that is as much as one PHRM professional for each group of fifty employees which is four times greater than the all industry average. In the personal and commercial services it is lower, mainly because of the private sub-sector of that sector. For transportation and manufacturing sectors, it is average, while it is higher than average in the finance and mines sectors (seven/one thousand). Those two sectors, however, and especially the latter, represent a small part of the total economic activity.

On the overall, it seems that, traditionally, for each increase of one hundred thousand jobs in Canada, five hundred jobs were created in the PHRM field. In the future, that will not necessarily be the

Table 2-6 Employment in Personnel Occupations by Industry, Canada 1981

	Total Employment	Personnel Occupations	Personnel in Total	% of Total Employment in Personnel
Public Administration	908 115	18 605	20/1000	32,0
Personal and Commercial Services	3 477 245	14 365	4/1000	27,7
Finance, Insurance and Real Estate	636 070	4 700	7/1000	8,1
Trade	2 004 135	4 510	2/1000	7,8
Transport Communication and Public Utilities	960 770	4 715	5/1000	8,1
Construction	767 105	675	1/1000	1,2
Manufacturing	1 641 365	8 770	5/1000	15,1
Mines	216 445	1 435	7/1000	2,5
Fishing, Hunting and Trapping	37 790	20	1/1000	0,03
Forestry	102 960	255	2/1000	0,4
Agriculture	486 995	40	1/1000	0,06

Source: *Census Data*, Cat. no. 92–923, 1981.

case, given the expected decreasing role of governments in the economic activity, (perhaps with the exception of the health sub-sector). The prediction of accelerated growth for the PHRM professions might still hold, however, but not in the traditional sectors where it did in the past.[6] Some adjustments might be needed. First, new graduates may have to revise their expectations about the role of governments and the relative importance of traditional industrial relations approach. Second, university programs might need some revisions. But another reason for an accelerated growth for business and I.R. graduates is that they can get a larger share of the market. As indicated in Table 2–7, there is room for that move even though the competition is tight.

The Supply of PHRM Professionals

Table 2–7 shows that among the university educated PHRM professionals, only 26.7 percent graduated from business and/or industrial relations schools. Close to seventy-five percent of the profession comes from other disciplines or fields of specialization. The main competition comes from social sciences and humanities. Close to twenty-five percent of the PHRM professionals graduated in psychology, sociology, economics and political science alone. Education, history, english and arts (general) also represent another twenty-five percent of the profession. Thus, in the future, there is room for securing a larger share of the market, as long as the quality of the formation is adapted to the new contingencies of the profession and provides good comparative advantages. One way to analyse that question is by looking at recent trends in the labour market, and seeking the most likely qualifications in demand in the future.

RECENT TRENDS AND QUALIFICATIONS IN DEMAND

The available data for examining recent trends is generally poor in Canada, except for the province of Quebec where some extensive questionnaires are regularly sent to graduates two years after their graduation. Two such surveys will be compared over time: one for the 1975 graduates, surveyed in 1978, and another for the graduates of 1980 which were surveyed in 1983. The comparative results are presented in Table 2-8.

In the survey of 1978, the rate of unemployment was as low as zero percent. This was one of the very few cases where unemployment was so low. The time period needed for finding their first employment was also reasonably low (four to seven weeks). The 1980 graduates, on the other hand, faced a very different situation. Their unemployment rate reached the average of the total graduate student population (two years after their graduation) of twelve percent, and the period of unemployment before their first employment reached a level of twenty-four weeks. That is close to six months.[7] Their

Table 2-7   Distribution and Incidence of PHRM Professionals by Field of Origin

		No. 6145	% 100,0%	Total cumul	Sub-totals
	Nb. Total				
Administration	Adm., commerce and industrial relations	1 640	26,7%	26,7	26,7
Social sciences	Psychology	530	8,6%	35,3	
	Sociology	345	5,6%	40,9	23,3
	Economics	250	4,1%	45,0	
	Sc. political	245	4,0%	49,0	
Humanities	Education	535	8,7%	56,7	12,4
	History	230	3,7%	60,4	
	English	205	3,3%	63,7	18,3
	Philosophy	160	2,6%	66,3	
Engineering and applied sciences	Engineering and applied sciences	270	4,4%	70,7	4,4
Arts (general)	Arts	605	9,8%	80,5	9,8
Other sciences, religion, french, etc.		1 130	19,5%	100,0	19,5

(Highly Qualified Manpower Survey, Statistics Canada, 1973)

Table 2-8   Recent Trends for Industrial Relations Graduates in Quebec

Unemployment rate	1978	0.0%
	1982	12,0%
Weeks unemployed before	1978	4 to 7
1st employment	1982	24 (males)
Relative wages 1982: I.R. graduates	24074/23192	(males/females)
Employment and formation adequacy index (100= average)		80
Exclusivity index		70

Source: *Relance à l'Université*, Ministère de l'Education, Gouvernement du Québec, 1983.

wages, however, were kept slightly above the average. But the new graduates complained about the inadequacy and the lack of exclusivity of their formation. While the indexes of adequacy and exclusivity are set at one hundred for the average graduates of all fields of specialization, it worths only eighty and seventy respectively for industrial relations graduates in the field of business administration in the 1983 survey.

The danger of a mismatch between training and employment, however exaggerated by underemployment or overqualification of new graduates might be real in so far as the competition between different types of training is concerned. This raises an important question: Is traditional I.R. training the answer to the challenges of the future or should the emphasis be placed on human resource management?

A survey among I.R. graduates from the University of Montreal (Simard and Lévesque 1983) shows that PHRM professionals constitute a larger proportion of the profession in the most recent years. While for the 1947–69 graduates, eleven percent of them found work in that field, it grew to thirty-one percent in 1970–75 and to forty-five percent for the 1976–81 period. In the industrial relations field however, there was a peak in 1970–75 but the proportion of jobs in that field fell down dramatically subsequently.

Table 2-9   Distribution of Graduates, (Industrial Relations, University of Montreal) by Field of Activity

	1947–69	1970–75	1976–81
Human Resources	11,1%	31,0%	45,2%
Industrial Relations	28,9%	37,5%	23,0%
3 Activities or More (managers)	44,4%	14,5%	14,0%
Administration	4,4%	4,5%	4,5%
Other Activity (Health and Security, etc.)	11,2%	12,5%	13,3%
Total	100,0%	100,0%	100,0%

Source: Marcel Simard and Christian Lévesque (1983) p. 31.

Another point that might have some importance in the future is the growing importance of computers. Clearly, the respondents in the same questionnaire (Simard and Lévesque 1983), raise that question and suggest that computer use will be much more important in the future. Nonetheless, they also mention that university graduates' past training was inadequate for that purpose. Thus, it seems that the computerized use of personnel data training programs, compensation policy, manpower planning, etc., is becoming more significant. It brings new material for manager and analysts that express their need for guiding practice to command the precise work to be done and to adequately analyse the results that come out of that process. Mathematics, quantitative methods and methodology do clearly emerge from this new decision-making technology. It is not surprising, therefore, to find that past graduates insist on the needs for an improved and larger share of such training in the business and industrial relations university programs.

Communication is another skill on which past graduates insist (Guérin 1979). This means, they require above average oral and writing abilities, in their mother tongue as well as in a second language. It is clear that in the future, such skills will also be increasingly in demand.

CONCLUSION

In conclusion, we have seen that the labour market is in constant evolution both on the supply and demand side, and that the market for PHRM professionals is a promising field and offers both activity and job openings for the future. Their employment and wages have grown fast in the past, and are expected to grow rapidly in the future.[8] Even in times of general high unemployment in Canada, there are many regions where there still exists an excess demand for personnel managers.

Some adjustments must be made however. First, the private sector may function as a more important employer than it has in the past. Second, new technologies as well as changing laws and environment will mean more uncertainty and greater pressures for adaptation. Thus some emphasis should be placed on a better understanding of the theory and basic mechanisms of social organization (principles of sociology, psychology, economics, etc.), instead of standard information on traditional administration recipes.[9]

Third, human resource management will also employ a larger share of university graduates as well as it may represent a larger share of the current activity of the present managers. Both students and university managers should take notice of these changing trends.

Fourth, given the pressures already noted for adaptation in the future, reinforced attention should be given to general training which can be defined by the four keys of access to knowledge. That is to say: mother tongue, second language, mathematics, and computer training. One way to achieve the goal of improved general training is to provide specific courses of that type at a university level. Another way is to use those elements as criteria for assessing the students in most of the specific specialized courses of that same program. While specialization gives access to the first job, general training, as previously defined, maximizes the chances of a job for the rest of one's life.

Endnotes

1. PHRM titles and activities may be defined as follows: personnel recruiter—in-

terviews and administers tests to job applicants, assess their qualifications for classification, selection, referal and job openings; training programmer—organize and evaluate training and educational needs and programs for purpose of employee development and performance; job analyst—develops occupational data concerning job qualification and characteristics of workers to perform jobs; wage and/or fringe benefits administrator—establishes, coordinates and administrates wages and/or fringe benefits in conformity with law requirements, collective agreements, or company policy; labour relations officer—assist employees and appraise their interests, prepare collective bargaining, participate in the grievance procedure . . . ; and labour relations adviser—strategic planning, health and security programs, absenteeism and turnover studies, quality circles, semi-autonomous groups, ... Personnel managers do cumulate at least three of those functions or coordinate the activity of personnel officers and participate more directly in the decision-making process.
2. Following the analysis of the Brookings Institute, professor Julien suggested that such a change is linked to the observed structural decrease in the growth of productivity in most of the occidental economics over the 1970s. The capacity of the traditional Taylor approach for improving productivity being exhausted.
3. For example see Kumar (1975), Glueck (1979) and Caroll and Schuler (1983).
4. The data have been appropriately standardized for comparison between the two census by Statistics Canada.
5. That kind of data is not available for Canada as a whole.
6. Professor Fabi suggested interestingly that the development of small counselor firms might well constitute an important expanding sector of activity in the future.
7. Those results are valid for males only. It is shorter for females (15 weeks) but the female unemployment rate is higher than for males.
8. A comparison with the United States thus shows similar patterns of growth and upgrading but the challenges may differ given the different degree of unionization in Canada (more than a third of the labour force in 1985).
9. Whether training, instrumental courses or instrumental information provided in theoretical courses is the better way to acquire such a necessary complement is still an open question however.

References

Caroll, S. and R. Schuler, eds. 1983. Professional HRM: Changing functions problems. In *Human resources management in the 1980s*. Washington, D.C.: The Bureau of National Affairs.

Cousineau, J. M. 1979. *Le marché du travail des diplômés universitaires au Québec*. (November). Dossier no. 3. Conseil des Universités, Gouvernement du Québec, Québec.

Freeman, R. and J. Medoff. 1984. *What Do Unions Do?* New York: Basic Blackwell.

Glueck, W. 1979. "PAIR in Canada." In *professional PAIR*, ASPA Handbook of Personnel and Industrial Relations, 8. Washington, D.C.: The Bureau of National Affairs.

Guerin, G. 1979. Formation-emploi des diplômés en relations industrielles. *Relations Industrielles/Industrial Relations*. 34(4): 740–67.

Kochan, T. 1985. "Perspectives on Industrial Relatives" Seminar given at McGill University in March 1985, Montreal.

Kumar, P. 1975. *Personnel management in Canada*. Kingston: Industrial Relations Centre, Queens University.

Megginson, L.C. 1985. *Personal management. A human resource approach.* 9–27. Richard, D. Irwin.

Ministère de L'education. 1979. *Relance à l'Université*. Gouvernement du Québec, Québec.

Ministère de L'education. 1983. *Relance à l'Université*. Gouvernement du Québec, Québec.

Ministère de la Main-D'oeuvre et dè la Sécurité du Revenu. 1984. *Surplus et pénurie de main-d'oeuvre au Québec pour 1985*. Québec, (March).

Northrup, H. R. 1984. "Labor market trends and policies in the 1980s." In *Readings in personal and human resource management.* Edited by Schuler, R. S., Youngblood, S. A. St. Paul: West Publishing Co.

Simard, M. and Lèvesque, C. 1983. "Marché du travail et formation en relations industrielles." (November). Ecole de relations industrielles, Université de Montréal.

Statistique Canada, 1981. *Recensement du Canada.* Various catalogue numbers.

Strauss, G. 1984. "Industrial relations: Time of change." *Industrial Relations* 23(1) (Winter): 1–15.

Weiler, P. C. 1983. "Promises to keep: Securing workers' rights to self-organization under the N.L.R.A." *Harvard Law Review* 96(8) (June): 1769–1827.

Section II
Planning For Human Resource Management

The four readings in this section describe information that influences human resource planning at the macro as well as the micro levels. In order to facilitate the expansion of human resource planning, Ulrich addresses himself to answer the questions of "what", "why", and "how". The article summarizes published research trends concerning the linkages between strategy and human resource planning. This is targeted at answering the question of what application domains have been emphasized. Posing and responding to why questions, the author attempts to answer: Why do linkages between strategy and HRP lead to positive organizational outcomes? and, why PHRM helps implement strategies whereby it benefits both individuals and organizations. Often, managers know what needs to be done, but they do not know how to go about it. Ulrich concludes the paper by exploring practical ways to help managers translate human resource planning into action. Furthermore, his exploration consists of examining research models, and developing relevant hypotheses and designs for improving strategic human resource planning.

The second article provides a federal overview of human resource planning in Canada. Canada Employment and Immigration Commission (CEIC) is engaged in a massive macro planning. Jacques, who is the Director General of Labour Market Services (CEIC) explains the multiple roles and activities of the federal government concerning human resource planning. In addition to thorough information about these activities, Jacques provides examples illustrating some of the initiatives which have been undertaken by the public and private sectors in support of the federal policies regarding HRP.

Human Resource Information System (HRIS) is being introduced at an accelerated rate in many Canadian firms. HRIS helps managers to plan better by enabling instant access to information. It is being used in improving many PHRM functions. Marier, in the third article, provides a microscopic example of a no-nonsense-approach, to illustrate the many advantages of implementing HRIS in an organization. By emphasizing the experience of Provigo Inc., the author takes an historical perspective depicting the process of HRIS implementation. Both operational and strategic concerns during the various phases of the implementation are covered in this article. Marier concludes his article by asserting that the computerization process is certainly cost-effective and it definitely contributes to the overall company's profitability and long-term growth.

Although job analysis is critical to the management of human resources, and serves so many purposes, there are still many misconceptions about its conduct and usage, according to Sparks. In the fourth article, Sparks provides a state of the art review concerning the dilemmas and problems associated with job analysis. He also summarizes the techniques that can be used to improve the accuracy or ease of the data collection and/or interpretation of job analysis outcomes (job description and job specification).

3. Strategic Human Resource Planning: Why and How?

Dave Ulrich, University of Michigan

Human resource (HR) planning practices have undergone dramatic transitions over the last decade. Scholars and practitioners have called for greater attention to and tighter linkages between HR planning practices and organization strategies (Tichy, Fombrun, and Devanna 1982; Dyer 1984; Schuler 1987). Research and practice have indicated that matching manager characteristics (Gupta and Govindarajan 1984), reward systems (Lawler 1984; Kerr 1985), and development programs (Tichy et al. 1982) with strategies increase the probability that strategy will happen. The increased attention to HR practices in general has heightened awareness and development of strategic HR planning as a distinct research and application topic.[1]

However, for both scholars and practitioners, the rhetoric has surpassed action. More talk about what research might be done on linking strategy and HR plans has occurred than actual research. More discussions of what frameworks show the integration of strategy and HR planning have been proposed than actually implemented. The tendency for rhetoric may be due in part to the recency of the discipline. Most new disciplines require time to focus on key conceptual and practical issues. As current research to test linkages between strategy and HR planning expands, relevant applications may follow.

To facilitate that expansion, new questions about HR planning merit posing. Traditionally, the dominant questions underlying both research and application domains have emphasized *what*. What research frameworks define linkages between strategy and HR? What research designs and propositions may be generated to test the research frameworks? What have organizations done to implement a strategic HR planning focus? What applications have been more successful than others? *What* questions lead to description of research frameworks and application programs. To complement the existing descriptions, two new questions need posing: *why* and *how*.

Linkages between strategy and HR planning often focus on the *what*, not the

This article appears simultaneously in R. S. Schuler, S. A. Youngblood, and V. L. Huber (eds.) *Readings in Personnel and Human Resource Management* (3rd edition). West Publishing Company, 1987. Text was modified for Canadian readers.

why. Focusing exclusively on *what* may lead to action without substance. Many people or productivity improvement programs highlight *what* needs to be done without a full explanation of *why*. Setting goals of *X* number of quality circles, team building sessions, or participants in training may accomplish the *what*, or program goals; but without understanding the *why*, or program philosophy and theory, these programs may fade from fad to farce.

Posing and responding to *why* questions (e.g., why bridge strategy and HR planning?) explore how the bridge between strategy and HR planning builds organizational competitiveness (see Schuler and MacMillan 1985). For example, at Disneyworld in Florida, new employees undergo extensive socialization programs so that they learn to think and feel about Disneyworld like Walt Disney, the founder. For the Jungle Cruise ride nine pages of script must be memorized. Six of those nine pages review the material to repeat during the ride; three of the nine pages reviews the philosophy of the ride, and *why*. The emphasis on the *why* in Disneyworld's training activities has helped Disneyworld orient and commit new employees to Disneyworld's strategies.

For those interested in research on the strategy/HR planning linkages, *why* questions (e.g., why do linkages between strategy and HR planning lead to positive organizational outcomes?) explore the theoretical foundations of strategy/HR planning linkages. These *why* questions go beyond frameworks which show what HR practices relate to different strategies to explain why PHRM helps implement strategies and to integrate PHRM into broader theories of individuals and organizations. From posing *why* questions, researchers develop theory, or sets of interrelated propositions about strategy and PHRM.

How questions emphasize usefulness of strategic HR plans for both application and research domains. For application domains, *how* questions encourage the translation of frameworks into managerial behaviours. Often, managers know what needs doing, but not *how* to go about doing it. A football coach once asked for advice about how to win more football games. After extensive analysis of offensive and defensive tendencies, player strengths and weaknesses, and training schedules, the following advice was offered, "Coach, to win, your team must score more points". This response emphasized the *what* (score more), when the real challenge was *how*. Likewise, *how* questions force managers to explore practical ways to translate strategic HR planning frameworks to individual and organizational actions.

For research domains, *how* questions encourage exploration of research models, hypotheses, and designs to test theories of strategic HR planning. Posing *how* questions requires that scholars not only develop and espouse frameworks, but do research to test the frameworks. This reading complements other readings by explicitly exploring the *why* and *how* questions of strategic HR planning for both application and research domains. The goal of this reading is to encourage and direct application and research domains to pose and explore answers to *why* and *how* questions about strategic HR planning.

WHY DO STRATEGIC HR PLANNING?

Why questions address the underlying rationale, philosophy, and theory supporting linkages between strategy and HR planning. While responses to *why* questions may vary by practitioner or scholar, posing and responding to why questions leads to better understanding of strategic HR planning for both application and research domains.

Application Domain

In the application domain, *why* questions justify efforts to implement strategic HR planning. Two why questions may be posed: (1) Why are people so critical about organizations gaining a competitive advantage? and (2) Why do strategic HR planning efforts help organizations gain a competitive advantage?

Why are people so critical about organizations gaining a competitive advantage? Gaining a competitive advantage has become a major national and organizational challenge. Evidence indicates that productivity in Canada has been declining. Many scholars have suggested reasons for the Canadian productivity decline including government regulations and taxes, national industrial policies, technological deficiencies, inadequate support of education systems, and lack of cooperation between industry and government. An argument has been made that a leading cause for the decline in national productivity has been the ineffective management of people resources (Ouchi 1981; Thurow 1984; Dolan and Schuler 1987). Societies which have been gaining in productivity, such as Japan and Germany, better manage their people resource (Dolan and Schuler 1987, ch. 18).

In organizations, people affect gaining a competitive advantage from two perspectives. First, some organizations may view people as costs, and calculate and track people costs as a percent of the operating budget. In some organizations, the ability to reduce costs becomes a critical competitive advantage. Organizations which compete on price and have a high percent of their operating budget tied to people costs may easily document the importance of people to competitive advantage. Firms in the U.S. airline industry, since deregulation in 1978, have experienced tremendous competitive pressures. Firms which have entered the market and grown quickly since deregulation have found that the ability to control people costs derives a major competitive advantage. Major costs which affect price may be classified into equipment, maintenance, fuel, and people categories. Of these four, people costs become the major manageable cost category since equipment, maintenance, and fuel are relatively fixed costs which each competitor must bear equally. Donald Burr, founder of People Express, argued that by maintaining lower people costs through staying nonunion, paying lower salaries, having broad job categories, and working within teams People Express would gain a competitive advantage. Other airlines including New York Air, Continental, TWA, United, and Southwest Air have followed the lead of People Express and worked to gain a competitive advantage by cutting people costs. Organizations which compete on prices and in which people costs represent a major portion of operating budgets may view people as costs and justify the importance of people as a means to gain competitive advantages.

Second, some organizations may view people as resources which must be managed and modified to gain a competitive advantage. Competitive advantage may come to organizations through a number of strategies and organizational practices (Porter 1985). To a great extent, each strategy which leads to a competitive advantage depends on people who understand and implement the strategy. For example, technology may enhance competitive advantage because technological leaders move quickly down a learning curve, pioneer new products before competitors, and have first mover advantages in going to market with new products (Porter 1985, ch. 5). However, identifying technology as a competitive advantage may be like telling the coach to score more points; it highlights *what* needs to be done, not *how*.

To gain a competitive advantage through technological leadership requires efficient use of people and people management systems. Hiring individuals who have technological abilities, rewarding development of technology through bonuses and promotions, and offering training in implementation of technologies become the *hows* of using technology as a competitive advantage. A senior executive of the new Saturn division for General Motors commented that technology was not the key competitive advantage to building the new Saturn car as many observers presumed. He reasoned that the technology which would be used to build Saturn cars—including state-of-the-art robotics, inventory controls systems, and management information systems—was equally available to GM's competitors. He said that technology was a necessary, but not sufficient condition for GM's successful development of the Saturn car. The key ingredient, he argued, was the ability to hire and manage people who would understand and implement the technology. Likewise, other strategies to develop competitive advantage, quality, productivity, differentiation, mergers, and globalization require management of people to implement the strategy to gain a competitive advantage.

Why do strategic HR planning efforts help organizations gain a competitive advantage? Once the relationship between people and competitive advantage has been established, discussions about how to systematically manage people to attain the competitive advantage follow. Most managers acknowledge the critical value of people within an organization; fewer realize the alternative people management programs which may be used to systematically manage human resources for a competitive advantage. The design and delivery of people management programs becomes a primary agenda for strategic HR planning. People management programs exist within organizations as HR systems (e.g., selection, development, appraisal, rewards). Many efforts to do strategic PHRM attempt to integrate strategies with PHRM. Unfortunately, much of this work views the bridge between strategy and PHRM as the end, or goal, when the end might more effectively be building a competitive advantage, and the bridge between strategy and PHRM a means to that end. Strategic HR planning helps organizations acquire a competitive advantage, when linkages between strategy and PHRM serve as a means to the end of building competitive advantage, and when five transitions occur in thinking about strategic PHRM (Ulrich 1986a) (see Table 3–1).

First, often integrating strategy and PHRM comes through complex models which lay out decision paths or establish multidimensional matrices to describe how PHRM may match with strategies.

Table 3–1   Transitions From Strategic Human Resource Planning as Ends to Means

Strategic Human Resource Plans As

Ends	Means
Develops complex models	Uses simple, straightforward models
Leads to rhetoric	Leads to action
Emphasizes and measures success	Emphasizes and measures success with business performance
Directed by human resource	Directed by line managers
Provides answers	Asks questions

While development of such complex frameworks gives an overview and informs strategic PHRM, these frameworks may not lead to organizations being more competitive. When considering strategic HR planning as a means to building competitive organizations, HR plans need to be framed in simple, business language.

Second, a goal of integrating strategy and PHRM often encourages rhetoric to explain the complex frameworks. Such rhetoric leads to interesting discussions of ways in which PHRM corresponds with strategies. When strategic HR planning becomes a means to building competitive organizations, action replaces rhetoric. PHRM linkages with strategies focus more on resource allocation decisions than on rhetoric.

Third, when the goal is to integrate strategy and PHRM, administering, completing, and coordinating the completion of forms may become the focus of strategic PHRM. When strategic HR plans build competitive advantage, improved business performance, not completion of forms becomes the primary focus.

Fourth, using strategic HR planning to build a competitive advantage encourages a shared responsibility between operations and HR professionals. Distinctions between line and staff become blurred as both groups collaborate to develop HR plans which build competitive advantage.

Fifth, when strategic HR planning builds competitive advantage, answers to difficult HR issues may not be as forthcoming as the questions. Many people issues cannot be solved in the short term, so efforts which find simple solutions to difficult people questions may not build competitive advantage as much as continually posing challenging people questions.

Gaining a competitive advantage through people and strategic HR planning responds to the national pressure for increased competitiveness. With people representing costs and critical resources, and strategic HR planning programs representing the means to manage people resources, strategic HR plans may be drafted which provide organizations a competitive advantage. For the application domain, such competitive advantages respond to the question: *Why* do strategic HR planning?

Research Domain

In the research domain, *why* questions emphasize the philosophy and theory underlying strategic HR planning: Why does strategic HR planning explain individual and organizational behaviour? Over the past twenty years, transitions in strategic HR planning parallel transitions in the underlying theory. Three phases of the transition in strategic HR planning suggest responses to the above *why* question; each phase having a distinct concept, goal, metaphor, responsibility, and activities for HR professionals (see summary in Table 3–2).

Phase I: Regulation. Traditional HR planning frameworks emphasized the regulatory role of HR planning. HR plans existed to ensure compliance with governmental regulations such as employment equity, wage and salary, and labour laws. HR plans led to managerial behaviour and organizational systems which generated compliance with regulations. HR professionals assumed primary responsibility for the compliance by becoming the organizational police force. HR professionals translated governmental regulations into corporate policies, then enforced compliance to corporate policies. In the regulatory phase of HR planning, HR policies were seen as barriers to implementing strategic plans. This historical phase of HR planning, which predominated through the 1960s and 70s and persists in some organizations through the 1980s, responds to the *why* question by focusing on regulation and

Table 3-2   Transitions in Strategic HR Planning

Phase	Concept Guiding HR Planning	Goal of HR Planning	Metaphor of HR Planning	Responsibility for HR	Activities for HR Professionals
I	Regulation	Compliance with regulations and policies	Policeman	HR Professionals	Translate government and corporate regulations into corporate policies, e.g., EEO
II	Control	Match HR practices with strategies	Professional	HR and strategic planning staffs	Modify HR practices to implement strategies
III	Shape	Create a competitive advantage through HR	Partner	Operations managers and HR professionals	Create strategic unity throughout an organization by using HR practices to shape behaviour, information, and rewards

compliance as the primary explanation of individual and organizational behaviour. With regulation as the primary explanation, HR planning emphasized operational rather than strategic practices.

Phase II: Control. As interest in strategic PHRM expanded, the role of HR planning shifted from regulating behaviour to matching PHRM with strategies. In this phase, HR planning processes explained individual and organizational behaviour by establishing and maintaining control systems. Control occurred as HR plans directed individuals to behave in ways consistent with organizational strategies. Reward systems such as pay for performance or management by objectives were designed so that individuals behaved to accomplish organizational strategies. In addition to using reward practices to control behaviour, selection, development, and appraisal, practices were modified to match PHRM with strategic plans (Tichy et al. 1982). Using HR planning to ensure control, popular in the 1980s, has lead many organizations to identify HR practices which may be modified to make strategies happen. HR planning assumes a professional role, since it becomes involved in implementing strategic plans. HR professionals collaborate with strategic planners to form a team which has the capacity to implement strategic plans. In this phase, HR planning assumes a more strategic focus, with the emphasis on implementation. Individual and organizational behaviour coincides with controls established through HR practices. HR planning explains behaviour through establishment and monitoring of control systems.

Phase III: Shape. While many organizations continue to use HR planning as a means of controlling managerial behaviour, some organizations have begun to use strategic HR planning to create a competitive advantage. Creating a competitive advantage through HR plans requires that HR plans shape, not merely regulate or control, behaviour. Shaping behaviour implies that HR plans create strategic unity. Strategic unity occurs when stakeholders to an organization—including employees, customers, suppliers, financiers, unions, and distributors—agree on the philosophy, vision, and goals of an organization. From this agreement accrues a commitment of each stakeholder to move an organization to accomplish its strategic goals.

Brockbank and Ulrich (1986) discuss three means of attaining strategic unity: management of behaviour, information, and rewards. Strategic HR planning influences each of these three methods. Research on commitment (Salancik 1977) indicates that when individuals behave as if something is valued, they come to value the behaviour. Runners who spend hours preparing for a marathon come to value the exercise much more than observers who may not participate in or understand the reasons for running. In marketing, research indicates that after a product is purchased, the buyer comes to value the purchased product much more than alternative products, even though before the purchase the products had relatively equal value. Having invested time in buying the product, the purchaser becomes even more committed to the decision by valuing more highly the purchased product. In an organization, when stakeholders behave consistent with an organization's strategy, they become more likely to accept the strategy. HR planning may be used to elicit stakeholder behaviour consistent with an organization's strategy by ensuring that individuals spend time in appraisals setting standards and asking questions about organizational strategies or in promotion and staffing practices establishing hiring criteria consistent with strategic goals. Using HR plans to shape individual behaviour consistent with strategic goals, builds strategic unity which leads to a competitive advantage. Likewise, HR plans may be structured so that information which employees receive—through newsletters, bulletins, training programs, salary reviews—reinforces an organization's strategy, thus building strategic unity. Finally, reward systems may be explicitly designed to link rewards with organizational strategies. For example, a percent of managerial bonuses at Westinghouse Corporation depends on the performance of the organizational unit in which the manager worked over the previous five years, thus reinforcing managers who build long-term effectiveness rather than short-term profits.

Using strategic HR planning to create strategic unity explains individual and organizational behaviour by exploring processes which generate commitment. Commitment to organizational strategies—as engendered by strategic HR plans which modify behaviour, information and rewards—creates a strategic unity where stakeholders within an organization share philosophy, values, and goals. Shared values, in turn, may provide a competitive advantage as separate stakeholders collaborate to accomplish organizational strategies. HR professionals in this phase become strategic partners, not merely implementing, but also playing a primary role in shaping strategies. Organizations which have allocated resources to a core culture and create strategic unity exemplify use of HR planning as a means of building a competitive advantage. International Business Machines (IBM) has established a core culture based on values of excellence, customer service, and respect for employees. These values have been institutionalized through HR plans and practices such as rewards based on service and sales, development programs which review and espouse IBM core values, and hiring programs which admit only employees to share the core values (Sobel 1983). With employees experiencing strategic unity, firms like IBM have been able to gain a competitive advantage in distribution, research, technology, and marketing. In each of these areas, when employees understand *why* their work relates to overall corporate success, they increase commitment and dedication to achieve organizational goals, thus building a competitive advantage.

In the research domain, understanding *why* strategic HR planning affects individual and organizational behaviour offers theory to explain research findings. Rather than rely on anecdotal data of what some organizations have done, theoretical explanations describe *why* strategic HR planning builds a competitive advantage. As reviewed in Exhibit 3–1 theories of HR planning have transitioned through three phases, from a regulation focus on compliance, to a control focus on matching HR plans with strategies, to a shape focus on creating strategic unity and competitive advantage.

For both application and research domains, *why* questions explore the underlying rationale, philosophy, and theory supporting linkages between strategy and HR planning.

Exhibit 3–1   Subsets of Human Resource Activities

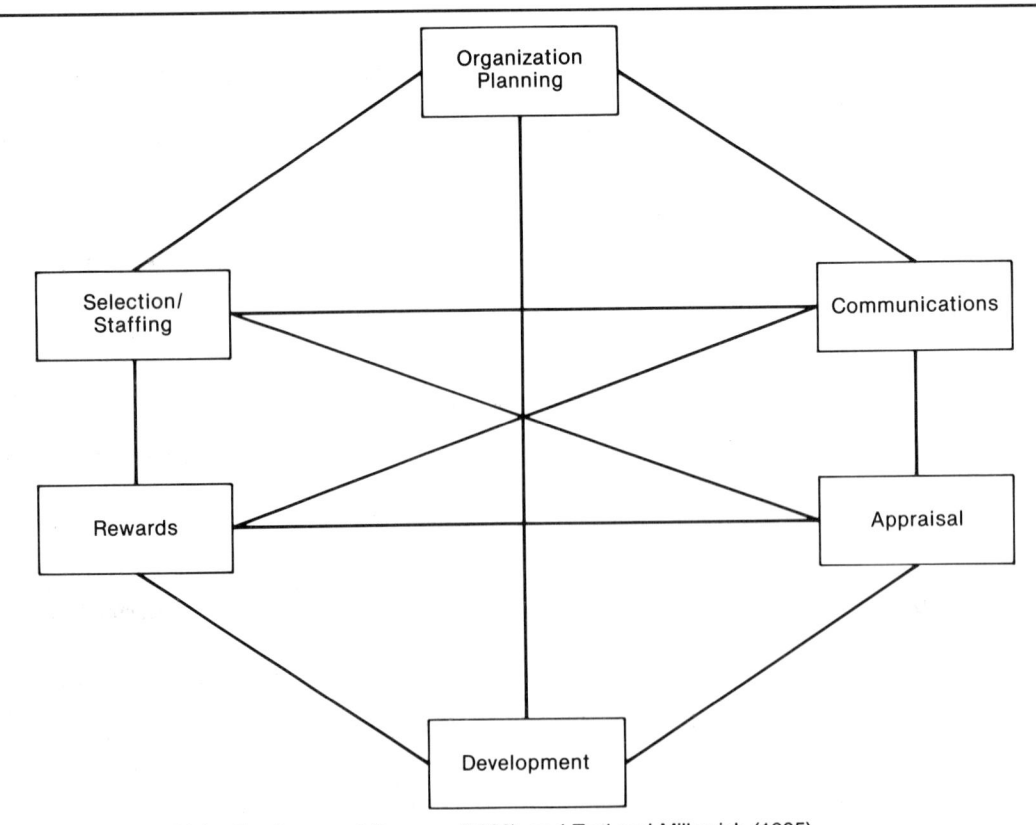

Based on work by Tichy, Fombrun, and Devanna (1982), and Tsui and Milkovich (1985).

HOW TO DO STRATEGIC HR PLANNING?

Why questions offer philosophical rationale; *how* questions lead to specific guidelines for implementation. Many strategic PHRM frameworks describe what needs to be done, but leave the challenge of application to the individual practitioner or scholar. Knowing *what* needs to be done may not lead to action; answering *how* questions offers guidelines for application and research domains.

Application Domain

In the application domain, *how* questions translate strategic HR planning frameworks into managerial actions. Managerial actions relative to strategic HR planning may be divided in content and process issues. Content actions address the questions: How can strategic HR plans be prepared to ensure that issues in the plan build competitive advantage? The content, or substance, or plan needs to be such that it includes key choices which build competitive advantage. Process action addresses the question: How can strategic HR plans be prepared to ensure that the act of preparing the plans focuses attention and generates commitment to the competitive advantage? By responding to these two questions, we address *how* strategic HR plans build competitive advantage.

Content Actions: How can strategic HR plans be prepared to ensure that issues in the plan build competitive advantage? Strategic HR plans apply to both operational units and HR departments. Operational units which prepare strategic plans may build competitive advantage by adding a section dedicated to strategic human resources to existing strategic plans. The HR section of a strategic plan ensures that human resource factors both shape and implement the strategy. At IBM, strategic plans for each operational unit must include a section dealing with human resource issues. This section of the strategic plan may help shape the content of the plan, when, for example, a particular competitive strategy may be more successful given existing human resources. For example, rather than reduce a technical work force when sales in a product line decline, the technical work force may be redeployed to a new product line. Recognizing the technical skills within the existing work force may influence the development of new products. For HR departments, strategic HR plans clarify a vision, define goals, organize, and commit the department to building a competitive advantage. For both operational units and HR departments, strategic HR plans respond to *how* to build competitive advantage when characterized by the following five components.

Encompass a Large Variety of HR Activities. Generally, when companies work on HR plans, the energy focuses on one aspect of human resources, such as succession, career development, markov chain, forecasting, or skill inventory planning (Butensky and Harari 1983). Strategic HR plans may include a wider array of human resource activities. Frameworks which categorize PHRM practices classify HR practices into similar HR systems (Tichy et al. 1982; Tsui and Milkovich 1985). Based on these typologies, six HR systems may be identified, each of which merits inclusion in building a strategic HR plan leading to competitive advantage.[2]

Organization planning. Organization planning explores the alternative ways work may be organized to accomplish strategic goals. Alternative organization types such as functional, division, product, or matrix organization designs may be matched with strategies (Galbraith 1977). In addition to determining the organization design, organization planning might address such issues as:

——What, if any, jobs, titles, or levels might be added, deleted, or modified to create a competitive advantage for the organization? For example, organizations where new product development becomes the key ingredient for competitive success may want to consider adding jobs in other areas.

——What reporting relationships might be modified to create a competitive advantage? For example, critical departments may need to report more directly to senior management, or having a sales and marketing department report through one manager may increase discussion between the departments which may build competitive advantage.

——Where should primary responsibility for accomplishing work be assigned? Work in organizations may be performed at corporate, group, division, or business units levels. Choices about where to allocate primary responsibility for work may affect competitive advantage.

——What ad hoc work groups (e.g., quality circles, task forces, etc.) may be organized to develop a competitive advantage?

Considering these organization planning issues and ensuring that organization plans accomplish strategies may build a competitive advantage.

Selection/staffing. Selection and staffing practices may also be included in preparing strategic HR plans. Many frameworks recommend matches between managerial characteristics and organizational strategies (Gupta 1984; Olian 1984; Szilagyi and Schweiger 1984). Two sets of selection and staffing issues need to be considered: who is hired and who is promoted. In hiring new employees, a number of choices must be considered including:

——What skill level to hire? Choices may be made about hiring employees who already have skills versus hiring new college graduates. This choice depends in part on the time frame of the organization's strategies and resources available to the organization to pay for existing skills. This issue has played a major role in American sports as choices are made to build through farm systems or buy talent through free agency.

——Who to involve in the hiring process? At times, hiring occurs by HR professionals enacting requests from diverse operational groups. Other options exist. At Hewlett-Packard, engineers work in short-term assignments as college recruiters of new engineers. This not only helps recruit new engineers, it also commits employed engineers because the engineers become representatives of the company on the college campuses, and their behaviour reinforces their acceptance of the company values.

——What types of skills to hire, specialists or generalists? Some organizations focus new hiring on specialists who will fill a specific need. Other organizations search for generalists who will fit into the organization and fill into a number of positions over time. Along the continuum anchored by specialists and generalists, choices may be made to hire employees who build competitive advantage. A baseball team, for example, with twenty-four players requires that some employees be specialists who play few positions (pitchers, catchers, other starting players); other employees must fill a generalist role and be a utility infielder, able to play a number of positions. Having exclusively specialists or generalists would weaken a baseball team's ability to compete over an entire season. Likewise, organizations must balance specialists and generalists in hiring decisions.

Once employees are hired, decisions about who to promote must be considered. To tie promotion decisions to competitive advantage, choices must be made about:

——What ratio of insiders to outsiders should be promoted? Promotion practices may feature exclusively insider promotions. Such practices may add to internal morale, but may hinder an organization's competitiveness. For example, a United States firm with ninety-five percent of its sales within the United States decided to enter the global market. When selecting an individual to direct the international operations, the firm maintained its policy of promotion from within and promoted a candidate who had succeeded in many corporate functions, but had no experience in international operations. This firm may have been able to compete in international markets more quickly had it hired an outsider to head the international function.

——What career paths are followed within the organization? Some organizations elect to promote within a single career path; others systematically encourage promotions across functional lines. Promoting within a career track may develop better specialists; movement across functional areas may develop better generalists. Decisions about movement within or across functional areas may be considered as replacement plans are made.

——Who becomes corporate versus division property? The choice of being corporate or division property underlies the philosophy of many succession plans. Some organizations allow divisions to control careers of all employees within the division; others state that above a certain level, employees become corporate property, thus they may be moved according to corporate succession plans.

These questions about who to hire and who to promote affect an organization's competitive advantage. In preparing strategic HR plans for either operational units or HR departments, these issues merit discussion.

Reward Systems. Research has indicated that individuals generally do what they are rewarded for (Lawler 1984; Kerr 1985). Strategic HR plans analyse and review options for using reward systems to direct employee behaviour. A number of choices about how rewards may be used to gain a competitive advantage exist:

——How can both financial and non-financial rewards be used to gain a competitive edge? Generally, when rewards are considered, the focus rests exclusively on compensation. While compensation choices exist (see the following), so also do choices of non-financial rewards. Nonfinancial rewards might include office space, titles, or other working conditions. While often discounted, the symbolic value of these factors influences behaviour. Nonfinancial rewards might also include autonomy, challenging work, or the work itself. Creatively adding these nonfinancial rewards into a strategic HR plan expands reward options beyond financial compensation and, in many cases, may influence behaviour more than compensation.

—How to set criteria for compensation? Decisions about how much to pay may be derived from many criteria, including position or time in the organization, performance according to standards, or job skills. Each option might induce individual behaviour consistent with strategic goals.

—How to allocate compensation? Financial compensation may come in a variety of forms, including base salary, incentives based on annual performance, incentives based on long-term performance, stock options, or deferred salary. Again, choices on how to allocate compensation may instill a competitive advantage. Small firms with high growth strategies often use the lure of equity as an incentive to motivate employees and to gain a competitive advantage.

—How to determine and distribute benefits? Benefits, representing up to forty percent of salary, may be seen as a right of employment or as a tool to increase employee commitment and organizational competitiveness. Providing employees options for benefit packages may instill within employee's a sense of autonomy and a greater dedication toward an organization's strategies.

—How open to be with the salary system? Public organizations often must be open with salary structures, where all salaries are known. Private organizations have the choice of being open or closed. Open salaries may be used to motivate employees by everyone knowing the individuals who are financially compensated and learning from this information what behaviours are encouraged.

In preparing strategic HR plans, choices exist about financial and nonfinancial rewards. Making these choices influences individual behaviour which in turn influences an organization's competitiveness.

Development Systems. Development programs may be tools to gain a competitive advantage. Development includes both formal training and on-the-job development activities. In preparing strategic HR plans, a number of choices about development programs may be made:

—Who to include in a formal development program? Development programs may include individuals at all levels of the organization. Development programs may be used to orient new employees, to provide technical training for specialists, to offer managerial skills for managers, and to generate a strategic perspective for executives.

—What outcomes should result from the development program? Development programs may serve a variety of outcomes, depending on who participates. Development programs may be designed to build conceptual understanding of organizational goals and practices, learn managerial and/or technical skills necessary for organizational success, build team unity among participants, solve on-going business problems, or create a strategic focus for the organization. As development programs move from the individual cognitive to organizational strategic purposes, more efforts must be spent linking off-site development programs with ongoing work challenges. Development programs which emphasize the strategic focus of an organization examine consequences of the program in a longer time frame than programs emphasizing cognitive or skill development.

—Who to use in designing and delivering the development program? A number of choices exist in creating a development program. At one extreme, organizations may rely exclusively on sending participants to outside programs. At the other extreme, organizations may design and deliver programs with no outside support. Between these extremes are choices about using outside versus inside faculty, involving line managers as presenters, and establishing advisory groups to oversee the program.

—How to use nontraining activities as development programs? Individual counseling, job rotation, task force assignments, cross-functional transfers, and special project assignments (for example presenting a speech about company goals to an outside group) may all serve as development programs. Systematically designing and managing these nontraining development activities may play a major role in strategic HR plans.

Development programs receive a great deal of attention at many companies. In 1985, IBM spent approximately $500 million on training programs, which represented approximately one percent of the corporation's total sales volume. This expense was not to make employees feel good about their jobs, but to ensure that employees at all levels of IBM possessed the technical, conceptual, managerial, and executive skills to keep IBM ahead of domestic and foreign competition. Jack Welch, chairman of General Electric Corporation (GE), uses GE's executive training facility as a platform to communicate his vision and goals for the corporation. He meets often with participants to share his ideology and respond to questions. Through the development programs, he is able to personally communicate with large numbers of employees. Development programs may play a central role in creating strategic HR plans.

Appraisal Systems. Appraisal systems may be used to build a competitive advantage. At the most generic level, appraisal systems establish standards and offer feedback on performance. In dealing with standards and feedback, many key choices may be considered as components of strategic HR plans:

—What criteria may be used to establish standards? Standards for individual performance may be set according to outcomes (accomplishing an objective) or behaviours (doing the right things). Ideally, employees attain outcomes and practice the right behaviours, but at times choices may exist where employees attain outcomes, but do not follow prescribed behavioural patterns (meeting objectives, but always coming late to work); or, employees may follow prescribed behavioural patterns, but not attain desired results (always working hard and doing what is expected, but not reaching established objective). Criteria for both outcomes and behaviours may be short or long term. In these cases, choices about criteria may be made and communicated through a strategic HR plan.

—How often are appraisals given? Feedback occurring from a formal appraisal which surprises an employee indicates that insufficient feedback is being given. Most parents understand that being limited to annual performance reviews with children would be disastrous, yet managers may fall into the trap of deciding to have a formal feedback session when the earth rotates 360 degrees around the sun. Criteria other than rotation around the sun might appropriately govern feedback which comes from appraisals.

——How do appraisals link with other HR systems? Appraisals may link with reward systems (pay for performance) or with development systems (identify needed development). Choosing to link appraisals with these systems requires that appraisals be used honestly and consistently.

Appraisal systems are often the black hole of HR systems. Resources are consumed revising and updating performance appraisal forms in search of an ideal appraisal. More realistically, appraisals which build a competitive advantage emphasize the process of establishing standards and giving feedback, not the content of the forms. Strategic HR plans use appraisal systems to identify standards which may be added, deleted, or modified so that individual behaviours are directed toward building a competitive advantage.

Communication Programs. As strategic HR plans are established, employees throughout an organization deserve continual access to and understanding of *why* programs exist. Communication programs deal with how to disseminate information, including who presents the information, how it is presented, when it is presented, and what is presented. Strategic HR plans which build a competitive advantage specify communication programs which disseminate information to ensure that employees know not only what changes are occurring, but why.

Strategic HR planning often equates with only one of the six HR systems in Exhibit 3–1. Relying on only one of the six HR systems may limit HR's contribution to competitive advantage. A strategic HR plan assesses and upgrades practices within each of the six systems.

Remain Simple. Strategic HR plans become more effective when they synthesize the complex HR issues reviewed above into relatively simple action plans. One organization had a philosophy of "dummy it down" when drafting HR plans and kept plans to a maximum of two pages. The rationale for this philosophy was that the organization could probably not do all the nice things which had to be done. Forcing strategic HR plans into simple formats requires prioritization. When high priority items are identified, actions may be taken to resolve those high priority items. Another organization prioritizes two HR issues each year. Buy focusing on only two issues a year, executives require that resolutions to each of the two issues occur during the year. Their position is that not everything which needs to be can be done with equal rigor, so they prioritize those key issues which must be managed and ensure that those priority issues are resolved.

Simplicity involves length, it also involves presentation and language. Like all professions, HR is mired in jargon. When HR plans use jargon, the plans become useful for only a limited audience. Simple language encourages application. When the content of strategic HR plans remains simple, plans are more likely to be used.

Identify Specific HR Activities Which May Be Used to Accomplish Strategies. Strategic HR plans offer decision makers menus of HR practices and the implications of those choices (Schuler 1987). The more specific the practices in an HR plan, and the more tightly the linkage between HR practices and strategies, the more likely the HR practices will be implemented. The systems and choices reviewed above identify specific HR practices which might be implemented to accomplish a particular strategy.

Rely on Business Rationale and Language. Strategic HR plans justify HR practices based on business logic, generally financial data. Costs of adding to or detracting from the work force, of designing and delivering a training program, of modifying benefit packages, of changing compensation programs, or of modifying corporate personal policies (e.g., relocation) may be identified and calculated. With financial information about HR practices, decision makers may make cost/benefit analyses to decide which HR practices lead to a competitive advantage.

Upjohn Corporation quantifies estimated costs and benefits of hiring professional employees. When a manager needs a new hire, the manager working with an HR professional performs a job description to specify the duties of the new position. Then, the cost of the new hire is calculated for one, three, and five years. In this calculation are assumptions about direct costs of salary and benefits and indirect costs of training time, relocation costs, and support costs (secretary, office space, etc.). On the other side of the ledger, the manager requesting the position must identify potential financial benefits of the new position (time savings, ability to meet goals more effectively). These costs and benefit figures must be reviewed by three layers of management before approval of new hires. By relying on business logic and quantifying HR costs, HR plans become meaningful for operations managers.

Raise More Questions. Strategic HR plans depend heavily on discussions of important questions. Ensuring that the right questions are posed and discussed may allow answers to be generated which build competitive advantage. By creating HR plans which raise critical questions, in lieu of providing answers to all the choices reviewed previously forces discussions which may lead to more informed HR decisions. There are few right or wrong answers for most PHRM issues. What works in one setting may not apply equally to other settings. Emphasis on questions rather than answers maintains the flexibility necessary for building a competitive advantage through HR plans.

Based on these five practices, the content of strategic HR plans may vary dramatically from traditional HR plans. Strategic HR plans which build a competitive advantage include more than staffing or replacement plans, prioritize key issues, link directly to strategic plans, communicate in business language, and raise more questions than answers.

Process Actions: How can strategic HR plans be prepared to ensure that the act of preparing the plans focuses attention and generates commitment to competitive advantage? Strategic HR plans require a different process than traditional HR plans where an HR planning staff assesses environmental and organizational strengths, weaknesses, opportunities, and threats, and then devises strategies to respond to these trends. Managing the process of creating and implementing an HR plan becomes a primary predictor of how likely the plan will be implemented. When emphasizing the process of designing strategic HR plans, four practices merit consideration.

Redefine the Role of HR Planners. HR planners assume new roles as process managers when designing strategic HR plans which build a competitive advantage. Rather than be a part of the strategic planning process, they become strategic partners. As strategic partners, they spend time learning and understanding technical, organizational, and strategic plans. As they come to understand these plans, they begin to behave as strategic partners by spending more time with line and other staff executives, by assessing critical human resource issues and their relationship to strategy, and by collecting and disseminating HR information which may affect an organization's competitiveness (Parker and Ulrich 1986).

As strategic partners, HR planners also play a more proactive role by ensuring that meetings to develop HR plans include key decision makers throughout the organization, by orchestrating meetings to ensure that agendas force discussion and resolution of priority issues, by facilitating involvement in the planning process to generate commitment to plans from important political players, by sharing information about plans with key stakeholders, by managing an iterative process of revising an HR plan to meet specific business needs, and by clarifying and communicating specifically how HR plans build a competitive advantage. HR planners assuming this role spend equal time managing the process of creating, communicating, and generating commitment to the plan, as they do on assuring that the content of the plan matches strategic needs.

Redefine the Role of Users of The HR Plan. Users of an HR plan—including general managers and directors of engineering, marketing, manufacturing, and other functions—assume new roles in the process of developing strategic HR plans. Rather than passively wait for plans to emerge from an HR department, these users become active participants in conceiving, formulating, drafting, and implementing HR plans.

Early involvement in the human resource planning process ensures that users of HR plans understand why and how human resource practices directly influence business success. Once users become involved, they need role clarity to shape strategic HR plans. As discussed above, strategic HR plans must be broad, simple, specific, business-justified, and raise more questions than answers. HR planners provide users frameworks for assessing how HR practices may be modified to attain strategic goals. Based on the six HR systems reviewed in Exhibit 3–1, users may be encouraged to ensure that for each objective in a strategic plan HR practices be formed to help reach the strategic objective. This process may be accomplished by users learning to ask HR questions for each strategic objective. The questions which users might ask to ensure that competitive HR plans exist include:

——*Organization Planning:* To reach the strategic objective, what organization design needs to be in a place in the division or function?

——*Selection/Staffing:* To reach the strategic objective, what types of people with what types of skills need to be in which jobs in the organization?

——*Appraisal:* To reach the strategic objective, what types of performance review information needs to be monitored and communicated with employees?

——*Rewards:* To reach the strategic objective, what reward systems need to be in place to motivate employee performance toward strategic goals?

——*Development:* To reach the strategic objective, what types of development programs need to be in place to prepare employees with adequate skills?

——*Communication:* To reach the strategic objective, what communications need to occur within the organization?

As these six questions are raised and discussed with each strategic objective, users become sensitive to HR practices which may be modified to create a competitive advantage. By working through these straightforward, but challenging questions, users also become invested in shaping the essential elements of a strategic HR plan.

After discussing the questions and reaching consensus on *how* to use HR plans to build competitiveness, users assume the role of doers. Within divisions or functions, users ensure that necessary HR practices are initiated, implemented, and monitored. As users assume increased responsibility for creating, communicating, and generating commitment to human resource plans, they implement plans to build a competitive advantage.

The process of developing and implementing strategic HR plans requires a great deal of attention from HR planners and users. As HR planners and users accept and act on revised roles, they collaborate to design and deliver strategic HR plans.

Share Information With Public Commitments. To focus attention and generate commitment to strategic HR plans, information about the HR plan needs to be shared. Once the plan is prepared, a wide dissemination of the plan allows many individuals to review the plan. These individuals begin to expect that actions suggested by the plan will occur. These expectations increase pressure for actions to occur based on the plan.

In addition, public commitments by operation and HR managers increases the probability that attention and commitment to the plan will translate the plan from concept to action. In one organization, an HR Planner who had received agreement from the CEO about the HR plan realized that public commitment from the CEO would be critical to acceptance and implementation of the plan. To create an image of public commitment by the CEO, the HR planner made sure that CEO speeches, as transmitted through videos and newsletters, referred to the importance of the HR plan. In addition, when the HR planner learned that the CEO was making a world-wide tour, the HR planner requested that the CEO ask two questions of each country manager: (1) How effectively was the manager deploying the corporation's HR assets? (2) How could the country manager use the corporation's HR practices, specifically development and appraisal, to build a competitive advantage within the country. During the CEO's world-wide tour, he met with many country managers and posed these two questions. Two months later, when the HR planner approached each country manager about using HR as a competitive advantage, he received very favourable receptions. This HR planner recognized the importance of public commitments by senior operations executives. Realizing this, he devised strategies to evoke the public commitments. Sharing information and evoking public commitments to HR plans increases the probability that strategic HR plans become action oriented.

Ensure Measurement and Assessment of HR Effectiveness. Including ways to measure HR effectiveness in strategic HR plans forces the plan to become a reality. Four benefits come from measuring HR effectiveness. First, measurement justifies the value of HR practices since relationships between HR practices and organizational competitiveness may be assessed. Second, measurement focuses attention on key HR practices by identifying which HR practices build a competitive advantage. Third, measurement assigns responsibility for making HR practices a reality. Fourth, with clear measures of effectiveness and responsibility, measurement may generate commitment to implementing PHRM. Often measures of HR effectiveness rest on intuition rather than data because approaches to HR measurement are not clearly understood. Three approaches to measuring HR effectiveness exist: stakeholder, index, relationship (Ulrich 1986b).

Stakeholder approaches to measuring HR effectiveness rely on perceptions of users to assess the value of HR practices. By surveying or interviewing users, HR practices which most favourably build a competitive advantage may be identified and emphasized. Also, by involving stakeholders in assessment of HR practices, stakeholders become more aware of and committed to implementing HR practices.

Index approaches to measuring HR effectiveness translate HR practices into financial indices. These indices indicate the costs and benefits of HR practices such as turnover, counseling, development, compensation programs, and internal versus external promotions. For each HR practice, direct and indirect costs may be calculated and equations devised to create indices which measure HR effectiveness. Monitoring these indices assigns responsibility for HR practices and ensures that HR practices build toward a competitive advantage.

Relationship approaches measure HR effectiveness by showing how HR practices relate to strategies. Organizations which accomplish strategies may engage in different HR practices than organizations which fail to accomplish their strategies. Identifying which HR practices coincide with organizations that accomplish strategies may lead to better understanding of relationships between strategies and HR practices. Relationship approaches have not been as widely used as stakeholder and index approaches, but efforts to measure HR effectiveness through assessing relationships exist (Ulrich et al. 1984; Ulrich 1986b).

Each of these three approaches to measuring HR effectiveness justified the value of HR practices for gaining a competitive advantage. When efforts to measure HR effectiveness are included in strategic HR plans, the plans receive more individual attention because plan proposals are assessed and individuals are responsible for accomplishing the stated objectives.

Managing the process of preparing strategic HR plans requires new roles for HR professionals and users of HR plans, encourages public sharing of information, and forces assessment of HR effectiveness to monitor success. Managing these processes responds to the *how* question and moves from concepts about strategic HR plans to implementation.

Research Domain

In the research domain, *how* questions translate theory into research designs and analyses. Only recently have research efforts on strategic HR planning emerged (Schuler 1987; Smith-Cooke and Ferris 1986). These efforts go beyond suggesting that strategic HR planning may be important and identify specific hypotheses which test the relationships. The paucity of research may exist for a number of reasons. First, as discussed previously, a theory which explains why strategic HR planning works has been lacking. The summary in Table 3-2 suggests phases of theoretical development which may now be used to generate specific hypotheses. Lacking theory, approaches to strategic HR planning have emphasized frameworks integrating strategy and HR practices without suggesting specific hypotheses and research models. Work by Schuler (1987) begins to offer hypotheses which assess linkages between strategy and HR practices.

Second, research may be lacking due to insufficient measures of strategy and HR practices. Before research tests relationships between strategy and HR practices, explicit measures of strategy and HR practices must be established. These measures emerge from the theory and identify types of strategies and HR practices and the relationships between them.

Third, after measures of strategy and HR practices are prepared, difficulties arise in selecting organizational units of analysis. Research may be lacking because collecting data from many organizational units requires extensive time and resources. Fourth, a difficulty exists in collecting the types of data required by strategic HR research. Data needs to be collected on strategies, HR practices, and measures of organizational effectiveness. This requires involvement of many individuals within an organization; it also requires that organizations divulge confidential information, for example, strategies or financial information.

These four reasons indicate the conceptual and practical barriers to research on strategic HR planning. Overcoming these barriers begins with a clear understanding of theory underlying strategic HR planning. This reading begins that effort. Building on theory, four steps may generate research models, designs, and assessments of strategic HR planning.

Step 1: Define Variables and Models to Test Variables. Three sets of variables need to be defined to research strategic HR planning. First, typologies of strategies need to be defined. Schuler (1987), building on work by Gerstein and Reisman (1983), identifies five strategic types. Other strategy researchers identify four generic strategies: cost leadership, cost focus, differentiation, and differentiation focus (Porter 1985). Regardless of the typology used, a strategic typology identifies strategic positions and choices organizations make to respond to competitive pressures.

Second, typologies of HR systems and alternative HR practices within each HR system need to be identified. Exhibit 3-1 presents a typology of HR systems. Within each system, specific HR practices or choices may be specified. Third, typologies of organizational outcomes need to be identified. These typologies may include traditional financial outcomes (e.g., return on investment, liquidity or return on assets) and nonfinancial outcomes (e.g., innovation or productivity).

After typologies of strategies, HR systems and practices, and organizational outcomes are specified, models can be derived which suggest hypotheses between strategies, HR systems and practices, and organizational outcomes. Schuler (1987) suggests a series of propositions about relationships between strategy types and HR choices. Two modeling approaches may be used to explore relationships among strategies, HR systems and practices, and organizational outcomes. First, regression models may be developed to predict how changes in strategies or organizational outcomes may be predicted by HR systems and practices. These models analyse how the variance in strategies or organizational outcomes may be explained by HR systems and practices. For example, a model predicting an organizational outcome or strategy might be:

$$\hat{y} = x_1\beta_1 + x_2\beta_2 + x_3\beta_3 + x_4\beta_4 + \text{error}$$

where $\hat{y}$ refers to the outcome of interest, either an organizational outcome or a strategy, and x_1 refers to selection practices, x_2 refers to reward practices, x_3 refers to appraisal practices, and x_4 refers to development practices.

This type of model partitions the variance in the outcome variable according to the differing influences of the predictor variables. A more elaborate model of the same genre might include strategic types as a set of predictors. With this model, the relative impact of strategic types versus HR practices on organizational outcomes could be assessed.

Second, models may identify matches between strategic types and HR practices. Schuler's (1987) propositions represent this type of model. These models hypothesize matches between strategic types and HR practices. When appropriate matches occur, organizational outcomes should be positive; when mismatches occur, outcomes would be less positive. Either type of modeling offers the first step of transitioning between theory and research.

Step 2: Define Appropriate Unit of Analysis. After variables and models are specified, decisions about the organizational level of analysis for data collection must be made. These decisions are not simple. Many organizational units must be included in a data collection so that refined statistical analysis of the proposed models may occur. Choices exist about collecting information on variables at an organization or organizational unit level of analysis. Using the organization as the unit of analysis may be appropriate with smaller organizations where one predominant strategy exists for the entire organization. For larger organizations with more than one strategy, the unit of analysis needs to occur at an organizational level where strategies differ. For example, aggregating General Electric's diversified business into one unit of analysis would mask their distinct strategies and HR practices. For diversified organizations, information on strategic type, HR practices, and outcomes needs to be collected at an organizational unit of analysis. An organizational unit may be characterized by having a distinct strategy, unique set of customers and competitors, dedicated support staff who work for the organizational unit, and a profit center mentality where organizational outcomes are aggregated. Organizational units are often labeled division or business units.

In addition, information also needs to be collected by industry. Different industries have different requirements of HR practices. Some industries are heavily people intensive (e.g., banking, retail, and other service industries), others are capital intensive (e.g., utility or oil industries). The information that is collected by industry helps to control people practices, which may differ by industry.

Step 3: Collect Data on Strategies, HR Practices, and Organizational Outcomes For Organizational Units. Having specified variables and identified appropriate units of analysis, data may be collected on strategic types, HR practices, and organizational outcomes. Collecting this information involves a number of functional areas within an organizational unit. Strategic planners may provide strategic position and choice data; HR professionals may provide information about HR practices; and financial staffs may provide data on organizational outcomes. Collaboration among these diverse groups requires coordination to ensure that each group provides the necessary information. In addition, in collecting data, it is important to manage the highly confidential nature of the information collected. Much of the strategic type and financial data, particularly when collected at an organizational unit level, are proprietary. Researchers must adhere to strict standards of confidentiality to ensure that proprietary information remains proprietary.

Collecting such complex data consumes many resources. It requires that researchers have access to many organizational units; it requires that researchers communicate research goals to diverse functional groups within an organization; it requires that researchers make extensive commitments to guarding proprietary information. However, as practical research issues are faced and resolved, data collection may occur to create data bases of strategy, HR, and outcome variables.

Step 4: Analyse Results of Data. Analysis follows data collection. If variables are measured and models specified accurately, data analysis follows the logic proposed by the models and hypotheses. To fully assess complex relationships between strategic types, HR practices, and organizational outcomes requires large data bases with many organizational units. Currently, such data bases do not exist and will probably require collaboration among many researchers to collect data which assess strategic HR plans.

Following these four steps will not ensure that research on strategic HR planning occurs, but these four steps respond to the *how* question. Research which tests complex relationships among strategic types, HR practices, and organizational outcomes has not occurred for good reasons. However, as beginning efforts (Schuler 1986; Ulrich et al. 1984; Smith-Cooke and Ferris 1986) continue, research strategies may lead to better explanations of how strategic HR plans build a competitive advantage.

CONCLUSION

This reading asks two simple questions about strategic HR plans: why and how. Within both application and research domains, the responses to these two questions may further understanding of strategic HR planning. Responses to these two questions move the discipline beyond *what* to do, to expanded understanding of *why* strategic HR plans build organizational competitiveness, and *how* to prepare and research strategic HR plans. This reading begins an effort which merits further discussion and elaboration. As such discussions occur, strategic HR plans may become primary levers for building an organization's competitive advantage.

Endnotes

1. In the reading, a distinction is made between HR systems, HR practices, and human resource management. HR systems refers to sets of practices. Exhibit 3–1 identifies six HR systems. Within each HR system exist a number of HR practices. When referring to both systems and practices, the term PHRM will be used.

2. For each of the six HR systems, we identify choices to consider in creating strategic HR plans. Schuler (1986) reviews menus of similar choices available to HR professionals. The author of this reading has prepared the choices reviewed in this reading into a decision tree which reviews step-by-step what HR practices to consider in building a competitive advantage. This decision guide is available from the author on request.

References

Brockbank, W. and D. Ulrich. 1986. Strategic unit: A theory of strategy implementation. Working paper, University of Michigan.

Cameron, K. and D. Ulrich. 1986. "Transformational leadership in colleges and universities." In *Higher education: Handbook of theory and research*. Vol. 2. Edited by J. Smart. New York: Agathon Publishing.

Butensky, C. and O. Harari. 1983. Models vs. reality: An analysis of twelve human resource planning systems. *Human Resource Planning*, 11–12.

Dolan, S. L. and Schuler R. S., *Personnel and Human Resource Management in Canada*. St. Paul: West Publishing Co. 1987.

Dyer, L. 1984a. Linking human resource and business strategies. *Human Resource Planning*, 79–84.

Dyer, L. 1984b. Studying human resource strategy: An approach and an agenda. *Industrial and Labor Relations Review* 23: 156–69.

Galbraith, J. 1977. *Organization Design*. Reading, Mass.: Addison-Wesley.

Gerstein, M. and H. Reisman. 1983. Strategic selection: Matching executives to business conditions. *Sloan Management Review* (Winter): 33–49.

Gupta, A. K. 1984. Contingency linkages between strategy and general manager characteristics: A conceptual examination. *Academy of Management Review* 9:399–412.

Gupta, A. K. and V. Govindarajan. 1984. Business unit strategy, managerial characteristics, and business unit effectiveness at strategy implementation. *Academy of Management Journal* 9:25–41.

Kerr, J. L. 1985. Diversification strategies and managerial rewards: An empirical study. *Academy of Management Journal* 28: 155–179.

Lawler, E. E. 1984. "The strategic design of reward systems." In *Readings in personnel and human resource management*. 2d ed., edited by R. S. Schuler and S. A. Youngblood, 253–69. St. Paul: West Publishing.

Mahler, W. R. and R. Gaines, Jr. 1984. *Succession planning in leading companies*. Midland, New Jersey: Mahler Publishing Company.

Olian, J. D. and S. L. Rynes. 1984. Organizational staffing: Integrating practice with strategy. *Industrial Relations* 23:170–83.

Ouchi, W. G. 1981. *Theory Z*. New York: Addison Wesley.

Parker, D. and D. Ulrich. 1986. From human resource strategies to strategic human resources. Working paper, University of Michigan, Graduate School of Business.

Porter, M. E. 1985. *Competitive advantage: Creating and sustaining superior performance*. New York: Free Press.

Salancik, G. 1977. "Commitment and the control of organizational behavior and belief." In *New directions in organizational behavior*, edited by B. M. Staw and G. R. Salancik. Chicago: St. Clair Press.

Schuler, R. 1987. "Personnel and human resource management: choices and organization strategy." In Canadian *Readings in personnel and human resource management*. Edited by S. L. Dolan and R. S. Schuler. St. Paul: West Publishing, 1987.

Schuler, R. and I. C. MacMillan. 1984. Gaining competitive advantage through human resource management practices. *Human Resource Management* 23(3):241–55.

Smith-Cooke, D. and G. Ferris. 1986. Strategic human resource management and firms effectiveness in industries experiencing decline. *Human Resource Management* 25(3).

Sobel, R. 1983. *IBM: Colossus in Transition*. New York: Bantam Books.

Szilagyi, A. A. and D. M. Schweiger. 1984. Matching managers to strategies: A review and suggested framework. *Academy of Management Review* 9:626–37.

Thurow, L. 1984. Revitalizing American Industry: Managing in a competitive world economy. *California Management Review* 28(9): 9–41.

Tichy, N., C. Fombrun, and M. A. Devanna. 1982. Strategic human resource management. *Sloan Management Review* (Winter): 47–61.

Tsui, A. and G. Milkovich. 1985. Dimensions of personnel department activities: An empirical study. Paper presented at Academy of Management.

Ulrich, D., A. Geller, and G. DeSouza. 1984. A strategy, structure, human resource database: OASIS. *Human Resource Management* 23(1) (Spring): 77–90.

Ulrich, D. 1986a. Human resource planning as a competitive edge. *Human Resource Planning*, forthcoming.

Ulrich, D. 1986b. Measuring human resource effectiveness: Stakeholder, index, and relationship approaches. Working paper, University of Michigan.

4. Human Resource Planning— A Federal Perspective

Allan Jacques, Labour Market Services, Canada Employment and Immigration Commission

This article provides a federal overview of human resource planning practices in Canada and provides examples to illustrate some of the initiatives which have been undertaken by the public and private sectors in support of human resource planning.

The Canada Employment and Immigration Commission (CEIC), is the federal agency responsible for employment, unemployment insurance, and immigration programs. In the CEIC, there is a recognition that human resource planning involves several stakeholders (business and labour, government agencies, educational institutions and interest groups) in a multilateral effort to ensure that labour market problems and opportunities are effectively managed.

Human resource planning in this context attempts to contribute to the achievement of three results: a labour force which meets the nation's occupational needs; an economy capable of growth the adaptation without undue burden on individuals, groups and regions; and, equality of opportunity for all Canadians to compete for and have access to jobs.

Macro-level estimates of the demand for and supply of labour are an important part of our labour market information. In our free labour market, forecasts of supply and demand influence investment and career decisions. The federal government leaves most of the responsibility for the management of our human capital to the private sector.

What does the federal government expect of the private sector in respect of human resource planning? The CEIC has explicitly stated its policy that it is the responsibility of the private sector to do human resource planning. It is thus viewed as a normal part of the management responsibilities of competitive industry. No corporate plan is considered complete unless it includes a human resource plan.

Against this general background let us review some of the initiatives taken by public and private sector organizations to encourage human resource planning.

This article represents the personal views of the author. Credit is due to the staff of the Canada Employment and Immigration Commission who provided much of the background information for this article.

THE FEDERAL GOVERNMENT

The recent history of federal government interest in and promotion of the concepts of human resource planning goes back to the 1950s when there was so much concern about the disruptive effects of technological change. One focus for this attention was the introduction of the diesel locomotive. Railway unions fought hard to protect the interest of the redundant firemen. This resulted in some of the earliest technological change provisions in collective agreements in Canada.

By 1963, the federal government put in place a Manpower Consultative Service—MCS program, now known as the Industrial Adjustment Service—IAS, to make available a small cadre of public servants, with skills in labour-management relations, to help companies and their workers develop joint action plans to cope with mass layoffs and plant closures. By 1974, the service was expanded to encompass human resources planning in situations of plant expansion. Financial incentives were, and still are, made available to reimburse employers for a portion of the costs of establishing joint labour-management committees to do research and planning related to worker adjustment. Shared costs include remuneration for an independent chairperson selected by the committee, compensation for loss of wages, and committee administrative expenses. Employment and Immigration Canada (EIC) 1983 WH–3–831; EIC, 1983 MPH 3–146, and EIC 1985).

The CEIC spends about $6 million per annum on this type of joint planning initiative to help about 600 employers and their workers. The service is also used at the industry sector level to deal with more general adjustment needs. An article in the *Harvard Business Review,* July–August 1983, refers to the IAS program as "Canada's good example with displaced workers". (Batt 1983).

The CEIC has increased its efforts in recent years to promote human resource planning. In July 1984, a chapter on human resource planning was introduced into the employment manuals, four thousand copies of which are used by the 460 Canada Employment Centres to help local staff promote the CEIC's policy of encouraging private sector human resource planning. The CEIC has also recognized the crucial link between economic and human resource development. There are examples of the CEIC applying the principles of leverage to promote human resource planning. These include, among others, provisions in federal procurement reviews for the CEIC to comment on employers' employment plans and, if necessary, recommend conditions to be attached to procurement contracts. There is similar provision for the CEIC to review and comment under the Investment Canada program. There are provisions built into the Industry and Regional Development Program (IRDP), administered by the federal department of Regional Industrial Expansion, which require that firms receiving major financial assistance under the IRDP do human resource planning. The CEIC can and does require employers who are granted permission to recruit temporary foreign workers to undertake human resource planning measures to maximize opportunities for Canadians by reducing or eliminating the need for foreign workers. It is evident that the CEIC is not promoting human resource planning for its own sake, but rather as a means to maximize employment and career development opportunities for Canadians and to ensure economic development is not impeded by a lack of skilled labour.

Measures taken to promote human resource planning demonstrate how much the federal government, as a stakeholder, is involved with its various economic partners. A variety of complementary approaches is needed to establish the labour market conditions necessary for economic growth. Federal programming includes:

1. The delivery of programs and services which address specific labour market situations, including:
   —The Canadian Jobs Strategy
      Job Entry
      Skills Shortages
      Skill Investment (and the Industrial Adjustment Service)
      Job Development
      Community Futures
      Innovations
   —Mobility/Relocation Assistance
   —Labour Exchange Services;
2. the establishment of long-term relationships with economic partners to anticipate and devise solutions to emerging labour market problems, including:
   —Industry sector human resource planning agreements
   —Employment equity provisions
   —Canadian Occupational Projection System
   —Human Resource Planning Boards
   —Canada Farm Labour Pool System;
3. the integration of the CEIC's human resource development priorities into the programs and initiatives of other federal department/agencies:
   —Economic and regional development agreements
   —Canada Oil and Gas Act
   —Major crown projects and procurements
   —Investment Canada
   —Industrial and Regional Development Program
   —Other federal business assistance programs, and
4. seizure of ad hoc opportunities to encourage economic partners to engage in human resource planning, including:
   —Foreign worker approval process
   —Advertising and direct mail campaigns.

The linkages with CEIC's economic partners are crucial to the success of CEIC's efforts. These processes also depend, in turn, on the willingness of business and labour to develop and implement human resource plans.

PROVINCIAL/TERRITORIAL GOVERNMENTS

Canada's ten provinces and the territories have been active promoters of human resource planning. In Quebec, for example, the province typically joins with the federal government when dealing with plant closures. Provincial labour codes provide for workers to receive advance notice of layoff. Officers of the federal Industrial Adjustment Service work with their provincial colleagues and business and labour representatives on the committees set up to find jobs for the workers affected by plant closures. In Ontario, there is also close collaboration between the federal and provincial staff in promoting human resource planning. The Ontario Manpower Commission (OMC) has sponsored employer seminars to explain the good business sense of doing human resource planning. Officers of the OMC and the CEIC's Industrial Adjustment Service work together as resource staff in the seminars as case studies are undertaken to add reality to the learning process.

PRIVATE SECTOR SUPPORT

Studies and surveys over the past fifteen years have shown that human resource planning is still not widely practised in most Canadian businesses. Relatively few corporate plans include provisions for comprehensive human resource planning to be done. At the same time, recognition of the importance of human resource planning is widespread in the business community.

Evidence shows that the commitment to human resource planning within key parts of the private sector is growing. Since 1981, some twenty national human resource planning agreements have been signed between major industrial and professional associations and the federal minister of employment and immigration. These agreements cover some 6,200 firms and 795,000 workers as well as 193,000 workers in professional and technical associations. Some of the sectors include aerospace, mining, electronics, engineering, shipbuilding, plastics, pulp and paper, and agriculture.

The intent of these agreements is to focus each industrial sector's attention on the need to identify its current and future human resource constraints and to develop appropriate solutions. The agreements are flexible and do not impose contractual obligations. Nevertheless, they are an instrument each party can refer to over the long term as a reminder of a joint commitment to cooperative action. These agreements point to the various actions industry and the CEIC may choose to take to address labour market imbalances. These include: development of work force inventories and regular surveys of supply and demand, the application of training in industry and institutions, planning for the implementation of employment equity, more effective utilization of government programs and services, improved liaison with educational and training institutions, and, publicity promoting careers on selected occupations and industries.

The joint human resource planning agreements signed between industry and government are not limited to the national level. Provincial level industry and professional associations and individual firms have signed hundreds of human resource planning agreements since 1983. Many other private sector organizations also actively promote the value of human resource planning. For instance, the Conference Board of Canada had devoted considerable study and publicity to the need to closely integrate human resource planning into overall strategic corporate planning. Such views are echoed in a wide range of academic and business research.

Organized labour has not, historically, played a major role in promoting human resource planning, although several unions have been signatories to government-industry human resource planning agreements in situations involving technological change and economic adjustment. Some major labour organizations, concerned about world-wide competition and productivity, now appear to be more receptive to human resource planning.

THE PRACTICALITIES OF APPLIED HUMAN RESOURCE PLANNING

As those who have tried to develop human resource plans know, one must make some strategic decisions to balance the costs of doing human resource planning with the anticipated benefits. Invariably, this results in a process of selective intervention. Firms try to plan in advance for key staffing, classification, training, relocation, or other personnel actions, but without getting bogged down in the process. The same principles apply to the governmental bodies which promote human resource planning. Scarce resources require that they focus the human resource planning effort at the extremes of labour market activity. That is, they must consciously choose to assign the highest priority to severe layoff, job growth, and technological change situations. The principles of *incrementality* suggest that government assistance is most justified when bottlenecks or major dislocation would occur without such help. When employers and workers are not able, themselves, to smooth out the turbulence in the labour market, the potential social and economic costs provide a sound rationale for government help.

This principle of requiring private initiative first, and selective application of government support is not new, but it is being given increased emphasis in the federal government. The Nielsen Task Force reviews of government spending are causing a fundamental re-thinking of government assistance to business. The 1986 federal budget and the 1985 First Ministers Conference in Regina asserted that adjustment assistance should have the highest priority applied to helping workers. Help to firms would have a lower priority.

Just as human resource planning is a process, the key to progress in its adoption is process. In government, programs which involve the expenditure of massive amounts of funds get lots of publicity. Human resource planning does not involve the direct expenditure of massive amounts of money, either by the private sector or governments, so it is not surprising that little attention is given to the efforts being made to promote human resource planning practices.

Good examples show that much can be done, and is being done, without spending massive amounts of money, simply by making the effort to do human resource planning.

——Unpleasant though it was, when Uranium City was so hard hit in 1982–83 by the closure of the Eldorado Nuclear mine, the collective joint planning of the workers, the company, all levels of government, and other affected parties, resulted in successful adjustment for the vast majority of the displaced workers.

——Joint government-industry initiative in the aerospace sector led to the formation of Human Resource Planning Boards. These boards were formed to deal with skill shortages and have been flexible enough to address the more severe downside adjustments flowing since the recession of the early 1980s.

——In the summer of 1985, the Canada Employment and Immigration Commission undertook a series of informal consultations in an effort to identify needs and constraints for CAD/CAM (Computer Assisted Design and Manufacturing) related human resource planning. Some 104 participants from industry (both management and labour), research groups, associations, universities and colleges, and other government levels made their views known. The findings were reported in December 1985, under the title *Towards Options for Human Resource Planning with Respect to CAD/CAM and Related Technologies*. (Rochow 1985).

——Each year, hundreds of firms and their workers engage in joint planning efforts to address employment growth, technological change, productivity, and new plant situations.

CONCLUSION

Human resource planning is reaping benefits to more stakeholders each year. Although the prime responsibility for doing human resource planning rests with the private sector, there are many sources of help for firms and their workers. With continued collaboration between government, industry and educational institutions, both economic and social objectives will be achieved.

References

Batt, William L., Jr. 1983. Canada's good example with displaced workers. *Harvard Business Review* (July–August): 6–22.

Employment and Immigration Canada. 1983. Guidelines for the preparation of a Human Resource Plan. *WH–3–831*, 7/83.

Employment and Immigration Canada. 1983. Human Resource Planning—A Guide for Employers. *Cat. No. MP43–146*/1983.

Employment and Immigration Canada. 1985. The Human Resource Plan—Some Details for Employers. *Cat. No. MP–43–161*/1985.

Rochow, Gunter. 1985. Towards Options for Human Resource Planning With Respect to CAD/CAM and Related Technologies. *Employment and Immigration Canada Report.*

5. Human Resource Information System: The Case of Provigo

Claude Marier, Corporate Director Human Resources, Provigo Inc.

INTRODUCTION

The long-term profitability and growth of a company depend primarily on the combined efficiency of its wealth of resources and the data it has access to. To be completely effective, the data must be accurate, precise, easy to obtain and analyse, and must be fully integrated into the culture and the goals of the organization.

The early '70s gave rise to the massive introduction of management information systems in companies of all sizes. Their purpose was essentially to digest the masses of internal corporate data and to present it in a form useful to managers. These systems were mainly designed to manipulate information of a financial nature, which is one of the reasons why human resources has been one of the last sectors to gain from the many advantages of information systems.

Human resources management consists of a series of distinct yet complementary functions. The payroll function is historically the first, if not the only one, to have benefited from the opportunities offered by the computer. This is normal, given that payroll operations generally involve routine.

Of course, some of the information gathered for the payroll function would serve other purposes and other functions of the human resources department. However, potential usefulness of the information proved limited, because of its small volume and the fact that it was designed to serve a single function.

By restricting the use of data processing, business was depriving itself of a very precious tool for improving the efficiency of its human resources management. As penetration and use of information systems increased in the most strategic business sectors, human resources departments began to develop and play a more important role in modern corporations. Social change, the recent economic recession, and the proliferation of laws and regulations made the task of the manager, and of the human resources professional, more difficult and more complex, and they still had no technology really suited to these new requirements. Files were still updated manually and data transmitted by archaic and traditional means.

Nowadays, information systems are more sophisticated and more accessible in terms of cost. They have also proven extremely useful in almost all business sectors. The question is why have they not been adopted to human resources management? Provigo decided to take up the challenge.

SIRHUM, the system we designed, is not a solution to all the problems a manager encounters. Nor is it a perfect machine. It is rather a concrete example of a tool that can still be improved on and that can help the manager to be more efficient or, in current parlance, to excel.

DECIDING TO COMPUTERIZE

At Provigo, the need for a specific information system for the human resources department stemmed from both the size of the firm and the extent and diversity of its resources.

Presentation of the Company

Provigo is becoming a North American leader in the distribution of consumer goods and services at the wholesale and retail levels. Its mission is to offer consumers the best value and the most extensive choice. The result is a formal commitment to excellence, a superior financial performance, innovation, profitability, and growth in Canada as well as in the United States.

Provigo was formed in 1969, out of the merger of three Québec food companies: Denault Limitée of Sherbrooke, Couvrette et Provost Limitée of Montréal, and Lamontagne Limitée of Québec City. Today, this sector still accounts for nearly eighty percent of corporate sales in Québec, as well as Ontario, Alberta, Virginia and California. Provigo's other activities are concentrated mainly in the pharmaceutical and oil industries and in sports and leisure goods. Overall, Provigo reported slightly less than $5 billion CAN in sales for the fiscal year ending January 26, 1986.

The operating units working within the same industry are structured into homogeneous groups with clearcut strategies and policies that remain a constant concern of the management teams. Presently, five such groups exist: food, convenience stores, pharmaceutical and health products, non-food, and the United States market. Each group has its own mandate and precise strategic goals. Coordinating the groups is the responsibility of a small team of managers at the head office of Provigo Inc., based in Montréal.

The initiave described in this chapter took place in Provigo Distribution Inc., Provigo's operating company involved in the wholesale and retail distribution of food in the province of Québec. At the time of the study, there were approximatively 7500 employees in this Company, most of which were unionized. There were about eighty collective agreements governing the working conditions of the union employees and twenty other sets of policies for those of the remaining employees.

The human resources department which is responsible for labour relations, among other things, is essentially decentralized and each human resources manager reports to a divisional general manager. Functionally speaking, however, the department comes under the vice-president of human resources. The payroll centre is the responsibility of the department of finance and administration. In Provigo Distribution Inc., there were ten human resources departments and five payroll centre at the time the experience began.

Nature of Problems

Of course, managing a company of the scope of Provigo is not always an easy task. It is understandable and indeed inevitable that problems will arise, all the more so since Provigo's extremely rapid growth and diversified activities necessarily entail more numerous and more complex administrative standards. When management first considered computerization, the problems inherent in human resources were of two orders: there were those relating to payroll and then, those more specifically part of the human resources department. In the case of the payroll, the problem was finding out where costs originated and how to control them, especially those generated by the various fringe benefits.

In addition, integrating changes brought by new collective agreements into the Company's new collective agreements administrative procedures was a long, hard process and errors were frequent and very costly.

The payroll centre lacked the flexibility and rigor essential to its orderly functioning. Also, because there existed four payroll systems in the company at the time, all incompatible, there was no uniformity in the management of the payroll.

Another problem encountered was the significant variations observed in the data contained in various interim reports. In the human resources department, hand-compiled files were often incomplete, and updating was long and arduous. It was practically impossible to analyse the information because rapid compilation of company data was unrealistic. Finally, exerting effective controls over human resources management was almost unthinkable.

Objectives of Computerization

It was therefore decided to provide the human resources and payroll departments with a reliable and efficient set of tools to build a permanent computerized data base containing all the necessary information for personnel management and production of the company payroll.

To accomplish this, management set objectives that aimed, first of all, to provide each human resources department and payroll centre with a complete management tool that would be specific to each but integrated to the whole. The second aim was to reduce to a minimum the manual work required to develop, update, and consult employee records, and produce the payroll.

The aim was also to facilitate follow-up of employee records and minimize the involvement of the data processing department in data updating and report production. Finally, the system had to be flexible enough for speedy integration of the employees of any company eventually acquired by Provigo. Apart from solving identified problems, these objectives would equip Provigo with a powerful management tool capable of providing all the information needed to improve its efficiency.

DEVELOPING AND IMPLEMENTING THE SYSTEM

The introduction of an information system adapted to the needs of human resources managers cannot be done overnight. It must rather proceed by precise stages which may here be divided into three distinct categories, namely the preliminary, the development, and the implementation phases.

PRELIMINARY PHASE

Towards 1980, the director of human resources for the five Montréal regional divisions, who was in a position to pinpoint unfulfilled needs with regard to useful information for managers, began to inquire into what it would take to build the ideal human resources system. Having worked previously for a year as an organizational development specialist helping to design the so-called office of the future, he was already aware of the numerous possibilities offered by data processing. As this was not a task imposed on him in any way, there was no pressure to perform according to a pre-established schedule. Ideas slowly matured and led to the conceptualization of a system.

After this step, a systems analyst was assigned the task of analysing the various functions of the human resources department and their interrelationship. For example, this consisted in determining exactly what is involved in the recruitment function and how it relates to the remuneration function and so on for each of the functions.

Once this study was completed, an organic analysis was conducted simply to dissect the internal mechanics of each function. The results were to form the very basis for developing a system that would be truly adapted to the human resources department.

DEVELOPMENT PHASE

The setting up of an information system must be planned in order to obtain the maximum performance from every individual involved in the project. Consequently, tasks must be clearly and precisely assigned and schedules established in order to meet predetermined objectives.

Here is how the scenario unfolded at Provigo.

Operational Structure

In order to implement and pilot the project, the sector of food distribution in Québec was chosen and in the first decision, the director of human resources was relieved of his regular responsibilities for a year. Considering his position in the company, this decision publicly demonstrated the company's commitment to the project. For the purposes of this mandate, he worked under the authority of a steering committee which reported to the information systems committee presided by the president and chief operating officer of Provigo. The steering committee's job was to approve the budgets, phases, and objectives of the project as well as the personnel required to see it through.

The people appointed to the project were assigned to four sections, namely coordination of users within the human resources department, coordination between the EDP and human resources departments, coordination between EDP and the payroll centres and, finally, coordination of users within the payroll centre.

Each team member had a precise job description specifying, among other things, what he or she had to report on periodically and at the end of the project.

It was agreed from the start that formal meetings of the steering committee, including agenda and minutes, would be held once a month. As the project advanced, meetings became less frequent and, towards the end, were held approximately every three months.

Organizational Development Approach

Developing an information system involves numerous decisions that must be made if project is to materialize. Some of these deserve special mention here as they, in our opinion, contributed directly to the project's success.

Thus, although there already existed a favourable atmosphere and good team spirit in the human resources departments, a graduate in industrial psychology was called in to evaluate the degree of staff resistance to change. The purpose of this was to ensure that every detail supported the development and implementation of the new system.

Since information had to be gathered regarding the users' reactions and attitudes toward the impending new information system, the graduate was commissioned to accomplish the following: identify the factors of resistance to change by means of sample interviews, and develop an implementation strategy in accordance with the resulting diagnosis. This organizational development approach was, we think, one of the most influential elements in the successful outcome of the project.

Major Trends

In general, analysis of the results revealed the following trends:

1. Everyone involved viewed the project as a very useful contribution to the organization since it would significantly improve the efficiency, quality, and quantity of the services rendered by the different divisions of the human resources department.
2. Some individuals nurtured high expectations regarding the new information system. Their subsequent evaluation of the change could prove unfavourable if their expectations remained high and promises did not materialize.
3. Most administrative regions seemed cautious regarding the new system. Certain remarks led us to believe that some people were particularly skeptical.

This skepticism concerned the EDP's ability to conclude the project quickly and produce the expected results. They wondered whether the computer experts could be of real support to the regions during implementation. Finally, there was also a question about the system's specific advantages vis-à-vis the existing systems.

Important Aspects of the Strategy

It appeared that the change process would be greatly facilitated if the implementation strategy emphasized certain aspects such as:

1. taking into account individual pace and ability with respect to organizing work and learning the system
2. planning training sessions using real-life situations
3. setting up an information-sharing
4. establishing a support structure to compensate for difficulties caused by the extra work load and the users' lack of technical knowledge
5. offering consulting processes for parties concerned whether the system will be adapted to the characteristics of each division.

Positive Aspects

Several aspects favoured the implementation of the new system. First, the system was unanimously perceived as capable of performing efficiently and quickly. More specifically, numerous remarks were made within the company to the effect that the system would reduce manual controls, standardize various procedures, simplify tasks, considerably improve the quality of work, and speed up access to information.

In sum, although the people surveyed were not unconditional relative to the planned change, they remained very receptive. This was a long-awaited change that many considered a necessity for the company.

Aspects to Follow-Up

Nevertheless, certain aspects tied to the development and implementation of the new system needed careful attention.

Reliability of Information and Communication. The need for information on the real capabilities of the system and on its impact on work had been clearly expressed all through the administrative regions. The information sought was more precisely related to the following items:

1. the capabilities, operation, and flexibility of the new system
2. the process of accessing information given the confidential nature of the data
3. effects of the system on working conditions namely, job security, task assignment, working atmosphere, quality of human relations between employees, and job satisfaction
4. method used to diagnose users' needs
5. knowledge of the present state of the project
6. knowledge of the projected implementation process, its stages and timetable

Apprehension of Change. Although the need for change was an acknowledged fact, caution was still required as, in many regions, past data processing modifications had not been a positive experience for users and had even generated mistrust among them. The changes made were often inefficient and, in certain cases, did not respond to the real needs.

Guarantees of Job Satisfaction. As mentioned previously, there was some anxiety as to the effects of the system on job security, task assignment, and the quality of working life. The regions also explicitly expressed a need for real consultation and adequate training.

Indeed, for certain people, change is often synonymous with layoffs. For others, it is a sign of the company's intention to centralize its operations. The problem was also posed in terms of the system's tangible effects on work and pointed to such preoccupations as:

—What would replace the manual work?
—Who will be assigned to the printer?
—How many hours a day will we spend working on the machine?

While a number of people considered the change a challenge, others continued to worry and expressed little enthusiasm at the thought of the possible monotony, routine, and alienation caused by long hours in front of a screen. The same respondents were also apprehensive of the impact of the new system on employee relations and the atmosphere at work.

The employees were unanimous in their wish to be consulted before the completion of the system in order to ensure that it met their needs. While a lack of consultation could have threatened the acceptance of the system by the users, it was more than appropriate to use this potential of positive energy by recognizing the employees' skills and experience with the environment.

Finally, for most, the need for adequate tools to help them maintain the high level of service prevailed. To what extent would the training given enable the managers and users to resume their supervisory or executive role with as much competence as before? How is it determined whether users would be sufficiently informed to spot errors themselves and to correct them? To what extent could the risk of data losses be mitigated?

With these questions in mind, it became essential to approach training from a practical angle using case studies. Similarly, it was necessary to adapt it to the concerned parties, that is, to their educational background, their role in the organization and their work experience. This way, the feeling of incompetence tied to difficulties in adapting to change would be reduced. If they knew where they were headed, users would be able to take over the system more easily.

Need for Employee Support. The need for support during implementation was evident in all divisions. In fact, personnel was hoping to work in close cooperation with the computer professionals. Users wanted, first to have the consultants available and, second, to have the option of conducting preliminary tests on the system. They also stressed the importance of knowing their interlocutors. When some people voiced their concerns about being evaluated during the implementation phase, it became appropriate for supervisors to offer the human support that would promote a climate of trust, free of any intolerance to errors all through the crucial adjustment period.

Implementation Strategy

Given the previous comments, the implementation process could be considered in relation to the positive and negative forces at play, that is, those favoring change and those slowing it down. The strategy was supposed to reduce the impact of the negative elements and increase that of the positive ones.

Other Essential Decisions

Other decisions and activities have also contributed to the success of the project. Given the fact that the output of one system is used as input for another, it was important to organize data in such a way that the other systems of the company could use it in an efficient and profitable manner. For instance, the responsibilities of the human resources department and the payroll centre were clearly defined and delimited and the relationships between the human resources' integrated system and the other information systems of the company.

One of the wisest decisions taken was the creation of a technician position at the onset of the development phase, as it seemed fundamental to have someone on hand who was familiar with users' expectations and the requirements of their jobs.

A clerk already working in the human resources department at file handling was assigned to this position, being the most capable of interpreting the users' needs on a day-to-day basis. This employee participated directly in designing the system and transposing into the users' language the documentation meant for them. He also helped set up training programs for various user groups and acted as main instructor during training sessions. To summarize, the key role played by this employee was extremely valuable during the development phase and even more so during implementation.

Another decision that proved helpful was to use data processing for its own ends. It should be noted that the development phase comprised more than six hundred distinct activities that were the responsibility of both the users and the data processing personnel. To manage the scheduling of these activities better, a computer program was designed to provide updated information on the status of the project without delay.

The development phase was consequently divided into blocks, activities, and sub-activities to help clearly identify the starting and ending dates, the estimated number of hours, actual and revised, the variation between the revised and estimated times, and the name of the person responsible for accomplishing each task.

Every Monday afternoon, the progress report on the project was reviewed and an appropriate plan of action determined. By keeping management informed on the status of the project, this approach was doubtless instrumental in keeping the development phase within budget.

IMPLEMENTATION PHASE

The last phase of the project but not the least was the progressive implementation of the system. To follow the same logical path established from the start, a committee of individuals in high-level positions in the payroll centre and human resources department of each administrative region was set up to supervise the orderly implementation of the system.

The committee members were to play an active role in the selection of future users of the new system. They were also to decide on when the system would begin operating in their division, on the resources to be allocated and on the priorities.

Once the committee was formed, a key user was appointed to become the leading expert on the system in each region. His duties included acting as resource-person and trainer for the other users, as well as liaison between his division and the people at head office who were responsible for the system and for deciding on the pace of implementation in the regions.

In an effort to minimize the time required for developing the new computer files, a program was designed to convert the data in the old payroll department files. The new system would validate and recycle the old data and automatically generate new data. For example, the designation Mr and Mrs could be computerized from the sex code entered in the file.

The job was further simplified by the use of a microcomputer program for planning and controlling some 450 activities pertaining to implementation. It was a matter of setting up a master plan adapted to the needs of each region. In short, as in the development phase, information systems were heavily relied on to set up the information system.

A list of steps and an order of priorities were defined to add the essential data missing from the files and a schedule was established for each division according to its available resources. As expected, the decision to include one data set rather than another depended on the overall priorities of the company, as well as on the needs of each division.

Motivating and Training Users

Firstly, employees were reassured as to the continuation of their employment within the department. They were informed that the content of their tasks would most probably change but that there would be no layoffs directly resulting from this technological change. In fact, no jobs were eliminated and two new positions were even created.

Secondly, personalized programs were established adapted to the individual's learning pace, and the on-the-job training period was officially recognized by the awarding of diplomas, which represented a gratification for the employee.

The training program was designed as a four-part module with each part destined to a specific group of users. The key users followed a ten-day program while other users followed one lasting six days. Both were led by the technician mentioned before and progressed according to each person's learning pace.

There was also a third program for human resources managers who were sent general information on the system along with a user's manual for the report generator program, a tool specifically developed for their benefit. More will be said about it later.

As for the general managers and department heads (the main clients of the human resources department), instead of formal training they received information on the capabilities of the system and how to benefit from them. Training sessions were and are still held at the head office, a mysterious location highly valued by the regional clerical staff who rarely have access to it. Apart from these, periodic meetings are also held with users at the same location. The purpose of these meetings is to create a team spirit among employees working at similar jobs in different regions and to completely review the system with the people who use it on a constant basis.

For example, these two issues have been discussed at such meetings. The first, entitled "SIRHUM: So easy", aimed to demystify the new system by presenting the users with a simplified profile of a very complex system. The second topic theme was "SIRHUM: Let's use it". The intended purpose was to change old working habits and to reassure users that the information would not disappear when they shut off their screen.

The ideas expressed told us how the system was perceived and what improvements were required. At the same time, the meetings were an opportunity for users to talk about the problems they encountered, to discuss and to develop a feeling of pride in the system.

DESCRIBING SIRHUM

Why is the system so well adapted to the human resources department? This is easy to answer. It was entirely designed by the main parties concerned and is based on their needs. But let's take a look at what makes it an indispensible management tool.

The system is designated by the initials SIRHUM, which stand for *Système intégré des ressources humaines* (Integrated Human Resources System). It is a complex system developed from a simple model whose elements and modules are arranged in a flexible, complete, and reliable whole.

The first thing to note is that SIRHUM has a regulatory file comprising all the codes, static and dynamic tables, and reference data used by the system. As such, SIRHUM is a centralized data bank which contains useful information for managers in their administration of the company's human resources.

In fact, each employee file is composed of more than 350 elements of information. Some of these elements are regarded as historical and are kept according to user management needs such as the employee's salary adjustments since his first day with the Company. Other elements are non-historical such as the employee's home address. The bank also contains all the data supplied or computed by the payroll module which are entered in the employee file and are easily accessible to the user.

SIRHUM Application Modules

SIRHUM-payroll is nothing more than an application module for production and management of the employee payroll. Its advantages are numerous since it works without prior calculations or any of the usual limitations. It applies the payroll regulations specific to the company no matter their diversity or their complexity. To these advantages should also be added the fact that the system instantly accepts all changes to employee records and transmits all the legal or other documents that the user may need.

SIRHUM data base, SIRHUM-payroll, and a file of appropriate regulations are presently in operation in all of Provigo Distribution Inc. However, a series of other modules have already been outlined which will draw information from the data base or regulatory file to respond to the specific needs of human resources. In the next two or three years, it is expected that eleven modules will go into operation; some of them are already under development.

SIRHUM collective agreements will be especially designed to help the labour relations experts manage their activities better by gathering all information pertaining to collective agreements. There is also the possibility of adding a word processor to facilitate the writing and updating of our many collective agreements.

SIRHUM-simulations will be used to make projections or simulate situations based on the monetary clauses in one or more collective agreements while SIRHUM-pensions will be specially designed to manage the company's various retirement plans. SIRHUM-fringe benefits, as the name implies, will be used to manage the fringe benefits and, specifically, the group insurance plans.

SIRHUM-budgets will deal with labour and salary budgets, while SIRHUM-functions will include a list of the hierarchical positions as well as the job description and a profile of skills required for each of the positions.

SIRHUM-organization chart will contain graphic representations of the company's organizational structures; and SIRHUM-human resources planning is meant to simplify the development of back-up plans based on simulated organization charts.

The objective of SIRHUM-health and safety will be to help define the physical features of the various jobs and monitor the employees' work environment. It will also identify the individual equipment used and the products handled by employees. Finally, this module will enable us to maintain the existing electronic links with the C.S.S.T. (Québec's Occupational Health and Safety Commission).

Lastly, SIRHUM-medical services will contain complete employee medical records which will be accessible only to the attending physician.

Main Features of the System

The integrated human resources system operates mainly in the conversational on-line mode except for the production of reports which is in the batch mode. On request, SIRHUM will generate an individual card which is part of each employee's physical file. The card contains all the information most frequently requested by the user.

Updating data is safe and easy. The coding step has been simplified as much as possible and strict and efficient controls introduced. The system must at all times prevent the transmission of erroneous information which would introduce inconsistencies into the file and render it unusable. It also features a whole range of messages in order to inform the user immediately when errors are made. Updating principles are simple so the user can converse easily with the computer and so that necessary changes to a file can be made promptly and be available instantly.

The diversity of the information in the file and its essentially dynamic nature mean that SIRHUM must be flexible. Changes can be made if necessary but will not affect programs. They must be executed with ease and within a set time limit to prevent confusion and downgrading of the system. In fact, the documentation used in data capture is designed according to the users' needs, it can be modified independently of the programs.

The SIRHUM-payroll application module offers several special features as well. It will fully automate payroll and post-payroll activities: calculation of the payroll, payment, payroll entry, payroll analysis, monitoring of absences and productivity, etc. The module is also flexible enough to modify the payroll regulations recorded in the system, as well as the results already computed.

These module programs are organized in such a way that updating is fast and simple. The main programs are the master program, the gross and net salary programs, and the data entry and dissemination programs. Each program works in an independent but complementary manner.

Computing of the payroll is based on three information sources which are, in ascending order of priority:

—the annex file with the regulations specific to the Company
—SIRHUM where the permanent information on each employee is stored
—the variable elements of the pay period (for example: overtime)

Calculation of the payroll includes the automatic management of annual cumulative data. The system makes progressive adjustments to deductions, interrogates files, analyses results, and computes the salary forecasts needed to plan budgets.

The entire system and its administrative procedures were reviewed by our internal audit staff which reported that SIRHUM-payroll meets the generally recognized and accepted audit standards for this type of system. With reference to the preceding features, I would now like to draw your attention to certain major applications for the manager.

Follow-up Management

The system can schedule the activities to be accomplished with regard to the file of an individual or of a group of employees. In fact, a future date referring to a task to be done or a decision to be made can be input to an employee's computer file. Whether a salary increase, the end of a probation period, the opening date of a pension file, or the date when a disciplinary notice should be removed from the physical file, SIRHUM will automatically remind the user of the date of the activity, even one or two weeks in advance. This lapse of time has been determined sufficiently long to make a decision and intervene if necessary.

There is, therefore, no need for the traditional cardex or notebook to remind the user of important events or activities or things to do in the coming weeks. SIRHUM's reliable memory considerably reduces the stress caused by omissions and eliminates delays in file maintenance. It should be noted that the machine cannot make decisions in the user's place; it simply reminds the user of what must be done and when.

Report Management

The system has another feature that delights managers. It is the report generator or PRAP (for Personnel Report). The expression refers to a function that enables the user to produce all the reports needed with the information chosen and according to the desired format.

The report request is made directly on the screen by the user and the report, printed overnight, is available the next morning. No more waiting lines where the personnel report is the twentieth priority.

With reports on request, the computer professionals rarely have to intervene and the absence of intermediaries makes the user feel more comfortable with the system since the user can change his or her mind and is no longer afraid of making mistakes.

Managing Absenteeism

Among the many problems encountered by companies, one of the most common is employee absenteeism. We are not trying to make the reader believe that an information system can solve the problem at its source. However, it could prove extremely useful in analyzing various dimensions of the problem whether the nature, frequency, or length duration of absences.

With SIRHUM, the manager can display each employee's time card directly on the screen and access all the management reports he or she may need. Some are automatically produced and others may be obtained by means of the report generator.

Data Protection

Despite the definite advantages of such a system, many managers do without because they are afraid of leaks or unrestricted access to confidential information. There are obviously no foolproof computer systems but, often, the very people who worry about leaks are the ones who leave a file open on their desk or forget to lock the filing cabinet.

SIRHUM provides the necessary guarantees to restrict data dissemination to authorized individuals only. Thus, it is possible to determine who has access to what without risk of error. Passwords made up according to a predefined hierarchy determine the access to data. This hierarchy is established in terms of the users' level of specific responsibilities within the company. The user may change passwords as required and at any time.

Furthermore, the data base is structured so that the human resources department of an administrative region has access to the employee records for region only. However, the system will permit the temporary loan of a file between regions, for consultation purposes only. Finally, each file has its own confidential code and each user also has a code to access files bearing confidential codes of an equal or lower level.

DEFINING PRINCIPLES OF SUCCESS

Our experience with computerizing the human resources department allowed us to realize how important certain basic principles are in ensuring the successful design and implementation of a management information system, no matter the business sector it applies to.

First Principle

The project must have the full support of the company's top management.

The person responsible for the project must make sure management is aware of the scope of the project, sees its real benefits and is ready to authorize the necessary resources for its conclusion.

Second Principle

The cost/benefit analysis must take into account the impact of data processing on the quality and availability of management information, as well as its impact on direct operating costs.

It is sometimes difficult to measure some of the advantages of computerization with any precision. The project's profitability must therefore be viewed in a perspective wider than that of the immediate benefits.

Third Principle

Responsibility for the project must be assigned to a competent and available manager who has the required authority.

Computerization is a complex and costly task. The person chosen to head the project must have an overall view of the company's culture, stategies, objectives and management mode, and must be capable of making decisions and committing the company to a given path.

Fourth Principle

Responsibility for the project must always be shared by the user.

The manager should not blindly trust or abdicate responsibility to the computer expert. To avoid this, the manager must supervise the computer expert regularly and appropriately and act in such a way that the latter is the one who responds to the former's needs and not the opposite.

Fifth Principle

The ones who will be using the system should be directly involved in its design and implementation.

The users' participation will reduce their resistance to change to a minimum and ensure their needs are met.

Sixth Principle

The planning and control of the development and implementation stages are essential to the successful completion of the project.

The manager who engages in a computerization process like the one described above should know exactly where he wants to go, and when and how to get there. As a rule, he will know very little about managing a project involving so many different activities. He must take the time to acquaint himself with these techniques or turn to a person competent in the field.

Seventh Principle

The time spent preparing detailed documentation is an investment that yields enormous dividends.

An information system is the result of an almost endless series of actions and decisions. It is therefore important to document each precisely so the manager can see his way clear and bring the project to its successful completion.

CONCLUSION

The management of Provigo firmly believes that the system discussed above will meet managers' expectations as to their need for fast, complete and accurate information in the field of human resources.

We can also state without risk of error that SIRHUM is a tool essential to the efficient management of human resources, an instrument that will contribute positively to our company's profitability and long-term growth.

6. Job Analysis

C. Paul Sparks, Serendipity Unlimited

There are so many misconceptions about this topic that it is necessary to begin this discussion with a definition. The one that will be used in this chapter is: *Job analysis is the process of determining the characteristics of an area of work according to a prescribed set of dimensions.* The dimensions to be used may come from one of the many standardized job analysis systems that have been developed, or they may be a unique set prepared to illuminate a particular constellation of needs. Job analysis is generally discussed under one of two major headings: *methods* or *applications*. Confusion frequently arises when a specific technique, for example methods analysis or time-and-motion study, is treated as if it encompassed the entire field. Similarly, end products such as job descriptions or job evaluations are frequently treated as if they were the job analyses. Part of this confusion is due to the fact that studies of work and workers are found in many disciplines—anthropology, compensation management, economics, industrial engineering, labour relations, occupational medicine, physiology, psychology, sociology, and training. This variety of disciplines also causes an extreme fragmentation of the literature on job analysis. Articles appear in all kinds of professional journals. The serious student will find it quite difficult to assemble a sufficiently comprehensive library within a small number of sources. McCormick (1979) covers more aspects of job analysis than does any other recent textbook. However, even his treatment is becoming dated with the advent of more and more researched or tailored systems. Bemis, Belenky and Soder (1983) contains an excellent summary of job analysis methods prefatory to presentation of their own method, Versatile Job Analysis System (VERJAS). They conclude with a very extensive bibliography. Gael (in press) assembled original papers from almost one hundred authors in an attempt to cover the entire field in a *Job Analysis Handbook*. Many of the authors describe their own work in developing a system, per-

Appears simultaneously in R.S. Schuler, S.A. Youngblood, and V. L. Huber (eds.) Readings in Personnel and Human Resource Management. 3e. (St. Paul: West Publishing Co., 1987). Text adapted for Canadian readers.

forming research, or making an application.

The concept of division of labour predates written information. Anthropologists tell us that ancient peoples had very strict rules for the distribution of work between the sexes and, later, of work that was deemed appropriate to the individual's status in the tribal hierarchy. Historians tell us that guilds with masters and apprentices date back at least as far as Babylonia in the time of Hammurabi (about 2100 B.C.). These guilds even fixed prices and wages. Similar guilds were present in China before the advent of the Christian Era. Philosophers and religious leaders were concerned with the meaning of work. The Greek and Roman philosophers held that work was evil, punishment by the gods. Leisure was to be preferred so that the individual could exercise mind and spirit. The Hebrew philosophers held that work was atonement for sin, but was also necessary in order to create a better world. The early Christians generally adopted the Hebrew beliefs but later Christians taught that work was good for man and idleness was sinful. Since the education of the leaders of the countries fell to these philosophers and clerics, their power and influence extended far beyond their immediate constituencies.

The Industrial Revolution brought about a marked change in the meaning of work. A much larger proportion of the populace could attain significant material possessions. A new type of leader emerged, one whose power was derived from an ability to produce goods and services at a profit from an interaction between workers and equipment or raw materials. Yet, the teachings and preachings of the past had some influence. Laws to protect individuals from exploitation were passed. For example, in 1802 the British Parliament adopted the *Health and Morals Act to Regulate the Labour of Bound Children in Cotton Factories*. Among other things, it prohibited the employment of such children if they were under nine years of age. As time went by more and more changes were made. The working day was shortened, working conditions were improved, living standards rose, and public education was made available to almost everyone. The Industrial Revolution was also a primary contributor to the labour movement. The worker now had something to sell a prospective employer—skills and time. But, as one individual the worker had little power or influence. On the other hand, a collection of such individuals acting as one could greatly affect the enterprise. The union provided the vehicle for bargaining with an employer. Not surprisingly, the bargaining frequently turned into conflict, with many excesses committed by both employers and unions. Laws were enacted to curb most of these excesses. Labour unions were among the first organizations to espouse job analysis.

The capitalist system of free enterprise pits employers with similar offerings against each other, unless some form of collusion is effected. Such combinations in restraint of trade are illegal. Yet, employers are constantly seeking legal ways of obtaining a competitive edge. Attempts have run a very large gamut, too many to list here. A few broadly defined examples will give some feeling for the scope—industrial engineering, personnel psychology, motivation theory, management practice, training, compensation and benefits systems, work simplification, job enrichment, quality circles, profit sharing, employee ownership, and many, many more. Several of these virtually demand some form of job analysis prior to adoption.

USES OF JOB ANALYSIS

It will become apparent shortly that job analysis techniques should be chosen on the basis of their applicability to a particular need. Among the more common uses of job analysis are the following.

Writing Job Descriptions

Organizations need job descriptions for a variety of purposes. Ordinarily, job titles convey very little information on what the employee does or why he or she does it. A good job description can convey to employment agencies, prospective employees, and recruiters the demands of the job and result in a significant lessening of processing time occasioned by obviously unsuitable applicants. In this age of emphasis on fair employment it can stem some cries of bitterness resulting from failure to employ members of a particular race, ethnic group or sex. Beyond entry level jobs these job descriptions are extremely valuable in developing lines of progression where prior experience is an asset.

Developing Job Families

Despite differences in job title, many jobs have the same or similar underlying requirements. Techniques exist for combining jobs into families where job analysis provides an adequate data base. Such information is important for selection, job retraining, job enrichment, and classification. Pearlman (1980) contains an excellent review of the literature on the development of job families and includes an extensive set of relatively current references.

Job-Related Interviews

Employment office interviewers frequently have had training in interviewing skills. They are less likely to have had exposure to the factual content of the jobs for which they are interviewing. Specifications provided by operating supervisors are often highly idealized. The interviewer is typically inclined to compromise by trying to evaluate traits instead of skills and abilities. A file of documented tasks and the underlying knowledge, skill, and ability requirements can minimize this tendency. The resulting interviews should be demonstrably more job-related, a very important consideration in complying with federal and state guidelines on employee selection.

Test Development, Selection, and Validation

Some years ago your author was employed to develop and validate a selection program for use in the hiring of installer-repairmen in a large telephone company. With only limited knowledge of actual job requirements, I envisaged tests of fine manual dexterity and color discrimination. Little written job information was available and it was necessary to add observations and interviews with incumbent employees. It turned out that the first requirement was translation of notes taken by an operator to whom the malfunction was reported. This was followed by reference to a manual that included in order of frequency of occurrence the most probable reason for the particular malfunction. The malfunction was generally corrected by replacing the offending component with one that had been certified as operable. The defective part was then returned to the factory. At no time was the dexterity level higher than that required to oppose thumb and forefinger. No colour discrimination was required. Good job analysis can prevent such false starts as these.

Where the validity of selection procedures is in question, the job analysis information plays a dual role. Where a *content* strategy is to be used (there is a close similarity between the measurement employed and the job itself as in a typing test) the job analysis can provide evidence that the performance measured by the test is actually used on the job. Where a *criterion-related* strategy is to be used (there is a significant correlation between the measurement used and job performance) the job analysis can provide evidence that the evaluation of job performance was based on essential elements of the job and avoided peripheral considerations.

Development of Training Programs

Recommendations for training usually come from a perceived need. The need is identified by the accumulation of symptoms—sales are down, customer complaints are increasing, defective products are piling up in the scrap bin, time schedules are not being met, grievances are more frequent, absence and turnover are up, etc. Symptoms seldom telegraph the underlying cause. Among the first investigations should be a training needs analysis to establish whether there are deficient skills, knowledge, equipment, systems, attitudes, etc. If the situation suggests that training may contribute to a solution, a next step should be the construction of training performance objectives (TPOs), specifics as to what the training is expected to accomplish. Job analysis information is almost a necessity for this step, particularly if the training is to be geared to a specific level of performance.

The legitimacy of selection procedures is frequently studied by comparison of scores on the selection program instruments with later success in a training program. Sparks (1981) summarized regulatory and judicial arguments in this area and noted the extent to which consideration was given to the relevance of the content and level of the training program when compared to the actual requirements for successful job performance. The value of a good job analysis is demonstrating that this relationship is obvious.

Performance Appraisals

Many organizations use some system of evaluation of performance or job contribution as contributing or controlling with respect to personnel actions—merit pay increases, promotions, layoffs, separations, etc. Many such systems have been successfully challenged in the courts as not being sufficiently related to actual job requirements. Ratings that emphasize traits such as reliability, loyalty, cooperation, etc., without some kind of job performance tie-in have been particularly suspect. Where appraisals have been based on job behaviour or job outcomes the employer's defense has had a much greater likelihood of success. Here, again, a good job analysis can make a major contribution.

Appraisal of the performance of subordinates by supervisors is perhaps the most commonly used criterion for validation of selection procedures. Appraisal with a form based on a job analysis is much more likely to be viewed favourably.

Job Structuring and Restructuring

Organizations are frequently faced with the necessity of staffing a new facility without benefit of a comparable existing facility. Sometimes there is a limited knowledge of the skills and capabilities of persons in the area from which new employees will be recruited. Detail available from an analysis of the specific requirements of the projected jobs can frequently spot job overlapping or insufficient coverage.

Much attention has recently been given to a procedure known as *job enrichment* as a means of improving productivity of employees. This job restructuring is espoused as lessening boredom and resulting inattention and increasing job satisfaction. Detailed study of the characteristics of the original job is crucial to know how to enrich jobs without simply making them more difficult and risking demands for higher pay.

Job Evaluation

Numerous systems exist for establishing appropriate relations between the perceived value of jobs and the pay that is offered for their performance. Almost all of these systems have a base in the identification of different requirement levels of some facets of the job—education required, number of employees under a supervisor, physical exertion required, working conditions, etc. Though classification of these characteristics by levels can be made on the basis of general information, it is far better to be able to tie them back to specific requirements.

Canadian Human Rights Act and the Equal Wage Guidelines of the Canadian Labour Code requires that men and women be given equal pay for equal work and defines both the bases of comparison and the exceptions to the rule. This principle has received wide acceptance in the employer community and in the courts. It seems to have worked well within job families, for example, clerical, mechanical, technicians, professional, and lower level management. Across job families comparisons have been difficult. This has been due in large part to the fact that different job factors have been valued differently in applying them to the jobs in different families. A raging controversy exists today over the proposition that the law should read, equal pay for work of comparable worth. Except to note that the root cause of the controversy is the fact that jobs predominated by women pay less than do jobs predominated by men, discussion is beyond the scope of this chapter. Further information can be found in Blumrosen (1979), Livernash (1980), Treiman and Hartman (1981), and Williams and Kessler (1984).

Occupational Research

It is certainly worth noting that much of the theoretical research and developments in such areas as job satisfaction, motivation, training techniques, occupational or vocational choice, and managing employees is rooted in some form of job analysis. Standardized instruments or well defined systems have been devised for use in a wide variety of investigations. Examples include the Job Diagnostic Survey (Hackman and Oldham 1975), the Job Description Index (Smith, Kendall, and Hulin 1969), and The Self-Directed Search (Holland 1973). For an overview of many of the systems that have been advocated for managing employees, the reader is invited to consult Hersey and Blanchard (1982).

Legal and Quasilegal Concerns

At the present time there is no provincial or federal statutory mandate for any form of job analysis. However, implementing regulations in many of the equal rights areas demand the development of job information in detail that can be provided only by a good job analysis. Examples have been given earlier. For further details see Dolan and Schuler (1987, Ch. 3).

PLANNING FOR A JOB ANALYSIS

Given the multiple uses of job analysis, it should be fairly obvious that no single technique or system will satisfy all of them. The first step in planning is thus to identify the objective(s), or the use(s) to which the job information will be put. This should include both a first use and subsequent uses. For example, if the job analysis information is used to build a performance appraisal form, will the results of the performance appraisal be used in merit pay administration, promotability assessment, analysis of training needs, employee counseling, test validation, or some other purpose? If the job analysis information is used to develop a job classification system for base pay purposes, will it also be considered as usable for salary surveys of competitors? Once these questions have been answered, a study of techniques and their requirements can begin. This can be a mind boggling task as job analysis systems continue to proliferate. Levine, Ash, Hall, and Sistrunk (1983) conducted a study to determine the relationship between methods and objectives. They selected seven different job analysis methods and had experienced job analysts evaluate each of them by using a standardized questionnaire. The seven job analysis methods were chosen on the basis of their widespread use and/or the extent to which they were methodologically different. The analysts were asked to rate each method on *effectiveness* as it might be used for each of eleven different organizational purposes and to rate each method's *practicality* against eleven different concerns. The actual findings of the seven methods are not discussed here. Suffice it to say that a statistically significant difference among the seven job analysis methods was found for each of the organizational purposes. Four different methods ranked as the first choice (mean rating) for at least one organizational purpose. The specified purposes parallel closely those discussed in this chapter: job description, job classification, job evaluation, job design, personnel requirements/specifications, performance appraisal, worker training, worker mobility, efficiency/safety, manpower/work force planning, and legal/quasilegal requirements. Similar findings resulted for ratings of the seven methods on practicality concerns. These involved: occupational versatility/suitability, standardization, respondent/user acceptability, amount of job analyst training required, operational, sample size, off-the-shelf reliability, cost, quality of outcome, and time to completion. Unfortunately, from the point of view of the potential user, the most effective systems were not necessarily the most practical and vice versa.

Searching For the Right System

From my own work and study I have identified nineteen methods of job analysis reported in the literature or otherwise publicized. Each of these is listed here along with a key reference. Not included are systems developed for use in a single organization or for a unique situation. I am sure that the list is not exhaustive. Description of even the principal features of these nineteen systems is beyond the scope of this book.

Ability Requirements Scales (ARS), Fleishman (1975)

Brief GOJA: A Two Hour Job Analysis, Biddle (1977)

Comprehensive Occupational Data Analysis Program (CODAP), Christal and Weissmuller (1977)

Critical Incident Technique (CIT), Flanagan (1954)
Functional Job Analysis (FJA), Fine and Wiley (1971)
Health Services Mobility Study Method (HSMS), Gilpatrick (1977)
Job Components Inventory (JCI), Banks, Jackson, Stafford, and Warr (1983)
Job Element Method (JEM), Primoff (1971)
Job Information Matrix Systems (JIMS), Stone and Yoder (1970)
Management Position Description Inventory (MPDI), Tornow and Pinto (1976)
Occupational Analysis Inventory (OAI), Cunningham, Tuttle, Floyd and Bates (1970)
Physical Abilities Analysis (PAA), Fleishman (1977)
Position Analysis Questionnaire (PAQ), McCormick, Jeanneret, and Mecham (1972)
Skills and Attributes Inventory (SAI), Baehr (1971)
Task Inventories (TI), Melching and Borcher (1973); U.S. Department of Labor (1973)
Threshold Traits Analysis (TTA), Lopez, Kesselman, and Lopez (1981)
Versatile Job Analysis System (VERJAS), Bemis, Belenky, and Soder (1983)
Work Performance Survey System (WPSS), Gael (1983)
Worker Elements Inventory (WEI), Baehr, Lonergan, and Potkay (1967)

Some of these systems or methods provide a standardized form for use in collecting job information. Others provide a system or method for organizing the job information, regardless of how it is collected. There is a growing tendency to modify and combine the various methods and analytical techniques, due in large part to experiences such as those reported in the Levine et al. (1983) study.

Choosing Job Descriptors

All job analyses culminate in a set of job descriptors. Among the more common descriptors found are: education or training requirements; supervision exercised or received; dollar assets employed in the job; specific aptitudes, skill, or knowledge required; amount of prior experience; tools or other equipment used; physical demands reflecting needs for skill or agility; exposure to harsh or noxious working conditions; tasks performed or behaviours demonstrated; and job outcomes. Some descriptors involve information readily available in personnel files. Some involve information that can be obtained by direct observation. Some involve information that can be inferred from knowledge of or inspection of job outcomes. Some involve prior research, the judgment of presumably knowledgeable persons, or some form of inference. All should eventually rest on a foundation of tasks performed or behaviours demonstrated.

Task statements describe operations that can be observed—"mixing mortar for bricklaying." Such task statements generally culminate in a composite description of the *job-oriented content* of the job being analysed. Behaviour statements describe demands made on the worker or anticipated outcomes—"building a brick wall." These behaviour statements generally culminate in a composite description of the *worker-oriented content* of the job being analysed. These distinctions often become fuzzy in practise but they are useful in deciding on what basic data to accumulate.

Frequently, information on several descriptors will be developed in the same job analysis, particularly if multiple uses of the data are contemplated. The U.S. Department of Labor, Manpower Administration (1973) published a volume entitled *Task Analysis Inventories: A Method for Collecting Job Information*. Forms were provided for use in inventorying twenty-two separate and highly diverse occupations. Despite the title of the publication, the items encompass much more than tasks. All items are not included for all occupations, but the basic list includes:

—What the worker does
—Education and training
—Licensure, certificates, rating, etc.
—Communication responsibilities
—Area of responsibility
—Work aids used
—Machines and equipment
—Techniques used
—Specializations
—Products
—Services
—Registry and association requirements
—Union affiliations
—Environmental setting

Even this list is far from exhaustive and the reader will no doubt think of items that should be added when a particular organization or system is under consideration.

COLLECTING DESCRIPTOR INFORMATION

Three major aspects of collecting information need to be considered: (1) how will the necessary information be obtained, (2) who will perform the recording or interpretation of the information, and (3) what form of cataloguing or scaling will be used, if any? Decisions will obviously be made on the objectives of the job analysis, the system to be used, and the facilities available to the organization.

Methods

The method to be used is likely to vary with the kind of information to be collected. However, there may be more than one method for any one type and the choice may well depend on such factors as cost, availability of competent agents, accessibility of employees, the type of data analysis planned, etc.

Observation of the worker doing the job is one obvious method. It is highly suitable where performance of specific tasks is the principal component of the job and where the operations performed, the equipment used, and the end products are readily apparent. It is poorly suited to jobs where the operations and end products are heavily dependent on the integration of knowledge or of cognitive or artistic skill. "Makes marks on paper with a felt-tipped pen" hardly describes an advertising copy-writer.

Interview with the job incumbent is applicable to a wide variety of jobs, including jobs at almost all levels of the occupational hierarchy. It is extremely time consuming and costly. It also suffers from the fact that the interviewer may not be able to separate the idiosyncratic aspects of the job, as performed by a particular incumbent, from the basic activities of the job as preformed by a number of incumbents. Since the only remedy for this is to interview multiple incumbents, the gross inefficiency of the method becomes readily apparent.

Conference with experienced personnel is also applicable to a wide variety of jobs. It lessens the risk of recording examples of idiosyncratic behaviour, but the seeming consensual agreement may be only generalizations at a higher level than specific examples of behaviour.

Open-ended or unstructured questionnaires are frequently used with professional, staff, or managerial personnel. The job holder or some other knowledgeable person writes a narrative in response to a topical outline or to a series of questions. The quality of the instructions is tremendously important for this method. The responses may vary from minutiae to broad generalizations unless strong control is provided.

Structured questionnaires may be used with jobs of all types and at all levels. The content of the forms may be varied to fit the objectives of the job analysis. The response mode may be varied to obtain information along different dimensions of the job. The questionnaire is most often completed by job incumbents, but it may also be completed by others who are familiar with the job, for example immediate supervisors. Standardized forms are commercially available, some of which are applicable to a variety of jobs and some of which are tailored to a specific job family.

A diary maintained by the worker is sometimes used for jobs that have very little structure. The job incumbent simply keeps a chronological record of activities or events. A variant of this method is a stratified sampling procedure. At specified times the job incumbent records what he or she was doing.

Film records of the worker doing the job are often used where the elements of interest are the physical movements performed. An example is found in industrial engineering where realtionships between persons and machines are being investigated. Athletic coaches use the technique extensively, though they might not think of it in terms of job analysis.

Inspection of transactions performed can provide a wealth of information on certain kinds of jobs, for example, delivery-salespersons. Some organizations couple written information with a tachometer that records vehicle movements.

Obviously, many of these methods may be used in combination. One method may frequently be the starting point in preparation for the eventual use of some other. A limited number of interviews or observations may be the first step in preparation of a questionnaire that will be administered to a large number of job incumbents and/or their supervisors. A conference of experienced personnel may be used to develop topics or questions for use in conducting interviews or for use in an open-ended questionnaire.

Agents

A great deal of attention has been given to the subject of the type of person required to obtain the job analysis information. Three classes of individuals come immediately to mind: (1) analysts, (2) incumbents, and (3) supervisors. Each class provides advantages but also has disadvantages. Method constraints must also be taken into consideration. A diary can hardly be maintained by anyone other than the job incumbent. Observation cannot be accomplished except by someone external to the worker.

Job analysts are trained in the systematic recording and the interpretation of the material collected. No amount of carefully written material can substitute for this training and experience. The job analyst is most often needed where the organization's own experience with job analysis is limited and in-house personnel are naive. If the method chosen is based on observation or interview, and the number of jobs to be analysed is large, the time and expense required for complete coverage may be almost prohibitive. A compromise is sometimes effected by having in-house personnel specialists or even operating personnel trained to be analysts and having them supervised by a skilled analyst. With other methods, for example, questionnaires, the analyst may be used in the designing of the questionnaire and the analysis of the results, while in-house personnel handle the administrative detail of obtaining the basic data.

Job incumbents are most likely to have the best information on what is actually done on the job. However, the incumbent may not be in a position to evaluate properly the importance of the many tasks and behaviours that make up a typical job. Some job analysts have been concerned about the possibility that incumbents would tend to inflate their jobs in order to make them seem more important than they really were. There is little published research on this proposition and it is mixed. Employers with union contracts have frequently expressed a concern that having incumbents describe their jobs might result in a freezing of job content or even in jurisdictional disputes over the work to be done by different categories of workers. Certainly, the use of job incumbents is the most efficient way to obtain multiple descriptions of the same job, particularly when questionnaires are used to collect the basic information.

Job supervisors should generally be in a position to know what their subordinates do and be able to judge the importance of different activities. There are exceptions. For example, it is the custom in many organizations for generalists to supervise the professional or technical specialists or for engineers to supervise craft workers. In many instances, they are not expected to know the working details of the job, but are considered to be better planners and administrators. It has been suggested that supervisors have a tendency to give idealized versions of the job. That is, they are likely to give a description of the job as it should be performed, instead of describing the job as it is actually performed.

Obviously, these agents can be mixed. Many organizations have found that having the job incumbent and his or her supervisor compare independently prepared job analyses is an excellent way to communicate with each other. Sometimes the choice is dictated by considerations external to obtaining the best or most efficient job analysis. Management may consider that employees should not be permitted to determine the content of their jobs. Unions may be averse to having their members contribute information. Your author was treated to a curious situation where long service employees were reluctant to admit that they had developed various labour saving devices. For example, in one refinery the employees had been able to devise a way to use a pair of binoculars instead of climbing a ladder in order to measure the contents of a tank. This fact was revealed at a neighborhood bar and not at the plant.

Cataloguing and Scaling

At some point in the analysis, all of the information that has been accumulated must be brought together in some kind of summary. This generally means fleshing out a previously prepared outline of the major considerations being investigated—content, location, educational demands, physical demands, tools or equipment, supervision, working conditions, etc. Narrative descriptions of the activities performed and/or their meaning in terms of job requirements may be sufficient. However, for most objectives it is important that some form of qualifier be added. For example, a typewriter may be used by the receptionist and by a secretary. The former may be using the typewriter for a simple forms-finishing job while not engaged in his or her primary job. The latter may spend the majority of his or her time in the preparation of correspondence that will go outside the company. "Uses a typewriter," without further qualification is obviously not an adequate piece of job information. If the basic data have been properly recorded, the summary should provide information necessary to rate typewriter usage on a scale such as *essential, important, useful,* and *unimportant*. Scales chosen for rating must reflect the degree of importance of a particular activity or a particular qualification. A commonly used scale involves rating the *relative time spent* in different activities. This may or may not be a good reflection of relative importance. A firefighter may spend eighty percent of the working hours cleaning and repairing equipment or even playing pinochle. Answering alarms and fighting fires are still the essential parts of the job.

Numerous headings in a job analysis summary involve areas that conventional wisdom, market place values, or tradition have scaled. For example, education required is frequently scaled as years of schooling through high school graduation and degree level beyond. The working conditions scale runs from the most disagreeable and noxious to quiet, air conditioned surroundings. When judgments on these scales are required it is essential that actual information be used. Generalizations can get one in trouble. The fact that all incumbents are highly qualified in advanced mathematics is a false lead if the job does not require the exercise of such training. A large petrochemical complex air conditioned a huge hanger-like structure so that its machinists, welders, etc. would not be exposed to the brutal deep south weather.

TECHNIQUES FOR STRUCTURING INFORMATION

Some jobs are so nearly identical that they might have been stamped out with the same cookie-cutter. However, much more common are jobs that have the same primary content, but vary slightly in terms of such factors as ancillary duties, job surroundings, size of the operation, etc. Management needs to know at what point such differences suggest variations in training, classification, pay, etc. The process to be used will depend on several factors—the way in which the basic information has been collected, the objectives of the job analysis, the extent to which the desired result is an indication of similarities or differences, etc. The judgments that have been made as to placement on different scales may be all that are necessary for comparison among jobs. For example, ability to read blueprints at the fabrication level may be a necessary factor in several craft jobs but not in others, even though a factor such as reading operational manuals is essentially identical in all of the craft jobs. Meeting such objectives as designing and validating a selection program, or developing a training program, could be an important reason for differentiating among the craft jobs. On the other hand, such a differentiation might be relatively unimportant if the objective is a job evaluation to establish appropriate wage levels for the different jobs.

Current job analysis techniques rely heavily on one or more statistical techniques. It is hard to say which was the driving force. Modern statistical techniques and improved capabilities of computer manipulation have made the handling of masses of data possible in ways that rational judgment does not permit. Almost simultaneously the advent of masses of questionnaire data and/or more systematic recording of the most elemental job data has created a demand for more sophisticated techniques of analyzing similarities and differences. Examples of these are necessary for understanding these developments.

Standardized Instruments

Basic data are collected by having the job incumbent or someone else intimately familiar with the job use a standardized questionnaire. This may be analyzed according to the instructions of the author. The questionnaire may also be used as a basic research device on the presumption that the author has been able to cover all of the salient aspects of the jobs to be analysed. Two instruments stand out as having a substantial research base. One is the *Position Analysis Questionnaire* (McCormick, Jeanneret, and Mecham 1972). The other is the *Occupational Analysis Inventory* (Pass and Cunningham 1977).

The Position Analysis Questionnaire (PAQ) is a structured job analysis questionnaire containing 187 job elements. These elements are worker-oriented and so might be characterized as behaviour statements, as opposed to task statements. McCormick (1979) notes that the PAQ is organized in six divisions. These are:

——*Information input* Where and how does the worker get the information he or she uses in performing the job?
——*Mental process* What reasoning, decision-making, planning, and information-processing activities are involved in performing the job?
——*Work output* What physical activities does the worker perform and what tools or devices does he or she use?
——*Relationships with other persons* What relationships with other people are required in performing the job?
——*Job context* In what physical or social contexts is the work performed?
——*Other job characteristics* What activities, conditions, or characteristics other than those described above are relevant to the job?

Each of the 187 job elements is rated on one of six different types of rating scales: extent of use, importance to the job, amount of time, possibility of occurrence, applicability, and a special code that is used for only a few very specific job elements. Except for applicability which is dichotomous, all scales have five steps that range from some version of very low to some version of very high, plus a provision for noting that the element does not apply to the job being analysed. The authors provide a scoring system which develops a quantitative profile of the job. Basic dimensions of this profile were developed through extensive factor analyses. The PAQ has been a favourite with job analysis researchers, both applied and theoretical. Its structure lends itself readily to many types of study. For example, McCormick, DeNisi, and Shaw (1979) used the PAQ to derive job-related aptitude requirements for establishing job-related selection tests. Robinson, Wahlstrom, and Mecham (1974) used the PAQ to develop job evaluation points for determining pay scales and job classifications. Arvey and Mossholder (1977) used the PAQ in development of a job analysis procedure for determining similarities and differences among jobs. The interested reader will find these and a host of other

PAQ based articles in the professional literature.

The Occupational Analysis Inventory (OAI) was started from an interest in the possibility of occupational clustering in order to develop efficient occupational education programs. The OAI is a long instrument, containing 602 work elements grouped into five categories, some with subcategories:

> Information received
> > Information content
> > Sensory channel
>
> Mental activities
>
> Work behaviour
> > Physical work behaviour
> > Representational work behaviour
> > Interpersonal work behaviour
>
> Work goals
>
> Work context

One of the reasons for the large number of elements in the OAI is the inclusion of specific activities associated with a particular occupation. The OAI was researched on 1,414 jobs selected to represent five major classifications contained in the *Dictionary of Occupational Titles* (U.S. Department of Labor 1965). Like the PAQ, the OAI can be used without the structure developed by the authors, with reasonable assurance that the job coverage has been systematic and complete.

Standardized Formatting

As noted earlier, job information may be obtained by a variety of methods or techniques. It is often highly desirable to summarize this information in a standardized fashion. One way of accomplishing this is to have the analyst interpret the information according to a predetermined, standardized format. That is, the analyst uses specified scales and uses the job information deducted from the appropriate placement on the scales. Some methods of information collecting are easier to handle in this way than are others. Task statements are ordinarily the easiest.

Functional job analysis is the prime example of standardized formatting. It was developed during research performed in preparing for the 1965 edition of the *Dictionary of Occupational Titles* (U.S. Department of Labor). The research identified three primary classifications of activities—those associated with data, those associated with people, and those associated with things. Furthermore, these were posited as existing in a hierarchy from an activity of low value to an activity of high value. In addition to these three primary considerations, the FJA system included four other scales—worker instructions, reasoning development, mathematical developments, and language development (Fine 1973). Each step of the functional scales is carefully defined so that consistency of level assignment is maintained. A complete listing of the steps in each of the scales is given here. Note that alternatives are provided for some of the steps in each.

Data Function Scale

1.	Comparing	4.	Analysing
2.	Copying	5A.	Innovating
3A.	Computing	5B.	Coordinating
3B.	Compiling	6.	Synthesizing

People Function Scale

1A.	Taking instructions—helping	4A.	Consulting
1B.	Serving	4B.	Instructing
2.	Exchanging information	4C.	Treating
3A.	Coaching	5.	Supervising
3B.	Persuading	6.	Negotiating
3C.	Diverting	7.	Mentoring

Things Function Scale

1A. Handling	2B. Operating—controlling
1B. Feeding—offbearing	2C. Driving—controlling
1C. Tending	3A. Precision working
2A. Manipulating	3B. Setting up

Fine and his associates used task statements to gather the data to be used in scaling. However, any method may be used if it provides sufficient information for making reliable and valid judgments.

The job element method was developed by the U.S. Civil Service Commission (Primoff 1971). It was developed as a basis for the establishment of standards for employment in the federal government. It has since been adopted by many state and local government agencies. The method uses a set of carefully defined criteria and systematic procedures for determining critical worker requirements and then examining for them. The job elements of the system are the various knowledges, skills, abilities, and other personal characteristics (KSAOs) necessary for workers to perform the jobs. Panels of job incumbents and their supervisors are frequently used to develop a list of possible KSAOs. These are then evaluated through the application of four rating scales. Paraphrased, these are:

——What proportion of barely acceptable workers are now on the job?

——How important is the element in picking out acceptable workers?

——How much trouble is likely if the element is not considered?

——How many openings can be filled if this element is demanded?

The important or critical job elements are identified by the use of index scores obtained from ratings on these scales. The item index is constructed by multiplying the superior worker's value by the practicality value (openings can be filled) and adding the trouble value. Since the method begins with identification of the KSAOs, selection characteristics are identified almost immediately. Primoff (1972) has proposed the *J-coefficient* as a way of making this translation.

The Physical Abilities Analysis (PAA) was developed to analyse the special subset of abilities and job demands identified as requiring physical proficiency (Fleishman 1964, 1975, 1979). The importance of identifying physical proficiency requirements at a level of almost unchallengeable accuracy is growing daily with the pressures to employ women in nontraditional jobs, employment of handicapped persons, and protection for older workers. Physical demands rated on the PAA are nine, and the job being analysed can be profiled for each of these dimensions. These are:

——*Dynamic strength* This is defined as the ability to exert muscular force repeatedly or continuously over time.

——*Trunk strength* This is a derivative of the dynamic strength factor and is characterized by resistance of trunk muscles to fatigue over repeated use.

——*Static strength* This is the force that an individual exerts in lifting, pushing, pulling, or carrying external objects.

——*Explosive strength* This is characterized by the ability to expend a maximum of energy in one or a series of maximum thrusts.

——*Extent flexibility* This involves the ability to extend the trunk, arms, and/or legs through a range of motion in either the frontal, sagittal, or transverse planes.

———*Dynamic flexibility* This contrasts with extent flexibility in that the ability involves the capacity to make rapid, repeated flexing movements, in which the resilience of the muscles in recovering from distention is critical.

———*Gross body coordination* This is the ability to coordinate the simultaneous actions of different parts of the body or body limbs while the body is in motion. This ability is frequently referred to as agility.

———*Gross body equilibrium* This is the ability to maintain balance in either an unstable position or when opposing forces are pulling.

———*Stamina* This is synonomous with cardiovascular endurance and enables the performance of prolonged bouts of aerobic work without experiencing fatigue or exhaustion.

The analyst rates the demands of the job task on a seven-point scale in which the top anchor is a well-known task agreed upon as representing maximum performance on the particular scale, and the bottom anchor is a well-known task representing minimum performance on the scale. Other levels are tasks slotted appropriately. Many of the scaled tasks are from sports, household activities, or other ordinary life activities.

Statistical Programming

The advent of sophisticated software that will handle large amounts of data has led to development of several techniques for determining similarities and differences among jobs. All of these depend on some kind of numerical input (binary data will generally be sufficient). The format for collection of data is generally unimportant if the data can be scaled.

Factor analysis is the most venerable of the statistical techniques and is still widely used. It requires a correlation matrix that shows the interrelationships among items or profiles for the jobs in question. For example, data for secretaries, file clerks, computer programmers, repair persons, salespersons, and the supervisors of each could be factor analysed. The result would be a matrix of factor loadings. Inspection of these loadings would indicate similarities and differences among the jobs. Early factor programs required reduction of data (development of average or mean scores where several observations were made). Currently, the software will permit the handling of multiple observations of the same job. The factor structure obtained must still be interpreted. Ordinarily, several different solutions will attain approximately the same level in explaining the underlying dimensions. A choice is frequently made on the basis of the rationality of the solution or the extent to which it meets the objective of the job analysis.

The Ward and Hook hierarchical grouping procedure (Ward and Hook 1963; Feild and Schoenfeldt 1975) is an iterative clustering method that can be used to develop the most parsimonious explanation of the number of groups that can be formed from a large number of observations. The essence of the technique is the successive clustering of individuals (jobs) into groups that contain members who are more like that group than they are to members of any other group. For example, starting with the presumption that all of the observations belong to the same group, one is likely to find that there are numerous outliers, persons who obviously do not fit. Continuing the procedure, one will ordinarily find that more persons will fit into two groups, three groups, etc. If the groups become too specialized, there is essentially no grouping. Judgment must frequently be used in determining when to stop the iterative process. The technique is widely used in job analysis. The reader is referred to Tryon and Bailey (1970) for a more complete discussion of cluster analysis.

Analysis of variance has been proposed as one method of looking at the degree of similarity among jobs (Arvey and Mossholder 1977). Discussion of statistical techniques is beyond the scope of this chapter. Essentially, an analysis of variance compares variation among jobs thought to be similar with data from jobs that are not so considered. For example, job *A* has ten incumbents and there are minor variations in their tasks and duties. Is this variation less or more than is found when they are compared with incumbents in job *B*? Results may well depend on the specificity of the information.

The Air Force Comprehensive Occupational Data Analysis Program (CODAP) was developed over a period of many years by Christal and his associates at the Personnel Research Division, Air Force Human Resources Laboratory, Lackland Air Force Base, Texas (Christal and Weissmuller 1977; Archer and Giorgia 1977). The system is now used outside the Air Force (Trattner 1979) and training programs in the use of CODAP are being offered across the country, notably by the International Personnel Management Association. The heart of the CODAP program is a task analysis. Tasks and duties involved in a particular job are developed by incumbents, supervisors, or other knowledgeable persons. After the listing of tasks included in a particular occupation has been prepared, incumbents are asked to indicate whether or not they performed the task listed. If yes, they are asked to indicate the relative amount of time spent in performing the particular task relative to other tasks performed. A judgmental scale is used rather than actual amounts of available time. The CODAP scale has seven points, anchored at the top by 7—Very much above average and at the bottom by 1—Very much below average. Each task rating of each job incumbent is summed across all tasks and each task summation is then summed and divided by the sum to give an estimated percentage of the total job. The total of these percentages accounts for the total job. The total for the critical jobs represents the extent to which the analysis has accounted for the total job.

EVALUATING THE ANALYSIS AND/OR THE END PRODUCT

Once the job analysis has been completed and the descriptions, profiles, classifications, families, etc. can be determined, the adequacy of the analysis or the end products should be evaluated. Several points should be considered. The end result of a job analysis is a measurement and is subject to evaluation in terms of its psychometric adequacy.

Reliability

This is a measure of the consistency of the results obtained. Within reasonable limits, two different analysts should obtain the same results from an analysis of the same job, or an analyst should obtain the same results from an analysis of the same job on two different occasions, unless the job has materially changed in the meantime. There is no professional consensus on what constitutes an acceptable degree of reliability, but attention to the concept is vital.

Validity

This is a measure of the accuracy of the results. It is quite possible for two analysts to agree completely and for both to be wrong as a result of incomplete information, biased reports, and so on. There is no way of showing that a job analysis is or is not valid. This is particularly true as one moves from the simple operational type jobs to those demanding a high level of cognitive skills or a high degree of interaction with others. The most common methods of ensuring accuracy is the use of multiple reporters or analysers or the use of more than one method of job analysis.

Comprehensiveness

The job analysis may be both reliable and valid, for what it covers. The description of a secretarial job in terms of shorthand, typing, filing, etc. may be highly accurate, but it is certainly not complete unless it includes such activities as answering the telephone, making quick copies, accepting and relaying messages, etc. A simple listing of tasks performed may fail to cover the context in which these tasks are carried out. CODAP, and some other systems, provide an indication of the extent to which the listed activities provide an indication of the size of the total job. At a less sophisticated level, incumbents can be asked to estimate the coverage of the total job that is covered by the listed elements.

WHAT OF THE FUTURE

It should be obvious from the foregoing discussion that no one system of job analysis available at the present time will meet all of the possible objectives. Many employers are routinely using two or three and trying to meld the results. In the meantime, research on ways to improve the accuracy or ease of data collection and/or interpretation is underway. For example, Hogan and Fleishman (1979) had subjects rate the effort required to complete tasks whose actual metabolic costs were known. They found a high degree of agreement between the judged amount of effort and the actual metabolic costs.

Additional systems will undoubtedly continue to proliferate as the amount of money to be made in the field increases because of the stance of the regulatory agencies and the importance of job analysis in litigation. In all probability there will be instances in which expert witnesses for the plaintiff and for the defendant will argue as to whether the right or best technique was used. In any case, tomorrow's human resource manager had better be prepared to develop in-house expertise or find a consultant with appropriate credentials.

References

Arvey, R. D. and K. M. Mossholder. 1977. A proposed methodology for determining similarities and differences among jobs. *Personnel Psychology* 30:363–74.

Baehr, M. E. 1971. *Skills and attributes inventory.* Chicago, IL: The University of Chicago, Industrial Relations Center.

Baehr, M. E., W. G. Lonergan, and C. R. Potkay. 1967. *Work elements inventory.* Chicago, IL: The University of Chicago, Industrial Relations Center.

Banks, M. H., P. R. Jackson, E. M. Stafford, and P. R. Warr. 1983. The job components inventory and the analysis of jobs requiring limited skill. *Personnel Psychology* 36: 57–66.

Bemis, S. E., A. H. Belenky, and D. A. Soder. 1983. *Job analysis: An effective management tool.* Washington, DC: The Bureau of National Affairs.

Biddle, R. E. 1977. *Brief GOJA: A two hour job analysis.* Sacramento, CA: Biddle and Associates.

Blumrosen, R. G. 1979. Wage discrimination, job segregation, and Title VII of the Civil Rights Act of 1964. *University of Michigan Journal of Law Reform* 12:397–502.

Christal, R. E. and J. J. Weissmuller. 1977. New Comprehensive Data Analysis Programs (CODAP) for analyzing task factor information. JSAS *Catalog of Selected Documents in Psychology* 7:24–25 (Ms. No. 1444).

Cunningham, J. W., T. C. Tuttle, J. R. Floyd, and J. A. Bates. 1970. *Occupational Analysis Inventory.* Raleigh, NC: North Carolina State University, Center for Occupational Education.

Dolan, S. L. and R. S. Schuler. 1987. *Personnel and Human Resource Management in Canada.* St. Paul, MN: West Publishing Co.

Feild, H. S. and L. F. Schoenfeldt. 1975. Ward and Hook revisited: A two-part procedure for overcoming a deficiency in the grouping of persons. *Educational and Psychological Measurement* 35:171–73.

Fine, S. A. 1973. *Functional Job Analysis Scales: A Desk Aid.* Kalamazoo, MI: Upjohn Institute for Employment Research.

Fine, S. A. and W. W. Wiley. 1971. *An Introduction to Functional Job Analysis: Methods for Manpower Analysis.* Kalamazoo, MI: Upjohn Institute for Employment Research.

Flanagan, J. C. 1954. The critical incident technique. *Psychological Bulletin* 51:327–58.

Fleishman, E. A. 1964. *Structure and measurement of physical fitness.* Englewood Cliffs, NJ: Prentice-Hall.

Fleishman, E. A. 1975. Toward a taxonomy of human performance. *American Psychologist* 30:1127–49.

Fleishman, E. A. 1977. *Physical abilities analysis manual.* Washington, DC: Advanced Research Resources Organization.

Fleishman, E. A. 1979. Evaluating physical abilities required by jobs. *Personnel Administrator* 24(6): 82–92.

Gael, S. 1983. *Job analysis: A guide to assessing work activities.* San Francisco, CA: Jossey-Bass.

Gael, S., ed. In press. *Job analysis handbook.* New York, NY: John Wiley & Sons.

Gilpatrick, E. (1977). *The Health Services Mobility Study method of task analysis and curriculum design—Concepts, task identification, skill scales and knowledge system.* Research Report No. 11, Vol. 1. Springfield, VA: National Technical Information Service.

Hackman, J. R. and G. R. Oldham. 1975. Development of the Job Diagnostic Survey. *Journal of Applied Psychology* 60:159–70.

Hersey, P. and K. H. Blanchard. 1982. *Management of organizational behavior: Utilizing human resources.* Englewood Cliffs, NJ: Prentice-Hall.

Hogan, J. C. and E. A. Fleishman. 1979. An index of the physical effort required in human task performance. *Journal of Applied Psychology* 64:197–204.

Holland, J. L. 1973. *Making vocational choices: A theory of careers.* Englewood Cliffs, NJ: Prentice-Hall.

Levine, E. L., R. A. Ash, H. Hall, and F. Sistrunk. 1983. Evaluation of job analysis methods by experienced job analysts. *Academy of Management Journal* 26:339–48.

Livernash, E. R., ed. 1980. *Comparable worth: Issues and alternatives.* Washington, DC: Equal Employment Advisory Council.

Lopez, F. M., G. A. Kesselman, and F. E. Lopez. 1981. An empirical test of a trait-oriented job analysis technique. *Personnel Psychology* 34:479–502.

McCormick, E. J. 1979. *Job analysis: Methods and applications.* New York: AMACOM.

McCormick, E. J., A. S. DeNisi, and J. B. Shaw. 1979. Use of the Position Analysis Questionnaire for establishing the job component validity of tests. *Journal of Applied Psychology* 64:51–56.

McCormick, E. J., P. R. Jeanneret, and R. C. Mecham. 1972. A study of job characteristics and job dimensions as based on the Position Analysis Questionnaire (PAQ). *Journal of Applied Psychology* 56:347–68.

Melching, W. H. and H. D. Borcher. 1973. *Procedures for constructing and using task inventories.* Columbus, OH: The Ohio State University.

Pass, J. J., and Cunningham, J. W. 1977. *Occupational clusters based on systematically derived work dimensions: Final report.* Raleigh, NC: North Carolina State University, Center for Occupational Education.

Pearlman, K. 1980. Job families: A review and discussion of their implications for personnel selection. *Psychological Bulletin* 87: 1–28.

Primoff, E. S. 1971. *Summary of job-element principles: preparing a job-element standard.* Washington, DC: U.S. Civil Service Commission, Personnel Measurement and Development Center.

Primoff, E. S. 1972. *The J-coefficient procedure.* Washington, DC: U.S. Civil Service Commission, Personnel Measurement and Development Center.

Robinson, D. D., O. W. Wahlstrom, and R. C. Mecham. 1974. Comparison of job evaluation methods: A "policy capturing" approach using the Position Analysis Questionnaire (PAQ). *Journal of Applied Psychology* 59:633–37.

Smith, P. C., L. M. Kendall, and C. L. Hulin. 1969. *The measurement of satisfaction in work and retirement.* Chicago, IL: Rand McNally.

Sparks, C. P. 1981. Success in training as a criterion for test validation. *Journal of Policy Analysis and Information Systems* 5: 31–41.

Stone, C. H., and D. Yoder. 1970. *Job analysis.* Los Angeles, CA: California State College.

Tornow, W. W., and P. R. Pinto. 1976. The development of a managerial taxonomy: A system for describing, classifying, and evaluating executive positions. *Journal of Applied Psychology* 61:410–18.

Trattner, M. H. 1979. Task analysis in the design of three concurrent validity studies of the Professional and Administrative Career Examination. *Personnel Psychology* 32: 109–19.

Treiman, D. J. and H. I. Hartman, eds. 1981. *Women, work, and wages: Equal pay for jobs of equal value.* Washington, DC: National Academy Press.

Tryon, R. C. and D. E. Bailey. 1970. *Cluster analysis.* New York: McGraw-Hill.

U.S. Department of Labor. 1965. *Dictionary of occupational titles.* Washington, DC: U.S. Government Printing Office.

U.S. Department of Labor, Manpower Administration. 1973. *Task analysis inventories: A method for collecting job information.* Washington, DC: U.S. Government Printing Office.

U.S. Equal Employment Opportunity Commission, U.S. Civil Service Commission, U.S. Department of Labor, and U.S. Department of Justice. 1978. Adoption by four agencies of uniform guidelines on employment selection procedures (1978). *Federal Register* 43:38290–38315.

Ward, J. H., Jr. and M. E. Hook. 1963. Application of an hierarchical grouping procedure to a problem of grouping profiles. *Educational and Psychological Measurement* 23:69–81.

Williams, R. E. and L. L. Kessler. 1984. *A closer look at comparable worth.* Washington, DC: National Foundation for the Study of Equal Employment Policy.

Section III
Staffing

In the first article, Janz attempts to demonstrate that the use of scientific methods of selection, as opposed to traditional methods, could significantly benefit the Canadian economy. Once considered an art, selection nowadays is becoming a science. According to Janz, the proper use of scientific selection methods can benefit the average firm far beyond the costs associated with the development of rigorous selection procedures. Using a mathematical model, Janz is able to demonstrate this assertion. In a brief reference to selection fairness, Janz concludes that scientific selection not only promotes efficiency, but it also contributes to selection fairness.

The next three articles highlight the growing concern over issues of employment equity in making staffing decisions. Canadian National Railways was the first company in Canada forced to undertake a mandatory affirmative action program in order to promote equal employment opportunities for its female employees. First, Piché elaborates on the development of strategies by CN in order to comply with the affirmative action requirements. In a detailed analysis the author explains how the system works. Next, Jain provides a state of the art review of equality of employment in Canada within the framework of the Charter of Rights and Freedoms, and the Employment Equity Act. Jain concludes that employers should develop employment equity policies not only for reasons of compliance with the various laws, but also for an increase in efficiency. In the last article in this sub-section on employment equity, White explains the evolution of the equal employment opportunity program at the Royal Bank of Canada. Today, the EEO program at the Royal Bank is well integrated within the personnel and human resource management practices. White provides details about the operational aspects of the program and concludes with a look into the future.

The next three articles by Janz, Broadhurst and Cronshaw examine components of the staffing process. While Janz and Cronshaw provide an academic analysis of the selection interview and the psychological testing respectively, Broadhurst comments on the practicality of using these and other selection devices. The article by Janz begins with a quick look at the received wisdom emerging from research on the selection interview. Then he contrasts old theories with the new research findings especially with regard to the validity of certain types of interviews. Janz ends his paper with some practical suggestions regarding the use of the interview in making staffing decisions. Broadhurst looks at some practical concerns facing PHRM officers who make staffing decisions. They are subject to pressures arising from economic forces, technological forces, societal and political forces, and legal pressures. These pressures, according to Broadhurst result in new employee selection and placement systems. The author discusses the characteristics of this new evolving system. Given the frequent use of tests in large Canadian companies, Cronshaw begins his paper by identifying the characteristics of valid and reliable tests. He then suggests three approaches to either finding or developing good tests. He concludes with an example of a successful Canadian testing program developed by the Life Insurance Marketing and Research Association.

The final article in this staffing section addresses the leading edge of research on new and some controversial methods surrounding staffing practices. Tziner's article on the assessment center, highlights selected facets regarding the manner in which it is being used and its contribution to selection. More specifically, the article focuses on such topics as: the assessment process outcomes, the predictive validity of the ratings and the comparison to more traditional selection methods.

7. Forecasting the Costs and Benefits of Traditional Versus Scientific Employment Selection Methods in Canada to the Year 1990

Tom Janz, The University of Calgary

The past few years produced major advances in the science of employment selection. In the late seventies, Frank Schmidt, John Hunter, and their colleagues in the United States Office of Personnel Management injected new life into the selection utility formulae developed earlier by Cronbach and Gleser (1965). They attacked the tough parameter estimation problems head on, offering new approaches for estimating the population accuracy or validity of selection methods (Schmidt and Hunter 1977; Hunter, Schmidt, and Jackson 1982), and suggested novel methods for estimating the annual standard deviation of performance in dollars (Schmidt, Hunter, McKenzie and Muldrow 1979; Hunter and Schmidt 1983). While debate continues, especially on the dollar spread in performance issue, their vigorous efforts place scientists in a much better position to forecast net benefits for selection policy alternatives.

This paper applies the formulae they derived to forecast the net dollar benefits of scientific versus traditional selection methods for the Canadian economy to the year 1990. The results project how much it will cost Canadians to upgrade employment selection systems to state-of-the-art levels. It also projects how much it will cost Canadians not to. We can choose to spend the money on upgrading now, or on poor performance and low productivity later. It truly remains an investment decision.

CALCULATION OF COSTS, BENEFITS, AND SAVINGS

Adding up the costs of selection programs, from the money spent to recruit the applicants through to the last dollar spent on the last interview has never been the fundamental costing problem. Cost accountants capable of the task abound. The problem has been producing reasonable dollar estimates for the benefits. Traditionally, selection program benefits have been captured by such words as acquiring the cream of the crop or maintaining a tradition of outstanding personnel. Whose annual report does not emphasize that, "our human resources are our greatest asset?" Yet, throughout human resource activities, practitioners have been unable or unwilling to put a dollar value on that asset.

The basic mathematical relationships among selection program characteristics and the benefits they produce have been available since the 1950s (Cronbach and Gleser 1965). Recent years yielded a bumper crop of research articles exploring the utility formulae in detail (Cascio 1982; Landy, Farr, and Jacobs 1982; Arnold, Rauschenberger, Soubel, and Guion 1983; Schmidt, Hunter, and Pearlman 1981; Janz 1982; Boudreau and Berger 1985; Janz and Etherington 1985).

This paper applied formula six from the Schmidt et al. (1979) paper to the task of projecting bottom line savings for investing in scientifically proven selection methods. In symbolic form, the formula is:

$$U = t\, Ns\, (r2 - r1)\, SDy\, (O/p) - Ns(C2 - C1)/p \text{ where:}$$

U is the gain in dollars for the improved interviewing

t is tenure of those selected in years

Ns is the number of openings

$r2 - r1$ is the difference in accuracy between the two techniques stated as validity correlation coefficients

SDy is the annual standard deviation of performance in dollars

O/p is the normally scaled advantage of selecting from more than one applicant for each opening

p itself is the selection ratio (openings/applicants)

$C2 - C1$ is the difference in selection costs per applicant of the old versus improved selection system

In words, the part of the formula left of the minus sign calculates the elusive benefit side of the cost-benefit comparison. Dollar benefits are the multiplication of the number of hires by the average tenure in years, by the dollar value for the annual performance difference between top, middle, and bottom third workers, by the accuracy of selection decisions by the advantage gained from looking at more than one applicant for each opening.

Costs include recruiting costs, costs of developing new selection skills or systems, time and overhead in pre-screening, time in interviews, test scoring, and time taken to reach a decision after it all.

Other literature addresses how each of the terms of the utility equation can be measured. The benefit side presents the major challenge. Of the five terms on the benefit side, the number of applicants, the number of openings, and the average tenure, pose minor difficulties. Hunter and Schmidt (1983), Hunter and Hunter (1984), McDaniel and Schmidt (1985), and Weisner and Cronshaw (1986) applied meta-analysis to the task of estimating the population accuracies or validities of alternative prediction methods. Table 7-1 summarizes their findings.

Scientific methods have demonstrated superior job validity based on many hundreds of individual research studies involving a combined data base containing over one hundred thousand individual people.

The one term of the utility equation not discussed so far remains a thorn in the side of selection practitioners—the annual standard deviation of performance in dollars (labeled SDy). This statistic summarizes the dollar value of job performance differences among top, middle and bottom third performers on any given job. We all intuitively know that top third performers produce more returns for their organizations in terms of goods sold, cases handled, or taxes collected. This statistic (SDy) tells us how much more top third performers return in dollars.

Three major approaches have been suggested for deriving SDy: (1) the cost accounting method (Roche 1965), (2) the direct method (Schmidt et al. 1979), and (3) the forty percent rule (Schmidt and Hunter 1983). The cost accounting method requires a detailed accounting of all input materials, capital costs, energy costs, along with a market valuation of the goods produced. These costs can be estimated for routine production jobs such as Roche's drill press operators, but become problematic for managerial and professional jobs requiring team effort.

Schmidt et al. (1979) introduced the direct estimation method as an alternative. They asked supervisors of computer programmers to directly estimate the annual dollar value of the total goods and services produced by average (defined as fiftieth percentile), top (defined as eighty-fifth percentile), and poor (defined as fifteenth percentile) programmers. Recalling that the eighty-fifth percentile corresponds to one standard deviation of the normal distribution, Schmidt et al. estimated SDy by averaging the top minus average, and the average minus poor performer annual dollar return. They reasoned that individual managers might be off in their perceptions, but that their errors would cancel out over a large enough sample. This approach lacks logical precision, and the empirical results find supervisors in such wide disagreement that the central limit theorem provides me little comfort.

To make it even easier for selection practitioners to conduct utility analysis, Hunter and Schmidt (1983) introduced the forty percent rule. Oversimplifying their arguments, they observed the variation in worker set production rates reported for twenty-three studies. Variation in output volume plotted fairly steadily at around twenty percent of wage. Then Hunter and Schmidt argued that when adding quality considerations to mere counts of volume, the variation or spread of performance in dollars plotted predictable between forty to sixty percent of wage. Thus, they advocated selection practitioners use a forty percent rule in setting SDy—forty percent of wage. Again, the logic remains unconvincing. Surely the routine production jobs reviewed cannot be taken to adequately sample all jobs. The weak logic calls for skepticism, but before we reject this or the direct estimation method altogether, I review how they perform in empirical studies. Recall that bumblebees are not supposed to fly.

Bobko, Karren, and Parkington (1983) offered empirical evidence in support of the direct estimation method. They asked managers of insurance sales staff to estimate the sales performance of eighty-fifth, fiftieth, and fifteenth percentile performers. They compared the esti-

Table 7-1   Meta-analytic Corrected Validities for Selection Methods

Traditional Methods	Validity Findings
Traditional, unstructured interview	.30
Training and experience ratings	.14
Reference check	.26
Education	.10

Scientific Methods	Validity Findings
Cognitive ability composite	.53
Work sample test	.54
Behaviour consistency ratings	.49
Interviews structured by formal job analysis	.82

mate of SD_y formed by averaging the eighty-five to fifty and fifty to fifteen percentile comparisons with the actual standard deviations computed from sales records. They found strong agreement, reporting the direct estimate of SD_y at $56,900 versus the actual archival SD_y of $52,300. Janz and Etherington (1983) found highly similar results when comparing direct versus detailed behavioural estimates for forty-two supervisors of staff accountants in public accounting firms. Here, the forty percent rule fell within the same range as the other two methods.

Burke and Frederick (1984) suggested minor revisions to the direct estimation method. They had supervisors rate average performance first, and then once the average return for average performers is known, rate eighty-fifth and fifteenth percentile performers as deviations from a common base. This new procedure reduced the wide swings from one supervisor to the next somewhat.

Reilley and Smither (1985) compared the direct estimates, the forty percent rule, and yet another SD_y technique named CREPID (Cascio-Ramos Estimate of Performance in Dollars). The CREPID technique uses job analysis to identify key job components and is based on a market definition of the value of an individual person's labour. They use wages as a baseline against which to measure the relative value of individual job performance to the firm. Reilley and Smither's subjects participated in an organizational simulation of a pharmaceutical firm. They completed direct estimates of SD_y for yearly repeat sales, new product sales, net sales revenue after expenses, and overall worth of a pharmaceutical detailer (the job title under study). They also completed the CREPID procedure for overall SD_y.

Reilly and Smither (1985) report direct estimates of the SD_y for repeat and new sales fall close to actual values, but the direct estimate of net sales doubled the actual value, substantially inflated by outlier data. The same problems with high outliers cropped up for the overall estimate of SD_y. The CREPID procedure produced a more conservative overall estimate that avoided the outlier problem, and agreed fairly well with the forty percent rule.

Summing up, the cost accounting method places strict accounting demands on the practitioner and applies to a limited subset of jobs. Neither the direct nor the forty percent rule methods offer logical elegance, but empirical research suggests that they can fall close to SD_y as calculated from records. We need more empirical comparisons of all methods, and perhaps new methods entirely before this issue settles down. Still, research so far demonstrates that a reasonable band of SD_y estimates bounded on the low end by twenty percent and the high end by fifty percent of salary has a high probability of including the true SD_y.

POTENTIAL SAVINGS FOR THE CANADIAN ECONOMY

This section applies the utility formula to the task of forecasting potential savings across the Canadian economy for hiring predicted to take place during the years 1987, 1988, 1989, and 1990. First, I explain the rationale behind my selection of key utility equation parameter ranges.

Number of Openings

Total job openings includes both new jobs and openings created by quits or terminations. For the past two years, the number of new jobs created has averaged around

330,000. I chose the number of 200,000 new jobs per year as a conservative estimate of annual new jobs created throughout the projection period.

For quits or terminations, I selected two, four, and six percent of currently employed Canadians as conservative, likely, and favourable values. The higher percentage, the more openings and the greater the importance of improving selection procedures.

Tenure

I did not find Canadian statistics on tenure. A recent American article (Hall 1982) suggests that average tenure may be longer than commonly thought. For males over thirty, for example, average tenure in the United States exceeds twenty years. He reports the median eventual tenure across all categories of United States workers for 1978 as 7.7 years. I selected overall tenure values of four, six and eight years. In view of the American statistics, the eight year value may not be biased on the high side.

SDy

In view of the doubts expressed in the literature and the logical problems associated with the forty percent rule, I selected a conservatively biased range of twenty, thirty and forty percent of average annual wage as the estimates of SDy.

Selection Gain

Selection gain derives from the characteristics of the normal distribution. The selection ratio, the number of openings divided by the number of applicants, determines selection gain. I chose six, eight, and ten applicants per opening as the range of possibilities likely to occur over all jobs throughout the projection period.

There may be more applicants now for many openings, but I chose again to bias my parameter estimates in a generally conservative direction to anticipate possible shifts over the next several years.

Validity Difference

Reviewing Table 7-1, the combination of reference checks and unstructured interviews takes the lion's share of current selection practise. Comparing those validities with values possible, using carefully structured interviews based on job analysis, combined with ability tests or job sample tests, yields a range of validity gains from .2 to .4.

Cost Increases

I include two kinds of cost increases. First, I estimate the startup cost of applying currently published job analyses plus new analyses to the task of generating structured interview patterns and appropriate job tests for all jobs. Much of this work could be carried out through a centre for selection research and application, jointly funded by industry and government. Expertise would draw from some centres in industry, government, and the armed forces, but mainly from the universities through a series of grants. The $20 million figure probably falls on the high side, but it hardly matters, as we shall see.

Second, I include the increased costs of operating thorough, systematic, selection methods. Again, my cost estimates fall clearly on the high side. I allow an increase of one hundred dollars per short listed applicant and twenty dollars per screened applicant. The extra time spent interviewing and thoroughly testing applicants would certainly cost no more than this.

FORECASTED NET BENEFITS AND ROIs

Table 7–2 contains the forecasted outcomes given three scenarios: (1) conservative—a lower bound of reasonable outcomes, (2) likely—the expected outcome (still using conservative values for some equation components), and (3) favourable—the best outcome realistically possible if parameters go our way.

Even under the conservative column in a generally conservative table of forecasts, the net benefit of 9.3 billion for an expenditure of 653 million stands as a good investment in and for the people of Canada. The likely column, using parameter estimates within, if not below empirically derived values, forecasts a 55.6 billion dollar net benefit for spending a total of 1.3 billion. The favourable column finds a possible 186 billion dollar saving for a 1.9 billion dollar expenditure—an amazing 96.4 times return on investment.

The numbers merely support what people of good will and common sense know already—the crucial importance of matching people to jobs that suit their talents and temperaments. Research already cited proves that traditional, unstructured selection methods fail to produce a good match. This research lays out the costs of continuing to ignore systematic, scientific selection procedures.

We can choose to pay the twenty million investment now plus the increased selection costs of 1.3 billion over the next four years, or we can choose to pay the 55.6 billion over the next ten years for

Table 7–2 Forecasted Net Benefits for Scientific Versus Traditional Selection Methods for Hiring Projected for Canada in the Years 1987 Through 1990

	Conservative	Likely	Favourable
Annual new jobs	200 000	200 000	200 000
N of years	4	4	4
Turnover rate	.02	.04	.06
N currently employed	12 000 000	12 000 000	12 000 000
N short list per opening	3	4	4
N screened per opening	3	4	6
Total openings	1 760 000	2 720 000	3 680 000
Tenure	4	6	8
SDy	4 700	7 050	9 360
Selection gain	1.51	1.65	1.71
Validity difference (Scientific—Traditional)	.2	.3	.4
Dollar benefit increase	9 992 576 000	56 952 720 000	188 481 945 600
Increased costs:			
Selection-startup	20 000 000	20 000 000	20 000 000
Selection-process	633 600 000	1 305 600 000	1 913 600 000
Total	653 600 000	1 325 600 000	1 933 600 000
Net benefit	9 338 976 000	55 627 120 000	186 548 345 600
ROI ratio	14.2	41.9	96.4

missed opportunities, absenteeism, alcoholism, poor performance, accidents, and waste. But be sure of one thing. In an era of free trade and world markets, we will not be able to pass the 55.6 billion on to those who purchase our exports. Canadians will pay through a reduced standard of living.

WHY ARE THEY SO LARGE?

Table 7-2 demonstrates the magnitude of the savings possible for applying what we know from research on scientific selection. The dollars are as large as they are because management has not invested in the past. Productivity is the current focus, but productivity is driven by investment, not faddish attentions.

Canada's high productivity in agriculture is no accident. It happened through investment in developing appropriate genetic strains and efficient farm implements. Managing the productivity of human resources is no different. The reality is under investment. The result is that modest investments to apply technology recently developed can produce major gains.

For a long time, the opportunity costs of staying with the traditional, easy selection interview were not clear. Managers could have argued that better selection is a noble goal, but does not show a clear bottom line return. Now that the bottom line returns are clear and often large, managers sharing the goal of selecting top performers will opt for advanced, proven techniques.

But for some organizations, having the clear dollar impacts for modern selection methods may not be enough. Webster (1982) argued that the interview is a complex social process. Different managers interview for different purposes. Some managers are trying their best to identify top performers. Other managers use the interview in a different way, selecting applicants who have demonstrated servility and loyalty. For these managers, the unstructured interview is a mechanism for maintaining their power. They are unlikely to give up this source of power easily. Showing them dollar savings for better interviewing has no impact, since their agenda is focused on power and not high quality selection decisions. For power-oriented managers, only when top management strives to eliminate the political route to corporate success will managers be willing to give up the power of personal choice. Only then can the substantial savings from implementing scientific selection methods be realized.

SCIENTIFIC SELECTION AND FAIRNESS

I close with a brief reference to the issue of selection fairness. Does scientific selection mean the reduction of personal choice, or systematic unfair discrimination against minorities? The answer is no to both valid concerns.

On the issue of personal choice, many people resent taking employment tests, none more so than professionals. They report feeling more in control during an interview—a feeling not born out by research. The probability of being made an offer given that the applicant would make a top performer is much less for an unstructured interview versus a structured interview coupled with an appropriate job knowledge test.

Recent developments in work sample and trainability tests yield tests with a high face validity and applicant acceptance. A new form of structured interview called the behaviour description interview has received rave reviews from applicants, especially the high performers (Janz, Hellervik, and Gilmore 1986). Applicants view BD interviews as tough, but also as providing the interviewer with a sound basis for making the selection decision.

The issue of unfair discrimination has also been clarified. Schmidt and Hunter (1981) reviewed several old myths and the recent research evidence finding that cognitive ability tests do not unfairly discriminate against identifiable minority groups. In other words, when population group differences between a minority and majority group emerged, they were matched by group performance differences as well.

The common experience base of some minority groups leads group members on the average to be more or less suited for some job families. For example, subgroups that ridicule or avoid the study of advanced mathematics will send fewer of their members on to success as engineers or physicists. If society wishes to redress a given minority group *performance* difference, it must address the experience base that leads to the difference, not attack the selection method that senses the job performance difference accurately.

A retreat from scientific selection procedures to imposed quotas for target minority groups may well create larger problems than the minority group performance differences were in the first place. First, quotas alone do not increase the job skills or competence of anyone. Thus, meeting quotas increases the chances of placing minority group members on jobs beyond their competence level. The results include job stress for the group member and for others that depend on or work for that person—never mind the costs to the organization as a whole.

A better solution involves diagnosing the causes underlying group performance differences, and aiming interventions directly at those causes. This may mean changes in role stereotypes, educational cirriculae, or specialized training programs.

I suggest we begin by making sure that our public and private organizations understand the consequences of the choices they face in setting selection policy. Then, improvements in selection methods will lead to human resource savings that could provide the resources to solve social problems arising from minority group job performance differences.

References

Arnold, J. D., J. M. Rauschenberger, W. Soubel, and R. M. Guion. 1983. Validation and utility of a strength test for selecting steel workers. *Journal of Applied Psychology* 67:588–604.

Bobko, P., R. Karren, and J. J. Parkington. 1983. Estimation of standard deviations in utility analyses: An empirical test. *Journal of Applied Psychology* 68:170–176.

Boudreau, J. W. and C. J. Berger. 1985. Decision theoretic utility analysis applied to employee separations and acquisitions. *Journal of Applied Psychology* 70:581–612.

Burke, M. J., and J. T. Frederick. 1984. Two modified procedures for estimating standard deviations in utility analyses. *Journal of Applied Psychology* 69:482–489.

Cascio, W. F. 1982. *Costing human resources: The financial impact of behavior in organizations.* Boston, MA: Kent.

Cronbach, L. J., and G. Gleser. 1965. *Psychological tests and personnel decisions.* Urbana, Ill.: University of Illinois Press.

Hall, R. E. 1982. The importance of lifetime jobs in the US economy. *The American Economic Review* 72:716–724.

Hunter, J. E., and R. F. Hunter. 1984. Validity and utility of alternative predictors of job performance. *Psychological Bulletin* 96:72–98.

Hunter, J. E., and F. L. Schmidt. 1983. Quantifying the effects of psychological interventions on employee job performance and workforce productivity. *American Psychologist* 38:473–478.

Hunter, J. E., F. L. Schmidt, and G. B. Jackson. 1982. *Advanced meta-analysis: Quantitative methods for accumulating research findings across studies.* Beverly Hills, CA: Sage.

Janz, J. T. 1982. Personnel decisions: Costs, benefits, and opportunities for the energy industry. *Journal of Canadian Petroleum Technology,* (Sept.–Oct.): 80–84.

Janz, J. T., and L. E. Etherington. 1983. Comparing methods for assessing the standard deviation of performance in dollars. Proceedings of the Annual Conference of the Administrative Sciences Association of Canada, Vol. 4. Pt. 5.

Janz, J. T., and L. E. Etherington. 1985. Using forecasted net benefits in designing improved recruitment and selection systems. *International Journal of Forecasting* 1: 287–296.

Janz, J. T., L. E. Hellervik, and D. C. Gilmore. 1986. *Behavior description interviewing: New, accurate, cost effective.* Newton, MA: Allyn and Bacon.

Landy, F. J., J. L. Farr, and R. R. Jacobs. 1982. Utility concepts in performance measurement. *Organizational Behavior and Human Performance* 30:15–40.

McDaniel, M. A., and F. L. Schmidt. 1985. A meta-analysis of the validity of training and experience ratings in personnel selection. Technical report no. OSP-85-1. United States Office of Personnel Management, Office of Staffing Policy. Washington, DC: U.S. Government Printing Office.

Reilly, R. R., and J. W. Smither. 1985. An examination of two alternative techniques to estimate the standard deviation of job performance in dollars. *Journal of Applied Psychology* 70:651–61.

Roche, W. J., Jr. 1965. "The Cronbach-Gleser utility function in fixed treatment employee selection." In *Psychological Tests and Personnel Decisions*, edited by C. J. Cronbach and G. C. Gleser. Urbana, Ill.: University of Illinois Press.

Schmidt, F. L., and J. E. Hunter. 1977. Development of a general solution to the problem of validity generalization. *Journal of Applied Psychology* 62:529–40.

Schmidt, F. L., and J. E. Hunter. 1981. Employment testing: Old theories and new research findings. *American Psychologist* 36:1138–47.

Schmidt, F. L., J. E. Hunter, R. C. McKenzie, and T. W. Muldrow. 1979. Impact of valid selection procedures on work force productivity. *Journal of Applied Psychology* 64:609–26.

Schmidt, F. J., J. E. Hunter, and K. Pearlman. 1981. Assessing the economic impact of personnel programs on work force productivity. *Personnel Psychology* 35:333–45.

Weisner, W. H., and S. F. Cronshaw. 1986. The moderating impact of interview format and degree of structure on interview validity. Unpublished manuscript, Department of Psychology, University of Waterloo.

Webster, E. C. 1982. *The employment interview: A social judgment process.* Schomberg, Ontario: S.I.P. Publications.

8. Employment Equity at Canadian National Railways: Initiatives and Proactive Measures

Louise Piché, Canadian National

INTRODUCTION

Employment equity used to be called affirmative action and, before that, it was known as equal employment opportunity. Judge Rosalie Silberman Abella[1] presents the definition of equality in employment in Canada in Part 1, Chapter 1, of the report of her Royal Commission into this matter, in November 1984. This definition is now regarded by the federal government and those employers of federal jurisdiction as most contemporary and appropriate for use in public policy and legislation. It is defined through the goal of removal of discriminatory barriers to employment that negatively affect identifiable groups, particularly women as the largest disadvantaged group, for example, fifty two percent of the Canadian population. The novelty of the term is, in some ways, unfortunate. It suggests that a new idea is represented when, in fact, the idea has been with us for decades and is one that commands a broad societal consensus in Canada, as revealed in many surveys; the most recent one by Decima Research in December 1985.[2]

There is no serious debate today about the desirability of equality of opportunity; there is, however, a good deal of discussion about the means to achieve this goal, the effects it will produce in the economy, and the risk of reverse discrimination, as indicated also in this survey.

Consequently, this concept of employment equity deals with older principles and newer techniques of implementation. The older principle is as stated: equality of opportunity. The newer techniques are management tools, or communications techniques, that might be applied to other, and quite different, objectives related to the implementation of major changes in large organizations.

There are people who find employment equity mysterious, not that the notion is new (our Canadian societies and corporations have made it a goal for quite a few years), but because there is some history of failure in implementation as reported by Judge Abella.[3] Failure encourages people to suppose either that the task is impossible or that they are dealing with supernatural forces.

EMPLOYMENT EQUITY: DEVELOPMENT AND STRATEGIES

Strategies for implementing an employment equity program can be discussed in precisely the terms one might use to talk about any other human resources program.

Before examining strategies for successful implementation of employment equity, it may be useful to briefly analyze some failures. Ten years ago, a number of large Canadian corporations believed that equality of opportunity for women would be accomplished through enlightenment, awareness, and education of our work force and management. It was recognized that old prejudices were at play and it seemed reasonable to believe that by stripping them away and by encouraging more open attitudes, the environment would tend naturally and inevitably toward equality and fairness. Through awareness, behaviours would change. Between 1975 and 1978, Canadian National had a very extensive training program for all its managers and all its female employees dealing with the issue of women in the workplace.

Much of this was beneficial to individuals and to corporations. Some women, for instance, took charge of their career in a much more assertive manner as a result of a career planning seminar they attended in that period. High potential women were recognized and placed in positions where their contribution to the organization was valuable. But, on the whole, equality of opportunity for working women was not achieved; some progress for exceptional women, quite often due to the foresight of certain men, was the only concrete realisation of this voluntary approach.

Hindsight, the herald of humility, provided us with a simple explanation: If you want to change behaviour, you will have to work on behaviour. This issue should not be a mission where the goal is to convert all officers to take on a morally correct attitude; it must be a corporate objective where the corporate expectations are clear and the rewards for a job well done forthcoming.

Corporations did not stumble over this insight unassisted. Social science theory and research led the way and corporations paid close attention. Organizations are now more concerned with actions than attitudes; they are looking for measurable, quantifiable results. In human resource management, as much as any other corporate division, the bottom line is the criteria. All activities must contribute to the achievement of the strategic goals of the business. The practitioner and the milieu are more business oriented, more hard headed.

Communications in the organization have changed. In retrospect, it seemed that communication had the primary goal of making everybody feel good; sharing was the operative word and the process was deemed almost more important than the substance. As society in general and the business world in particular increase their reliance on information, communications are more important, more directly competitive than ever before as was detailed in the best-selling thesis, *Megatrends*, in 1982.[4] Communications become one of the most strategic tools to the achievement of corporate goals.

These changes can and should be seen as improvements. They result in improved human resource management which contribute to better management and leads to new things. Employment equity is one of those new things.

Not only does employment equity result in improved human resource systems, but it also is a desirable and inevitable product of better human resource systems. On the one hand, allegations of discriminatory impact of a given traditional practise may stimulate questioning of this practise and spur its review to reduce this risk while improving the quality of the decision-making process. On the other hand, defensible, valid, and objective approaches which enshrine the principles of fairness and job-relatedness most likely produce equitable results.

New processes are emerging to ensure that all decisions in the employment relationship rest on criteria that are job-related. Hiring processes are more objective, their validity measured. Performance appraisal is based on behavioural, measurable criteria, and the scales are reliable. Promotion is based on measurable ability to perform the work required. More and more, the objective criteria related to the position requirements and assessed with a fair instrument is replacing the traditional systems which relied extensively on personal knowledge of people, subjective measurement through the interview process, and social assumptions based on gender, role or age.

Employment equity means fair employment practises and, as Judge Abella [5] reminds us, it entails the recognition that certain groups of people have experienced less-than-fair treatment in the work place. Such discrimination creates barriers to employment and advancement of women and minority group members. In Canada, the political and legislative process has determined that these barriers must be removed and corrective measures implemented until the proper balance in the work force is reached. Since 1975, all provinces in Canada have passed human rights laws and established commissions to monitor compliance to these laws. The most recent development is the federal initiative to make employment equity mandatory in those businesses under federal jurisdiction employing more than one hundred employees, and to make contract compliance a reality with federal contractors. At this point in time (April 1985), the bill is in the third reading and about to be passed.

The adoption of an employment equity program by a corporation represents a deliberate exercise in the management of change. By definition, change means going *from* something *to* something else. The changes sought by the corporation in implementing employment equity will occur, or fail to occur, in the context of that corporation and its culture. Corporations have different characters. They have different sizes, structures, compositions, capabilities, and goals. They have different traditions, priorities, and needs. And they find themselves in different circumstances. Corporations are no more alike than *Madame Bovary* is like *Moby Dick* although both are novels, or than hockey is like chess although both are games. The management of those changes, therefore, requires a thorough knowledge of the particularities and peculiarities of that corporation before the appropriate and effective tools can be selected, let alone used. Before describing those tools and techniques used in Canadian National Railways to introduce the acceleration measures or the affirmative action steps, it must be emphasized that right for CN does not necessarily mean right for any other corporation, and that the first and indispensible task in the management of change generally, and the implementation of employment equity particularly, is a detailed analysis of the environment in which change is to take place.

In effect, what employment equity has to do is conceptually straightforward;

to achieve this goal, what it has to undo is complicated. Attitudes and prejudices may be at the root of the discriminatory practises that employment equity seeks to correct, but our past experience of the mid-1970s with awareness programs on the role of women in the work place has shown that it takes us to no known destination, that progress is no more tangible than the attitudes themselves. This approach is not practical.

What is practical is an effort to ensure that anyone who has or wants a job has a fair chance to do it or get it. It is practical to analyse job criteria, to correct for entrenched discrimination and to ensure neutrality in hiring and promotion. Since 1979, Canadian National has been modifying all its selection systems. The first initiative was aimed at entry-level jobs through a thorough and extensive content-validation process resulting in in-house test and structured interview development. CN is dealing with approximately twenty-five job families at the entry levels, and each review requires up to sixty person-weeks of work. A full-time team of a dozen professionals has been assigned the task and is aiming at a 1988 completion date. Obviously, this work results in extensive user-training to ensure consistency and appropriate delivery. Since 1981, similar work is being done in relation to promotion from within, performance appraisals and assessment of future potential; each project is different and unique in the strategy selected (content approach, predictive or criterion-related), but the goal remains the same: a fair job-related system ensuring work force quality. In fact, the goal pursued through these activities is to make CN an equal employment opportunity employer where discrimination has been neutralized.

At Canadian National, analysis in preparation for an employment equity program produced a profile of the company that identified opportunities and constraints at the end of 1984. Further, it led to realistic and shared expectations for the program. While CN had its women's program from 1975 to 1978, the base representation of women still hovered around six percent at the end of the seventies. A complaint of systemic discrimination against women in blue-collar occupations, filed in 1979 when the representation in those ranks was less than one percent, resulted, in the summer of 1984, in the first affirmative action program to be imposed on a Canadian corporation. This decision by a human rights tribunal included a hiring quota of twenty-five percent and an ultimate goal of a thirteen percent representation of women in the occupations of brakeman, coachcleaner, labourer, track construction gang, etc. Even if this decision was taken by CN to the Federal Court of Appeal and the quota subsequently annulled in the summer of 1985, the executive of the corporation announced in November 1984 a voluntary program aimed at matching the internal representation of women at all levels in the company to the level of available female labour pool.

The analysis of the situation as it stood then produced a strategy aimed at getting measurable and visible results quickly. Although this priority was clear enough to those in the corporation who had lived through the previous trials and tribulations since 1979, it shook conventional human resource practises. Conventional practise takes plenty of time and occupies sequential stages: conception, planning, development, experiment, adjustment, implementation, monitoring, and reporting. This process is time-tested and perfectly valid. CN decided to short-circuit the process.

Two complementary strategic paths were adopted; one to implement, monitor and report, the other to carry communications and information to facilitate—or, if necessary, force—development and adjustment in scope, focus and fine-tuning. Each path would carry two-way traffic. On the implementation path, goals and techniques would go top-down; initiatives and reporting, bottom-up. Communications tools and techniques would be top-down; program needs and information, bottom-up.

Corporate management supported and gave commitment to the employment equity program on both strategic lines: immediate implementation and communications.

Communication lines were pursued in in-house publications with an article on the program in every issue; public meetings with each of the thirty-five top executive officers across the CN system and their respective staffs for a total of approximately five hundred managers, within the first quarter of 1985; the production of audio-visual materials such as a video of the press conference with the president announcing the program and a brochure on employment equity for employees; and advertising norms soliciting qualified women in particular to apply at CN. Each of the departments at Canadian National was provided with details about the program and departmental-specific needs identified with respect to implementation. Departments were asked, one by one, to set realistic goals and timetables to produce the measurable results required.

It became practical to set specific goals aimed at improving the representation of groups who are clearly underrepresented wherever, whenever, and to the extent that this underrepresentation is or may be a function of discriminatory practise. Moreover, it is practical to establish those goals in the context of timetables. In CN, these measures, akin to affirmative action, were introduced.

In order to achieve this, the corporate role was to develop new instruments to be used by the departments and to provide training at three-day workshops focusing on neutralizing processes and content, with designated employment equity coordinators from all parts of the organization. The forms used in developing and monitoring action plans are included in Appendix 1 to illustrate some of the principles. These exchanges sharpened our understanding of different employment conditions within CN, identified the tools and techniques required by the conditions, and helped to entrench the goals of the program in standard employment practises.

Accordingly, a series of ad hoc measures to employ and promote women was undertaken. CN is making deliberate efforts to recruit women by directing employment information in newspapers and educational publications, or concerning internal job postings, to their specific attention. In 1985, as a result of these actions, twenty-five percent of CN Rail's blue-collar hirings were women, twenty-three percent of the company's new engineers were women, and forty percent of hirings in management were women. This brings the total representation across CN to 8.9 percent, with ten percent in management. This compares to something in the area of five percent in 1975 in the total work force in the company.

An example of these measures is described here. As a major employer in Canada, CN receives about 150,000 unsolicited job applications every year. Therefore, there has been limited need to spend money on recruitment campaigns. In fact, the only form of recruitment was by word-of-mouth which has resulted in a traditional pool of applicants. This pool does not contain sufficient qualified women for blue-collar positions. Should CN decide to rely on this form of recruitment, changes in its blue-collar work force would be, at best, very slow if at all. CN now advertises its vacancies and stresses that "qualified women in particular are invited to apply" which, in fact, has produced a more significant pool of applicants increasing the probability of selecting greater numbers of women for these occupations.

CN's short-term measures are backed up with three-year work plans which generate statistical information, scrutinize it for underrepresentation of women, outline remedial measures, and set goals for each group. These work plans take account of employment equity goals in relation to every group of positions at Canadian National such as brakeperson, trade worker, lineman, telephone operator, senior officer, lawyer, etc. Special initiatives in training and development are expected to broaden opportunities for women.

To that end, in 1985, Canadian National's employment equity coordinators in the field performed work force analyses comparing the available female labour pool (external and internal) to CN's female representation in 339 occupational groupings to determine if and where underrepresentation exists. Out of this work, 159 action plans have been approved to bridge these gaps within a given time frame taking into account the realities of the organization. It is practical to require the active collaboration of all the persons engaged in the employment process: the hiring officers, the line managers, the personnel staff. Finally, it is practical to monitor and measure results as CN implements these action plans. The goal of these measures is to accelerate the rate of change through active intervention.

CN's program has exploited its advantages, one of which is momentum in the wake of the tribunal's decision. This has given us news value and regular appearances in CN in-house publications as well as posters dealing with different aspects of the program and brochures outlining their features and objectives, all of which are being distributed throughout the organization.

Regular communications from the field permits the monitoring of progress. In this regard, it is worth mentioning that after several months into our program, it was discovered that a device to record initiatives which might or might not eventually bear fruit was required. This had not been anticipated and, without clear communications channels, probably would have remained unattended.

In such a decentralized implementation context, corporate sponsored initiatives have been symbolically and materially important to this program. The first was the adoption of the program and the assignment of a high profile for it. CN offers scholarships to women registering in non-traditional training programs at post-secondary educational institutions in Canada. In addition, CN is providing paid leaves of absence for a limited number of women employees who have demonstrated potential and motivation and who wish to pursue advanced studies. In 1985, the first five recipients were selected for leaves ranging from one to four years. In 1986, the total complement will come to ten. When these corporate measures were made public, some people claimed they were creating reverse discrimination situations. This issue was dealt with in one of the articles in our in-house newspaper where it was explained that the measures being required to redress past disadvantages were in place only temporarily and would not be pursued any longer than necessary to achieve a fair balance in the representation of qualified women in CN's work force. These initiatives are akin to catch-up measures and, as such, are recognized as legal in the Canadian context not only in the human rights legislation, but in Canada's constitution itself, the Charter of Rights and Freedoms.

Maternity benefits to CN employees were improved according to different formulas, depending on their employee status of unionized, nonunionized or management. A pilot project for an on-site day care facility in Montreal is in development.

Targets and goals are a separate and important tool in the employment equity program at Canadian National. Short-term targets helped establish an upbeat, proactive perception of the program; long-term targets reflect a commitment to employment equity as business as usual from here on in.

EMPLOYMENT EQUITY: STRUCTURE AND ORGANIZATION

Initially, the employment equity core staff was made up of three people and was exclusively concerned with the women's program. The responsibilities have expanded to include the other target groups contemplated by proposed legislation, for example, disabled persons, visible minorities, and aboriginal people; the company's youth employment program; and human rights compliance. Integration has strengthened the numbers in the unit, and resulted in better coordination and net productivity gains.

The program also required setting up an infrastructure throughout the CN network to ensure every unit's commitment to the overall goal through its own program, targets, and timetable. CN's work force is approximately 55,000 people working in the ten Canadian provinces, the Yukon, and Northwest Territories. Eighty-two percent of all workers are members of one of the twenty or so unions representing them. The Canadian operations are made up of the following businesses: freight transportation, hotels, communications, real estate, trucking, exploration, and international consultants. The transportation group is by far the largest employer (eighty percent). A coordinated decentralized strategy based on the identification, training, and monitoring of thirty-four field coordinators, most of whom assume this responsibility over and above their regular duties, entrenched the process in each unit of the corporation.

The deficiencies or absence of data has been a major difficulty in the program. External data on the available pool of women is approximate at best and an unreliable guide to appropriate representation. Nor is there an adequate internal employee data base or an external availability data base with respect to the disabled, aboriginal people, and members of visible minorities. CN is now launching a total work force survey to remedy this lack of internal data.

CONCLUSION

It is imperative to recognize an important feature of the techniques described in CN's program. None exists in isolation, each is interdependent, all have been developed as measures to mutually support and enhance one another. The work in communications supports and is supported by corporate initiatives. Each of these elements informs and validates the efforts and emphasis the corporation has committed to targets and timetables. Good data is essential to be effective in each of these areas; at the same time, prompt initiatives in these areas are important to the prospects of acquiring good data, and so on.

It is possible to describe these techniques separately, but they do not work separately. It is possible, especially given CN's focus on goals, to suppose that these techniques produce a linear progression toward a fixed and orthodox end. In fact, progress is fragile and uneven. It is a product of the techniques CN uses but depends on factors formally external to the employment equity program and inherent in conditions prevailing at Canadian National.

Such developments will call for modified or new techniques which, in turn, will derive from continued study of the nature and direction of Canadian National overall. That is the starting point, the framework and, finally, the arbiter of success.

And that sweeping generalization is the only formula, the only recipe, I have to offer. Fortunately, the rest is not mysterious; just plain, hard work.

Endnotes

1. Abella, Rosalie S. Equality in Employment. *Report of the Royal Commission.* (Ottawa, 1984).
2. Decima Research and Public Affairs International Report, unpublished Preliminary Results, December 1985.
3. Abella, *Equality in Employment* 125.
4. Naisbitt, J. *Megatrends: Ten New Directions Transforming Our Lives.* (New York: Warner, 1982).
5. Abella, *Equality in Unemployment*, 1.

Appendix 1

EMPLOYMENT EQUITY PROGRAM
PROGRAMME D'ÉQUITÉ EN MATIÈRE D'EMPLOI
ANALYSIS / ANALYSE

REF. NUMBER
RÉFÉRENCE _____

TARGET JOB/LEVEL
POSTE/NIVEAU CIBLE _____

DATE _____

LOCATION
LIEU _____

INITIATOR
REPONSABLE _____

ORG. UNIT
UNITÉ ORG. _____

BONA FIDE OCCUPATIONAL
REQUIREMENTS / EXIGENCES
NORMALES DU POSTE _____

NUMBER AND % OF WOMEN EMPLOYEES IN TARGET JOB/LEVEL (SOURCE AND DATE)
NOMBRE ET % DE FEMMES AU POSTE/NIVEAU VISÉ (SOURCE ET DATE)

N	RATIO	%

OPENINGS (GROWTH-RETRENCHMENT-TURNOVER-ATTRITION) (SOURCE AND DATE)
DÉBOUCHÉS (AUGMENTATION-DIMINUTION-ROULEMENT-ATTRITION) (SOURCE ET DATE)

APP. NUMBER OF OPENINGS FOR NEXT (5) YEARS
NOMBRE APPROX. DE DÉBOUCHÉS
POUR LES CINQ PROCHAINES ANNÉES

1986	1987	1988	1989	1990

AVAILABILITY: (NUMBER OF WOMEN / TOTAL POPULATION)
DISPONIBILITÉ : (NOMBRE DE FEMMES / POPULATION TOTALE)

INTERNAL:
INTÉRIEUR :

EXTERNAL:
EXTÉRIEUR :
- WOMEN IN OUTSIDE LABOUR FORCE (IDENTIFY SEGMENT)
- FEMMES OEUVRANT DANS CE SECTEUR D'ACTIVITÉ (PRÉCISER)
- GRADUATES/DIPLOMÉES
    CURRENT/ACTUELLEMENT
    PREVIOUS/ANTÉRIEUREMENT
- ASSOCIATIONS
- OTHER SOURCE (IDENTIFY) / AUTRE SOURCE (PRÉCISER)

N	RATIO	%

122 STAFFING

ADVERSE IMPACT ANALYSIS
ANALYSE DES EFFETS D'EXCLUSION

$$\frac{\%\ OF\ CURRENT\ REPRESENTATION}{\%\ OF\ AVAILABILITY} = \text{"GAP"}$$

$$\frac{\%\ DE\ LA\ REPRÉSENTATION\ ACTUELLE}{\%\ DE\ FEMMES\ DISPONIBLES} = \text{"ÉCART"}$$

EXTREME/EXTRÊME (0-.29) ☐

VERY SIGNIFICANT/TRÈS GRAND (.30-.59) ☐

SIGNIFICANT/GRAND (.60-.79) ☐

NON/AUCUN (.80 AND OVER/ET PLUS) ☐

IDENTIFY LIKELY REASONS FOR CURRENT ADVERSE IMPACT
IDENTIFICATION DES CAUSES VRAISEMBLABLES DES EFFETS D'EXCLUSION ACTUELS

DEVELOP STAFFING SCENARIOS
ÉLABORATION DE SCÉNARIOS DE DOTATION EN PERSONNEL

	GOAL / OBJECTIF	TIMEFRAME FOR CATCH-UP SITUATION / ÉCHÉANCIER DE RATTRAPAGE	SELECTED RATIO / RATIO CHOISI
SCENARIO I / SCÉNARIO I			
SCENARIO II / SCÉNARIO II			
SCENARIO III / SCÉNARIO III			

COMMENTS:
OBSERVATIONS :

CN

EMPLOYMENT EQUITY PROGRAM
PROGRAMME D'ÉQUITÉ EN MATIÈRE D'EMPLOI

IMPLEMENTATION 86/86 MISE EN OEUVRE

REF. NUMBER _____
RÉFÉRENCE _____

TARGET JOB/LEVEL
POSTE/NIVEAU CIBLE _____

DATE _____

LOCATION
LIEU _____

PREPARED BY:
PRÉPARÉ PAR: _____

ORG. UNIT
UNITÉ ORG. _____

APPROVED BY:
APPROUVÉ PAR: _____

SELECTED STAFFING SCENARIO
SCÉNARIO CHOISI DE DOTATION EN PERSONNEL

GOAL/OBJECTIF PRINCIPAL

    SUB GOALS/OBJECTIFS SECONDAIRES

NUMBER AND % OF WOMEN EMPLOYEES IN TARGET JOB/LEVEL
NOMBRE ET % DE FEMMES AU POSTE/NIVEAU VISÉ

| JAN. 1/86 | APRIL 30/86 | AUG. 31/86 | DEC. 31/86 |
| 1 JAN./86 | 30 AVRIL/86 | 31 AOÛT/86 | 31 DÉC./86 |

N	RATIO	%		N	RATIO	%		N	RATIO	%		N	RATIO	%

NARRATIVE: COMMENT ON PROGRESS/NON-PROGRESS TOWARDS GOAL RELATING BACK TO ACTION PLAN.
REMARQUES: COMMENTAIRES SUR LES RÉSULTATS POSITIFS OU NÉGATIFS VIS-À-VIS LES OBJECTIFS FIXÉS EN RÉFÉRANT AU PLAN D'ACTION.

CN

EMPLOYMENT EQUITY PROGRAM
PROGRAMME D'ÉQUITÉ EN MATIÈRE D'EMPLOI
SPECIAL INITIATIVES 1986 / **INITIATIVES SPÉCIALES** 1986

Rationale (why):
Justification rationnelle (pourquoi ?) :

Objective (what):
Objectif (lequel ?) :

Specific Group (who):
Groupe spécifique (lequel ?) :

Specific Actions (how):
Mesures spécifiques (comment ?) :

Location/Organizational Unit (where):
Lieu/unité organisationnelle (où ?) :

Date/Timetable (when):
Date/échéancier (quand ?) :

Results Expected/Achieved:
Résultats escomptés/atteints :

Officer(s) Involved:
Cadre(s) en cause :

Equity Coordinator: _____
Coordonnateur - Équité en matière d'emploi: _____

Date: _____

EMPLOYMENT EQUITY PROGRAM
PROGRAMME D'ÉQUITÉ EN MATIÈRE D'EMPLOI
ACTION PLAN / PLAN D'ACTION

CN

REF. NUMBER
RÉFÉRENCE _____

TARGET JOB/LEVEL
POSTE/NIVEAU CIBLE _____

DATE _____

LOCATION
LIEU _____

INITIATOR
REPONSABLE _____

ORG. UNIT
UNITÉ ORG. _____

BONA FIDE OCCUPATIONAL
REQUIREMENTS / EXIGENCES
NORMALES DU POSTE _____

SELECTED STAFFING SCENARIO
SCÉNARIO CHOISI DE DOTATION EN PERSONNEL

GOAL/OBJECTIF PRINCIPAL

SUB GOALS/OBJECTIFS SECONDAIRES

MEASURES TO ACHIEVE GOAL
MESURES ENVISAGÉES POUR RÉALISER L'OBJECTIF

REMEDIAL CORRECTIVES	SUPPORT SOUTIEN	DESCRIPTION	WHO RESPONSABLE	DATE

STAFFING

(Continued / Suite)

REMEDIAL CORRECTIVES	SUPPORT SOUTIEN	DESCRIPTION	WHO RESPONSABLE	DATE

CONTIGENCY PLAN:
PLAN DE CONTINGENCE :

POLICY ISSUES:
QUESTIONS DE POLITIQUE :

PREPARED BY:
PRÉPARÉ PAR :

DATE SENT TO COORDINATOR:
DATE D'ENVOI AU COORDONNATEUR :

PROGRESS REPORT DATES
DATES DES RAPPORTS D'ÉTAPE

APPROVED BY:
APPROUVÉ PAR :

9. Equality in Employment

Harish C. Jain, McMaster University

In the last several decades employment discrimination against certain groups has become an important social and political issue. Several government commissions (Daudlin report 1984; Abella report 1984) have documented widespread discrimination against minority groups in the work place. These groups include women, racial minorities, natives, and the disabled. Human rights statutes have been enacted in all jurisdictions in Canada and the equality section of the Charter of Rights and Freedoms, a part of the Canadian Constitution, has come into effect as of April 1985. The purpose of these statutes is to eliminate discriminatory practises and to provide equality of opportunity. The federal government has recently (June 1985) introduced the Employment Equity Act in the Parliament to increase employment opportunities for minorities.

The federal government has designated four target groups in the employment equity legislation as well as in the affirmative action program for its employees. The status of each of these groups is described below.

WOMEN

Female participation in the work place has increased steadily since the early 1950s. Their proportion in the labour force will continue to rise substantially over the 1980s and approach the male participation rate by the year 2000 (Affirmative Action 1985). In 1982, fifty-two percent of all Canadian women of working age were in the paid labour force. They constituted fortyone percent of the entire work force (Abella report 1984). Despite their increased involvement in the work place, there is continued inequity in their pay and employment. They continue to be concentrated in relatively few occupations and industries. Only one of every ten females (or ten percent) work in areas other than service industries. According to the census in 1981, sixty-two percent of working women were located or ghettoized in clerical, sales, and service occupations and another 14.4 percent were engaged in teaching, medicine, and health. Thus, women are over-represented in the low-pay and low-skill jobs with little or no opportunity for advancement.

Male average earnings exceed female average earnings in all occupational groups, even those dominated by women. A number of empirical studies, where the male-female differences in the occupational distribution, experience, and education, etc., are controlled, have revealed that an unexplained differential between male and female wages persists. It is not hard to conclude that discrimination accounts for the differential; and that discrimination accounts for about twenty percent of earnings differentials between males and females.

A part of the explanation is that societal values have not encouraged women to enter nontraditional fields such as skilled trades and male-dominated professions. Some of the other reasons include lack of female role models, and preemployment and postemployment job barriers.

VISIBLE MINORITIES

The term visible minorities is ambiguous and euphemistic. Essentially, visible minorities are nonwhites whose origins are in Africa, Middle East, China, India, Pakistan, South East Asia, Japan, West Indies, Korea, Philippines, Latin America, and the Pacific Islands. Some of the racial minorities such as Canadians of Chinese, East Indian, and Japanese origin and Blacks have been in Canada for several generations. It is relatively recently (since the late 1970s), however, that a majority of new immigrants to Canada have come from Third World rather than European countries. Approximately seven percent of the population (Daudlin report 1974) and more than four percent of the labour force (1981 Census) is comprised of visible minorities.

Some groups face more serious employment barriers than others. While many nonwhites face employment discrimination, the incidence of discrimination differs by group and region. Some of the problems faced by a majority of the nonwhite immigrants include (1) inadequate language and skill training, (2) lack of bias free mechanisms for determining the validity of foreign credentials and experience, and (3) employers making Canadian experience as a job requirement, when it is not related to job performance (Daudlin report 1984; Abella report 1984).

Both recent nonwhite immigrants and other nonwhites have few role models in key public positions, and in key decision-making positions. Many groups are unjustifiably excluded from the opportunity to compete as equals based on their racial origin or colour (Abella report 1984).

Several studies have reported that the Third World immigrants (relative to other immigrants) experienced higher rates of unemployment, earned less money, and were more frequently unable to find work in their chosen fields (Saunders 1975; Marr 1976; Reitz 1981; Ginzberg and Henry 1985; Billingsley and Musyznski 1985).

NATIVE PEOPLE

The native working age population and labour force participation are expected to increase in the 1980s. Their working age population will increase by approximately two hundred thousand in the 1980s and their participation is expected to increase in the 1980s due to relocation from reserves into urban areas and as resource projects accessible to reserves create new employment opportunities. They are expected to constitute over twenty percent of Saskatchewan and Manitoba labour force growth and up to thirty percent in Regina and Winnipeg in the 1980s. By 1990, about thirteen percent of Saskatchewan's labour force is expected to be of native ancestry (Labour Market Developments 1981; Axworthy 1981). Thus, the native working age population is increasing faster than during any earlier time. However, their labour force participation rate continues to be much lower than the national rate. Their unemployment rate is more than twice that of other Canadians. Similarly, the average wages and income of those that are employed are well below national levels. They are concentrated in low-paid, low-skill jobs, since a vast majority of natives are employed in primary economic activity, such as agriculture, fishing, forestry, wildlife, etc., (Jain 1985).

Native people face major pre-employment barriers due to low educational achievement, lack of training, and lack of job experience. They also face language and cultural barriers (Affirmative Action 1985).

DISABLED PERSONS

According to the federal Department of Health and Welfare, 2.3 million Canadians of working age have physically or mentally disabling conditions. One million of these people are partially disabled, but they are capable of performing major employment tasks. National volunteer agencies estimate that approximately five hundred thousand disabled persons are employable. However, there is persistent unemployment (as high as eighty-five percent) and underemployment among them. Those that are employed are primarily concentrated in low-income jobs; their number in career jobs is chronically small (Affirmative Action 1985; Jain 1979).

One of the most important reasons for the continued inequality faced by women and minorities in the work place is both pre- and post-employment discrimination. Both of these types of discrimination are outlined in the following discussion.

ENTRY–LEVEL JOB BARRIERS

A requirement that is unrelated to actual or potential job success or performance on the job is called a *job barrier*. Job barriers include recruitment, application forms, educational requirements, employment tests, and interviews.

Recruitment channels and procedures can contribute to discrimination against minorities and women. Many organizations tend to follow established channels of recruitment. If employee referral methods, such as word-of-mouth, have been used in the past, only friends and relatives can hope to obtain employment to the exclusion of women, natives, Third World immigrants, or disabled workers since the firm may have traditionally employed only a few of these minorities or employed them in low-level jobs.

Recruitment Advertising

Traditionally major employers have placed their recruitment advertising in the major English-speaking newspapers, or have recruited via the old boys network of word-of-mouth. However, this traditional source of advertising may not be the best way to communicate staffing needs to minorities. A recent attempt (1983) by the CBC to hire a few visible minorities met with overwhelming positive response from Canada's racial and ethnic minorities. This occurred because the CBC placed advertisements in ethnic newspapers, magazines, or journals.

Employee Organizations and Trade Unions

These organizations can sometimes impose restrictive entry requirements such as control of hiring through union hiring halls, high levels of education and training, tests of ability, entry fees, and giving preference to members' sons and other relatives. In the case of professional associations, licensing bodies sanctioned by governments may impose qualifications for entry into an occupation which are higher than performance on the job requires.

Credentialism or educational qualifications requirements that are higher than necessary for effective job performance, tend to have a disproportionate impact on minorites. For example a requirement of a high school diploma screens out a majority of natives. As average educational levels have gone up, credentialism has also increased with an increased impact on minorities (Jain 1974).

Tests can also act as barriers to minority employment. Many tests which have been used to make selection decisions have been found to be poor predictors of job success. Some tests which require physical ability or dexterity to complete them tend to screen out physically handicapped applicants who are otherwise able to do the job. Similarly, there might be sexual and cultural barriers in some standardized tests which have a differential impact on women, racial and ethnic minorities, and natives (Jain 1983a).

Job Interviews are used by almost all organizations as an important pre-screening device. The interview process can screen out a disproportionate number of minorities because of personal bias, prejudice, or stereotyping on the part of the interviewer. For instance, females are generally given lower evaluations than males with identical qualifications (Arvey 1979).

Similarly in job interviews, studies have found that job applicants are more likely to be hired if they look straight ahead rather than down. People who look the interviewer straight in the eye are rated as being more alert, assertive, dependable, confident, responsible, and having more initiative. Moreover, applicants who demonstrate greater amounts of eye contact, head moving, smiling, and other non-verbal behaviors are rated higher than applicants who do not (Jain 1983b).

The effect of all the above-mentioned restrictions will be to limit opportunities for minority workers, since they may, on average, fare less well on these requirements than the rest of the population. This is especially true of the native people who are denied entry into courses in skilled trades since these can only be taken upon completion of grades 11 or 12. Thus, a majority of natives receive no training in the trades such as carpentry and plumbing since their educational attainment level, in most cases, is too low. Furthermore, existing employees in such occupations will resist any attempts to remove such indirect discrimination which reduces competition for their jobs and hence enables them to maintain artificially high wages.

Entry level discrimination against the disabled includes the presence of barriers, in addition to unfavourable attitudes. There is a general lack of ramps and special walkways at private and public institutions to enable a disabled person to navigate and to perform effectively.

Levitan and Taggart (1977) have summarized the barriers faced by the disabled this way: "Employer surveys evidence a general reluctance to hire the disabled when nondisabled workers are available. Many employers believe that there are higher costs, such as increased worker's compensation expenses or inflated medical and life insurance premiums. Although most believe that the disabled will be more reliable, they (employers) fear involuntary absenteeism and turnover. Another consideration is the lack of flexibility in job assignments and the difficulty of promoting." To these can be added absence of company policies governing recruitment of the disabled and the lack of flexible work schedules (Sampson 1981). Since the disabled as a group are likely to have lower educational and training attainments than the nondisabled, several of the employment hurdles (i.e., screening, credentialism, etc.) discussed above, have a disproportionate effect on their employment even though they might be able to perform some of the jobs.

Post-Employment Practices

Discrimination can also occur after an individual has been hired. It can take the form of poor performance evaluation, lack of promotions, transfers, and/or salary increase. Women, visible minorities and the disabled could be assigned to lower level jobs at lower salaries relative to nonminorities despite similar qualifications, (Malkiel and Malkiel 1973; Chiplin and Sloane 1976).

Minority group workers may be denied promotion by restrictive promotion criteria, by limitations upon the posting and bidding arrangements for internal recruitment, by restricting both minorities and women to the lower paying job classifications and mobility clusters, and by discriminatory seniority systems.

Seniority systems in unionized companies, for example, may discriminate against women. If males have more seniority than females, they will naturally have higher earnings, larger fringe benefits, easier access to overtime, preferred jobs and operation of last-in-first-out systems. Seniority systems, therefore, have the serious disadvantage of perpetuating existing unfavourable minority employment patterns. If women are the last to be hired during the recovery phase of the business cycle, they will be the first to be laid off in the recession phase (Jain and Sloane 1983).

LEGAL APPROACHES

In order to overcome the discriminatory practices outlined above, all Canadian jurisdictions have enacted human rights laws. In addition, Section 15 of the Charter of Rights and Freedoms, a part of the Canadian Constitution, also prohibits discrimination in employment as of April 1985. These statutes have been influenced by the human rights instruments and numerous conventions of the United Nations (UN) and the International Labour Organization (ILO) that have been ratified by Canada. These include the two UN Conventions on the elimination of all forms of racial discrimination and discrimination against women, and the ILO convention on discrimination in employment and occupation, just to cite a few.

HUMAN RIGHTS STATUTES

All jurisdictions in Canada have equal employment provisions in their human rights legislation. These laws seek to promote equality of opportunity and treatment in employment in order to prevent discrimination in the recruitment and staffing practices of employers. These statutes apply to employers, employment agencies, and trade unions. Discrimination is prohibited with respect to advertising, and terms and conditions of employment including promotion, transfer, and training.

PROHIBITED GROUNDS FOR DISCRIMINATION

The prohibited grounds in employment include race, colour, national or ethnic origin, sex, marital status, religion, and age; age groups protected vary among jurisdictions, with the most common being between the ages of eighteen and sixty-five, and forty-five and sixty-five. Physical and mental disability is proscribed in several jurisdictions. Other prohibited grounds include sexual orientation in Quebec and pardoned offences in the federal, Ontario, and Quebec jurisdictions.

LEGAL DEFINITION OF EMPLOYMENT DISCRIMINATION

Direct or intentional discrimination involves searching for a motive or an intention to discriminate on any of the prohibited grounds of discrimination above by an employer. It means having to prove prejudicial treatment namely harmful acts motivated by personal antipathy towards the group of which the target group was a member. Thus, intent to discriminate must be proved.

Increasingly, however, there has been a realization that employment discrimination in most cases does not result from isolated, individual acts of bigotry, but rather from historical assumptions and traditions which have become embedded in the normal operations of employment and industrial relations systems.

SYSTEMIC, INDIRECT, UNINTENTIONAL, OR CONSTRUCTIVE DISCRIMINATION

The Canadian Human Rights Act as well as numerous decisions by boards of inquiry in several provinces have borrowed the legal definition of discrimination from the United States case law and the relevant British legislation. In the United States the concept of indirect or systemic discrimination was articulated by the Supreme Court in *Griggs* vs. *Duke Power Co.* case in 1970. The court unanimously endorsed a results-oriented definition of what constitutes employment discrimination. The court indicated that intent does not matter; it is the consequences of an employer's actions that determine whether it may have discriminated under Title VII of the Civil Rights Act. In this case, the court struck down educational requirements and employment tests on two grounds. (1) These requirements could not be justified on the grounds of business necessity since they were not valid or related to job performance. Moreover, (2) they had adverse impact since they screened out a greater proportion of blacks than whites. However, if business necessity could be proved, for example, if the educational and testing requirements that had disproportionate or adverse impact on minorities were in fact related to job performance, then the practise was not prohibited. Thus, disproportionate impact is not sufficient to outlaw credentialism, tests, and other hiring standards. Business necessity is the prime criterion in hiring and promotion decisions.

The approach adopted in the *Griggs* case has been adopted in Canada. One of the leading cases which changed the intent to discriminate situation involved a member of the Sikh faith. He complained to the Ontario Human Rights Commission after he was refused a job as a security guard. The dress and grooming regulations of the firm to which he had applied required employees to be clean shaven and to have their hair trimmed. The Sikh applicant wore a turban and had a beard as required by his religion and therefore, was unable to comply with the firm's regulation. In this case, *Ishar Singh* v. *Security and Investigation*, (1977), the Ontario Board of Inquiry found that the "employer bore no ill will towards Sikh people ... had no intention to insult or act with malice ... and did not have the intention or motive of discrimination." The board, however, found that the effect of the employer's policy which required that their security guards be clean-shaven and wear caps, was to deny employment to Sikhs. It ruled that intention was not necessary to establish a contravention of human rights legislation.

A similar concern is reflected in a January 1979 board of inquiry case. In the case of Ann Colfer against Ottawa Police Commission, the board decided that the commission's minimum height requirement of five feet, ten inches "virtually eliminates women as police constables," as only five percent of females in Canada are that height or taller. This height and weight (160 pounds) requirement, the board declared, had a disproportionate effect upon female gender relative to the male gender.

In December 1985, the Supreme Court of Canada, in a *unanimous decision* in *O'Malley* v. *Simpson-Sears Ltd.*, upheld the systemic approach. In the *O'Malley* case, Mrs. O'Malley had worked full-time for Simpson-Sears for seven years as a sales clerk in the ladies wear section. She accepted working on two out of three Saturdays as a normal part of her job until she joined the Seventh Day Adventist Church. Because of the religious requirement, of observing Sabbath from sunset on Friday evening to sunset on Saturday, she informed the store that she was unwilling to work on Friday evenings or Saturdays. The personnel manager explained that the Saturday work requirement applied to all salespeople. She was asked to resign, but she refused to quit. She was therefore transferred to part-time employee status. This caused reduction in her pay by almost one-half and loss of some fringe benefits, only available to full-time employees. She filed a complaint with the Ontario Human Rights Commission (OHRC) on the basis of religious discrimination.

Since the OHRC could not affect a settlement between the parties, a board of inquiry was appointed. The board concluded that the Saturday work condition amounted to unintentional discrimination. Therefore, the board decided, the Simpson-Sears store had a duty to offer her reasonable accommodation.

The Ontario Divisional Court and the Ontario Court of Appeal both decided that intention was essential to employment discrimination as defined by the old Ontario code; in addition, they decided that the old code did not have an indirect discrimination provision and that the Saturday requirement was a bonafide occupational requirement. The Supreme Court of Canada rejected the intentional discrimination approach adopted by the lower courts and decided that:

an employment rule, honestly made for sound economic and business reasons and equally applicable to all to whom it is intended to apply, may nevertheless be discriminatory if it affects a person or persons differently from others to whom it is intended to apply. The intent to discriminate is not a governing factor in construing human rights legislation aimed at eliminating discrimination. Rather, it is the result or effect of the alleged discriminatory action that is significant ... In a case of adverse effect discrimination, the employer has a duty to take reasonable steps to accommodate short of undue hardship in the operation of the employer's business.

Thus, the employer must make an effort to provide reasonable accommodation to the religious beliefs of his employees.

Enforcement

Almost all jurisdictions have human rights commissions which enforce human rights laws. Enforcement in all jurisdictions relies primarily upon the processing of individual complaints. However, in some jurisdictions, human rights commissions may file a complaint or commence an investigation on their own initiative.

All the acts provide for the settlement of complaints, if possible, by conciliation and persuasion. They provide for an initial informal investigation into a complaint by an officer who is directed to endeavour to affect a settlement. If conciliation fails, a board of inquiry may be appointed in all jurisdictions except Quebec. Such a board may issue orders for compliance, compensation, etc. This order may be appealed to the supreme court of the province on questions of law or fact, or both. The federal jurisdiction allows an appeal by either the complainant or person complained against, to a review tribunal, where the original tribunal had fewer than three members.

In actual practise, the emphasis has been to "concentrate rather less on the issues of legal guilt than on the issue of effectuating a satisfactory settlement", according to Dr. Hill, the former chairman of the Ontario Human Rights Commission (Hill 1979). This is also true in Canada as a whole, where the Ontario legislation has been the prototype of statutes in most other jurisdictions.

LEGAL DECISIONS AND CONCILIATED SETTLEMENTS PERTAINING TO VARIOUS GROUNDS OF DISCRIMINATION

Race, Colour, Ancestry, Place of Origin, National or Ethnic Origin, Nationality or Citizenship

These characteristics have not been defined with any precision by either the legislators, or boards of inquiry, or courts. The latter have done so for limited purposes and generally only when necessary to decide a specific issue. These characteristics form the basis of the largest number of employment discrimination complaints and cases that have come before human rights commissions, boards of inquiry and courts.

In *F. W. Woolworth Company Ltd.* v. *Dhillon*, (1982), an Ontario board of inquiry decided that providing a proper working environment was a condition of employment. Dhillon, who had worked for two years as a warehouseman for the company was of East Indian ancestry. He was subjected to racial insults and was subsequently dismissed. While management was aware of racial tension in the warehouse, they were ineffective or indifferent to the situation.

In the case of *Dr. M. A. Rajput* v. *Dr. Donald Watkins and Algoma University College and its Agents*, (1976), an Ontario board of inquiry found that Dr. Rajput was not offered re-employment on the basis of "nationality" or "place of origin".

In *Mears et al.* v. *Ontario Hydro*, (1983), a board of inquiry decided that discrimination against blacks was an aspect of assessment of the four complainants at the time of the layoffs by Ontario Hydro's foremen, even though the layoff of twenty-three employees was motivated by financial circumstances. That was because the foreman's previous actions towards these four employees indicated a discriminatory attitude towards black persons. Evidence indicated that the foremen kept no written records about the productivity or quality of work of their crew members, and did not use objective, standardized criteria to assess their members on a day-to-day basis.

The board also concluded that Ontario Hydro was directly responsible for the discrimination against the complainants since the company "must assume responsibility for the actions of its foremen ... because of both the authority it vested in these employees and the ineffective personnel policies that were in force in South Pickering."

Sex

Employment practises which differentiate between men and women without justifiable business necessity have been declared illegal. For instance, several boards of inquiry have held that stereotypes and misconceptions held by employers about male and female jobs have no bearing upon ability to perform the job. In *Stairs* v. *Maritime Cooperative Services Ltd.*, (1975), in New Brunswick, Mrs. Stairs had applied for a position as a cost accountant trainee. She was told by the interviewer that she would lose her "feminity" if hired. In a second interview, she was told that "I was the best qualified for the job, but he could not see having a woman in his department." In *Francis Perry* v. *Robert Simpsons Ltd.*, (1976), in Nova Scotia, Mr. Perry applied for the position of a copywriter with the company. When visiting the employment office at the company to apply for the position, he was told it would be a waste of his time, since the company only hired women for the position. Subsequently, a woman was offered the job. In *Betty-Ann Shack* v. *London Drive-Ur-Self Ltd.*, (1974) in Ontario, the rental truck agency refused to hire an inexperienced woman as a rental clerk because the employer thought the work was "too arduous" for a woman, and that she would occasionally be alone in the office at night. The chairman of the board held that "this is merely one of the 'stereotyped' characterizations of the sexes ... this factor would have no bearing whatsoever upon her ability to perform the job in question."

Similarly, women cannot be denied a job because of heavy duty janitorial work according to an order of a BC board of inquiry. In two private settlements, the Federal Human Rights Commission has decided that women cannot be refused work because of night work or shift work.

Another aspect of sex discrimination is the disparate impact of minimum height and weight requirements. For instance, height and weight requirements for a police constable's job in the *Ottawa Police Force*, (1979), weight requirement for a labouring job in *Sechelt Building Supplies Ltd.*, (1971), in BC (1979) and height requirement for an entry level labouring job in a sawmill, *BC Forest Products Ltd.*, (1979) were declared illegal by boards of inquiry in Ontario and BC. These requirements were held to have an adverse impact on females as a group. In the *BC Forest Products Ltd.* case, the BC Supreme Court upheld the decision of the board of inquiry. The Canadian Human Rights Commission reports that the CNR and the Greyhound Lines of Canada have agreed to abolish height requirement for the job of a trainman and for a job as a bus driver respectively; in both cases, a woman had complained to the commission that height requirement discriminated against females.

Marital Status

Marital status is defined in Ontario as the status of "being married, single, widowed, divorced or separated" and expressly includes "living with a person of the opposite sex in a conjugal relationship outside marriage."

In *Kerry Segrave* v. *Zellers Ltd.*, (1975), the complainant alleged that he was refused employment and refused training because of his sex and marital status by Zellers Ltd. The applicant arranged for an interview with Zellers in response to an advertisement in the Hamilton Spectator for personnel manager trainees and credit management trainees positions. He was interviewed by a female personnel manager trainee who told him that there were only women in the position of personnel management trainees in the Zellers Company and that the wage scale was too low for the complainant to consider. She also told him that they did not hire men because women would not go to them with their problems. The applicant then expressed interest in the credit manager trainee position. He was given a preliminary interview for the position, but was not processed further because of "undesirable" marital status. He had been divorced three months ago and Zellers took this as "a sign of instability in his background which could cross over into his business life as well." The board of inquiry found that Zellers had discriminated against Segrave on both sex as well as marital status grounds.

Religion or Creed

Judicial and board of inquiry decisions have given no clear indication whether religion and creed include only beliefs in a supreme being or a broad spectrum, including personal philosophy, political beliefs, agnosticism, atheism, and others. Rather, legal decisions have thus far addressed a narrow range of issues such as dress and safety requirements as in Ishar Singh, and sabbath observance and staffing requirements as in O'Malley.

Age

Canadian laws set varying protected age groups: forty-five to sixty-five, forty to sixty-five, eighteen to sixty-four, nineteen and over, and nineteen to sixty-four. Pension and benefit entitlement based on actuarial computations and related to an individual's age are uniformly exempted from prohibited discriminatory practices. The Supreme Court of Canada has (1982) ruled that in order for employers to deny employment on the basis of age, two standards must be met. One is based on production and economic reasons, and the other is related to the concern for public safety. In either case, more than impression and belief must justify the employer's practises. There must be some objective evidence relating to safe, efficient performance in order to claim exemption as a bona-fide occupational requirement.

Bona-fide Occupational Qualification (BFOQ)

All jurisdictions have a bona-fide occupational qualification exemption in respect of several prohibited grounds of discrimination. This exemption has generally been narrowly construed. The burden of proof in seeking to declare the existence of a BFOQ rests with the employer in most jurisdictions.

On 9 February 1982, the Supreme Court of Canada in a unanimous award established a subjective and an objective standard for a BFOQ, as noted earlier. First, the Supreme Court declared, a BFOQ must be imposed honestly, in good faith, and in the sincerely held belief that such limitation is imposed in the interests of the adequate performance of the work involved with all reasonable dispatch, safety, and economy and not for ulterior or extraneous reasons aimed at objectives which could defeat the purpose of the code.

Second, in addition, the Court held, it must be related in an objective sense to the performance of the employment concerned, in that it is reasonably necessary to assure the efficient and economical performance of the job without endangering the employee, his fellow employees and the general public. This judgment was rendered in the Borough of Etobicoke and the *Ontario Human Rights Commission* v. *Dunlop, Hall, Gray*.

The issue under appeal was whether the Borough discriminated against firefighters Hall and Gray in imposing mandatory retirement at age sixty. The court found that while the requirement was honestly imposed, there was not sufficient evidence that it was objectively based.

Sexual Harassment

It has become an important issue in recent years. Human rights commissions across Canada have reported an increase in the number of complaints on this ground. Numerous boards of inquiry have also ruled on this issue. Beginning with the precedent setting case, *Ann Korchzak and Cherie Bello* v. *Ernest Lada and the Flaming Steak House Tavern Inc.*, (1980), boards of inquiry across Canada have consistently ruled against sexual harassment.

In the *Ann Korchzak et al.* case, the board chairman Owen Shime declared that "... there is no reason why the law, which reached into the work place so as to protect the work environment from physical or chemical pollution or extremes of temperature, ought not to protect employees from negative, psychological and mental effects where adverse gender-directed conduct emanating from a management hierarchy may reasonably be construed to be a condition of employment." In 1983 in the *Kotyk and Allary* v. *Canadian Employment and Immigration Commission and Chuba* case, the tribunal chairman found that one of the employer's managers had engaged in sexual harassment on a consistent and deliberate basis for a period of months and that the effect of this conduct had been to "poison" the work environment. The chairman ruled that an employer's failure to: (1) recognize that sexual harassment is prohibited conduct, (2) deal with complaints as serious matters, (3) advise their employees that sexual harassment that affects the employment relationship is improper, and (4) establish mechanisms and to make both supervisors and employees aware of the significance and consequences of sexual harassment, will lead to direct liability attaching to the employer. This is what happened in this case. In another case, *Olarte* v. *Commodore Business Machines Ltd. and DeFilippes*, (1983), an Ontario board of inquiry also considered the issue of employer liability. In this case, the board found that the foreman had been guilty of sexual harassment. It ruled that while the employer could not be held vicariously liable for the foreman's conduct, it could be held personally liable to the complainants. This is because the foreman had managerial authority and therefore his acts of sexual harassment became those of the corporation. Moreover, all of the acts complained of occurred in the course of carrying on employer's business. This decision was upheld by an Ontario Court.

EMPLOYMENT EQUITY OR AFFIRMATIVE–ACTION PROGRAMS

Judge Abella, in her Royal Commission Report (1984) has called affirmative action as employment equity since affirmative action arouses emotional response. In this chapter, we will use these terms interchangeably.

One of the most important features of the Canadian human rights statutes is their provision of special programs known as affirmative-action programs. The rationale for such programs is that because of the effects of pre- and postemployment job barriers discussed above, the minority groups have not had and do not currently have the opportunity to obtain training and experience in order to qualify for better jobs. Affirmative-action programs are designed to correct the consequences of past and continuing discrimination.

Affirmative-action is a deliberate, structured approach to improving work opportunities for minority groups and women. This approach involves a series of positive steps undertaken by employers to remove barriers to employment and achieve measurable improvement in recruiting, hiring, training, and promoting qualified worker groups who have in the past been denied access to certain jobs.

Voluntary affirmative programs are legal in all jurisdictions. In Alberta, the cabinet can approve such a program. Such programs are also legal under Section 15(2) of the Canadian Charter of Rights and Freedoms. In Saskatchewan and at the federal levels, boards of inquiry can order affirmative-action programs if discrimination is found.

A tribunal under the Canadian Human Rights Commission recently (22 August 1984) ordered the Canadian National Railways to undertake a mandatory affirmative-action program. The tribunal, after three years of hearings and deliberations, found that the company had discriminated against women in its hiring practises in the St. Lawrence region. In the landmark decision, the tribunal ruled that the company is required to hire women for one in four non-traditional (blue-collar) jobs in the region until they hold thirteen percent of such jobs. The CN was also required to implement a series of other measures, ranging from abandoning certain mechanical aptitude tests to modifying the way it publicizes available jobs.

It is an important decision in several respects. It arose from a complaint laid against CN in 1979 by a Montreal women's lobby group, *Action Travail des Femmes*. It is the first time that goals have been specified; the goal of thirteen percent roughly corresponds to the proportion of women in blue-collar work in industry generally. The Federal Court of Appeal in a split decision, upheld the finding of discrimination but rejected the quota (thirteen percent) requirement. The decision has been appealed to the Supreme Court of Canada.

Voluntary affirmative-action programs have been adopted by some business organizations at the federal level, in Nova Scotia, Saskatchewan and Ontario. However, a majority of organizations in Canada do not have such programs. The existing programs have resulted in very limited progress for minorities and women. It is also true of affirmative-action programs in the Federal and the Ontario Public Service.

It is for this reason that the federal government has introduced the Employment Equity Act (Bill C–62) in the Parliament. The legislation, when enacted, will require some crown corporations and federally regulated businesses, with one hundred or more employees, to publicly report their work force data. Employers will be required to report on the representation of the four designated minority groups by occupation and salary groupings. Companies doing business with the federal government worth more than $200,000.00 will be asked to make some commitment to employment equity.

LEGAL EVIDENCE

A study by the author (Jain 1982b) of seventy-four decisions of boards of inquiry, including some court cases from 1975 to 1980 in Alberta, British Columbia, New Brunswick, Nova Scotia, Ontario and Saskatchewan revealed that: (1) discrimination was found in seventy-three percent or every seven out of 10 cases that went before a board, (2) a majority (seventy-six percent) of cases in which discrimination was found pertained to sex discrimination, (3) systemic discrimination was becoming the prevailing view in Canada in an increasing number of cases, (4) a majority (forty percent) of the cases analysed pertained to employers in the community, business and personal services industrial sector including such enterprises as hospitals, universities, school boards, etc. One-fifth of the cases pertained to trade as well as manufacturing sectors, (5) most of the complainants (more than seven out of ten) were white-collar workers, (6) in the white-collar occupational category, more than half were in the secretarial and service occupations, one-quarter were professionals and one-fifth were in technical occupations.

REMEDIES

In most cases that went before a board of inquiry, in which discrimination was found, more than one remedy was ordered. The most frequent remedy was compensation for lost wages. The other remedies in order of frequency were an order to employers to (1) display the relevant human rights code in predominant places in employer premises, (2) stop their unlawful conduct, (3) compensate for general damages, (4) compensate for expenses incurred by the complainant, (5) compensate for pain and humiliation suffered by the complainant, (6) reinstate the complainant, (7) write a letter of apology to the complainant, (8) offer employment or opportunity for employment or interview etc. at the next available job opening, (9) allow the relevant human rights commission to conduct human rights workshop for company executives, (10) amend application form and/or other selection tools, (11) write a letter of apology to the relevant human rights commission, and (12) provide separate facilities for women (Jain 1982).

CONCLUSIONS AND IMPLICATIONS

Employers should develop clear equal opportunities policies for the sake of both equity and efficiency. Such policies will help ensure that employers are not discriminating by default of appropriate action and provide safeguard in the event of their policies being challenged. Organizations should remove job entry and post-employment barriers by removing systemic discrimination. For instance, employers can issue clear instructions regarding the employment interview through their personnel departments. Interviews should be structured as much as possible, and only questions of direct relevance to the job should be asked. Similarly, choices of predictors such as tests, references, and recommendations etc. should be governed by the nature of the job and the validity of the predictors. Staffing systems can be improved considerably by standardization, to obtain reliable information and by the validation process.

References

Abella, R. S. 1984. "Equality in Employment." *A Royal Commission Report*. Minister of Supply and Services. Ottawa, October.

Affirmative Action: Technical Training Manual, Employment & Immigration Canada, Ottawa, March 1985.

Arvey, Richard D. 1979. *Fairness in selecting employees*, Reading: Mass., Addison-Wesley, 1979.

Axworthy, L. 1981. "Notes for an Address," Regina Chamber of Commerce, Regina, Sask. June 10.

Billingsley, Brenda and L. Muszynski. 1985. *No Discrimination Here? Toronto Employers and the Multi-Racial Work Force*, Social Planning Council of Metropolitan Toronto, Toronto.

Canada. House of Commons. 1984. "Equality Now! Daudlin Report." *Report of the Parliamentary Committee on Visible Minorities*. March.

Chiplin, B. and P. Sloane, 1976. Personal characteristics and sex differentials in professional employment. *Economic Journal* (December).

Employment and Immigration Commission. 1981. Labour Market Developments in the 1980s. Ottawa, Canada. July.

Ginzberg, E. and F. Henry. 1985. Who gets the work? A test of racial discrimination in employment, Social Planning Council of Metropolitan Toronto. Toronto.

Hill, D. G. 1979. The role of the Human Rights Commission: The Ontario experience. *University of Toronto Law Journal* 19.

———. 1974. "Is education related to job performance?" In *Contemporary issues in Canadian personnel administration*, Scarborough, Ontario: Prentice-Hall Canada, Inc.

Jain, H. C. 1983a. "Staffing: recruitment and selection," in *Human resource management in Canada*. Scarborough, Ontario: Prentice-Hall Canada, Inc.

———. 1983b. Communication difficulties in the workplace. Affirmation (September).

———. 1984. "Discrimination in the workplace," in *Human resource management: Contemporary perspectives in Canada*, edited by K. Srinivas. Toronto: McGraw-Hill Ryerson.

———. 1979. *Disadvantaged groups on the labour market and measures to assist them*, Paris: OECD.

Jain, H. C. and P. J. Sloane 1981. *Equal employment issues: Race and sex discrimination in the United States, Canada and Britain*. New York: Praeger.

———. 1981. "Discrimination against Indians: Issues and policies." In *Work in the Canadian context: Continuity despite change*, edited by K. Lundy and B. Warme. Toronto: Butterworth.

———. 1982a. "Employment and pay discrimination in Canada: Theories, evidence and policies." In *Union-management relations in Canada*, edited by J. Anderson and M. Gunderson, Don Mills. Ontario: Addison-Wesley.

———. 1982b. Race and sex discrimination in Canada. *Relations Industrielles* 37.

———. 1983. The impact of recession on equal opportunities for minorities and women in the United States, Canada and Britain. *The Columbia Journal of World Business* (Summer).

———. 1984. *Anti-discrimination staffing policies: Implications of human rights legislation for employers and trade unions*, Ottawa: Dept. of the Secretary of State.

Levitan, S. and R. Taggar. 1977. *Jobs for the disabled.* Baltimore: John Hopkins University Press.

Malkiel, B. G. and J. A. Malkiel 1973. Male and female differentials in professional employment. *American Economic Review* (September).

Marr, W. 1976. Labour market and other implications of immigration policy for Ontario. Ontario Economic Council, Toronto. November.

Reitz, J. 1981. *Ethnic inequality and segregation in jobs.* Toronto: University of Toronto. May.

Sampson, F. *Issues relating to the labour force position of the disabled in Canada*, Ottawa: Employment and Immigration Commission. July.

Saunders. G.S. 1975. The labour market adaptation of Third World Immigrants. University of Alberta, Sept. 5.

Statistics Canada. 1981. Census. Ottawa, Ministry of Supply and Services Canada.

Young, D. M. and E. G. Beier. 1977. The role of applicant nonverbal communication in the employment interview. *Journal of Employment Counselling* 14.

10. Equal Employment Opportunities—Challenges and Practices for Canadian Companies: The Royal Bank Experience

Lynda J. White, The Royal Bank of Canada

When women first began working in banks close to one hundred years ago, they were hired as typists because men didn't know how to operate the new invention. Few among those first women realized the challenge ahead and the progress that would be made.

In 1910, it is estimated that women made up six percent of bank employees. Women were beginning to enter the political arena, and the suffrage movement was gaining momentum. The twenties brought a new era of personal freedom and some of the first appointments of women to public office. This, in conjunction with an acceptance of higher education for women, brought increasing numbers into the work force. Most aspiring career women, however, were still limited to very traditional positions set aside for females. The overwhelming majority of women still held clerical, low-level positions.

In the thirties, feelings that working women took jobs away from men intensified, however, the outbreak of World War II saw this trend reverse, and women were encouraged to take jobs traditionally held by men. Women took over in areas of greater responsibility, and for the first time, many of the conventional stereotypes of women's work were challenged.

By the early fifties, women were seen as well suited for clerical jobs, however, the debate as to their suitability as appointed officers was underway. A 1953 article in *The Canadian Banker* stated that matrimony was probably the most "disturbing element in the employment of women." Since work was seen as a stopgap measure between school and marriage, banks like other employers, were reluctant to train women if they were going to marry and leave the service of the company in a few years.

Nevertheless, the changes of the forties would not be reversed and the number of women working for banks by the late fifties had increased to sixty percent of total staff. In 1958, Miss Gladys Marcellus became the first Canadian female branch accountant at the Bank of Nova Scotia in Chesterville, Ontario, and four years later, in 1962, she and Mrs. Shirley Gilles were appointed managers of the Bank of Nova Scotia in Ottawa and Toronto, respectively. The Royal Bank appointed its first female branch manager in 1968 when Georgette St. Cyr became manager at Place Longueuil, Montreal.

During the late sixties, the Royal Bank also began to respond to the changing expectations of women. Reviews were undertaken of policies regarding training and advancement opportunities and benefits. A work force analysis began in order to establish the number and location of female employees and to track their progression. As well, senior management and personnel started to investigate the reasons for segregation of the work force and began looking for solutions.

In November 1963, the bank's pension plan had finally been opened up to women albeit at entry age of twenty-four for women as compared to twenty-one for men, and at a retirement age of sixty for women versus a comparable age of sixty-five for men. May 1974, as a result of the overall policy reviews instituted earlier, saw final elimination of all discrimination towards women in the area of compensation and benefits policy, with benefits (e.g., pensions, insurance, medical) extended equally in all respects to men and women.

The sixties saw legislation in both Canada and the United States begin to recognize the right of women to equal access in employment, and it was firmly established that women were in the labour force to stay. The seventies would see much action at the Royal.

In the early seventies, realizing the lack of women in management, a catch up measure was introduced in the form of a special management training course for women. This program commenced in 1973 and over approximately three years, about 150 women completed the management development program. Steps were taken in each district field unit to identify women with management potential as candidates for this training. While there are many success stories, and some of the most senior women in our organization today are graduates of this program, there were also some failures. The pressures and demands were such that a few women did not succeed when given greater responsibility. They ended up returning to positions similar to those held prior to the management training and preferred to stay in such areas.

In early 1974, at our annual meeting of shareholders, Mrs. Laura Sabia, prominent in the women's movement in Canada, spoke on the status of women in relation to the Royal Bank's organization and business. Mrs. Sabia played a part in the creation of the Federal Royal Commission on the Status of Women in 1967 and at the time was Chairman of the Ontario Status of Women's Council, an advisory board appointed by the Ontario government. The following day, acting as a representative of the council, Mrs. Sabia met with our chairman, Mr. W. Earle McLaughlin and a number of Royal bankers to discuss such matters as the equality of employee benefits, how banks treated women as customers, what opportunities existed at senior levels for women in the Royal, and the representation of women in the bank's advertising. Following the meeting, Mrs. Sabia gave a telephone interview to the *Toronto Globe & Mail*, and wire service versions of this article appeared in some other Canadian newspapers. She stated that her overall impression of the bank's efforts to advance the position of women within the organization was that while the situation with regard to women was not yet satisfactory, she recognized that these things take time and that the bank was doing a "more than fair job." This meeting was followed internally by a communication to all bank staff and a further commitment to ensure all employees rightful and equal access to opportunities within the bank.

By the late seventies, we had come a long way—but still had a long way to go. A group of female bank employees calling themselves the Women's Action Committee approached Mr. Frazee (then executive vice president and chief general manager) with a presentation indicating their concerns that despite policy statements, their perception was that they were still facing subtle and pervasive discrimination at each stage of the advancement process. They recommended a more comprehensive review of the systems and practices of the bank.

Mr. Frazee agreed and in response established in early 1977, a Task Force on the Status of Women. An outside consultant and ten employees (six women and four men) from across the bank worked together over the next year and concluded "that while there is no discrimination in the bank's policies, there are in fact inequities in practise." To eliminate the inequities and gaps that existed between written policies and actual application, the task force made some significant and far reaching recommendations. In the words of the force, these included the following:

Mobility

Mobility was one of the most difficult issues addressed by the task force. It interrelates with many other areas and is perceived to be a major cause of concern by the staff, male and female, at all levels. The task force views consultation as the key to an equitable mobility policy and made the following recommendations:

1. Consult staff before transferring them
2. Employees who restrict their mobility will, on the basis of merit, qualify for training leading to middle management
3. Give the opportunity annually for all staff to state their level of mobility

Training

Research conducted by the task force indicates that in spite of the fact that increasing numbers of women are participating in the Institute of Canadian Bankers educational program, access to many internal programs may yet be blocked, whether as a result of numerical restriction of the programs themselves, a lack of knowledge on the part of women, mobility restriction, or because women are not encouraged to participate. The task force made the following recommendations with respect to training:

1. Implement the self-nomination concept for training
2. Amend the district management training program to include more women
3. Develop a training module to help women gain confidence
4. Develop awareness/assertiveness training to be incorporated into all the bank's training programs
5. Encourage women's participation in external management courses
6. E.E.O. coordinator must take an active part in the selection and progress of women in training courses
7. Establish as a high priority key result area, the ongoing promotion of women into management

Assessment of Potential

The key to achieving the corporate goal of assimilating more women into the management and executive ranks of the bank is the ability to properly identify those with sufficient potential to promote and train. The task force is aware of potential at all levels. However, it felt that some steps must be taken immediately to improve the present system. Accordingly, the following recommendations were made:

1. Amend immediately the mechanism for assessing potential pending the introduction of a more sophisticated system. To do this, the performance appraisal green card must be revised
2. Collect all relevant information on each employee, which may be generated from various reports, in one file
3. Arrange regular interviews for all employees to discuss their careers with personnel officers from the districts or head office
4. Establish a resource pool in each district of the ten percent of staff in each pay grade with the highest potential

Job Opportunities

Through the results of a survey conducted, the task force found that women do not know what positions are available in the bank, nor how to obtain them, nor what training is needed. Additionally, the task force stated that career counselling is virtually non-existent. To improve job opportunities, the task force recommended that the bank: Establish at once a program which provides a mechanism for employees to apply in advance for positions which may become open.

Equal Employment Opportunity

Now that the bank has created and staffed the post of equal employment opportunity coordinator as recommended in their interim report, the task force recommended that the bank:

1. Establish an E.E.O. advisory group
2. Pinpoint E.E.O. accountability in districts
3. Appoint a consultant to work with the E.E.O. coordinator for at least one year

Awareness Sessions

An important prerequisite in the effort to improve the position of women in the bank is that management at all levels understand the issues and attitudes surrounding equal employment opportunities for women. To ensure this, it was recommended that the bank:

1. Ensure that all supervisory staff participate in awareness sessions as soon as possible
2. Incorporate appropriate awareness sessions in all training programs

Public Relations

Although the position of women in the bank has improved over the past few years and continues to improve, this is not readily perceived by women in the bank. To stress both inside and outside the bank the importance of the bank's role as a fair employer of women, the task force recommended that the bank:

1. Distribute a summary of the final report of the task force to staff, the media, and others who are interested
2. Keep employees and the media informed of progress on women's issues in the bank

Accountability

Corporate objectives are more easily achieved with clear-cut accountability for results. For this reason, the task force recommended that the bank build accountability for equal employment opportunity into mandates and key result areas.

Targets for the Future

The task force strongly supports the bank's policy of promoting and developing from within. However, in light of the present pool of women, it will take time to prepare them for senior levels and as promotion is preferable to parachuting, the task force recommended that the Bank review resources available in each district and set objectives for promoting women. The objectives will be reviewed by the chief general manager's committee.

The task force reports were widely publicized, cassette tapes were used to allow the chief general manager and task force members to speak directly to all staff, as well, the task force report summary was distributed to each and every bank employee.

As the seventies came to a close, important changes had taken place and included the following:

- Two women held directorships on the board
- The first woman executive had been appointed
- All senior management had participated in awareness sessions conducted by Rosabeth Moss Kanter to examine their own attitudes and biases
- The job opportunities program was operational across Canada
- A task force was studying further the issue of mobility
- Training programmes were being monitored to ensure the participation of women
- All high potential women were identified
- The performance appraisal system was updated
- The second equal employment opportunity coordinator was in place
- All field units across the bank were required to complete and submit equal opportunity status reports on a quarterly basis

Most significantly, attitudes had changed, fears of quotas, tokenism, and reverse discrimination had been replaced by the comfort of familiar ideas, promotion based on merit, maximization of our human resources, and matching the right people with the right jobs.

THE EQUAL EMPLOYMENT OPPORTUNITY PROGRAM TODAY

Policy and Responsibility

It is the policy of the Royal Bank to accept applications and fill positions without regard to sex, ensuring that the male and female composition within the bank reflects the qualified candidates available in the work force population. In addition and in keeping with our promotion from within policy, promotions will also reflect the representation of men and women in our internal feeder work force.

The objective of the equal employment opportunity program is to ensure areas of underutilization and concentrations of women are identified and appropriate corrective action is taken. We are reaching this objective through policy dissemination, analysis and monitoring of our work force, and an ongoing results-oriented equal opportunity program.

The policy of equal employment opportunity is continually emphasized through both internal and external communication channels.

1. *Internally* this is accomplished by the following methods:
   a. A statement of our policy is in the personnel administration manual. This manual is available in all units and accessible to employees at any time.
   b. An annual statement and update is provided through the annual report to staff.
   c. A videotape presentation is available discussing the nature of opportunity, power, and numbers in the context of equal opportunity.
   d. Employees are kept updated of important equal employment opportunity changes through the distribution of the bank news bulletin *Between Ourselves* to each and every employee.
   e. Articles pertaining to equal employment opportunity issues are frequently published in such internal communication vehicles as *Interest* magazine and *ChequeMarks*. Women are also portrayed in staff publications and video communications. The public affairs department has developed editorial guidelines to ensure language and editorial treatment is unbiased.
   f. Orientation packages for new employees contain information regarding our policy on equal employment opportunity.
   g. Regular discussions are held with individual personnel departments and more formal presentations included at personnel courses and conferences.
   h. Our annual recruitment strategy provides guidelines for recruiters and personnel departments that ensure equal opportunity for all applicants.
   i. Senior management and the E.E.O. coordinator address groups across the bank to discuss equal employment opportunity issues.

2. *Externally* the equal opportunity policy is communicated in the following ways:
   a. The bank's equal employment opportunity policy and posture is often published externally through newspapers and magazine articles.
   b. The bank takes an active role in talking with and counselling other companies about affirmative action.
   c. Women as well as men are portrayed in publications and advertising including those relating to employment practise.
   d. Written and verbal notification of our policy of equal employment opportunity is made to all recruiting sources.
   e. The bank's equal opportunity policy is included in recruitment brochures.
   f. Representatives from the bank who address community groups and other civic organizations reiterate our commitment to equal employment opportunity.

The senior vice president of personnel has overall responsibility for equal employment opportunity. The chief executive officer is directly involved with equal employment issues and is kept informed on the status and direction of the program. The equal employment opportunity coordinator reports through the vice president of personnel and is responsible for monitoring bankwide equal opportunity efforts as well as reviewing bank policies and programs.

Responsibility for ensuring equal employment opportunity rests with the bank's line management. All department heads, branch managers and supervisors are responsible for equal employment in their respective areas. Their responsibilities include but are not limited to:

1. Identifying equal opportunity problem areas
2. Ensuring women within their unit receive equal consideration for hires, promotions, transfers and opportunities for training
3. Providing career counselling for all employees including the identification and development of qualified women for positions with more responsibility
4. Ensuring that all interviews for openings are conducted in a nondiscriminatory manner
5. Ensuring that any documents placed in personnel files are fair, objective, and job related
6. Applying policies consistently and in a nondiscriminatory manner
7. Ensuring corporate targets and objectives are met within their own unit

The function of the personnel department is to ensure fair treatment of all bank employees. Personnel officers are responsible for providing staff support to all bank units on all matters relating to equal employment opportunity. Personnel works closely with other departments (human resource development, compensation, employee relations, corporate recruitment, and the equal employment opportunity coordinator) to ensure that all bank policies, practises and procedures comply with equal opportunity objectives. Their special responsibilities are:

1. Reviewing equal employment opportunity progress and problems quarterly
2. Providing assistance to department heads in identifying problem areas and recommending solutions
3. Providing advice on personnel decisions and how to document those decisions as they relate to equal employment opportunity
4. Investigating and resolving complaints of alleged discrimination filed by employees
5. Providing specialized ongoing training to all bank supervisors regarding equal employment opportunity
6. Ensuring that during personnel visits in branches and departments, personnel policies are communicated and enforced in a nondiscriminatory manner
7. Serve as a liaison between staff and equal employment opportunity coordinator in matters concerning equal employment opportunity
8. Communicate the bank's policies regarding equal opportunity and affirmative action both internally and externally

The coordinator works to ensure bankwide commitment to our equal employment opportunity objectives and works with individuals and departments in managing equal employment opportunity issues. The position provides a central source of information in this area, reviews the program's effectiveness, makes recommendations to senior management and is expected to:

1. Compile quarterly monitoring information and provide analysis of the data to senior management for review with field units
2. Review problems and concerns bankwide and recommend changes and implement corrective action
3. Handle and deal with complaints concerning discrimination
4. Ensure a continued awareness of all bank staff on issues related to equal employment opportunity
5. Represent the bank's position outside the organization
6. Gather information external to the organization on equal employment and affirmative action matters
7. Monitor the activities of personnel, human resource development, and compensation to ensure activities are in compliance with our objectives

Analysis

The equal employment opportunity coordinator maintains a listing by sex for job levels, divisions, and streams. The listing is produced and analysed on a quarterly basis and is reviewed with the heads of field units. Areas of concentration and underutilization of women are pointed out to the fields and appropriate recommendations are provided.

Utilization is monitored by comparing the estimated available female work force with the bank's actual female work force. To determine the availability of nonofficer positions and entrance level positions, we examine the external work force considering the following factors:

1. The size of the female work force
2. General availability of women with requisite skills in the area that the bank can reasonably recruit
3. Availability of women seeking employment

Most officer positions, however, are filled by promotion from within. Therefore, availability of women for the majority of management positions is determined by:

1. Examining the availability of women in the job groups below who possess the requisite skills necessary for the available opening
2. Availability of promotable and transferable women within the bank
3. Degree of training the bank can undertake to qualify women for the job

In cases where specialized technical and professional expertise is needed, availability is determined by surveying the marketplace.

Table 10–1 shows the progress of women as a percentage of those in management, as well as management including supervisory positions since 1976.

Management is defined as jobs with a 1985 base job rate (averaged nationally) of approximately $26,200, while the first line supervisory staff includes everyone with a base job rate for 1985 (again averaged nationally) of $20,800. These jobs would include branch administration officers and consumer loans officer positions, which are traditionally seen as stepping stones to management jobs.

Table 10-1   Women as a % of Total Group

	1985	1984	1982	1980	1978	1976
Management	20	18	16	12	9	7
Including Supervisory Staff	41	40	38	36	33	26

Current Personnel Practices

The bank's selection, promotion, transfer, compensation, benefit, and discipline practices are continually audited and reviewed by corporate personnel, human resource development, compensation, and employee relations to ensure policy and practice reflect our equal opportunity initiatives. This process includes the following.

Selection. The bank's objective is to select qualified applicants without regard to sex or other non-job related criteria. The process is monitored to ensure the selection is consistent from location to location, free from bias, and that the process does not have an adverse effect on women. Monitoring includes:

1. An analysis of position descriptions to ensure that they accurately and objectively reflect the duties and functions of the job
2. A salary scale tied to a position mandate which is rated in terms of know how, problem solving, accountability, and working conditions
3. An analysis of education, skill, and experience requirements upon which selection and placement decisions are made—if any of these should have a disparate effect on men or women, the requirements are validated as to their business necessity
4. A review of the employment application form and the employment interview and screening process to ensure that there are no hidden barriers to employment—an updated and revised application form was completed in 1983
5. An analysis of placement procedures to ensure women are not restricted to certain jobs, departments, or locations

Promotion and Transfer. Promotion and transfer procedures have been reviewed to ensure that individuals are placed in positions where they are optimally productive and that such decisions are made without regard to sex or other non-job related criteria. The review included the following:

1. The Opportunities Program was introduced in 1980 and has today been updated to enable all employees to apply for positions of interest to them. If an applicant is not accepted for a certain job, he/she is informed and counselled by the personnel department or immediate supervisor
2. Employee promotions and transfers are monitored by the E.E.O. coordinator and the personnel department
3. The performance appraisal card allows employees to express a career interest and indicate specific jobs and/or training desired
4. A flexible policy on mobility ensures qualified candidates with limited

mobility are not overlooked for promotional opportunities

5. On an annual basis, all staff members are reviewed and those with high potential identified and monitored. A review of the male/female ratio is examined to ensure equality and that a consistent standard is being applied

6. As a special measure, a review of all management women is done, to ensure that their careers are progressing as expected and career plans are established to ensure continued progress

Training. Training is key to upgrading all employees. Women are encouraged to take advantage of training opportunities through the Institute of Canadian Bankers and apply for training within the bank. Training programs are monitored closely to ensure women are fairly represented. Presently, corporate goals exist for career development training and we are committed to and achieving fifty percent representation of women on the branch administration and consumer loans officer training programme and are presently concerned with moving our management training program from approximately thirty percent to fifty percent women.

Compensation and Benefits. All employees receive compensation and benefits on the basis of performance and job responsibilities without regard to sex. The bank continually reviews employee benefits to ensure their equitable application to all employees.

Discipline. The bank ensures disciplinary procedures are applied appropriately and without bias through instruction in the personnel administration manual. An appeal process has also been established whereby an employee may make a submission to employee relations head office.

Sexual Harassment. The bank believes all employees have a right to work in an environment free of sexual harassment, and it is the bank's intent that no employee be subjected to such abuse. A complaint procedure is outlined in the personnel administration manual.

Special Programs

Career Counselling. Career counselling is available for all employees through their immediate supervisor or the personnel department. The bank encourages all employees to express their goals and aspirations on a regular basis, but at least annually, and to take a major responsibility in planning their own careers. Those female employees who work in departments where there is a concentration of women, are encouraged to take advantage of the counselling program to ensure they are aware of opportunities elsewhere in the bank, of training programs, and tuition assistance programs.

Summer Undergraduate Program. The summer undergraduate program provides summer employment and training on the branch administration officer training program for a limited number of university undergraduates in business or commerce programs. This program includes women and men.

Cooperative Program. The bank provides employment for a limited number of undergraduates as part of the work requirements for university cooperative programs. This program is available to men and women.

Muir Scholarship Program. The Muir program allows a limited number of employees to pursue full-time study, in a career related program at the university while receiving full salary. This program is currently occupied with fifty percent women.

RSVP. The RSVP program gives all employees the opportunity to voice complaints, raise questions or describe work related problems with complete assurance that the correspondent's identity will remain anonymous. Only the coordinator knows the individuals who write RSVP, and he/she will not reveal the identity without authorization from the individual.

Access. Access is an employee assistance plan providing information, counselling, and referral services, designed to help employees and their families with behavioral or medical conditions such as alcoholism, dependence on mood-altering drugs, or emotional disturbances.

Implementation and Follow Through. Through the human resource planning system, each planning unit can establish its own plan for reaching equal opportunity objectives.

Through human resource quarterly monitoring reports and in particular, the equal employment opportunity reports, corporate personnel and line management review progress on a quarterly basis. This review includes:

1. The recruitment quarterly and year-to-date for positions at each level, as well as recruitment directly into training programs
2. The number of promotions at each level, as well as lateral moves, developmental moves, and demotions
3. Turnover rates, with a particular look at reasons for resignations of both men and women
4. The number of men and women in training programs at both management and non-management levels
5. Predicted next moves against actual moves for all promising officers
6. A review of current issues and concerns in the equal employment opportunity area
7. The status of men and women at each management level, and within each occupational stream

Corporate personnel reports quarterly on affirmative action progress to senior management, with details of reports and discussions with field units. Corporate senior management reviews, with the senior line manager of each field unit, the outcome of these reviews.

THE EQUAL EMPLOYMENT OPPORTUNITY PROGRAM IN THE FUTURE

While we have been active in the field for some time, with positive results, we realize there is still much to be done. Today, with employment equity legislation in the offing, we anticipate that as a federally regulated corporation, we shall have to start filing reports with the government in 1988. These reports are to include internal work force analysis data based on the four identified target groups—women, native peoples, visible minorities and the handicapped. We do know that all of the groups are represented in our work force. At this time, due to interpretations of human rights legislation, we have data on women only, as is the case with most Canadian corporations. We foresee in the near future, the need for a self-identification survey of our staff to put us in a position to meet reporting requirements. Monitoring of all target groups will commence following receipt of survey results.

We have been active in outreach programs, both at the field unit and corporate levels, and are increasing communications with these groups to better understand how to successfully integrate their members into our work force.

Our message to staff today is that while we have come a long way and are considered a leader in the field of equal employment opportunity, we have a long way to go. Public accessibility to reports filed is an integral part of the proposed government legislation. We have long been public with our figures in the area of female representation, however, with an increased public profile, we shall have to strive even harder than we have in the past to continue our leadership role. The commitment to equal employment opportunity involves each and every one of us!

11. The Selection Interview: The Received Wisdom Versus Recent Research

Tom Janz, The University of Calgary

Employers make heavy use of personnel interviews in deciding who to hire from the pool of applicants available to staff job openings. Interviews fall second in frequency of use only to application forms as tools in the selection process (McDaniel and Schmidt 1985). Personnel and line managers give the interview a strong vote of confidence, both in terms of the frequency and importance accorded the interview (Glueck 1978). Given this high level of usage, one might expect that the interviewing literature abounds with careful, detailed research pointing up interview do's and don'ts so that the thoughtful student can learn to accurately predict applicant job performance. Sadly, clear guidelines to accurate interviewing based on firm evidence have surfaced only recently (Latham, Saari, Purcell, and Campion 1980; Janz 1982; Orpen 1985; Janz, Hellervik, and Gilmore 1986).

This chapter begins with a quick look at the received wisdom passed on in recent personnel management texts and reviews of the interviewing literature. Then, it contrasts these old theories with several new research findings investigating the validity of patterned, behaviour-based interviewing. A review of three recent meta-analyses bearing on improved interviewing follows, including the largest meta-analysis of the interviewing literature to date. The chapter ends with the practical implications offered by the recent research findings.

THE RECEIVED WISDOM

Most recent human resource management texts feature a section on the employment interview. What follows samples their evaluations of the accuracy or validity of interview assessments.

Werther, Davis, Schwind, Das, and Miner (1982) cite interview reliability and validity as notable flaws. They claimed that different interviewers commonly form different opinions about the same applicants. They suggested interview decisions may relate more closely to individual applicant characteristics than to future job performance.

Stone and Meltz (1983) conclude that the value of the interview is problematic, since different interviewers often disagree due to subjectivity and a lack of interview structure. While the authors waxed more enthusiastically about employment tests and weighted application blanks, they did not directly compare interview accuracy with reported accuracies for alternative methods.

Glueck (1978) painted a confusing picture of interviewing validity—again in the absence of any direct, numerical comparisons of accuracy. He contrasted the widespread use of interviews with the controversy over their reliability and validity. He pointed out that most research finds structured interviews more reliable (higher agreement among interviewers) than unstructured ones, but went on to say that other research questioned this conclusion.

Schuler (1984) stated that the interview is not a good procedure for making applicant assessments because it is too subjective. He preferred written tests or carefully developed situational tests. He went on to note that the continued popularity of interviews may stem from pressure for equality of opportunity at the expense of staffing accuracy.

Mathis and Jackson (1985) summed up a rather lengthy section on interviewing dos and don'ts by stating that, despite its frequent use, interviewing is likely one of the least accurate methods of predicting job performance. As with all the others, no direct comparisons among staffing techniques was presented.

Heneman, Schwab, Fossum, and Dyer (1983) round out our sampling of the received wisdom being passed on to today's students in management schools. Heneman et al. (1983) sounded most pessimistic on the value of interviews, stating that interrater reliability is low and validity, with the occasional exception, is very low. They concluded that the interview does not accomplish the purpose of identifying high performing applicants.

So far we know two things. Personnel and line managers use and trust the selection interview with the crucial task of deciding who will populate organizations. We also know that the received wisdom as expressed in personnel management texts almost uniformly derides the accuracy or validity of interviews, claiming they are too subjective to do the job. While these texts offer steps for improving the interview, the received wisdom turns thumbs down on interviewing in general.

The authors of these texts cite the scientific literature to support their views. Several key reviews of the literature on interviewing stand behind most of their statements. Arvey and Campion (1982) is the best place for the serious academic student to start, since that article contains reviews of all the previous reviews. From the first review by Wagner (1949) through Mayfield (1964), Ulrich and Trumbo (1965), Wright (1969), and Schmitt (1976), studies of interview accuracy often yielded poor results. There were important exceptions yielding high validities, but it seems it was easier to ignore them in favour of documenting why unstructured, spontaneous interviews did not work. Schmitt (1976) noted the trend to micro-research on poor interviewing and suggested that a return to finding effective interviewing methods was needed. It has been slow to happen.

RECENT RESEARCH: BEHAVIOUR-BASED METHODS

The recent research leading to more valid interview assessments began with an article by Maas (1965). He argued for critical incident analysis as basis for asking better interview questions. Maas suggested that the scaled behaviour expectation procedure created for measuring job performance be applied to developing benchmark answers against which to rate an applicant's interview answers. He reported high interviewer agreement in two data sets.

Latham et al. (1980) carried the behaviour-based notion a step further. They turned critical incidents—stories of effective and ineffective job behaviour—into interview questions. They call their approach situational interviewing. For example, one incident described an employee who called in sick because his wife was away and his kid came down with the flu. Latham et al. turned this into an interview question by asking applicants what they would do if their spouse was away visiting parents and their eight-year-old child came down with the flu?

The situational interview approach develops benchmark answers to these open-ended questions. Continuing the example, an answer like "I would stay home with my kid" is benchmarked low on the response scale whereas an answer like "I would phone a neighbor and ask her to check in on my kid so I could make my shift" is benchmarked at a high score. Latham et al. (1980) reported high interviewer reliabilities (.71 and .67) and significant correlations with job performance measures (.46 and .30).

The situational interview asks the applicant "what WOULD you do IF." The other approach to patterned, behaviour-based interviewing asks the applicant "what DID you do WHEN." I call this *behaviour description* interviewing (Janz 1982; Janz et al. 1986). Behaviour description interview patterns start with the same pool of critical incidents as the situational interview. Instead of forming questions that ask the applicant to provide hypothetical responses, the BD interview asks the applicant to describe the *most satisfying, most disappointing, most frustrating,* or *most recent* time in the applicant's past that recalls a situation described in one of the critical incidents.

Carry the illustration from the situational interview a little further. The situational interviewer asks applicants, "What would you do IF your spouse was away visiting her parents and your eight-year-old child came down with the flu?" To cover the same ground, the BD interviewer asks "Tell me about the most recent time you had to miss work and stay at home. What was the reason? What did you do?"

The situational interviewing improves over unstructured interviews or even structured interviews that dwell mainly on applicant opinions. Still, I argue that applicants with above average verbal reasoning, fluency, and presence respond with agility to the hypothetical questions posed by the situational interview. The applicant may *know* what to do, but will he or she do it when the time comes? BD interviews offer the clearest opportunity to cut through the marshmallow impressions created by applicants motivated to get jobs ill-suited to their abilities and temperament. Still, situational interviews do not require that the applicant has past experience that samples future settings, an advantage for some applicants.

Two research studies directly support the accuracy of the behaviour description method. Janz (1982) compared traditional, unstructured interviews with behaviour description interviews. One group of eight senior undergraduate business students was trained in traditional interview techniques, for example, establishing rapport, active listening, etc. Another group of students was training in BD interviewing. The position studied was teaching assistant. The criterion was the TAs student performance rating administered at the end of the semester.

Interviews were tape recorded and analysed. While the traditional interviewers obtained BD answers about four percent of the time, BD interviewers raised that percentage to fifty-six percent. The traditional interviewers agreed more reliably (.71 *versus* .46), but on the wrong applicant. BD interview accuracy or validity was a substantial .54 *versus* .07 for traditional interviews, both statistically and practically superior.

The relatively small sample size, the academic setting, and the nonrandom assignment of subjects to interview conditions weakened the Janz (1982) study. Orpen (1985) corrected these deficiencies in a replication of the Janz (1982) design conducted for predicting life insurance sales success. He randomly assigned potential interviewers to two conditions: (1) behaviour description training and (2) traditional interview training. He ensured that both training programs took the same length of time and offered similar opportunities to practice. Orpen measured two job criteria: (1) value of insurance sales and (2) supervisor's ratings. The results echoed the Janz (1982) finding remarkably, and offered even stronger support where they differed.

For the criterion of supervisor's ratings, Orpen (1985) reported the BD validity at .56 *versus* .08 for traditional, unstructured interview. For the criterion of value of policies sold, he found a BD interview validity of .72 *vs.* .10 for unstructured interviews. It takes a determined skeptic to downplay the power of behaviour description interviews in the light of these findings.

Taking stock so far, a line of research that applied the critical incident method to developing behaviour-based interview questions led to the situational and BD interview methods. These methods produced interview validities approaching levels reported for cognitive ability tests, work sample tests, and carefully developed bio-data forms (Hunter and Hunter 1984). Taken together, these studies stand in stark contrast to the received wisdom still passed on to naive business students today—the interviewers of tomorrow. The next section of this chapter examines two recent meta-analyses that bear on the search for more accurate interviewing methods.

RECENT META-ANALYTIC RESEARCH

In the past, a practitioner trying to figure out what *we know* about a given topic could either sift through several journals to dig out the individual studies, or read a review of the studies written with a particular point of view. Meta-analysis emerged recently (Glass 1976) and has been refined (Hunter, Schmidt, and Jackson 1982) as a method of statistically combining the existing research literature on a given question. However, as the three meta-analyses reviewed below illustrate, even meta-analysis can be misleading depending on the studies the researcher selects for inclusion in the analysis.

Hunter and Hunter

Hunter and Hunter (1984), examined the accuracy or validity of alternative predictors of job performance—alternative, that is, to their favoured cognitive ability tests. Their list of alternative predictors included: (1) peer ratings, (2) bio-data, (3) reference checks, (4) college GPA, (5) the interview, and (6) the Strong Interest Inventory. Hunter and Hunter review previous reviews, and then report meta-analyses of their own conducted on 202 studies. They do not describe in detail how the studies were selected for inclusion.

Hunter and Hunter report an uncorrected population correlation for interview predictions of eventual supervisory ratings of .11. When corrected for unreliability of the criterion, the validity estimate rises to .14. This finding suits them well, and falls clearly within the bounds of the received wisdom, but it was based on only ten coefficients. Since we do not know how they were selected, it is hard to know, just from their own findings, whether those ten coefficients sample all interviewing research in a biased or unbiased way.

McDaniel and Schmidt

The second meta-analytic study bears indirectly on the value of behaviour-based approaches to predicting job performance. McDaniel and Schmidt (1985) compared different methods for evaluating applicant training and experience. They compared the point, job element, task, and behaviour consistency methods. The point method assigns the applicant points for years of experience and for specific training programs. The job element method assigns points to specific job elements rated to be present in the applicants' past jobs. The task method asks applicants to rate their experience at several tasks.

The behaviour consistency method shares many similarities with BD interviewing. It asks applicants to describe their major achievements in several job-related performance areas. The performance areas are identified via a behavioural job analysis. Interviewers rate the applicant's achievement statements against behaviourally-anchored rating scales.

The mean true validities across all studies was .14 for the point method, .23 for the job element method, .32 for the task method, and .49 for the behaviour consistency method. This result falls cleanly within the range of substantial validities reported for behaviour-based interview methods, offering further evidence for the value of improved interviewing.

Weisner and Cronshaw

The most convincing meta-analytic review appears last. The Weisner and Cronshaw (1986) meta-analysis captures the widest range of published and unpublished research, including 134 usable validity coefficients. It carefully teased out key interview characteristics that make the difference between accurate and inaccurate interview methods.

Weisner and Cronshaw (1986) reported the mean uncorrected validity for all studies at .27, based on a combined sample size of 50,130. Validity rose to .48 when corrected for the estimated effects of range restriction and criterion unreliability. Clearly, this study based on 134 coefficients paints a different picture than the Hunter and Hunter (1984) meta-analysis, based on only ten coefficients.

Weisner and Cronshaw compared structured *versus* unstructured interviews, finding mean uncorrected validities of .34 and .16 respectively. When corrected for range restriction and criterion unreliability, validities rose to .62 for structured (combined sample size of 9,905) *versus* .29 for unstructured interview methods (combined sample size of 4,698). These results show strong support for interview structure, yielding much higher population validities than the received wisdom suggests.

Finally, Weisner and Cronshaw (1986) examined the role of job analysis as a further moderator of the validities reported for structured interviews. They were able to divide studies of the structured interview into three categories: (1) formal job analysis, (2) "armchair" job analysis, and (3) unknown job analytic method. They hypothesized that formal job analysis yields better interview pattern questions that focus directly on job-related applicant performance.

They reported the following mean corrected population validities with the sample sizes in parentheses: (1) formal—.87 (1,265), (2) armchair—.59 (4,943), and (3) unknown—.56 (1,602). While Weisner and Cronshaw (1986) may have overcorrected somewhat by using general estimates of range restriction and criterion unreliability, even the uncorrected finding of .48 soundly denounces the received wisdom of poor interview decision accuracy. The corrected value of .87 for structured interviews based on formal job analysis, both characteristics of patterned behaviour-based interviews, argues strongly for the continued use of these interviewing methods.

THEORETICAL IMPLICATIONS OF THE NEW RESEARCH

How did the received wisdom get off track and then remain derailed for so long? I speculate that the answer lies in our human failings rather than a fatal flaw in scientific procedures. Before meta-analysis, researchers reviewing the literature would gather together all published studies and perform a mental evaluation of each study. The big picture supposedly emerged from this mental review of the documented evidence.

Of course, researchers are people too, and possess no special immunity to personal biases, hunches, selective perceptions, and elaborate rationalizations. Also, those familiar with the publication game recognize how much easier it is to publish yet another restatement of the received wisdom than it is to publish a contrary finding.

So how did we get off track? Wagner (1949) conducted the first major review of the interviewing literature. He reviewed many studies—some that reported poor validities and others that reported remarkably high ones. He reported an average uncorrected validity of .25, remarkably similar to the Weisner and Cronshaw value of .27. Thus the seed of the derailment lay not in the data, but in it's interpretation.

All previous academic reviews of the interviewing literature preceded meta-analysis and the debate on validity generalization (Schmidt and Hunter 1977). Authors did not correct for criterion reliability or restriction of range. They lacked the insight, provided in the early '80s, into large versus small sample estimates of effect size. They looked at the interviewing research averaging validities of .25 and concluded that interviews were inaccurate. They suggested that structured patterns and job analysis seemed to help, but they were unable to quantify their advantage.

As Schmitt (1976) noted, the focus on interviewing research then turned to process studies aimed at revealing why traditional, unstructured, interviews fail. That line of research kept academics occupied but off track for several years. At the end of it all, we knew a lot more about why unstructured interviews don't work, but very little more about how to make structured, job-relevant interviews work better.

Meta-analysis greatly reduces problems with interpreting individual validity studies, but as Hunter and Hunter (1984) attest, does not eliminate them. With only ten coefficients, Hunter and

Hunter drew the same negative conclusions about interviewing as before. Clearly, their sample of ten studies did not reflect the much larger and nearly exhaustive analysis of Weisner and Cronshaw. Future researchers should endeavour to gather the population of published and unpublished research before drawing meta-analytic conclusions on this or any other topic.

PRACTICAL IMPLICATIONS OF THE NEW RESEARCH

By now, the practical implications should be clear. They are summarized briefly below. A more detailed treatment appears in Janz, Hellervik, and Gilmore (1986).

1. Carefully structured interviews based on a thorough job analysis result in selection decisions that match and often out-perform alternative predictors of job performance.
2. Unstructured interviews that dwell on applicant opinions about topics not directly related to the job do a poor job of predicting job performance.
3. A systematic job analysis that clearly spells out effective and ineffective job behaviour forms the first step towards implementing an accurate interviewing system.
4. Interview questions that probe what the applicant has *actually done in the past* in situations similar to those described in the job analysis predict future performance accurately.

References

Arvey, R. D. and J. E. Campion. 1982. The employment interview: A summary and review of recent research. *Personnel Psychology* 27:519–33.

Glass, G. V. 1976. Primary, secondary, and meta-analysis of research. *Educational Researcher* 5:3–8.

Glueck, W. F. 1978. *Personnel: A diagnostic approach.* Dallas, Texas: Business Publications Inc.

Heneman, H. G., D. P. Schwab, J. A. Fossum, and L. D. Dyer. 1983. *Personnel/human resource management.* Homewood, Ill.: Irwin.

Hunter, J. E. and R. F. Hunter. 1984. Validity and utility of alternative predictors of job performance. *Psychological Bulletin* 96: 72–98.

Hunter, J. E., F. L. Schmidt, and G. B. Jackson. 1982. *Advanced meta-analysis: Quantitative methods for cumulating research findings across studies.* Beverly Hills, CA: Sage.

Janz, J. T. 1982. Initial comparisons of patterned behavior description interviews versus unstructured interviews. *Journal of Applied Psychology* 67:577–80.

Janz, J. T., L. Hellervik, and D. C. Gilmore. 1986. *Behavior description interviewing: New, accurate, cost effective.* Newton, MA: Allyn and Bacon.

Latham, G. P., L. M. Saari, E. D. Purcell, and J. E. Campion. 1980. The situational interview. *Journal of Applied Psychology* 65:422–27.

Maas, J. B. 1965. The patterned scaled expectation interview. *Journal of Applied Psychology* 49:431–33.

Mathis, R. L. and J. H. Jackson. 1985. *Personnel human resource management.* St. Paul, Minn.: West Publishing Co.

Mayfield, E. E. 1964. The selection interview: A re-evaluation of published research. *Personnel Psychology* 17:239–60.

McDaniel, M. A. and F. L. Schmidt. 1985. A meta-analysis of the validity of training and experience ratings in personnel selection.

Technical Report OSP-85-1. Washington, DC: US Office of Personnel Management, Office of Staffing Policy.

Orpen, C. 1985. Patterned behavior description interviews versus unstructured interviews: A comparative study. *Journal of Applied Psychology* 70:774-76.

Schmidt, F. L. and J. E. Hunter. 1977. Development of a general solution to the problem of validity generalization. *Journal of Applied Psychology* 62:529-40.

Schmitt, N. 1976. Social and situational determinants of interview decisions: Implications for the employment interview. *Personnel Psychology* 29:79-101.

Schuler, R. S. 1984. *Personnel and human resource management*. St. Paul, Minn.: West Publishing Co.

Stone, T. H. and N. M. Meltz. 1983. *Personnel management in Canada*. Toronto, Ontario: Holt, Rinehart, and Winston.

Ulrich, L. and D. Trumbo. 1965. The selection interview since 1949. *Psychological Bulletin* 63:100-116.

Wagner, R. 1949. The employment interview: A critical summary. *Personnel Psychology* 2:17-46.

Weisner, W. H. and S. F. Cronshaw. 1986. The moderating impact of interview format and degree of structure on interview validity. Unpublished manuscript, Department of Psychology, University of Waterloo.

Werther, W. B., K. Davis, H. F. Schwind, T.P.H. Das, and F. C. Miner. 1982. *Canadian personnel management and human resources*. Toronto, Ontario: McGraw-Hill Ryerson Ltd.

Wright, O. R. 1969. Summary of research on the selection interview since 1964. *Personnel Psychology* 22:391-413.

12. Employee Selection and Placement: Practice, Problems, and Future Trends

Peter Broadhurst, Litton Systems Canada

INTRODUCTION

Over 2,300 years ago Plato proposed a series of tests for the guardians of his ideal Republic. He had considerable advantage over present day executives inasmuch that ideal organizations are, by definition, long-lasting whereas today's organizations are changing rapidly and dramatically.

Corporate success is assured if each key person is relatively successful at his or her task. This success pattern is situational; it involves an individual, a situation, a specific point in time, and a known, attainable goal. In a large measure for most people, the organizational structure is a large part of the situation. It is the structure and its associated environment that over a period of time attracts and holds one group of people, and repels those who are not comfortable with its culture. Thus, the function of management is to decide on the kind of people the company needs, select them properly, and then create the type of environment in which they can be fully effective.

All organizations are currently being influenced by four major forces—economic, technological, societal, and political. These forces result in at least six major changes in North American society affecting the type of work, work places, workers, organizations, relationships, and compensation (Hall 1981). All these forces and changes impact directly on the employee selection and placement function and its efforts result directly in the development of the organization culture.

Economic Forces

In very general terms the economic forces are leading to efforts to increase productivity. With the full paraphernalia of our welfare state, this can only be achieved by the increasing use of technological capital and a reduction in the direct labour component. This is leading to the next trend where labour is moving into the indirect and support functions. In the limit this will result in labour being treated as an asset rather than an expense item, especially in highly automated manufacturing operations where the direct labour costs will be less than five percent of the total costs. However, success in the future will depend on the effective management of the people side of the business.

Technological Forces

The spread of computer technology in organizations is having several major effects. The whole experience of automation techniques to date has confirmed that this technology increases the productivity of the skilled, trained and highly educated, and leads to the elimination of unskilled and semi-skilled jobs. The second major impact has been the elimination of the processing and analysis functions of middle management into the software of management information systems. This is leading to the reduction in the levels between the working levels and top management, together with a major change in function of the remaining intermediate levels.

From a management point of view, the very considerable capital investments in the new technology, often in the order of six to ten percent of sales, together with the associated lead times for its acquisition and implementation, is leading to a considerable emphasis on strategic planning as a necessity for organization survival. The management of this technological change within an organization is the major concern of senior management. Historically, employee selection and placement has been based on previous experience of what was appropriate for its operations. Now technological change is forcing emphasis on the ability to recruit, select, and place a whole new breed of talents and skills required to implement the new corporate strategies and their associated cultures.

The same technology that forces these changes also bears the seeds of the solution. The computer and newly developed software allows the generation of significant data bases, provides the ability to use mathematical and statistical techniques, and allows modelling of present and future situations.

Against these technological and economic imperatives the human resource function is also faced by the societal developments and political reactions.

Societal Forces

A recent Decima Research report (Gregg 1984) has identified three major trends in Canadian society. Canada has had the fastest growing labour force in the Western industrialized world since World War II. There is also a significant age skew in the Canadian population due to the Baby Boom or Big Generation that came between 1946 and 1966. There has been no echo boom as this group reached maturity and married, so that they remain a unique characteristic of the Canadian demographic scene. For example, in the 1984 federal election forty percent of the electorate could not have voted in 1974 due to being under the voting age. This is the most educated generation ever in Canada, and as a result of the recession, the most disillusioned with the effectiveness of traditional ways of running the country. As a group, they are willing to experiment and try new approaches when their perceptions and reality do not coincide.

The second major trend is female participation in the work force. In 1966 this participation rate was thirty-eight percent and by 1984 it had reached fifty-six percent, and the trend was still accelerating. In addition the participation rate of females in post secondary education was reaching fifty percent for most disciplines. As a result of this activity the country was looking at reduced fertility rates compared to historical rates. Under current conditions and without immigration, the Canadian population will fall from 24 million to 11.4 million in 2050.

In reviewing the makeup of the Canadian population the marginally active—that is, those under twenty or over sixty—would increase from forty-six percent to fifty-nine percent of the population. Those at or nearing retirement would increase from fourteen percent to fifty percent, and most disturbing less than ten percent of the population—those under the age of twenty about to enter the work force—would be saddled with the problem of supporting this population. Under these constraints it is obvious that Canada will have to revert to its historical policy of encouraging immigration.

This gives rise to the third long-term trend that will dominate the Canadian scene. In 1961, ninety percent of the immigrants came from Europe or the United States. In 1977, this had dropped to forty-seven percent with fifty-three percent coming from the West Indies, Asia, and other third world countries. In the event that immigration quotas were increased, it is unlikely that this trend would be reversed, so Canada will become increasingly a multi-cultural society. One of the results of immigration is that the new arrivals bring much of the intellectual baggage of other cultures to add to the already large supply of misconceptions and suspicions in Canadian society. Canada is a country that has adopted as a policy the concept of distinctive multi-culturalism rather than the melting pot or the development of a singular Canadian identity.

Political Forces

The impact of the economic, technological, and social changes lead in the macro sense to political changes. As far as an organization is concerned four major stages in the development of political issues can be discerned (Hale 1981), and it behooves the human resource executive to monitor and track these stages, bearing in mind that significant organizational change is at least an eight-year process to ensure a lasting change in the corporate culture.

The first stage of a political issue is that of societal perceptions. These perceptions are moulded by a variety of educational, media, and experiential situations. This is probably the most amorphous area, but one that requires attention from the human resources function in its role as the early warning system for the organization. The problem is that most organizations tend in themselves to be closed societies, with their own perceptions and culture, which often can be out of phase with the society in which they exist.

The second stage is where the perceptions of significant elements of society become politicized in the platforms of political parties at both the federal and provincial levels of government. This is followed, if the idea receives either consent or consensus, in the third or legislative phase where the concepts are defined in law and approved. And finally the fourth and final stage of litigation where the courts interpret, define, and build a body of practice and precedent that radically alters the previous operating methods.

Over the past few years no aspect of the human resource function has been more subject to political attention than the selection and placement activities of organizations.

Litigation

Currently three major areas of litigation are now before the courts or various tribunals. The first of these is in the area of human rights discrimination where taking all jurisdictions into account, some twenty-seven prohibited grounds can be cited. This activity has caused organizations to review their recruitment, selection, and placement procedures in depth and to institute more costly processes and procedures to eliminate these problems. The second major area has been costs associated with terminating employees, which has again led to establishment of internal procedures, checks, and balances to minimize costs. A final area in which litigation has just started is in cases where alleged infringements on the Canadian Charter of Rights are the basis for a suit. Section 15 of this legislation is currently being cited to eliminate mandatory retirement in several jurisdictions. One of the unresolved points at this time is the civil action consequences of a breach of the Charter. It can, therefore, be predicted that the legislation will lead to very expensive cases as each one will be considered as setting new precedents.

Legislation

While the system is digesting the present developments, legislators at both the federal and provincial levels are passing more legislation associated with employment equity. The Federal Bill C-62, an Act Respecting Employment Equity, became a law in April 1986. Essentially it tables the concept and leaves the aspects that affect business to bureaucratic regulations. This makes it difficult and expensive to plan permanent systems to meet the requirements of the act. Employment equity is a term that will have increasing importance to Crown corporations, federally regulated companies, and businesses tendering on federal government contracts. The legislation which is very brief will impose on affected employers an obligation to implement employment equity and to report specified data. This will be in the form of an annual report tabled in June of each year beginning in 1988. The information will cover five categories.

1. The industrial sector and location in which employees are employed
2. The total number of employees and the participation rates of designated group members—currently defined as women, handicapped, native people, and visible minorities
3. Occupational distribution of designated group members
4. The total number of employees and representation of designated group members in various salary ranges and subdivisions of each range
5. Representation of designated group members in respect of hiring, promotions, and terminations

The form, content, and instructions for completion of the report will be prescribed by regulation, and a fine of $50,000 can be imposed if the employer does not file or certify the accuracy of the data submitted. The federal government has indicated that the 1986 census may also be used to compare an employer's data to national data concerning the availability of designated groups for employment. Beginning in 1988 the employer's data will be tabled in Parliament in a consolidated form. There may be analysis of the data, and the results will be available for review by the public who may file complaints based on these results with the Canadian Human Rights Commission.

Legislation requiring employers to pay their male and female employees equally for work of equal value performed in the same establishment exists only at the federal level and in Quebec and will, in the near future, be law in Ontario.

The value of work is determined by the composite of values assigned to four criteria: skill, effort, responsibility required in the performance of the work, and the conditions under which the work is performed. In addition, the Canadian Human Rights Commission has proposed additional guidelines covering:

1. Methods for applying the four criteria to determine the value of work
2. Criteria for determining when a group of employees is to be considered predominantly male or predominantly female
3. Procedures in the investigation and, if appropriate, settlement of group complaints
4. Definition of establishment

As previously mentioned, mandatory retirement policies may be challenged under human rights legislation in some provinces and under Section 15 of the Canadian Charter of Rights and Freedoms which prohibits discrimination on the basis of age without specifying any limit. The employer may, however, terminate an employee working beyond the normal retirement age for "good and sufficient cause." These acts aggravate the problems of youth unemployment. They will result in more harsh appraisals of older employees if the effects of aging have to be dealt with as a disciplinary problem, thus eliminating the present tolerance and dignity as retirement age approaches.

Politicization

As a result of the high costs associated with regular full-time employees and their associated benefit costs, together with the complexities and costs associated with termination, many organizations have been moving to increased use of part-time employees. Concurrent with this trend there is now political pressure to provide constraints and additional benefit provisions to this class of workers. This topic has been included in several political party platforms.

Furthermore, there is the political reaction to increased use of high technology in organizations. This is brought on by the perception that technology is driving organizations into a bi-polar configuration—a highly paid, technical, elite management group and a larger techno-peasant group. This second group is also purported to be largely female. It is apparent that if the public perceptions are in phase with this scenario, then a significant political issue is developing.

A subset of these public concerns is the topic of retraining to meet the new challenge. The magnitude of the retraining required is leading to pressures for skill development leave funded by the employer in a similar fashion to existing vacation entitlements.

Perceptions

In the short term, the Canadian public has been traumatized by the recession (Gregg 1984). As a result, as a society it is leaner, meaner, and more self-reliant. There is a greater willingness to sacrifice present pleasure for perceived long-term stability. People are willing to participate in problem solving if they think it will contribute to a solution. They are more supportive of authoritative measures to reduce dislocation and uncertainty in our society.

There are signs of the development of a post-survival mentality. This mentality associates the old rules of conducting business and government with the recent problems. Recessionary or cautious financial behaviour is considered to be the smart approach, which accounts for the nonappearance of the consumer spending boom economists have been forecasting, based on previous experience. This mentality sees fundamental changes being required in our institutions. Both business and government are under critical scrutiny.

However, the approach to work is still good. Ninety-seven percent need pride in their work for full satisfaction, and eighty-two percent look forward to going to work. Only eleven percent disagreed with the statement that they are proud of the company they work for. The commitment to work endures, but many find it difficult to realize that commitment; their work doesn't exercise their skills and abilities, jobs are structured in such a way as to reduce the challenge. As a result seventy-six percent want access to more practical training with a view to getting into a more interesting job. They also view the achievement of status at work in a different light. Salary is no longer the prime mover, eighty-four percent would trade security in lieu of wage increases, eighty-one percent would choose a safer and more enjoyable work environment, sixty percent would choose access to further training over salary. For those over fifty-five, the majority would choose improved pensions over salary increases, and for those under twenty-five increased vacations were more attractive than salary alone.

The commitment to conventional employment practices is changing. Sixty-one percent would prefer a ten-hour day and four-day work week compared to an eight-hour day and five-day work week. Seventy-one percent would trade dollars for a thirty-two-hour work week. Work sharing is not considered particularly threatening; only twenty-six percent actively disliked the idea. Sixty-six percent were willing to work half the normal work week for seventy-five percent of their present pay.

Basically, the underlying tone is individuals' desire to take control over their own destiny and to seek in some way to control change in their lives. Traditional ways and institutions have in their minds proven inadequate, and they are less and less inclined to rely on the decisions of the various elites in business, finance, and government who have not been effective in the recent past. There is a growing demand for worker participation and say in their work environment. Sixty-six percent would like to take part in decisions, and eighty-five percent think companies would be more successful if they did listen to their employees' insights into their operations.

CHARACTERISTICS OF FUTURE EMPLOYEE SELECTION AND PLACEMENT SYSTEMS

As a result of the techno-economic and socio-political factors discussed previously, it is possible to predict the characteristics of future selection and placement systems. Four key factors can be identified as essential to meeting the evolving mores of Canadian society:

1. Equitable access to opportunities generated by an organization
2. Elimination of systemic discrimination
3. Selection due to inherent ability as the sole criteria
4. Placement as the process that allows all individuals to use their abilities according to their potential

In reviewing present systems, and planning future systems these factors should be borne in mind and used to screen all proposals for future policies.

In general, the optimum utilization of human resources requires the attention to seven major topics (Scott 1983) namely:

Job analysis
—What work needs to be done
—How is the work divided

Job evaluation
—What is the job worth to the company
—How competitive are we

Employment process
—Who are we looking for
—When do we need them
—Where do we find them
—How do we select them
—What do we need to know about them

Job clarification
—What is expected of the employee
—What resources are available—training, etc.

Goal setting
—What are we trying to accomplish
—How does this fit with employee aspirations
—What support is available

Performance appraisal
Salary review
—How well did we do
—What are the rewards
—When

Job Analysis

Present practice is largely based on past experience. This has been a valid approach where new jobs tended to be variations on a basic theme. The job description emphasized functions not activities, and listed qualifications in knowledge, skills and behaviour. Under favourable conditions, its preparation takes at least ten hours of expensive analyst time.

In the future, as jobs tend to be new or unique, with few precedents in an organization, there is a trend toward the use of structured questionnaires and greater emphasis on employee participation and input. The focus is on quantifiable and verifiable information in a standard format to allow effective use of data processing, word processing, and data storage. This allows flexibility for planning, changes, and the production of new job descriptions to reflect the dynamic situation in most organizations.

The job analysis now becomes the first step in identifying new opportunities within the organization. As such, it must be recognized that it may be subject to review by external agencies to ensure that it meets the requirements of equitable access and lack of systemic discrimination.

Job Evaluation

Job evaluation techniques usually fall into one of two broad categories—quantitative or nonquantitative (Morden 1983). In the nonquantitative area the methods include the following.

Ranking. A process whereby all jobs in an organization are ranked from top to bottom with respect to their usually undefined worth or value. These systems can rarely stand outside scrutiny for lack of bias and cultural stereotypes leading to allegations of discrimination.

Classification. A process whereby an idealized hierarchical structure is predetermined, with categories defined on the basis of skill and responsiblity thought to be required by various jobs. All jobs in the organization are then placed by comparison with the idealized levels describing each category. Again this system is usually hard to defend against allegations of bias and cultural perceptions of the management group.

In the quantitative area the methods include the following.

Factor Comparison. This method divides jobs into elements of compensable factors, for example, skill, effort, responsibility, or working conditions. Each of these factors are quantified in benchmark jobs. Comparisons are then made, factor by factor, for all other jobs in the organization relative to the benchmark jobs. A final hierarchy of jobs results when the total values are compared. Under current Canadian law, this method is the essential minimum that can stand up to outside scrutiny. However, most companies using this approach are usually open to litigation on the details of their methodology and process.

Factor Point. This approach provides for the selection of compensable factors which are measured by a scale of points representing increasing levels of worth. Each job is rated on each factor separately and is assigned the corresponding number of points for the rated level of each factor. The points are totaled to yield the job-worth score.

These conventional approaches are not necessarily accurate, objective, understandable, equitable, or defensible. They are usually expensive, cumbersome, and antiquated. However, with the advent of the computer and improved knowledge in psychometrics, statistics, and data processing we can improve on the conventional approaches to job-to-job comparison. Structured questionnaires have been used increasingly to collect and update job information as a replacement for the detailed interview. This method of collecting information focuses on quantitive, verifiable information in a standardized format. As a result, job evaluations are comparative rather than descriptive.

Typical of this approach is the system generally referred to as the Position Analysis Questionnaire (P.A.Q.) system. This questionnaire requires specific responses to 194 PAQ topics, which are then scored statistically by computer to provide a job profile of some forty-five job dimensions. This job profile can then be compared to and statistically serviced against a large data base using the whole world of work to establish a job value in PAQ points. Further structured processes allow the development of job families and job levels. Systems such as this allow organizations to establish equitable job evaluation and classification and provide definitive results economically for organization groups having over five hundred job classifications. Because of the large data bases and rigorous statistical procedures, it is better able to defend its results from fair employment and equal pay litigation. Internal evaluation committees have always been suspected of contributing to bias and discrimination in setting job levels, especially where women and other minorities are involved.

The output of the system is a relative number of points which decide the ranking of the job for purposes of determining job grades. The pay range is determined by local and industry wage surveys.

Ultimately, job grades are intended to be both externally competitive with local employers and comparable employers in the industry, and internally equitable making certain that all jobs are ranked according to their relative value to the organization. Additionally, job evaluation and ranking of jobs helps the organization get a better understanding of the allocation of payroll dollars.

Employment Process

Dr. Tupper Cawsey has identified three fundamental recruiting strategies (Cawsey 1984):

1. Tight screening, rigorous entry standards
2. Low entry screens, vigorous follow-up on the job
3. Identify specific groups and attract them to the organization

Strategy 1. This is very similar to that proposed by Peters and Waterman in their book *In Search of Excellence*. It assumes that there is a large waiting list of people wishing to join the organization. A tight screening process reduces the amount and cost of on-the-job training for new recruits. The success of this strategy depends on the organization's ability to select people with the qualities to do the job well, both in the short- and long-term. Incorrect criteria mean poor selection decisions. This is the major risk of this strategy. This strategy is appropriate when the hiring criteria are clear and the prediction of performance is not difficult. This strategy becomes attractive as the costs of on-the-job mistakes increases. It requires a disciplined approach if equitable access and systemic discrimination complaints are to be prevented.

Strategy 2. The advantages of this strategy are with its potentially low recruiting costs. As well, line managers are involved in the screening which increases their commitment to those who succeed. The drawback to this strategy is the cost of poor performance, particularly if the costs of training or poor performance are high. Also as costs of dehiring become costly, messy, and difficult this strategy becomes less attractive. It requires intensive supervisor training to reduce its susceptibility to systemic discrimination and biased appraisal systems.

Strategy 3. This strategy relies on being able to clearly identify desirable candidates in the marketplace. Thus specific individuals or groups can be targeted and a campaign designed for them. The principal advantage of a selective appeal is that costs can be minimized by narrowing the recruitment activities while not lessening the probability of attracting desirable candidates. The main problems are being able to attract enough candidates or having to pay too much for them. This strategy can be appropriate when there is a distinctive characteristic which allows for the easy identification of the desired groups. This strategy can lead to susceptibility for litigation in the areas of equitable access, systemic discrimination, biased methods of ability determination, and promotion prospects.

It is apparent that all these recruiting strategies require definitive policies and procedures, vigorously followed and documented to operate in the developing legal environment of the Canadian labour market.

Employment Process: Labour Market Data

For effective planning of selection and placement needs, the characteristics of the labour market require review.

Most published data is derived from macroeconomic studies and large scale demographic studies. Typical is the Canadian Occupational Projection System which attempts to draw conclusions on supply and demand using the *Canadian Compendium and Dictionary of Occupations* (CCDO) job classifications. In general, this data is too broad gauge to be of use in targeting recruiting efforts. Companies these days are looking for specific skills and experience, and this can lead to perception of shortages by company management, even though the macrodata indicates surpluses. In many cases, the total number of appropriate candidates for a specific job in Canada may not exceed one hundred people, even though published statistics indicate a large supply surplus for a particular job. When this is further probed, and relocation, present job satisfaction, compensation, and relevant experience factors are taken into account, the selection pool has dropped to less than five.

This fact has led to the market for the services of recruiting firms and agencies specializing in specific areas of the market. In the city of Toronto there are over seven hundred such agencies covering areas from clerical help to chief executive officers. In general, there is a substantial minority who have very aggressive business tactics. Most organizations have found it necessary to develop a relationship with a selected few and resist the approaches of the rest. In some high technology and computer classifications, the shortages have lead to situations similar to guerrilla warfare. This is caused to a large extent by the fact that the high-tech business tends to be project oriented with immediate large requirements for skills when a contract is issued. Company recruiting success, therefore, tends to be measured on the net increase, new recruits, and retention of existing personnel.

Similarly, recruiting advertising is becoming more specialized, specific, and focused on the target group. Generalized advertisements can lead to discrimination complaints. For example, the use of the word aerospace technician can cover a large field of technical specialties. Unsuccessful candidates can therefore claim they are qualified and because of their race or sex, etc., were not given due access to the opportunity. The time wasted on defending these decisions can increase the recruiting costs significantly.

It is a necessity that the recruiting system be able to draw the largest possible net in order to ensure that the organization can meet its employment equity commitments and its economic goals. This will be an area where human resource specialists will be involved in both counselling line functions and in carrying out the initial screening. The whole subject of cross-cultural communications will increase in importance. Three major factors affect cross-cultural communication (Audvicon Associates 1984):

Language factors
—Accent and dialect
—Pitch stress volume and tone factors
—Politeness/abruptness
—Pausing patterns

Cultural elements
—Use of gestures and facial expressions
—Status relationships
—Formality and informality
—Frankness
—Time conciousness
—Spatial consciousness/ physical intimacy
—Stereotyping

Job related
—Degree of competitiveness
—Priorities

It is apparent from the above that this subject will have to be part of a supervisor's training and skill set. The objectives of the training will be successful if the participant realizes that:

——Cross-cultural factors affect communication

——Communication problems resulting from cultural differences are not the fault of the people involved
——Communication problems can be overcome with patience, recognition of real difficulties, and willingness to listen
——Communication can be defined as perceptions, expectations, and involvement

Employee Selection and Placement Selection Methods

Historically four general methods have been utilized (Odiorne 1971) namely the following.

Personal Preference. Still the most commonly used method, even when disguised by the apparatus of science; the hunch of the manager, his or her biases, or his or her likes and dislikes determine the selection of employees. This is becoming a high-risk and high-cost strategy, rarely able to justify its decisions to public agencies.

The Occupational Characteristics Approach. Earliest of the scientifically-based methods, this method applied aptitude measurements to applicants and attempted to predict success on the job. The thing sampled in aptitude tests is, in most cases, human behaviour. Specifically, a psychological test is the measurement of some phase of a carefully chosen sample of an individual's behaviour from which extrapolations and references are made. In its simplest terms, aptitude testing rests on a correlational relationship between a normally distributed predictor variable (which may or may not be related to the skills and abilities required on the job) on the one hand, and another normally distributed measure of satisfactory performance on the other hand. The simple matching task is to eliminate, on the basis of the relatively inexpensive predictor variable, those individuals with little likelihood of success in the job—easy in theory, but beset by complexities in practice. This approach has been the subject of much litigation in the areas of equitable access and systemic discrimination, and a considerable body of negative opinion exists on its validity to establish the inherent ability of potential employees. This whole area is currently under attack on the grounds that I.Q. and scholastic tests such as GMATS are more culturally biased than objective measures of inherent ability (Fallows 1985).

The Behavioural or Skills Approach. Behaviour—activity which can be seen and measured—has been the subject of measurement and observation in this cluster of tests. The simplest form is the achievement test for a typist. Her work was timed, checked for errors, and if performed well, the typist was hired.

The use of such tests are useful screening devices. Attempts have been made to extend such testing to selection of managerial candidates or candidates for sales, professional, or technical positions. The distinctive feature of this approach is that it presumes that a pattern of behaviour is the key ingredient in hiring. Reference checks, intensive attention to past behaviour, and the reports of past observers about the behaviour of individuals, are coupled with the hardest probing into every aspect of the applicant's past behaviour to create an extensive dossier. This approach currently reaches its highest development form in the use of assessment centres, which represent a combination of achievement tests and behaviour modelling techniques.

The Background Approach. This approach has resulted in the dramatic increase in the campus recruiting out of the unstated and sometimes unconscious assumption that a college degree is needed for most management and staff positions. It is assumed that a person who has a degree learned something in college, that it is learning that he or she will carry to first and subsequent positions, and that the learning will convert into behaviour on the job and will produce results that could not be produced by a noncollege graduate. The suggestion here is not that background is not useful information, but rather that as a single predictor it has the limitations of all single-cause explanations for multiple-cause outcomes. This approach is currently in decline due to the perceptions during the recent recession that the relationship between academic prowess and business survival was tenuous if not fallacious. Similarly, it is hard to defend on equity grounds.

Placement Practices: Job Clarification

This function of human resource management will become more important as the full impact of the employment equity legislation is felt. This topic covers the whole range of topics from employee indoctrination, counselling, and career planning to internal and external job training and job rotation. It is apparent that to meet the requirements of establishing women, native peoples, handicapped, and visible minorities, in higher levels organizations will have to ensure that the excessive costs of tokenism do not inhibit their growth.

Based on industry experience, the counselling and career planning aspects are the essential first step in this program.

Goal Setting

Goal setting is based on two fundamental beliefs (Gibb 1985). The first belief is that performance planning and appraisal are factors in the same equation. It is impossible to carry out performance appraisals unless established and agreed benchmarks are in place. A second belief is that organizational goals and individual objectives are compatible. As was indicated previously it is impossible to implement strategic change successfully if this is not recognized.

Goal setting has two major objectives—to promote individual productivity and to increase the efficiency and harmony of the work group.

The first goal development process has five major steps:

1. Define organizational constraints and mandates affecting the work group.
2. Negotiate team goals in three major areas:
   a. Maintenance goals—usually good operating goals to essentially consolidate gains from the previous round
   b. Problem-solving goals—these are goals to eliminate problem areas either internally or externally induced on the organization
   c. Innovative goals—the introduction of new techniques and strategies to obtain a competitive advantage
3. All goals must be measurable in quantifiable terms such as dollars, time, percentages, units, etc. They must be attainable within the capabilities of the group within a specified time. Finally and most importantly, they must be mutually acceptable to both management and the group.
4. Negotiate an individual's goals ensuring compatibility with the group goals.

5. Agree that the individual's goals will be the basis for performance reviews.

The linked performance planning and appraisal system effectively administered can:

—— Promote understanding and acceptance of organizational goals
—— Articulate problems in a supportive environment
—— Enhance individual skill assessment and growth within the group

Performance Appraisal

When examining approaches to performance appraisals in most corporations, one is struck by the similarity to the scholastic report card. It is a questionable ritual in both organizations.

Performance appraisals fall into two broad categories. The first can be defined as the closet approach where the supervisor privately rates the employee and writes a summary of his or her perceptions of the subordinate's performance. The review is filed away to be used as a justification for future personnel actions. Manager and subordinate never sit down to review the summary together, and in some cases the subordinate has no access to the report without initiating complicated personnel or legal action.

The second category is defined as collaborative reviews and comes in various stages of participation. The first subset can be defined as the big brother model where the manager writes the performance review and then presents it to the subordinate. The manager may also access peer groups, and there is also an appeal process if the subordinate feels the evaluation is unjust. This model meets the minimum demands for a performance review system. The next stage of participation is the coach model where the subordinate initially completes some form of self-evaluation. This model signals to the supervisors that the organization expects employee input in these reviews. This performance appraisal moves beyond a report card and into a plan for growth and teamwork. Supervisor communication skills become all important. There is a subtle but significant difference between the coach model and the next most collaborative scheme—the partnership model. This model, although acknowledging the supervisor's final decision-making responsibility, gives increased emphasis to the fact that the relationship is fundamentally a team relationship. The final model is the fully developed team relationship where the evaluation is essentially a peer review process. This is not appropriate for every organization. It is usually effective for groups used to working closely together in which a healthy degree of trust has already been established, for example, in a small research and development team.

It is apparent, however, that the traditional report card performance appraisal in the context of the new legislative environment is a loose cannon from a litigation point of view. Most organizations will have to move to the appropriate version of the collaborative models if they are to defend themselves against charges of systemic discrimination and biased appraisal and promotional procedures. This will place considerable costs on supervisory training on communications and familiarization with employment legislation.

Salary Rewards

This is the area that under employment equity will be the basis for public review and judgment of the effectiveness of an organization's employee selection and placement efforts. As discussed earlier, the reporting mechanisms proposed are essentially linked to the salary ratios of the affected groups. The major challenge for the human resource function in the 1980s is to maintain the economic viability of the organization by the selection and placement of the appropriate human skills and talents, while at the same time operating within the legal and cultural constraints of Canadian society.

References

Audvicon Associates. 1984. Report for Ontario ministry of citizenship and culture, (March).

Cawsey, T. 1984. Recruiting: A strategy perspective. *P.A.T. Reporter* (May).

Fallows, James. 1984. The case against credentialism. *The Atlantic Monthly* (December).

Gibb, P. 1985. Appraisal goals and controls. *Personnel Journal* (August).

Gregg, A. 1984. The changing public and its working environment. Decima Research Ltd., 8 May.

Hale, L. (Chairman). 1981. United Way of America Long Range Planning Committee Report.

Morden, D. L. 1983. Job evaluation: Yesterday and today. *Benefits Canada* (November/December).

Odiorne, G. S. 1971. *Personnel administration by objectives.* Homewood, Ill.: Richard D. Irwin Inc.

Peters, T. J. and R. H. Waterman, Jr. In Search of Excellence. New York: Harper and Row Publishers, 1982.

Scott, S. 1983. Finding the right person. *Personnel Journal* (November).

13. Employment Testing in Canada: Strategies for Higher Organizational Productivity and Human Rights Compliance

Steven F. Cronshaw, The University of Guelph

Many Canadian organizations use employment tests to make individual employee assessments, particularly for hiring purposes. Jain's (1972) study showed that approximately twenty-eight percent of Canadian manufacturing firms surveyed used employment tests in hiring managers, although such testing was more frequent in large companies. Given this volume of testing activity, it is important for personnel managers to recognize and use good employment tests. This chapter is intended to assist personnel managers in two ways. First, the characteristics of good employment tests are detailed. Second, three approaches to either finding or developing good tests are identified. An example of a successful Canadian testing program accompanies the description of each approach.

Employers should develop a greater familiarity with employment testing for two reasons. First, effective human resource management, including proper use of employment tests, can produce major improvements in organizational productivity (Schmidt, Hunter, McKenzie, and Muldrow 1979). These improvements translate into improved national productivity and increased competitiveness in international markets (Janz 1986). Second, federal and provincial human rights commissions increasingly require personnel managers to demonstrate the business necessity of their assessment procedures, including employment testing (Cronshaw in press-a; Jain 1983). This critical examination of business necessity occurs when an assessment procedure adversely affects an aggrieved member of a group protected under human rights legislation. Under such circumstances, human rights commissions are more likely to permit use of a reliable, valid test (i.e., a good test) than a test with questionable or unknown technical characteristics.

CHARACTERISTICS OF A GOOD EMPLOYMENT TEST

Thus far, the importance of using good employment tests has been emphasized. Next is a detailed and precise, technical explanation of what is meant by a good test follows. Industrial psychologists generally agree that a good test is both reliable and valid. Reliability and validity are in turn technical concepts discussed at length in one Canadian and three United States professional pronouncements of employment testing. They are listed as supplementary references at the end of this chapter. The Canadian *Guidelines on Educational and Psychological Testing*, now being prepared by the Canadian Psychological Association (working draft), describe proper development and use of employment tests in this country. These *Guidelines*, which deal extensively with reliability and validity, should be consulted as the primary reference whenever employment tests are developed or adapted in Canada.

In addition to reliability and validity, I will discuss utility as the third characteristic of a good test. Although the *Guidelines* deemphasize utility, this concept is gaining prominence in the employment testing literature. At this point, a brief (if oversimplified) explanation of reliability, validity, and utility is necessary. Then I will discuss ways to find or develop tests possessing these characteristics.

Reliability

A good test must be reliable in that it yields stable and consistent measurement. Although a person's test score can never be perfectly consistent from one occasion to the next due to various sources of error (e.g., fatigue or shifts in focus of attention), the reliability of the test must be adequate for employment testing purposes. The empirical index of reliability is referred to as the reliability coefficient.

Four methods of empirically determining reliability are available. *Test-retest reliability* assesses the stability of scores on a test administered before and after a time interval. *Alternate forms reliability* measures the consistency of scores on alternative forms of a test constructed to assess a common content domain. *Split-half reliability* involves dividing the test into two equivalent parts (e.g., by summating odd- and even-numbered items) and relating the scores on the two parts of the test. *Internal consistency reliability* measures the degree to which the test items assess the same underlying attribute (i.e., the extent to which the item scores are homogeneous). The appropriate method of reliability estimation (e.g., test-retest versus internal consistency) depends on the type of test used, purpose of testing, and the psychometric model of reliability assumed by the test developer (Ghiselli, Campbell, and Zedeck 1981).

Reliability places an upper bound on validity (Nunnally 1978). Adequate reliability is therefore a necessary, but not sufficient, precondition for a valid test. Test users can determine reliability by referring to test manuals or by collecting and analyzing test scores.

Validity

Testing authorities unanimously agree that an employment test must be valid. However, they agree less readily on exactly what validity is. Although validity is a complex and multi-faceted concept, the definition provided in the 1985 United States standards (see supplementary references) best captures professional consensus: "Validity ... refers to the appropriateness, meaningfulness, and usefulness of the specific inferences made from test scores." (American Psychological Association 1980, 9). Simply put, validity reflects the extent to which the personnel manager can produce the evidence necessary to justify a particular use of the test scores (e.g., in selection). The personnel manager thereby becomes accountable for a rational and empirical defence of the way that the organization uses test scores to make decisions about people. (Note that human rights commissions are ever more insistent on exactly this kind of accountability.)

Professional testing standards, including the Canadian *Guidelines*, identify three primary types of validity. These types are listed below, with a brief discussion of each.

Criterion-related validity is demonstrated when a set of test scores can be statistically related to a job-related outcome (i.e., a criterion) of interest to the organization. Criteria often identified as appropriate to validation efforts include job performance, training success, absenteeism, and job tenure. Criterion-related validity is further differentiated into two major types. Predictive validity requires a demonstration that test scores of job applicants relate statistically to criterion measures collected after these people have been on the job for some time. Concurrent validity requires that test scores of job incumbents statistically relate to criterion measures taken for this same job incumbent group. For example, a group of secretaries presently on the job are asked to take a clerical test, then the test scores are matched to job performance data taken from performance appraisals of these same people.

Validity generalization is an important variant of criterion-related validity that gained much popularity after its introduction ten years ago (Schmidt and Hunter 1977). Validity generalization calls for the accumulation and statistical combination of all available criterion-related validities for a particular test and job. Statistical artifacts operating to confound the results of individual validity studies are adjusted for so that a comprehensive, and often stable, pattern of criterion-related validity emerges. Frequently, real differences in validities across organizations for a given test and job are trivial or nonexistent (Schmidt, Hunter, and Caplan 1981; Schmidt, Hunter, and Pearlman 1981). Proponents of validity generalization claim that the test can then be used for selection into the same job *in a completely new setting* without the necessity to collect criterion-related validation data again. The Canadian *Guidelines* in fact recognize validity generalization as a form of criterion-related validity. Validity generalization, if used appropriately, with full knowledge of its limitations, offers a feasible and defensible validation strategy for many Canadian organizations lacking the financial resources, technical expertise, or large samples necessary to undertake other forms of validation.

Content validity requires that the employment test representatively samples the content domain of job performance or the knowledge, skills, or ability necessary for performance on the job. Content validity is demonstrated using two types of evidence: (1) that each component of the test reflects the content domain, (2) that the components cover the domain in a representative fashion (Ghiselli et al. 1981). Work samples, job knowledge tests, and achievement tests are often developed using content validation procedures.

Any conclusion of content validity is based on the subjective judgment of experts who have carefully scrutinized all technical stages of test development. Unlike criterion-related validity, test validity is not summarized by statistical indices representing the direction and magnitude of the relationship between employment test scores and criterion scores. Note however, that certain statistical analyses (e.g., individual item statistics) can be an important part of the accumulated evidence leading to a conclusion of content validity.

Construct validity focuses on how adequately the test scores reflect a psychological attribute of interest. Construct validity is important to theory-testing research generally because social scientists must use valid empirical indicators of the constructs that they incorporate into their theories (Dubin 1978). For selection purposes, an employment test is considered construct valid if it conforms to two basic criteria: (1) the test reflects the construct of interest, (2) the construct in turn is important to job performance. For example, we might hypothesize that the construct of mechanical aptitude underlies job performance for automotive mechanics. If we can collect sufficient empirical evidence to support this hypothesis, then we can defend the use of the mechanical aptitude test on grounds of construct validity.

Personnel psychologists involved in selection rarely use a pure construct validation strategy. To do so would require the psychologist to painstakingly and systematically collect large volumes of data in a series of studies over many years. Exclusive reliance on the construct validity approach, while it leads to rich understanding of the processes determining effective job performance, is infeasible in most applied settings.

The reader should note that psychologists have compartmentalized validity into three types (i.e., criterion-related, content, construct) in order to simplify application of validation procedures. In fact, validity is a unitary concept. Most simply put, the available data either demonstrate that the test is valid or they do not. For example, we might defend use of a mechanical aptitude test primarily through criterion-related validation by demonstrating that the test scores correlate to job performance criteria. However, the items in the test were originally chosen because they relate to the domain of mechanical aptitude (content validity). In addition, construct validity evidence might support the contentions that the test actually reflects the mechanical aptitude construct, and that this construct is an important component of job performance. We might reasonably conclude from the accumulated weight of evidence that the test is valid. Importantly, the practitioner must gather, combine, and weigh validity evidence from whatever sources are appropriate under the circumstances rather than mechanically apply a single validation procedure recommended in the *Guidelines*.

Utility

The third characteristic of a good employment test is closely related to the first two. Test utility represents the benefit to the sponsoring organization of using the employment test. For example, utility could be expressed in terms of dollar productivity gains resulting from use of a selection test compared to random selection or use of an alternative selection device. A good test should have utility for the organization with reference to whatever index of gain or benefit that the organization deems appropriate. The organization may identify one or more of the following as appropriate measures of benefit accruing to an employment testing program: productivity gain in dollars (Cronbach and Gleser 1965; Schmidt et al. 1979), net present value of dollar gains (Boudreau and Berger 1985), or any of a number of capital budgeting indices (Cronshaw and Alexander 1985). Note that test utility is predicated on the use of a reliable, valid test. An unreliable, invalid test cannot assess people in any way that produces benefit to the organization.

THREE APPROACHES TO FINDING OR DEVELOPING GOOD EMPLOYMENT TESTS IN CANADA

So far, the characteristics of a good employment test in terms of reliability, validity, and utility have been described. Regrettably, practitioners often view these characteristics as too abstract or academic for real-world use. *This belief is totally false.* In more specific terms, three approaches could be used by practitioners to find (or develop) good employment tests. All three approaches will be illustrated with examples from Canadian organizations who are successfully using the employment tests. Importantly, all three of these testing programs rely heavily on the reliability and validity concepts discussed in the previous section.

The Test Transportation Approach

Here an employment test developed outside the organization is adopted for operational use, sometimes with minor adaptations of test content or format. Often these transported tests are purchased from American test developers. The test transportation approach has obvious advantages. Our smaller Canadian organizations often lack the necessary technical expertise or financial resources to develop their own employment tests, even if this strategy were advisable. American test developers offer a wide variety of ability, aptitude, personality, and interest tests along with technical assistance for test administration, scoring, and interpretation.

Tests should never be transported without careful assessment against the standards of reliability and validity discussed in the *Guidelines*. Some tests marketed by test developers and consultants do not meet these standards of reliability and validity. Prior to using a test, thoroughly examine the reliability and validity data in its accompanying test manual (with the assistance of an industrial psychologist where necessary). If the test has no manual, or if reliability/validity evidence is deficient or nonsupportive, do not use the test. Even where the test is valid in another situation, the *Guidelines* require empirical evidence of job similarity before the test is transported between settings. Local validation may be required unless sufficient data are available to support validity generalization.

Test transportation obviously involves much more than simply buying a test from a salesperson or test publisher. The burden of responsibility rests on the employer to ensure that the test is appropriate for its intended use and that it is used properly.

An Example of Test Transportation. The Canadian Forces (CF) has used test transportation with considerable success. Although the CF pioneered selection testing in Canada with the famous *M* test developed during World War II, a review of available test batteries during the 1970s led to a decision to adapt the United States Army Classification Battery or ACB for use by the CF. The initial test battery for research purposes, comprised of subsets of items drawn from the ACB, was designed as the Classification Battery Men-Experimental or CBM-X. The operational equivalent, the Canadian Forces Classification Battery, or CFCB, was implemented in 1981 for selection of applicants into CF trades (Miller and Argus 1985).

The CF tests fare well on all three criteria of a good test. Ellis and Saudino (1980) report internal consistency *reliability* on eight CBM-X subtests using an Anglophone sample of recruits as ranging from .64 to .82 with a median of approximately .73. With 1.00 representing perfect reliability, these reported reliabilities are adequate to justify the operational use of the test. The *validity* inference is made from two sources. Ellis and Saudino (1980), in a series of criterion-related validity studies within individual trades, found generally adequate CBM-X validities. Cronshaw and Gowans (1986) combined the CBM-X and CFCB test data using validity generalization procedures. They found that when a test from either battery was used for selection in a trade group for which it was designed (e.g., the mechanical comprehension test in the mechanical trade group), the tests were nearly always valid. Further, Mattinson and Cronshaw (in press) found that test validities held up well when the tests were transported from the United States to Canada. Finally, Cronshaw (in press-b) calculated that the *utility* of using a test composite from the CFCB for the clerical/administrative trade group in the CF was fifty million dollars for a single year of testing. The CF offers a model for proper test transportation (including the necessary supporting research) that is worthy of emulation.

The In-house Test Development Approach

Here employment tests are developed and validated by staff psychologists for specific jobs within the organization. Any of the three validation strategies previously mentioned are appropriate for in-house test development, although content validation is frequently used. However, relatively few Canadian organizations have the large-scale staffing requirements and technical resources to make in-house test development viable. Where the approach is feasible, it has at least two important advantages. First, an in-house test is usually developed to assess the specific requirements for an identified job or set of jobs in the organization. As a consequence, job applicants and testing critics find it easier to see the linkages between test scores and job requirements. Second, local norms are often generated during in-house test development. These norms have important uses within the testing program (e.g., for setting cut-off scores or interpreting test results).

An Example of In-house Test Development. The Public Service Commission (PSC) of Canada has developed a group-administered intelligence test called the General Intelligence Test (GIT) which provides similar results to the individually-administered Wechsler Adult Intelligence Scale. The GIT, consisting of six subtests, is used mainly as a pre-selection screening device and a measure of educational equivalency for promotional purposes. Two series of GIT's were developed, one for university level and the other for secondary school level. Each of the two series contains three alternate forms of the test at that level (Anderson and Slivinski 1971). The PSC has also developed and validated clerical tests, administrative and managerial knowledge tests, management simulations, and assessment centres (Personnel Psychology Centre 1983).

The GIT does well on reliability and validity. O'Neill (1977) reports internal consistency *reliability* for the GIT ranging from .92 to .94. These reliabilities are more than adequate for operational use. *Validity* inferences come from two sources. Construct validity is suggested by moderate to high correlations of the GIT with other measures of intelligence (O'Neill, Slivinski, Grant, Pederson, and McDonald 1978) combined with evidence of lower correlations with non-intelligence measures such as personality or leadership (Anderson and Slivinski 1971). Criterion-related validity is indicated by relationships of GIT scores to educational and job performance (O'Neill 1977). This author could find no *utility* data on the GIT. Given the predictive efficiency and utilities of general cognitive tests similar to the GIT reported by Hunter and Hunter (1984), one would expect the utility of the GIT to be quite high. As would be expected, the normative information available on the GIT (using Canadian samples) is extensive. Because PSC test development procedures conform so closely with professional standards, they are a good example of how in-house test development should be conducted.

The Cooperative Test Development Approach

Here, two or more organizations jointly develop and validate a test for a common job or set of jobs. The organizations involved might be Canadian or a consortium of Canadian and foreign partners. Cooperative test development, while rare in Canada, can offer significant economies of scale because the fixed costs of test development and validation are shared by the participants. In fact, a consortium can acquire expensive technical resources cooperatively that none of the participants could afford individually. Where data are collected in participants' field offices, local norms become available as a byproduct of test development.

An Example of Cooperative Test Development. The Life Insurance Marketing and Research Association (LIMRA), which was established by American and Canadian life insurance companies to conduct research into marketing and agency management, has carried out cooperative test development since the 1920s. The LIMRA program produced a series of biographical data (biodata) instruments for selecting life insurance agents. Biodata questionnaires require applicants to describe themselves on multiple-choice items measuring such variables as demographic characteristics, experience, attitudes, or personality (Owens 1976). The items in the biodata questionnaire are chosen to maximally discriminate between high and low job performers.

LIMRA used their first biodata instrument, called the *Aptitude Index* (AI) (LIMRA 1961), in Canada during the 1930s. The AI was subsequently replaced by the *Aptitude Index Battery* (AIB) (LIMRA 1969). Both the AI and AIB were transported tests in that they were primarily developed from American samples. In the late 1970s, LIMRA developed a uniquely Canadian biodata form called the *Inventory of Insurance Selling Potential-Canada* (IISP-C) (LIMRA 1978–a) to comply with provincial legislation on human rights. A second Canadian biodata form called the *Career Profile* (CP) (LIMRA 1984) replaced the IISP-C in 1983.

LIMRA personnel have conducted a large volume of biodata research over many years. Although *reliability* is not yet available for the IISP-C and CP, the test-retest reliability for the items in the AIB is a highly satisfactory .9 (William D. Love, personal communication, March 5, 1986). Note that the AIB has the same type of scoring key and items as the IISP-C and CP. Therefore, the two Canadian forms should have reliabilities comparable to the AIB. Biodata relies to a great extent on criterion-related *validity* based on large samples. The available LIMRA research demonstrates that for all four biodata forms used in Canada (AI, AIE, IISP-C, and CP), low biodata scores are associated with poorer job performance for new life insurance agents. Low biodata scores are also consistently associated with decreased survival rates on the job (LIMRA 1947, 1948, 1961, 1969, 1978a, 1981, 1984). LIMRA has also documented substantial dollar savings resulting from use of biodata in Canada. *Utility* analyses on the IISP-C showed that a company hiring one hundred new agents using the optimal score cut-off on the IISP-C realized increased profits of over $1 million in discounted 1978 dollars (LIMRA 1978b). As in the previous two examples, careful test development has produced a reliable, valid selection instrument. The instrument also has considerable utility for the participating organizations.

THE NEW GROUND RULES FOR EMPLOYMENT TESTING IN CANADA

Two realities face Canadian personnel managers in the 1980s. First, they must manage human resources more productively. Second, they must be prepared to defend their employment tests on the grounds of business necessity before human rights commissions and courts. Reliable, valid employment tests of the type described here fulfill both functions. Less rigorous assessment procedures, such as unstructured interviews (Wiesner and Cronshaw 1986), do not yield comparable utilities and certainly offer a poor defence against charges of employment discrimination. The tools described in this chapter can be used to greatly improve employment testing. Personnel managers should use them to maximum effect.

References

Anderson, K. and L. W. Slivinski. 1971. *General intelligence test manual*. Ottawa: Personnel Assessment & Research Division, Personnel Psychology Service & Research Centre, Public Service Commission.

Boudreau, J. W. and C. J. Berger. 1985. Decision-theoretic utility analysis applied to employee separations and acquisitions [Monograph]. *Journal of Applied Psychology* 70:581–612.

Cronbach, L. J. and G. C. Gleser. 1965. *Psychological tests and personnel decisions*. Urbana, IL: University of Illinois Press.

Cronshaw, S. F. In press–a. The status of employment testing in Canada: A review and evaluation of theory and professional practice. *Canadian Psychology*.

Cronshaw, S. F. In press–b. The utility of employment testing for clerical/administrative trades in the Canadian military. *Canadian Journal of Administrative Sciences*.

Cronshaw, S. F. and R. A. Alexander. 1985. One answer to the demand for accountability: Selection utility as an investment decision. *Organizational Behavior and Human Decision Processes* 35:102–18.

Cronshaw, S. F. and S. R. Gowans. 1986. Validity generalization of Canadian Forces selection tests. Working paper, Toronto: Canadian Forces Personnel Applied Research Unit.

Dubin, R. 1978. *Theory building*, revised edition. New York, NY: The Free Press.

Ellis, R. T. and D. A. Saudiro. 1980. Selection and trade assignment (Men) project: Status report. Working paper 80–13. Toronto: Canadian Forces Personnel Applied Research Unit.

Ghiselli, E. E., J. P. Campbell, and S. Zedeck. 1981. *Measurement theory for the behavioral sciences*. San Francisco: W. H. Freeman and Company.

Hunter, J. E. and R. F. Hunter. 1984. Validity and utility of alternative predictors of job performance. *Psychological Bulletin* 96:72–98.

Jain, H. C. 1972. A study of managerial recruitment and selection in the Canadian manufacturing industry. Paper presented at the Annual Conference of the Association of Canadian Schools of Business, June, at McGill University, Montreal.

Jain, H. C. 1983. "Staffing: Recruitment and selection." In *Human resources management in Canada*, 25,011–25,060. Toronto: Prentice-Hall.

Janz, T. 1986. Forecasting the costs and benefits of traditional versus scientific employment selection methods in Canada to the year 1990. Symposium paper presented at 47th Annual Convention of the Canadian Psychological Association, June, Toronto.

Life Insurance Agency Management Association 1947. 2300 Recruits: Experience with 2308 new agents appointed in 1945 by 31 companies operating in Canada. Hartford, CT.

Life Insurance Agency Management Association. 1948. 2300 recruits a year later: A study of new agents appointed in 1945 by companies operating in Canada. Hartford, CT.

Life Insurance Agency Management Association. 1961. Early results from centralized scoring, A preliminary report on Form 7 of the Aptitude Index: A selection study. Research Report 1961-3, File No. 424. Hartford, CT.

Life Insurance Agency Management Association. 1969. Predicting success with the Aptitude Index Battery, Form 1: A selection study. Research Report 1969-5, File 424. Hartford, CT.

Life Insurance Agency Management Association. 1978a. The new Canadian agent selection-rejection tool, Inventory of insurance selling potential-Canada: A selection study. Research Report 1978-4, I/R Code 86.16. Hartford, CT.

Life Insurance Agency Management Association. 1978b. Profits and the inventory in Canadian ordinary companies: A selection study. Research report for companies operating in Canada 1978-6, I/R Code 86.16. Hartford, CT.

Life Insurance Agency Management Association. 1981. Re: Using the Inventory profitably in Canadian ordinary operations. I/R Code 86.16. Hartford, CT.

Life Insurance Agency Management Association. 1984. Career profile validity and rating distributions for Canadian operations. I/R Code 86.16. Hartford, CT.

Love, W. D. Personal Communication, with author. 5 March 1986.

Mattinson, G. and S. F. Cronshaw. In press. A transnational validity generalization study: Transportability of employment tests between the United States and Canada. *Canadian Journal of Administrative Sciences*.

Miller, D. L. and R. J. Angus. 1985. *A revalidation model for the Canadian Forces Classification Battery*. Working Paper 85–2. Toronto: Canadian Forces Personnel Applied Research Unit.

Nunnally, J. C. 1978. *Psychometric theory*, 2d ed. New York: McGraw-Hill.

O'Neill, B. 1977. *General intelligence test 310: Technical manual*. Ottawa: Test Development and Services Division, Personnel Psychology Centre, Public Service Commission of Canada, Staffing Branch.

O'Neill, B., L. Slivinski, K. Grant, L. Pederson and V. McDonald. 1978. *Predicting managerial performance with the General Intelligence Test (GIT 310)*. Ottawa: Test Development and Services Division, Personnel Psychology Centre, Public Service Commission of Canada, Staffing Branch.

Owens, W. A. 1976. "Background data." In *Handbook of industrial and organizational psychology*, edited by M. D. Dunnette. Chicago: Rand McNally College Publishing.

Personnel Psychology Centre, Public Service Commission of Canada, Staffing Programs Branch 1983. *Catalogue of tests*. Ottawa: Minister of Supply and Services Canada.

Schmidt, F. L. and J. E. Hunter. 1977. Development of a general solution to the problem of validity generalization. *Journal of Applied Psychology* 62:529–40.

Schmidt, F. L., J. E. Hunter, and J. R. Caplan. 1981. Validity generalization results for jobs in the petroleum industry. *Journal of Applied Psychology* 64:609–26.

Schmidt, F. L., J. E. Hunter, R. C. McKenzie, and T. Muldrow. 1979. The impact of valid selection procedures on work force productivity. *Journal of Applied Psychology* 64:609–26.

Schmidt, F. L., J. E. Hunter, and K. Pearlman. 1981. Task differences and validity of aptitude tests in selection: A red herring. *Journal of Applied Psychology* 66:166–85.

Wiesner, W. H. and S. F. Cronshaw. 1986. The moderating impact of interview format and degree of structure on interview validity. Paper submitted for publication.

Supplementary References

American Educational Research Association, American Psychological Association, and National Council on Measurement in Education. 1985. *Standards for educational and psychological testing*. Washington, DC: American Psychological Association.

American Psychological Association, Division of Industrial-Organizational Psychology. 1980. *Principles for the validation and use of personnel selection procedures*, 2d ed. Berkeley, CA.

Canadian Psychological Association. 1986. *Guidelines for educational and psychological testing*. Working draft. Ottawa.

Equal Employment Opportunity Commission, Civil Service Commission, Department of Labor, and Department of Justice. 1978. Adoption by four agencies of uniform guidelines on employee selection procedures (1978). *Federal Register* 43:38290–38315.

14. The Assessment Centre Revisited: Practical and Theoretical Considerations

Aharon Tziner, Bernard M. Baruch College (CUNY) and Tel-Aviv University

Assessment centres are an increasingly popular approach to the complexities of staff selection. Their methodological emphasis on observed behaviour reflects the distinction which Wernimount and Campbell (1968) make between the use of signs and samples in the prediction of future job behaviour. Signs refer to such traditional indices of general work predispositions as ability tests, personality inventories, and biographical background, while samples refer to the observation of activities on-the-job or in job-like settings. The belief that sampling offers better prediction of actual job performance has lead to assessment centres' predilection for observation in simulations provided by role playing, business games, in basket techniques, and in leaderless discussion groups.

Early examples of assessment centre techniques can be traced back to Biblical times and the heavenly prescription to Gideon for choosing the best soldiers by their behaviour at the water hole. "... and the Lord said unto Gideon: 'Every one that lappeth of the water with his tongue, as a dog lappeth, him you shall set by himself; likewise everyone that boweth down upon his knees to drink.'"

Presumably, this situational exercise was designed to winnow out potentially disloyal idol worshippers since their bowing down to idols had engrained in them a general tendency to stoop over—even in the simple act of getting a drink. As such, Gideon was utilizing the central assessment centre notion of situational tests aimed at eliciting behaviours related to preselected target criteria.

In more modern times, assessment centre techniques were first used by the military in both World Wars. It is widely believed that German psychologists used assessment centre procedures to select officers in World War I (Thornton and Byham 1982). A better documented example in World War II is the Office of Strategic Services (OSS) center set up to screen and evaluate intelligence agents (MacKinnon 1977). Indeed, this OSS centre served as the prototype of initial industry applications of centres, such as the research-oriented management progress study conducted by American Telephone and Telegraph in 1956 (Cohen, Moses, and Byham 1974).

Industrial use of assessment centres for actual staff selection sprang up following the example of Michigan Bell in

1958. The early Sixties saw the entrance of such major firms as Standard Oil, IBM, General Electric, Sears, Wickes, and J. C. Penney (MacKinnon 1975). Spillover of assessment centres into the U.S. Federal arena started with the IRS in 1969, but spread quickly into almost all branches of government (Byham and Wettengel 1974). States have not lagged far behind in their own use of the approach.

Recently, Thornton and it Byham (1982) have offered an authoritative recounting of the rapid spread of assessment centre programs around the world. For example, the Canadians Slivinski and Ethier (1973) and Slivinski, Grant, Bourgeois, and Pederson (1977) offer interesting examples of centre applications and research within a governmental framework. These international works present an exciting counterpart and extension to the field.

The phenomenal growth and deployment of assessment centres has, of course, generated considerable research and debate regarding the manner of their implementation and the nature of their contribution to selection. The present article attempts to highlight selected facets within this compendium of knowledge and opinion. In particular, it focuses on such topical areas as:

1. Assessment process outcomes
2. Predictive validity of ratings
3. Comparisons to traditional selection methods

ASSESSMENT PROCESS OUTCOMES

The assessment process yields a variety of outcomes, ranging in number, breadth, and scope. These include individual ratings for each dimension observed in differing exercises, overall performance evaluations for each situational exercise, and final consensus ratings made after assessors have discussed candidate performance between themselves. Not surprisingly, this panoply of outcome measures has raised a number of questions regarding their reliability as well as their possible reduction. These concerns in turn have raised more fundamental issues regarding the judgemental process itself.

In terms of reliability, it is important to note that significant differences appear in interrater reliability obtained before and after case discussions between assessors. The literature suggests that before discussion, median interrater reliability across dimensions falls below satisfactory levels. Specific figures range from between .50 (Tziner and Dolan 1982) to .67 (Schmitt 1977) and .76 (Borman 1982). Reliability improves remarkably after assessors discuss individual candidates' performance. Coefficients of .80 or higher reappear consistently (Sackett and Dreher 1982; Thornton and Byham 1982; Tziner and Dolan 1982; Tziner 1984).

The changes in reliability may, of course, reflect simple artifactual effects of conformity and group persuasion. Yet, it would be somewhat hasty to overlook the possibility that the differences may be reflecting more basic judgemental biases which assessors face. For example, each assessor may collect different types of information for a given subject or evaluate them differently, due to a priori differences in interpreting a dimension. Alternately, differential placement, cue perception, or allocation of attention may all lead to differences in observations collected. As such, the heightened reliabilities following discussion may simply reflect the fact that only by combining data and perceptions can the assessor team get to a comprehensive collective image.

A second notable trend is the moderate level of intercorrelations found between exercise ratings. Turnage and Muchinsky (1984) found a fairly low average of .43. The figures reported by Sackett and Dreher (1982) or Tziner and Dolan (1982) are only slightly higher, falling around .60. These moderate intercorrelations may arise from a number of causes. On the one hand, they may be pointing to an underlying common *structural* component—something on the order of Spearman's G. On the other hand, they may be evidence of undesirable appraisal biases such as the artifact of halo effects. Halo involves the carryover of judgements in such a way as to make uncorrelated factors appear related. Although the former possibility might be considered a theoretical issue deserving of greater attention, the latter artifact should be considered a methodological problem which must be redressed.

A recent empirical finding by Sackett and Hakel (1979) raises question marks regarding the individual assessment dimensions and their summation into overall assessment ratings (OAR). Regression of OAR on dimension ratings for given assessor and assessor teams revealed that a small subset of dimensions were sufficient to explain the vast majority of variance. The remaining dimensions added negligibly to the prediction of OAR. Subsequent findings of a similar nature have been reported by Tziner (1984). These findings of course draw into doubt the manner to which assessors draw all dimensions into their summative considerations and raise the possibility that some dimensions could be dropped from analysis.

Thornton and Byham (1982) have argued against dropping dimensions on a number of counts. First, at a statistical level, they note that regression analyses assume linear relationships. However, if dimensions had a curvilinear association with OAR, their importance may have been underestimated. Second, even if the dimensions contribute little to the prediction of OAR, they may still be important factors contributing to the predictive validity of OAR scores. Third, even if the laggard dimensions are of little importance to prediction, they may still have important diagnostic value and permit accurate feedback to assess once observations have been concluded.

Individual dimension ratings figure in a second disquieting finding which calls into question basic assumptions regarding the assessment centre approach itself. The assessment centre method and its emphasis on behaviour sampling rest eventually on the hypothesis that people exhibit consistent patterns of behaviour across situations. If this assumption is correct, Sackett and Dreher (1982) conclude that correlations across exercise ratings of a dimension would have to be at least moderately high. Thus, it is somewhat surprising to find that correlations between exercises on a given dimension are often lower than correlations between dimensions for a given exercise.

Clearly, a number of alternate explanations may be offered for these findings before dismissing the basic assessment centre tenet of behavioural stability. For example, the current literature on contingency theories (for example, Naylor, Pritchard, and Ilgen 1980) would lead one to conclude that a major portion of performance efficacy is situationally determined. This situationality could be expected to override at times the forces of consistency.

Yet taken as a whole, the differing empirical results suggest that the reliability and necessity of the varying assessment outcomes is far from clear. In many cases, these inconsistencies seem linked to even deeper issues related to our limited understanding of the judgemental processes at work in the arena. Among the many avenues of future research, particular scrutiny could be usefully directed to the dynamics of impression formation and decision making within the framework of the group assessor process.

PREDICTIVE VALIDITY

For many, the central data regarding assessment centres is that of predictive validity: Do assessment centre methods, based upon behavioural sampling predict one's later performance on the job? No wonder then that so many studies have addressed the issue of predictive validity nor that a substantial literature of reviews have sprung up on the topic (Cohen et al. 1974; Dreher and Sackett 1982; Thornton and Byham 1982). Evidence of the research mass is reflected in the fact that Huck (1977) reviewed nearly fifty studies, while Klimoski and Strickland (1977) tap additional others. They conclude that there is a median .40 correlation coefficient between overall assessment ratings and such criteria as career progress, salary advance, supervisor ratings, and evaluations of potential progress. More recently, reviews by Thornton and Byham (1982) and Tziner (in press) arrive at equally positive estimations of predictive validity, based on latest findings.

Yet positive pronouncements notwithstanding, problems and questions regarding the evaluation of predictive validity have arisen. Some relate to the appropriateness of the performance criteria employed, the possible contamination of assessment and performance, and the timing of prediction. Other criticisms have related to the overall assessment ratings themselves and their summarization by mechanical/statistical or clinical/judgemental means.

In regard to performance criteria, research findings suggest that OAR predicts some better than others. In particular, reviewers (Dreher and Sackett 1982; Thornton and Byham 1982) note that OAR predicts measures of advance (e.g., promotions, salary likes) better than actual performance ratings. These findings of course raise the possibility that assessment centres do not improve performance selection so much as identify candidates which organizational decision makers are likely to promote. In other words, assessors at the centre may be judging promotability and not competence or efficacy. This charge finds support in Turnage and Muchinsky's (1984) article which shows that OAR scores were better at predicting subjective supervisory appraisals than objective on-the-job outcomes.

It should be recognized that prediction of organizational success is not necessarily bad. Indeed, there may be great value in the early identification of candidates with high promotion potential. Yet, this surrendipitous state of affairs cannot be considered evidence of centres' utility in performance prediction. Indeed, some organizations turn to assessment centres precisely because of their dissatisfaction with their internal promotion procedure and a desire to use more objectively considerations of competence.

Yet, before one concludes that assessment centres are indeed failing to predict performance, it is important to consider the myriad difficulties inherent in their primary index—supervisory ratings. Thornton and Byham (1982) astutely note that the limitations of subjective supervisor ratings are legion: leniency, halo, range bias restriction, and more. These difficulties are further exacerbated by researchers' tendency to average supervisor ratings, since many hold widely divergent views of success. The error and vagary introduced by averaging is highlighted by Schmidt, Noe, Meritt, and Fitzgerald (1984), who report low correlations between different supervisors assessing the same worker (.20 to .40). Thus, one might conclude that subjective job performance ratings are simply poorer methodological indices of job efficacy than objective data concerning transfers, quits, and discharges.

One additional problem overhanging interpretation of predictive success is the possibility of criterion contamination. In particular, there is a potential dependence between OAR scoring and such criteria as promotion. For example, favourable candidate evaluations may lead supervisors to more positively perceive them later. This impression in turn can influence subsequent promotion recommendations (i.e., self-fulfilling prophecies). Such contamination patterns may lead to artifactual overestimates of predictive success.

Contamination is related to another concern regarding timing. Over what time period are predictions being made? If criteria are collected a short period after assessment, candidates may not have had sufficient chance to reach or display their potential. Yet, if too much time has passed, many extraneous factors will have begun to account for candidate performance. This issue of optimal timing between assessment and prediction of collected criterion deserves additional research attention.

These issues surrounding the predictive criteria are complemented by similar ones surrounding the formulation of OAR scores as well. As noted in the previous section, assessment centre procedures yield a wide and varying range of dimensional scores. This has given rise to a long standing debate regarding the preferable method by which to combine them into a predictive index. Two opposing stances have appeared, one favouring statistical mechanical compilation and the other favouring clinical judgemental processes.

The data to date point consistently to the fact that OAR which are clinically formed have high predictive validity (Borman, Eaton, Bryan, and Rosse 1983; Ritchie and Moses 1983; Tziner and Dolan 1982).

This has frequently been taken to mean that the clinical judgemental approach is the one of choice. Indeed, just such a stand is taken by Thornton and Byham (1982).

Yet a number of researchers (Borman 1982; Sackett and Wilson 1982; Tziner and Dolan 1982; Tziner 1984) have shown that mechanical statistical procedures can also lead to a successful integration of data. Indeed, this technique has often been found to predict better than the clinically-based formulation. These findings, suggest that the debate is far from settled.

Apologists for the mechanical statistical technique are often willing to admit the potential advantages of the clinical method in certain limited instances. Thus for example, the subtleties of performance in higher occupational echelons may require an attention to complex behavioural nuances more amenable to clinical hands than rote formula. Yet, even within these grounds of acceptance, doubts remain regarding the well-known shortcomings of judgemental processes (Dolan and Roy 1982) which mechanical methods mitigate.

In the absence of unequivocal evidence, it seems reasonable to suggest that the best approach would be a combination of the two methods. Judgemental procedures would seem best suited to the formulation of the cross-situational dimensional ratings since this requires comparison and contrast of cues over a variety of settings. Yet the combination of the resultant dimensional scores into an overall predictive index would seem most suited to the statistical mechanical method. Surprisingly, the possible combination of techniques has not yet been the focus of research and remains an option for further study.

In review, it appears that assessment centres do offer support for the predictive validity of their results. Yet, close analysis of the literature points to important areas of future development, on an empirical as well as a theoretical level. In spite of the vast literature in the area, there is a strong possibility that renewed attention to the issues of criteria for success, the criteria for prediction, and the predictive methods themselves can further enhance the efficacy of the assessment centre approach.

COMPARISON TO TRADITIONAL SELECTION METHODS

As noted earlier, assessment centres represent one pole of the sample versus sign distinction in selection. Thus, review of the approach should naturally involve a comparison with its contrasting competitor, namely, traditional selection methods. How well do assessment centres stack up against personality inventories, ability tests, internal staff assessments, and the like?

Conventional wisdom suggests that the assessment centre compares very favourably indeed. Initial support for the supposition was based on Byham's (1977) review of twenty-two studies which demonstrated the preferential predictive strength of the approach. Later researchers such as McNutt (1979) have gone so far as to assert that the most impressive feature of assessment centres is the fact that their predictive validity exceeds that of more traditional methods.

Yet a number of discordant notes regarding the preferential status of assessment centre techniques have also been sounded. Klimoski and Strickland (1981), for example, have found that preassessment potential ratings are more correlated with later performance ratings than assessment centre scores. In a similar vein, Hinricks (1969, 1978) finds that managerial predictions of future potential based upon personal file reviews did a better job predicting performance one to eight years later. The challenge to a monolithic view of overwhelming statistical benefits from the assessment centre approach is clear. The differences may be smaller than were first thought.

In light of the major costs associated with assessment centres, it seems reasonable to ask to what extent increased success in prediction is cost beneficial. Tziner and Dolan (1982) for example, found that assessment centre ratings were indeed substantially more valid than such traditional tools as interview ratings, potential ratings, or even paper and pencil ability tests administered by the centres themselves. However, the statistical difference did not necessarily translate itself into an economically significant return on the greater investment in assessment centre techniques.

The possibility arises that a well designed system of ability tests, biographical data, structured interview evaluation, supervisor ratings, and similar traditional tools may well offer an economically satisfactory substitute for the assessment centre approach. Clearly, the specific answer is dependent on the task at hand. In certain job classifications, the cost of selection error may far outweigh the additional outlay. Moreover, the benefit of the psychological value of greater predictive certainty is not always clear. In this regard, it is important to note that rates of prediction error have consistently been shown to be more stable in assessment centre tools than in traditional methods (Dreher and Sackett 1983; Thornton and Byham 1982). The difference in certainty may itself carry a premium.

Finally, it should be noted that comparisons between methods frequently overlook the possibility that the differing techniques are by no means incompatible and that two may be better than one. A Canadian study by Slivinski and Bourgeois (1977), for example, demonstrated that combination of assessment centre and traditional methods offered a notable increment in the predictive success of either method alone. They concluded that both methods should be viewed as complementary parts of a total evaluation package.

In sum, the comparison of assessment centre and traditional means seems far from straightforward. The conventional wisdom that assessment centres may be more valid is true, but the economic benefits are not necessarily certain. In this light, arguments for the integration of assessment centre techniques with well-formulated, traditional methods take on added weight. The form and content of these hybrids remain an avenue for future exploration and analysis.

CONCLUSION

Frequent mention has been made throughout this article concerning the large amounts of empirical data which have been collected to date around the assessment centre approach. The three central focuses addressed here reflect in large part those appearing within this larger mass. Reasonably, issues of reliability, predictive validity, and comparison with traditional methods have dominated the concerns of those in the field.

To students of assessment centres, the very number of studies is not surprising. Indeed, assessment centres have from the start reflected an empirical and practical attempt to improve through better selection means the fit between people and their occupations. This attempt has generally been fueled by debate and concerns arising from the evaluation of implementation within the marketplace.

Yet the number of empirical works tended to overshadow, at times, central theoretical issues of critical relevance to future improvement of assessment centre techniques. Throughout the article, reference has been made to basis underlying problems and lacuna in our understanding of such theoretical issues as the nature of the assessment-making process, combination of multiple information sources, or the consistency of behaviour across settings. Resolution of the empirical problems in the field must ultimately progress hand-in-hand with the clarification of these theoretical issues.

An example of the interplay between theory and assessment centre practice will suffice. Thus far, most assessments of managerial candidates are based upon performance dimensions obtained by practically derived job analysis methods. At the same time, it is commonly believed that leadership forms a central facet of management success. However, little attempt has been made to employ current understanding of situationally contingent facets of leadership in order to devise more appropriate assessment centre elements.

The dialectic between empirical and theoretical advance is a recurrent theme in all branches of scientific endeavour.

Thus, the call here to further integrate the two represents a recognition that empirical work in the field has advanced far enough to turn assessment from an art into a science. The practical success of an assessment centre can only further benefit from the development.

Acknowledgement. The author is deeply indebted to Michael Hoffman for his invaluable editorial assistance.

References

Borman, W. C. 1982. Validity of behavioral assessment for predicting military recruiter performance. *Journal of Applied Psychology* 67:3–9.

Borman, W. C., N. K. Eaton, J. D. Bryan, and R. L. Rosse. 1983. Validity of army recruiter behavioral assessment: Does the assessor make a difference? *Journal of Applied Psychology* 68:415–19.

Byham, W. C. and C. Wettengel. 1974. Assessment center for identifying and developing management potential in government operations. *Public Personnel Management* 3: 352–65.

Byham, W. C. 1977. "Application of the assessment center method." In *Applying the assessment center method*, edited by J. L. Moses and W. C. Byham. New York: Pergamon Press.

Cohen, B. M., J. L. Moses, and W. C. Byham. 1974. *The validity of assessment centers: A literature review.* Monographs 2. Pittsburgh, PA: Development Dimensions Press.

Dolan, S. and D. Roy. 1982. *Managerial selection.* Monograph, Montreal: University of Montreal.

Dreher, G. F. and P. R. Sackett. 1983. *Perspectives on employee staffing and selection: Readings and commentary.* Homewood, Ill.: Richard D. Irwin.

Hinrichs, J. R. 1969. Comparison of "real-life" assessments of management potential with situational exercises, paper-and-pencil ability tests and personality inventories. *Journal of Applied Psychology* 53:425–32.

Hinrichs, J. R. 1978. An eight-year follow-up of a management assessment center. *Journal of Applied Psychology* 63:596–601.

Huck, J. R. 1977. The research base. In *Applying the assessment center method*, edited by J. L. Moses and W. C. Byham. New York: Pergamon Press.

Klimoski, R. J. and W. J. Strickland. 1977. Assessment centers—Valid or merely prescient? *Personnel Psychology* 30:353–61.

Klimoski, R. J. and W. J. Strickland. 1981. A comparative view of assessment centers. Unpublished manuscript.

MacKinnon, D. W. 1975. An overview of assessment centers (CCL Tech. Rep. 1). Berkeley, CA: University of California, Center for Creative Leadership.

MacKinnon, D. W. 1977. From selecting spies to selecting managers. In *Applying the assessment center method*, edited by J. L. Moses and W. C. Byham. New York: Pergamon Press.

McNutt, K. 1979. Behavioral consistency and assessment centers: A reconciliation of the literature. *Journal of Assessment Methods in Psychology* 2:1–8.

Naylor, J. C., R. D. Pritchard, and D. R. Ilgen. 1980. *A theory of behavior in organizations.* New York, NY: Academic Press.

Ritchie, R. R. and J. L. Moses. 1983. Assessment center correlates of women's advancement into middle management: A 7-year longitudinal analysis. *Journal of Applied Psychology* 68:227–31.

Sackett, P. R. and M. D. Hakel. 1979. Temporal stability and individual differences in using assessment information to form overall ratings. *Organizational Behavior and Human Performance* 23:120–37.

Sackett, P. R. and G. F. Dreher. 1982. Constructs and assessment center dimensions: some troubling empirical findings. *Journal of Applied Psychology* 67:401–10.

Sackett, P. R. and M. A. Wilson. 1982. Factors affecting the consensus judgment process in managerial assessment centers. *Journal of Applied Psychology* 67:10–17.

Schmitt, N. 1977. Interrater agreement and dimensionality and combination of assessment center judgments. *Journal of Applied Psychology* 62:171–176.

Schmidt, N., R. A. Noe, R. Meritt, and M. P. Fitzgerald. 1984. Validity of assessment center ratings for the predominant performance ratings and school climate of school administrators. *Journal of Applied Psychology* 69: 207–13.

Slivinski, L. W. and L. Ethier. 1973. *Development of the assessment centre for the career assignment program: Descriptive summary of the senior executive population.* Public Service Commission of Canada, Managerial Assessment and Research Division.

Slivinski, L. W., K. W. Grant, R. P. Bourgeois, and L. D. Pederson. 1977. *Development and application of a first level management assessment centre.* Ottawa, Canada: Managerial Assessment and Research Division of the Personnel Psychology Centre.

Slivinski, L. W. and R. P. Bourgeois. 1977. "Feedback of Assessment Centre Results" in *Applying the Assessment Centre Method*, ed. J. L. Moses and W. L. Byham. (New York: Pergamon Press.

Thornton, G. C. and W. C. Byham. 1982. *Assessment centers and managerial performance.* New York: Academic Press.

Tziner, A. and S. Dolan. 1982. Validity of an assessment center for identifying future female officers in the military. *Journal of Applied Psychology* 67:728–36.

Tziner, A. 1984. Prediction of peer rating in a military assessment center: A longitudinal follow-up. *Canadian Journal of Administrative Sciences* 1:146–60.

Tziner, A. In press. Personnel selection (in Hebrew). Ramat-Aviv; University Press.

Turnage, J. J. and P. M. Muchinsky. 1984. A comparison of the predictive validity of assessment evaluations versus traditional measures in forecasting supervisory job performance: Interpretive implications criterion distortion for the assessment paradigm. *Journal of Applied Psychology* 69:595–602.

Wernimount, P. F. and J. P. Campbell. 1968. Signs, samples and criteria. *Journal of Applied Psychology* 52:372–76.

Section IV
Appraising and Compensating

The five articles in this section describe several issues and methods in appraising and compensating employees in organizations. Schwind begins by providing an overview of the field of performance appraisal. He examines the past, present, and future trends in performance appraisal. A special emphasis throughout the review, is placed on the major obstacles in the PA system and hints are suggested insofar as overcoming some of these pitfalls.

Dipboye highlights in the second article some neglected variables in research on discrimination during the appraisal process. He points out that unfair discrimination in subjective appraisals is mostly attributed to raters' stereotypes of the ideal occupant of a job and that their evaluations reflect their perceptions of the goodness of fit of the ratee to the job.

The third article by Theriault, discusses key issues in designing compensation systems. The linking pin in designing sound and effective compensation systems, according to Theriault, is the simultaneous consideration of three facets: clear objectives, explicit wage and pay policies, and attention to various forms of equity. Theriault elaborates on these issues in his paper.

In the following article Podsakoff, Greene, and McFillen point out some difficulties in effectively using compensation systems especially to motivate and enhance performance. Their article is particularly applicable in helping PHRM and line managers understand why pay does not always motivate performance. The authors identify several factors that may prevent the establishment of a link between pay and performance, including a failure to create contingencies, creating inappropriate contingencies, and employee opposition. Podsakoff et al. conclude with management implications by suggesting how pay-performance contingencies can be established and properly administered.

The final article in this section is by Kanungo who discusses how reward systems can be strategically designed to influence the major PHRM objectives of attraction, retention, motivation, and an increase in employee's attendance. The paper begins with a review of the motivation theories of work behaviour with a particular examination of the use of the intrinsic-extrinsic dichotomy. Then he describes alternative basis for rewards classification which can provide coherent and practical guidelines for effective rewards management.

15. Performance Appraisal: The State of the Art

Herman Schwind, Saint Mary's University

INTRODUCTION

This chapter gives an overview of the state of the art of performance appraisal (PA) and takes a look at what the future is most likely to bring. It should be emphasized that it is an overview and not an in-depth treatment of the topic. Readers who are interested in detailed discussions of the subtopics are directed to the list of references at the end of the chapter.

First we will take a look at some critical issues regarding PA and then address the problem of how to develop and maintain an effective PA system.

If one looks at PA systems currently in use one has to assume that their development and utilization is based on the following assumptions:

— For a PA system to work a PA form and perhaps a training session for the supervisors is needed
— the personnel manager is the best person to develop an appraisal form

"We don't know what we're doing but we we're doing it very carefully and hope you are pleased with our unintelligent diligence" (Wherry, 1957, 1, as quoted in Bernardin and Beatty, 1984).

— the supervisor is the best rater because she knows
  a. The job, and
  b. How the employee performs
— Traits are practical and relevant PA criteria
— An overall rating (all scores added up) is useful to indicate performance differentials
— Feedback once a year is sufficient
— Jobs are independent
— Once management is behind a PA system it will work

It will be shown in the subsequent discussion that all these assumptions, although not publicly stated, but practised, are in urgent need of revision.

CRITICAL ISSUES

The Popularity of PA as a Management Tool

Several surveys show that PA is a widely used management tool in North America. Lazer and Wikstrom (1977) in their survey study found that seventy-four percent of their respondents used PA while

Locher and Teel (1977) reported a figure of ninety-eight percent. The difference in these findings is probably based on company size since the first study included more small companies. Another survey (Colby and Wallace 1975) which included Canadian companies showed that ninety-three percent used PA. In a Canadian study, seventy-five percent of large companies and fifty-five percent of medium-sized companies used PA for their clerical, professional, supervisory, and management employees (Royal Commission 1976). A study on thirty-nine United States government agencies indicated that one hundred percent utilized PA (Feild and Holley 1975).

Effectiveness of PA

The Colby/Wallace (1975) study mentioned previously contains an interesting finding. Only ten percent of the personnel managers surveyed felt that their PA system was effective. The author recalls a remark by a personnel manager who worked for fifteen years with several large companies in the United States and Canada. His words were: "I have not seen a PA form which was worth the paper it was printed on." Thompson and Dalton (1970) and Winstanley (1972) report similar negative attitudes expressed by personnel managers. DeVries (1984) surveyed 972 managers and professionals in a major United States corporation about their PA practices. What he found was a group of "uninformed participants" (p. 7). What are the reasons for these frustrating experiences? Here are some of the more important ones.

Insufficient Funding. Many companies are just not prepared to invest sufficient funds and manpower into the development of an adequate, well-developed, and executed PA system which, admittedly, can be costly. Most of the presently used systems have too many shortcomings to be effective. (DeVries, Morrison, Shullman, and Gerlach 1980).

One PA Instrument Is Expected to Serve too Many Objectives. PA usually is utilized for several purposes (listed in sequence of popularity) (Locher and Teel 1977):

1. Reward decisions (compensation, promotion)
2. Individual development decisions (performance improvement, feedback, training)
3. Employment decisions (documentation, manpower planning)

However, it is highly unrealistic to expect one instrument or scale to be equally useful for such diverse purposes as mentioned above (DeVries et al. 1980)

Managers' Overconfidence of Rating Ability. Several studies have demonstrated that many supervisors lack sufficient rating skills to make valid judgments regarding the performance of their employees. Variables which may affect a rater's ability to judge an employee's performance include:

1. Personal characteristics (sex, race, age, level of education, self-confidence, cognitive complexity, job experience, performance level, and leadership style)
2. Type of rater (supervisor, peer, self, or subordinate)
3. Rater knowledge of ratee and job (level of supervision, familiarity with job, rater-ratee acquaintance-ship and friendship).

(See Landy and Farr 1980, for a detailed discussion of these variables).

Unwillingness of Raters to Give Negative Feedback. Much has been written on this topic. Supervisors are perceived to be unwilling to play the role of the bad guy or the role of God (McGregor 1957). Others mention the built-in conflicts in the PA process (Smith and Brouwer 1977).

The Nature of Managerial Work. Mintzberg (1973) in his now classical study found that managerial work can be characterized by variety, brevity, and fragmentation. He points out that fifty percent of a manager's activities last nine minutes or less, and only ten percent last over an hour. This is quite contrary to the requirements of an effective PA system which concentrates on past behaviour, and, depending on the degree of formalization, represents a structured and routine activity.

Organizational Factors. PA is often tied to merit pay. However, Lawler (1971) found that in many organizations supervisors had little discretion in allocating pay increases. Many other factors, for example, seniority, COLA clauses, and across the board adjustments limit a manager's ability to reward individual performance. Assessing employees' performances assumes, also, that their jobs are independent of other jobs. However, several studies confirm that most managerial jobs are interdependent (McCall, Morrison, and Hannan 1978; Mintzberg 1973; Lorsch and Morse 1974). In addition, it has been pointed out that profit and losses in an enterprise are rarely determined by a single person (Campbell, Dunnette, Lawler, and Weick 1970).

These are some of the factors which are obstacles in the effective use of a PA system, even if it has been developed according to the rules. To summarize the introduction: It has been shown that PA is an important and very popular management tool, but despite its popularity most personnel managers have doubts regarding its effectiveness. Even a well-developed PA system faces so many obstacles—organizational and human—that its proper functioning is never assured. It should be pointed out, however, that there are ways to increase the probability that a PA system actually will work. These ways will be discussed subsequently.

THE PAST

In the past, research on PA has concentrated on the development of formal evaluation methods and the reduction of rater error through rater training. Typically, studies would be concerned with the validity and relevance of criteria and the appropriateness of evaluation procedures (Borman and Dunnette 1975; Campbell et al. 1970; Cascio and Valenzi 1977; DeCotiis 1977), and secondly, with the elimination or reduction of rater errors, such as halo, leniency, and central tendency (Bernardin, Alvares, Cranny 1976; Borman 1975, 1979; Cooper 1981). However, a consensus seems to have emerged among researchers that the focus on evaluation methods and rater errors did not significantly improve the effectiveness of PA systems (Cooper 1981; DeVries et al. 1980).

For the reasons mentioned previously, the emphasis of research has shifted more recently to the rater and the rating process. A number of researchers recognized that the personality of the rater and the work environment had a significantly larger impact on the validity and accuracy of performance ratings than the instrument or method itself (Bernardin 1979, 1981; Borman 1978; Cooper 1981; Feldman 1981; Ilgen and Feldman 1983; Landy and Farr 1980; Schneier 1977).

The following part will very briefly discuss the earlier concerns—performance criteria, measurement methods, and rater errors—and then, in more detail, the new approaches.

Performance Criteria

Nagle (1953) defines a criterion as a measure of the degree of success by an individual on a given activity. If we accept this definition, it follows that a criterion is an operational definition of the extent to which an employee exhibits desirable job behaviours. This is in line with the Campbell et al. (1973) definition of work performance which is described as "work related behavior which has been evaluated as to its contribution to organizational objectives" (p. 16).

Three types of criteria are utilized in PA systems:

——Traits (honesty, aggressiveness, etc.),
——Behaviour (lifting the package, answering the telephone),
——Results (number of widgets, words per minute).

Traits. There seems to be agreement among researchers in the personnel field that traits have low validity and little relevance as performance criteria (Bernardin and Beatty 1984; Campbell et al. 1970; Kane and Lawler 1979). Their major shortcoming is that they are difficult to measure since they are not visible and have to be inferred from behaviour (How does one know whether a person is honest?). They are also difficult to define and are interpreted differently from person to person, resulting in low interrater reliability (consistency). The strongest criticism of the use of traits as performance criteria comes from Kane and Lawler (1979). They state:

Even though traits may relate in predictable ways to more nearly ultimate criteria of performance, this no more qualifies them as surrogates for such criteria than it qualifies IQ scores as surrogates for school grades. (P 445)

DeVries (Rice 1985) takes a different, more pragmatic view. He says:

... in business, ... traits are very important, subjective or not. Executives make personnel decisions based on them all the time. If they do, then those traits should be evaluated, and we researchers can't afford to ignore them. (P. 36)

The best solution probably is to include traits in a PA system, but to inform managers of the problems associated with them.

Behaviour. According to Latham and Wexley (1981) behaviour-based appraisal measures account for more job complexity, relate more to what the employee actually does, and more likely minimize irrelevant factors not under the control of the employee. Behaviour criteria of job performance became more popular during the last three decades, beginning with Flanagan's (1954) critical incidents technique, modified by Smith and Kendall (1963) and Campbell et al. (1970), and expanded by Blanz and Ghiselli (1972), Kane and Lawler (1980), and Kane (1981).

The behavioural approach to PA reduces much of the ambiguity of the trait-rating method by reducing the performance construct to the job itself (Dunnette 1966; Harari and Zedeck 1973). As Latham and Wexley (1981) put it:

Good cost-related outcomes (e.g. profits) do not come about through osmosis. Someone must do something to make them good or bad. Behavioral measures based on a job analysis indicate precisely what is being done by an employee to warrant recognition, discipline, transfer, promotion, demotion, or termination. (P. 45)

Results. Undoubtedly, immediate outcomes of a job are the most objective performance criteria, given that the job outcomes can be clearly specified and that it has been established that they are under the control of the employee (Campbell et al. 1970). Unfortunately, many objective measures relate more to unit than to individual performance, causing a vague relationship between individual job performance and objective performance criteria (DeVries et al. 1980). In addition, it is often very difficult, if not impossible, to obtain objective measures of job performance for many job titles (Landy and Farr 1980).

THE PRESENT

The change in focus of research on PA began in the middle seventies. Schwab, Heneman, and DeCotiis (1975), in their review of the literature on behaviorally anchored rating scales concluded that so far all attempts to improve rating scales had met with limited success. They suggested that research efforts may be better invested in the understanding of what is going on in a rater's mind, how information is gathered for the evaluation process, and what factors may influence a rater's judgment.

In line with above recommendations, Schneier (1977) in his studies on cognitive complexity found that raters' ability to make valid judgments was related to their cognitive ability to interpret complex information.

While the first discussions of the importance of cognitive processes, such as memory and recall, in PA took place in the early fifties (Wherry 1952), more elaborate models were proposed by Stone and Slusher (1975) and Landy and Farr (1980). The Landy and Farr model (see Figure 15-1) demonstrates the complexity of the performance evaluation process, taking into account thirteen variables. An excellent review of the cognitive phases of the evaluation process occurring in a rater's mind has been provided by Feldman (1981).

Feldman based his model on contributions from a variety of sources, mostly from the area of social psychology. He divides the PA process into four steps: attention, categorization, recall, and information integration. He suggests that these processes are carried out either automatically or in a controlled way.

In the automatic process a rater will observe an employee's behaviour and categorize it, but not monitor it consciously. Feldman maintains that the automatic process is dominant except when decisions are problematic. In such a case the categorization is done willfully.

If the rater is required to make a judgment on the performance of a specific employee, and tries to recall the information stored in his memory, the image of the employee which will appear will be biased according to the category (stereotype) used to classify the employee's behaviour.

According to Feldman, several factors, such as personal disposition and environment, will influence the type of categories chosen during the initial judgment and subsequent recall. All subsequent search for information about the employee will also be biased and be influenced by the job task to result in halo, leniency/stringency biases, as well as racial, sexual, ethnic, and personalistic biases. On the other hand, the same automatic and controlled processes are also responsible for the accuracy of a performance evaluation. Personal motivation of the rater to perform a valid assessment is apparently an important factor in the PA process.

For human resource managers the implications of Feldman's model are that any performance judgment by a supervisor is hopelessly biased. Biased yes, hopelessly no. Feldman argues that good deci-

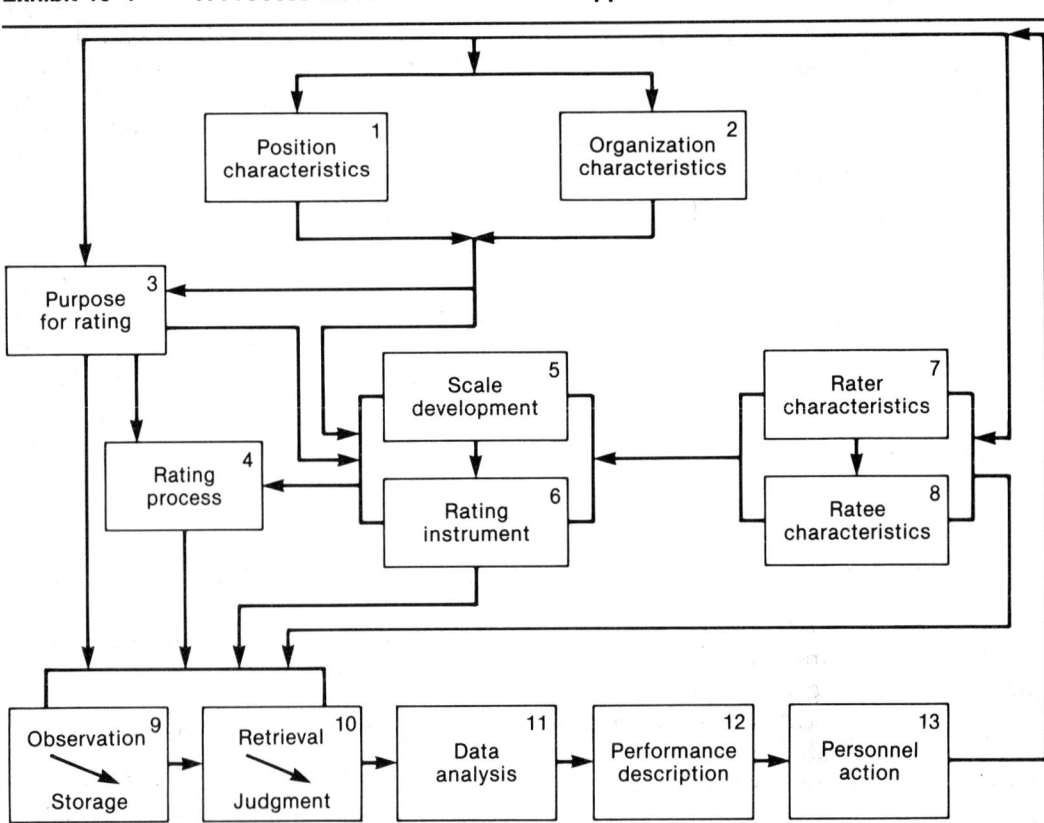

Exhibit 15-1 A Process Model of Performance Appraisal

```
                    ┌──────────────────┐     ┌──────────────────┐
                    │ Position       1 │     │ Organization   2 │
                    │ characteristics  │     │ characteristics  │
                    └──────────────────┘     └──────────────────┘

        ┌──────────┐ 3
        │ Purpose  │
        │ for rating│
        └──────────┘
                          ┌──────────┐ 5          ┌──────────────┐ 7
                          │  Scale   │            │    Rater     │
                          │develop-  │            │characteristics│
                          │  ment    │            └──────────────┘
        ┌──────────┐ 4    └──────────┘
        │  Rating  │      ┌──────────┐ 6          ┌──────────────┐ 8
        │ process  │      │  Rating  │            │    Ratee     │
        └──────────┘      │instrument│            │characteristics│
                          └──────────┘            └──────────────┘

  ┌─────────┐ 9   ┌─────────┐ 10   ┌────────┐ 11  ┌──────────┐ 12  ┌──────────┐ 13
  │Observation│   │Retrieval │     │  Data  │     │Performance│    │Personnel │
  │          │   │          │     │analysis│     │description│    │ action   │
  │ Storage  │   │Judgment  │     └────────┘     └──────────┘     └──────────┘
  └─────────┘   └─────────┘
```

Source: F. J. Landy and J. L. Farr, "Performance Rating," *Psychological Bulletin* 87(1): 72–107. Copyright 1980 by the American Psychological Association. Reprinted by permission of the author.

sions are made in organizations and mentions several reasons for it. It can be assumed that experienced evaluators have developed relatively accurate categories of acceptable and unacceptable job performance, thus enabling them to come up with relatively valid performance evaluations. Feldman further points out that if the quality of job performance is specifiable in terms of observable behaviours, the judgment process should be relatively easy and valid. He mentions too that often consensual standards exist against which performance can be measured and which assist in prototype formation. He cautions, however, that many evaluation procedures currently in use may not allow evaluators to make more than a good-bad judgment.

Feldman's recommendations for the improvement of current PA systems include:

——The use of behaviour-based scales. Feldman perceives them as an attempt to define a more valid prototype of the successful and unsuccessful employee.

——Training in the use of these scales. Such training can be seen as an attempt to familiarize raters with com-

mon prototypes of successful and unsuccessful employees.
— Explicit definitions of prototypes of employees to provide for higher validity.
— Use of multiple raters to overcome individual biases.
— Use of hard criteria wherever reasonable.
— Use of job samples as decision tools for promotions and transfers.
— Training of raters to make behaviour sampling a routine part of a supervisor's job to avoid memory-related biases.
— Avoidance of trait ratings.
— Creation of positive consequences of PA for both the rater and ratee.

Cooper (1981) adds some interesting insights into factors which affect raters' judgments. He suggests that raters believe in what he calls illusory correlations between job dimensions which cause haloed ratings (see also Hamilton 1979). The six sources of halo described by Cooper are:

— Undersampling (insufficient sampling of job behaviour and resulting greater reliance on guessing)
— Engulfing (ratings affected by single, salient characteristic)
— Insufficient concreteness (occurs when scale anchors are too vague)
— Insufficient rater motivation and knowledge (raters are not aware of potential sources of bias)
— Cognitive distortion (raters lose and add information in the process of storing and recalling information)
— Correlated true scores (in reality most performance factors or dimensions are correlated to some degree)

The models and factors discussed above offer a glimpse at the complexity of the rating process and an insight into the difficulties researchers and practitioners face if they attempt to develop a PA system that is expected to be valid and effective.

THE FUTURE

As the saying goes, nothing is more difficult to predict than the future. On the other hand, it is possible to look at the demands which will be made on PA and PA systems and to draw conclusions on most likely trends. Legal constraints will have a stronger impact in the future; the nature of the labour force has to be taken more into account when developing and implementing new PA systems, and, last but not least, when the probable transition from a manufacturing to a service society occurs.

Legal Requirements

There can be little doubt that legal requirements will have a major effect on the development of PA systems. The Federal Charter of Rights and Freedoms and federal and provincial human rights laws require selection procedures be valid (nondiscriminatory), implying that an applicant will be judged on job-related criteria, and nothing else. However, the only way a selection procedure can be proven valid—meaning nondiscriminatory—is by demonstrating through a **valid** PA system that it has concurrent or predictive validity (Cascio and Bernardin 1981).

Employees also increasingly contest layoff, dismissal, and even promotion cases. Many employers found out the hard way that because they were without valid and carefully documented performance evaluations, courts, arbitrators, and arbitration boards awarded compensation settlements which in some cases went into the millions of dollars (Cascio and Bernardin 1981; Holley and Feild 1975).

Valid in this context means to use performance criteria which are clearly job related, for example, job behaviour and/or results. These criteria have to be developed from a job analysis which describes job-related activities, defines the outcomes, and, ideally, spells out the standards according to which the activities described are to be performed (Campbell et al. 1970).

Carefully documented means the use of well-developed and standardized appraisal instruments by well-trained observers who record effective and ineffective job behaviours whenever they occur and who do not rely on memory (Bernardin and Beatty 1984).

A significant change in the legal status of PA systems will come when the mandatory retirement requirements are declared discriminatory. Especially profit-oriented organizations will be forced to monitor much more closely the performance of their older employees. They will need air-tight proof to show to the satisfaction of arbitrators or courts that the performance of an employee has deteriorated so much that further employment is not justified and that the employee has to retire.

Expectations

Clearly, the nature of the work force has changed and will change even more in the future. The new type of employee is characterized by higher education, interest in a career rather than just a job, and a much higher interest in accepting responsibilities and willingness to question managerial decisions (Renwick and Lawler 1978; Yankelovich 1979; although both are United States studies, there are no reasons to believe that these findings are not generalizable to Canada).

The implications for the personnel practitioner are significant. As research has shown, most PA systems have been developed and implemented by management with little or no input from employees. If management is serious with the so often expressed expectation that it prefers a motivated and committed work force, then it is essential that employees be involved in the development and the implementation of PA systems (DeVries et al. 1980; Meyer 1976) and even in the PA training process (DeVries et al. 1980).

Changing Economy

If the predictions of some futurists come true, then we will have a service rather than a manufacturing industry, and the majority of our work force in Canada will be white-collar rather than blue-collar (Task Force on Employment Opportunities in the 80's 1981). It is usually more difficult to assess the work performance of a white-collar employee because of the greater job complexity. It means that PA systems in the future have to be more sophisticated to enable supervisors to assess the contributions of their employees (DeVries et al. 1980).

CHARACTERISTICS OF AN EFFECTIVE PERFORMANCE APPRAISAL SYSTEM

From the discussions so far it has become quite clear that the PA process is very complex, that it is difficult to develop an appropriate and effective PA system, that PA system developers and users have to be thoroughly trained and informed, and that management has to be strongly committed to a PA system to really make it work. This last part of the chapter will look at the necessary and the desirable attributes of a PA system, one with a high probability of success.

The following characteristics of an effective PA system expand on literature reviews and suggestions by Burke, Weitzel, and Weir (1978), and Schwind (1980).

Valid and Reliable Measurement of Job Performance

Validity has to be the top requirement for any measuring instrument (Campbell et al. 1970; Kane and Lawler 1979). If it is not known what the instrument is measuring, no conclusions can be drawn. Reliability, although highly desirable, is difficult to achieve in an organizational setting because of different raters, different instruments, and changing work environments. As a consequence, reliability can be looked at only as a distant aim (Kane and Lawler 1979).

Employee Input into the Development of a PA System

Employee participation in the development of the PA instrument and PA system increases significantly the acceptance of the system by both supervisors and employees (Campbell, et al. 1970; Friedman and Cornelius 1976; Schwind 1978).

Employee Input into the Interview Process

Allowing employees to have a high level of participation in the appraisal process increases employee satisfaction and morale (Cummings 1973; Greller 1975; Nemeroff and Wexley 1977).

Frequent Feedback

Most appraisals take place once a year. Ideally, performance feedback would be given immediately after effective or ineffective job behaviour has been observed (Meyer, Kay and French 1965), which is unrealistic in a real world setting. A compromise may be feedback sessions on a monthly, quarterly, or at least on a twice a year basis.

Rater Training

Bernardin and Beatty (1984) suggest that raters should be trained mainly to improve their observation and categorization skills, specifically through frame-of-reference training and diary keeping. Frame-of-reference training aims at raters with idiosyncratic (person specific) work standards which are not in line with organizational norms. Such raters are grouped with raters who rate closer to the organizational norm. With group problem-solving techniques the training attempts to change the norms of the off-standard raters, apparently with good success (Bernardin 1979; Bernardin, Orban, and Carlyle 1981). A second, quite effective way of standardizing observations is through the use of diaries (Bernardin and Walter 1977; Buckley and Bernardin 1980).

Goal Setting

Latham and Yukl (1975) found that when supervisors set specific goals, performance improved twice as much than when they discussed general goals (see also a literature review on "Goal Setting and Task Performance: 1969–1980," by Locke, Shaw, Saari, and Latham 1981).

Constructive Criticism

Two studies (Maier 1958; Meyer and Kay 1964) found that when supervisors discussed work-related problems with employees and tried to find solutions, it led to significant performance improvements. Conversely, the more job behaviours were criticized, the less likely was there any improvement, but the stronger was the defensive reaction (Kay, Meyer, and French 1965; Nemeroff and Wexley 1977).

Different Sources of Appraisal

Different sources of appraisal refers to evaluations from different raters, for example, superiors, self, peers, and/or subordinates. Borman (1974) and Lawler (1967) make a strong case for the use of multiple raters. They suggest that raters from different levels of the organization will have different, but valid views of a job and the performance of the incumbent. Similar evaluations will strengthen a case, while differences in judgments should lead to an analysis of the variance to find the reasons. Blood (1974) sees such potential discrepancies as a useful way to assess organizational policies, for example, they could indicate ineffective channels of communication.

Appraisal Consequences

Experts in the field agree that a PA system without consequences (e.g., training, pay, or promotion) will lose its effectiveness very quickly (Ivancevich 1972; Lawler 1971; Porter, Lawler, and Hackman 1975). Employees, as well as supervisors, have to see that appraisal results are taken seriously by management and are followed up on. All too often evaluation results end up in the personnel file unread, leading to cynical employees and frustrated supervisors (DeVries and McCall 1976).

A Nurturing Organizational Environment

That the social climate in an organization may have a significant impact on the effectiveness of a PA system has been suggested by Lawler (1971). He goes so far as to recommend that in organizations with low trust levels performance appraisals should not be done. Bernardin, Orban, and Carlyle (1981) found that raters with low trust in the appraisal process rated their subordinates significantly higher (with greater leniency) than raters with high trust in the process. In a treatise on PA, DeVries (1984) points out that whenever a new or revised PA system is implemented in an organization, a change process has been started. He suggests that the field of organizational development—although only emerging now as a discipline—may provide management with the tools for preparing people and organizations for change. He says: "Designing a successful PA system for use in an organization is as much an exercise in organizational development as it is a study of performance measurement" (p. 8).

Only the first characteristic is a necessary one, but the more the others will be present in a PA system, the higher will be the probability that it will succeed.

SUMMARY

This chapter tried to describe the state of the art in the area of performance appraisal by discussing the highlights of its evolution. If it sounds somewhat discouraging in the beginning, the reader can be assured that despite the negative picture of the PA process and all the obstacles described, there are PA systems in place which seem to work quite well (see for example, Beer and Ruh 1976). The secret lies, as so often in life, in knowing about the possible obstacles for, the potential pitfalls with, and the most likely consequences of a system one wants to use. In short, the development and implementation of a PA system requires considerable expertise.

As long as managers have insufficient knowledge in matters of criterion development, rater and ratee training, and the effect of the organizational environment on PA, any attempt of creating an effective PA system is most likely an experience in frustration.

The advice to use behavioural scientists and consultants is, of course, self-serving, but, in most cases, probably appropriate. As has been shown, too many variables have to be taken into account. As mentioned in the introduction, one of the problems with the use of PA systems was the lack of sufficient investment of manpower and financial resources in its development. A PA system of high quality may not be cheap, but the potential benefits will make the investment worthwhile.

References

Beer, M. and R. A. Ruh. 1976. Employee growth through performance management. *Harvard Business Review* 54(4): 59–66.

Bernardin, H. J. 1979. Rater training: A critique and reconceptualization. Proceedings of the Academy of Management, 216–20.

Bernardin, H. J. 1981. Rater training strategies: An integrative model. Paper presented at the annual meeting of the American Psychological Association.

Bernardin, H. J. and R. W. Beatty. 1984. *Performance Appraisal: Assessing Human Behavior at Work*. Boston, Mass.: Kent Publishing Co.

Bernardin, H. J., K. M. Alvares, and C. J. Cranny. 1976. A recomparison of behavioral expectation scales to summated scales. *Journal of Applied Psychology* 61:564–70.

Bernardin, H. J., J. A. Orban, and J. J. Carlyle. 1981. Performance ratings as a function of trust in appraisal, purpose for appraisal, and rater individual differences. *Proceedings of the Academy of Management*, 311–15.

Bernardin, H. J. and C. S. Walter. 1977. The effects of rater training and diary keeping on psychometric error in ratings. *Journal of Applied Psychology* 62:64–69.

Bianz, F. and E. E. Ghiselli. 1972. The mixed standard scale: A new rating system. *Personnel Psychology* 25:185–99.

Blood, M. R. 1974. Spin-offs from behavioral expectation scale procedures. *Journal of Applied Psychology* 59:513–15.

Borman, W. C. 1974. The rating of individuals in organizations: An alternate approach. *Organizational Behavior and Human Performance* 12:105–124.

Borman, W. C. 1975. Effects of instructions to avoid halo error on reliability and validity of performance evaluation ratings. *Journal of Applied Psychology* 60:556–60.

Borman, W. C. 1978. Exploring upper limits of reliability and validity in performance ratings. *Journal of Applied Psychology* 63:135–44.

Borman, W. C. 1979. Format and training effects on rating accuracy and rater errors. *Journal of Applied Psychology* 64:410–21.

Borman, W. C. and M. D. Dunnette. 1975. Behavior-based versus trait-oriented performance ratings: An empirical study. *Journal of Applied Psychology* 60(5): 561–65.

Buckley, M. R. and H. J. Bernardin. 1980. An assessment of the components of an observer training program. Paper presented at the annual meeting of the Southeastern Psychological Association.

Burke, R. S., W. Weitzel, and T. Weir. 1978. Characteristics of effective employee performance review and development interviews: Replication and extension. *Personnel Psychology* 31:903–19.

Cafferty, T., A. DeNisi, B. Meglino, and S. Youngblood. 1981. A cognitive view of the performance appraisal process. Paper presented at the American Psychological Association Convention, Los Angeles, CA., August.

Campbell, J. P., M. D. Dunnette, R. D. Arvey, and L. V. Hellervik. 1973. The development and evaluation of behaviorally based rating scales. *Journal of Applied Psychology* 57:15–22.

Campbell, J. P., M. D. Dunnette, E. E. Lawler, and K. E. Weick. 1970. *Managerial behavior, performance, and effectiveness.* New York: McGraw-Hill.

Cascio, W. F. and H. J. Bernardin. 1981. Implications of performance appraisal litigation for personnel decisions. *Personnel Psychology* 34:211–26.

Cascio, W. F., and E. R. Valenzi. 1977. Relations among criteria of police performance. *Journal of Applied Psychology* 62:301–10.

Colby, J. D., and R. L. Wallace. 1975. Performance appraisal: Help or hindrance to employee productivity. *Personnel Administrator* 26(6): 37–39.

Cooper, W. H. 1981. Ubiquitous halo. *Psychological Bulletin* 90:218–44.

Cummings, L. L. and D. P. Schwab. 1973. *Performance in organizations: Determinants and appraisal.* Glenview, Ill.: Scott, Foresman.

DeCotiis, T. A. 1977. An analysis of the external validity and applied relevance of three rating formats. *Organizational Behavior and Human Performance* 19:247–66.

DeVries, D. L. 1984. Viewing performance appraisal with a wide-angle lens. *Issues & Observation*, 6–9.

DeVries, D. L. and M. W. McCall, Jr. 1976. Performance appraisal: Is it tax time again? Paper presented at a conference at the Center for Creative Leadership, Greensboro, N. C.

DeVries, D. L., A. M. Morrison, S. L. Shullmann, and M. L. Gerlach. 1980. Performance appraisal on the line. Technical Report #16. Greensboro, N.C.: Center for Creative Leadership, December.

Dunnette, M. D. 1966. *Personnel selection and placement.* Belmont, California: Brooks Cole.

Feild, H. S. and W. H. Holley. 1975. Performance appraisal—an analysis of state-wide practices. *Public Personnel Management* 7: 145–50.

Feldman, J. M. 1981. Beyond attribution theory: Cognitive processes in performance appraisal. *Journal of Applied Psychology* 66: 127–48.

Flanagan, J. C. 1954. The critical incident technique. *Psychological Bulletin* 51:327–58.

Friedman, B. A. and E. T. Cornelius. 1976. Effect of rater participation in scale construction on the psychometric characteristics of two rating scale formats. *Journal of Applied Psychology* 61:21–216.

Greller, M. M. 1975. Subordinate participation and reaction to the appraisal interview. *Journal of Applied Psychology* 60:544–49.

Hamilton, D. L. 1979. "A cognitive-attributional analysis of stereotyping." In *Advances in experimental social psychology* (Vol. 12), edited by L. Berkowitz. New York: Academic Press.

Harari, O. and S. Zedeck. 1973. Development of behaviorally anchored scales for the evaluation of faculty teaching. *Journal of Applied Psychology* 58:261–65.

Holley, W. H. and H. S. Feild. 1975. Performance appraisal and the law. *Labor Law Journal* 26:423–30.

Ilgen, D. R. and J. M. Feldman. 1983. "Performance appraisal: A process focus." In *Research in organizational behavior* (Vol. 5), edited by B. Shaw and L. L. Cummings. Greenwich, Conn.: JAI Press.

Ivancevich, J. M. 1972. A longitudinal assessment of management by objectives. *Administrative Science Quarterly* 17:126–38.

Kane, J. S. 1981. Improving the measurement basis of performance appraisal. Paper presented at the annual meeting of the American Psychological Association.

Kane, J. S. and E. E. Lawler. 1980. Performance appraisal effectiveness: Its assessment and determinants. *Research in Organizational Behavior* 1:425–78.

Kay, E., H. H. Meyer, and J. R. P. French, Jr. 1965. Effects of threat in a performance appraisal interview. *Journal of Applied Psychology* 49:311–17.

Landy, F. J. and J. L. Farr. 1980. Performance rating. *Psychological Bulletin* 87(1): 72–107.

Latham, G. P. and K. N. Wexley. 1981. *Increasing productivity through performance appraisal*. Reading, Mass.: Addison-Wesley.

Latham, G. P. and G. A. Yukl. 1975. A review of research on the application of goal setting in organizations. *Academy of Management Journal* 18:824–45.

Lawler, E. E. 1967. The multitrait-multirater approach to measuring managerial job performance. *Journal of Applied Psychology* 51:369–81.

Lawler, E. E. *Pay and organizational effectiveness: A psychological view*. New York: McGraw-Hill.

Lawler, R. I. and W. S. Wikstrom. 1977. *Appraising managerial performance: Current practices and future directions*. Conference Board Rep. No. 723. New York: Conference Board.

Locher, A. H. and K. S. Teel. 1977. Performance appraisal—a survey of current practices. *Personnel Journal* 56:245–47, 254.

Locke, E. A., K. N. Shaw, L. M. Saari, and G. P. Latham. 1981. Goal setting and task performance: 1969–1980. *Psychological Bulletin* 90:125–52.

Lorsch, J. W. and J. J. Morse. 1974. *Organizations and their members: A contingency approach*. New York: Harper & Row.

Maier, N. R. F. 1958. *The appraisal interview: Objectives, methods, and skills*. London: Wiley.

McCall, M. W., Jr., A. M. Morrison, and R. L. Hannan. 1978. Studies of managerial work: Results and methods. Tech. Rep. No. 9. Greensboro, N.C.: Center for Creative Leadership.

McGregor, D. 1957. An uneasy look at performance appraisal. *Harvard Business Review* 35(3): 89–94.

Meyer, H. H. 1976. Format for a constructive annual performance review discussion. In D. L. DeVries and M. W. McCall, Jr. (coordinators), Managerial performance feedback: Appraisals and alternatives. Paper presented at the Center for Creative Leadership, Greensboro, N.C., January.

Meyer, H. H. and E. A. Kay. 1964. Comparison of a work planning program with the annual performance appraisal interview approach. Behavioral Research Report No. ESR 17, General Electric Company.

Meyer, H. H., E. A. Kay, and J. R. P. French, Jr. 1963. Split roles in performance appraisal. *Harvard Business Review* 43:123–29.

Mintzberg, H. 1973. *The nature of managerial work*. New York: Harper & Row.

Nagle, B. F. Criterion development. *Personnel Psychology* 6:271–88.

Nemeroff, W. F. and K. N. Wexley. 1977. Relationships between performance appraisal interview outcomes by supervisors and subordinates. Paper presented at the annual meeting of the Academy of Management, Orlando, Florida.

Porter, L. W., E. E. Lawler, and J. R. Hackman. 1975. *Behavior in organizations*. New York: McGraw-Hill.

Renwick, P. A. and E. E. Lawler. 1978. What you really want from your job. *Psychology Today*, May, 53–58, 60, 62, 65, 118.

Rice, B. 1985. Performance review: The job nobody likes. *Psychology Today*, Sept., 30–36.

Royal Commission on Corporate Concentration. 1976. Personnel administration in large and middle-sized businesses. Study No. 25:61. Ottawa: November.

Schneier, C. E. 1977. Operational utility and psychometric characteristics of behavioral expectation scales: A cognitive reinterpretation. *Journal of Applied Psychology* 62:541–48.

Schwab, D. P., H. Heneman, and T. A. DeCotiis. 1975. Behaviorally anchored rating scales: A review of the literature. Academy of Management Proceedings, 222–24.

Schwind, H. F. 1978. The development and evaluation of a new performance appraisal and training evaluation instrument: The behavior description index. Unpublished Ph.D. dissertation, The University of British Columbia, Vancouver.

Schwind, H. F. 1980. Obstacles to effective performance appraisal systems. Paper presented at the Atlantic Schools of Business Conference, Sydney, Nova Scotia, October.

Smith, H. P. and P. J. Brouwer. 1977. *Performance appraisal and human development.* Reading, Mass.: Addison-Wesley.

Smith, P. C. and L. M. Kendall. 1963. Retranslation of expectations: An approach to the construction of unambiguous anchors for rating scales. *Journal of Applied Psychology* 47:149–55.

Stone, T. H. and E. A. Slusher. 1975. Attributional insights into performance appraisal. JSAS Catalog of Selected Documents in Psychology, MS #964, 5:253.

Thompson, P. H. and G. W. Dalton. 1970. Performance appraisal: Managers beware. *Harvard Business Review* (Jan.–Feb.): 149–57.

Wherry, R. J. 1952. *The control of bias in rating: A theory of rating.* Washington, D.C.: Department of the Army, Personnel Research Section.

Wherry, R. J. 1957. The past and future of criterion evaluation. *Personnel Psychology* 10:1–5.

Winstanley, W. B. 1972. Performance appraisal: Another pollution problem? Conference Board Report.

Yankelovich, D. 1978. The new work psychology. *Review* (August): 27–29, 60–64.

Yankelovich, D. 1979. Yankelovich on today's workers: We need new motivational tools. *Industry Week*, Aug. 6, 61–65, 68.

16. Some Neglected Variables in Research on Discrimination in Appraisals

Robert L. Dipboye, Rice University

Any discussion of discrimination should begin with the reality that major segments of American society are economically disadvantaged. Women occupy lower status jobs than men and are paid less than men occupying similar jobs. Also, black, Hispanic, physically handicapped, and older persons must contend with discrimination that places them at an economic disadvantage. There are several factors that contribute to this problem. The present paper is concerned with one potential barrier to the upward mobility of women and minorities, unfair discrimination in performance appraisals.

Recent analyses of court cases indicate that courts are carefully scrutinizing the appraisal systems of organizations as sources of unfair discrimination (Cascio and Bernardin 1981; Feild and Holley 1982). Furthermore, field research on discrimination in appraisals has shown that performance appraisal systems are vulnerable to claims of unfair discrimination. Kraiger and Ford (1983), in a meta-analysis of forty-nine published and unpublished field studies with a cumulated

Source: *Academy of Management Review*, 1985, Vol. 10, No. 1, 116–127. Reprinted by permission.

N of 13,706, found a correlation between race of the employee and performance ratings of .192. Their findings indicate a small but consistent tendency for white employees to receive higher ratings than black employees. Cleveland and Landy (1981) found that older employees received lower ratings than young employees on appraisals of self-development and interpersonal skills. In contrast to the research on race and age, the published field research on sex bias has shown that female employees are rated the same (Cascio and Phillips 1979; Dreher 1981; Elmore and LaPointe 1974, 1975; Harris 1975; Moses and Boehm 1975; Pulakos and Wexley 1983; Wexley and Pulakos 1982) or higher (Mobley 1982) than male employees. Nevertheless, Fernandez (1981) recently found in a national survey that female managers tend to believe that they are discriminated against in the appraisal of their performance.

The findings of field research show that unfair discrimination is at least a potential problem in the appraisal systems of many organizations. It is impossible, however, to determine from the findings of the typical field study whether differences (or lack of differences) in the appraisals of blacks and whites, men and women, and the young and old reflect the biases (or lack of biases) of the rater or a myriad of factors that are confounded with sex, race, and age. Because of the difficulties involved in interpreting field data, some researchers have taken the phenomenon of unfair discrimination into the laboratory. Much of this research is guided by a cognitive framework, which here is called the stereotype-fit model of discrimination. The essential aspect of this model is that appraisals reflect the rater's perceptions of the fit of the ratee to the perceived requirements or stereotype of the job. Reflecting the idea that discrimination is primarily a cognitive bias, the typical experiment places the rater in the role of a passive-observer who evaluates the ratee solely on the basis of information provided by the experimenter.

The many laboratory experiments on the topic appear not to have contributed significantly to the understanding and elimination of unfair discrimination in performance appraisals. This author's thesis is that this research is limited by an overdependence on the stereotype-fit model and passive-observer research methods.

THE STEREOTYPE–FIT MODEL

Raters possess a variety of cognitive structures, including implicit theories, schemata, and prototypes. A stereotype is a particular type of implicit theory consisting of the characteristics that raters attribute to a category of persons. According to the stereotype-fit model, which is depicted in Exhibit 16-1, raters tend to attribute to an individual ratee characteristics consistent with their stereotype of persons similar to the ratee. In like manner, raters tend to attribute to a particular position requirements that are consistent with their stereotype of successful occupants of the position. For instance, some jobs are considered man's work requiring masculine characteristics whereas other jobs are considered woman's work requiring feminine characteristics (Krefting and Berger 1979). The current incumbents in the job and other characteristics of the context make salient particular stereotypes of the ratee (1 in Exhibit 16-1) and the job (2 in Exhibit 16-1). For example, there is some evidence that raters are more likely to describe female ratees with stereotypic female traits when there are more female ratees in a situation than when there is an equal number of male and female ratees (Heilman 1980). Similarly, raters may be more likely to stereotype a job as a man's job or a woman's job depending on the proportion of men and women currently in the job. The expectations that raters hold for the ratee's performance in a job depend on the extent to which the stereotype of persons similar to the ratee is perceived to fit the stereotype of the ideal job incumbent (3 and 4 in Exhibit 16-1). Furthermore, the stereotypes of the ratee guide the raters' encoding and retrieval of information on the ratee's performance (7 in Exhibit 16-1) so that information consistent with these stereotypes is more likely to be noticed and recalled than information that is inconsistent with these expectations (Feldman 1981). Raters then compare the behaviour and accomplishments of the ratee to the stereotype of the ideal incumbent and form an opinion of that ratee's fit to the job (8 in Exhibit 16-1). The stereotype-fit model predicts that raters evaluate a ratee's performance favourably to the extent that their perceptions of the individual ratee fit their stereotype of the

SOME NEGLECTED VARIABLES   213

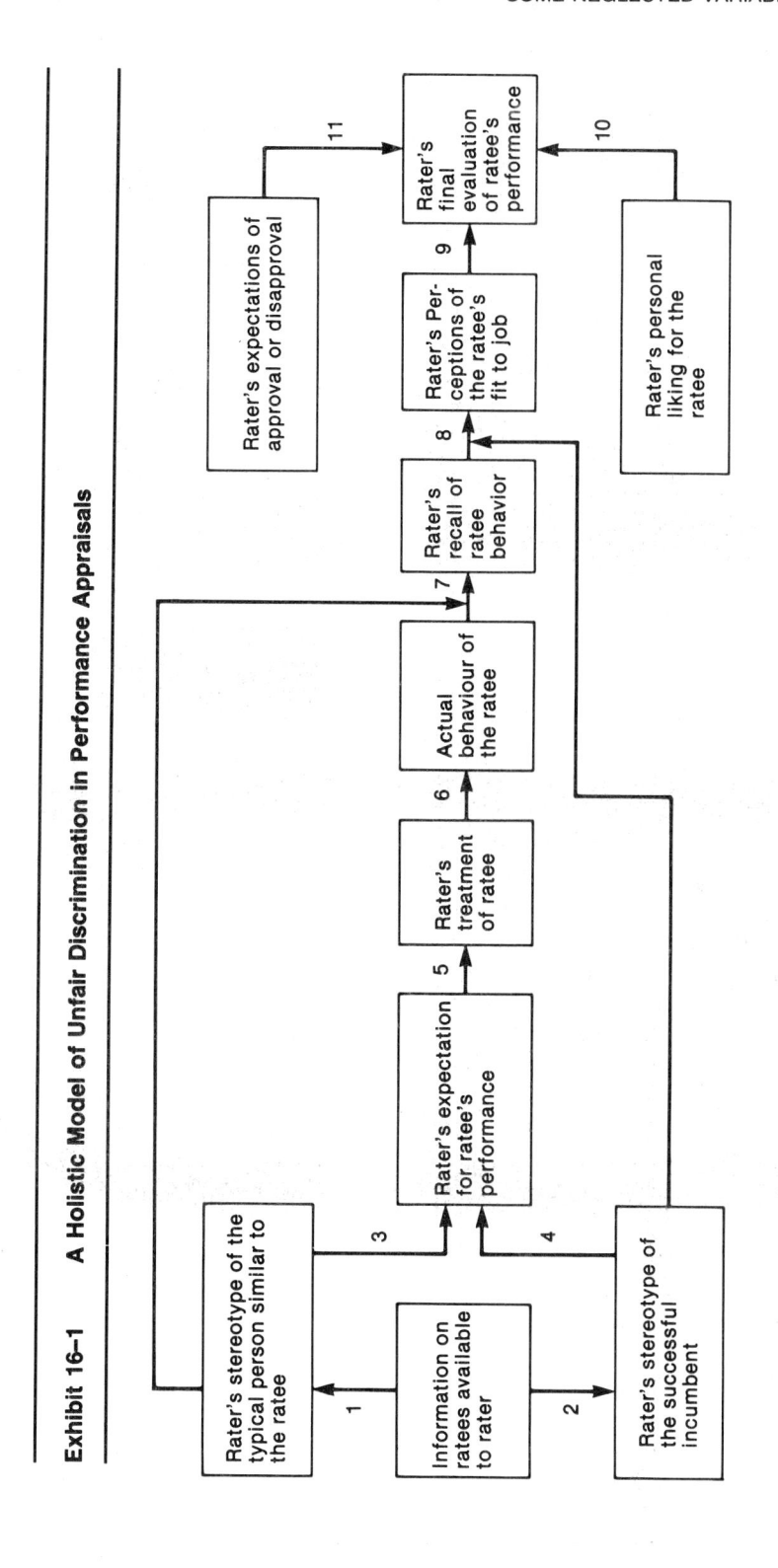

Exhibit 16–1   A Holistic Model of Unfair Discrimination in Performance Appraisals

job (9 in Exhibit 16–1). Thus, raters who discriminate unfairly against a ratee do so for what they believe to be rational reasons, that is, the ratee lacks the requisite characteristics.

PREVIOUS LABORATORY RESEARCH

The Passive-Observer Procedure

Underlying the stereotype-fit model is the assumption that unfair discrimination results primarily from biases in the individual rater's processing of information on the ratee. Consistent with this assumption, a typical passive observer study presents a hypothetical ratee in the form of paper credentials or a videotaped performance to raters under instructions to assume the role of evaluator of the ratee. The effects of variations in the characteristics of the ratee such as age, sex and race, on appraisals of the ratee's performance are assessed, either holding constant or independently varying objective performance. Unfair discrimination is operationally defined as different evaluations given to ratees with the same objective performance.

Passive-Observer Research on Ratee Race, Sex, and Age

The few experiments examining race effects have yielded inconsistent findings, with some studies showing bias against blacks (Hamner, Kim, Baird, and Bigoness 1974), others reporting slight biases in favour of blacks (Bigoness 1976), and still other studies showing no differences in the ratings as a function of race (Hall and Hall 1976; Maruyama and Miller 1980). Yarkin, Town, and Wallston (1982) found that college students rated successful black performers as less able and more motivated than successful white performers. Brugnoli, Campion, and Basen (1979) found that black performers were rated lower than white performers on global performance scales but the same as whites on specific behavioural dimensions. In their meta-analysis of the research on race effects, Kraiger and Ford (1983) found a mean correlation of .032 between race of the ratee and appraisal in an analysis of ten laboratory studies containing a total N of 992. There was a large amount of variation around this mean, however, with the 95 percent confidence interval ranging from –.25 to .32.

The research on ratee sex has yielded findings as mixed as the race research (Nieva and Gutek 1980). Bias against female ratees has been found in ratings of the quality of their essays (Cline, Holmes, and Werner 1977; Goldberg 1968; Isaacs 1981; Toder 1980), how well they relate to customers and other employees (Cohen and Leavengood 1978; Rosen and Jerdee 1974), the skill with which they shelve library books (Schmitt and Lappin 1980), and their contributions to a group discussion (Taylor and Falcone 1982). Bias against females also has been shown in causal attributions of their performance (Deaux and Emswiller 1974; Garland and Price 1977). Finally, several studies have found bias against women who act out of role by being directive (Haccoun, Haccoun, and Sallay 1978; Rosen and Jerdee 1973; Wiley and Eskilson 1982) or aggressive (Costrich, Feinstein, Kidder, Maracek, and Pascale 1975).

Despite the evidence of bias against women, a substantial number of investigators have found no differences in the ratings of men and women (Frank and Drucker 1977; Hall and Hall 1976; Heilman and Guzzo 1978; London and Stumpf

1983; Penley and Hawkins 1980; Rose and Stone 1978; Stumpf and London 1981) or have found that higher evaluations are given to women (Bigoness 1976; Hammer et al. 1974; Norton, Gustafson, and Foster 1977). To complicate the picture further, several studies have found that women are rated as highly as, or higher than, men when they both exhibit high levels of performance and less favourably than men when they both exhibit mediocre or poor levels of performance (Abramson, Goldberg, Greenberg, and Abramson 1978; Jacobson and Effertz 1974; Madden and Martin 1979; Pheterson, Kiesler, and Goldberg 1971). Also, Rosen and Jerdee (1975) and Mai-Dalton, Feldman-Summers, and Mitchell (1979) have found that females who act out of role by behaving aggressively are evaluated more favourably than those who comply with conventional sex role stereotypes.

The few laboratory experiments on age have yielded more consistent findings than either the research on sex or race bias. These studies have found that older ratees are typically rated less favourably than younger employees (Rosen and Jerdee 1976, 1979; Rosen, Jerdee, and Lunn 1981). Schwab and Heneman (1978) have found that bias against older raters is more likely to occur among older than among younger raters.

Limitations of Passive-Observer Research

In summary, the laboratory research on race and sex bias is quite inconsistent in showing bias against blacks and women, and even when bias is found, the effects typically are small. Indeed, if one accepts the findings of laboratory research as accurate estimates of the extent of the problem, a logical conclusion is that there is little reason for concern that women, minorities, and the older employee are unfairly discriminated against in performance appraisals. Such a conclusion is unwarranted. Not only is the laboratory an inappropriate setting for determining the prevalence and strength with which a phenomenon occurs in the field, but some doubts exist as to the internal and external validity of this research.

The most frequently mentioned problem is that the findings of laboratory research using college students are not generalizable to experienced raters. Even those laboratory experiments using experienced raters, however, often rely on too few stimuli to allow generalization of findings, and they inappropriately treat stimuli as a fixed effect rather than as a random effect in statistical analyses (Fontenelle, Peek, and Lane 1983). Past research has given little attention to the possible moderating effects of the task on evaluations of performance, despite the findings of several studies that task type is an important moderator of the effects of ratee sex on appraisals (Cohen, Bunker and Burton 1978; Deaux and Emswiller 1974; Isaacs 1981). Another problem is that investigators continue to use analysis of variance to make group comparisons and ignore the considerable differences that exist among raters in their attitudes and stereotypes (Madden 1981). Finally, many laboratory experiments on unfair discrimination appear transparent and laden with demand characteristics (Newman and Krzystofiak 1979).

The aforementioned problems are potentially serious flaws that researchers should take into account in future laboratory experiments. More fundamental than these methodological frailties, however, is the rather limited conceptualization of unfair discrimination underlying laboratory research. Although there is little reason to doubt that stereotypes are important determinants of unfair discrimination, there are behavioural, affective, and social determinants of discrimination as well (Allport 1954; Fromkin and Sherwood 1974). For research on unfair discrimination in appraisals to yield findings that are both theoretically important and useful, researchers must take a more holistic view of the determinants of discrimination.

TOWARD A HOLISTIC MODEL

The holistic model of discrimination presented in Exhibit 16-1 represents an initial attempt to broaden the view of discrimination in appraisals by incorporating the behavioural, affective, and social determinants of discrimination within the stereotype-fit model. According to the model, the rater's personal feelings enter into the appraisal process and influence evaluations independently of perceived fit to the job requirements (10 in Exhibit 16-1). Also, raters are not passive observers but interact with the ratee and influence the performance of the ratee (5 and 6 in Exhibit 16-1). Finally, raters in organizations occupy social roles, and their evaluations reflect a compliance to expectations communicated by other persons in the organization as much, if not more, than they reflect the private beliefs of the rater (11 in Exhibit 16-1). Corresponding to the emotional, behavioural, and social determinants of appraisals, respectively, bias in the appraisal of employees occurs in the form of personal disliking for the ratee, self-fulfilling prophecies, and conformity to social pressures. Moreover, raters experience ambivalence in their evaluations of ratees to the extent that there are inconsistencies among the affective, cognitive, behavioural, and social components.

Biased Appraisal as Personal Disliking

As indicated earlier, underlying passive-observer research and the stereotype-fit model are the implicit assumptions that discrimination in appraisals is relatively free of affect and has the semblence of rationality. In contrast to this view of the appraisal situation, rater and ratee typically interact face-to-face, and in the process of interacting they form relationships that vary in intimacy and attachment. As stated in Exhibit 16-1(10), raters can be biased in their appraisals of a ratee simply because they dislike the ratee, independent of more objective information on the ratee's performance (Cardy 1982; Dobbins 1982; Keenan 1977; Smith, Meadows, and Sisk 1970). A face-to-face interaction seems likely to evoke stronger liking or disliking for a ratee, however, than is likely to occur in passive-observer research because of the larger number of auditory and visual cues (Shapiro 1966; Washburn and Hakel 1973) and the greater motivational pressures on raters in realistic appraisal situations. For example, raters can find their self-esteem threatened by a high performing female (Grube, Kleinhesselink, and Kearney 1982), can feel embarrassed and tense in the presence of a physically handicapped person (Kleck 1966), can fear and distrust ratees of different nationalities and skin color (Allport 1954), and can feel angered and frustrated over the anticipated failure of a minority ratee (Kipnis, Silverman, and Copeland 1973).

In contrast to the wide range of emotions that raters experience in face-to-face interactions, raters are unlikely to react with much emotion to the pale and bloodless evaluation tasks performed in most passive-observer studies. Consequently, biases emerge in face-to-face interactions that remain dormant when raters are relegated to the role of passive observers. Some evidence of this was reported by Hagen and Kahn (1975), who found that male subjects were more attracted to a competent female than to an incompetent female when they merely observed her performance than when they interacted with her. Also, they were more attracted to both competent and incompetent females when they observed them than when they competed against them.

Biased Appraisal as Self-fulfilling Prophecy

The stereotype-fit model and passive-observer research is well described by Neisser who, in criticizing social cognition research, noted that it deals with "an essentially passive onlooker, who sees someone do something (or sees two people do something) and then makes a judgment about it. He (this is the generic passive he) doesn't do anything—doesn't mix it up with the folks he's watching, never tests his judgments in action or in interaction. He just watches and makes judgments" (1980, 602). Raters in most realistic appraisal situations obviously interact with those they evaluate, and biases against a minority, female, older, or handicapped ratee often are manifested in the behaviour of the rater toward that ratee. Consequently, unlike the passive-observer situation, the rater is a potential cause of the ratee's performance in most organizational appraisals. In some cases, the appraisals of a ratee are the consequence of self-fulfilling prophecies. For example, raters expect a ratee to perform poorly; this expectation leads them to treat the ratee in a biased manner (5 in Exhibit 16–1); this biased treatment evokes ratee performances confirming the original expectations of the rater (6 in Exhibit 16–1). Thus, unfair discrimination in appraisals in this case result largely from unfair treatment of the ratee.

There are several ways in which rater treatment of the ratee can mediate self-fulfilling prophecies in the appraisal process. Raters typically gather information rather than simply receive information, and previous research has shown that information gathering often is biased in the direction of confirming the information gatherer's expectations (Snyder 1981). Additionally, most raters supervise the ratee, and biases in supervision have been shown to mediate self-fulfilling prophecies (Eden and Ravid 1982; Eden and Shani 1982). The extent to which such self-fulfilling prophecies occur in the supervision of black, female, handicapped, or older employees has not been fully documented. Nevertheless, white male managers have been found to treat white male subordinates as the in-group (Fernandez, 1981) and to employ referent and expert power more frequently in managing them (Ayers-Nachamkin, Cann, Reed, and Horne 1982; Kipnis et al. 1973; Richards and Jaffee 1972; Rosen and Jerdee 1977) than they do with black and female subordinates. Furthermore, Eden and Shani (1982) and Eden and Ravid (1982) found that military trainees who were falsely described to their instructors as highly competent actually performed better than trainees in a control group for whom there was no information. Apparently mediating the effects of instructor expectations and trainee performance, instructors treated the competent trainees with more support and consideration (Eden and Shani 1982), and the competent trainees felt more self-confident and overrewarded (Eden and Ravid 1982). A logical extension from these findings is that low expectations for minority, women, handicapped, and older subordinates lead to inconsiderate supervision from the rater and, consequently, to low self-esteem, feelings of under-reward inequity, and poor performance in the ratee.

A third category of behaviour mediating self-fulfilling prophecies is the nonverbal, paralinguistic, and verbal behaviour that accompanies a particular style of supervision and may unintentionally leak the attitudes of the supervisor. Kleck and his associates (Kleck, Ono, and Hastorf 1966) have shown that subjects exhibit more motoric inhibitions and terminate interactions sooner with persons confined to a wheelchair than they do with physically normal persons. Both Word, Zanna, and Cooper (1974) and Weitz (1972) found that white interviewers displayed more negative nonverbal behaviour with black interviewees than with white interviewees. Word et al. (1974) also found that the negative nonverbal behaviours exhibited by the white interviewers (low eye contact, backward lean, physical distance) appeared to have a detrimental effect on the interview performance of the black interviewees. Although they suggest possible mediators of self-fulfilling prophecies, the interpretation of these effects and the extent to which they generalize to appraisal contexts are still undetermined.

Biased Appraisal as Conformity to Social Pressures

Another assumption that seems to underly the stereotype-fit model and passive-observer research is that unfair discrimination is based on the private beliefs of the individual decision maker. With the possible exception of experimental demand characteristics, social pressures are given little opportunity to influence appraisals in the typical passive-observer study. In organizational appraisals, however, evaluations are conducted by occupants of organizational roles. The frequency and severity with which raters discriminate unfairly are influenced by a variety of social pressures, including the formal policies of the organization and the expectations of subordinates, clients, and managers.

Past research has shown that the evaluations of individual ratees are influenced by the sex and race of the other ratees (Schmitt and Hill 1977; Toder 1980). Kraiger and Ford (1983) found in a meta-analysis of field research that bias against blacks declined as the percentage of black employees in the work group increased. A cognitive interpretation of these context effects is that the sex and race composition of a group of ratees serves as informational cues that make salient stereotypes, which, in turn, bias the evaluation of particular ratees (1 and 2 in Exhibit 16–1). The social context in a realistic appraisal situation, however, consists of more than informational cues. It also consists of interacting persons, who are actively communicating their expectations to the rater and reinforcing and punishing the rater for complying or failing to comply with these expectations. Moreover, raters in organizations usually are sensitive to the expectations of others and the disapproval that violations of these expectations incur. Consequently, biased appraisals often reflect the conformity of raters to organizational norms in addition to, or instead of, the personal prejudices of raters (10 in Exhibit 16–1).

Quinn, Tabor, and Gordon (1968) provided some evidence of the powerful influence of social pressures on discrimination in appraisals in a 1968 study of anti-Semitism. They found that social pressures to discriminate against Jewish employees could lead even those managers who were relatively egalitarian in their private views to discriminate against

Jewish employees in evaluations of promotability. Of those managers in their sample who expressed a low level of anti-Semitism and who believed that no third parties would be upset by the hiring or promotion of a Jew, fifteen percent were inclined to discriminate against Jews in promotion decisions. Of those managers who believed that two or more third parties would feel uncomfortable with the hiring or promotion of a Jew, fifty-six percent said they would discriminate against Jews in promotions. Perceived pressures from third parties also appeared to amplify the bias of those who were already anti-Semitic in their private beliefs. Of the anti-Semitic managers, fifty-three percent said they would discriminate against Jews if they believed that no third party would feel uncomfortable, but seventy-seven percent were inclined to discriminate if they believed two or more third parties would feel uncomfortable. Similarly, Bowman, Worthy, and Greyson (1965) found that the reluctance of managers to promote women to supervisory roles was largely the result of anticipated resistance by coworkers.

The Ambivalent Rater

Unfair discrimination in appraisals is manifested in more ways in realistic appraisals than in the artificial circumstances of most passive-observer studies. This is not to suggest, however, that rampant prejudice is the typical state of affairs and that the primary problem with passive-observer research is that it has failed to capture this bias. With increasing legal and social prescriptions against unfair discrimination, raging bigotry probably is far less common among raters in organizations today than is ambivalence. A primary problem with passive-observer research is that it fails to capture this ambivalence.

Katz and Glass (1979) use the term ambivalence in its psychodynamic sense to refer to conflicts between a person's self-image as fair and unprejudiced and feelings of aversion for a disadvantaged person that threaten this self-conception. Ambivalence is used more broadly here to refer to instability in the behaviour and attitudes of raters resulting from inconsistencies among the cognitive, behavioural, social, and affective determinants of their appraisals. For instance, the personal feelings of raters regarding the ratee can conflict with their cognitive appraisals of the ratee's qualifications, as is the case in male supervisors who recognize that a female employee's assertiveness meets the requirements of the job but, nevertheless, personally dislike her for her assertiveness. Ambivalence also might result when the stereotypes and feelings of raters conflict with the policies of the organization, as happens in managers who are convinced that women are unqualified for managerial jobs but who must comply with the formal equal opportunity policy of the organization.

According to Katz and Glass's theory of ambivalence, subjects evaluate a good performance more favourably and a poor performance less favourably to the extent that they are ambivalent in their feelings for the ratee. The effects of rater ambivalence appear moderated by the extent to which there are socially desirable excuses available to raters for their actions. Several experiments have shown that subjects are biased in favour of minority persons when actions against them are likely to appear prejudiced. When there are socially desirable excuses for discriminating against them, however, subjects openly discriminated against these minority persons (Gaertner and Dovidio 1977; Katz and Glass 1979; Rogers and Prentice-Dunn 1981; Snyder, Kleck, Strenta, and Mentzer 1979). In addition to showing instability in their ratings and treatment of a minority person, raters who are ambivalent toward minority persons may find it particularly difficult to give them negative feedback on their performance. For instance, Feild and Holley (1977) found that the poorer the performance rating given by white supervisors to black subordinates, the less likely the supervisors were to tell them about this appraisal. On the other hand, the poorer the performance of white subordinates, the more likely they were to give them the feedback. Similarly, Hastorf, Northcraft, and Picciotto (1979) found in a laboratory simulation that supervisors were more likely to give unrealistically favourable performance feedback to handicapped subordinates than to normal subordinates. At this time one can only speculate as to the antecedents and consequences of rater ambivalence in organizational contexts, but enough evidence exists to suggest that unfair discrimination in performance appraisals is more complex and subtle than is indicated by the stereotype-fit model and passive-observer research.

Implications for Practice and Research

One obvious implication of the holistic model is that field research is needed that goes beyond the simple group comparisons dominating past field studies and explores the behavioural, cognitive, social, and emotional factors in Exhibit 16-1. Although the focus of attention in this paper is on the frailties of laboratory research, it is not the laboratory per se that is the problem but the passive nature of the procedures used in this research. Passive-observer research appears poorly suited for capturing the affective, behavioural, and social components of unfair discrimination and the ambivalence associated with these components. Rather than simply replacing paper-people with videotaped stimuli, laboratory researchers must end their dependence on passive-observer procedures and investigate face-to-face interactions between raters and ratees.

A practical implication of the model is that the particular intervention one chooses to eliminate unfair discrimination in a situation should depend on the relative influence of the affective, social, behavioural, and cognitive factors in that situation. If faulty stereotypes are indeed the cause, then one might train raters to think with more complexity about ratees (Gardiner 1972) or provide relevant information on the ratee to counteract these stereotypes (Locksley, Borgida, Brekke, and Hepburn 1980). One also might focus the attention of raters on job relevant information through the use of behaviourally based rating scales (Brugnoli and Campion 1979) and instructions to avoid biases in using these scales (Latham and Wexley 1981), although these two approaches appear somewhat ineffective in improving the accuracy of ratings (Bernardin and Buckley 1981; Schwab, Heneman, and DeCotiis 1975). If discrimination is rooted in the personal needs and feelings of raters, then cognitive approaches such as these may be ineffective, and one may need to make raters aware of their own prejudice (Bass, Cascio, McPherson, and Tragash 1976; Rokeach 1971) and provide them with self-insight into its causes (Katz, McClintock, and Sarnoff 1957).

Biases in the evaluations of performance resulting from biased treatment of the ratee may require training to improve the skill and sensitivity with which raters communicate verbally and nonverbally with female, minority, handicapped, and older employees. Such social skills training appears effective in clinical (Waxer 1979) and classroom (Wolfgang 1979) settings and may prove useful as a component of supervisory training. Intercultural training, in which the supervisor is instructed in the norms of the subordinate group (Mitchell and Foa 1969), also may prove effective in eliminating biases in the supervision of subordinates. Finally, to the extent that unfair discrimination results from social pressures, management needs to counteract these pressures by clearly communicating equal opportunity policies and by rewarding raters for compliance. Quinn et al. (1968) found that even managers with strongly anti-Semitic views were unlikely to discriminate against Jews if they believed that higher management supported equal opportunity.

In conclusion, appraisals in organizations have multiple determinants, and the most effective attempts to understand and reduce unfair discrimination are likely to be holistic. Laboratory research on unfair discrimination in appraisals is likely to make a much more significant theoretical and practical contribution if raters are viewed not only as information processors, but as occupants of social roles, whose feelings and behaviours influence the appraisal process.

References

Abramsom, P. E., P. A. Goldberg, J. H. Greenberg, and U. M. Abramson. 1978. The talking platypus phenomenon: Competency ratings as a function of sex and professional status. *Psychology of Women Quarterly* 2: 114–24.

Allport, G. W. 1954. *The nature of prejudice.* Reading, MA: Addison-Wesley.

Ayers-Nachamkin, B., C. H. Cann, R. Reed, and A. Horne. 1982. Sex and ethnic differences in the use of power. *Journal of Applied Psychology* 67:464–72.

Bass, B. M., W. F. Cascio, J. W. McPherson, and H. J. Tragash. 1976. Prosper-training and research for increasing management awareness of affirmative action in race relations. *Academy of Management Journal* 19:353–69.

Bernardin, H. J. and M. R. Buckley. 1981. Strategies in rater-training. *Academy of Management Review* 6:205–12.

Bigoness, W. J. 1976. Effect of applicant's sex, race, and performance on employers' performance ratings: Some additional findings. *Journal of Applied Psychology* 61:80–84.

Bowman, G. W., N. B. Worthy, and S. A. Greyson. 1965. Problems in review: Are women executives people? *Harvard Business Review* 43(4): 52–67.

Brugnoli, G. A., J. E. Campion, and J. A. Basen. 1979. Racial bias in the use of work samples for personnel selection. *Journal of Applied Psychology* 64:119–23.

Cardy, R. L. 1982. *The effect of affect in performance appraisal.* Unpublished doctoral dissertation, Virginia Polytechnic Institute and State University.

Cascio, W. F. and H. J. Bernardin. 1981. Implications of performance appraisal litigation for personnel decisions. *Personnel Psychology* 34:211–26.

Cascio, W. F. and N. F. Phillips. 1979. Performance testing: A rose among thorns? *Personnel Psychology* 32:751–66.

Cleveland, J. N. and F. J. Landy. 1981. The influence of rater and ratee age on two performance judgments. *Personnel Psychology* 34:19–29.

Cline, M. E., D. S. Holmes, and J. C. Werner. 1977. Evaluations of the work of men and women as a function of the sex of the judge and type of work. *Journal of Applied Social Psychology* 7:89–93.

Cohen, S. L. and S. Leavengood. 1978. The utility of the WAMS: Shouldn't it relate to discriminatory behavior. *Academy of Management Journal* 21:742–48.

Cohen, S. L., K. A. Bunker, A. L. Burton, and P. D. McManus. 1978. Reactions of male subordinates to the sex-role congruency of immediate supervision. *Sex Roles* 4:297–311.

Costrich, N., J. Feinstein, L. Kidder, J. Maracek, and L. Pascale. 1975. When stereotypes hurt: Three studies of penalties for sex-role reversals. *Journal of Experimental Social Psychology* 11:520–30.

Deaux, K. and T. Emswiller. 1974. Explanations of successful performance on sex linked tasks: What is skill for the male is luck for the female. *Journal of Personality & Social Psychology* 29:80–85.

Dobbins, G. H. 1982. *The effect of leader performance and leader likableness upon ratings of leader behavior.* Unpublished master's thesis. Virginia Polytechnic Institute and State University.

Dreher, G. F. 1981. Predicting the salary satisfaction of exempt employees. *Personnel Psychology* 34:579–89.

Eden, D. and G. Ravid. 1982. Pygmalion versus self-expectancy: Effects of instructor- and self-expectancy on trainee performance. *Organizational Behavior and Human Performance.* 30:351–64.

Eden, D. and A. Shani. 1982. Pygmalion goes to boot camp: Expectancy, leadership, and trainee performance. *Journal of Applied Psychology* 67:194–99.

Elmore, P. B. and K. A. LaPointe. 1974. Effects of teacher sex and student sex on the evaluation of college instructors. *Journal of Educational Psychology.* 66:386–89.

Elmore, P. B. and K. A. LaPointe. 1975. Effect of teacher sex, student sex, and teacher warmth on the evaluation of college instructors. *Journal of Educational Psychology* 67:368–74.

Feild, H. S., and W. H. Holley. 1977. Subordinates' characteristics, supervisors' ratings, and decisions to discuss appraisal results. *Academy of Management Journal* 20:315–21.

Feild, H. S. and W. H. Holley. 1982. The relationship of performance appraisal system characteristics to verdicts in selected employment discrimination cases. *Academy of Management Journal* 25:392–406.

Feldman, J. M. 1981. Beyond attribution theory: Cognitive processes in performance appraisal. *Journal of Applied Psychology* 66:127–48.

Fernandez, J. P. 1981. *Racism and sexism in corporations.* Lexington, KY: Toronto.

Fontenelle, G., A. Peek, and D. Lane. 1983. Generalizing across stimuli as well as subjects. Unpublished manuscript, Rice University.

Frank, F. D. and J. Drucker. 1977. The influence of evaluatee's sex on evaluations of a response on a managerial selection instrument. *Sex Roles* 3:59–64.

Fromkin, H. L. and J. Sherwood, eds. 1974. *Integrating the organization.* New York: Free Press.

Gaertner, S. L. and J. R. Dovidio. 1977. The subtlety of white racism, arousal, and helping behavior. *Journal of Personality and Social Psychology* 35:691–707.

Gardiner, G. S. 1972. Complexity training and prejudice reduction. *Journal of Applied Social Psychology* 2:326–42.

Garland, H. and K. H. Price. 1977. Attitudes toward women in management and attributions for their success and failure in managerial positions. *Journal of Applied Psychology* 62:29–33.

Goldberg, P. A. 1968. Are women prejudiced against women? *Trans-Action* 5(5): 28–30.

Grube, J. W., R. R. Kleinhesselink, and K. A. Kearney. 1982. Male self-acceptance and attraction toward women. *Personality and Social Psychology Bulletin* 8:107–12.

Haccoun, D. M., R. R. Haccoun, and G. Sallay. 1978. Sex differences in the appropriateness of supervisory styles: A nonmanagement view. *Journal of Applied Psychology* 63:124–27.

Hagen, R. L. and A. Kahn. 1975. Discrimination against competent women. *Journal of Applied Social Psychology* 5:362–76.

Hall, F. S. and D. T. Hall. 1976. Effects of job incumbents' race and sex on evaluations of managerial performance. *Academy of Management Journal* 19:476–81.

Hamner, W. C., J. S. Kim, L. Baird, and W. J. Bigoness. 1974. Race and sex as determinants of ratings by potential employers in a simulated work sampling task. *Journal of Applied Psychology* 59:705–11.

Harris, M. 1975. Sex role stereotypes and teacher evaluations. *Journal of Educational Psychology* 67:751–56.

Hastorf, A. H., G. B. Northcraft, and S. R. Picciotto. 1979. Helping the handicapped: How realistic is the performance feedback received by the physically handicapped? *Personality and Social Psychology Bulletin* 5:373–76.

Heilman, M. E. 1980. The impact of situational factors on personnel decisions concerning women: Varying the sex composition of the applicant pool. *Organizational Behavior and Human Performance* 26:386–95.

Heilman, M. E. and R. A. Guzzo. 1978. The perceived cause of work success as a mediator of sex discrimination in organizations. *Organizational Behavior and Human Performance* 21:346–57.

Isaacs, M. B. 1981. Sex role stereotyping and the evaluation of the performance of women: Changing trends. *Psychology of Women Quarterly* 6:187–95.

Jacobson, M. B. and J. Effertz. 1974. Sex roles and leadership perceptions of the leaders and the led. *Organizational Behavior and Human Performance* 12:383–96.

Katz, I. and D. C. Glass. 1979. "An ambivalence-amplification theory of behavior toward the stigmatized." In *The social psychology of intergroup relations*, edited by W. G. Austin and S. Worchel, 55–70. Monterey, CA: Brooks/Cole.

Katz, D., C. McClintock, and D. Sarnoff. 1957. The measurement of ego defense as related to attitude change. *Journal of Personality* 25:465–74.

Keenan, A. 1977. Some relationships between interviewers' personal feelings about candidates and their general evaluations of them. *Journal of Occupational Psychology* 50:275–83.

Kipnis, D., A. Silverman, and C. Copeland. 1973. Effects of emotional arousal on the use of supervised coercion with black union employees. *Journal of Applied Psychology* 57:38–44.

Kleck, R. E. 1966. Emotional arousal in interactions with stigmatized persons. *Psychological Reports* 19:12–26.

Kleck, R., H. Ono, and A. H. Hastorf. 1966. The effects of physical deviance upon face-to-face interaction. *Human Relations* 19:425–36.

Kraiger, K. and J. K. Ford. 1983. A meta-analysis of ratee race effects in performance ratings. Paper presented at the American Psychological Association, Anaheim, California.

Krefting, L. A. and P. K. Berger. 1979. Masculinity-feminine perceptions of job requirements and their relationship to job-sex stereotypes. *Journal of Vocational Behavior* 15:164–174.

Latham, G. P. and K. N. Wexley. 1981. *Increasing productivity through performance appraisal.* Reading, MA: Addison-Wesley.

Locksley, A., E. Borgida, N. Brekke, and C. Hepburn. 1980. Sex stereotypes and social judgments. *Journal of Personality and Social Psychology* 39:821–31.

London, M. and S. A. Stumpf. 1983. Effects of candidate characteristics on management promotion decisions: An experimental study, *Personnel Psychology* 36:241–59.

Madden, J. M. 1981. Using policy-capturing to measure attitudes in organizational diagnosis. *Personnel Psychology* 34:341–50.

Madden, J. M. and E. Martin. 1979. An indirect method of attitude measurement. *Bulletin of the Psychonomic Society* 13:170–72.

Mai-Dalton, R. R., S. Feldman-Summers, and T. R. Mitchell. 1979. Effects of employee gender and behavioral style on the evaluations of male and female banking executives. *Journal of Applied Psychology* 64:221–26.

Maruyama, G. and N. Miller. 1980. Physical attractiveness, race, and essay evaluation. *Personality and Social Psychology Bulletin* 6:384–90.

Mitchell, T. R. and U. G. Foa. 1969. Diffusion of the effect of cultural training of the leader in the structure of heterocultural task groups. *Australian Journal of Psychology* 21(1): 31–43.

Mobley, W. H. 1982. Supervisor and employee race and sex effects on performance appraisals: A field study of adverse impact and generalizability. *Academy of Management Journal* 25:598–606.

Moses, J. L. and V. Boehm. 1975. Relationship of assessment center performance to management progress of women. *Journal of Applied Psychology* 60:527–29.

Neisser, V. 1980. On "social knowing." *Personality and Social Psychology Bulletin* 6:601–605.

Newman, J. and F. Krzystofiak. 1979. Self-reports versus unobtrusive measures: Balancing method variance and ethical concerns in employment discrimination research. *Journal of Applied Psychology* 64:82–85.

Nieva, V. F. and B. A. Gutek. 1980. Sex effects on evaluation. *Academy of Management Review* 5:267–76.

Norton, S. D., D. P. Gustafson and C. E. Foster. 1977. Assessment for management potential: Scale design and development, training effects and rater/ratee sex effects. *Academy of Management Journal* 20:117–131.

Penley, L. E. and B. L. Hawkins. 1980. Organizational communication, peformance, and job satisfaction as a function of ethnicity and sex. *Journal of Vocational Behavior* 16:368–84.

Pheterson, G. T., S. B. Kiesler, and P. A. Goldberg. 1971. Evaluation of the performance of women as a function of their sex, achievement, and personal history. *Journal of Personality and Social Psychology* 19:110–14.

Pulakos, E. D. and K. N. Wexley. 1983. The relationship among perceptual similarity, sex, and performance ratings in manager-subordinate dyads. *Academy of Management Journal* 26:129–139.

Quinn, R. P., J. M. Tabor, and L. K. Gordon. 1968. *The decision to discriminate: A study of executive selection.* Ann Arbor, MI: Institute of Survey Research.

Richards, S. A. and C. L. Jaffee. 1972. Blacks supervising whites: A study of interracial difficulties in working together in a simulated organization. *Journal of Applied Psychology* 56:234–41.

Rogers, R. W. and S. Prentice-Dunn. 1981. Deindividuation and anger-mediated interracial aggression: Unmasking regressive racism. *Journal of Personality and Social Psychology* 41:63–73.

Rokeach, M. 1971. Long range experimental modification of values, attitudes, and behavior. *American Psychologist* 26:453–55.

Rose, G. L. and T. H. Stone. 1978. Why good performance may (not) be rewarded: Sex factors and career development. *Journal of Vocational Behavior* 12:197–207.

Rosen, B. and T. H. Jerdee. 1973. The influence of sex role stereotypes on evaluations of male and female supervisory behavior. *Journal of Applied Psychology* 57:44–48.

Rosen, B. and T. H. Jerdee. 1974. Influence of sex-role stereotypes on personnel decisions. *Journal of Applied Psychology* 59:9–14.

Rosen, B. and T. H. Jerdee. 1975. Effects of employee's sex and threatening versus pleading appeals on managerial evaluations of grievances. *Journal of Applied Psychology* 60:442–445.

Rosen, B. and T. H. Jerdee. 1976. The nature of job-related age stereotypes. *Journal of Applied Psychology* 61:180–83.

Rosen, B. and T. H. Jerdee. 1977. Influence of subordinate characteristics on trust and use of participative decision strategies in a management simulation. *Journal of Applied Psychology* 62:628–31.

Rosen, B. and T. H. Jerdee. 1979. Influence of employee age, sex, and job status on managerial recommendations for retirement. *Academy of Management Journal* 22:169–73.

Rosen, B., T. H. Jerdee, and R. O. Lunn. 1981. Effects of performance appraisal format, age, and performance level on retirement decisions. *Journal of Applied Psychology* 66:515–19.

Schmitt, N. and T. E. Hill. 1977. Sex and race composition of assessment center groups as a determinant of peer and assessor ratings. *Journal of Applied Psychology* 62:261–64.

Schmitt, N. and M. Lappin. 1980. Race and sex as determinants of the mean and variance of performance ratings. *Journal of Applied Psychology* 65:428–35.

Schwab, D. P. and H. G. Heneman, III. 1978. Age stereotyping in performance appraisal. *Journal of Applied Psychology* 63:573–78.

Schwab, D. P., H. G. Heneman, III, and J. D. DeCotiis. 1975. Behaviorally anchored rating scales: A review of the literature. *Personnel Psychology* 28:549–62.

Shapiro, J. G. 1966. Agreement between channels of communication in interviews. *Journal of Consulting Psychology* 30:535–38.

Smith R. E., B. L. Meadows, and T. K. Sisk. 1970. Attitude similarity, interpersonal attraction, and evaluative social perception. *Psychonomic Science* 18:226–27.

Synder, M. 1981. "Seek and ye shall find: Testing hypotheses about other people." In *Social cognition: The Ontario symposium on personality and social psychology*, edited by E. T. Higgins, C. P. Herman, and M. P. Zanna. Hillsdale, NJ: Erlbaum.

Synder M. L., R. E. Kleck, A. Strenta, and S. J. Mentzer. 1979. Avoidance of the handicapped: An attributional ambiguity analysis. *Journal of Personality and Social Psychology* 37:2297–2306.

Stumpf, S. A. and M. London. 1981. Capturing rater policies in evaluating candidates for promotion. *Academy of Management Journal* 24:752–66.

Taylor, S. E. and H. T. Falcone. 1982. Cognitive bases of stereotyping: The relationship between categorization and prejudice. *Personality and Social Psychology Bulletin* 8:426–32.

Toder, N. L. 1980. The effect of the sexual composition of a group on discrimination against women and sex-role attitudes. *Psychology of Women Quarterly* 5:292–310.

Washburn, P. V. and M. Hakel. 1973. Visual cues and verbal content as influences on impressions formed after simulated employment interviews. *Journal of Applied Psychology* 58:137–41.

Waxer, P. 1979. "Therapist training in nonverbal behavior: Toward a curriculum." In *Nonverbal behavior: Applications and cultural implications*, edited by A. Wolfgang. Orlando, FL: Academic Press.

Weitz, S. 1972. Attitude, voice, and behavior: A repressed affect model of interracial interaction. *Journal of Personality and Social Psychology* 24:14–21.

Wexley, K. N. and E. D. Pulakos. 1982. Sex effects on performance ratings on manager-subordinate dyads: A field study. *Journal of Applied Psychology* 67:433–39.

Wiley, M. G. and A. Eskilson. 1982. The interaction of sex and power base on perceptions of managerial effectiveness. *Academy of Management Journal* 25:671–77.

Wolfgang, A. 1979. "The teacher and nonverbal behavior in the multicultural classroom." In *Nonverbal behavior: Applications and cultural implications*, edited by A. Wolfgang. New York: Academic Press.

Word, C. O., M. P. Zanna, and J. Cooper. 1974. The nonverbal mediation of self-fulfilling prophecies in interracial interaction. *Journal of Experimental Social Psychology* 10:109–20.

Yarkin, K. L., J. P. Town, and B. S. Wallston. 1982. Blacks and women must try harder: Stimulus persons' race and sex attributions of causality. *Personality and Social Psychology Bulletin* 8:21–24.

17. Key Issues in Designing Compensation Systems

Roland Thériault, Université de Montréal

INTRODUCTION

One of the most important functions work organizations perform for their members is to offer them many possibilities for satisfying a whole range of human needs. Whether in the form of opportunities for using their knowledge and skills, or opportunities for challenge, personal development, recognition, and security, or opportunities for satisfying various physiological needs, the work organization, by virtue of the array of rewards at its command, constitutes a meaningful, potentially satisfying action environment for its members. However, as high in reward potential as the organization may be, it also may be an important source of frustration.

The list of components that could be included in the organization's reward system is a relatively long one: the intrinsic nature of the work, the responsibilities to be assumed, recognition by colleagues, salary, promotions, challenges to be taken on, titles, social benefits, job security, participation in decision making, special privileges, and so on (Lawler 1977; Beer et al. 1984; Von Glinow 1985). The systems required to manage each one of these reward components, as well as their possible consequences, could easily be the subject of an entire chapter. However, in view of the space limitations, the text which follows will deal only with a single reward system component, *compensation*, focusing specifically on the management of compensation systems.

Although compensation is an important concern to managers, the technical complexities involved often prompt them to shunt the task of compensation management to human resources specialists. As managers, their preoccupations in compensation matters are often narrowly focused on the costs involved. Inevitably, in times of crisis or austerity, given the importance of labour costs as a component of overall production costs, the reactions of managers are often limited to cost-reduction techniques such as cutting pay raises, freezing wages, and eliminating bonuses (Frank 1984).

As a partial response to this form of tunnel vision, this chapter offers a broad overview of compensation management approaches, with particular attention to the principal underlying concepts and the possible consequences flowing from the ways in which these management tools are used. Discussion in this chapter is not addressed to the one-minute manager (Blanchard and Johnson 1982) or to those in search of quick fix solutions.

Schematically the major facets of the compensation design process may be illustrated as in Exhibit 17–1.

Each of the facets will be discussed in the following sections of this chapter.

THE GOALS OF THE COMPENSATION

The many and varied compensation systems designed and implemented for work organizations have a number of underlying objectives (Belcher 1974; Thériault 1983; Milkovich and Newman 1984). Typically, these goals are of three broad types: attracting the desired quality of personnel in sufficient numbers, maintaining a certain degree of manpower stability, and stimulating employee performance. Although objectives such as these represent imposing challenges to management, they can hardly be said to exhaust the list of goals which organizations try to achieve through the reward system. In fact, there are as many different formulations for these goals as there are employers. Moreover, in some highly diversified organizations, the objectives being pursued by the reward system may even vary from one unit to another (Salscheider 1981; Chakravarthy and Zajac 1984; Milkovich 1983).

By virtue of their impacts on the nature and design of programs, determining what the organization's goals are to be regarding compensation represents a critically important strategic decision. As in most areas of endeavour, it is not possible to do everything—choices must be made, priorities must be established. In one case, the organization may wish to encourage innovation while also recognizing exceptional employee contributions, in another case, the organization is primarily concerned with maintaining its competitive position in the labour market. Similarly, one organization might do its best to foster the development of a genuine esprit de corps among employees, while another clearly tries to promote a spirit of competitiveness among its organizational units. From these few examples, it is evident that not only can the organization's compensation goals be multiple, but they can also be conflictual, in the sense that achieving one may prevent the realization of another.

At times, coordination in the area of personnel and human resources (P/H.R.) management is so poor that it actually appears as if the right hand has no idea what the left hand is doing. For example, an organization anxious to recruit employees who are risk-takers and innovators may nonetheless have compensation practices designed to achieve quite another objective, such as protecting the firm's competitive edge in bidding for qualified personnel. Another form of incongruity can be seen in the case of the firm that gives high priority to attaining its long-term goals, but actually operates with compensation practices geared more to rewarding employee performance in the short-term.

A survey conducted recently brought to light many of the difficulties that can arise when formulating goals related to compensation (Gosselin and Thériault 1985). P/H.R. vice-presidents from medium-size firms and large corporations, participating in a workshop on managerial compensation, were asked their opinions concerning a lengthy list of possible compensation-related objectives. Specifically, for each objective on the list, they were asked to indicate (1) the relative importance given to that goal by their own organization, and (2) the relative importance they felt *should be* given to each. Next, participants were presented with a list of potential problems relating to compensation and asked to rank-order them in terms of their importance in their own organization.

The following schema (Exhibit 17-2) summarizes the results of that survey. Recognition of individual performance heads the list of objectives. Not only is recognition believed to be the most important goal actually pursued, but it is felt that this goal *should be* the most important. Moreover, the list of goals actually pursued corresponds to that which has traditionally been associated with business organizations and that which has been conveyed by textbooks in compensation management (Belcher 1974; Nash and Carroll 1975; Henderson 1979). However, since the beginning of the 1980s business competition has gotten stiffer and problems with productivity are mounting. Considering the goals the organization *should* pursue, the results of this survey suggest that senior human re-

Exhibit 17-1   Major Facets of the Compensation Design Process

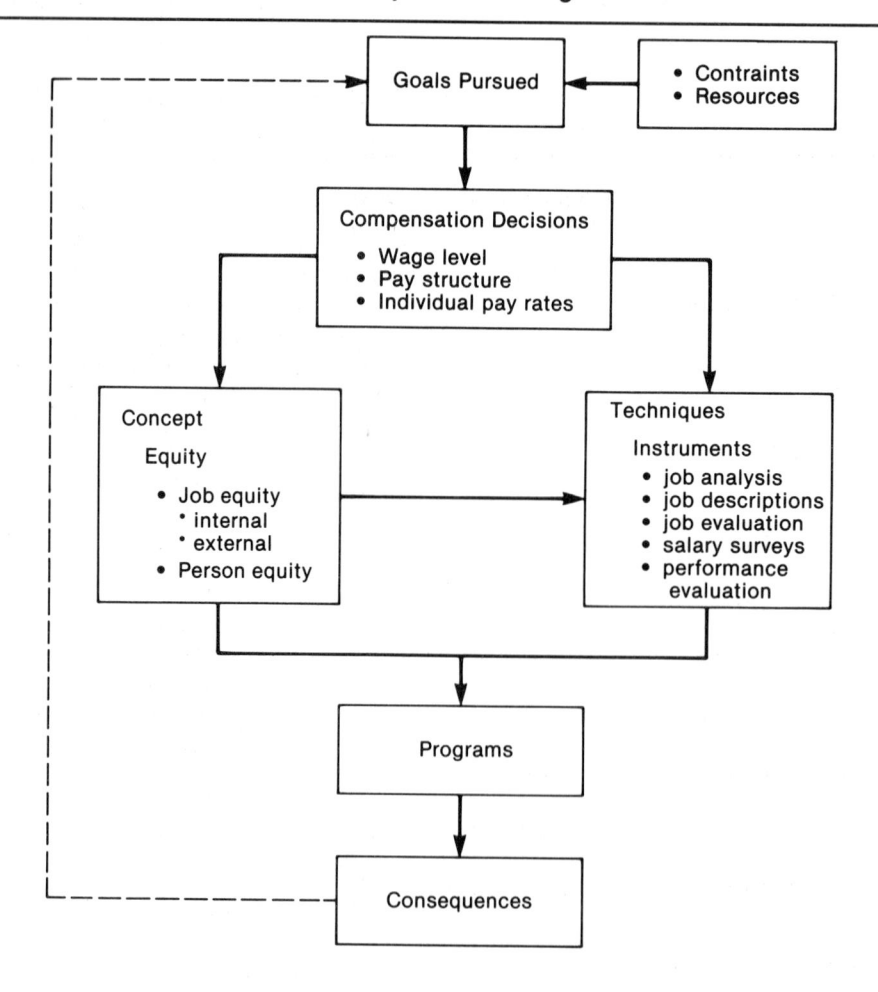

```
                    ┌──────────────┐      • Contraints
         ┌─────────▶│ Goals Pursued│◀───  • Resources
         │          └──────┬───────┘
         │                 │
         │                 ▼
         │       ┌────────────────────┐
         │       │Compensation Decisions│
         │       │ • Wage level        │
         │       │ • Pay structure     │
         │       │ • Individual pay rates│
         │       └──┬──────────────┬──┘
         │          │              │
         │          ▼              ▼
         │   ┌──────────┐    ┌──────────────┐
         │   │ Concept  │    │ Techniques   │
         │   │ Equity   │    │ Instruments  │
         │   │ • Job equity│─▶│ • job analysis│
         │   │   • internal│  │ • job descriptions│
         │   │   • external│  │ • job evaluation│
         │   │ • Person equity│ │ • salary surveys│
         │   │          │    │ • performance│
         │   │          │    │   evaluation │
         │   └────┬─────┘    └──────┬───────┘
         │        │                 │
         │        └────────┬────────┘
         │                 ▼
         │          ┌──────────┐
         │          │ Programs │
         │          └─────┬────┘
         │                ▼
         │          ┌─────────────┐
         └──────────│ Consequences│
                    └─────────────┘
```

sources managers are quite conscious of the changes taking place. However, it also appears that these changes in managers' thinking have not as yet made themselves felt in day-to-day compensation practices. Given the discrepancy between what exists and what is desired, we can hardly be surprised at the kinds of problems work organizations are experiencing in managing their compensation programs.

A similar study involving United States compensation managers raised a similar issue: Managers' close involvement with employee issues may cause them to value employee concerns more highly than basic organizational concerns (Freedman, Montanari and Keller 1982).

THE NATURE OF COMPENSATION DECISIONS

As a general rule, the formulation of objectives, in addition to providing a basis for controlling existing practices, serves first and foremost as a guide for action. This is no less true where compensation programs are concerned. However, in addition to the guidance provided by these objectives, decisions concerning the nature and form of the organization's diverse compensation programs must take

Exhibit 17–2 Actual Compensation Goals, Preferred Goals, and Problems Relating to Compensation Management

Goals Actually Pursued	Rank-ordered by a Sample of VP's for Human Resources Goals that Should be Pursued	Problems Experienced
1. Individual performance	1. Individual performance	1. Does not favour attainment of strategic objectives
2. Attract competent managers	2. Recognize exceptional contributions	2. Does not develop the organizational culture
3. Remain competitive	3. Stimulate innovation	3. Weak relationship between compensation and performance
4. Reinforce norms and values	4. Remain competitive	4. Compensation insufficient to motivate performance
5. Attain short-term goals	5. Assure internal coherence	5. Fails to take fiscal legislation into account
6. Assure internal coherence	6. Favour implementation of strategies	6. Does not stimulate productivity increases
7. Favour implementation of strategies	7. Attain long-term goals	7. Emphasizes quantity over quality
8. Recognize exceptional contributions	8. Attract competent managers	8. Does not favour implementation of strategies
9. Pay equity	9. Attain short-term goals	9. Does not encourage innovation
10. Stimulate innovation	10. Job satisfaction	10. Does not recognize exceptional contributions

into account a certain number of considerations.

Apart from determining the content of the social benefits program and deciding what part it will play in the overall compensation package, there are three basic decisions the organization must make with respect to compensation: (1) what wage level it can offer, (2) how the pay structure will look like, for example how pay will be distributed among the different occupational categories (job clusters or job families), and (3) how much will individual employees be paid.

Wage Level

The organization's wage level can have a more or less marked impact on its profitability, depending upon the sector of activity in which it operates, since the proportion of total operating costs taken up by the pay component varies enormously from one sector to another. For example, in a store belonging to a large supermarket chain, wages and salaries may account for only ten percent of operating costs, whereas they may account for sixty percent or more of a service organization's costs of operation. This might seem to suggest, a priori, that compensation management is more critical to the profitability of organizations in the latter sector than it is to those in the former. This is not necessarily the case. Indeed, in some sectors, flexibility is almost nonexistent. For example, in supermarket chain stores, because costs not related to pay are virtually immutable, a deviation of plus or minus two percent from the ten percent norm can mean the difference between a profitable and an unprofitable operation.

In addition to economic sector variable, there are other factors the organization must consider when determining its wage levels. These factors have to do as much with the characteristics of the organization itself as with the characteristics of the operating environment.

As for the environment, factors such as geographic location, fiscal and labour standards legislation, the degree of union strength, and the supply-and-demand situation with respect to categories of personnel all combine to influence the degree of flexibility an organization enjoys when setting rates of pay for its jobs (Mahoney 1979; Wallace and Fay 1981). Although these factors do not, by any means, constitute totally inflexible constraints, they do impinge in important ways on employer decisions, notably when the firm decides where to set up operations. Moreover, these factors evolve over time. A case in point: the changes that have been occurring in recent years in Alberta and on Quebec's North Shore, where significant alterations in the economic climate have stifled pressures for growth in wage levels of the businesses in those regions (Booth 1984).

Organizations' characteristics also have a vital role to play in determining the funds that can be made available for compensation. Among the most critical of these are the organization's size, its short-term and medium-term ability to pay, and the ease or difficulty it has in recruiting and holding competent personnel. Employers may also be influenced in decisions about the size of the compensation budget by such factors as prestige (for example, they want to be seen as a company that pays well) or habit (they have always paid well) (Nash and Carroll 1975; Thériault 1983).

By way of illustration, consider organization size. All other things being equal, the larger the organization, the higher the wage level it will have to set. This is no doubt due, at least partly, to the existence in large organizations of greater numbers of hierarchical levels and to the pay differentials which must be maintained among them. The size of the organization also determines, to a considerable extent, the availability of financial resources and the prestige the employer commands in the labour market, and these, in turn, influence the rates of pay it establishes for its employees (Lester 1967; Ingham 1970).

The Pay Structure

A second key component of the compensation program is its pay structure, which establishes a hierarchical ordering of pay rates for the organization's repertory of jobs.

In designing the pay structure, three considerations are particularly crucial: (1) the differential requirements (job specifications) associated with each job and the worth of that job to the organization, (2) the pay structure prevailing in the labour market for different jobs, and (3) the degree of incentive the organization wants to build into the compensation system in order to encourage employees towards upward mobility. Although these considerations will be discussed separately, each one should be regarded as inextricably linked to the other two.

The diverse jobs within any given organization differ, to one degree or another, in the kinds and levels of skills and knowledge required to perform them, just as they may have different requirements with respect to mental or physical effort. Different jobs may also involve very different responsibilities (financial, technical, and human), or they may be performed in surroundings which are more or less favourable in terms of noise levels, temperature, risk of accidents, and the like. Therefore, to the extent that an organization wishes to assure itself a stable supply of qualified manpower, it will have to make certain that its pay structure reflects these differentials in job requirements (Thériault 1983; Milkovich and Newman 1984).

This is not to suggest that the relationship between job requirements and pay levels is necessarily a linear one. In some cases, jobs having the same level of requirements do not have the same power to attract job applicants. This may simply be due to the fact that people are drawn more to some activities than to others (Bergmann 1974). An example of this can be seen in the differential success rates which various university faculties have in recruiting personnel—some just seem to attract more candidates than others. In a context such as this, the going rates of pay in the marketplace come to play a significant role in the employer's deliberations concerning the pay structure.

For a number of years, the use of the labour market as a criterion in setting pay is debated (Livernash 1980; Treiman and Hartmann 1981; Remick 1984). The controversy revolves, in part, around the fact that pay rates in the marketplace do not reflect manpower supply-and-demand alone; they also reflect pay discrimination which exists with regard to certain groups in society. Thus, the argument suggests that by allowing the marketplace to regulate pay rates, it encourages organizations to perpetuate discrimination. Obviously, a problem of this magnitude and complexity does not lend itself to easy solutions.

The third major consideration is the degree to which the organization incorporates monetary incentives into its pay structure. Since some jobs are by nature more demanding than others, and must be filled by relatively more qualified employees, the compensation system must allow for financial and other kinds of incentives to encourage those employees to seek the more demanding positions. Understandably, if the organization fails to provide such incentives, it could experience serious difficulty in filling its upper echelon positions. Certain norms have been developed that can assist employers in knowing when to expect trouble in this regard. For example, it has been clearly demonstrated that whenever the pay differential between a foreman or a clerical supervisor and his or her highest paid subordinate is less than ten to fifteen percent, the employer will have a serious problem keeping foremen and clerical supervisors on the payroll (Mahoney 1979). Similarly, at the very top of the ladder in a large corporation, the minimum differential should be on the order of fifty percent or more.

Three important qualifiers should be made regarding the use of monetary incentives. First, the determination of pay differentials cannot be made without taking into account the differentials in job requirements existing at different hierarchical levels. Since it is well known that some organizations are more hierarchical than others (of the same size), it is obvious that the norms mentioned earlier cannot be applied blindly. Second, differentials built into the pay structure cannot be established without taking into account opportunities for promotion. If such opportunities are restricted, monetary incentives to climb the job ladder can only generate frustration (Thériault 1983). Third, within every organization, it is crucial that a clear distinction be drawn between the pay structure for management personnel (i.e., line) and professional and technical employees (i.e., staff). An organization that subordinates the pay structure for its professionals to the management pay structure runs a high risk of losing the better part of its professional staff. In recent years, a number of employers seem to have recognized this fact, so that it is now possible for professionals and technical employees to better their status and pay position while continuing to work in their chosen fields. No longer is it necessary for them to leave their fields in favour of management jobs in order to obtain worthwhile improvements in compensation. Furthermore, it is no longer rare to see cases where professionals are earnings as much, if not more, than their bosses.

Setting Individual Pay Rates

The third category of decision the employer must make in the compensation area involves the setting of pay rates for individual employees. To do this, the employer must decide whether to take into consideration the characteristics of individual jobholders, and, if so, it must then determine which characteristics will figure in the decision and how. With the exception of jobs in certain skilled trades (e.g., plumbing and carpentry), recognizing certain personal characteristics is a fairly common practice (Thériault 1983; Milkovich and Newman 1984). Attributes such as length of service and level of performance constitute important criteria in setting pay rates. And, in certain cases, variables such as the employee's potential and his or her negotiating skills and leverage also play a role in determining compensation outcomes (Dyer, Schwab and Thériault 1976; Dyer and Thériault 1976; Thériault and Payette 1981).

It goes without saying that seniority with the organization, or sometimes seniority in the job, is a sacred cow as far as unions are concerned. The seniority principle has also come to be an important decision factor in setting pay for nonunionized (managerial or nonmanagerial) employees as well, regardless of formal disclaimers by top management (Thériault and Dyer 1977; Thériault and Payette 1981). The relevance of this factor can be explained in several ways. First, rewarding seniority is a way for the employer to give formal recognition to the experience acquired by the employer. It thus assumes that there is a maturity curve and that the senior employees contribute more to the organization. Second, it may be seen as a way for the employer to recognize someone's past performance. Finally, another possible explanation of the seniority principle in setting pay is that it is a way to give formal recognition to an employee's years of devoted service to the organization.

The particular meaning given to the seniority criterion has implications for the pay-setting process. For example, when the criterion is intended as a mechanism for recognizing acquired experience, the wisest course of action would be to avoid awarding pay increases at regular time intervals, since the acquisition of experience tends not to progress according to such regular intervals. On the contrary, the learning process more closely resembles a hyperbolic function than a forty-five degree angle. In other words, once the employee has gone beyond the initial break-in period of intense learning, longer and longer periods of time are normally needed to acquire equivalent increments of experience. Beyond a certain point, there may be a ceiling on the amount of further experience that can be accumulated. Moreover, learning curves do not unfold independently of the learning possibilities inherent in the job itself or the aptitudes and attitudes of the individual jobholder. Therefore, whenever pay increases based on seniority are intended to reward experience, they ought to be awarded at a fairly rapid pace in the beginning, subsequently tapering off to longer and longer intervals between raises, until a ceiling is attained. Ideally, the number of years required to reach the ceiling for each job should take into account the amount of learning required by that job relative to others. (For more details, see Thériault 1983; Milkovich and Newman 1984).

In contrast, when seniority increases are used to acknowledge length of service, common sense suggests that such increases be granted at fixed time intervals and, possibly, for an unlimited span of years.

In reality, it is often difficult to understand the logic underlying the pay structures of many organizations. Indeed, it is common practice for employers to distribute seniority increases at fixed intervals (once a year) for a fixed time period (e.g., seven years, ten years, or more), and to do so more or less universally, regardless of the nature of the jobs involved.

Another highly pertinent criterion used in setting individual pay rates, which is being invoked with increasing frequency, is that of individual performance. If the seniority principle is sacred in union circles, the performance criterion is virtually so in management circles (at least at the level of formal policy). In practice, however, the situation is riddled with ambiguity. From what has been said by some (Meyer 1975; Mickalachki 1976), one could say that in North America merit pay is one of the greatest myths there is in the compensation field. However, more realistic views have usually been expressed (Thériault 1983; Heneman 1984).

Finally, some brief observations should be made regarding two other criteria which play a role in fixing individual pay rates: the employee's potential and the individuals' negotiating leverage.

Individual potential, as measured by the employee's particular knowledge and skills, can have an effect on the pay level at the initial hiring. However, whether or not this potential ultimately translates into long-term benefits for the employee depends on what happens after hiring: this potential had better make itself felt in performance terms rapidly if the employee hopes to benefit monetarily in relation to colleagues.

There is another formula for monetarily rewarding potential which has been in vogue for some years, notably in the manufacturing sector and involving mainly unskilled workers. According to this formula, an employee is no longer compensated in terms of the specific job performed at a given point in time, but rather in terms of the number of different jobs he or she has mastered over time. The greater the number of different jobs mastered, the higher the compensation. This strategy can claim a number of salutary side effects, most notably the fact that it encourages employees to develop their skills, counteracts monotony, and introduces a degree of flexibility into the way that jobs can be allocated. (For examples see the Topeka plant of General Foods in Lawler 1978).

It is sometimes said that individuals (not only organizations) have negotiating power that can be used to affect their pay rate, either at hiring time or during the pay revision process (Tarrant 1976). As a practical matter, however, this factor is rarely operative for a number of reasons. On the one hand, in order to bargain effectively, one has to have something to bargain with—that is, the individual must possess certain qualities and capabilities which are in short supply and in great demand, which is rare. In addition, the compensation policies of the organization must be such that they can deal effectively with these unique cases, and this is also rare.

CONCEPT AND TECHNIQUES

The Equity Concept

In the compensation context, equity, which is usually defined as a form of justice, consists of rewarding all parties in accordance with their contributions and in a manner which takes into account the rewards given to others for similar contributions (Adams 1965; Carrell and Dittrich 1978; Cosier and Dalton 1983). This definition raises several important points. First, what is meant by contribution? A contribution may be defined, in general terms, as those attributes the individual brings to the organization and those acts performed on behalf of the organization. Contributions may take two forms: (1) those which are required by the nature of the job and the performance context (job equity), and (2) the attributes of employees themselves (employee equity) (Milkovich and Newman 1984).

Second, the concept of equity requires that certain comparisons be made in order to evaluate the fairness of a specific act of compensation. Since rewards for contributions differ in nature and substance from the contributions themselves, assessments of fairness must use other people and the rewards they receive as the point of reference. In other words, for an employee to determine whether he or she is being compensated fairly, will usually depend on comparisons he or she is making with other employees in the same or similar situation. These referent persons may work for the same employer or for another (Goodman 1974; Beatty and Rhyne 1977). In the former case, the comparison involves internal equity, the latter involves external equity (Belcher 1974).

Third, in the definition used here, the numerator of the reward/compensation ratio includes only tangible forms of compensation. In practice, of course, employees receive more than financial rewards for their contributions; they may also receive job security, prestige, a sense of accomplishment, and so on. For this reason, the design of compensation programs must also take into account intangible forms of rewards (Belcher 1974; Thériault 1977).

Finally, and perhaps most important, the concept of equity is essentially a cognitive, subjective phenomenon—what is equitable for one person may not be equitable for another. Moreover, a particular contribution may be perceived as valuable by one person but not by another, just as people may disagree as to the value of a given reward or the appropriateness of the referents used to assess fairness (Thériault 1977).

Internal Job Equity

Internal job equity consists of determining the work requirements associated with each of the organization's jobs so that compensation can be commensurate with the demands of the work being performed. In order to determine what these job requirements are, the content of each job must first be identified and described in a precise and clear manner.

Developing the data required to achieve internal job equity requires three types of operations: (1) job analysis, (2) job description, and (3) job evaluation. A brief description of each of these operations follows.

Job Analysis. Simply stated, job analysis is a process by which data is compiled relative to each job in the organization, with a view toward identifying the various job components and the characteristics required of each job's incumbent. The components of job content may include the tasks, activities and responsibilities required in the performance of the work (McCormick 1979).

There exist a number of procedures and techniques for collecting job data, such as observation of the work being performed, administration of questionnaires, and interviews with workers or their supervisors (Thériault 1983; Milkovich and Newman 1984). As a practical matter, however, the observation technique, because of the constraints associated with it (e.g., the impossibility of recording mental tasks or tasks requiring long periods of time to complete) is reserved almost exclusively for the analysis of production jobs (Thériault 1983). As a general rule information gathered through observation is supplemented by questionnaire and interview data (Wortman and Sperling 1975).

Questionnaires used for job analysis purposes are usually of the open or unstructured variety. Unstructured questionnaires offer the twin advantages of flexibility and adaptability to virtually any type of job. However, one drawback to the use of questionnaires is the possibility that respondents will give different meanings to certain terms (e.g., supervise, direct, control, plan). Another disadvantage is that motivation and skill in dealing with questionnaires vary from one respondent to another (Thériault 1983). In light of this, job analysists often feel that the interview is the technique of choice, despite the fact that the interview process can be a time-consuming and onerous one (Wortman and Sperling 1975). It is common practice in job analysis to use the questionnaire and interview methods in tandem, thereby maximizing the strengths and offsetting the weaknesses of each.

Job analysis may be carried out by one of the organization's own analysts or by an external consultant whenever its own resources are insufficient to the task.

Job data may be collected from jobholders themselves, from their immediate supervisors, or from both. Although it might seem, a priori, that using supervisors as informants would cut down on the time needed to compile information, studies have shown that supervisors are rarely able to provide complete operational data (Thériault 1983). Including employees themselves in the data-gathering process offers the double advantage of improving the quality of the information developed and increasing the likelihood that employees will identify with and have confidence in the program. For these reasons, job data are nowadays typically collected using the following three-step process: (1) completion of a questionnaire by each employee, (2) interviews with employees, in order to clarify or fill gaps in information, and (3) interviews with each employee's immediate supervisor, in order to validate information given in the first two steps.

Job Descriptions. The information painstakingly gathered during the job analysis phase is eventually recorded in the job description, a document which presents pertinent data on each job surveyed in an easily usable form.

In order to be useful as an information tool, the job description must be complete and explicit. Since the document will be used at some point as a basis for comparing different jobs, it must be, above all, operational. This requirement is a source of considerable difficulty. For example, it is easier to state that a particular employee manages the personnel under his or her direction than it is to specify what managing involves from one supervisory context to another. Indeed, managing subordinates is a responsibility shared by supervisory personnel at many levels of the hierarchy from foreman to chief executive officer. However, while the management components of one job description may include responsibility for hiring and firing, in another case, it may imply only the power to make recommendations to that effect.

A good job description should enable the user to respond in operational terms to the following questions: What does the incumbent do? How does he or she do it? Why is it done? (McCormick 1975).

Finally, it should not be forgotten that organizations are in a sense living tissue. As open systems, they are constantly called upon to evolve, to adapt to ever-changing internal and external challenges which require them to make adjustments and modifications in their objectives, strategies, structures, and jobs. As a result, the content of job descriptions cannot be cast in concrete—they too, should evolve and be modified periodically to keep pace with changing organizational realities. Unfortunately, it is an all too common practice for system designers to create a job description document which responds to a particular set of objectives at a particular point in time. Once the initial objectives are met, the document is often relegated to the archives or to the bottom of someone's drawer. This seems to be a high price to pay for an instrument which ends up simply gathering dust—especially when, for a marginal supplementary investment, if could continue to be useful (Thériault and Payette 1981).

Job Evaluation. Job evaluation can be defined as a process by which the jobs in an organization are ordered hierarchically in terms of their respective requirements, so that pay rates commensurate with those requirements may be set for each job.

Although the definition used here refers to job requirements (job specifications) as an evaluation criterion, it is common for analysts to substitute for this the terms job worth, or job value. Legislation dealing with pay discrimination also uses these latter terms (Niemann 1984). Following the example of certain provinces, federal wage legislation establishes four test criteria for ascertaining the worth of a given job: (1) qualifications of the incumbent (training and experience), (2) effort (physical and mental), (3) responsibilities (financial, technical, human), and (4) job conditions (Canadian Human Rights Act, 1978). Given this usage, the expression requirement would seem to be more appropriate and to the point. Indeed, the term worth seems to refer more precisely to the measurable character of the contributions a particular job makes to organizational performance, contributions which, strictly speaking, relate more to the jobholder than to the job itself. If we wish to avoid the pitfalls of reductionism (basing compensation decisions solely on the outcomes of job evaluation), this distinction is worth making and remembering.

Job evaluation is carried out by using a number of methods which may be grouped into two categories: whole job methods and compensable-factors methods (Henderson 1979). The first of these categories includes, most notably, the ranking and the market-pricing methods. Position classification, factor comparison, and point methods are examples of the compensable-factor approach. Compensable-factor methods, although more complicated to use than the whole job variety, are advantageous mainly because it is usually easier to arrive at a consensus on job requirements. Furthermore, demonstrating compliance with legislative requirements is also a much more straightforward matter when jobs have been evaluated using compensable-factor rather than whole-job methods.

The job evaluation approach most widely used is the point method, which involves essentially the following steps:

— Selecting the factors and evaluation criteria to be used, which entails identifying and defining in operational terms the requirements of each job. (These factors typically focus on the four universal factors embodied in law: qualifications, effort, responsibilities, and job conditions.)

— Determining, for each chosen factor, the number of degrees (different levels of intensity) and their respective meanings

— Indicating the degrees of each factor for each job

— Weighing each factor (distributing a certain number of points among the various factors according to the relative importance of each.)

— Deciding how these points are to be apportioned among the degrees of each evaluation factor. (This distribution is customarily arithmetic.)

— Adding together, for each job, the points obtained on all factors

— Establishing the requisite pay grades (ordering jobs according to equivalencies in their respective requirements, taking into account both the number of points obtained and the subjective character of the judgments involved) (For further details, see Thériault 1983; Milkovich and Newman 1984)

It is worth noting that the mathematics involved in these and other methods can sometimes impart a spurious impression of exactitude or impartiality to the evaluation process. However, despite claims to the contrary by certain compensation specialists, job evaluation is a process which remains essentially subjective, regardless of the method chosen (Treiman 1979).

The task of job evaluation is customarily conducted by specialists. These specialists consult with the immediate supervisors of the employees whose jobs are being evaluated prior to finalizing their evaluations and recommendations. However, given the subjective nature of the evaluation process, together with the importance of feelings about equity in compensation, this approach may appear questionable to some observers (Belcher 1974; Thériault 1983). For this reason, the task of job evaluation is being assigned more and more often to joint committees, where employee representatives sit down with compensation specialists. This appears to be having a salutary effect on the credibility of the entire process.

External Job Equity

Assuring external job equity basically involves compiling as much relevant information as possible about compensation practices prevailing in the labour market with respect to the categories of personnel the organization employs. When an employer's pay rates are, to the extent possible, pegged to the going rate for particular kinds of services rendered, employees tend to feel fairly compensated and the organization improves its ability to bid successfully for the personnel it needs.

The concept of external job equity requires some clarifications. It is important to realize that, as a practical matter, it is impossible to obtain relevant data for all jobs being evaluated. A number of jobs are organization specific and have no satisfactory equivalent in the labour market, for example, hospital nursing jobs. For this reason, the compensation survey must focus on what is called key or benchmark jobs, those jobs which are most likely to exist in the marketplace.

Despite the difficulties involved, if external job equity is to be achieved, equivalencies must be established. So, for each job, the primary task of the analyst is to determine the degree of comparability. The validity of the data depends on it. (For further readings on wage and salary surveys, see Thériault 1983; Milkovich and Newman 1984. For those directly interested in the characteristics of different surveys in Canada, see Compensation Data Sourcebook 1983).

Although data are required on the wages and salaries paid in the marketplace, assessments of comparability must also include other components, such as bonuses, benefits, job security, and promotion opportunities, elements which may vary from one employer to another. Adopting the all other things being equal perspective may have convenience to recommend it, but it does not represent a realistic approach to compensation issues (Thériault 1983; Milkovich and Newman 1984).

Finally, establishing equivalency is further complicated by the fact that the relevant market varies from one occupational category to another. For office workers, it may be sufficient to survey only the city in which the employer operates, while for managerial personnel it may be necessary to broaden the scope to include the region or the province. In certain cases, such as top executives or highly specialized professionals, the relevant market may be national or even international.

In sum, compensation survey is only as good as its data and that, no matter what statistical procedures are used, the interpretation of its findings remains a subjective matter. Moreover, the findings from one or even several surveys are only one of the elements to be considered in the pay-setting process.

Once the findings from the compensation survey and the job evaluation process are in, the organization decides how its compensation dollars are to be spent (i.e., how much and what forms of compensation are to be paid). It is at this stage that the resource and constraint factors mentioned earlier (e.g., ability to pay, manpower stability, ease or difficulty of recruitment) come into play. To the extent that these variables differ in their effects from one personnel category to another, their impact on specific decisions will also vary.

Employee Equity

In the majority of cases, pay rates reflect certain personal characteristics, usually seniority or performance, as suggested before. Individual differences on seniority and performance criteria are customarily recognized by means of pay increase differentials. Recognition for performance may take the form of merit pay, although this is by no means the only approach. Another method uses the bonus system to reward performance (Heneman 1984).

Pay-for-Performance

Of all the compensation issues, pay-for-performance is without a doubt the one which has been, and still is, the most controversial (Meyer 1975, 1976; Lawler 1976; Heneman 1984). The following remarks will briefly comment the facets of this debate.

Pay increases are commonly used to reward employees for performance above and beyond the norm. Performance, however, is not the only criterion that is reflected in a pay increase. Adjustments are sometimes made in recognition of years of service, and factors such as fluctuations in the consumer price index (CPI) and the organization's ability to pay.

Given the various criteria, it is often difficult to identify the specific contribution of each criterion to the overall increase. For example, when the CPI rises by five percent, and when the employer has decided that pay increases may vary between zero and 10 percent, but total wages must not rise above 6.5 percent, the share of the increase attributable to performance is rather meager. Furthermore, given the terms of this formula, one can hardly expect things to be otherwise. Indeed, at revision time, employers must face the fact that, whenever they award a three percent pay hike, they will be living with its cumulative effects for a long time to come, not to mention its implications for costs in social benefit programs (e.g., retirement or insurance).

Another major drawback to the merit pay approach is its lack of flexibility. According to the present formula, when performance improves, pay increases. However, if performance declines, pay does *not* decrease. On the contrary, it often continues to increase, although less rapidly.

The message from this situation is that if organizations wish to reward excellence and extra effort in a meaningful way, they will have to abandon the present pay-for-performance formula in favour of one that will enable them to avoid incongruities and inequities. A more desirable alternative would be the bonus formula, which establishes more direct, explicit links between compensation and individual performance (Thériault 1983; Lawler 1983).

Finally, one should note that, whatever formula is used to reward performance, its efficacy will ultimately depend upon the quality of the performance evaluations on which merit increases are based and on the rigor with which the system is managed. (For further readings on performance evaluations, see Latham and Wexley 1981; Landy and Farr 1983; Bernardin and Beatty 1984.)

CONCLUSION

The purpose of this paper was to identify and discuss some of the key issues that must be considered in designing compensation systems. In particular, the various goals which organizations seek to accomplish through their compensation policies and practices were reviewed. An examination of some of the basic decisions employers must make when designing employee reward systems followed, briefly touching upon issues, such as constraints and resources, which shape the outcomes of these decisions. Finally, a description was made of the design and implementation of compensation programs, with particular emphasis on the key notion of equity. In concluding this paper, a brief review of certain contemporary trends and developments in compensation management in Canada is provided. Much of these trends are based on clinical observations rather than systematic research.

Participation in Productivity Gainsharing Programs

Over the past few years, in order to promote greater employee involvement in their work, a number of employers have set up programs whereby employees, either as individuals or members of work groups, may share in some way, in the gains resulting from improvements in productivity (Brown 1982; Nightingale 1983).

An example of a participatory approach which focuses on the individual rather than the group is the revival of the suggestion box program in a number of companies. Unfortunately, experience has shown that, despite its laudable intentions, this approach is fairly ineffective in increasing employee participation. What typically happens is that, although numerous suggestions are generated at the beginning, the frequency and quality of employee input falls off quite rapidly. Many factors probably account for this: the system is often poorly administered (e.g., response to suggestions are slow in coming), there is no built-in mechanism for fostering esprit de corps among employees, the financial pay-off for the employee is low, etc.

Other organizations have chosen to encourage participation through programs based on work-group or total employee involvement. Generally speaking, the various group-based productivity gainsharing programs (e.g., the Scanlon Plan, the Rucker Group Incentive Plan, Improshare) have had considerably more success than the individual regimes. Although programs of this type differ in several respects (the type and extent of participation required, the incentive mechanisms for encouraging and sustaining participation, the way in which employee shares are computed, etc.), they share a number of important advantages; they encourage the development of esprit de corps, they provide for the formulation of performance targets, and they are profitable for those who participate. On the debit side of the ledger, however, there are some hazards and pitfalls connected with these plans, such as the formulation of objective production standards, the communication by management of potentially sensitive information (i.e., regarding the computation of gains) to its employees, and the acceptance by everyone of the need to modify production standards over time (Brown 1982; Nightingale 1983).

The Declining Importance of Seniority

Until recently, it was a common practice for employers to build automatic seniority increases into the pay structure. Increasingly, this practice is falling into disfavour, as evidenced by the number of organizations which are rethinking their philosophy and redesigning certain aspects of their pay plans. In some cases, the solution has been to reduce the period of time during which an employee is eligible to receive seniority increases. In other cases, the pay plan is redesigned so that such increases are no longer granted automatically. Still other companies have adopted the approach of subtracting from the CPI component of the pay increase an amount equivalent to the seniority component. To illustrate, let us assume that there has been a five percent rise in the CPI and that the company had budgeted a two percent seniority increase. Instead of offering a five percent cost-of-living increase, the company reduces that component by the amount of the seniority increase (two percent). Even if the CPI component is reduced, the company can still keep its employees whole because the combined amount of the increase will still be five percent.

The Growing Importance of Performance

More and more organizations are basing part or all of pay increases on individual performance. This seems to be the trend as much in the public sector as in the private sector (Frank 1984). Where such practices exist, there are growing doubts about the efficacy of the approach. This has prompted stricter controls over the implementation of these programs and serious reviews of existing performance evaluation programs.

The Increasing Use of Bonuses

Recognition of individual performance may take the form of either pay increases or bonuses. More and more employers seem to be leaning toward the latter method of stimulating employee contributions (Frank 1984). Under this system, an employee whose performance is at least satisfactory will benefit from the general pay increase, while those whose performance surpasses the predetermined standards can expect to receive bonuses.

The Growing Relevance of Organizational Performance

As was argued in the discussion on compensation goals, the short-term and long-term performance of the organization itself is coming to be an increasingly crucial determinant in compensation decisions. This is particularly true for policies affecting lower-level managers and top executives. For managers, individual performance in terms of work objectives constitutes only one of the criteria used in computing their bonus payments. Just as important is the organization's ability to realize its short-term and long-term performance targets.

Dual Pay Scales

Because of the difficulties involved in reducing existing levels of pay and benefits, and because of increasing competition for jobs, the past few years have witnessed the negotiation of reductions in many compensation packages and the emergence of a certain parallelism in the personnel structures of affected organizations. In one category we find the existing employees who continue to enjoy work and pay conditions prevailing before the rules of the game were renegotiated. And, in a parallel category, we have those employees hired following the revision who must make do with the terms of a scaled-down compensation package World of Work Report 1984a and 1984b.

This tendency toward the "downsizing" of compensation plans, and the concomitant parallelism in personnel structures, is more typical of organizations where organized labour has had a significant impact on compensation outcomes and where the employer's competitive posture is in danger. Obvious examples of this can be found among the large supermarket chains and the aviation industry.

While this approach may appear to offer an attractive solution in the short run, it promises to pose serious problems for management over the longer haul, particularly concerning the work climate in affected organizations.

Pay Discrimination

The trend is irreversible, as much for private sector employers as for the public sector, top management must make greater efforts to reduce existing levels of wage and salary discrimination (Canadian Human Rights Commission 1984; McDougall 1985; Abella 1985). This will be accomplished by reinforcing existing equal employment opportunity programs, and putting in place new programs designed to enforce more effectively the equal pay for equal work principle enshrined in legislation. Accompanying these affirmative actions will surely be a move toward greater involvement of employee representatives in the job evaluation process, coupled with a trend toward more rigorous scrutiny of compensation structures.

References

Abella, R. S. 1985. Toward employment equity for women. *Canadian Business Review.* (Summer): 7–14.

Adams, J. S. 1965. "Inequity in social exchange." In *Advances in experimental social psychology.* Vol. 2, edited by L. Berkowitz, 267–99. New York, NY: Academic Press, 1965, pp. 267–299.

Beatty, J. R. and G. T. Rhyne. 1977. Evaluating comparison standards of employees regarding equity in employment exchanges. Text presented at the National Convention of the American Psychological Association, San Francisco, August.

Beer et al. 1984. *Managing human assets.* New York, NY: The Free Press.

Belcher, D. 1974. *Compensation administration.* Englewood Cliffs: New Jersey: Prentice Hall.

Bergmann, B. 1974. Occupational segregation, wages, and profits when employers discriminate by race or sex. *Eastern Economic Journal* (April/July): 103–10.

Bernardin, H. J. and R. W. Beatty. 1984. *Performance appraisal: Assessing human behavior at work.* Boston, Mass.: Kent Publishing Co.

Blanchard, K. and S. Johnson. 1982. *The one minute manager.* New York, NY: William Morrow and Co.

Booth, P. L. 1984. Compensation planning outlook: Historical supplement to special report no. 3. Ottawa: Compensation Research Centre, Conference Board of Canada, Nov. 19.

Brown, H., ed. 1982. *Profit sharing: An innovation approach to effective management.* Don Mills, Ontario: Profit Sharing Council of Canada.

Canadian Human Rights Act. 1978. Equal wages guidelines. *Canada Gazette*, Part II, vol. 112, no. 18, (September 27).

Canadian Human Rights Commission. 1984. Cases of wage disparities 1978–1984. Ottawa.

Carrell, M. R. and J. E. Ditrich. 1978. Equity theory: The recent literature, methodological considerations, and new directions. *Academy of Management Review* 3:202–10.

Chakravarthy, B. S. and E. J. Zajac. 1984. Tailoring incentive systems to a strategic context. *Planning Review* 12(6): 30–35.

Compensation Data Sourcebook. 1983. Compensation Research Centre. The Conference Board in Canada, Ottawa.

Cosier, R. A. and D. R. Dalton. 1983. Equity theory and time: A reformulation. *Academy of Management Review* 8(2): 311–19.

Dyer, L., D. P. Schwab and R. Thériault. 1976. Managerial perceptions regarding salary increase criteria. *Personnel Psychology* 29(2): 233–42.

Dyer, L. and R. Thériault. 1976. Correlates of managerial preferences for selected salary criteria. "Visiting Scholar" Series, Industrial Relations Center, University of Minnesota.

Frank, J. G. 1984. Pay planning 1985: Survey results and implications. Paper presented at the Western Compensation and Human Resources Conference, Conference Board of Canada, November 8.

Freedman, S. M., J. R. Montanari, and R. T. Keller. 1982. The compensation program: Balancing organizational and employee needs. *Compensation Review* (2nd Quarter): 47–54.

Goodman, P. S. 1974. An examination of referents used in the evaluation of pay. *Organizational Behavior and Human Performance* 12:170–95.

Gosselin, A. and R. Thériault. 1985. Designing strategically oriented reward systems. Working paper, Ecole des H.E.C., University of Montreal, Montreal.

Heneman, R. L. 1984. *Pay for performance: Exploring the merit system.* New York: Pergamon Press.

Henderson, R. I. 1979. *Compensation management.* Reston, Virginia: Reston Publishing Co.

Ingham, G. K. 1970. *Size of industrial organization and work behavior.* London: Cambridge University Press.

Landy, F. J. and J. L. Farr. 1983. *The measurement of work performance.* New York: Academic Press.

Latham, G. P. and K. N. Wexley. 1981. *Increasing productivity through performance appraisal.* Readings, Mass.: Addison-Wesley.

Lawler, E. E. 1976. Comments on Hubert H. Meyer's, The pay for performance dilemma. *Organizational Dynamics* (Winter): 73–75.

Lawler, E. E. 1977. "Reward systems." In *Improving life at work*, edited by J. R. Hackman and J. L. Suttle, 163–236. Santa Monica, California: Goodyear Publishing Co.

Lawler, E. E. 1978. The new plant revolution. *Organizational Dynamics* 6:305–10.

Lawler, E. E. 1983. "Merit pay: An obsolete policy?" In *Perspectives on behavior in organizations*, edited by J. R. Hackman, E. E. Lawler and L. W. Porter, 305–10. New York: McGraw-Hill.

Lester, R. A. 1967. Pay differentials by size of establishments. *Industrial Relations* 4:57–67.

Livernash, E. R., ed. 1980. *Comparable Worth: Issues and alternatives.* Washington, D.C.: Equal Employment Advisory Council. 1980.

Mahoney, T. A., ed. 1979. *Compensation and reward perspectives.* Homewood, Illinois: Richard D. Irwin.

Mahoney, T. A. 1979. Organizational hierarchy and position worth. *Academy of Management Journal* 22(4): 726–37.

McCormick, E. J. 1975. *Job Analysis: Methods and applications.* New York: AMACOM.

McDougall, B. 1985. Here comes equal pay. *Small Business*, (October): 35–38.

Meyer, H. H. 1976. Reply to Edward E. Lawler III. *Organizational Dynamics* (Winter): 75–77.

Meyer, H. H., The pay for performance dilemma, *Organizational Dynamics* (Winter): 55–61.

Mikalachki, A. 1976. There is no merit in merit pay. *Business Quarterly* (Spring): 46–50.

Milkovich, G. T. 1983. Pay systems in a highly diversified organization. Working paper, ILR School, Cornell University, Ithaca, New York.

Milkovich, G. T. and J. M. Newman. 1984. *Compensation.* Plano, Texas: Business Publications Inc.

Nash, A. N. and S. J. Carroll. 1975. *The Management of compensation.* Montery, California: Brooks/Cole Publishing Co.

Niemann, L. 1984. Wage discrimination and women workers: The move towards equal pay for work of equal value in Canada. Discussion paper series, Women's Bureau Series A: no. 5. Ottawa: Labour Canada.

Nightingale, D. V. 1983. *The Profit-sharing handbook.* Don Mills, Ontario: Profit Sharing Council of Canada.

Remick, H., ed. 1984. *Comparable worth and wage discrimination.* Philadelphia: Temple University Press.

Salscheider, J. 1981. Divising pay strategies for diversified companies. *Compensation Review* (2nd Quarter): 15–24.

Tarrant, J. J. 1976. *How to negotiate a raise.* New York: Van Nostrand Reinhold Co.

Thériault, R. 1977. Equity theory: An examination of the inputs and outcomes in an organizational setting. Unpublished doctoral thesis, Cornell University.

Thériault, R. and L. Dyer. 1977. Critères d'augmentation de salaires chez les cadres canadiens-français, canadiens-anglais et américains. *Relations Industrielles* 32(1): 18–34.

Thériault, R. and S. Payette. 1981. *Politiques et pratiques en rémunération dans les sociétés au Québec.* Montréal: Association of Human Resource Professionals of the Province of Quebec.

Thériault, R. 1983. *Gestion de la rémunération: Politiques et pratiques efficaces et équitables.* Chicoutimi, Québec: Gaëtan Morin.

Treiman, D. J. 1979. *Job evaluation: An analytic review.* Washington, D.C.: National Academy of Sciences.

Treiman, D. J. and H. I. Hartmann, eds. 1981. *Women, work, and wages: Equal pay for jobs of equal value.* Washington, D.C.: National Academy Press.

Von Glinow, M. A. 1985. Reward strategies for attracting, evaluating, and retaining professionals. *Human Resource Management* 24(2) (Summer): 191–206.

Wallace, M. and C. Fay. 1981. Job evaluation and comparable worth: Compensation theory Basis for modeling job worth. *Proceedings of the Acadamy of Management,* 296–300.

World of Work Report. 1984a. Dual pay scales on the rise. (October): 1.

World of Work Report. 1984b. Two-tier pay plans. (September): 8.

Wortman, M. S. and J. Sperling. 1975. *Defining the manager's job.* New York: AMACOM.

18. Obstacles to the Effective Use of Reward Systems

Philip M. Podsakoff, Indiana University

Charles N. Greene, University of Southern Maine

James M. McFillen, Bowling Green State University

THE TREND AWAY FROM PERFORMANCE-CONTINGENT PAY SYSTEMS

Recent research suggests that among the most prominent factors which affect employee performance and satisfaction is the way in which rewards are administered.[1] Rewards that are administered contingently (that is, according to performance) cause increases in subsequent employee performance and expressions of satisfaction among high performers. Similar findings have also been obtained in the case of social rewards such as the praise, recognition, and social approval provided by one's supervisor for his or her good performance. On the other hand, rewards administered noncontingently, or without regard to performance, have been shown to have little effect on subordinate performance, but to have many dysfunctional effects on the work attitudes of high performers.

Modified with permission from: R. S. Schuler and S. A. Youngblood (eds.) *Readings in Personnel and Human Resource Management.* 2d (St. Paul, Minn.: West Publishing Co.) 1984.

These particular results logically lead to the expectation that organizational reward systems should be designed to facilitate managers' use of performance-contingent rewards. Unfortunately, this simply has not happened. Data obtained from a number of government and industry sources, in fact, reveal a very clear trend away from the use of such reward systems.

While industrial surveys of specific segments of the labour force often do not provide such dramatic evidence, they do reveal more about the basic problem. For example, Evans' survey of *Fortune's* "500" firms[2] reports that only one-fourth of the organizations sampled consider performance as a primary determinant of blue-collar compensation. Less than half (or seven percent) of these firms even utilized a formal appraisal system for compensation decisions. Other studies[3] provide still further documentation of the trend away from performance-related compensation plans—a trend which began in the blue-collar work force as early as the mid-1940s. Additional evidence suggests that compensation for executives may not be performance-related either. A recent article in *Fortune*[4] entitled

"The Madness of Executive Compensation" indicates little correspondence exists between CEO compensation and organization performance as measured by stockholder equity. Taken together these findings suggest the pervasiveness of the trend away from performance-contingent rewards.

A Specific Example of the Effects of the Trend

A more detailed illustration of the adverse effects of this trend on productivity is provided in a recent field experiment conducted by Greene and Podsakoff[5] in two paper mills employing over 1,100 managers and operative level personnel. Both mills are part of the same company division and were comparable in size, unionization, and geographic location. The only significant difference between the two mills (A and B) was that mill A was about to discard the four-year old performance-contingent pay system in favour of a flat-rate, cost-of-living pay plan while mill B was to retain it. Performance declined by twenty percent in mill A within a year of the time the performance-contingent pay system was removed. Interestingly, satisfaction with both pay and supervision actually increased for low performers, but decreased significantly for high performers. The increased satisfaction of the low performers may have been expressions of relief at no longer being under pressure to produce. Employee turnover in mill A went down slightly, but now sixty-five percent of the turnover consisted of high performers leaving mill A. Similarly, grievances were down by forty percent, but most complaints were now from high performers objecting to the loss of opportunity to earn more money.

OBSTACLES TO EFFECTIVE REWARD SYSTEMS

The findings of this study and the aforementioned surveys raise several questions. If the use of noncontingent monetary and social rewards systems produces such undesirable effects, why do we find so much evidence that rewards are generally not tied to performance? And why do we find such a widespread movement away from use of performance-contingent reward systems? Indeed, why would supervisors relinquish their control over those events that have been demonstrated to be so effective in achieving higher performance from all workers and satisfaction from the most valued employees; that is, the high performers?

Providing answers for these questions is not an easy task. There are, however, several obstacles that managers encounter in trying to link rewards to employee performance which provide at least partial answers to these questions. The obstacles are (1) problems in specifying and assessing good performance, (2) difficulties in identifying valued rewards, and (3) difficulties in establishing appropriate contingencies between rewards and performance. In this paper, we examine these major obstacles and their implications for managers.

Difficulties in Specifying and Measuring Performance

If rewards are to be linked to employee performance levels, a manager first must be able to identify and define good performance. Thus, the first requirement of developing an effective performance-contingent reward system is to have valid and reliable measures of desirable behaviours. Unfortunately, there are several factors which generally limit a manager's ability to identify and assess functional task performance—(1) changes in the nature of work performed by many employees, (2) the multidimensional nature of work, (3) technological advances in the work place, and (4) lack of managerial training in how to assess good performance.

Changes in the Nature of Work. At the turn of the century, most jobs in American industry were directed at the production of material goods or products. Measuring the performance of employees who produced a quantifiable unit of work was quite easy. Recent trends, however, have changed the nature of work. The American economy has evolved from a product to a service orientation. Service jobs differ from those that are product oriented in that generally no quantifiable material good is produced that can be utilized to assess subordinate performance. For example, should the performance of an employment counselor be evaluated by number of people placed, percentage placed, number of clients processed, or should performance be defined as some combination of these criteria? If so, how are the criteria to be combined to represent total performance? No simple measures of quantity or quality of performance exist for such occupations. Inevitably, measurement of performance in these jobs becomes more subjective and thus linking rewards to performance becomes problematical.

The percentage of white-collar, managerial, and professional jobs has also increased. The performance of managers, in particular, is notoriously difficult to measure. Of course, various attempts have been made to utilize objective measures of managerial performance and some progress has been made through development of results-oriented appraisal systems. These appraisal systems involve the setting of managerial goals, development of an action plan to obtain these goals, and the periodic evaluation of goal attainment as a measure of performance. The success of these programs is, however, not unequivocal. For example, few organizations actually employ any performance criteria as determinants of managerial pay decisions. [6]

Finally, the tasks performed by many managers, white-collar workers, and professionals today are more complex and interdependent than their counterparts a few decades ago. Many organizations have become vast systems which require levels of integration never imagined a few years ago. For example, managerial decisions, long considered a basis for judging manager performance, are now supported by a wide variety of staff inputs and analysis. As a result, managerial jobs have become more differentiated, varied, and complex. Thus, considerable ambiguity may exist regarding a task's description, and the potential for disagreement about what constitutes good or poor performance may increase within an organization.

Multidimensionality of Work. Only belatedly has it been recognized that performance is a multidimensional rather than a unidimensional construct. The more complex the job, the greater the number of criteria or dimensions that are required to assess performance. Unfortunately, many performance assessment procedures utilized today fail to acknowledge the multidimensional nature of work—that is, all of the dimensions and their relative importance to the performance of a particular job. If critical job performance criteria cannot be specified and weighted, linking rewards to performance becomes little more than pure guesswork.

Technological Development. Technological innovations have created still other problems of measuring performance. The recent advent of computerized technologies increased the ability of many firms to manufacture goods more efficiently. However, such systems have had some dysfunctional effects on the administration of reward systems. First, technological change often results in the use of new and untested methods in which performance is difficult to measure. Second, machine-paced work permits little variation in employee behaviour. When work flow is controlled by factors outside the influence of the employee, few differences in performance exist that can be distinguished by a manager. Under these circumstances, managers evaluate subjective characteristics of employees as opposed to their actual productivity, or simply appraise all subordinates as equal in terms of performance.

The Manager's Own Personal Value System. Some managers don't see or don't want to see differences, particularly evaluative differences, among subordinates. To do so and to administer rewards accordingly creates dissatisfaction among low performers. Furthermore, the manager often is forced to defend his or her appraisals, particularly from criticisms of the low performers. Most managers prefer not to be cornered into such a position, especially when dealing with subjective performance criteria. Many managers simply do not feel comfortable playing an active role in evaluating and reinforcing differences in the performance of others.

Lack of Supervisory Training. If performance ratings are to be both reliable and valid, they must be conducted by managers with the requisite evaluative skills. Unfortunately, new or inexperienced supervisors rarely automatically possess such skills. Even seasoned managers often have difficulty assessing performance because they never have received the training necessary to reduce the errors that frequently occur in performance evaluations. Perceptual errors or biases that limit a supervisor's ability to assess a subordinate's behaviour accurately include:

——*Implicit Personality Theory*—The tendency to evaluate people on the basis of our attitudes toward them, instead of their actual behaviour. For example, we tend to overevaluate the performance of people we like and underevaluate those whom we dislike.

——*Projection*—The tendency to perceive in other people traits or characteristics (particularly undesirable traits) that we ourselves possess.

——*First Impressions*—The tendency to evaluate individuals by giving more weight to the impressions we developed from our first interactions with them than to later interactions.

——*The Halo Effect*—The tendency to see one trait in a person because he or she possesses some other trait. For example, we may evaluate someone as honest because he or she is friendly toward us.

——*Stereotyping*—The tendency to attribute to an individual the traits which we believe are characteristic of a particular group with whom we associate the individual. For an example, an accountant, because he or she is an accountant, must have good quantitative skills but probably lacks interpersonal skills.

——*Perceptual Readiness*—The tendency to see in another either what we want or expect to see, even if it means ignoring contradictory information.

——*General Evaluative Set*—The tendency to be either overly tough or lenient in our evaluations of others.

When managers lack training in the evaluation process, the reward system is doomed to failure.

Problems in Identifying Valued Rewards

For rewards to be effective, they must be valued by the person who receives them. Rewards not valued by employees, even when tied to performance, are not likely to have positive effects. But, the identification of those events that prove rewarding to subordinates is not always easy. Furthermore, there is little guarantee that events which prove reinforcing for one individual will prove to be equally so for another.

Identifying Different Types of Rewards. Because of the important role that rewards play in determining employee behaviours and attitudes, much effort has been expended in trying to identify the characteristics of rewards that determine their value. As a result of this research, environmental events have been divided into two categories—extrinsic and intrinsic—which presumably reflect differences in their reinforcing potential.[7] Extrinsic rewards are rewards administered by other people. Included are financial incentives as well as the praise, approval, and attention received from supervisors or coworkers. Intrinsic rewards, on the other hand, are rewards that an individual receives directly from performing his or her job. Originally, the rewards in this category included feelings of competency experienced from completing a difficult task and the sense of autonomy associated with controlling one's work. Recent research has suggested that the intrinsically rewarding characteristics of tasks may be divided further into several dimensions.[8] Among these are:

—— *Job Variety*—The range of operations the individual must perform and the variety of equipment he or she must use in the work he or she does.

—— *Job Autonomy*—The degree to which the individual controls the work scheduling and the procedures to be followed in the job.

—— *Product Identity*—The degree to which the individual can identify the results of the efforts of his/her work.

—— *Task Feedback*—The extent of information the individual receives about how he or she is doing in the job.

—— *Task Significance*—The extent to which the individual's task is perceived as important to the success of the organization.

Intrinsic rewards often have been assumed to be more highly valued by organizational participants than extrinsic rewards. This has led to the suggestion that managers would be more effective in improving subordinate performance and satisfaction if they increased the amount of responsibility the subordinates had in their work and enriched the tasks they performed. Common sense and a substantial amount of empirical evidence, however, suggests that this view of intrinsic rewards is probably oversimplified for several reasons. First, not all individuals are reinforced by being given added responsibilities. Some workers do not desire increased responsibility and some actively avoid it. Second, job enrichment programs do not always produce the intended effects and in some cases have had dysfunctional consequences for the organization.[9] Finally, extrinsic rewards such as verbal praise or money remain quite potent rewards.[10] Taken together, the evidence indicates that intrinsic rewards are not universally more effective than extrinsic rewards. A manager must be able to identify the rewards that work most effectively with each individual and tailor them accordingly. Thus, while the distinction between intrinsic and extrinsic rewards may be used conceptually to differentiate between rewards that are received from the job and those mediated by others, this distinction should not be taken as an indication that intrinsic rewards are necessarily more valued than extrinsic rewards.

Reward Magnitude, Size, and Timing. The identification of those events that may serve as potential rewards does not necessarily insure that they will be effective in increasing an individual's performance and satisfaction. Even when a manager identifies those events that may serve as rewards, other factors associated with the way they are administered may severely limit their effectiveness.

One problem involves the size or magnitude of the rewards received by subordinates. Rewards must be of sufficient magnitude if they are to be motivating. Unfortunately, even when managers know that their employees are reinforced by salary increases, they may be unable to effectively use salary because of a lack of company resources or because of company policy, or both. During inflationary periods, workers feel they deserve cost of living increases to compensate for their reduced buying power and organizations feel compelled to provide them. While the manager's ability to control the size or magnitude of other rewards such as praise and approval may not likewise be restricted by company policy or resources, the value attached to these rewards may nevertheless diminish if subordinates learn that they are not associated with subsequent increases in pay, promotions, or other tangible rewards.

If significant merit raises are to be added to cost-of-living adjustments (COLA), the financial strain may be more than the budget can withstand. As the cost-of-living adjustments grow in size, the amount of money necessary to represent a significant merit raise also rises. A three percent merit raise compared to a five percent COLA looks good, but compared to a ten percent COLA the three percent merit raise would be much less significant. In most situations, managers are forced to sacrifice differentials between high and low performers in order to provide reasonable cost-of-living raises for all.

A second problem has to do with the timing of rewards. Generally speaking, the more quickly rewards follow desirable behaviour, the more potent they are. Rewards which are delayed often have many undesirable effects, including the possibility of (1) decreasing the desired behaviour, (2) increasing dissatisfaction and frustration expressed by high performers, and (3) increasing undesired behaviour which occurs during the interval between the desirable response and the delayed reward. Far too frequently, however, rewards administered to employees are delayed. As firms increase in size and complexity, they develop more formalized and standardized procedures for providing feedback to employees. While often unintended, the result of these practices is to remove the manager's ability to reward a subordinate appropriately without going through much red tape. Even in those instances when the manager acts promptly to administer rewards, a rather substantial delay may still occur.

Difficulties in Establishing a Link Between Rewards and Performance

Overcoming the obstacles associated with providing a clear, unambiguous definition of performance and identifying valued rewards is a necessary prerequisite for the design of effective reward systems. The ability to assess performance and specify rewards, however, is not sufficient to guarantee that the manager will, in fact, successfully administer rewards. Another obstacle that may prevent the implementation of an effective reward program has to do with establishment and maintenance of a link between rewards and performance.

Failure to Create Contingencies. Even when managers effectively identify rewards and are able to assess performance adequately, they still may fail to establish the necessary link between rewards and performance. Among the major problems is the belief held by some supervisors that administering rewards according to performance levels is not important. Despite the evidence to the contrary, some managers believe that subordinates are intrinsically motivated to either work or not work and that no amount of effort on their part is likely to improve either the productivity or satisfaction of these individuals. If this assumption were an accurate one, it would mean that the way rewards are administered should have little or no effect on subordinate behaviours and attitudes. This simply is not true. Rewards administered appropriately do have significant effects on employees performance and the satisfaction expressed by high performers.[11]

Even when a manager believes rewards are important to subordinate performance and satisfaction, however, other factors may limit his or her ability to establish effective contingencies. One of these factors is the skill of the supervisor. Some supervisors simply lack the knowledge, skills, or experience necessary to design and administer effective performance-reward contingencies. Thus, while some managers almost intuitively allocate rewards appropriately, others must be trained if they are expected to be effective. Another factor is the difficulty associated with the administration of such reward systems. When a supervisor wants to link performance to rewards, (s)he must specify what good performance is, identify rewards, monitor the subordinates' performance levels and reward them accordingly. This takes time and effort that some supervisors are not willing or able to invest. Consequently, we find some managers who pay little attention to the performance of a subordinate unless that subordinate performs poorly. This practice of greasing the wheel only when it squeaks simply reinforces squeaking behaviour and presents numerous other problems. First, individuals who are not rewarded for performing will have little incentive to sustain their good performance. Second, since the only feedback people receive from a manager who employs this strategy is negative feedback, turnover and absenteeism are the likely result.

Creating Inappropriate Contingencies. Reward systems may suffer not only from a lack of ability to create or establish reward contingencies, but from managers who unintentionally establish inappropriate contingencies. In part, this may result from the fact that when the criteria of good performance goes unspecified, behaviour which does not increase performance may be rewarded. In addition, many rewards administered in organizations are delayed and thus unproductive behaviours may be unintentionally reinforced. However, there is an even more substantive reason as to why inappropriate contingencies are often established. As Kerr[12] has noted, organizations often reward one behaviour while really hoping that another behaviour will occur. He cites as one example:

It is *hoped* that administrators will pay attention to long-run costs and opportunities and will institute programs which will bear fruit later on. However, many organizational reward systems pay off for short-run sales and earnings only. Under such circumstances it is personally rational for officials to sacrifice long-term growth and profit (by selling off equipment and property, or by stifling research and development) for short-term advantages. This probably is most pertinent in the public sector, with the result that many public officials are unwilling to implement programs which will not show benefits by election time.

Of course, to the extent supervisors only wish for good behaviour but don't explicitly reward it, they cannot expect it to occur.

Nullifying Intended Contingencies. One method organizations have utilized to improve the probability that good performance will be rewarded is to develop formal performance appraisal (PA) systems. These programs may be quite flexible and often permit the appraisal of an individual's performance even when it does not involve quantifiable output. The implementation of a performance appraisal system, however, is not without its difficulties. One problem is that many PA systems employ rating forms which evaluate vaguely defined traits or characteristics of the subordinates rather than observable behaviours or the outcomes of their performance. Such practices increase the potential that the perceptual biases of a manager affect the evaluation process and that rewards will not be allocated according to performance. A second problem is that many managers use the information gathered from the PA systems inappropriately—that is, if it is utilized at all. If managers merely go through the motions of appraisal solely to meet the requirements of a yearly evaluation or to justify reward allocation decisions after the fact, then appraisal will be of little value. A third problem involves the consistency with which PA programs are applied. In many organizations, performance evaluations are utilized by some managers but not by others. And in some instances, managers use appraisals for some subordinates but not for all. These practices often lead to some subordinates being evaluated on the basis of performance while the criteria utilized to evaluate others is left unclear. The differential treatment accorded to subordinates in such situations is perceived as inequitable and unjust by many employees. Such practices are seldom effective.

Employee Opposition. Among the difficulties faced by managers who wish to utilize performance-contingent pay systems is the potential lack of acceptance of such plans, particularly by blue-collar workers:

One reason pay is not related to performance in many organizations may simply be that employees object to this way of handling pay. If employees object to seeing their pay tied to performance, there can be real problems in trying to implement any kind of merit pay system, since it could be and, in fact, would probably be undermined by the employees themselves ... (Lawler 1971, 159) [13]

In part, this opposition may be attributable to the attempts by employee unions to obtain assured incomes for their members and to minimize the differences between, and increase the comparability of, blue-collar and white-collar workers' pay. However, much of the resistance to these plans results from the lack of trust employees have regarding management's concern for their well-being. For example, a large steel producer used a complex incentive bonus plan in its tubing department. The plan involved multiple standards designed for different machines and different products. Management assumed that the plan was too complex to be explained to the hourly workers and thus provided little explanation of it. As a result, very few workers understood the plan. Since the workers normally worked on several different machines and products over a given period of time, they perceived little relationship between their performance and pay. Not surprisingly, they suspected that the bonus was in fact arbitrarily set by management without regard to production. For the individual, such mistrust often leads to feelings of inequity and a lack of fairness. At the group level, it often results in restrictions in productivity due to the fear that once the group starts earning too much under the new incentive system, management will either change the performance standards or lay off workers. With this in mind, it is not surprising that many employees express doubts about incentive systems and unions generally avoid them—striving for pay based upon equality rather than performance.

Exhibit 18-1 summarizes the obstacles to the implementation of effective reward systems discussed previously and their causes. In the section that follows this discussion, we will consider implications that these obstacles have for practicing managers.

MANAGEMENT IMPLICATIONS

Specifying and Measuring Performance

Our previous discussion underlines the essential role of performance measurement in the process of rewarding employee behaviour. Three related issues must be addressed by organizations: (1) development of the measurement instrument, (2) the training of managers in its use, and (3) motivating managers to use the instrument effectively.

Create Performance Dimensions. Organizations need to create specific, unambiguous performance dimensions. Typically, organizations have relied upon trait descriptions such as creativity, innovativeness, perseverance, knowledge, dependability, initiative, adaptability, and reasoning ability as measures of performance. Traits are assumed to be stable qualities of the subordinate that have a direct relationship to observed performance. However, trait measures fail on three issues. First, trait measures lack reliability. Indeed, managers are notoriously poor in making trait assessments and frequently fail to agree as to what traits are being exhibited by given behaviour. Second, trait measures lack validity. In other words, traits rarely relate directly to performance on the job. Third, traits lack generalizability. Even if traits were valid and could be measured reliably, different jobs potentially would require different traits and yet organizations frequently employ the same trait measures across broad classes of jobs. Performance measurement, therefore, should rely on assessing the performance and/or behaviour of the employee and not his/her personal qualities. In order to develop adequate performance measurement, organizations must:

—Develop effective performance appraisal instruments based on an analysis of the requirements of the job, not on the traits of the individual

—Utilize evaluation procedures which acknowledged the multidimensional nature of performance

Train Managers to Appraise. Good measurement also requires trained appraisers. Most managers have little, if

Exhibit 18–1   **Obstacles to the Design of Effective Reward Systems and their Implications for Management**

Obstacles	Causes	Implications for Management
A. Specifying and measuring performance	1. Changes in the Nature of Work —Increase in service oriented jobs. —Increase in white-collar, managerial, and professional jobs. —Increases in the interdependencies and complexity of work. 2. Multidimensional Nature of Work —Single item measures of performance are often inadequate. —In many jobs today, multiple criteria are necessary to assess performance. 3. Technological Developments —Technological developments often result in new and untested methods of work. —Machine-paced jobs permit little variation in performance. 4. Lack of Supervisory Training —Use of untrained, inexperienced supervisors in the evaluation process. —Perceptual biases. 5. The Manager's Value System —Lack of interest in or inability to differentiate among high and low performers. —Failure to see long range outcomes of differential rewarding.	1. Develop techniques for specifying desirable behaviours and clarifying the objectives of the organization. 2. Utilize evaluation procedures which recognize the multi-dimensional nature of performance. 3. Develop a valid and reliable performance appraisal system based on results and/or behavioural standards. 4. Train supervisors to utilize the PA system appropriately and to understand potential sources of bias. 5. Clearly define long term consequences of performance-contingent and noncontingent reward practices.
B. Identifying valued rewards	1. Choice of Rewards —Choosing a reward that is not reinforcing. 2. Utilizing Rewards of Insufficient Size or Magnitude —Lack of resources. —Company policy. 3. Poor Timing of Rewards —Size of organization: bureaucracy. —Standardization/formalization of feedback mechanisms. —Complexity of feedback system.	1. Make managers aware of the effects of rewards on employee performance and satisfaction. 2. Train managers to identify rewards for their subordinates. 3. Administer rewards of sufficient magnitude. 4. Administer rewards as quickly after desirable responses as possible.

Continued on next page

OBSTACLES TO THE EFFECTIVE USE OF REWARD SYSTEMS 255

Exhibit 18-1—*Continued*

Obstacles	Causes	Implications for Management
C. Linking rewards to performance	1. Failure to Create Appropriate Contingencies Between Rewards and Performance —Lack of knowledge, skill, experience. —Belief system. —Difficulty of administration. 2. Creating Inappropriate Contingencies —Rewarding behavior which does not increase performance. —Rewarding behavior A, but hoping for B. 3. Nullifying Intended Contingencies —Using improper PA instrument. —Improper use of PA instrument. —Failure to use information obtained. —Inconsistently applied. 4. Employee Opposition —Individually: mistrust, lack of fairness, inequity. —Socially: restrictions due to fear of loss of work. —Outside intervention: union.	1. Train manager to establish appropriate contingencies between rewards and performance. 2. Use information obtained from appraisals of employee performance as basis for reward allocation decisions. 3. Administer the reward system consistently across employees.

any, understanding of the appraisal process, often employ radically different interpretations of measurement dimensions, and apply significantly different standards of performance. Therefore, organizations must:

——Make managers aware of the importance of objectively evaluating employee performance

——Train managers on the use of the performance appraisal system

Motivate Managers to Appraise. Finally, managers must be motivated to observe and assess performance, and personal biases against the use of appraisal systems need to be overcome. Organizations must make managers aware that the performance measurement system is important to the effective functioning of the organization. This would entail rewarding managers themselves for their involvement and performance in the appraisal process.

Organizations can obtain greater commitment to the appraisal process and overcome some of the manager's personal biases against appraisal if:

——Managers are made aware of the long-term consequence of both rewarding and failing to reward differentially on the basis of individual performance

—Performance data are used to justify administrative decisions, for example, promotions, salary increases, and training assignments

—Performance data are used to provide feedback to employees regarding their progress and development

—Performance data are used to evaluate the contribution and value of personnel programs and policies, for example, employee selection and training

—managers are held accountable for appraising performance by including their appraisal activities in their own performance evaluation

—Managers are rewarded for their appraisal and development role

Identifying Valued Rewards

In selecting rewards that are relevant both to an organization's purpose and to the employee recipient, four issues stand out: types of rewards available, value to employees, applicability to organizational purpose, and magnitude.

Identify Potential Rewards. Organizations have a wide range of rewards from which to choose (see Exhibit 18–2). Managers must become aware of the potential rewards and the ability of the firm to make certain rewards available. Greater creativity in identifying potential rewards will be required of management to fit the wide variety of individuals and situations that will evolve over the next decade. A short list of rewards, whether created by organizational policy or lack of creativity and awareness, will hamper an organization's ability to respond effectively to employee performance. In order to identify rewards they might use, managers should:

—Investigate rewards utilized in other organizations or by other managers

—Brainstorm potentially relevant rewards

—Explore constraints

—Eliminate (where possible) policies which limit the variety of rewards

—Identify rewards or rewarding events that are *not* available or over which they have no control

Match Individuals and Rewards. Not all rewards are equally relevant to or valued by all employees or by a given employee over time. Managers must be cognizant of significant individual differences among employees or groups of employees. Although some rewards, for example money, may have salience to a wide range of employees, other rewards may have much less universal appeal.

Knowing employees, that is, taking the time to identify those particular events that are rewarding to one subordinate but not to another, is perhaps the most critical action managers can take. Often, it can be done very simply. For example, managers must think about a subordinate (subordinate X) they know well. They must look back over the past three months, six months, or as far as they can with respect to subordinate X's behaviour and then ask the following questions: "When I have observed subordinate X working particularly hard, exerting considerable effort (e.g., working late hours, coming into the office on weekends, taking work home), what happened? What was X working on? What have I or coworkers done to X? When in the past has subordinate X expressed obvious satisfaction with what s/he was involved in at work? What has subordinate X requested from me, either directly or indirectly, in the past?" The answers to these questions should provide a long list

Exhibit 18-2 Organizational Rewards

Material Rewards, Including Fringe Benefits	Status Symbols	Social Rewards	From the Task-Self Rewards
Pay	Office size and location	Friendly greetings	Interesting work
Pay raise	Office with window	Informal recognition	Sense of achievement
Stock options	Carpeting	Praise	Job of more importance
Profit sharing	Drapes	Smile	Job variety
Bonus plans	Paintings	Evaluative feedback	Job-performance feedback
Christmas bonus	Watches	Compliments	Self-recognition
Provision and use of company facilities	Rings	Nonverbal signals	Self-praise
Deferred compensation, including other tax shelters	Formal awards/recognition	Pat on the back	Opportunities to schedule own work
Pay and time-off for attending work-related training programs and seminars	Wall plaque	Invitations to coffee/lunch	Working hours
		After-hours social gatherings	Participation in new organizational ventures
Medical plan, including free physical examinations			Choice of geographical location
Company auto			Autonomy in job
Pension contributions			
Product discount plans			
Vacation trips			
Theater and sports tickets			
Recreation facilities			
Reserved company parking			
Work breaks			
Sabbatical leaves			
Club memberships and privileges			
Discount purchase privileges			
Personal loans at favorable rates			
Free legal advice			
Free personal financial planning advice			
Free home protection-theft insurance			
Burglar alarms and personal protection			
Moving expenses			
Home purchase assistance			

Adapted and modified from Sims, H. P., Jr., "Managing Behavior Through Learning and Reinforcement," In D. Hellriegel and J. W. Slocum, Jr., *Organizational Behavior*, 2nd ed., New York: West Publishing Co., 1979.

of events, both extrinsic and intrinsic, that X finds rewarding. Some of the answers to these questions will be the same or similar for some subordinates while some will be quite different. This indicates that individual differences must be recognized when rewards are to be administered to different subordinates.

As organizations find their labour pools becoming more diverse due to changing population demographics, geographic dispersion of plant sites, or to internationalization of operations, the problem of matching rewards to individuals will increase. A greater variety of people will have to be accommodated with a greater range of alternative rewards. Organizations will have to create and tolerate situations in which reward systems possess considerable diversity. In order to facilitate the individual/reward match, managers should:

—— Know their employees
—— Involve employees in developing relevant alternative rewards
—— Create a smorgasbord of rewards from which can be selected the rewards that are most appropriate to selected individuals or groups

Match Rewards and Purpose. The choice of rewards to be used by organizations also will be constrained by the purpose for which the reward will be applied. Some rewards can be allocated incrementally and, therefore, can be adjusted to levels of performance. Other rewards are of an all or nothing character and can be applied only to some defined performance threshold. A related issue is whether the reward can be administered to individuals or must be allocated to groups of employees. Although rewards permitting individual allocations (for example, praise or money) can be utilized to reward group performance, rewards that require group allocations (for example, profit sharing) cannot be adapted easily to the rewarding of individual performance. Managers, therefore, must be careful to match the rewards to the intended purpose. Providing rewards which fail to recognize individual variations in performance when such recognition is appropriate results in equality of rewards among unequal recipients and therefore inequity. This suggests that managers should:

—— Identify the type of performance to be rewarded
—— Decide whether performance thresholds or performance increments are more relevant
—— Consider whether individual contributions can and should be recognized or whether group contributions are more relevant
—— Evaluate whether equity or equality is the more critical issue

Achieve Sufficient Reward Magnitude. The final consideration in choosing rewards is magnitude. Even though a reward may have potential value, the amount of the reward is critical in determining perceived significance. A manager's estimates of magnitude, however objective they may be, must be tempered by employee perceptions. Their perceptions are affected by factors external to the organization (for example, inflation, alternative employment, etc.) as well as factors internal to the organization (for example, profits, past reward allocations, etc.). Organizations are constrained in their ability to respond to these perceptions; organizational resources are limited. Managers must select and allocate rewards such that sufficient magnitude can be attained. Therefore, they should:

—Consider alternatives to rewards currently employed which permit greater magnitude at lower cost

—Utilize rewards that provide visibility for the recipient

—Avoid the upward ratcheting effect by using rewards that do not create ongoing, long-term obligations in response to current performance (for example, use performance bonuses rather than salary increases)

—Increase usage of nonmonetary rewards where relevant and applicable

—Incorporate job design elements which provide intrinsic rewards as a function of job performance

Creating Performance-Reward Linkages

In creating performance-reward linkages, managers must design and apply systems that reward what is intended and avoid rewarding what is undesired or unintended. Organizations can create stronger linkages by:

—Being specific and inclusive in stating what is to be rewarded

—Relying on performances as the determinant of rewards and by being consistent in responding to performance across time and employees

—Providing employees with performance feedback at the time of reward allocation to strengthen the association

—Being timely in rewarding desired performance by acknowledging good performance when it occurs and expediting formal organizational rewards

—Making managers aware of the critical role of contingencies in determining desired employee behaviours such as those associated with quantity and quality of performance, attendance, commitment, and cooperation

CONCLUSION

Effective reward systems require a high level of effort directed toward several key issues. Although this proactive approach to employee motivation may be viewed as demanding a significant increase in management involvement, the alternative is generally reduced levels of employee motivation, commitment, and productivity. Management has spent the last twenty-five years giving other approaches a fair test as management strategies. Perhaps the time has come to fundamentally review management's position as it relates to the issues of motivation and performance. Management has the responsibility to provide employees with the incentive to perform. Management must meet that responsibility with a renewed involvement.

Endnotes

1. See, for example, L. S. Baird and W. C. Hamner, Individual versus systems rewards: Who's dissatisfied, why, and what is their likely response? *Academy of Management Journal*, 1979, 22, 783–792; D. J. Cherrington, H. J. Reitz and W. E. Scott, Effects of contingent and non-contingent rewards on the relationship between satisfaction and task performance. *Journal of Applied Psychology*, 1971, 55, 531–536; C. N. Greene, P. M. Podsakoff, Effects of removal of a pay incentive: A field experiment. In J. C. Susbauer (Ed.) *Proceedings of the 1978 Meeting, National Academy of Management*, 1978, 206–210; P. M. Podsakoff, W. D. Todor and R. Skov, Effects of leader contingent and non-contingent reward and punishment behaviors on subordinate performance

and satisfaction. *Academy of Management Journal,* 1982, *25,* 810–821.

2. W. A. Evans, Pay for performance, fact or fable. *Personnel Journal,* 1970, *49,* 726–731.

3. E. E. Lawler III, Managers' attitudes toward how their pay is and should be determined. *Journal of Applied Psychology,* 1966, *50,* 273–279; M. Haire, E. E. Ghiselli and M. E. Gordon, A psychological study of pay. *Journal of Applied Psychology Monograph,* 1967, *51,* (4), (Whole No. 636); H. H. Meyer, E. Kay and J. R. P. French, Split roles in performance appraisal. *HBR,* 1965, *43,* 123–129; E. L. Stelluto, Report on incentive pay in manufacturing industries. *Monthly Labor Review,* 1969, *92,* 49–53; J. H. Cox, Time and incentive practices in urban areas. *Monthly Labor Review,* 1971, *94,* 53–56.

4. Carol J. Loomis, The madness of executive compensation. *Fortune,* July 12, 1982, 42–52.

5. See C. N. Greene and P. M. Podsakoff, Effects of withdrawl of performance-contingent reward on supervisory influence and power, *Academy of Management Journal,* 1981, *24,* 327–342 and Ending incentive pay hurts a plant's productivity and bosses' morale, *The Wall Street Journal,* Tuesday, November 24, 1981, page 1.

6. Ibid.

7. D. McGregor, *The Human Side of Enterprise* (New York: McGraw-Hill, 1960); E. E. Lawler III and L. W. Porter, The effect of performance on job satisfaction, *Industrial Relations,* 1967, *7,* 20–28.

8. A. N. Turner and P. R. Lawrence, *Industrial Jobs and the Worker.* (Boston: Harvard University Graduate School of Business Administration, 1965); J. R. Hackman and E. E. Lawler III, Employee reactions to job characteristics. *Journal of Applied Psychology,* 1971, *55,* 259–286; H. P. Sims, A. D. Szilagyi and R. T. Keller, The measurement of job characteristics. *Academy of Management Journal,* 1976, *19,* 195–212.

9. See M. Fein, Job enrichment: A re-evaluation. *Sloan Management Review,* 1974, *15,* 69–88; M. Fein, The myth of job enrichment, in *Humanizing the Workplace.* Roy P. Fairfield (Ed.) (Buffalo: Prometheus Books, 1974); W. Gomberg, Job satisfaction: Sorting out the nonsense. *AFL–CIO American Federationist.* June, 1973; J. R. Hackman, Is job enrichment just a fad? *HBR,* 1975, 129–139; J. R. Hackman, On the coming demise of job enrichment, in E. L. Cass and F. G. Zimmer (Eds.) *Man and Work in Society* (New York: Van Nostrand-Reinhold, 1975); C. N. Greene, Effects of job enrichment: A field experiment, *1981 Proceedings of the Academy of Management.*

10. Baird and Hamner; Cherrington, Reitz and Scott; Greene and Podsakoff; Podsakoff, Todor and Skov; loc. cit.

11. Ibid.

12. See S. Kerr, On the folly of rewarding A, while hoping for B. *Academy of Management Journal,* 1975, *18,* 769–783.

13. E. E. Lawler III, *Pay and Organizational Effectiveness: A Psychological View.* (New York: McGraw-Hill, 1971.)

19. Reward Management: A New Look

Rabindra N. Kanungo, McGill University

INTRODUCTION

The effective management of human resources is invariably viewed as a very formidable task by both management researchers and practitioners, primarily because of its complexity and the imponderables involved in it. Yet, if one focuses on the basic objective in this task, one finds that it becomes reasonably manageable. What is the objective of the management of human resources? It is to put into place ways and means of promoting among employees a specific set of beliefs, attitudes, and behaviours which are conducive to achieving the organizational goals of production and customer service. To achieve this objective, every organization institutes a variety of policies and programs, of which the compensation or reward program is certainly the most expensive—if not the most important. The justification for a reward program is based on the universally accepted assumption that rewards have a powerful, if not decisive, influence on the attitudes

The author is grateful to Mr. Manuel Mendonca, Sessional Lecturer, Faculty of Management, McGill University for helpful comments.

and behaviours of organizational members. To understand the precise validity of this assumption, it would be fruitful to explore the exact nature of rewards, their purpose, and the specific circumstances and conditions under which they are effective—because, despite their high costs, rewards do not always achieve their intended purpose.

Basically various components of a reward system are designed and administered within an organization to achieve four major behavioural objectives. First, reward systems are *designed to attract* to the organization individuals with the knowledge, ability, and talents demanded by specific organizational tasks. Second, reward systems are *designed to retain* valued, productive employees who must perceive them as fair and equitable relative to the market. Third, reward systems are *designed to motivate* individuals and groups within the organization *to maintain regular attendance and a high standard of performance on the job.* Finally, reward systems are designed *to promote among its members certain favourable attitudes toward the organization itself, including its various socio-technical components* such as supervision, coworkers, administrative practices, the assigned jobs, and its technology. Such attitudes and beliefs are often reflected in the employee's loyalty and commitment to the organization, high job involvement and job satisfaction.

Besides the previously mentioned behavioural objectives, the manner in which various components of a reward system are administered may influence the overall organizational culture or climate and reinforce the prevailing structure within the organization. For instance Lawler (1984) argues that different organizational climates such as human resource oriented, entrepreneurial, participative etc., are dependent upon how reward systems are designed and managed. Competence or skill-based reward systems may promote an entrepreneurial climate. Encouraging employee participation in the design of reward systems may create a participative climate. However, achieving such broad organizational objectives through systemic influences of reward systems has been more fully discussed elsewhere (Lawler 1981, 1984) and is not the focus of this paper. Rather, the paper deals with the nature or characteristics of specific organizational rewards, the way the rewards are classified, and the way they affect employee behaviour.

More specifically, the paper begins with a review of the motivation theories of work behaviour with a particular examination of the use of the intrinsic-extrinsic dichotomy, which has proved most unsatisfactory in the classification and management of rewards. Following a discussion of the findings of the Kanungo and Hartwick (1985) study of the attributes of rewards, the paper presents an alternative basis for rewards classification which is conceptually sound and provides clear, practical guidelines for effective rewards management.

PROCESS AND CONTENT APPROACHES TO REWARD MANAGEMENT

Our understanding of the nature of organizational rewards and their influence on the beliefs, attitudes, and behaviour of employees is derived from the theories and empirical research in the area of work motivation. Motivational theories of work behaviour can be grouped into two relatively separate and independent categories—mechanical or process theories, and substantive or content theories (Campbell, Dunnette, Lawler and Weick 1970; Campbell and Pritchard 1976). Process theories attempt to describe and explain *how* individual work behaviour is energized, directed, sustained, and stopped. Examples of such theories include the reinforcement and behaviour modification theories (Hull 1943; Luthans and Kreitner 1975; Skinner 1953), the various forms of expectancy theory (Atkinson 1964; Fishbein and Ajzen 1975; Lawler 1973; Vroom 1964), and the recent cognitive information processing theories (Salancik and Pfeffer 1978). In contrast, content theories are more interested in specifying *what* it is that energizes and sustains individual behaviour. In doing so, such theories typically develop taxonomies, or classifications of individual needs (Alderfer 1972; Maslow 1954; McClelland 1961; Murray 1938), and of work rewards (Deci 1975; Herzberg, Mausner and Snyderman 1959).

In recent years, much of the work motivation research has dealt with questions of process, testing the various forms of the expectancy theory. According to a popular version of the expectancy theory, the strength of a person's motivation to perform effectively is influenced by the person's belief that (1) efforts would lead to a desired level of performance and (2) level of performance would lead to valued organizational rewards (Lawler 1981). In other words, a person will be motivated to perform at a given level, if a person believes that he or she has the necessary ability to perform at that level *and* if a person believes that such performance will, in fact, bring rewards that person values. For the most part, research work on the expectancy theory must be considered successful. Mitchell (1979), for example, claims that the "expectancy theory has generated considerable research and most of the results have been supportive. In general, people work hard when they think that working hard is likely to lead to desirable organizational rewards" (p. 255). Expectancy theories have not only given us a good start at understanding how behaviour is initiated, directed, and sustained, but its sound theoretical base also permits us to formulate practical courses of action which every manager, with a little training, can easily apply for the benefit of both the employees and the organization. It follows from expectancy theory that: (1) an organization should offer rewards that have a *high valence*—that is, rewards that workers value; (2) the rewards are made *contingent on performance*—that is, the rewards are linked to performance; (3) the rewards are made *salient*—that is, the existence of the rewards and the contingencies attached to them are uppermost in the minds of the employees. Thus, to motivate good performance, the organization should ensure that the employees receive valued rewards when they perform well, and do not receive them when they perform poorly. On the other hand, to attract new employees or to reduce turnover, one should administer to all members of the organization certain valued rewards they might not otherwise obtain.

Most managers view such recommendations either as simple common sense or as ivory tower speculations, which provide little insight into the improvement of management practice. This is probably because their concerns are with a different set of questions. For example, they want to know what specific type of rewards they should give to motivate their employees. Such an approach seems to be seeking for a contraption with an omniscient intelligence built into it. Of course, the process theories do not provide such a contraption. Many believe that the content theories, with their simple distinction of intrinsic-extrinsic rewards, were an answer to the manager's prayer! We explore the content theories to determine if they are indeed the panacea for every motivational woe.

THE INTRINSIC-EXTRINSIC DICHOTOMY

In an attempt to be practical—to describe specifically what rewards do or do not motivate the desired work behaviour—content theorists have developed various ways of classifying rewards. The most popular classification has been based on the characteristics of the rewards as intrinsic or extrinsic. This distinction, which currently holds a prominent spot in the theory and practice of human resource management, was first popularized by Herzberg (Herzberg et al. 1959). Herzberg claimed that there were two basic classes of factors which affected work behaviour: intrinsic factors and extrinsic factors. He described intrinsic factors as all those rewards (or outcomes) which are built into or inherent in the job and form part of the job content. Consequently, the individual receives the intrinsic rewards by the very act of performance. For example: the satisfaction experienced by doing well a job with a considerable degree of autonomy and responsibility; or the sense of accomplishment and growth one experiences in doing well a demanding and challenging job. Extrinsic factors, on the other hand, are all those rewards (outcomes) which are external to the job and form part of the job context or environment. Examples of extrinsic rewards are: pay, working conditions, job security. According to Herzberg, if the extrinsic factors are absent, the individual is dissatisfied; if the extrinsic factors are present, the individual is not dissatisfied. The extrinsic factors do not generate satisfaction, they only prevent dissatisfaction. On the other hand, the intrinsic factors generate satisfaction. Assuming that satisfaction with outcomes results in increased motivation to perform, Herzberg concludes that the intrinsic factors alone are the true motivators; the extrinsic factors do not motivate, but only function as hygiene factors which must exist before the motivators can begin to operate. Hence, Herzberg's two-factor theory of motivator-hygiene factors.

More recently, the distinction between intrinsic and extrinsic rewards has been incorporated into a variety of process theories of motivation, most notably in a number of versions of expectancy theory (Lawler 1973; Staw 1976). Some of these theories, contrary to Herzberg, postulate that both intrinsic and extrinsic rewards act as motivators. However, the intrinsic and extrinsic rewards differ in the manner or process in which they influence motivation. The influence of extrinsic rewards on an individual's motivation to perform depends on (1) whether the individual expects such rewards to directly follow performance and (2) the value the individual attaches to such rewards. For example, an extrinsic reward, such as money, will motivate an individual if he values the monetary reward highly and has high expectation of receiving the reward for his performance. When his expectation and value for the reward are low, his motivation consequently will be low. Thus, for extrinsic rewards, these variants of the expectancy theory (Lawler 1973) invoke the traditional expectancy theory concepts and process, namely, extrinsic rewards. To be of motivational value, they must have valence and must be contingent on performance. However, for intrinsic rewards, the traditional expectancy concepts of valence and contingent on performance are not used. These variants of expectancy theories have assumed that an intrinsic reward, being an inherent part of the job content, will automatically result from performance. For example, if the job has elements of autonomy built into it, then the satisfaction of an autonomous job will automatically be experienced by the individual in the course of his performance. The expectancy (i.e., the probability that performance will lead to a desired outcome) of an intrinsic reward will always be high (or equal to one in a scale of zero to one). In such theoretical formulations, the expectancy of intrinsic rewards will always be equal to or greater than the expectancy of extrinsic rewards. As a consequence, despite their avowed disagreement with Herzberg's two-factor theory, these neo-expectancy theorists come to a rather similar conclusion: that intrinsic rewards, per se, are more important than extrinsic rewards in influencing motivation. Other versions of the expectancy theory (e.g., Fishbein and Ajzen 1975; Warshaw, Sheppard and Hartwick, in press) have incorporated intrinsic outcomes without the use of a separate explanatory mechanism. Such theories utilize expectancies and valences of all outcomes, intrinsic or extrinsic, suggesting that both types of rewards influence motivation through the same sort of psychological processes.

While the distinction between intrinsic and extrinsic rewards has had a major influence on motivational theory, this impact pales in comparison to its impact on management practice. Here, the influence is most pervasive in the manager's vocabulary, thinking, and approach to developing compensation programs. The reason for this lies in the relatively straight forward answer the distinction provides to practical questions which beset every manager. What rewards should a manager give to motivate workers? The obvious answer is: intrinsic rewards. How should intrinsic rewards be given? By redesigning jobs. Not only is the answer new, it is specific and provides the manager the challenge and the satisfaction of being creative and innovative. Indeed, much of today's work in job and work design is derived from a long tradition of interest in the intrinsic aspects of the job, stemming from Herzberg (Staw 1984).

Critique of the Intrinsic-Extrinsic Dichotomy

The intrinsic-extrinsic dichotomy is not, however, without its critics. One persistent problem has been the use of different definitions of intrinsic and extrinsic rewards. Some theorists (e.g., Herzberg et al. 1959; Staw 1976) have focused on the *relation between the activity and the reward*. Using such a distinction, intrinsic rewards are considered to be those rewards that derive directly from or are inherently connected to the task, such as: recognition, responsibility, achievement. In contrast, extrinsic rewards are considered to be those rewards which are seen as being external to or separate from the task, such as: pay, praise from supervisor, reserved parking. Other theorists (e.g., Deci 1972; Lawler 1973) have focused on the *person who administers or mediates the reward*. From this perspective, rewards that are self-mediated are denoted as intrinsic, for example, interesting and meaningful task, or pride in the job. Rewards that come from others are called extrinsic, for example, pay, promotion, or praise from supervisor.

It is obvious that the same reward can be classified either as intrinsic or extrinsic depending upon whether the focus of your definition is on the task or on the person who administers the reward. Thus, from the point of view of the task dimension, recognition could be classified as intrinsic, whereas from the point of view of the person who administers the reward, recognition could very easily be classified as extrinsic. The extent of the acute disagreement over the definitions of intrinsic and extrinsic rewards has been most clearly demonstrated by Dyer and Parker (1976). In a survey of members of Division 14 of the American Psychological Association, they found a wide range of definitions being employed. The two definitions based on the criterion of task and mediation of reward were most popular, with approximately forty-seven percent and twenty-nine percent of the responses respectively. Moreover, when asked to classify an extensive list of rewards as intrinsic or extrinsic, there was again considerable disagreement among the respondents. Indeed, only seven out of twenty-one rewards were classified as intrinsic or as extrinsic by more than seventy-five percent of the respondents. These results prompted Dyer and Parker to suggest a serious re-examination of the entire intrinsic-extrinsic issue.

Guzzo (1979) did precisely that. In his paper, Guzzo reviewed four methods typically employed to dichotomize intrinsic and extrinsic rewards. His conclusion was unambiguous:

... I conclude that this dichotomy of reward types, regardless of the specific criterion on which it is built, is not fruitful for understanding the nature of different work rewards. Specifically: (a) there is not unambiguous definitional separation of intrinsic and extrinsic rewards, whether the definitional statements are highly conceptual or highly operational; (b) there is no clear demarcation of reward types based on the level of need served; (c) two types of rewards do not usefully differentiate themselves on the basis of a reciprocal influence of reward effects; and (d) two types of rewards are not distinguishable on the basis of differences in the hypothesized cognitive consequences of rewards. Thus, if a further understanding of work motivation is to be gained, it is imperative that characteristics of work rewards be conceived of in other than intrinsic-extrinsic terms ... (P. 82)

The various theories utilizing the intrinsic-extrinsic distinction have also not escaped unscathed. In the late '60s and early '70s, Herzberg's two-factor theory was surrounded with controversy. Most reviews (e.g., King 1970) concluded that there was little empirical support for the theory, prompting Campbell et al. (1970) to suggest that it was time to lay the theory to rest. It would appear that researchers have done just that (Mitchell 1979). The use of the intrinsic-extrinsic dichotomy by the neo-expectancy theorists has been less criticized. However, as noted earlier, a number of researchers (e.g., Fishbein and Ajzen 1975; Warshaw et al. in press) have incorporated intrinsic outcomes without the use of a separate explanatory mechanism. Such theories utilize expectancies and valences of all outcomes, intrinsic or extrinsic. Thus, all rewards are seen as influencing motivation through the same sort of psychological processes.

Several researchers have argued in favour of maintaining intrinsic-extrinsic reward distinction because the two types of rewards tend to meet two different categories of needs. It is suggested that extrinsic rewards meet lower-order needs and intrinsic rewards meet higher-order needs as conceptualized by Maslow (1954). This argument is very weak when one considers that an extrinsic reward like pay can satisfy both lower-order needs—food and shelter—and higher-order needs—as a symbol of recognition or ego-status (Lawler, 1981).

The arguments are indeed overwhelming against the suitability of the use of intrinsic and extrinsic rewards as theoretical constructs in theories of worker motivation. But, how effective have been the practical applications of these theoretical constructs in the work place? Job and work designs, incorporating various improvements in the intrinsic aspects of work, have had mixed reviews. The most common of these designs has been job enrichment. Some reviews of various applications of job enrichment programs have concluded that they are for the most part successful (e.g., Davis and Cherns 1975; Lawler 1969). Others (e.g., Fein 1974), have questioned the data on which such conclusions are based. Moreover, there exist a number of critiques of such programs, coming from all interested parties. For example, Champagne (1979) has argued that in explaining the effects of job enrichment, "attention must be redirected from the presumed impact of intrinsic motivation to a more explicit reinforcement approach" (p. 34). Success of job enrichment programs is often attributed to employee reactions to "more interesting, exciting and challenging work. While this reasoning makes sense, a better rationale may be found by examining the tangible consequences employees face as a result of their performance" (Champagne, 1979, 24). Luthans and Reif (1973) noted that job enrichment programs are applicable to only a narrow spectrum of jobs, that the economic dividends in such jobs are minimal, and that workers frequently prefer unenriched jobs. Supporting this latter point, Winpisinger (1973) states that unions would prefer that management instead focus on providing extrinsic rewards such as good pay, working conditions, and job security. In a recent article on effective use of rewards, Podsakoff, Greene, and McFillen (1984) observed that the managerial advocacy for job enrichment programs is based on a commonly held assumption that intrinsic rewards are more highly valued by employees than extrinsic rewards. However, their review of empirical evidence indicates that intrinsic rewards are neither "necessarily more valued" nor "universally more effective than extrinsic rewards" (pp. 274–275).

Persistence of the Intrinsic-Extrinsic Dichotomy

In light of the cited conceptual and empirical shortcomings, one might wonder why the intrinsic-extrinsic dichotomy has remained so popular. Perhaps, it persists because of certain cultural values inherent in our society. The idea that our own behaviour is intrinsically motivated is pleasing to us. It provides us with a sense of freedom. Moreover, it is seen as separating humans from lower animal forms which operate solely for the acquisition of extrinsic rewards.

Intrinsic and extrinsic motivation have also become part of the layman's lexicon. They represent an important basis for a good deal of our intuitive or common sense theorizing about the causes of individual behaviour. For example, we tend to distinguish phenomena in terms of internal—whose cause is within our control—and external—whose cause is not within our control. Given this constant use in our everyday lives, it is only natural that this distinction extends to our practical and scientific endeavours.

Very often, a lack of perceived clarity of environmental forces, such as organizational goals, rewards, constraints, etc., makes us explain our behaviour in terms of intrinsic motivation.

There is one additional reason for the persistence of the intrinsic-extrinsic dichotomy. We do not have at the present time a popular alternative classification or taxonomy of work rewards. And, as Kuhn (1970) has pointed out, it takes more than contradictory research findings to eliminate a theory from consideration; it takes an alternative theory that is perceived to be better than what one has at present. The section which follows is an attempt to present one such alternative theory.

PROCESS APPROACH: AN ALTERNATIVE CLASSIFICATION

Campbell and Pritchard (1976) pointed out that in spite of several theoretical attempts at developing job-related, reward classification in content theories, "empirical taxonomic work is amazingly sparse" (p. 63). Very few studies provide empirical validation of reward taxonomies such as the intrinsic-extrinsic classification. Furthermore, in his critical review of existing reward classifications, Guzzo made the following observations:

There is tremendous variety in the properties of work rewards, and any one reward can be characterized by multiple attributes displayed in varying degrees. An expanded understanding of work rewards requires identification and analysis of their many attributers as well as some means of classification according to shared attributes. ... It is evident that additional inquiry into the nature of work rewards is warranted, with both inductive and empirical investigations of the attributes of work rewards needed. (P. 82–83)

This task was accomplished in a recent study by Kanungo and Hartwick (1985).

They investigated respondents' perceptions of forty-eight work rewards typically offered by organizations using the following ten attributes:

1. Is the reward intrinsic (i.e., related to or derived from the task) or extrinsic (i.e., not related to or not derived from the task)?
2. Is the reward intrinsic (i.e., self-administered or mediated) or extrinsic (i.e., other-administered or mediated)?
3. Saliency: is the reward salient?
4. Valence: is the reward valued?
5. Is the reward contingent on high performance?
6. Is the reward contingent on low performance?
7. Is the reward considered to be concrete or abstract?
8. The time of administration of the reward; how soon after one's performance is it administered or received?
9. Is the reward typically given to reward the mere completion of task activities or to reward the successful outcomes of task activities?
10. The frequency of administration, how often is the reward typically used by organizations?

The first two attributes corresponded to the two most popular definitions of intrinsic and extrinsic rewards. The next four attributes corresponded to various expectancy theory constructs. The next three attributes were included because they have in the past been linked to the intrinsic-extrinsic dichotomy. In contrast to extrinsic rewards, intrinsic rewards are frequently considered to be intangible, subjective, and lead to the satisfaction of higher-order needs (e.g., Deci 1972; Lawler 1969). More tangible objects, on the other hand, are considered to be extrinsic rewards. One reason often given for the effectiveness of intrinsic rewards is their immediacy. Either because they are directly related to the task or because they are self-administered, intrinsic rewards are likely to be administered or received earlier than extrinsic rewards. The ninth attribute relates to Staw's (1976) expectancy formulation. According to Staw, intrinsic rewards are received for both task behaviour (mere completion of activities) and task performance (successful outcomes of task). Extrinsic rewards, on the other hand, are given for task performance only. The final attribute, frequency of administration, was included simply because it was thought to capture an important aspect of work rewards not found in the other measures.

Together, the ten attributes were thought to assess a wide variety of ways in which work rewards could be perceived. Answers to such questions could be put to a variety of uses. However, the bulk of the attention in the study was focused on two key questions.

First, the study took a close look at the intrinsic-extrinsic dichotomy. In particular, it examined the construct validity of the distinction. The following questions were asked: Can workers consistently classify work rewards as intrinsic or extrinsic using the two definitions—that of relation to task and that of mediation? Does the intrinsic-extrinsic classification using these definitions relate to the other attributes of work rewards in similar and meaningful ways? Does the intrinsic-extrinsic dichotomy capture a significant amount of the variance among workers' perceptions of rewards?

There was a second key component to the study. It explored what other dimensions in fact characterize workers' perceptions of rewards. It was hypothesized that the expectancy theory constructs of valence, expectancy or contingency, and salience would form the basic dimensions. If the results of the study confirmed the hypothesis, then these constructs could be used to categorize work rewards.

The results of the Kanungo and Hartwick (1985) study revealed that respondents were unable to consistently classify work rewards as intrinsic or extrinsic. Their inability was clearly noticeable when they classified rewards using the task-relation definition. Only three out of forty-eight rewards were classified as either intrinsic (derives directly from the task) or as extrinsic (does not derive from the task itself) by more than seventy-five percent of the respondents. On the other hand, respondents were more consistent when they classified rewards according to the person who administers or mediates the reward. When this latter definition was used, twenty-two out of forty-eight rewards were classified as intrinsic (self-administered) or as extrinsic (other-administered) by more than seventy-five percent of the respondents. Overall, then, the results revealed a lack of response consistency. However, if we consider the two intrinsic-extrinsic attributes mentioned previously, then the use of the mediation definition (i.e., self- or other-administered) is superior to the task-related definition in separating intrinsic from extrinsic rewards.

Assuming that the two definitions, task-relation and mediation, of the intrinsic-extrinsic dichotomy refer to the same psychological construct, several predictions based on it were tested in the study.

It was predicted that rewards classified as intrinsic or extrinsic using the task-relation definition will be similarly classified using the mediation definition. However, the results showed that thirteen out of the forty-eight rewards were differentially classified as intrinsic/extrinsic under the two definitions, as illustrated by the following data:

1. Promotion, authority, responsibility, participation, praise from supervisors and from coworkers, recognition, and awards for superior performance were classified as intrinsic using the task-relation definition (perceived as deriving directly from the task) and were also classified as extrinsic using the mediation-definition (perceived as administered by others).

2. Pride in the success of the company and opportunity to make friends were classified as extrinsic using the task-relation definition (perceived as not deriving from the task itself) and were also classified as intrinsic using the mediation-definition (perceived as self-administered).

The data in the previous illustrations not only form coherent groupings, but also demonstrate a good sense of classification. Herzberg et al. (1959), using the task-relation definition, classified recognition, responsibility, and advancement as intrinsic rewards. However, it is clear that such rewards are mediated by others a good deal of the time.

These results do not confirm the prediction that when the two definitions, task-relation and mediation, are used rewards will be similarly classified as intrinsic or extrinsic. Therefore, these results raise the question whether the two definitions of the intrinsic-extrinsic dichotomy do indeed refer to the same psychological construct.

It was predicted that responses to each of the intrinsic-extrinsic scales should be related in similar ways to each of the other reward attributes assessed in the study. The results show that although the two intrinsic-extrinsic scales were found to be significantly related to one another, the relationship was not particularly strong for the two measures purported to assess the same construct. Moreover, there was a good degree of inconsistency in the pattern of relations between these scales and those assessing other constructs in the study.

Together, these results suggested the presence of serious problems with the construct validity of the intrinsic-extrinsic dichotomy. While scales based on the two definitional distinctions were found to relate to other work reward attributes in meaningful ways, very different patterns of correlations were found for each. Furthermore, it was found that a fairly large number of work rewards were differentially and meaningfully classified by the two distinctions. At the very least, then, the results of the study suggested that the intrinsic-extrinsic dichotomy, as currently conceptualized, does not reflect a single unitary psychological construct.

Given that the intrinsic-extrinsic dichotomy does not seem to represent a single strong coherent dimension in the workers' classification of rewards, one might ask how such rewards could in fact be classified. Based on the results of a factor analysis of their data, Kanungo and Hartwick (1985) reported three different dimensions (or clusters of attributes) on the basis of which work rewards can be classified. The first and the most important dimension was described as a *high performance contingent, valued and salient* reward dimension. On this dimension, rewards at one extreme are salient, frequently given to or received by high performers, and highly valued by them. Examples of rewards high on this dimension include pay, promotion, interesting work, and feelings of worthwhile accomplishment. Such rewards, according to expectancy theory, will definitely lead to a strong motivation to perform well at one's work tasks. Rewards at the other end of the dimension are, of course, less salient, infrequently given to high performers and less valued. Examples include a paid parking space, cafeteria subsidies and discounts on the purchase of company products. Such rewards are unlikely to motivate task performance.

A second dimension was described as *reward generality* or *performance noncontingent, frequent* rewards. On this dimension, rewards at one extreme are given frequently by organizations, even to low performers, and have little connection with one's work activities. Examples include vacations, coffee breaks, accident and sickness insurance, sick pay, and retirement benefits. Such rewards, then, represent those items generally given to all organization members regardless of performance. At the other end of the dimension are rewards that are less frequently given and more connected to one's work tasks. Examples include an expense account, use of a company car, and a uniform/clothes allowance. Such rewards are generally given only to those employees whose job functions or status demands it. The third dimension represented an *intrinsic-extrinsic mediation* dimension. Four reward attributes characterized this intrinsic-extrinsic dimension: mediation, abstract/concrete, administration to reward activities or outcomes, and time of administration. On this dimension, rewards at one extreme are abstract and self-administered during or soon after performance. Examples include personal challenge, feelings of worthwhile accomplishment, pride in work, and personal growth and development. At the other end of the dimension are rewards that are concrete, administered by others for various performance outcomes, and are received well after performance. Examples include profit-sharing, promotions, awards for long service, and retirement benefits.

IMPLICATIONS FOR REWARD MANAGEMENT

The results of the Kanungo and Hartwick (1985) study confirmed several observations of earlier critiques of the intrinsic-extrinsic dichotomy of work rewards (e.g., Dyer and Parker, 1976; Guzzo, 1979). Specifically, the results highlighted three problems with the dichotomy.

First, workers were unable to classify various work rewards into intrinsic and extrinsic categories with a high degree of consistency, even though they were given detailed definitional distinctions. This was especially true of the intrinsic-extrinsic distinction based on the relation to task definition.

Second, and of greater importance, the construct validity of the intrinsic-extrinsic dichotomy was found to be suspect. A substantial number of work rewards were classified in one way according to the task-relation definition and in exactly the opposite way according to the mediational definition. Not only does this result suggest the presence of two distinct constructs, it also provides an explanation for inconsistent reward classifications noticed in the literature on work rewards. The study further questioned the intrinsic-extrinsic dichotomy's construct validity. Scales reflecting the two definitional distinctions were found to relate to other reward attributes in very different ways, pointing to the presence of two distinct psychological constructs, instead of a single intrinsic-extrinsic dimension.

These results suggest that a serious reappraisal of the usefulness of the intrinsic-extrinsic dichotomy is in order. As a starting point, we might consider the two definitional distinctions of intrinsic-extrinsic dichotomy.

One distinction, frequently used in both theory and research (e.g., Herzberg et al. 1959; Staw 1976), focuses on the relation between tasks and the work rewards received or experienced for those tasks. Intrinsic rewards are defined as those rewards deriving directly from the task; extrinsic rewards are defined as those rewards not directly related to the task. It was with this distinction that one encounters the greatest difficulty, because of its ambiguity. Using the distinction, the workers in Kanungo and Hartwick (1985) study were unable to classify the work rewards with a high degree of consistency. As a consequence, it may be recommended that the use of this definitional distinction be ceased. It does not clearly and consistently differentiate work rewards. On the other hand, the expectancy theory constructs of salience, performance contingency, and valence as reward attributes would seem to provide a much clearer explanation of motivation than the intrinsic-extrinsic construct based on relation to task dimension.

A second distinction used in past theory and research (e.g., Deci 1972; Lawler 1973) focuses on the person who mediates the reward. Intrinsic rewards are defined as those which are self-administered; extrinsic rewards are defined as those which come from others. In the Kanungo and Hartwick (1985) study, this definitional distinction fared reasonably well. This, then, is the definitional distinction that may be recommended for use in the future. However, it would be preferable to label work rewards classified according to this distinction as self-and other-mediated rewards. The terms intrinsic and extrinsic generate too much ambiguity, possibly due to the other unsatisfactory distinction, and therefore should be laid to rest.

Third, although work rewards could be classified according to the person who administers them, there would seem to be little reason to do so, especially when another dimension of work rewards, based upon expectancy theory constructs, offers a much stronger basis of classification. The constructs of salience, performance contingency, and valence have consistently been shown to explain differences in task motivation in a wide variety of research contexts. Furthermore, there appears to be no a priori reason why, for example, self-administered rewards should be considered to be superior to rewards administered by others. Such rewards would seem to be more effective *only to the extent* that they are more salient, more likely to be administered to high performers, and more valued.

From the results of the Kanungo and Hartwick (1985) study, a classification of the forty-eight work rewards, based on the three expectancy theory constructs, is presented in Table 18–1. To create this classification, mean attribute scores for the three attributes were split into equal thirds. In the table, the top sixteen rewards are labelled high, the middle sixteen are labelled medium, and the lowest sixteen rewards are labelled low.

According to expectancy theory, work rewards that are highly salient, administered to high performers, and highly valued will elicit the highest level of task motivation and performance. As Table 19–1 shows, there are eight such rewards—promotion, job security, pay, pride in work, feelings of worthwhile accomplishment, interesting work, recognition, and personal challenge. It is interesting to note that several of these rewards are among those that have frequently been incorporated in job and work design projects aimed at increasing the intrinsic aspects of work. However, pay and job security, the two rewards neglected by such projects, are also present in the list. According to the proposed classification, all of these rewards will be highly effective and should be considered as essential components of a compensation program.

At the other end of the spectrum, rewards that are not salient, infrequently given to high performers, and not valued highly cannot be expected to motivate task performance. In the present list, there are nine such rewards—mortgage financing, company-sponsored recreational activities, discounts on the purchase of company products, extended lunch periods, company-sponsored professional services, a uniform/clothes allowance, cafeteria subsidies, sick pay, and a paid parking space. It is interesting to note that all nine of these rewards would typically be labelled as extrinsic by most organizational researchers. In the past, extrinsic rewards have often been said to be less effective than intrinsic rewards (e.g., Deci 1975; Herzberg et al. 1959); however, little theoretical justification was offered to explain why this was so. The proposed classification tells us why—these rewards are low in salience, not given to high performers, and not valued highly by employees.

Although the effectiveness of the proposed classification system needs to be thoroughly tested in a variety of organizational settings, it is expected that this process classification of work rewards will prove to be quite useful, as is clear from the findings of the

Table 19–1 Work Rewards Classified According to Expectancy Theory Constructs

	Salience	Administered to High Performers	Valence
Promotion	high	high	high
Job security	high	high	high
Pay	high	high	high
Pride in work	high	high	high
Feelings of worthwhile accomplishment	high	high	high
Interesting work	high	high	high
Recognition	high	high	high
Personal challenge	high	high	high
Participation in decision making	medium	high	high
Awards for superior performance	medium	high	high
Vacation	high	medium	high
Paid personal time off	medium	medium	high
Opportunity to use special abilities	medium	medium	high
Cost of living increase	low	medium	high
Sick leaves	low	medium	high
Use of company car	high	low	high
Responsibility	high	high	medium
Personal growth and development	high	high	medium
Prestige	high	high	medium
Praise from supervisor	high	high	medium
Sense of belonging	medium	high	medium
Opportunity for creativity	low	high	medium
Pride in success of company	low	high	medium
Social status	high	medium	medium
Variety of job	medium	medium	medium
Holiday bonus	medium	medium	medium
Authority	medium	medium	medium
Accident and sickness insurance	medium	medium	medium
Praise from coworkers	medium	medium	medium
Profit-sharing plan	medium	low	medium
Retirement benefits	medium	low	medium
Expense account	low	low	medium
Achieving the organization's goals	low	high	low
Opportunity make friends	high	medium	low
Coffee breaks	low	medium	low
Awards for long service	low	medium	low
Company-sponsored life insurance	medium	low	low
Dental plan	medium	low	low
Paid absence for study	medium	low	low
Mortgage financing	low	low	low
Company-sponsored recreational activities	low	low	low
Discounts on purchase of company products	low	low	low
Extended lunch periods	low	low	low
Company-sponsored professional services	low	low	low
Uniform/clothes allowance	low	low	low
Cafeteria subsidies	low	low	low
Sick pay	low	low	low
Paid parking space	low	low	low

Kanungo and Hartwick (1985) study. A cursory look at various individual, group, or organization-wide incentive schemes (Lawler 1984; Podsakoff et al. 1984) would reveal that their success depends to a large extent on the inclusion of specific reward components that are perceived by employees as salient, valued and performance contingent. Thus it seems that with work rewards classified along the three basic expectancy theory dimensions, we can not only choose *what* rewards to administer, we can also readily explain *why* such rewards will be effective.

It should also be possible to look at the particular rewards already present in a job or within an organization to see how such rewards are typically perceived and to predict whether or not they will be effective. Of course, the perceived characteristics of the rewards have to be based on the classification scheme suggested in this paper. Variations in the salience, performance contingency, and valence of different rewards are apt to vary somewhat from setting to setting. However, this also suggests it should be possible to modify the typical characteristics of a given reward, at least in some cases. Salience of a given reward can perhaps, be increased through increased visibility or publicity. Performance contingency might be increased through contingent reward or incentive schemes and clear feedback. Valence could be increased through a variation in the amount or in the diversity of a particular reward. The proposed classification system provides clear, practical guidelines, based on an easily understood rationale, not only to identify the rewards most likely to influence work motivation, but also to increase the potential benefits of existing rewards.

References

Alderfer, C. P. 1972. *Existence, relatedness, and growth.* New York: The Free Press.

Atkinson, J. W. 1964. *An introduction to motivation.* Princeton, N.J.: Van Nostrand.

Brief, A. P. and R. J. Aldag. 1977. The intrinsic-extrinsic dichotomy: Toward conceptual clarity. *Academy of Management Review* 2: 496–500.

Campbell, J. P., M. D., Dunnette, E. E. Lawler, and K. E. Weick. 1970. *Managerial behavior, performance, and effectiveness.* New York: McGraw-Hill.

Campbell, J. P. and R. D. Pritchard. 1976. "Motivation theory in industrial and organizational psychology." In *Handbook of Industrial and organizational psychology*, edited by M. D. Dunnette. Chicago: Rand McNally.

Champagne, P. J. 1979. Explaining job enrichment. *Supervisory Management* (November): 24–34.

Davis, L. E. and A. B. Cherns. 1975. *The quality of working life. Vol. 2, Cases and commentary.* New York: The Free Press.

Deci, E. L. 1972. The effects of contingent and noncontingent rewards and controls on intrinsic motivation. *Organizational Behavior and Human Performance* 8:217–29.

Deci, E. L. 1975. *Intrinsic motivation.* New York: Plenum Press.

Dyer, L. and D. F. Parker. 1976. Classifying outcomes in work motivation research: An examination of the intrinsic-extrinsic dichotomy. *Journal of Applied Psychology* 60: 455–58.

Fein, M. 1975. Job enrichment: A reevaluation. *Sloan Management Review* 15(2): 69–88.

Fishbein, M. and I. Ajzen. 1975. *Believe, attitude, intention, and behavior.* Reading, Mass.: Addison-Wesley.

Guzzo, R. A. 1979. Types of rewards, cognitions, and work motivation. *Academy of Management Review* 4:75–86.

Heider, F. 1958. *The psychology of interpersonal relations.* New York: Wiley.

Herzberg, F., B. Mausner, and B. B. Snyderman. 1959. *The motivation to work.* New York: Wiley.

Hull, C. L. 1943. *Principles of behavior.* New York: Appleton-Centure-Crofts.

Kanungo, R. N. and J. Hartwick. 1985. A process approach to the classification of work rewards. Working Paper, Faculty of Management, McGill University.

Kelley, H. H. 1967. "Attribution theory in social psychology." In *Nebraska Symposium on Motivation*, edited by D. Levine. Lincoln, Nebraska: University of Nebraska Press.

King, N. 1970. Clarification and evaluation of the two-factor theory of job satisfaction. *Psychological Bulletin* 74:18–31.

Kuhn, T. S. 1970. The structure of scientific revolutions. Vol. 2 of *International Encyclopedia of Unified Science.* Chicago: University of Chicago Press.

Lawler, E. E. 1969. Job design and employee motivation. *Personnel Psychology* 22:426–35.

Lawler, E. E. 1973. *Motivation in work organizations.* Monterey, California: Brooks/Cole.

Lawler, E. E. 1981. *Pay and organization development.* Reading, Mass: Addison-Wesley.

Lawler, E. E. 1984. "The strategic design of reward systems." In *Readings in personnel and human resource management*, edited by R. S. Schuler and S. A. Youngblood. St. Paul, Minnesota: West Publishing, 1984.

Luthans, F. and R. Kreitner. 1975. *Organizational behavior modification.* Glenview, Illinois: Scott, Foresman.

Luthans, F. and W. E. Reif. 1973. Job enrichment: Long on theory, short on practice. *Organizational Dynamics* 3:30–43.

Maslow, A. H. 1954. *Motivation and personality.* New York: Harper & Row.

McClelland, D. C. 1961. *The achieving society.* Princeton, N.J.: Van Nostrand.

Miner, J. B. 1980. *Theories of organizational behavior.* Hinsdale, Illinois: The Dryden Press.

Mitchell, T. R. 1979. Organizational behavior. *Annual Review of Psychology* 30:243–81.

Murray, H. 1938. *Explorations in personality.* New York: Oxford University Press.

Podsakoff, P. M., C. N. Greene, and J. M. McFillen. 1984. "Obstacles to the effective use of reward systems." In *Readings in personnel and human resource management*, edited by R. S. Schuler and S. A. Youngblood. St. Paul, Minnesota: West Publishing.

Salancik, G. R. and J. Pfeffer. 1978. A social information processing approach to job attitudes and task design. *Administrative Science Quarterly* 23:224–53.

Skinner, B. F. 1953. *Science and human behavior.* New York: Macmillan.

Staw, B. M. 1976. *Intrinsic and extrinsic motivation.* Morristown, N.J.: General Learning Press.

Staw, B. M. 1984. Organizational behavior: A review and reformulation of the field's outcome variables. *Annual Review of Psychology* 35:627–66.

Vroom, V. H. 1964. *Work and motivation.* New York: Wiley.

Warshaw, P., B. H. Sheppard, and J. Hartwick. In press. "The intention and self-prediction of goals and behavior." In *Advances in Marketing Communication*, edited by R. Bagozzi. Greenwich, CT: JAI Press.

Winpisinger, W. W. 1973. Job satisfaction: A union response. *AFL–CIO American Federalist* 80:8–10.

Section V
Improving Employees Effectiveness and Motivation

The five articles in this section are included to illustrate ways PHRM can improve employees effectiveness and motivation. In the first article, Adams provides a macroscopic view of training and development in Canada. For illustrating the variety of ways in which Canadian employees are being trained, the article begins with a focus on five different occupations: clerk-typist, salesperson, manager, accountant, and tool and die maker. The author then describes the general characteristics of the Canadian training system. Comparisons to the United States, Germany, and Japan are mentioned. Emphasis is placed on the institutional and legal aspects of the Canadian system.

One particular difficulty in implementing a training program in the industry is the lack of a scientific and rigorous mechanism to assess the effectiveness of the training. The second article by Haccoun addresses itself to issues of training evaluation. The paper begins with a brief introduction to the processes involved in the development of training programs. Then Haccoun details out the types of evaluation measures which might be used in the assessment phase. The author clearly advocates the use of methods which land inferential sense such as experimental procedures or a time series design.

In the third article, Szawlowski speculates on the particular training needs in the high technology industry in Canada. Drawing on the challenges of the aerospace industry, Szawlowski begins with identifying the strategic purposes of training and development. He then works through the various phases of training to include assessment of needs, development of training objectives, implementing and selecting the training media and assessment. The author concludes the article by looking into the future. He suggests that training in the future would be part of the strategic management of the organization.

In the next article, Kolodney concentrates on innovations in Canadian organizations designed to promote employees effectiveness and satisfaction. A special emphasis is placed on innovations that have a quality of working life and/or sociotechnical systems philosophy inherent in their design and implementation.

The final article in this section deals with the management of absence from work. First, Johns takes a close examination of the extent, costs, and benefits of absenteeism. Then, the author reviews models of absence behaviour that help enhance our understanding of this phenomenon. Johns concludes with ideas to be used by managers in monitoring, diagnosing, and managing absenteeism.

20. An Overview of Training and Development in Canada

Roy J. Adams, McMaster University

THE SYSTEM OF TRAINING

The social mechanisms through which individuals acquire knowledge, understanding, and skills may be referred to as the education and training system. All advanced, industrial countries have extensive and complex arrangements, and Canada is no exception. Training systems do, however, vary considerably from nation to nation. In this essay my intention is briefly to describe the key elements of the Canadian system and to contrast it with approaches taken elsewhere. Special regard will be paid to those aspects of the system which are of particular relevance to labour and management at the level of the enterprise. I will not, however, limit myself to training in industry because the character of industrial training is very much dependent upon the nature of the broader system. In order to understand firm level training policy it is first necessary, it seems to me, to appreciate the system as a whole.

I would like to thank my colleagues, Naresh Agarwal and Harish Jain, for their useful comments on an earlier version of this paper.

THE SKILL FORMATION PROCESS

Training in Canada takes many different forms from formal to informal, from systematic to haphazard, and from classroom to on-the-job. In order to illustrate both the variety of ways in which working people acquire skills, and the distribution of training responsibilities between the various actors in the system, it will be useful to focus on a group of specific occupations required by Canadian industry: clerk-typist, salesperson, manager, accountant, and tool and die maker.

Clerk-Typist

There are several ways in which a person might acquire clerk-typist skills. Secondary schools generally provide courses in typing, filing, etc. In fact, clerk-typist is one of the few occupations where a substantial number of job seekers acquire the necessary entry-level skills in secondary school. Most secondary school education is general rather than vocational in nature although there has been a trend towards the expansion of vocational schemes in recent years (MacDonald Commission Report 1985).

Beyond high school, publicly financed community colleges typically offer relevant courses as do private business colleges. It is very rare for private companies or government agencies to train people to be clerk-typists, although upgrading or retraining (e.g., from clerk-typist to computer-based word processor) may be provided.

At the post-secondary level, the more expensive private business colleges have been able to compete with publicly funded community colleges because they are smaller, more specialized, and put greater emphasis on placing all graduates in suitable jobs. Towards that end they maintain very close ties with industry.

Salesperson

There are a variety of ways that people find their way into sales positions. In one pattern, common in parts of manufacturing industry, individuals begin their careers in production occupations and later switch to sales. However, in several industries (e.g., auto manufacture, chemicals, insurance) the new employee begins as an apprentice salesperson. Selling skills are most often gained through informal learning and through on-the-job experience. It is not uncommon for new or potential salespersons to enroll in short courses put on by various associations, colleges, and consultants. Such courses are typically presented in one-, two-, or three-day formats and are taught by professionals with considerable experience. Participants are typically permitted fully paid day releases or bloc releases by their companies in order to attend the courses.

An alternative pattern is for the individual to follow a course of studies in marketing at a university or a college leading to a degree or diploma. In such cases, potential salespersons are often rotated through production or marketing jobs before being assigned a territory to service. Informal, on-the-job learning of sales skills is the general training pattern throughout Canadian industry. Although a great deal of sales learning apparently takes place continuously, very little of it happens in the context of comprehensive formal programs provided by the employer.

Manager

A somewhat similar pattern may be found when one focuses on managers. Few employees begin their careers as manager. Instead, after a period of time within a specialty (e.g., sales, production, personnel, or research) they are promoted to management positions (Daly 1974). Quite often the transition is a difficult one because managerial skills are different from skills required in any technical specialty. Because of the importance of good management at all levels to the success of the enterprise, more attention has been focused by companies on management development than on any other aspect of training. Management development has also been the subject of more administrative science research than has other aspects of training. However, instead of being prepared for their positions via carefully planned training schemes, it is likely that most managers in Canadian industry acquire their skills through a combination of on-the-job learning and attendance at occasional courses conducted by associations, colleges, and universities.

Some large companies, however, do maintain formal, planned, training programs for managerial candidates, most of whom are recruited from a university.

During the past decade or so the number of Canadian managers with a university education has been increasing rapidly. It is probable, however, that the majority are still not university educated. Of those managers with degrees, most took courses in the university which were unrelated to commerce or administration, and thus had to be trained in those skills subsequent to university. Enrollments in commerce courses has, however, expanded greatly in the past few decades (MacDonald Commission Report 1985).

Accountant

Whereas sales and management skills are largely transmitted informally and through occasional short courses the training of accountants is more organized and systematic. There are three professional accounting associations in Canada. All of them have courses of study leading to a professional designation. For example, the Society of Management Accountants' program leads to a designation as a certified management accountant (formerly, registered industrial accountant). The society specifies the curriculum which must be followed, but individual courses are provided by colleges and universities. The society's curriculum may be and often is followed by individuals working full time in entry level financial positions (bookkeeper, for example) in order that they may qualify for more responsible jobs.

The other two associations are the certified general accountants and the chartered accountants. Graduates of the former association, which has a strong presence in western Canada, go into both public and private accounting. C.A. students are trained to be public auditors, but many eventually pursue careers as financial managers in industry.

Not all accountants in industry have professional designations, of course; indeed, it is likely that among smaller firms the majority do not have such qualifications. On the other hand it is common for those filling accounting positions in industry to have supplemented on-the-job learning with courses taken on a part-time basis at colleges and universities. Formal, systematic, in-house training is uncommon.

Tool and Die Maker

Another occupation where training is formalized is that of tool and die maker. The classic form of training is apprenticeship. The company provides on-the-job experience, as well as systematic supervisory instruction over a period of years. In addition to learning on-the-job, the apprentice also attends formal classes, usually in community colleges. The curriculum is typically regulated by a government agency with the aid of advice from representatives of labour and management. Some companies, however, prefer to administer their own programs separate from the government framework.

Apprenticeship training is expensive. Costs range from about twenty thousand dollars to forty thousand dollars to fully train an industrial craftsman (see, *Youth: The Forgotten Generation* 1982, vol. 3). Moreover, there is no guarantee that apprentices will stay with the firm once training has been completed. As a result, many companies are loathe to operate apprenticeship schemes. A much smaller portion of the labour force is trained via such schemes in Canada than is true of many European countries (*In Short Supply* 1982). Instead of training, historically, there has been a strong dependence by Canadian companies on immigration to fill skilled positions. One Ontario study carried out in the mid

1970s found that most industrial craftsmen in the surveyed firms had immigrated from Europe (Robertson, Nickerson Associates 1978; see also *Youth: The Forgotten Generation* 1982).

The combination of shortages of skilled workers in the midst of high unemployment was the most important factor giving rise to debate and research on training problems during the 1970s. That debate eventually produced the National Training Act of 1982 and several initiatives by government to induce industrial firms to engage in more apprenticeship-type training. As of 1983, however, the problem appeared to be still a substantial one. A study by the Ontario Manpower Commission found that twenty-one of fifty-one of the largest manufacturing and processing firms in the province did not have training adequate to their needs (*Industrial Training for High Level Skills* 1983). Instead of training they "poached" skilled workers from other firms. This policy in turn placed a burden on smaller firms who could not compete with large companies in the market for skilled labour. The commission also concluded that although government prodding had produced an expansion of skills training in industry, it did not appear that the increase was sufficient to fill anticipated future needs (*Industrial Training for High Level Skills* 1983).

GENERAL SYSTEMS CHARACTERISTICS

With that occupational tour in mind, some general characteristics of the Canadian training system may be noted. First, systematic vocational training is not a primary function of the schools at the secondary level. Less than fifteen percent of secondary school students take vocational training programs. Canada is similar to the United States and Japan in that regard but quite different from West Germany. In that country about one-half of all sixteen-year olds enter the apprentice system which provides systematic training in a wide variety of trades from machinist to retail sales clerk (Weiermair 1982; Adams, Draper, and Ducharme 1979).

Second, although a great deal of learning takes place in Canadian industry, most of it is the result of informal on-the-job experience. Comprehensive, systematic training in Canada is primarily provided by post-secondary educational institutions and to a lesser extent by professional and occupational associations. Such programs do exist in industry, but, with some notable exceptions, companies prefer that systematic, long-term training be done by universities and colleges.

Quite a different pattern exists in Japan (Ishikawa 1981). Usually Japanese companies recruit high school and university graduates with few vocational skills and train them to a high level of proficiency over a number of years. Large Japanese companies often teach new recruits all of the noted skills, although smaller companies do depend on post-secondary institutions for some of them.

A third outstanding characteristic of the Canadian training system is the extensive involvement of government. Post-secondary vocational education is largely underwritten by government funds. Only about fifteen percent of the operating expenses of universities and colleges are paid out of student fees (MacDonald Commission Report 1985). The preponderance comes from the government. Apprentice training is also assisted by government funds which subsidize the bloc release periods during which the apprentice studies theoretical and conceptual aspects of the trade. Industry is enticed to provide both long- and short-term training by the lure of government grants. The appropriate mix of responsibility for training between government, industry, and individuals has been a major focus of debate and controversy in recent years.

THE ENTERPRISE PERSPECTIVE

In regard to acquisition of human resources, organizations must decide whether to make or buy. As the introductory overview suggests, Canadian companies (and, it might be added, government bureaucracies as well) tend to buy to a much greater extent than they make. Heavy reliance is placed upon educational institutions, immigration, and the relatively small number of training-active firms for the production of skilled clerical, technical, administrative, and professional employees.

There are, however, certain types of training which companies generally do provide. Orientation training, for example, is very common. Such training consists of introducing new employees to the history and customs of the enterprise. The expectations which the organization has of the new employee, as well as the rights and benefits which the individual acquires as a new member of the work community, are subjects that are also part of the curriculum. In North America, this type of training typically lasts for a few days at most. In Japan, however, the process of socialization may last for several weeks or even months (Ishikawa 1981). Research suggests that it may have a substantial influence on the future behaviour and performance of the employee.

Many companies also provide incentives, opportunities, and occasional formal courses in order to have employees upgrade and renew their skills. For example, many large firms offer tuition refund schemes in order to encourage employees to continue developing their capacities (Draper and Alden 1978). Department managers often have discretionary funds which may be used to send subordinates to short courses put on by colleges, universities, and various specialized associations and consultants. In the context of technological change (e.g., a switchover from typewriter to word processor), the vendor commonly provides training as part of the package. Large firms not uncommonly have training departments who periodically conduct specialized training courses on a wide variety of topics from work safety to union contract administration.

In the typical North American firm a training strategy has the following elements: (1) identify training needs, (2) develop a training program carefully designed to match the needs, (3) execute the program, and (4) evaluate the results. Not only is this model common in industry, it is also universally taught in schools of business and commerce.[1] It is interesting to note, therefore, that companies in other countries may employ quite different strategies. In Japan, for example, employees are expected to continually broaden their skills throughout their organizational careers. Slack time should be filled with learning more about the present job as well as learning to do contiguous jobs. While such an expecta-

---

1. The actual practice in industry is much cruder than the carefully designed schemes called for in human resource management textbooks (see Jain and Murray 1985). Nevertheless, the general format, often implemented very informally, is widespread in the real North American world.

tion is common enough for managerial employees in the West, it is much less in evidence with regard to clerical and production workers. (Regarding similarities between the conditions of work of western managers and Japanese blue-collar workers, see Koike 1983). In the West, the unstated assumption behind conventional wisdom is that either a problem exists or it does not, and if no problem is evident no response is required. The Japanese believe that employees can never know too well how to do their jobs and can never possess too many skills. The Japanese do, of course, set up programs designed to meet specific defined needs. Those programs, however, are in addition to the primary training strategy which requires that all employees continually learn, grow, and improve.

Continuous learning in Japan is buttressed by other aspects of the Japanese employment system (Vogel 1979). Thus, low mobility between firms means that the employee is not likely to abscond with acquired skills. Moreover, the relative permanence of employment, for which Japan is famous, means that the well-being of the individual is highly dependent on the overall well-being of the enterprise, Japanese employees may, therefore, be more motivated to improve themselves in order to contribute better to enterprise performance.[2]

A still different training strategy exists in West Germany with regard to skilled workers. Each year firms train a given number of young people in industrial and commercial skills regardless of the current demand situation (Weiermair 1982; Adams et al. 1979). Even during periods when an oversupply of skilled workers exists, apprenticeship training continues. In the aggregate, German industry considers this commitment to be critical to its international competitiveness. Research in Germany has shown that apprentice graduates are less often unemployed than nongraduates, even though they may have switched into radically different occupations from those in which they were trained. Work habits and standards of industrial excellence acquired at a young age, it is widely believed, continue to pay dividends through subsequent decades.

In short, the German strategy does not call for identifying and responding to problems or matching demand with supply. Instead the proposition is that all young workers should be given sound, initial vocational training.

TRAINING POLICY DEVELOPMENTS

Corporate training efforts are necessarily dependent in part on developments in the broader education and training system. Since the mid 1960s, Canadian training policy has been in a state of almost continual flux.

The 1960s and 1970s saw a great expansion of the training and education system in Canada. Community colleges were created and university enrollments increased rapidly. However, the economic problems caused by the oil crises of the 1970s resulted in a reconsideration of priorities.

During the heyday of educational expansion the nature of the education being provided was rarely scrutinized closely by the public or by government agencies. In that milieu, general educational pro-

---

2. These comments, of course, do not apply to small firms in Japan which have high rates of turnover (see Taira and Levine 1985).

grams proliferated at the expense of vocational courses, which were considered to be less prestigious in academic circles. By the late 1970s, however, considerable pressure was being exerted on educational institutions to make their courses more relevant to the practical needs of the times. In response, secondary schools began to pay more attention to their vocational offerings. Ontario's Linkage Program, for example, aimed at preparing secondary school students for entry into practical, skilled trades training by offering them courses required of industrial apprentices (*The Linkage System* 1980; *Youth: The Forgotten Generation* 1982). Cooperative work-study programs also expanded.

As part of its active labour market strategy initiated in the late 1960s, the Canada Employment and Immigration Commission purchased seats in community college programs into which it placed unemployed people. The object was to improve the job prospects of the unemployed, but research in the 1970s indicated that some of the courses offered by colleges were not in line with market needs (*In Short Supply* 1982). As a result, graduates sometimes had as much difficulty finding jobs after training as before. In the early '80s, the Employment and Immigration Commission began to scrutinize its seat purchase policy more carefully, and the colleges were compelled to reorganize their programs in line with current needs. The government also provided funds which enabled post-secondary institutions to purchase state-of-the-art technology so that expensive, skilled, training schemes could be updated and expanded (Training Consultation Paper 1984).

Universities also reacted to the new demands by shifting resources to business, engineering, and computer science courses although at a pace many considered too slow. At the same time the proportion of students in Arts facilities declined (MacDonald Commission Report 1985).

Under the Adult Occupational Training Act (AOTA) of 1967, the federal government acquired the ability to support employer-centered training. Most of its funds, however, went into expanding the institutional training system. Employer efforts at providing systematic, long-term training were, as noted above, very modest. By the late 1970s the weight of opinion held that the balance between institutional and employer-centered training should be shifted. Private companies should know best what skills they required, and because they were primary beneficiaries of a highly skilled work force, should take more responsibility for its creation. In order to shift the balance, several initiatives were undertaken.

Enriched subsidies of wages and training costs were provided in order to encourage the expansion of longer-term, skills training. Under AOTA the federal government could provide funds for no more than one year, but that barrier was removed in the National Training Act of 1982. Currently employers may receive funding for up to three years (*Canadian Jobs Strategy* 1985). Within the context of these subsidy schemes, particular emphasis is placed by government on the training of certain disadvantaged groups: women, visible minorities, the handicapped, and native peoples. Indeed, concern for job prospects of the disadvantaged has been a focus of government policy equal in importance to, if not greater than, the concern for quantity and type of training offered. Many categorical subsidy programs in effect over the past decade have been aimed specially at the disadvantaged.

A second initiative taken by government to expand employer-based training was to encourage employers to engage in human resources planning. By doing so they would be able to identify their likely future needs and presumably take action to meet those needs. Moreover, research indicated that employer-based training, although expensive, was very often cost effective, contrary to a commonly held employer view that training was costly with uncertain benefits (Harvey 1980). Planning, it was hoped, might result in a reduction in this misapprehension.

To encourage planning, the federal government signed agreements with several industrial associations under which they would encourage their members to plan, and government would provide special assistance towards that end. The computer-based Canadian Occupational Projection System was developed in order to permit estimates to be made of labour supply three to ten years in future. Through computer links, users could gain access to a wide range of disaggregated data.

Ontario took the lead to establish Community Industrial Training Councils, comprised of representatives of employers, unions, and educators. The councils undertook to estimate skill needs and to take action to ensure that those needs were met. In its Canadian Jobs Strategy, unveiled during the summer of 1985, the federal government stated its intention to emulate this approach across the country. The Canadian Jobs Strategy also called for establishment of employer-based, training trust funds. These jointly administered funds would enable employees to upgrade their skills in the face of technological change. In order to encourage the establishment of such funds, the government agreed to contribute fifty percent of the amount paid by the participants up to four hundred thousand dollars over three years. Apparently, training trust funds are in lieu of Registered Educational Leave Plans (RELP's) called for by several commissions and task forces (see, for example, Adams et al. 1979 and MacDonald Commission Report 1985). Those plans would have allowed individual employees to put money into tax-sheltered accounts designed eventually to underwrite retraining expenses.

The concept of the training levy scheme was widely discussed during the 1970s and 1980s as a means of expanding employer-based training (Allmand Task Force 1982; Adams et al. 1979; Dodge Task Force 1981; and MacDonald Commission Report 1985). One of the primary reasons given by employers for not training was the fear that newly trained people would leave the firm carrying with them the investment of the employer. The training levy is designed to overcome that problem by assessing a training tax on all employers in order to create a fund from which training-active firms may be reimbursed. Although versions of such schemes were recommended by several commissions and task forces (e.g., Adams 1983; Allmand 1982), none have been adopted, in part because of opposition by powerful employer groups and in part because of doubts that the schemes would be effective. A good deal of attention has been directed to British training levy schemes whose effectiveness has been questioned (Dodge Task Force 1981; MacDonald Commission Report 1985). Unfortunately, little serious attention has been paid to schemes tailor made for the Canadian environment, such as the plan first proposed in 1979 by the Commission on Educational Leave and Productivity (Adams et al. 1979; Adams 1980).

Finally, initiatives taken in the mid 1980s have focused on the transition from home or school into work. In countries such as Germany and Japan, there are very well developed mechanisms, as previously noted, for moving school leavers into economic life.

In Canada, however, school leavers who do not go on to post-secondary school compete with each other for low paying, relatively unskilled jobs. Many jobs in that category are unstable, with the result that young people tend to wander from job to job and experience frequent periods of unemployment. Since only a small minority of firms offer systematic training, the skill acquisition process for young school leavers is very haphazard. Women who have been out of the labour force for several years face similar entry problems.

In order to smooth the transition from school (or home) to work, the federal government has recently unleashed a new scheme. Originally called the Youth Training Option, but now referred to as Job Entry, the scheme calls for entrepreneurs to establish and operate transition programs. Essentially, the entrepreneur (which could also be association, union, or college) identifies an employer or group of employers willing to participate, recruits a group of new labour force entrants, and designs and operates a training scheme composed of on-the-job experience and formal instruction. For his/her efforts a fee for service is provided by the government. After a pilot project in 1984, this scheme was substantially expanded in the Canadian Jobs Strategy of 1985. The Job Entry program also allows for the financing of more conventional work study schemes. Community colleges have been the most enthusiastic early participants in this scheme.

In concept, these innovations all seem to be sensible. One major problem with them is that they are all marginal in that the budgets allocated to them are restricted. For example, the training trust fund provision comes under the category of skill investment for which $100 million has been budgeted for 1985–86. If five hundred employers were to take advantage of the maximum yearly contribution available from government (i.e. $200,000 during the first year), skill investment would be exhausted. However, skill investment is designed to support not only training trust funds, but also other employer-sponsored training efforts. In short, the budget will permit only a small number of employers to establish trust funds. This marginal effort may be contrasted to France where all employers must spend a percent of payroll on training or be penalized financially by government (Adams et al. 1979).

The new transition program is likewise constrained. In several advanced, industrialized countries (e.g., France, Great Britain, West Germany), essentially all young people are guaranteed some form of relevant training in order to assist the transition to work. The Canadian scheme, however, will only affect a minority. The MacDonald Commission (1985) which favourably reviewed universal transition programs did not recommend a similar plan for Canada because of the costs involved.

CONCLUSION

As this essay has tried to indicate, the Canadian training system is not without flaws. It has, however, many strong points. Secondary and post-secondary education is probably as good as anywhere. Moreover, a larger percentage of Canadians participate in institutional post-secondary education than do citizens of any other nation except for the United States. Training in industry, however, continues to be problematic.

The most serious difficulty is the attitude of business towards training. Because people adequately trained in basic technical, administrative, and professional skills historically have been available either from abroad or from institutions, business has developed a minimalist training tradition. Training is to be done only as absolutely necessary. Such an attitude, if it persists, may prove to be detrimental to the ability of Canadian industry to successfully compete with nations whose companies place higher value on training for excellence.

References

Adams, R. J. 1980. Towards a more competent labour force: A training levy scheme for Canada. *Relations Industrielles* 35(3).

Adams, R. J. 1983. *Skills development for working Canadians—Towards a national strategy*. Ottawa: CEIC Task Force on Skill Development Leave.

Adams, R. J., P. Draper, and C. Ducharme. 1979. Education and working Canadians. *Report of the Commission of Inquiry on Educational Leave and Productivity*. Ottawa: Labour Canada.

Canada. 1981. Canada Employment and Immigration Commission. *Labour Market Development in the 1980's, Report of the Task Force on Labour Market Development* (Dodge Task Force).

Canada, House of Commons. 1982. *Work for Tomorrow*. "Report of the Parliamentary Task Force on Employment Opportunities for the 80's (Allmand Task Force)."

Canada. 1984. Canada Employment and Immigration Commission, Training Consultation Paper. December.

Canada. 1985. Canada Employment and Immigration Commission. *Canadian Jobs Strategy*. June.

Daly, D. J. 1974. "Managerial Manpower in Canada." In *Contemporary issues in Canadian personnel administration*, edited by Harish Jain. Scarborough: Prentice-Hall.

Draper, J. A. and A. Alden. 1978. The continuing education of employees—A review of selected policies in Ontario. Toronto: Ontario Institute for Studies in Education.

Harvey, E. B. 1980. Barriers to employer-sponsored training in Ontario. Toronto: Ministry of Colleges and Universities.

Industrial Training for High Level Skills. 1983. Toronto: Ontario Manpower Commission, June.

In Short Supply—Jobs and Skills in the 1980's, Ottawa: Economic Council of Canada, 1982.

Ishikawa, Toshio. 1981. Vocational training. Tokyo: Japan Institute of Labour.

Jain, H. and V. Murray. 1984. Why the human resources management function fails. *California Management Review* 26(4) (Summer): 95–110.

Koike, K. 1983. "Internal labour markets: Workers in large firms." In *Contemporary industrial relations in Japan*, edited by Tashiro Shirai. Madison: University of Wisconsin Press.

The Linkage System. 1980. Toronto: Ministry of Colleges and Universities.

Report of the Royal Commission on the Economic Union and Development Prospects for Canada (MacDonald Commission Report). 1985. Ottawa: Supply and Services Canada.

Taira, K. and S. B. Levine. 1985. "Japan's industrial relations: A social compact emerges." In *Industrial relations in a decade of economic change*, edited by Harvey Juris, Mark Thompson, and Wilbur Daniels, 247–300. Madison, WI: Industrial Relations Research Association.

Robertson, Nickerson Associates. 1978. Case Studies on Aspects of Training Upper Skilled Blue-Collar Industrial Workers. Report prepared for the Department of Employment and Immigration, Ottawa.

Vogel, E. 1979. *Japan as number one*. Cambridge: Harvard University Press.

Weiermair, K. 1982. Industrial training in Canada: An international perspective. *International Journal of Social Economics* 9(2).

Youth: The Forgotten Generation, A Study of Skill Training and Apprenticeship Programs in Metropolitan Toronto. 1982. Toronto: The Municipality of Metropolitan Toronto, February.

21. Improving Training Effectiveness Through the Use of Evaluation Research

Robert R. Haccoun, Université de Montréal

With the exception of small organizations, rare are the Canadian companies which do not have a group within the personnel department whose function it is to provide training to other employees. Additionally, many Universities,[1] consulting firms, and individuals gravitate around the prime organizations offering training assistance. In a real sense training is big business.

The purpose of training is to create planned change in people. The purpose of training evaluation is to establish if relevant change has in fact occurred, to test if the training has caused that change, and to pin point areas for further improvement in the training program. To accomplish these objectives one needs information and some guidelines for collecting that data. Hence this chapter is divided into four sections. A brief introduction to the processes involved in the development of training programs opens the chapter. The second section details out the types of measures which might be relevant to evaluation research. Then the discussion focuses on the experimental procedures which may be used to make inferential sense of the collected data. Finally, a detailed example of a series of evaluation studies executed by the author is presented.

TRAINING DEVELOPMENT

Training programs are presumably launched to ameliorate individual performance, in order to impact positively on collective performance.[2] The suggestion, then, is to insure that all training efforts be superceded by a thorough analysis of the deficiencies in need of correction.

In fact one can identify four broad classes of variables which may weaken individual (and consequently organizational) performance [3]: Individual performance may be suboptimal if (a) the individual lacks the abilities to perform, (b) lacks the motivation, (c) lacks the knowledge or skills to perform, or (d) is within a structure which inhibits performance. Notice that a training intervention is only profitable when the problem lies at the skills level, other interventions being required in other cases.

Assuming that the performance difficulty is indeed amenable to a training based corrective, organizations will typically design (or purchase) and implement the training program for those selected individuals or groups who presumably are most apt to benefit from it. Hence, the initial diagnosis serves to identify where problems lie, how they can best be corrected, and to whom the remedial actions will apply. As an end point to that process, organizations must (and many do) implement some sort of training evaluation. Minimally, the evaluations ought to be designed to ascertain if the problem is rectified. Hence, a complete training evaluation must provide information indicating the levels of learning achieved by trainees, the degree to which this learning is transposed into on-the-job behaviours, and the degree to which individual effectiveness has in fact improved.

In those cases where the performance problem is not resolved, the evaluation should also provide information as to the probable cause: the wrong people have been trained, the training techniques are inappropriate, the deficiencies presumably corrected by training are unimportant to performance, etc. Whereas a proper training evaluation should permit all of these inferences, it is obvious that few will actually be that extensive and well designed.

TRAINING EVALUATION— THE LEVELS OF MEASUREMENT

Evaluation suggests the need for information which is usually [4] collected from or about the trainee and which will take one or more of four forms: the reactions of participants to the training, the levels of knowledge and/or skills acquired by individuals, the actual on-the-job behaviours of the trainees, and finally, the degree to which the individual has become more effective in accomplishing the work tasks. This information may be visualised as levels of a staircase, as shown in Exhibit 21-1.

The easiest information to obtain is located on the first step in Exhibit 21-1, while the most difficult information to obtain is on the highest step. However, the overall quality and usefulness of the information increases with each additional data collection step taken. Generally, it will be the case that studies which measure the higher steps also obtain the lower information strata.

Step 1: Participant Reaction

Profoundly disliked training programs rarely survive in organizations. The converse is generally also true—well liked programs endure. Although positive reactions may be more motivating, this is not sufficient. The difficulty, of course, is that enjoyment and relevant learning are not necessarily synonymous.

Reactions are usually collected on questionnaires which are administered as

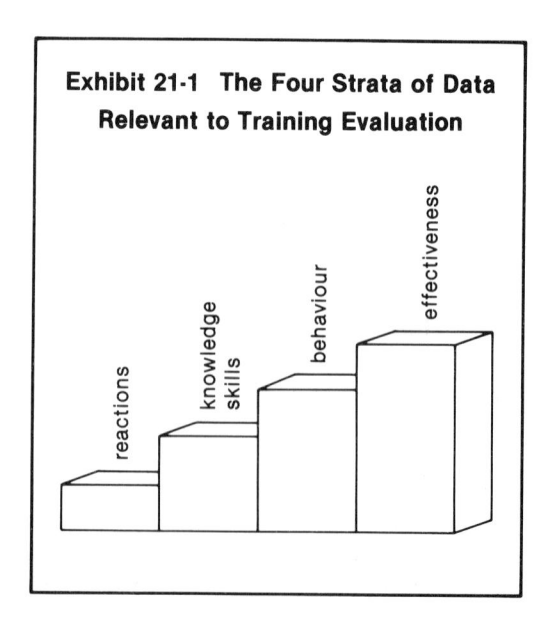

Exhibit 21-1 The Four Strata of Data Relevant to Training Evaluation

the last activity of the training program. Since the post-training measurement of participant reactions is relatively simple (the respondents are captive and rough questionnaires are easy to construct), rare are the programs which do not include such procedures. Unfortunately, it is often the case that such data represents the only training outcome information collected.

Typically, the immediate post-training reactions questionnaires will be anonymous and will consist of several sections including the perceptions held of the training leader, the perceived usefulness of the training, the perceptions of the depth and sequencing of training contents, the perceptions held of the physical locale of the training, and the overall levels of participant satisfaction.

Usually, the evaluator will use this information in a descriptive sense. For example, a frequency distribution might show that eighty percent of the trainees reported being highly satisfied with the course, while five percent might be very dissatisfied. Typically, this will be taken as strong evidence speaking for the quality of the training program. Unfortunately, for a number of reasons, such inferences are not warranted!

Generally, people will be very hesitant to pronounce extremely critical judgements about trainers or training programs with which they have spent a concentrated period of time. At the end of training, people often experience a warm glow. This will tend to produce satisfaction ratings that are very lenient. Haccoun, Garwood and Oeltjen (1982) point out that in the dozens of training evaluations they conducted they had yet to note a single one in which participants were not satisfied, even if the actual learning achieved was, in many cases, minimal. Consequently, very negative perceptions of training are rare, but can be most important when detected.

Second, to be effective, it must at least be the case that trainees acquire some relevant knowledge. Saying that one has learned a lot is hardly a demonstration that learning has indeed taken place.

Finally, such a descriptive approach can rarely provide for meaningful diagnostic information leading to course improvements.

Reaction questionnaires can be improved and Wexley and Latham (1981) provide some useful hints. Moreover, they can yield more powerful inferences when analysed by more sophisticated techniques. One can make better sense of the data by using the overall satisfaction question as a dependent measure against which all other perceptions are regressed. This will yield information about the aspects of training which are related to satisfaction and areas which are not. This is a way of identifying potential areas for improvement in the course. It might also be possible to construct an overall average score on all scales as a standard against which individual average scores for each section of the questionnaire might be compared. For example, it might be shown that the mean overall rating is 5.2 out of 7, but the training local section yields a mean of 2.4. Such a result would point out that the rooms in which the training takes place could advantageously be improved.

Finally, reaction information might be regressed against better outcome measures, hence pointing out possible correlates of learning a much more relevant criterion in judging training success.

These analyses might help draw more information from the reactions questionnaires but they will fail to answer the truly important question: Did training actually have a positive, job-relevant impact on participants? To begin to answer this question it is required to step up the information strata stairs in Exhibit 21-1.

Step 2: The Knowledge/Skill Strata

Following training, participants should have acquired some knowledge about the subject matter. The only way to test this proposition is to measure actual knowledge.

The commonest of knowledge measurement schemes will comprise the construction and administration of an easily scored multiple choice or true-false formatted paper and pencil examination. In chosing the specific questions to ask, one must be sensitive to the issues of content validity—the questions raised must be representative of a limited universe. Here a choice needs to be made. Is the universe the job, or the training contents? On the one hand, people should demonstrate that which they have been taught. Hence, the test items should be representative of the training content.[5] On the other hand, the training is presumably designed to help job performance. Consequently, the tested universe should be the job. In well designed programs, this is not a critical issue since the course is designed to reflect important job requirements.

The articulation of this choice can, moreover, be advantageously employed to create an a priori analysis of the quality of training. Performance on a test designed to measure training content retention should yield high scores for effective job performers and low scores for ineffective performers. If this is not obtained, the training may be irrelevant to effectiveness, or the test itself is a poor measure. If a new formulation of the test yields the same results, the training contents will need revisions, such that job contents are more closely modelled.

Knowledge is usually provided in order to alter skills. A most common way to assess skills levels is to place the trainee in a simulation which will elicit those skills if they exist. For example, a course designed to teach people how to program a computer using BASIC might ask of the trainees to write a BASIC program.

These procedures are usually administered immediately after training completion, but the critical elements for the evaluation are still wanting. Does the trainee apply this new knowledge and accompanying skills to the job, and do these skills make a difference in overall individual effectiveness? A manager who acquires some important human relations skills may not necessarily apply them to the day-to-day job behaviours. And if the manager does transfer them, they may not necessarily improve his/her effectiveness.[6]

Step 3: Behaviours

To really begin to assess training effectiveness, it is required that the actual work behaviours of trainees be measured. The individual who has mastered the safe operation of a machine in training, but who fails to demonstrate this on the job, is not well trained.

Behaviour observations are the most frequently used in a manner by which on-the-job actions are measured. One way would be for the supervisors of the trainee to note and describe specific examples of behaviour. Two examples may be offered: the supervisor might simply note the number of times in which a machine operator fails to wear his/her goggles or, the frequency with which a manager uses directive comments during meetings might serve as an index of the effectiveness of a program designed to teach participative decision skills.

Behaviours may also be collected in a less reactive manner. This is usually done by the collection of automatically recorded data. For example, the author conducted an evaluation of a program designed to help people make efficient use of a sophisticated telephone system. The system computer kept track of all applications activated by users. A simple tally of these usage frequencies showed that some telephone features were not used.

But it is not sufficient to know that trainees use the target skills and knowledges acquired. We must still know whether or not these make for a difference in actual job performance.

Step 4: Effectiveness

The measurement of post-training effectiveness is the touchstone of any training evaluation. Has the training experience finally led to improved performance on the job? As might be imagined, this is not a simple matter to decide, and consequently, this data strata is the least frequently employed in organizations.

When training on purely technical matters is at issue, it is generally easier to obtain performance information. For example, training provided on routine maintenance of equipment might be easily measured by perusing monthly or yearly repair records. An index of individual telephone operator performance might be constructed by dividing the average time spent answering a call into the overall office average time for a specific time period. This would serve as a handy tool for evaluating a training program designed to teach more efficient directory search procedures.

When training is less clearly technical, such as courses on leading group discussions or providing performance feedback to employees, the measurement difficulties are much greater. The key problem here is that a demonstration of the link between training contents and actual performance (having more efficient meetings or employees who are more apt to mend their ways) is considerably more tenuous. Performance tends to be a function of many variables, only a subset of which will actually be contingent on acquired skills and knowledge. The impact of training on overall performance is usually difficult to discern, though cumulative effects spread over years may be detectable. It is for this reason that few training evaluators will make use of overall performance appraisal ratings to infer the effectiveness of a specific training program.

Nonetheless, those organizations which have access to a more detailed and high-quality performance appraisal system can make use of it. Hence, one would expect greater levels of year to year changes on training-relevant dimensions than on irrelevant ones.

THE DESIGN OF TRAINING EVALUATION STUDIES

The basic question which training evaluation answers is whether or not it makes a difference (in knowledge, skills, behaviours, etc.). That simple statement carries with it the fundamental design parameter involved in evaluation research—evaluation requires comparison. The manner in which the comparisons are made determines the quality of the design. Exhibit 21–2 plots six, well-known evaluation designs.

The better designs in Exhibit 21–2 are those which make use of a control group. This consists of people who are not trained but who are measured. This provides for relevant training effectiveness comparisons.

The members of a control group must be highly similar to those in the trained groups, otherwise all comparisons become meaningless. Intergroup similarity may be assured in two ways. One method consists in matching those

Exhibit 21-2   Six Common Training Evaluation Designs: A. post only, B. pre-post, C. post only with control, D. controlled pre-post, E. time series, F. time series with control

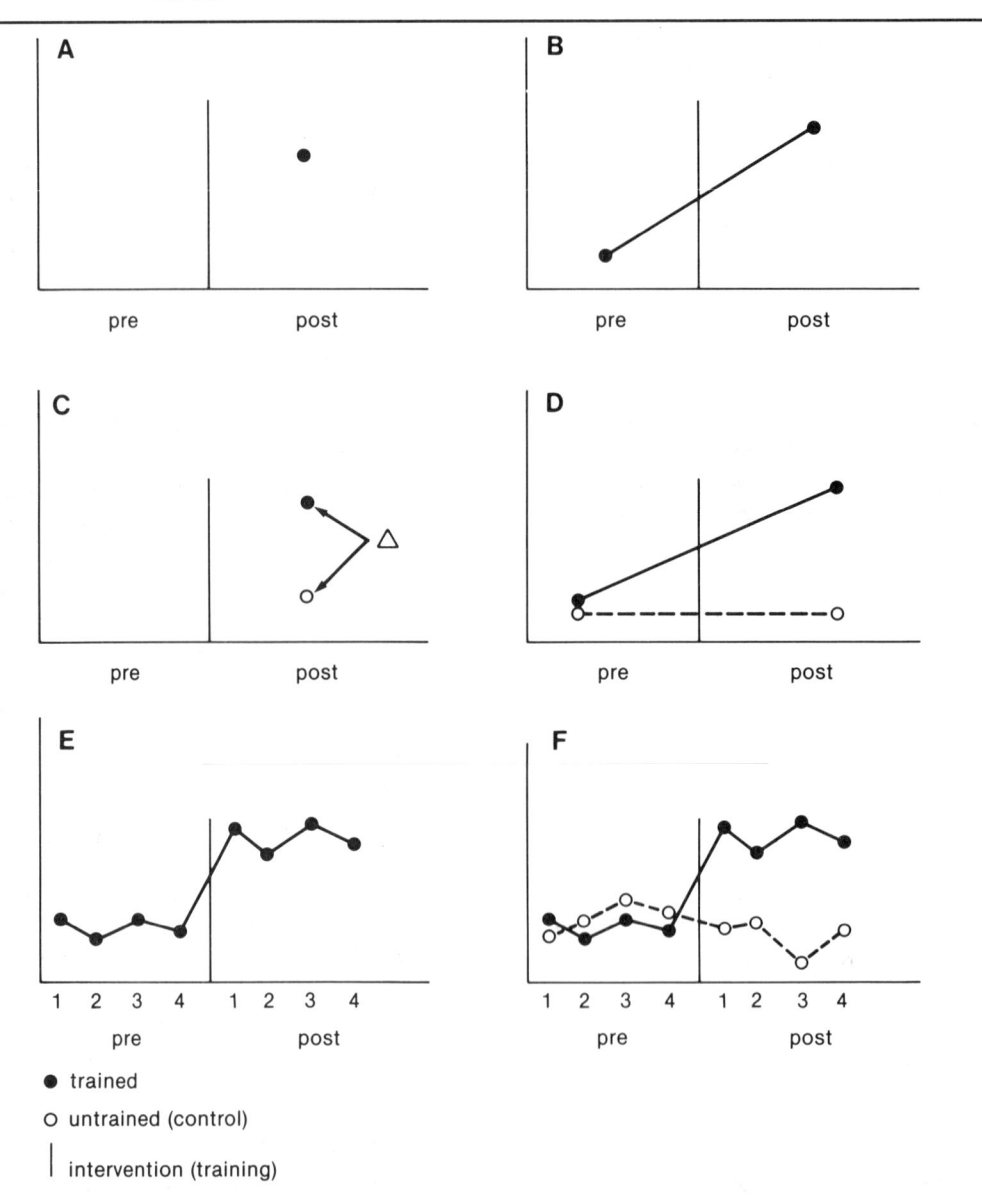

- ● trained
- ○ untrained (control)
- | intervention (training)

assigned to trained groups with individuals who serve as controls. For example, the two groups will consist of people who do the same work, are of similar age, educational levels etc. The second procedure relies on the laws of randomness. By randomly assigning individuals to untrained and trained groups, differences between them will tend to cancel out.

The matching procedure is risky in that its usefulness will hinge on the degree to which the subjects are matched on dimensions relevant to training. Since matching must be conducted on a limited set of variables, the risk of error can be high. There is no known method by which an a priori estimation of that risk can be calculated.

The random assignment procedure is technically better, provided that the initial group sizes are reasonably large (otherwise the concept of randomization loses its meaning). One common proposal for randomization involves the placement of the names of all candidates for training on a numbered list. A table of random numbers is then used to select those who will be invited for training, the balance being used as controls.

The use of control groups, however, is usually resisted in industrial settings. A list of commonly heard objections will include: that it is inconvenient for people to be taken from their jobs to answer questionnaires; that control group personnel will dislike being in the group which does not benefit from training, that it is inefficient to chose training participants on the basis of randomness, since the need for training is a much more relevant criterion for choice.

These are usually real constraints. Unfortunately, designs which do not include controls produce disappointing results or else involve procedures which can become rather complex. Although accommodations can be made to fit training evaluation designs into greater conformity with organizational imperatives, it remains that the levels of training evaluation efforts exerted bear a proportional relationship to the importance and practicality of the observed results. We now turn to a discussion of various designs which are used to evaluate training.

Design A: The Post-Only Design

Panel A in Exhibit 21-2 shows the most common design used in organizations today. It is also the poorest and, in effect, it lacks the basic quality which defines a worthwhile experimental design. Immediately after training reactions knowledge data [7] is sometimes gathered from the trainees. Mean reactions are calculated and if the scores obtained are sufficiently high the training program is judged to be adequate.

Quick perusal of Exhibit 21-1 will show a critical problem. There is no comparison point against which the data may be evaluated. Even if most people liked the course or scored well on the knowledge tests, nothing exists to confirm that training events were responsible for that result. It may be that the trainees would have scored just as well, if not better, had no training taken place.

Panel B: The Pre-Post Design

The obvious correction to the post-test-only design would be to get some information about the preliminary knowledge/skills levels of trainees prior to training. This would solve the major failing of the previous design by furnishing a comparison point, against which post-test results may be interpreted.

This is the second most common evaluation design used in industry. Typically, pretests are administered as the first activity in the training course. Post-tests may be taken immediately following training or some time thereafter. Whereas the design does provide a comparison, it is still a sorely deficient procedure.

Evaluation research must serve to identify if change occurs and to attribute that change to the training experience per se. Pre-post differences, when analysed statistically, can provide for reasonable certainty that change has occurred. However, that change could have been caused by anything including training. Could a change in work procedures contiguous with the training program actually be the cause of behaviour changes in the trainees? Can the mere passage of time be responsible for the post-training changes? Presumably a useful program is one which is responsible for changes. This design fails to shed practical light on this issue.

Panel C: The Post-Test-Only Design With Control

With this design, pretest measures are not taken. Rather, post-test observations are made on the trained individuals as well as on an independent, randomly selected, equivalent, untrained group. The basic comparison is then made between these two groups, where presumably, the trained group will score higher on relevant dimensions than the untrained group. A pretest is not required since a true control, permitting comparisons, is in place. This design compels the evaluator to be extremely careful about the composition of the control group. Either extensive matching or randomization is required, with the later being efficient only when large groups of individuals will be trained.

Panel D: The Full Pre-Test, Post-Test With Control

The full pre-post with control procedure is the classic experimental design. Two groups of equivalent people are administered both pre- and post-training measures. However, only one group is provided with the training. Evidence for program effectiveness is inferred when pre-post changes are greater for the trained than the untrained group. This design also places pressure on the correct choice of control trainees. However, the problem is less acute since pretraining differences between the groups may be adjusted statistically. A cost-benefit analysis would reveal that this model is most favourable, combining simple procedures with high quality information.

Panel E: The Time-Series Design

The time-series design provides for the collection of several initial (i.e., pretraining) measurements of the critical knowledge, skills, behaviours, and/or effectiveness dimensions relevant to the eventual training program.[8] After training, multiple observations are also collected to establish a new, post-training baseline measurement. Evidence for effectiveness is inferred by both a sharp break in the curves linking the pre- and post-training measurement points and the observation of a higher level of post-test scores as compared to pretraining measures. This design reduces the risks involved with the pre-post types of designs: that the pretest results obtained are abnormally too low or too high, relative to their true value. Further, since it is the number of data points rather than the number of trainees which are important in stabilizing the information series, this design is used when the number of people to be trained is small.

There are two fundamental justifications for the time series design. First, multiple pre-measures provide important estimates of the overall stability of the untrained behaviours. This will provide significant information relevant to the interpretation of post-training variability.

Second, multiple post-training measurements provide meaningful information about the longevity or decay of training effects. A significant droop in the post-measures would indicate that training effects lose their impact over time. This permits the generation of interesting hypotheses: Could it be that the work context discourages the use of the new skills? Could it be that learned skills are insufficiently entrenched during training? The design also pinpoints the need and the timing for any maintenance training.

The design is quite powerful, but it does suffer from the lack of a control (untrained) group. Technological changes coinciding with the onset of training, for instance, might be more salient explanations of the observed change than the training itself.[9]

Panel F: The Multiple Baseline Design, With Control

Panel F's design is identical to the multiple baseline design except that a control group is added. Sequential measurements taken at the same moment and on the same instruments can then be compared longitudinally with those results obtained with the trained group.

This is a very powerful model which can yield all of the information provided by the previous design, while removing from it all of its inherent ambiguities.

Two Final Designs

The Solomon four-group design is highly sophisticated and complex. It requires a basic pre-post design with control (panel D) to which are grafted two additional controls—one which is trained but not pretested, the other which is neither pretested nor trained. The comparisons between the results produced by these various groups will serve to infer training effectiveness while separating out the mere effect of being trained and of being sensitized by pretraining measures. Although some use has been made of the design (Bunker and Cohen 1977) it is generally too complicated to find consistent use in industrial applications.

The multiple baseline design is a powerful hybrid of the time-series procedure. It uses staggered groups to infer training effectiveness not at the individual level, but rather at the levels of groups. Simultaneous baseline performance measures are taken of different groups who will eventually receive training. One group is trained and the post-training measurement is pursued. While post-training information is gathered on this initial group, another group is introduced to the training intervention. This procedure is repeated with all groups. Effectiveness of training is inferred when a consistent pattern of pre-post changes is observed for all groups.

The design is particularly well suited for industrial applications where the intervention is relevant to several groups, and where practical realities prohibit the simultaneous training of all. Since all groups serve as both control and trained groups, the design furnishes a convenient solution to the independent control group problem with which all other techniques are afflicted. As with the other repeated measures designs, it is most suited to an analysis of effectiveness data (step 4).

Training Evaluation in Action: The SL-1 Telephone Example

A description will now be made of an extensive training evaluation research program conducted in the late 1970s by the author (Haccoun 1976a, 1976b, 1978). This will serve to show the link between training evaluation and the development of effective training.

Between 1976 and 1978, a series of studies were conducted on behalf of a very large telecommunications company—Bell Canada. That organization had developed a new communication system, the SL-1, which greatly expanded the range of functions normally associated with a conventional business telephone. The greater capabilities of the system, however, were associated with a commensurate complexity of the input-output procedures required to operate it optimally. The problem then, was to design a user training system such that inevitable implantation problems would be less frequently attributable to user error.

In total, seven studies were conducted, only some of which will be described here. Prior to the marketing of the SL-1 system, user training procedures solely consisted in having the customer service employees demonstrate telephone equipment to the end users.

The initial training evaluation study was conducted in two companies who had accepted the system on a trial basis. In one company, an audio-visual information package was added to the usual demonstration intervention. A second company (a matching procedure was used) was employed as a control. Here scant training was provided, although they were provided with an instructional booklet describing telephone operation.

The measures collected included: a reactions questionnaire, a knowledge test, a diary kept by users which charted SL-1 usage, and a second knowledge and reactions (to the system) questionnaire administered six weeks after training.

The major results of this study were that immediately after training people were relatively satisfied, but that actual learning was negligible. Those who received less extensive training (the controls) had some tendency to have less positive attitudes towards the system. This result held six weeks later. After six weeks, moreover, knowledge had dramatically and equally improved for all groups. It was concluded that the conventional training program may have served a public relations function, but that it failed dismally to teach telephone operation (i.e., no group differences were noted). However, the fact that knowledge had improved indicated that somehow people had learned. How? A qualitative study, based on personnel interviews (Conrath 1977) showed that people learned the system operation by trial and error and by informally sharing information and discoveries with each other. The management of the trial organizations were unhappy that people spent work time learning the use of this telephone.

Hence, immediate post-training learning levels were very low, learning improved greatly six weeks later, and there was dissatisfaction with the manner with which that learning was achieved. Consequently, it was decided that (a) another attempt be made to construct a better initial training program and (b) to develop a higher quality instruction booklet which, presumably may help people learn the system without the need to disturb other employees.

A second training evaluation study was launched in a different organization. Some of the training groups were led by Bell Canada service advisors, while others were led by specially trained personnel from the host organization (it was felt that in-house trainers might supply more relevant examples to their colleagues). Two versions of the audio-visual presentations were also prepared and each was administered to half the training groups. Hence, the design permitted a simultaneous comparison between different types of trainers and different types of training.

All measurement instruments and procedures used in the initial study were retained for this one, and the results were remarkably similar. Immediately after training people did not know how to use their telephones, but six weeks later they did know how.

Taking both studies together the conclusion is inescapable. Initial training procedures are ineffective, and in a sense, not really required since learning did in fact occur. This was taken to mean that given the complexity of the system, only continued practice on it would lead to reasonable levels of user knowledge. Rather than try again, it was thought more efficient to develop a better instructional booklet, to limit initial training to booklet usage, and to evaluate this new concept of user training.

A number of empirical studies were conducted to construct and evaluate the new booklet per se.[10] The booklet evaluation studies were essentially designed to ensure that, compared to the available alternatives, this booklet led to easier and more efficient learning. Modifications suggested by the results of one study were made and tested in follow-up studies. The end result was a booklet which achieved, at least experimentally, its fundamental objective—SL-1 learning.

The final question remaining was whether or not this booklet (a) would be used by end users and (b) reduced the user's dependency on other users. The pertinent evaluation study was conducted.

In this study (Dussolt 1977), a host company was divided into three experimental groups, all of which were provided with but minimal training. However, specific host employees were selected and trained as experts to answer post-training questions. The groups were given one or the other of three instruction booklets: the new, empirically constructed one, another which was prepared by technical experts in Bell Canada, and one which the manufacturer had developed. Reactions, behaviour, and effectiveness measures were collected. The reactions data showed that the empirically developed booklet was perceived to be *less* easy to consult. However, at a behavioral level this group consulted others to a very much lesser degree than did those who used other instruction manuals. Other perceptual data strongly suggested that the replacement of traditional user training with that booklet served to achieve the basic objectives hoped for—an effective and convenient means by which telephone operation could be taught.

These series of studies serve to exemplify several principles. The use of comparison groups quickly revealed that all efforts at initial training were futile. The use of repeated knowledge tests indicated that learning did go on after training. These two facts combined to yield the idea for a better self-instructional package. In this case, the evaluation studies provided specific hypotheses about the learning process of end users. It was with the recuperation of this knowledge that the pertinent insights about the training program required could be made.

Conclusion

Research on the effects of training in organizations derives its importance from two basic sources. Training programs represent the only formal manner with which organizations develop the knowledge and skills levels of the indigenous employees. As such, it is one of the major investments which the organization makes on its own work force.

From a philosophical or social responsibility point of view, it is evident that the organization ought to take this task seriously. Taking as criterion the organization's responsibility to itself, one reaches the same conclusion: through staff training, the organization is taking an important step in insuring its own continuance. The value of that investment must be monitored and periodically reviewed to insure that the objectives desired are being met.

For the student, training evaluation methods and procedures serve to highlight the major elements which are involved in applying and generating knowledge about the learning of human work. The most satisfying of training experiences are those which lead to important positive changes in the understanding which the employee has of his/her work. The most satisfying of all evaluation research are those which yield major improvements in the quality of training by relying on a new understanding of industrial learning, which the study permitted.

For the professional trainer, the evaluation process makes the link between those who develop and implement training and those upon whom they impact. In that link, lies the all-essential feedback required for learning. Feedback focuses human thought. Carefully designed training evaluation studies will contribute to the development of better training. The SL–1 studies exemplify this process.

Training programs, many of them poorly evaluated, are in use in organizations throughout the country. Most are at least minimally effective, while many are very good programs. All the more the pity, for without evaluations, knowledge about the better training programs is not desseminated. Hence, the overall levels of knowledge about human industrial learning is growing more slowly than might be the case.

Training is expensive, and such investments deserve monitoring and refinements. To date, it is only through the use of systematic and careful evaluation research that it becomes possible to achieve this amelioration in the training of organizational members.

Endnotes

1. The Université du Québec à Montréal, l'Ecole des Hautes Etudes Commerciales, and McGill University in Montreal make available to the business community a very active system of seminars and courses.
2. This chapter summarizes the basic fundamental concepts involved in evaluation research relevant to industrial training. The interested reader, desiring to deepen his/her understanding will find the perusal of the following books most profitable: Hamblin 1974; Struening and Guttentag 1975; Wexley and Latham 1981.
3. The use of the acronym "AMOK"—Abilities, Motivation, Opportunity (structure) and Knowledge represents an easy way to remember this grouping of variables.
4. It is occasionally relevant to collect data from others who might be influenced by the individual who has been trained. For example a programme designed to enhance human relations skills of managers may base part of its evaluative data on the post training experiences of subordinates.
5. Knowledge questionnaires might be improved by including questions which are relevant to training and questions which are related but directly relevant. If training is effective trainees should show more improvements on relevant as opposed to irrelevant sections of the test. Hamtiaux (1981) showed that such a procedure produces inferences which are

identical to those which a pre-post design with control yields.
6. In the 1950s Fleishman and his colleagues (Harris and Fleishman 1955) showed that human relations training does not impact on supervisory behaviours when that behaviour is to be exhibited in a context which does not permit it.
7. It is possible to collect all strata levels described in Exhibit 21-1 with this design. In practice however, organizations which make use of this procedure will generally not bother to evolve past step 1.
8. It is generally the case that measures of effectiveness are used in this design. Learning or skills tests are more difficult to use and more likely to be contaminated as the trainees may remember the items on the previous tests. Hence, the repeated observations are not independent. The use of parallel measures is theoretically possible but that greatly complexifies the test construction problems and, in any case, management and trainees may be resistant to repeated measurements. Effectiveness measures, such as absence rates, or actual performance data can often be tacitly collected.
9. Wexley and Latham (1981) report the interesting example of a multiple baseline design which showed no differences in pre-post measures of logger effectiveness even though the program was successful. Apparently, heavy rain falls contiguous with the post training periods reduced actual productivity. Had a control group been measured its performance would have showed a post-training drop! Hence the no difference result obtained was indicative of success, since the training weakened the impact of the weather on job performance.
10. The most difficult problem encountered was that the system generated a wide range of visual and auditory confirmatory signals which the user had to discriminate and which called for different and quick responses. Studies were conducted to identify graphic and mnemonic devices which could be meaningfully used in the booklet to describe these signals.

References

Bunker, K. A. and S. L. Cohen. 1977. The rigors of training evaluation: A discussion and field demonstration. *Personnel Psychology* 30:525–41.

Conrath, D. 1977. An investigation of organizational communication needs and a study of the impact of a business communication system (SL–1) on meeting these needs. Conrath Communications Ltd.

Dussolt, Y. 1977. Training program evaluation, SL–1 VL field trial, Northern Telecom, Montreal. Q.R. Market Planning, Bell Canada.

Haccoun, R. R. 1976. SL–1 user training in two companies—report on the training evaluation. Management Sciences Division, Bell Canada.

Haccoun, R. R. 1976. SL–1 user training in Dominion stores. Report on the training evaluation. Management Sciences Division, Bell Canada.

Haccoun, R. R. 1978. The SL–1 Telephone system: A summary of training development and evaluation research. Management Sciences Division, Bell Canada.

Haccoun, R. R., J. B. Garwood, and P. D. Oeltjen. 1982. La rentabilisation de la formation pour les années 80. *Revue Commerce*, mai.

Hamblin, A. C. 1974. *Evaluation and control of training.* Maidenhead Berkshire, England: McGraw-Hill.

Hamtiaux, T. 1980. Une nouvelle approche de l'évaluation de la formation: Le devis avec groupe à controle interne. Unpublished Master's thesis. Université de Montréal.

Struening, E. L., and M. Guttentag, ed. 1975. *Handbook of evaluation research.* Beverly Hills: Sage publications.

Wexley, K. N. and G. P. Latham. 1981. *Developing and training resources in organizations.* Glenview, Illinois: Scott-Foresman and company.

22. Training and Development in High Technology Industry: Present and Future Trends

Romi J. Szawlowski, Pratt and Whitney Canada

INTRODUCTION

Executives in high technology industry are facing the challenge of change in a dynamic environment. In this environment, they have to ensure that their organizations have adequate numbers of qualified people to carry out long- and short-term business objectives. There is an unwritten understanding that growing organizations grow people and in turn continue their own growth.

The information for this portion of the chapter was obtained from direct contact with the aerospace industry, educational institutions and government representatives over the past eighteen years. The relationship was cultivated as part of responsibilities for training and development for Pratt and Whitney Canada, Inc. The responsibility includes active participation in building networks of human resource professionals to respond to the needs of the Canadian aerospace industry for qualified employees.

There are some 165 companies which compose the Canadian aerospace industry. The companies provide a wide variety of products and services including aircraft, aircraft repair and overhaul, aircraft engines, unmanned airborne surveillance systems, avionics and electronics systems, satellites and ground stations, simulators, and many other specialized aerospace products and services.

The industry has developed a solid base over the years, is committed to excellence and innovation, and has an international reputation for providing high quality products and services for its customers. Canada ranks fifth in the aerospace league in the free world. The first four are the United States, United Kingdom, France, and West Germany. The industry is contributing significantly to the Canadian economy. The industry sales are expected to reach six billion by 1989, with some fifty thousand employees.

The major concentration of the aerospace manufacturing and services is located in Montreal, Toronto, and Winnipeg. Other locations include western and atlantic regions.

The industry faces future challenges in the world aerospace industry and as a contributor to the Canadian economy.

Contemporary Challenges in Training and Development

Contemporary challenges in training and development in the Canadian aerospace industry range across a wide variety of topics. Central among these, is the need to keep a competitive edge and prepare the people in organizations to meet the challenge of the changing business environment on all fronts.

Training directors in the industry are maintaining a careful contact with their organizations to determine training needs and to deliver quality programs to meet them.

There are myriads of outside resources which are ready to provide off-the-shelf or tailored courses or programs to those who are willing to engage them and who are able to pay the price.

Rapidly changing business conditions require the industry to produce higher quality products which are more reliable, with shorter lead times, faster response to customer needs, and with continuing health of the bottom line.

To add to the complexity, younger workers are bringing with them new attitudes which need to be taken into account. Older workers need to be trained or retrained to acquire new skills, knowledge, and attitudes so that they may remain included in the faster pace of doing work and making decisions.

These conditions require orienting new employees and training and retraining existing ones to ensure a common understanding of the business and what is required to make it successful.

Major challenges include: productivity improvement, upgrading supervisory and management personnel, upgrading skills of employees in new technology, and integrating the training function more effectively with the line organization. Central to these is the challenge of setting a climate of trust to develop an integrated system pulling together to attain organizational objectives with a high degree of satisfaction to the participants. The participants include customers, owners, suppliers, employees at all levels, and society in general.

Strategic Purposes and Importance of Training and Development

Traditionally organizations could afford to train informally on the job. As business grew and changes were becoming more rapid and complex, traditional ways were not adequate to match the high rate of change. Management of larger companies adjusted to include training and development in their strategic plans. They also started to monitor the performance of the function more closely.

The government continues to encourage and support the industry to include training of the work force. The assistance helps to provide job security to existing employees by preparing them to cope with new technology. Additionally, training provides for developing skills which are in short supply in the marketplace.

The introduction of new technology into the business requires careful planning, at least three to six years in advance of implementation. The introduction of a computer-integrated manufacturing facility, for example, using flexible machining systems may take some three years of careful planning by multidisciplined professionals before they decide which machines, equipment, systems, and configurations will be required. To transform the entire plant may take a total of ten years to complete. Furthermore, new technology requires new approaches to the management of people. More and more companies are now considering training as imperative for maintaining a competitive edge in the marketplace.

Senior management is reexamining the function in terms of purposes, effectiveness, resources, and structure.

Fitting Training and Development into the Systems Concept of the Company

The systems concept, with its fundamental components, includes, the purpose, objectives, standards, information flow, methods, resources, organization and feedback, and a monitoring network. New management attitudes require the inclusion of training as part of the total business system of the organization. If an organization wishes to improve its effectiveness, it almost always has to engage its employees in some kind of training. It may be orientation, briefings, workshops, seminars, courses or programs.

The strategic plans translated into tactical and operating plans invariably result in organizational and individual performance. On one side, there are requirements from the individual to work effectively. On the other, the management develops broad statements of what new skills, knowledge, and attitudes will ensure an effective organization. There is also the governmental influence to ensure adequate supply of critical skills which take time to develop. As supervision, management, and employees become aware of the business conditions, the training requirements and responses to them become evolutive in nature.

For instance, plans to improve productivity often involve replacing existing machines with new ones. As production engineers evaluate different suppliers, they become familiar with the features and pass on the information to the purchasing, finance, quality, production, and maintenance departments. Since, on the average, the time interval from ordering the machines to delivery is approximately one year, there is sufficient time for introducing front-end training for those involved.

Courses or Programs Given as a Result of Legal Requirements

For the most part, courses given as a result of legal requirements include those which are related to health and safety. These include emergency care, handling of hazardous materials, fire, and evacuation. Other courses include human rights, quality assurance, and managing equal opportunity practices.

Employer associations, such as the Canadian Manufacturers Association and the Aerospace Industries Association of Canada, frequently organize seminars or workshops to help with the interpretation of government regulations and with the approaches to implementing them. Government representatives serve as presenters and discussion leaders.

Meeting Organizational Needs With Training and Development

Training staff meets organizational needs by being in contact with line management and other specialists to keep on defining and redefining organizational needs for improving the ability of the work force to meet business objectives. Its relationship with the line organization is dynamic in that training programs and courses are continually being modified to suit immediate and more distant anticipation of future conditions. Basic needs translate themselves into three broad categories: Economics/finance, technology, and human relations. Although in the past some writers have insisted that human relations is dead, current events and discoveries indicate that good human relations are essential to effective organizational performance.

The aerospace industry has formed advisory boards to deal with a wide range of subjects concerning the assessment and availability of human resources for the industry. The boards have been formed on a regional basis in Ontario, Quebec, and the western provinces. The Human Resources Committee of The Aerospace Industries of Canada serves as the guiding and focusing unit for the boards. The primary purpose of the boards is to ensure that the industry has an adequate supply of qualified people. Members of the boards and the committee serve as a network of people who keep each other informed about what is going on and what should be done about it. They deal with a wide variety of issues and subjects ranging from forecasting of critical skills to preparing to implement employment equity plans. Trends in educational systems are identified, and representatives work with the schools to advise of curriculum changes or additions. Special conferences and symposiums are organized to meet special interests of the member companies.

Establishing the Needs for Training and Development

An emerging approach for determining the training and development needs for the company is to use corporate and divisional resources along with outside consultants.

Management is recognizing that this combination, with line management involvement, gives better results. Joint determination of needs makes the result more realistic and more complete. The consequence of joint effort builds commitment for sending people on programs and monitoring the progress and effectiveness of the training.

As an example, the corporate staff may recognize that a change is required in management development. They may call in a representative sample of divisional training directors to discuss an approach. Jointly they formulate a broad program outline and select a high caliber consultant to develop a portion of the program. The consultant starts with probe interviews of a representative sample of the organization. The interviews include one-on-one sessions and groups of representative managers. The interviewees are chosen for their competence in management. The results of the interviews are analysed and classified to managerial behaviour and conditions for decision making. From this information, the course is designed, tested, and implemented.

Traditional ways are to use off-the-shelf course-ware from existing internal sources or from outside organizations or consultants. This is no longer a satisfactory method because it does not meet the immediate and future needs of the incumbents. Moreover, higher level managerial input allow for the inclusion of future characteristics and higher performance standards for the incumbents.

Sometimes training staff members survey a particular section of the organization and develop specific courses to meet the needs of a group of employees. Examples of courses include communications, problem solving and decision making, report writing, delegation, and others.

Determining Training and Development Needs for the Individual

Performance appraisal, evaluation of results from in-company training programs, new technologies and equipment, long-range strategic plans, new businesses, customer requirements, career counselling, interviews, new jobs, new functions, marketing needs, and company strategy are sources of future skill requirements.

Performance appraisals and the goal-setting process gives management and the individual greater ability to reach a consensus on training objectives for the individual.

A number of organizations include developmental plans with performance appraisals and with the goal-setting process.

Some organizations use the assessment centre method to identify managerial potential. The method is a one-day simulation of the kind of work which an aspirant to supervisory position would eventually perform. A consequence of the simulation outlines for the individual strong points and areas which need to be developed, if they are to qualify for the supervisory positions to which they aspire.

The needs are determined by direct contact of the training staff with supervision, management, and individual employees. At least once a year, an annual budget is assembled to reflect felt needs of the organization for training and development. Training directors and their staff are required to live out the budget.

Categories of Training Needs Which Have Been Identified

Perhaps the most notable categories of training which are emerging are computers and computer software applications such as graphics, spread sheets, communications, word processing, data management, and the use of data banks.

In management, prevailing courses include strategic planning, general management, leadership, and performance appraising.

Human relations type courses continue to include communications, group problem solving, mutual goal setting, performance appraisal, negotiating, making presentations, and delegation. Some organizations provide assertiveness training and stress management.

There is evidence that nonsupervisory employees are potential for more general training regarding participative group action to give them an opportunity to make decisions about their own work. This type of training includes network planning, brainstorming, force field analysis, group problem solving, and functional charting.

Categories of Employees Which Training and Development Address

Major categories of employees which training and development address include shop workers, administrative staff, first line supervisors, middle managers, executives, and senior executives.

Categories of Persons Teaching In-Company Courses or Programs

Most large companies have their own dedicated staff to design and conduct courses. There are a number of companies which use consultants to complement internal resources. The consultants may be from outside or in-company specialists from the line organizations in addition to permanent staff.

University and college professors provide training services as well.

Teaching Media Used

A variety of popular teaching media includes inroads into computer-assisted instruction and the use of interactive laser video disks. Computer-assisted instruction, video presentations, films, texts, workbooks, slides, and so on are most commonly in use today.

Categories of Skills Being Taught

Three major categories of skills have been identified to be passed on to the employees regardless of the levels of responsibility. They are communications, doing the job, and relating effectively to others.

Communication skills pervade everything that people have to do in business. Communication skills help to promote understanding among those who have to achieve organizational objectives. Examples of communications sessions include listening, giving feedback, making presentations, and improving writing skills.

Job skills relate to the technical and administrative aspects of performance. Job skill development sessions include technical subjects, graphics and computers, planning, organizing, accounting and finance, goal setting, time management, and performance appraisal among others.

Human relations skills focus on the fundamental behaviour required for working together on a collaborative basis.

This category includes sessions on group problem solving, holding effective staff meetings, setting a motivational climate, leadership, work relationships, understanding human behaviour at work, negotiations, interviewing, developing employees, and stress management among others.

Design or Learning Factors Which Are Taken into Consideration When Developing Courses or Programs

The primary design factor is relevance to the work which needs to be performed. To determine relevance, the incumbents, may be interviewed to determine critical job dimensions and the behavioural characteristics required for them. The interviewees are selected for their competence and for being role models. Senior executives are interviewed as well, they add insights into higher levels of performance and into their own visions of future trends and requirements. Courses are designed to give the participants an opportunity to understand and practice new behaviour be it technical, administrative, or humanistic.

There is more emphasis on combining understanding the theory, practicing new behaviour, and planning back home projects. Large programs usually start at the top. This leads to the formation of groups focused on resolving specific problems or deliberately working out approaches to quality, styles of management, or changing the culture of the organization. The process involves reexamining current values and comparing them to future objectives.

This helps to discover the gaps and steps which need to be taken to fill them. This way the organization is able to realize its long-term goals in a realistic and resolute fashion.

Integrating Training into the Goal-Setting Process of Individuals and the Organization

The organizations which have a formal goal-setting and performance reviews are able to integrate training with organizational and personal goals. Those which do not, are driven by the decisions made as a consequence of pressures from the environment. They have to make training decisions reactively.

Leading organizations use strategic planning, goal setting, performance reviews, and special task forces or work groups to ensure that the integration of training and organizational objectives is made on a continuing basis. Since goal setting and performance appraisals are fundamentally negotiative in nature, training and development is seen by both the supervisor and the employee as being helpful. In each case the supervisor is required to identify a developmental profile for the employee and support its implementation over a planned period. The period may be anywhere from one to several years.

Individuals who have special problems may be asked by their supervisor to discuss their problems with training and development specialists. The consequence of the discussions will be a developmental plan for the person. Individuals have an option to follow the plan, modify it to their own needs, or reject it altogether. Most people choose to participate.

One leading company requires its training director to visit personally with senior executives to develop individual development plans for them. There is an underlying assumption that each one has a unique requirement as part of their unique situation. This approach ensures that developmental profiles and plans assure a dynamic management team.

The same organization has corporate office staff set model course outlines which the division uses to develop courses for its own requirements. Such corporate inputs provide standards of excellence which guide the decentralized units, but which provide enough freedom to meet local needs.

Industry representatives participate as members of advisory boards for universities and colleges. The boards are associated with different faculties depending on the need of the university. They may be concerned with research and development, educational technology, introduction of computer-integrated manufacturing, management studies or certificate programs to develop industrial trainers. The members may also decide to take action on common concerns.

The companies encourage self-development through continuing education on the individual's own time. The educational assistance programs available reimburse employees for successful completion of courses up to a maximum of one hundred percent. of the cost of tuition. Some organizations reimburse laboratory fees, as well as student service and registration fees.

Certain companies require and support specialized seminars or courses which are related directly to the person's job function. The organization pays full expenses for them.

Consultants and specialists may be brought in to provide specialized skills or knowledge to the work force.

On-The-Job Training Programs

Formal on-the-job programs are usually technical. They involve shop staff. The courses range from welding, machining, and soldering to the use of computers, graphics, and apprenticeship programs. The progress of the trainee is carefully monitored and recorded. Assistance is provided by the supervisor or the training staff member to the trainees. There is, of course, ongoing on-the-job training which is informal.

Types of Job Instruction

Job instruction usually involves coaching, counselling, demonstrating, and allowing the student to try out new behaviour under supervision. Eventually employees are allowed to perform duties and operations on their own. They are taught in maintaining high standards by monitoring and controlling their own operations.

Apprenticeship Programs

There are a variety of apprenticeship programs. They include electricians, electronic technicians, mechanics, machinists, sheet metal workers, air frame fitters and assemblers. The programs are usually designed to ensure that apprentices have a scheduled number of hours of class work as well as practical instruction.

Cooperative Programs

The companies enter into a cooperative relationship with universities, colleges, and secondary schools to give students an opportunity to obtain experience in industry as well as credits for their scholastic programs.

The participating schools include Sherbrooke University, Ecole de Technologie Superieure, University of Toronto, Waterloo University, and Georgian College, to name a few.

Training Methods Which Are Being Used

The methods used include case analysis, lectures, lecturettes, team assignments, simulations, computer assisted instruction, role plays, and hands-on use of information and equipment to perform actual work under supervision.

Assessment Criteria for Evaluating Training Programs

In technical subjects, for most cases training can be related to cost reduction. In management and supervisory training, no specific criteria have been established as a benchmark for evaluating the activities. There is evidence that training improves attitude and behaviour of the participants but, as yet, it has not been documented sufficiently well to predict outcomes.

At present companies are accumulating data, using computers, on absenteeism, scrap rate, grievances, complaints and incidence of maladies, and accidents. Eventually this information may be sufficiently integrated and interpreted to be of use in establishing criteria for evaluating training interventions. In the meantime, traditional estimates and interences are being used to relate training to productivity improvement and associated savings.

Chief Methods for Evaluating Training and Development Activities

The chief method for evaluating training and development activities includes participants' responses and feedback from supervision and management of the trainees. The training department staff use pre- and post-tests as well as various exercises to determine the extent of understanding and skills acquired by the trainees. These give some indication about the extent of learning, but do not ensure transfer of learning to the job. Relating training to savings and better employee relations are also indicators which help management evaluate the effectiveness of the training activities.

Membership in Professional Organizations

The training community lists some eight different associations which have members from the Canadian aerospace industry. Included among them are the American Society for Training and Development, the Ontario Society for Training and Development, and the Association for Human Resource Professionals of Quebec. The training professionals show a wide variety of interest in groups which meet their category of needs. No one professional organization seems to dominate the membership.

Future Changes

To keep pace with the changing business world, training function in aerospace industry is gearing to become more flexible in terms of delivering appropriate cost effective courses and programs to their organizations.

There are signs that indicate greater interest by top management in the process by which training interventions come about. Some companies are forming high-level task forces to provide impetus for interventions which have a long-term effect on the performance of individuals, departments, divisions, the corporation, and the industry. Modeling of technical systems points to the feasibility of developing models for the socio-technical systems as well. The availability of computers, to do so, makes this more likely. The general systems concepts are finding their way into the business world. This is making systems analysis and synthesis of the various functions possible. It also shows how to integrate them more effectively into a coherent whole.

Organizations are approaching the integration by considering the development of a systems model to include the people management system. More specifically future changes include:

—— More use of computers
—— Modular integrated packages for specific groups
—— More use of employees as trainers
—— Greater use of consultants
—— Greater emphasis on cost effectiveness
—— More stress on quality
—— More assistance from corporate staff
—— More integrated programs which include the entire organization with short-, mid- and long-term objectives
—— Certificate programs to professionalize the training staff
—— More cooperative projects with universities and colleges

Trends for the Next Five Years

The higher rate of change in the business world forces quicker response to business situations. This in turn requires speedier acquisition of knowledge, skills, and new attitudes to the way of doing business. Traditional ways of helping individuals and organizations to adapt will require radical changes. One device for doing this is the computer. Computer courses presently available allow for modularity and for relationships to a greater totality. Moreover, they can be available to the student on a twenty-four-hour basis. There will be, therefore, a continued growth in the computer-based training.

The introduction of sophisticated systems to engineering design, computer-integrated manufacturing, materials control, and information classification, storage and retrieval has created an inseparable need to train people in computer-aided methods.

The schools produce graduates with basic training in concepts and approaches, while industry has to provide operations-oriented instruction. There will be closer relationship between industry, government, and educational institutions to design learning systems which will enhance the effectiveness of education and training in all areas. Educational institutions will receive more guidance from industry through advisory boards. At the same time, industry will receive more benefit from applied research conducted in universities.

There will be a greater interchange of teachers with practitioners. More teachers will teach on location in industry and more practitioners will teach specialized courses in universities and colleges.

In addition to supporting individual courses or programs dealing with employability, upgrading, or retraining due to technological obsolescence, government will continue supporting major projects such as factory modernization programs. This will support a competitive edge for the industry in world-class marketing ventures. There will be greater cooperative efforts between government and private industry for long-term benefits to the industry and the country.

Competitive conditions are tending to maintain continuing focus on higher productivity and more efficient work methods. This will increase the proportion of time invested in training for all employees.

With a greater concern for personal growth and development by the younger work force, there will be a greater demand for personal development and career-oriented training.

Organizations will include professional career planning for all employees so as to prepare them for career changes. The training will include greater emphasis on job rotation so as to develop multiskilled persons more adaptable to changing conditions. The employees will be better equipped to understand how their function fits into the system. This will allow them to be better prepared to resolve problems.

There will be an increase in total training programs which include the entire organization. Such programs will start top down and continue evolving about some central value. The value may be quality, improved motivational climate, participative leadership style, or greater concern for the welfare of the individual.

Management is realizing that training does not only include class work and on-the-job instruction such as showing and coaching. Training is also personal contact with management and a demonstration of effective behaviour in deed as well as in philosophy. There will be, therefore, more tendency to use participative methods involving people in the decision-making process.

There is also an increasing realization that due to the complexity of modern industry individuals at their work place are bound to know more about their situations than persons at higher levels.

Participative management not only provides opportunities for employee involvement, but gives management an oppotunity to demonstrate effective ways of behaving. They lead while giving an example of organizational values.

There will be a greater emphasis on leadership and its effect on the organization. The nature of leadership will be reexamined to determine in what way it is different from management.

There are forces at work which require the reexamination of the difference between management and leadership. Management tends to be seen as a maintaining function while leadership appears to be transformational in nature. The characteristics of leadership include the generation of a vision and helping the members of the organization to understand it and commit themselves to work towards its attainment. The attaining process includes initiative, empowering others to take personal responsibility to do what they believe ought to be done and reiterate planning and achieving which will bring the organization closer to the vision. Since leadership can be taught, there will be a greater abundance of courses on the nature of leadership and how to acquire it.

As organizations become more aware of the potential of deliberate plans to improve their effectiveness through training and development, they will perceive training as an investment and a very real contributor to the bottom line. There will be greater interest in measuring the effect of training in accounting terms to show the relationship as adding to the capabilities of people to respond more effectively to business conditions. This will bring about greater interest in the organization of the function, what objectives it should have, what information it needs, what methods it uses, what resources are adequate for it and what feedback and monitoring network is required to ensure that the function is performing effectively. Additionally, there will probably be a reexamination of where the function fits in the organization and what communication networks make it more effective.

23. Canadian Experience in Innovative Approaches to High Commitment Work Systems

Harvey F. Kolodny, University of Toronto

INTRODUCTION

North Americans have experimented with innovative approaches to work organization for several decades. If we refer to scientific management as the base, the first significant innovations were applications of the humanistic psychology of Abraham Maslow. Distinguishing between items that motivated and others that only satisfied, Herzberg applied Maslow's psychology by encouraging the enrichment of individual jobs. There were other proposals to improve the narrow jobs that emanated from scientific management, for example, by having people enlarge their tasks to add variety to their activities, or by having them rotate jobs to experience that variety. This concern with the characteristics of jobs soon expanded and more items were added to the list of constituents of a good job, for example: autonomy, opportunities to learn, meaningfulness, respect (Emery and Thorsrud 1976). Comprehensive models were developed that included: different psychological states; a range of outcomes such as satisfaction, absenteeism and turnover; and some attention to individual differences (Hackman, Oldham, Jensen, and Purdy 1975).

At the organizational level, innovations from classical management theory were more frequently implemented and more successfully applied. Alfred Sloan's (1964) proposals for divisionalization at General Motors took root throughout North America. As environmental turbulence (Emery and Trist 1964) and uncertainty (Lawrence and Lorsch 1967) increased, the hierarchical coordination of traditional organizational forms was augmented with task forces, teams, project organization, and matrix organizational designs (Galbraith 1973).

In the 1970s, the focus on individual jobs expanded to a more holistic focus that took account of the effect of managerial values and peer groups on individuals at work. This perspective came to be called quality of working life (Davis and Cherns 1975). It developed from a systemic approach to organizational analysis and design that originated in the United Kingdom and was entitled sociotechnical systems theory (Emery and Trist 1960). Sociotechnical systems theory evolved from an increased recognition that organizations were open systems because they were imbedded in environmental contexts that constantly changed so that they too had to change. This was a marked departure from the closed systems perspectives of scientific and classical management theory.

This chapter concentrates on that set of work organization innovations that have a quality of working life and/or sociotechnical systems philosophy inherent in their design and implementation. In recent years they have acquired a newer terminology: high commitment work systems (Davis 1983; Walton 1985). Reference to work innovations here will mean innovations of these types only.

THE ROLE OF SOCIAL ACTORS

Government Quality of Working Life (QWL) Programs

Work innovation came to Canada in an organized way in 1978 through the initiatives of the QWL unit of the Employment Relations Branch of Labour Canada. The QWL unit was advised by Eric Trist who moved to York University in Toronto in 1978. To commence their initiatives, an outside consultant was hired to explore the interests of academics, consultants, managers, and trade unionists. Then they held a series of workshops across the country and invited interested representatives of all these constituencies to attend. They invited well-known members of the International Council for the Quality of Working Life to participate. They produced and widely distributed a newsletter of QWL events, articles about different initiatives, and books of QWL readings.

The academics and consultants came to these workshops willingly. The managers and trade unionists came reluctantly, if at all, and for the most part, it was only those involved in early QWL projects who did show up for these events. And when they did, they generally came to talk about their own company experiences.

Nevertheless, the process appeared to be an effective way to diffuse sociotechnical and, particularly, QWL ideas. Labour Canada's QWL Unit kept a steady stream of activities going across the country that maintained a high level of momentum until other efforts arose.

One other large scale, innovative effort actually preceded the establishment of Labour Canada's QWL unit. It was initiated by the Treasury Board of Canada on the advice of an Advisory Committee on Personnel Administration which recommended, in 1975, that "quality of working life approaches be tried on a limited scale in the Federal Public Service" (Mears and Brunet 1983, 7). Experiments based on the creation of semi-autonomous work groups were undertaken in 1975 in three departments with the cooperation of three different public sector unions, despite some misgivings of the latter. These first generation experiments, of eighteen months duration each were soon followed by a second generation series of experiments in two other departments (Cameron 1983) in 1978. Three other experiments commenced through the initiatives of three different departments themselves. Only one of these seven experimental sites has continued in the direction established (Jones 1983). It grew from a small unit of twenty-four keypunch operators to encompass the entire department of over two hundred employees.

One of the early nongovernmental promoters of QWL activities was York University, through the initiatives of Professor Eric Trist. Through seminars, courses, research and, particularly, community development efforts, this set of activities became the best known of the university-based efforts in Canada. Professor Trist attracted a body of interested students to York's Faculty of Environmental Studies and they, in turn, diffused the ideas about organizational innovation into the organizations that they were affiliated with.

In Vancouver, a QWL Forum was created under the umbrella of the British Columbia Research Council. At McGill University, a QWL unit began to offer courses to undergraduates, seminars to corporate personnel, and consulting services to those interested in changing their organization.

In the Province of Ontario, the Department of Labour had begun to research innovative work arrangements in the late 1970s and in 1978 published a survey of innovative work arrangements in Ontario. At the end of that same year, the government of Ontario created the Ontario Quality of Working Life Centre. It became immediately the best funded and most professionally organized of the QWL activities in Canada.

The Ontario QWL Centre began its formal life on the recommendation of a joint union-management committee comprised of four labour leaders, four corporate presidents, and the Deputy Minister of Labour. Its mandate was to consult interested organizations, carry out field projects, educate, inform, and research QWL. The committee has recently enlarged its mandate to include macro-level considerations of the tripartite relationships between labour, management, and government.

The Canadian Labour Market and Productivity Centre was established in 1984 (though initiatives to create a Labour Market Board had begun as early as 1976). The CLMPC is well funded ($7 million per year for four years), but its mission is still not clearly established. It remains uncertain as to whether it will take an active role in promoting innovative work arrangements.

And Some Nongovernmental Initiatives

In 1981, in Toronto, the Second International Conference on the Quality of Working Life was held. One thousand seven hundred people from twenty countries attended the conference, including nine hundred Canadians. The conference stimulated a wide variety of QWL activity in Canada. It also spawned a new organization: the Canadian Council on Working Life (CCWL), a network organization with a mission to disseminate, foster, and diffuse QWL practice across Canada. It has regional organizations in Ottawa and Toronto and links with similarly dedicated units in Vancouver and Montreal.

Trade Unions

Trade union support for QWL in Canada has been positive, but irregular and not universal. It has also been subjected to the politics of trade union organization. Commitments to QWL support exist in the official platforms of many of the major Canadian industrial unions and some of the public sector unions. However, because QWL requires cooperation with management, it remains anathema to some unions, particularly those whose relations with employers are poor or who are strongly ideologically driven.

Because support is not universal, even in unions that have accepted QWL as an operating principle, senior trade union leaders tend to hedge in their public positions about QWL. Such is the politics of democracy. However, their support is often stronger than their public positions. This is witnessed by their membership in the Ontario QWL Centre's committee, by their attendance at a variety of QWL events, by occasional public statements, and most of all, by the sanction given by many unions to their members and locals to proceed with QWL activity, if they so wish to do. A more significant demonstation of trade union support is the number of union-involved QWL projects.

Management and Organizations

Support for QWL from this sector is more varied. In some cases, it approaches the large system support that Eric Trist has prophesied (Trist 1980) as companies and agencies have engaged in ever increasing programs of QWL activity. These range from ergonomic and environmental improvement to new sociotechnically designed factories and organizations. For the most part, however, widespread adoption of QWL concepts by management is yet to come. Management that understand the concepts generally have positive feelings. For two many managers, however, QWL is one management fad competing with many others; and when these managers do happen to choose QWL as their current fad, their level of commitment is often too low to sustain any innovative activity.

Hence, while support is general, it is only selectively high. But the level is increasing. The inventory of companies exploring, considering, and actually engaging in new sociotechnically designed plants is becoming broader every day. Redesign efforts also continue, but redesign is difficult, and the low level of success of many redesign projects serves as a kind of nonstimulant for others.

Most early initiatives in Canada were in the food processing and petrochemical sectors. In the last few years, mechanical and electrical manufacturing sectors, particularly automotive companies, have initiated different QWL projects (List 1985). There has also been a stream of small activities in the retail industry (in warehousing, in particular), in some service sectors, and in several government departments. Several Canadian locations have often been mentioned as showcase examples of innovative forms of work organization (e.g., Shell Canada's Sarnia, Ontario polypropylene plant [Halpern 1984] and Canadian General Electric's Bromont, Quebec aerofoil manufacturing plant [Arnopoulos 1985]).

Workers, Academics, and Researchers

Worker involvement in QWL is almost exclusively through their employers. There is some independent networking interest via the CCWL but the numbers are small. When QWL projects take place, the worker attitudes are almost universally positive (except where politics or poor management undermines a project). This is especially the case in new sociotechnically designed plants. The promise they offer for individual worker growth and development is very exciting.

Research into QWL in Canada is diffused across the country and is growing. Most major universities have at least a single person interested in the area and carrying out some research. Some have several such people. The research is often case-oriented and prescriptive, and is rarely quantitative, with the exception of several recent doctoral theses at the University of Toronto. Because that qualitative orientation is not in the mainstream of current academic research paradigms, it tends to limit the amount of research undertaken.

With support from Labour Canada's QWL unit, a book of Canadian cases of QWL and sociotechnical systems experiences was published (Cunningham and White 1984). Fourteen separate cases are described in considerable detail, making the book a comprehensive record of work innovation experiences in Canada. Almost all the cases are from the private sector. Some of the public sector experiences that were initiated by the Treasury Board of Canada are documented in Neil Herrick's (1983) book entitled *Improving Government: Experiments with Quality of Working Life Systems*. This book emanated from the public sector cases presented at the 1981 conference referred to previously, as did a second book (Kolodny and van Beinum 1983) that recorded the key addresses presented at that conference.

Two other extensive sources of Canadian QWL data exist. Labour Canada's QWL unit has published a series of cases and conceptual notes as well as a quarterly publication entitled *QWL: The Canadian Scene*. Ontario's QWL Centre has published an occasional paper series and produces a regular journal entitled *QWL Focus*. Canadian experience is also documented in Nightingale's (1982) comparative research study of ten innovative and ten traditional organizations.

THE DEVELOPMENT OF NEW CONCEPTS AND STRATEGIES

Technology and Investment as the Driving Force

Innovations in work organization rarely proceed merely because they have potential benefits for the people working in the particular organization. Until recently, economic arguments have been too weak for an innovative proposal to receive the necessary support within the organization's infrastructure. When organizational innovation does commence, it usually does so in concert with technological change or with some significant program of investment in a new plant and in new equipment. This has been the general pattern in Sweden (Aguren, Hansson and Karlsson 1976; Lindholm 1975) as well as in Canada (Davis and Sullivan 1980; Cunningham and White 1984).

Interestingly, when the proposed organizational changes are accompanied by technological change, it often lowers resistance to change on the part of key organizational members. For example, introducing new production technology makes it easier for production engineers to accept changes in work arrangements that allow work teams, parallelization and longer task cycles to be implemented. Not only is their resistance to work innovations lowered, but, understanding the apparent necessity of the technological change, they often become supportive of the accompanying organizational changes (Skinner 1979).

In Canada, in the late 1970s and early 1980s, the petrochemical industry was the source of major new capital investment in plant. It is not coincidental then, that it was in this industrial sector that the most exciting new organizational innovations took place (Cunningham and White 1984). Other industrial areas in Canada demonstrated a similar pattern, for example food processing where plants are small, the industry is extremely competitive, and new plants are often built to manufacture a single product or product line in a portfolio of constantly changing product lines. Innovation in this sector in Canada is generally patterned after American parent organizations, since many of the companies are Canadian subsidiary organizations.

Organizational innovation in Canada has also occurred several times in the design of new warehousing facilities. It is usually the introduction of new materials handling technology and/or the construction of a new facility that drives the introduction of new organizational designs. The facilities here have tended to be small, and the work innovations generally revolve around the development of one or two relatively self-regulating work teams.

One quite different Canadian sector also tends to fit this pattern: the area of office reorganization. Most innovations here came on the wings of newly installed data processing equipment. Some were considerably aided by (pushed might be a better statement) the previously described Treasury Board of Canada's desires to promote QWL in the public sector. The Treasury Board was the source of the funding for the supportive systems of external and internal consultants and organized evaluations of progress. However, insurance industries in the private sector also took advantage of newly installed computers to implement innovative work designs (Kiggundu 1984).

This pattern continues now in Canada as capital investment has shifted to new automated manufacturing technologies (AMT). These include computer integrated manufacturing, numerical control, group technology, computer-assisted manufacturing, new materials handling systems including pilotless vehicles, etc. It is in these mechanical manufacturing sectors that considerations of new work arrangements have begun to arise in concert with the new technology. They range from minimal QWL considerations to significant sociotechnical design.

Other Driving Forces

In the wake of intense global competition, particulary from the Far East, performance is another key factor that will drive North American organizations to adopt more participative sociotechnical structures. The data on the performance of these innovative work arrangements is beginning to appear now (Day 1984) and it is attractive enough to overcome the preoccupation and history that so many North American managers have with authoritarian and scientific management structures. In the late 1970s and early 1980s, North American managers sought productivity solutions in Japanese techniques (quality circles, just-in-time systems, etc.) They are still adopting the best of these manufacturing methods. However, as they glance about, sociotechnical systems approaches will probably appear as the only viable alternatives to traditional organization.

The recession of the early 1980s kept capital investment down. As it returns, it will bring the increasing comprehension about organizational design alternatives to the designer's table. In Sweden, very few organizations would build a new factory based upon unquestioned functional organizational concepts in the mid 1980s (Kolodny 1986). That same statement cannot be made in North America, as yet; however, the awareness of organizational alternatives is building. More and more organizations are either committed to sociotechnical systems design for their new plants or are planning one or two as prototypes and learning models.

Sociotechnical Systems Design and Genuine Participation: A North American Direction

While quality of working life activities in Canada and the United States are both pervasive and growing, the aspect of them that will most mark North American efforts for the future and will constitute a genuine set of significant innovations in work organizations will be the design of new plants to a sociotechnical systems philosophy. The experience of designs of this kind is accumulating (Walton 1980 and 1985; Pasmore, Francis, and Haldeman 1982; Day 1984; Kolodny and Dresner 1986). The conceptual basis for sociotechnical systems theory is better understood now (Cherns 1976; Emery 1978; Trist 1980; Davis 1982). The process of sociotechnical systems design is beginning to be documented (Davis 1981 and 1983; Mansell and Rankin 1983; Kolodny and Stjernberg 1986). Finally, the number of consultants who can advise organizations and the number of training courses for interested learners have begun to increase in Canada and the United States.

Several European countries have legislated participative systems within their industrial relations systems. For the most part, however, they function to the minimum of the legislation. Real participation demands a level of involvement of blue-collar workers in work organizational decisions that flies in the face of traditional status differences between blue- and white-collar workers. Those differences are far smaller in North America. The blue/white-collar gap is far easier bridged in Canada and the United States. A deep level of participation has begun to evolve in the new, sociotechnically designed plants. This will be one of the most important differences in the evolution of North American work organization innovation vis-a-vis similar European activity. Sweden's union and management organizations, however, have recently signed an Agreement on Efficiency and Participation (1982) that may take their participation beyond the minimum.

AN ASSESSMENT OF NORTH AMERICAN DIRECTIONS

High Commitment Work Systems

There are a wide range of quality of working life projects in process in North America. Some are significant in the way they are changing work patterns in established organizations, such as the automobile industry or some of the labour-management committee structures in some steel-making factories. However, the significant innovations in work organizations in North America are unquestionably in the development of high commitment work systems (Walton 1980 and 1985; Davis 1983). Such systems have a basic philosophy built on sociotechnical systems theory (Emery 1978; Trist 1980) and/or the involvement of people in the process—both the design process and the ongoing operations of the organizations.

Most such organizational innovations have been in manufacturing plants and almost all are greenfield sites (Emery 1980). They arise where there is significant new capital investment in an industrial sector, and these tend to be sectors where the investment per employee is very high (often in the order of $1 million to $2 million per employee). With those levels of investment, management is highly aware of their dependence on their employees and looks to organizational systems that will ensure a higher level of commitment from the plant personnel.

Most of the innovation has tended to be in factories with some degree of continuous process in the production arrangements (e.g., petrochemicals or food-processing and consumer goods where the front half of the manufacturing process is a continuous process). In such sectors, apart from high capital investment, the number of employees per factory is relatively small (since the production process is relatively independent of the employees). Organizations seem prepared to invest in the higher than normal front-end costs associated with the development of such high commitment work systems because the small number of employees makes that front-end cost small in comparison to total investment.

The North American examples of high commitment organizations are still relatively few, though some suggest they now number in the thousands (Walton 1985). In any event, their numbers are increasing because they promise significant productivity improvement and because management values about the importance of human resources are changing.

Union Versus Non-Union

Some of this is taking place in unionized plants, but much of it is in non-union settings. Some of it is part of the runaway factory syndrome or southern strategy of many companies; namely, to build small factories in the southern United States or in Canada, in rural areas where salary expectations are low, as are experiences with unionization. Since these plants are in any event small, they tend to be less likely to be unionized because management is closer to the employees and more quickly aware of employee dissatisfaction. For the firms making these moves, the essential drive is towards increased flexibility. Organized labour tends to signify to them an unwillingness to be flexible (which is sometimes a valid perception). Hence, while some managers make statements to the effect that a unionized plant is easier to manage because communications are smoother via both union and management sides, they still prefer a nonunionized structure that allows them more degrees of freedom to arrange and rearrange work.

Interestingly, many of these plants have a commitment to employment security as opposed to job security (hence, the desire to be able to flexibly move people about) because they recognize it as an essential component of developing a high commitment work system. It generally means that they build up their work force slowly so as not to have to engage in a layoff, and they often use temporary help to handle peak periods.

Many efforts are now underway to develop innovative work organizations in office areas and white-collar clerical organizations. They will lead to reductions in people, and it is doubtful if the protections of even unorganized manufacturing organizations will be built into the designs. This sector tends to be low in unionization and the best management has often been more paternalistic than equitable. Without the pressure and experience that comes from a highly unionized infrastructure in the industry, the systems that evolve here are likely to be less equitable and less advanced in their innovations. As a result, they are also likely to build less commitment. To date, the technology of this industry is more amenable to single work station development, rather than to arrangements that provide opportunities for group work. That factor alone could stand in the way of significant and interesting innovation. This area of activity also centres around existing organizations. It is in the area of new designs that designers have the most scope to be innovative. However, some authors have argued that office technology, based on computerized equipment, is very amenable to flexible arrangements that could provide considerable social choice, even in existing organizations (Walton 1983).

Product Focused Factories

There is a movement towards product focusing of factories in North America (Skinner 1974). The Swedes experimented with product shops some twenty years ago, but implemented them widely only in the last few years. Product shops have product-oriented organization all the way through the unit in question: group technology cells, assembly cells (and parallelization), and self-managing work groups. They are, in effect, factories-within-factories organized with the grain (Lindholm 1975) or plants-within-plants (Skinner 1974). A product orientation overcomes many of the dysfunctions of functional forms: worker alienation, long throughput times, high inventory levels. As such, it is structurally conducive to the enhancement of the quality of working life. Small, with larger task cycles, it is a form that promotes many organizationally desirable features for individuals and groups (Kolodny 1984; Kolodny and Armstrong 1985).

Product-oriented structural forms offer a higher rate of organizational responsiveness, but in becoming more dedicated, they also increase the vulnerability of the firm to economic cycles (Rohan 1982). Computerization of facilities is, however, returning to these small and relatively dedicated structures some of the flexibility they gave up in adopting forms that resulted in faster throughput. With increased computerization, the investment per employee in plant and equipment usually increases, the number of employees decreases, and even discrete or batch manufacturing begins to assume some of the characteristics of the continuous process industry. It follows that the logic that drove the continuous process sector to innovate organizationally is also causing the batch manufacturing sector to move in the same direction.

Assessing Progress

The movement towards innovative work organization arrangements in Canada is still slight. But there is movement. It comes on the wings of good economic times, which explains why activity in QWL and new plant design was high in the petrochemical sector in the late 1970s and early 1980s when the industry was thriving. It will soon surge ahead again in the manufacturing sectors as that domain, led by extensive computerization, begins to reinvest and refurbish the many old and inefficient factories across the land.

Progress in QWL tends to follow the path Trist has predicted (1980). It takes place now in large systems. Companies embrace innovative work arrangements broadly while governments commence comprehensive programs of change. The best measure of success is that they have chosen to do so. Like so many others, they experimented first with one or two change situations. That they expanded to include many new plants in their QWL framework or many different departments in the mandate of their governmental program is evidence that they feel confident about their direction and the results of their early experiences.

This is how we will probably mark QWL progress in Canada, not by identifying this plant or that department, but rather by pointing to the larger systems in which they are embedded citing the company or the branch of government as the innovators.

References

Agreement on Efficiency and Participation: SAF–LO–PTK. 1981. Stockholm: Swedish Employers' Confederation.

Aguren, S., R. Hansson, and K. G. Karlsson. 1976. The Volvo Kalmar plant, Stockholm. The Rationalization Council SAF–LO (produced by the Swedish Employers' Confederation).

Arnopoulos, S. 1985. Participative management in an advanced high technology plant: Canadian General Electric in Bromont. Montreal: McGill Human Resource Associates Inc.

Cameron, M. 1983. "A Crown corporation: Process versus outcome." In *Improving government: experiments with quality of working life systems*, edited by N. Q. Herrick. New York: Praeger.

Cherns, A. B. 1976. The principles of sociotechnical design. *Human Relations* 29(8) (August): 783–92.

Cunningham, J. B. and T. H. White. 1984. *Quality of working life: contemporary cases*. Ottawa: Government Publishing Centre.

Davis, L. E. 1981. "Evolving alternative organizational designs: Their Sociotechnical Basis." In Quality of working life, edited by R. Dorion, 32–42. Ottawa: Labour Canada.

Davis, L. E. 1982. Organization design. Chapter 2.1 in *Handbook of Industrial Engineering*, edited by G. Salvendy. Atlanta, Ga.: Industrial Engineering and Management Press.

Davis, L. E. 1983. "Learnings from the design of new organizations." In *The quality of working life in the 1980's*, edited by H. Kolodny and H. Van Beinum, 65–86. New York: Praeger Publishers.

Davis, L. E. and A. B. Cherns. 1975. *The quality of working life*. Vols. 1 & 2. New York: The Free Press.

Davis, L. E. and C. S. Sullivan. 1980. A labour-management contract and quality of working life. *Journal of Occupational Behaviour* 1 (January): 29–41.

Day, N. 1984. The coming age of commitment. *Harvard Business School Bulletin* (December): 58–69.

Emery, F. 1978. *The emergence of a new paradigm of work*. Canberra: Australian National University, Centre for Continuing Education.

Emery, F. and E. Thorsrud. 1976. *Democracy at work*. Martinus Neihoff International Series on the Quality of Working Life.

Emery, F. and E. Trist. 1960. Sociotechnical systems. In *Management Science*, edited by C. W. Churchman and M. Verhurst. *models and techniques*. Elmsford, New York: Pergamon Press.

Emery, F. and E. Trist. 1964. The causal texture of organizational environments. *Human Relations* 18:21–32.

Galbraith, J. R. 1973. *Designing complex organizations*. Addison-Wesley.

Hackman, J. R., G. R. Oldham, R. Jensen, and K. Purdy. 1975. A new strategy for job enrichment. *California Management Review* (Summer).

Halpern, N. 1984. "Sociotechnical systems design: The Shell Sarnia experience." In The quality of working life: Contemporary cases, edited by J. B. Cunningham and T. H. White, 31–75. Ottawa: Government Publishing Centre.

Herrick, N. 1983. *Improving government: Experiments with quality of working life systems*. New York: Praeger Publishers.

Jones, C. M. 1983. "Major obstacles to QWL's development in the Canadian Federal Public Service." In *Improving Government: Experiments with Quality of Working Life Systems*, edited by N. Q. Herrick, 21–29. New York: Praeger Publishers.

Kiggundu, M. 1984. "Participative work design and supervisory problems." In The quality of working life: Contemporary cases, edited by J. B. Cunningham and T. H. White, 387–433. Ottawa: Government Publishing Centre.

Kolodny, H. F. 1984. Product organization structures improve the quality of working life. Paper presented at the 1984 SME World Congress on Human Aspects of Automation, Montreal, Sept. 16–19.

Kolodny, H. F. 1986. Work organization design in Sweden: Some impressions from

1982–83. *Human Systems Management* forthcoming.

Kolodny, H. F. and A. Armstrong. 1985. Three bases for QWL improvements: Structure, technology and philosophy. Paper presented at 1985 Academy of Management National Meetings, San Diego, August 11–14.

Kolodny, H. F. and B. Dresner. 1986. Linking Arrangements and New Work Designs. *Organizational Dynamics* forthcoming.

Kolodny, H. F. and T. Stjernberg. 1986. The change process in innovative work designs: New design and redesign in Sweden, Canada and the USA. *Journal of Applied Behavioural Science* forthcoming.

Kolodny, H. F. and H. Van Beinum. 1983. *The Quality of Working Life and the 1980s*. New York: Praeger Publishers.

Lawrence, P. R. and J. Lorsch. 1967. *Organization and environment*. Cambridge, MA: Harvard Graduate School of Business Administration.

Lindholm, R. 1975. *Job reform in Sweden*. Stockholm: Swedish Employers' Conference.

List, W. 1985. When workers and managers act as a team. *Report on Business Magazine*, October, 60–67.

Mansell, J. and T. Rankin. 1983. Changing organizations: The quality of working life process. Occasional Paper No. 4. Toronto: Ontario Quality of Working Life Centre, September.

Mears, J. M. and L. Brunet. 1983. "Overview: QWL activities in Canada." In *Improving government: Experiments with quality of working life systems*, edited by N. Q. Herrick, 5–11. New York: Praeger Publishers.

Nightingale, D. 1982. *Workplace democracy*. Toronto: University of Toronto Press.

Pasmore, W., C. Francis, and J. Haldeman. 1982. Sociotechnical systems: A North American reflection on empirical studies of the Seventies. *Human Relations* 35(2): 1179–1204.

Rohan, T. 1982. Focussed factories. *Industry Week*.

Skinner, W. 1974. The focussed factory. *Harvard Business Review* (May–June): 113–121.

Skinner, W. 1979. "The impact of changing technology on the working environment." In *Work in America: The decade ahead*, edited by C. Kerr and J. M. Rosow, 204–230. Work in America series. New York: Van Nostrand Reinhold.

Sloan, A. P. 1964. *My years with General Motors*. New York: Doubleday & Co.

Trist, E. L. 1980. The evolution of sociotechnical systems. Occasional Paper No. 2. Toronto: Ontario Quality of Working Life Centre, June.

Walton, R. E. 1980. "Establishing and maintaining high commitment work systems." In *The Organizational Life Cycle*, edited by J. Kimberley and R. H. Miles, San Francisco, CA: Jossey-Bass.

Walton, R. E. 1983. Social choice in the development of advanced information technology. In *The quality of working life and the 1980s*, edited by Kolodny, H. F. and H. Van Beinum, 55–64. New York: Praeger Publishers.

Walton, R. E. 1985. From control to commitment in the work place. *Harvard Business Review* (March–April): 76–84.

24. Understanding and Managing Absence from Work

Gary Johns, Concordia University

When was the last time you were absent from work? When was the last time one of your coworkers was absent from work? Work absence is an interesting form of organizational behaviour. On the one hand, virtually everyone exhibits some absence from work during his or her career. Thus, absenteeism is a universal phenomenon. On the other hand, most people manage to get to work most of the time. Thus, most people are not absent very much. These basic facts conspire to lead employees and managers not to think very much about absence. However, if the day-to-day impact of absence is undramatic, its aggregate effects are powerful. Consider the following findings:

- In Canada, the cost of absenteeism to the economy has been variously estimated at somewhere between $3 billion and $8 billion (Mikalachki and Gandz 1982). In the United States, estimates run from $10 billion (Allen 1983) to $30 billion (Steers and Rhodes 1984). Although different methods of calculation produce different results, these estimates are expensive by any standard.

- In Quebec, over twenty-three million person-days a year are lost to absenteeism. This is many times the days lost to strikes and lockouts (Picher 1985).

- At Bank of Montreal locations across Canada, fifty-four thousand hours a week are lost to absenteeism. This costs $18 million per year in salaries alone (Absenteeism 1983).

- A United States study found that the majority of the employee discharge cases brought before arbitrators dealt with excessive absenteeism (Scott and Taylor 1983).

Despite the economic impact and disruption suggested by these examples, we will see that few organizations devote much attention to monitoring and managing absenteeism. In the sections that follow we will look more closely at the extent, costs, and benefits of absenteeism. Then we will examine some models of absence behaviour that help organize our thinking about why absence occurs. Following this, we will examine systems to monitor, diagnose, and manage absenteeism.

THE EXTENT, COSTS, AND BENEFITS OF ABSENCE

What is the average or typical amount of scheduled time lost due to absenteeism? The answer to this question is complicated by the general lack of consistent reporting systems both within and between nations. However, the United States Bureau of National Affairs sample of United States organizations provides one useful baseline. During the 1970s, this survey and others suggested that time lost due to absenteeism averaged around three to four percent across industries. This works out to seven or eight days per employee per year. However, during the recession of the 1980s, this figure moved closer to two percent (Steers and Rhodes 1984). Data from a variety of sources shows that Canadian absence levels generally parallel United States levels, being perhaps slightly higher due to climatic conditions.

Several points should be made about this two to four percent range. First, compared to many European countries, it is really very low. For instance, Steers and Rhodes (1984) note a fourteen percent rate for Italy. Despite this, given the cost figures cited earlier, it should be clear that even a small change in the rate of absence can represent big dollars in costs or savings. Also, it must be emphasized that averages can conceal tremendous variations among occupations and organizations. For example, between 1981 and 1983 absenteeism among General Motors auto workers ranged from nine percent to eleven percent, a figure well above the Bureau of National Affairs average for this period (Ruben 1983).

The figures cited earlier indicate that absence can be expensive for the employing organization. For example, Kempen (1982) estimates that a five percent absence rate costs a one-thousand-employee firm $1 million a year. How are such costs arrived at? The essence of the accounting is that a person is on the payroll, but not producing. Furthermore, the lost production can only be recovered by the efforts of others. Thus, most estimates of the cost of absence include some combination of the following:

—Value of lost productivity

—Salary or wages paid to the absentee (if the absence is paid)

—Fringe benefits paid to the absentee, including accrued vacation, disability insurance premiums, etc. (a factor whether or not the absence is paid)

—Overtime paid to replacement personnel

—Salary or wages and benefits paid for overstaffing to compensate for a chronic level of absenteeism

Of these variables, the hardest to anticipate and measure is the impact of absenteeism on productivity. This probably depends upon how unanticipated the absences are and how people proofed the production of the object or service has been made (Moch and Fitzgibbons 1985). For example, automation, job simplification, or extensive cross-training may reduce the impact of absenteeism on productivity. Offsetting this advantage, however, are a number of less tangible costs of absence that seldom find their way into the accounting ledgers. These include general disruption and confusion, conflict with supervisors, increased time in processing grievances, and the possibility that replacement workers are more prone to accidents on unfamiliar jobs (Goodman and Atkin 1984).

The Medical Model

It is both conventional and reasonable to attribute a portion of absenteeism to sickness, injury, or general ill health. In fact, many persons quite literally *equate* absenteeism with sickness when the term is mentioned in casual conversation ("Stanley is absent? You mean he's sick? What's the matter with him?"). People are especially likely to invoke a medical model to explain their *own* absence behaviour, even when they are freed from making excuses to their boss or employer. For example, Nicholson and Payne (1984) report the results of a household survey that asked respondents to describe the reasons for past work absenteeism. Even under these low-threat conditions, minor medical ailments were cited as the most frequent cause of absence.

Does this self-report data mean that most absence is random behaviour influenced by uncontrollable sickness? Probably not. If ill health were the predominant contributor to absenteeism, we might expect to see a reduction in absences over the years as health care techniques have improved. However, in a careful study of British postal workers that spanned the years from 1891 to 1980, Taylor and Burridge (1982) noted an increase in absence rates. In addition, even for the relatively stable absence period of 1960 to 1980, they observed changes in diagnostic patterns for sickness. This suggests that many workers interpret their own absence behaviour in medical terms that are currently in vogue (e.g., lower back pain). Going a step further, being labelled sick can lead to an increase in absence even when there is no objective reason for this increase. A study of Canadian steel workers found that those with diagnosed high blood pressure were absent more than those with undiagnosed high blood pressure. When the latter were informed of their medical condition, their absence level increased to that of those that knew they had high pressure (Taylor, Haynes, Sackett, and Gibson 1981). This occurred even though high blood pressure has no self-detectable physical symptoms in its early stages.

One study has shown that medically-diagnosed absence has nonrandom patterns similar to voluntary absence (Rushmore and Youngblood 1979). Similarly, another study found that workers who took a scheduled day off work reported doing essentially the same things off the job as those who took an unscheduled day off work (Haccoun and Dupont 1984). Presumably, the unscheduled day was more likely due to sickness, yet the free time was spent in basically the same way as a well person.

As a group, these studies suggest that employees frequently interpret and explain their own behaviour in medical terms. However, they also suggest that a fair proportion of absence that is attributed to medical causes may be due to other factors. This means that the medical model must be supplemented with other models of absenteeism.

The Deviance Model

If workers often resort to a medical model to explain their own absence, observers, especially managers, are more likely to invoke a deviance model. That is, absenteeism is seen to reflect some combination of laziness, malingering, disloyalty, and untrustworthiness. In detailed interviews with industrial workers, Nicholson (1975) found that the absence of workmates was often viewed in this negative light, even among those who themselves were often absent. Also, a comprehensive study of United States personnel managers by Scott and Markham (1982) showed that discipline and punishment systems were the predominant and favoured means of controlling absence, even though such systems often were put into gear only after an absence problem was detected. This post-hoc negative reaction is a common response to deviants, be they juvenile delinquents or worse (Nicholson and Johns 1985).

What factors give rise to the deviance model? For one thing, as the absence data cited earlier indicates, most people show up for work most of the time. This sets the absentee apart from his or her coworkers, and this unusual behaviour often provokes observers to provide explanations that are personal rather than situational (Kelley 1972). In addition, it is sometimes observed that a fairly large proportion of absence is attributable to a small core of workers. For instance, the Bank of Montreal study cited earlier attributed seventy-five percent of the bank's absenteeism to twenty percent of its employees (Absenteeism 1983). Again, this small concentration of high absentees tends to signal deviance to observers.

Is there any evidence for the deviance model? One strong form of evidence, that is simply unavailable, would demonstrate that high absence was associated with other negative behaviours such as low personal productivity, sabotage, insubordination, and so on. A much weaker form of evidence would demonstrate that workers exhibit consistent levels of absence across time and across jobs. In fact, past absenteeism is a good predictor of current absenteeism (Breaugh 1981), even when a change in job assignments has intervened (Ivancevich 1985). However, this finding does not rule out the effects of chronic ill health or stable, external constraints (e.g., severe family demands) on attendance.

As noted earlier, the deviance model suggests a discipline or punishment-oriented response to managing absence. We will review such systems shortly.

The Withdrawal Model

If workers have favoured medicine to explain their own absence, and managers have favored deviance, many researchers have been partial toward job dissatisfaction. The general idea here is that absenteeism is a method of temporary withdrawal from dissatisfying aspects of the job. By extension, the worker might withdraw completely and exhibit turnover if alternative jobs exist. After all, it only seems sensible to escape or at least avoid an unpleasant work environment.

A large number of studies of the relationship between job satisfaction and absence have been recently subjected to rigorous review (Hackett and Guion 1985; McShane 1984; Scott and Taylor 1985). The results can be summarized as follows:

——In general, the relationship between job satisfaction and absence is really very small.
——Satisfaction with the content of the work itself is a better predictor of absence than satisfaction with pay, supervision, and so on.
——Job satisfaction is more strongly associated with frequency of absence (how often the employee is absent, irrespective of duration) than time lost (how many days are missed in some time period).

Why is the relationship between job satisfaction and absence so small? Organizations are designed in part to get people to come to work whether or not they are satisfied. Thus, absence control systems and a loss of pay for absent days may reduce the connection between job satisfaction and absence (Garrison and Muchinsky 1977).

The fact that satisfaction with work content is the best predictor of absence suggests that work redesign, such as that accomplished through job enrichment, might help in managing absence.

The Economic Model

The old saying time is money is indicative of the idea underlying the economic model of absenteeism. In essence, leisure (or nonwork) time has value, value that competes with the pay and other rewards received for spending time at work. When the desire for leisure exceeds the desire for pay, workers may be absent. Also, patterning attendance to protect one's economic interests becomes an important strategy.

Youngblood (1984) used economic techniques to determine the marginal rate of substitution of wages for nonwork time among utility company workers. He did this by asking them to estimate the amount of dollars and the amount of leisure time that they would pay for various benefits. The research demonstrated that workers who valued their nonwork time more highly exhibited higher levels of absence hours.

A mixed bag of evidence provides some support for the strategic economic use of attendance. One study found that refinery workers who perceived their pay to be unfair tended toward absenteeism (most of these absences were paid absences) (Patchen 1960). Also, there is evidence that absence increases when highly paid overtime is available (Gowler 1969; Martin 1971). Thus, employees will often attempt to maximize their effective hourly pay through various attendance strategies. Finally, at the national, regional, and organizational level, absenteeism seems to decrease as unemployment increases (Markham 1985). This suggests that good attendance may be seen as a defence mechanism in times of economic threat.

Most straightforwardly, the economic model implies absence-management schemes that reward attendance directly or reward employees for not using sick leave. Indirectly, it also suggests systems such as flex-time or the short workweek modify the connection between work and nonwork time. We will explore these methods shortly.

The Cultural Model

The medical, deviance, withdrawal, and economic models of absence are essentially individual-oriented models. That is, they suggest that absentees act as independent agents, uninfluenced by how others act or what others say. However, there is growing awareness that much absenteeism may be the product of a complex web of *social* influence. This social influence involves what coworkers and supervisors do and say about absence, and this is partly a function of occupational factors, technology, and plant or office layout. The result is a distinctive absence culture (Chadwick-Jones, Nicholson, and Brown 1982; Johns 1984; Johns and Nicholson 1982; Nicholson & Johns 1985) for various occupations, departments, plants, offices, and organizations.

Some absence cultures may be fairly weak, in effect signalling workers to do their own thing when it comes to attendance. For example, a polyglot mixture of immigrants working under a piecerate pay system may see their attendance at work as an individual decision based on economic need and pay little attention to the behaviour of others. Strong absence cultures may involve the development of specific norms concerning attendance. Johns and Nicholson (1982, 163) explain how an absence culture that supports high absence among female factory workers might develop:

Family, friends, and female co-workers might support a norm that encourages womens' absence based on a common belief that such work is "only temporary" or that the organization treats women inequitably. Convinced that female absence is a "special case," supervisors may then apply existing sanctions less rigorously, implicitly sending a similar normative message. As a culmination of this process, women employees acquire empirical evidence of the attendance behavior that is expected of them via the resultant absence level. . . .

There is as yet no hard proof of the value of the absence culture concept, although some rich descriptions of apparent absence cultures exist (Edwards and Scullion 1984). The best statistical evidence for the operation of such cultures involves group differences in absence levels. Thus, it appears that managers and professionals exhibit less absence than operative workers (Taylor 1981). Also, there are striking cross-national differences in absence rates. For example, Italy has many times more absenteeism than Switzerland, even though they are geographically adjacent (Steers and Rhodes 1984), and this is surely unlikely to be the product of differences in health or job satisfaction. Finally, within many organizations, it is possible to see great differences in absenteeism across units. For instance, in one Canadian manufacturing organization, time lost due to absence varies from five percent to twelve percent across plants. Within various plants, department rates range from one percent to twenty percent. It is unlikely that any of the above models fully explain these differences, and that a cultural model would prove useful.

The implications of the cultural model for absence management are complex. They often involve management acceptance of their own role in influencing absence and the development of concerted attempts to renegotiate absence norms (Chadwick-Jones 1980).

MONITORING AND DIAGNOSING ABSENCE PATTERNS

An adequate system for monitoring and diagnosing absence patterns lies at the heart of understanding and managing absence. However, despite the cost of absence, experts never cease to be amazed at how few organizations have adequate systems. In a large study of Ontario firms, Robertson (1979) found that only seventeen percent assembled absence data for management review. In Scott and Markham's (1982) survey of 987 United States personnel managers, only around fifty percent claimed that their organizations maintained and analysed detailed attendance records (though seventy percent claimed they had a "consistently applied attendance policy"). Suffice it to say that organizations that are famous for generating reams of statistics about every other aspect of their operations often appear to ignore attendance at work.

Measuring Absence

The key factor in any absence measurement system is a complete, accurate attendance calendar for each employee. This means that we should be able to retrieve the *exact* days of the year any employee was or was not at work. This exact attendance calendar may be important in the case of employee grievances or claims of unjust dismissal. There are many methods of summarizing and reporting absence data. For absence management programs the two most important are time lost and frequency of absence.

Time Lost. Time lost is the number of hours or days absent divided by the number of hours or days of work scheduled. If this ratio is multiplied by one hundred, it provides a percentage of the scheduled working time for which scheduled employees were absent. The percentages given at the beginning of the chapter were time lost percentages. Time lost, when costed, provides a good estimate of the economic impact of absence. However, it is generally agreed that it tends to be biased by longer-term incidents of sickness or injury. Thus, it does not provide an especially good estimate of the extent of absence that may be susceptible to management influence.

Frequency. Frequency of absence is the number of absence incidents that occur in some time frame (e.g., a month or a year) irrespective of how long each incident lasts. In other words, it is the number of inceptions of absence disregarding their duration. For a group of employees such as a department, frequency can be calculated by dividing the number of absence incidents beginning in the time frame by the number of employees in the unit. Compared with time lost, frequency is biased toward reflecting short-term absences. This is important, because it is these one or two day absences that are most likely to be a casual absence that is susceptible to management intervention. Also, other factors equal, high frequency of absence may actually prove more disruptive to the organization than high time lost. Thus, the frequency measure is an important complement to the traditional time lost measure in diagnosing and interpreting absence patterns.

Both time lost and frequency measures should be calculated to exclude obvious cases when work was neither truly scheduled nor missed. This rules out vacations, long-term disability, and matters such as jury duty or attendance at off-site training programs.

Diagnosing Absence

An effective absence monitoring system might calculate and report time lost and frequency on a monthly, year-to-date (cumulative), and yearly basis. This permits the analysis of trends and allows for the observation of seasonal variation. Time lost and frequency can be calculated at the individual, subunit, or total organizational level. Subunits could refer to departments, divisions, levels, occupations, work groups, or geographical locations. In order to aid in diagnosis, it is useful to cost absence by subunit. In other words, do any individuals exhibit time lost or frequency that is much above the level of their department or work group? These persons will usually require some form of customized management, generally through the supervisor, the disciplinary system, or the personnel function. However, the core of any good absence diagnosis system generally resides at the subunit level of analysis. Which plants, departments, or levels are exhibiting elevated degrees of absence, either historically or comparatively? Logic suggests devoting primary attention to those subunits where high-cost time lost is accompanied by high frequency of absence (Johns 1980). Here, the potential for savings is great because absence is costly. Furthermore, elevated frequency suggests the potential for management intervention. Additional information on measurement and diagnosis can be found in Kempen (1982) and Mikalachki and Gandz (1982).

MANAGING ABSENCE

It would be pleasant to report that the careful measurement of absence leads to clearcut diagnoses that suggest which of the models discussed earlier best explains absence in a given setting. Then, managers would have a good idea of which absence management techniques to implement. Unfortunately, we do not have a good theory that links absence patterns with absence causes (Johns 1980, 1984). Thus, choosing an absence management strategy is more art than science. Having a feel for the absence culture is important. Is most absence concentrated among a few employees, or is every employee a contributor? An individually-oriented discipline system may solve the former problem but not the latter. Is absence concentrated among less, well-paid workers, single parents, or some other identifiable group? Each pattern suggests different solutions.

Traditional Absence Management Techniques

Discipline Systems. As noted earlier, discipline systems that punish absence (usually with progressively stronger sanctions) are the most common and most favoured absence management techniques among personnel managers. Given this fact, it is remarkable that there are so few studies of the actual effectiveness of the introduction or escalation of discipline systems. While some studies show that discipline systems used alone reduce absence, at least one showed that the style (frequency) rather than the amount of absence (time lost) was modified. Nicholson (1976) found that a crackdown preceded a shift from short-term absence spells to longer medically certified spells.

At least two other potential side effects to discipline systems should be noted. First, rigorous punishment is likely to lead to an increase in expensive, time-consuming grievances. Secondly, many rigorous discipline systems put supervisors in the position of having to monitor subordinates, evaluate excuses, and hand out punishment. Some improperly trained supervisors may find the system an excuse to play vigilante. Others may simply find it stressful (Johns 1980).

Reward Systems. If discipline systems punish absence, reward systems are designed to, in some sense, reward attendance. Thus, the focus is on positive behaviour rather than negative behaviour. Simple systems provide employees who have good attendance records over some time period with a reward or the opportunity to win a reward via a lottery. Rewards have ranged from cash, to time off work, to consumer goods, to discounts on company products. Good attendance usually means perfect attendance. In general, research shows that reward systems of this nature are effective in reducing absenteeism (Schmitz and Heneman 1980; Steers and Rhodes 1984). However, the cost effectiveness of the systems has seldom been reported, and any organization adopting such a plan is advised to determine if savings outweigh costs.

A word should be said about the size of the reward and the time frame over which good attendance is required. One company instituted a system that provided a day's pay for textile workers who missed no more than three hours work during a business quarter. An additional day's pay was provided for those who achieved the three-hour criterion four quarters in a row. The result was a slight *increase* in absence and $7,500 paid out in bonuses (Schneller and Kopelman 1983)! What happened? There was a small increase in the proportion of employees who qualified for the bonus over those who would have qualified before the plan was put into effect. However, this was evidently offset by workers who blew the chances for the bonus early in the quarter and were less conscientious about their attendance. The moral here should be clear—the time frame was too long for the amount of money involved. Successful programs have usually used shorter time frames for perfect attendance, ranging even down to one week for lotteries in which not every perfect attender gets a reward.

Attendance reward plans that coexist with so-called sick-pay plans may be especially difficult to design properly. In essence, the sick-pay plan rewards employees for being absent, while the accompanying attendance-reward plan hopes to encourage employees not to use their sick pay through some kind of reimbursement. Striking a cost effective balance here may be difficult. Harvey, Schultze, and Rogers (1983) describe a well-pay plan established to encourage employees not to use sick leave. As part of the plan, one-day absences were not granted sick pay. Consequently, workers more than doubled the average duration of their sick leave absences. The well-pay plan paid out over $38,000 for a net saving of only $1,200 over the previous year. Not all such plans are unsuccessful. Schlotzhauer and Rossè (1985) report a well-pay plan that allowed hospital workers to convert up to twenty-four hours of unused sick leave (out of ninety-six available annually) into additional pay or vacation time. The plan resulted in a saving to the hospital of $14 per employee per year, and would have saved $42,000 if extended to all hospital employees. This plan was applied on an annual basis. Others do not permit the conversion of unused sick leave into rewards until the end of the employee's career:

In 1983, the Illinois State Legislature passed a law, which became effective in 1984, enabling an employee to be paid one-half of a day's pay for every day of sick time accrued and not used. The award is given at retirement or separation from the university. (Ward and Hirsch 1985, 54)

The odds that this system will reduce absence are close to zero. What rational person would forego a day's absence for the promise of a half-day's pay many years in the future?

Modified Working Times. What is the impact of a compressed workweek or flextime on absenteeism? The compressed workweek generally involves the conversion from a five-day week to a four-day week with extended work hours. Flextime permits employees to choose their starting and quitting times, as long as they work the required number of hours and are present during certain core times. Both systems give employees the opportunity to do personal business (such as dental visits) during normal working hours. Thus, a constraint on work attendance is removed. In addition, flex-time could reduce the tendency to convert lateness into absence when transportation or the weather pose problems. The compressed workweek, on the other hand, provides extended weekends while penalizing hourly paid employees for two extra hours of pay if they miss a day. Both factors might be predicted to stimulate attendance (Johns 1980).

The evidence is fairly clear in indicating that flex-time tends to be accompanied by reduced absenteeism (Golembiewski and Proehl 1978). Since many firms also note decreases in overtime and turnover, it seems that there are few negative side effects to the improved attendance. The picture for the compressed workweek is less clear. In some cases absence reduction is seen, while in others it is not (Ronen and Primps 1981). However, fatigue is often noted to accompany the longer work days required under the compressed week, especially in manufacturing environments. Here, expected attendance gains may be offset by employees taking time off to recuperate (Johns 1980).

Emerging Trends in Absence Management

In concluding this chapter, it is useful to note several emerging trends in the management of absence. It is safe to say that most organizations currently manage absence with what might be called a weak discipline system. That is, in line with the deviance model they wait for an employee to exhibit a high level of absence and then clamp down with some post-hoc punishment. By definition, this after-the-fact approach has not prevented absence on the part of the high absentee, and it is simply irrelevant to the attendance behaviour of the majority of the work force. More organizations are beginning to implement *mixed consequence systems* that combine rewards for attendance with systematic, rigorous discipline for absence (Steers and Rhodes 1984). Such systems reward good attendance, encourage average attenders to improve, and confront poor attenders with clear negative signals about their behaviour. Implicitly, mixed consequence systems recognize the existence of different absence cultures within organizations.

Another emerging trend is the implementation of *no-fault absence systems* (Kuzmits 1984; Olson and Bangs 1984). Although these systems may vary in detail, most have the essential feature that no attribution is made about the cause of an absence. Except for vacations, jury duty, and bereavement, an absence is an absence, and supervisors are freed from the difficult task of deciding whether an absence was voluntary or involuntary. For their part, employees are clearly informed as to how many absences are tolerable and given the opportunity to earn back good grace with periods of good attendance. Although no-fault can be combined with other absence management systems to good effect, it has usually been seen as an adjunct to discipline. As such, absence occurrences are usually defined in terms of frequency rather than time lost in an attempt to deal with chronic casual absentees.

A final welcome trend in absence management is the increased reporting in management journals of the results of absence management programs, including those that were unsuccessful. This exchange of information is gradually bringing absenteeism out of the closet as a behaviour that *can* be managed. In addition, it is tacit admission that managers, as well as employees, help shape the absence culture of the organization.

References

Absenteeism costs bank $18 million a year: Survey. 1983. *First Bank News*, February, 2.

Allen, S. G. 1983. How much does absenteeism cost? *The Journal of Human Resources* 18:379–93.

Breaugh, J. A. 1981. Predicting absenteeism from prior absenteeism and work attitudes. *Journal of Applied Psychology* 66:555–60.

Chadwick-Jones, J. K. 1980. *Absenteeism in the Canadian context*. Cat. No. L31–22/1980E. Ottawa: Labour Canada.

Chadwick-Jones, J. K., N. Nicholson and C. Brown. 1982. *Social psychology of absenteeism*. New York: Praeger.

Edwards, P. and H. Scullion. 1984. Absenteeism and the control of work. *Sociological Review* 32:547–72.

Garrison, K. R. and P. M. Muchinsky. 1977. Attitudinal and biographical predictors of incidental absenteeism. *Journal of Vocational Behavior* 10:221–30.

Golembiewski, R. T. and C. W. Proehl. 1978. A survey of the empirical literature on flexible workhours: Character and consequences of a major innovation. *Academy of Management Review* 3:837–53.

Goodman, P. S. and R. S. Atkin. 1984. "Effects of absenteeism on individuals and organizations." In *Absenteeism: New approaches to understanding, measuring, and managing employee absence*, edited by P. S. Goodman and R. S. Atkin, 276–321. San Francisco: Jossey-Bass.

Gowler, D. 1969. Determinants of the supply of labour to the firm. *Journal of Management Studies* 6:73–95.

Haccoun, R. R. and S. Dupont. 1984. *Absence type and gender: An exploratory study of the off-work behaviours of absent hospital workers*. Unpublished manuscript, Université de Montréal.

Hackett, R. D. and R. M. Guion. 1985. A reevaluation of the absenteeism-job satisfaction relationship. *Organizational Behavior and Human Decision Processes* 35:340–81.

Harvey, B. H., J. A. Schultze and J. Rogers. 1983. Rewarding employees for not using sick leave. *Personnel Administrator* 28(5): 55–59.

Ivancevich, J. M. 1985. Predicting absenteeism from prior absence and work attitudes. *Academy of Management Journal* 28:219–28.

Johns, G. 1980. Did you go to work today? *Montreal Business Report* (4th Quarter): 52–56.

Johns, G. 1984. "Unresolved issues in the study and management of absence from work." In *Absenteeism: New approaches to understanding, measuring and managing employee absence*, edited by P. S. Goodman and R. S. Atkin 360–90. San Francisco: Jossey-Bass.

Johns, G. and N. Nicholson. 1982. The meanings of absence: New strategies for theory and research. *Research in Organizational Behavior* 4:127–72.

Kelley, H. H. 1972. "Attribution in social interaction." In *Attribution: Perceiving the causes of behavior*, (edited by E. E. Jones, D. E. Kanouse, H. H. Kelley, R. E. Nisbett, S. Valins, and B. Weiner, 1–26). Morristown, NJ: General Learning Press.

Kempen, R. W. 1982. "Absenteeism and tardiness." In *Handbook of organizational behavior management*, edited by L. W. Frederiksen, 365–91. New York: Wiley.

Kuzmits, F. E. 1984. Is your organization ready for no-fault absenteeism? *Personnel Administrator* 29(12): 119–27.

Markham, S. E. 1985. An investigation of the relationship between unemployment and absenteeism: A multi-level approach. *Academy of Management Journal* 28:228–34.

Martin, J. 1971. Some aspects of absence in a light engineering factory. *Occupational Psychology* 45:77–89.

McShane, S. L. 1984. Job satisfaction and absenteeism: A meta-analytic reexamination. *Canadian Journal of Administrative Sciences* 1:61–77.

Mikalachki, A. and J. Gandz. 1982. *Managing absenteeism*. London, Ontario: University of Western Ontario School of Business Administration.

Moch, M. K. and D. E. Fitzgibbons. 1985. The relationship between absenteeism and production efficiency: An empirical assessment. *Journal of Occupational Psychology* 58:39–47.

Nicholson, N. 1975. *Industrial absence as an indicant of employee motivation and job satisfaction*. Unpublished doctoral dissertation, University of Wales, Cardiff.

Nicholson, N. 1976. Management sanctions and absence control. *Human Relations* 29:139–51.

Nicholson, N. and G. Johns. 1985. The absence culture and the psychological contract—Who's in control of absence? *Academy of Management Review* 10:397–407.

Nicholson, N. and R. L. Payne. 1984. The relationship between absence inducing events, susceptibility and causes. Memo No. 598. Sheffield, U. K.: University of Sheffield, Medical Research Council/Economic Science Research Council Social and Applied Psychology Unit.

Olson, D. and R. Bangs. 1984. No-fault attendance control: A real world application. *Personnel Administrator* 29(6): 53–56.

Patchen, M. 1960. Absence and employee feelings about fair treatment. *Personnel Psychology* 13:349–60.

Picher, C. 1985. L'absentéisme coûte au Québec vingt fois plus que les conflits. *La Presse* (Montréal) May 27.

Robertson, G. 1979. Absenteeism and labour turnover in selected Ontario industries. *Relations Industrielles* 34:86–107.

Ronen, S. and S. B. Primps. 1981. The compressed work week as organizational change: Behavioral and attitudinal outcomes. *Academy of Management Review* 6:61–74.

Ruben, G. 1983. GM's plan to combat absenteeism successful. *Monthly Labor Review* 106(9): 36–37.

Rushmore, C. H. and S. A. Youngblood. 1979. Medically-related absenteeism: Random or motivated behavior? *Journal of Occupational Medicine* 21:245–50.

Schlotzhauer, D. L. and J. G. Rossè. 1985. A five-year study of a positive incentive absence control program. *Personnel Psychology* 38:575–85.

Schmitz, L. M. and H. G. Heneman, III. 1980. Do positive reinforcement programs reduce employee absenteeism? *Personnel Administrator* 25(9): 87–93.

Schneller, G. O., IV and R. E. Kopelman. 1983. Using incentives to decrease absenteeism: A plan that backfired. *Compensation Review* (Second Quarter): 40–45.

Scott, D. and S. Markham. 1982. Absenteeism control methods: A survey of practices and results. *Personnel Administrator* 27(6): 73–84.

Scott, K. D. and G. S. Taylor. 1983. An analysis of absenteeism cases taken to arbitration: 1975–1981. *The Arbitration Journal* 38(3): 61–70.

Scott, K. D. and G. S. Taylor. 1985. An examination of conflicting findings on the relationship between job satisfaction and absenteeism: A meta-analysis. *Academy of Management Journal* 28:599–612.

Steers, R. M. and S. R. Rhodes. 1984. Knowledge and speculation about absenteeism. In *Absenteeism: New approaches to understanding, measuring, and managing employee absence* edited by P. S. Goodman and R. S. Atkin, 229–275. San Francisco: Jossey-Bass.

Taylor, D. E. 1981. Absences from work among full-time employees. *Monthly Labor Review* 104(3): 68–70.

Taylor, D. W. R. B. Haynes, D. L. Sackett, and E. S. Gibson. 1981. Long term follow-up of absenteeism among working men following the detection and treatment of their hypertension. *Clinical and Investigative Medicine* 4:173–77.

Taylor, P. J. and J. Burridge. 1982. Trends in death, disablement, and sickness absence in the British Post Office since 1891. *British Journal of Industrial Medicine* 39:1–10.

Ward, R. H. and N. A. Hirsch. 1985. Reducing employees absenteeism: A program that works. *Personnel* 62(6): 50–54.

Youngblood, S. A. 1984. Work, nonwork, and withdrawal. *Journal of Applied Psychology* 69:106–17.

Section VI
Establishing and Maintaining Effective Working Relationships

The articles in this section address a variety of industrial relations issues in both unionized and nonunionized settings. The first article by Craig, describes and analyses some of the more important aspects of Canada's industrial relations system. The author describes the main actors in this system and the economic, cultural, and legal framework in which the rules of the game are being set. Then, Craig provides more detailed analysis of the nature of the bilateral negotiations in Canada as well as methods of conflict resolutions and third party assistance. The author concludes the article by commenting on the outcomes of the Canadian industrial relations system.

In the second paper, Dolan develops a conceptual framework for demonstrating that the industrial relations system at the plant level, is shifting from being more adversary to more cooperative. His scenario includes two major components: first, he argues that changes in the economic conditions in Canada are forcing the parties to behave in a more rationale and less militant fashion; secondly, he argues that economic and political changes in the 1980's impose new attitudes which tend to favour higher frequency in contact between the parties and more equality in their relations. Dolan concludes his paper by suggesting a number of strategies which will further this trend towards cooperative relations.

The article by Trudeau examines the antecedent and consequences of dismissal decisions from both an employee and an employer point of view. He discusses how the divergent interests of management and the employees have been dealt with by Canadian labour law. Trudeau first describes the unique features of the Canadian common law doctrine and the Quebec civil law regarding dismissal. He then analyses provisions for management rights settled upon in collective agreements. Finally, he describes the statutory protection against wrongful dismissal for nonunionized employees under the federal jurisdiction and in the provincial jurisdictions of Nova Scotia and Quebec.

The final article in this section addresses the issue of final-offer selection as a new technique in resolving wages impasse. Weiler begins his paper by criticizing the conventional interest arbitration. He then analyses the merits and pitfalls of the final-offer selection as an alternative to conventional arbitration. Based on recent experiences, Weiler concludes that final-offer has proven to be relatively successful in inducing compromising behaviour.

25. The Canadian Industrial Relations System

Alton W. J. Craig, University of Ottawa

INTRODUCTION

The purpose of this paper is to describe and analyse some of the more important aspects of Canada's industrial relations system for those persons who are involved in the practice of personnel/human resource management. In another context I have defined industrial relations as comprising a complex group of private and public activities, operating in an environment which is concerned with the allocation of rewards to employees for their services and the conditions under which services are rendered (Craig 1983, 1). In short, the framework comprises the actors and their goals, values and power as internal inputs, the environment within which the actors operate as conditioning inputs (the external inputs), the processes for converting the inputs into outputs, the outputs themselves and the feedback loop which links the industrial relations system to the wider society within which it operates. For present purposes, we shall discuss the actors and their goals, values and power (the internal inputs), the environment within which the actors function during the mid 1980s, the processes for converting the inputs into outputs, the outputs themselves, and the feedback loop which links the industrial relations systems outputs for the actors and the environmental subsystems.

THE MAJOR ACTORS IN THE CANADIAN INDUSTRIAL RELATIONS SYSTEM

By the major actors we mean unions, management, government and private agencies. These will be discussed in turn, beginning with a discussion of unions.

While union membership is only about eighteen percent in the United States, it is close to forty percent in Canada (Labour Canada 1985, xxv). The higher incidence of unionization in Canada is accounted for in large measure by the fact that unionism and collective bargaining are now practised not only in the private sector, but in the federal, provincial, and municipal public sectors, as well as in the parapublic sectors such as schools and hospitals. (The legislation covering these workers will be discussed briefly in a later section of this chapter.)

The Canadian labour movement is characterized by a substantial number of international unions, i.e., unions with their headquarters in the United States, but with members in Canada, as well as a substantial number of strictly Canadian unions, particularly those in the public and parapublic sectors. The largest central federation of workers in Canada is the Canadian Labour Congress, which in affiliation unions in 1985 represented about fifty-eight percent of unionized workers in Canada (Labour Canada, xxvi). While there are a number of other peak federations at the national level, and the Confederation of National Trade Unions (CNTU) in Quebec, the next highest percentage of unionized workers are in unions unaffiliated with a national body. (Labour Canada, xxvi). The latter include unions as diverse as the Teamsters Union, unions of professional and white-collar workers such as teachers, nurses, engineers, and both professional and nonprofessional workers in the public and parapublic sectors. A problematic question is whether or not these various groups will join the mainstream of the Canadian labour movement by joining one of the peak federations.

A lingering issue within the Canadian labour movement is the tension between some international unions and their Canadian components. While there have been a number of important Canadian breakaways from international unions in recent years, and while other arrangements have been made to give more autonomy to the Canadian sections of international unions (Thompson and Blum 1983, 71–86), perhaps the most unexpected and dramatic event was the withdrawal of the Canadian section of the United Automobile Workers Union to form a Canadian Automobile Workers Union in 1985–86. One of the major issues which brought this split about was the unwillingness of the Canadian section to follow the American parent union in giving concessions to employers during the depths of the recent recession. An articulate and dynamic Canadian leader of the Canadian section was also a contributing factor, as was the unwillingness of the president of the international union to allow Canadian workers to pursue issues as they wished rather than follow the international body's wishes. While there will undoubtedly be more such breakaway movements in the future, it is impossible to predict the unions which may be in the forefront of such a movement.

On the employer side, there is no one major organization which speaks for all employers in Canada, as there are in a number of European countries. The Canadian Chamber of Commerce, the Canadian Manufacturer's Association, the Business Council on National Issues, and the Independent Federation of Small Businesses each deals with industrial relations matters from their respective viewpoints, but they have no control over their affiliated members. Hence, with the exception of British Columbia where employers are fairly highly organized on an industry basis, and where there is a business council, there is no single or articulate voice acting on behalf of the business community in Canada.

The major public and private organizations consist of the various labour departments and labour relations boards across the country, as well as law firms which cater to the needs of employers or unions, and individuals who act as mediators and/or arbitrators. While unions are generally guided by the egalitarian norm, business organizations are generally guided by increased profits or a larger share of the market. Governments and private agencies are usually guided by the objective of obtaining settlements between the private parties and maintaining labour peace.

THE ENVIRONMENTAL SUBSYSTEMS AS EXTERNAL INPUTS

Industrial relations systems do not operate in a vacuum, but rather within the environment set by the ecological, economic, political, legal, and social subsystems. While space precludes a discussion of each of them here, we shall discuss some of the environmental constraints within which the actors in the Canadian industrial relations system have operated in recent years. Until 1984, the Canadian industrial relations system has been operating in an environment characterized by high levels of inflation, unemployment, and wage settlements. While inflation has dropped to around four percent and while wage settlements have levelled off at roughly the same figure, unemployment continues to be around ten percent. During the recession of recent years, wages have lagged slightly behind price increases so that real income has decreased. The federal government's public sector restraint program of six percent and five percent per year in 1982 and 1983 respectively, along with restraint programs of the provinces, have had a significant impact on wage increases not only in the public sector, but also in the private sector.

One of the major issues of the mid 1980s is that of job security, particularly as the recession has hit some industries fairly hard and as governments are attempting to deal with the problem of deficits by reducing their labour forces. Incentives for early retirement have helped some workers to cope with the reduction of labour in some organizations, but in others outright layoffs have occurred, as was the case with the federal government. Also, the inability of many Canadian companies to compete effectively in international markets has hit some industries fairly hard, particularly those which lost the protection they previously had under high tariffs. Clothing and footwear are examples of industries which have been badly hurt by the lack of government protection.

Given this brief summary of some of the major environmental factors which are affecting Canada's industrial relations system, it is easy to understand why job security has become a major issue in negotiations in both the private and public sectors. Given this background, we shall now proceed to discuss the legislation under which the private sector of the Canadian industrial relations system has operated from both an historical and a current perspective.

LEGISLATION GOVERNING PRIVATE SECTOR INDUSTRIAL RELATIONS IN CANADA

Legislation governing collective bargaining in Canada goes back as early as 1907 with the Industrial Disputes Investigation Act, which made it compulsory for organizations coming under it to submit their disputes to conciliation boards before strikes or lockouts became legal. The legislation covered mining, public utilities, and other industries and operated under the jurisdiction of the federal government. However, in 1925 the legislation was declared to be *ultra vires* of the federal government by the British Privy Council, the court of last resort in constitutional cases until 1949. (In cases brought before the Canadian courts, ten out of twelve judges felt that industrial relations were of sufficient national concern as to fall under federal jurisdiction [Matkin 1986, 13].) This declaration by the privy council relegated the federal government to jurisdiction over only ten percent of the labour force, while the remaining ninety percent falls under provincial jurisdiction. Hence, when one studies labour legislation in Canada, one is confronted by an analysis of the provisions of eleven jurisdictions, most of which have a multiplicity of statutes dealing with various aspects of labour.

The constitutional division of powers means that Canada has the most decentralized industrial relations system in the world. The federal government has jurisdiction over a number of industries such as transportation and communications, but manufacturing, mining and other industries fall under provincial jurisdiction even though companies may operate plants on a national basis. During times of a national emergency, the federal government may invoke the War Measures Act of 1918 to legislate in the industrial relations field for industries considered essential to the emergency. This occurred during World War II and gave the federal government jurisdiction over about eighty-five percent of the labour force (Woods and Ostry 1962, 24).

It was during this period that the most influential piece of labour relations legislation was ever passed in this country. Order-in-council P.C. 1003 of 1944 gave workers the right to join unions, made provision for the certification of unions as bargaining agents by a labour relations board, and required unions and management to negotiate in good faith in an effort to reach collective agreements. The legislation also contained a number of unfair labour practices by both unions and management, such as the interference by employers of the workers' rights to join unions of their own choosing and coercion by unions to force workers to join unions, among others. The legislation also contained a two-stage compulsory conciliation process which had to be complied with before strikes or lockouts became legal. The legislation also contained a provision that there would be no work stoppages during the life of the collective agreement and required that collective agreements contain provisions for dealing with grievances, the final stage of which was binding arbitration.

With the end of World War II, jurisdiction over labour relations returned to its prewar regime, with the provinces claiming jurisdiction over ninety percent of the labour force. For some years following World War II there was more or less a uniform legislation across the country since most of the provinces followed the federal government's Industrial Relations and Disputes Investigation Act of 1948. It contained essentially the same provisions as P.C. 1003 of 1944. However, beginning in the early 1960s, the various jurisdictions began to go their own ways with the result that while the basic pattern remained pretty much the same as during the 1950s, there are now important differences among jurisdictions.

One way of capturing the essential ingredients of the legislation across the country is to look at three or four classical types of labour relations disputes and how the legislation deals with them. These disputes may be classified as the *recognition*, the *contract negotiation*, *the contract interpretation* disputes, and *jurisdictional* disputes particularly as they apply to the construction industry.

Prior to the 1944 legislation, there were two ways by which unions could gain recognition from employers to bargain over the terms and conditions of employment for a bargaining unit of employees. One was to organize a majority of an employer's employees, and ask the employer to recognize the union as the exclusive bargaining agent for that group (unit) of employees. If the employer agreed, then we had what is referred to as *voluntary recognition*—a practice which is permitted by a number of jurisdictions today. However, if the employer refused to voluntarily recognize the union, the other way for the union to gain recognition was by use of the strike. The 1944 legislation, and all subsequent legislation, has made provision for the determination of appropriate bargaining units and the certification of bargaining agents, matters to be determined by labour relations boards. (Quebec abolished its labour relations board around 1960 and certification is now done in that province by certification officers and certification commissioners.) Legislation now makes it illegal for unions to strike over recognition disputes.

Legislation across the country in the 1950s required that unions have a majority of employees in a bargaining unit as members before they could apply for certification. In recent years, some jurisdictions have made the requirement less than fifty percent. In addition, the legislation during the 1950s required that over fifty percent of the members of the bargaining unit vote for the union in order for it to be certified. Today, most jurisdictions require fifty percent of *those voting*. Those who fail to cast ballots are no longer considered as voting against the certification of the union.

A major policy issue which differentiates the Canadian approach to certification from the American approach is that in Canada the majority of unions are certified without a vote if an officer of the appropriate labour relations board finds, on the basis of signed membership cards, that the union truly has the support of a majority of the members in the bargaining unit. In the United States, there is no such reliance on membership cards as support for a union, and every certification case must result in a vote. (Weiler 1980, 37–49). In 1984, British Columbia adopted the American approach by now requiring a vote in every case of union certification. The latter approach is seen as giving employers time to undermine the support which unions may claim when certification votes are conducted. (Weiler 1980, 39–40). In our view, British Columbia's legislation is a step backwards in terms of the general philosophy surrounding industrial relations in Canada.

With respect to contract negotiation disputes, or interest disputes as they are sometimes called, a variety of legislative approaches involving third-party neutrals exists among Canadian jurisdictions. Quebec, for example, has done away altogether with conciliation boards, and employees are free to strike ninety days after the union has requested the appointment of a conciliation officer. Most jurisdictions still have the compulsory two-stage conciliation approach on their statute books, which calls first for the appointment of a conciliation officer, who is usually a member of a government department. If the conciliation officer fails to effect a settlement, the legislation in most jurisdictions calls for the appointment of a conciliation board which is made up of a nominee of each of the parties and a neutral person chosen by the two nominees. In practice, however, conciliation boards are seldom used now since they have come in for a great deal of criticism in terms of the time involved and their lack of success.

Recent years have seen provision in many statutes for the appointment of mediators, usually private individuals such as judges, professors, and lawyers.

Mediators spend more time with the parties and take a more intensive approach than conciliation officers, thus making their efforts generally more productive. While there used to be a predetermined sequence with the compulsory two-stage conciliation process, the present legislation usually gives the appointing authority more discretion in the appointment of their party neutrals. For example, the federal legislation gives the minister of labour the authority to appoint a conciliation officer, a conciliation board, and a conciliation commissioner who has all the powers of a conciliation board or a mediator. In any dispute, any one or more of these procedures may be invoked or the minister may decide after receiving a conciliation officer's report to make no further appointments in the dispute. In these cases, the union acquires the right to strike seven days after receiving notice of the minister's action. However, the parties may pledge themselves in advance to be bound by the recommendations of any of the above procedures. In such instances, we have what is called voluntary arbitration, whereby both parties bind themselves with the recommendations in lieu of taking strike or lockout action.

Canadian legislation dealing with contract negotiation disputes is somewhat different from American legislation in that it requires that collective agreements include a number of procedural and substantive clauses. As noted above, collective agreements must contain no-strike and no-lockout clauses which are intended to provide a degree of stability during the life of the collective agreement. As a *quid pro quo* for the above clause, collective agreements must also contain a grievance procedure, the last step of which is a binding decision of an arbitrator or arbitration board. For example, if a worker feels that under certain conditions he/she should have received overtime pay, he/she may first discuss the matter with the foreman. If the foreman refuses to agree, the worker may then approach his/her shop steward (an elected member who represents the workers in the area in which he/she works) and the matter may be taken up by the worker and shop steward with the foreman. If the foreman still refuses to agree with the worker's version of the situation, the issue may be put in writing and submitted to the next step of the grievance procedure. Each step of the procedure involves successively higher levels of management and union representatives. If there is no agreement at the highest level between the parties, the matter must be referred to a single arbitrator or a tripartite arbitration board. The union and employer each nominate a member to the board, and the two nominees select a third person as chairman. After hearing the positions of the parties during an arbitration hearing, the arbitrator or arbitration board renders a decision which is binding on the union, the employer, and the employee.

There has been a fair amount of criticism of the regular arbitration process. It is a time consuming and costly process since the parties share the cost of the arbitrator or chairman of an arbitration board, plus any costs associated with the arbitration hearings, and any fees they may have to pay to their nominees. Two provinces, Ontario and Saskatchewan, have made legislative provisions for expedited arbitration, whereby an employee with a grievance may request the minister of labour to appoint arbitration a short period of time after the alleged infraction occurred. In both provinces, a regular member of the labour departments will try to resolve the issue, but if the attempt is unsuccessful, then an arbitrator may be appointed by the minister of labour. An important provision is that the arbitrator may be appointed sooner in cases of discipline and discharge than in other types of cases. Also, arbitrators must agree to hold a hearing within a short period of time, and they usually give their decisions on the spot or shortly after any hearing. They may give a short written statement for their decision rather than the often lengthy dissertations that may accompany an arbitration award under the regular arbitration process.

The jurisdictional dispute, one of the four classical ones we mentioned previously, is most often found in the construction industry where two unions disagree as to which union has the right to organize the workers by virtue of the *work being done*. For example, the installation of bathrooms in new homes involves the work of a plumber and a carpenter, and in such cases the unions representing these workers may disagree as to which union has the right to organize such workers. In some provinces, the labour relations boards have panels of members (at least three persons) who know the construction industry well, and these panels usually render decisions in such cases. Sometimes, however, the unions involved may not abide by the panel's decision, and some Canadian cases have been referred to the National Joint Board in Washington for final resolution. This board is composed of representatives of the construction unions and employers in the construction industry in the United States. The unions which are parties to the board agree to be bound by its decisions. A proposal has been made to have Canadian joint boards at the provincial level with a national board to ensure consistency among provincial board decisions (Dion 1968, 333–75). So far no action has been taken to set up any such board in Canada.

Having discussed the four classical disputes and the general approach to them in Canada, let us now look briefly at a number of recent initiatives in some Canadian jurisdictions which have no counterparts in American legislation. Under Part III of the Canada Labour Code, which covers employees under federal jurisdiction, an employee in a nonunionized organization may request the federal minister of labour to investigate a case where the employee feels that he/she has been discharged without just cause. Usually an officer of Labour Canada will first investigate the case, and if there appears to be some irregularity, he or she may recommend that the minister appoint an arbitrator to render a binding decision in such cases. Since its enactment, this legislation has been used quite often. In about one-third of the cases, the arbitrators have found that there was just cause for dismissal. In the other two-thirds of the cases, just cause has not been found, and in many cases employees have been reinstated with reimbursement for any monetary loses. Nova Scotia has a similar provision, but most of its decisions involve financial settlements. Also, Quebec has a rather broad statement of protection of employee rights, but there has been no analysis of its cases as far as the author knows.

Another recent innovation in the federal and a number of provincial statutes is the imposition of a first collective agreement where a union fails to negotiate one successfully with an employer. The idea behind this policy initiative is to enable weak unions to consolidate their position and become viable bargaining agents. Analysis of experience with the British Columbia provision shows that it has not been too successful in that province (Weiler 1980, 54). The agreements are imposed by the labour relations boards in three jurisdictions and by arbitrators in Quebec, since Quebec no longer has a labour relations board.

The issue of compulsory dues check-off has been the source of some bitter strikes in recent years, and a number of jurisdictions have passed legislation compelling an employer to agree to a compulsory dues check-off clause if requested to do so by the union. Hence, this substantive issue has been taken out of the strike area in some jurisdictions. A somewhat related issue is that workers in some jurisdictions may, for religious reasons, request that their union dues be paid to a charitable organization rather than to the union. They must support such claims by documenting that payment of union dues is against their religious beliefs, and the documentation must be signed by a clergy of their particular belief. In a recent case, the Ontario Labour Relations Board upheld a request that a portion of a union member's dues which go to the Ontario Federation of Labour be given to a charitable organization on the grounds that the federation supported abortions on demand which is contrary to the individual's beliefs. This case came under the Charter of Rights and Freedoms, and there are a number of cases involving a variety of issues which are now before the courts and which may have very serious implications for unions and collective bargaining in the future.

Having discussed a number of the many interesting issues of public policy in the private sector, let us now discuss briefly the negotiation process, particularly from its structural point of view.

The Structure of the Negotiation Process

Given the fact that ninety percent of workers in Canada come under provincial legislation, and that each province can only legislate for those workers and employees in their respective jurisdictions, the Canadian system of industrial relations is a very highly decentralized one. The single establishment-single union is the most common in terms of negotiating units, i.e., decision-making units, and close to two-thirds of employees are covered by this type of negotiating structure (Craig 1983, 152–53). This results primarily from the fact that federal and provincial public servants, who are part of various negotiation units, work in various locations across the country under the federal jurisdiction and various locations within provinces for those workers who fall under provincial jurisdiction.

Given the fact of such a high degree of provincial jurisdiction for the private sector, it is very difficult for employers and unions in industries under provincial jurisdiction to negotiate on a national basis. However, some incidents of multi-provincial negotiations take place in a number of industries. For example, while the main negotiations for the Steel Company of Canada (Stelco) take place at the company's large Hamilton plant, negotiators from other locations including the company's plant in Montreal and some of its other large plants also take part in these negotiations. Only when the terms of settlement reached in Hamilton are acceptable to the negotiators from Montreal and other locations are the negotiated terms of settlement accepted by negotiators at the Hamilton plant. Hence, what is lost due to company-wide bargaining may be gained through pattern bargaining, whereby one plant or company settles first and that becomes the pattern for other plants in the same industry and/or locality.

British Columbia is one province where bargaining takes place at a fairly centralized level. This is partly due to the fact that the British Columbia legislation allows employers' associations in any industry to be accredited and to bargain on behalf of all of their members. Accreditation in the other provinces is confined mainly to the construction industry. This scheme for the construction industry came about in the late 1960s and the objective was to try to equalize bargaining power on both sides of the bargaining table in that industry. So far, the concept has worked relatively well as one study indicates (Rose 1980). Negotiations in the construction industry are very highly centralized in the Province of Quebec where one employers' association bargains with the union having the majority of workers in the construction industry. It bargains on behalf of all types of construction work in the province.

A highly centralized bargaining structure has certain economies of scale for negotiating purposes, and allows unions and management to negotiate uniform or nearly uniform conditions of employment for all of their employees. However, centralized bargaining removes the decision-making process away from the workers affected by it; it may make it more difficult for employers to negotiate terms which are closer to local labour markets and to take into account the economies of scale of particular operations. One industry in which this has occurred is the meat packing industry, and particularly with Canada Packers, the largest Canadian company in the industry. Even since the company was first unionized during the early 1940s, the company and union negotiated nationally on an extra legal basis by using the Ontario negotiations to negotiate conditions covering plants from British Columbia to Prince Edward Island. In the recent recession years, however, there has been a shift to greater plant bargaining in order to gear settlements more to local labour market conditions and to take into account the different levels of efficiency of operations among various plants.

Having discussed the structure of negotiation units briefly, we shall now turn to a brief discussion of collective bargaining in the public and parapublic sectors.

Collective Bargaining in the Public and Parapublic Sectors

Saskatchewan public servants were the first to gain bargaining rights in Canada, and these were gained at the same time that bargaining rights were given to workers in the private sector in the early 1940s. However, the 1960s marked a real breakthrough in the public sector in Canada. While Quebec gave its public servants the right to collective bargaining with the right to strike in 1964, what has been described as the bold experiment in Canada was the introduction of collective bargaining rights for over two hundred thousand federal public servants in 1967 (Findelman and Goldenberg 1983). The Public Service Staff Relations Act (PSSRA) which governs collective bargaining for federal public servants introduced several new concepts in the collective bargaining system in Canada. One of the major provisions of the PSSRA is that the bargaining agent (union) may choose between two methods of dispute resolution in the event that the parties are unable to reach agreement at the bargaining table. The two routes are the conciliation/strike route and the arbitration route. Before the beginning of each round of negotiations, the union must choose which of the two routes it wishes to follow in the event of an impasse.

If it chooses the conciliation and strike route, there is a provision for designated employees who are prohibited from striking and who shall continue their services in the interest of national safety or security while their fellow workers are on strike. This system worked reasonably well from 1967 until 1981 with the unions and the employer (Treasury Board) usually agreeing on the number of workers to be designated in the event that a strike should occur. In the air traffic controllers group, the parties usually agreed that between ten to fifteen percent of air traffic controllers would be sufficient in the event of a strike. However, in 1981 the Treasury Board designated some eighty percent of the air traffic controllers since the Minister of Transport wanted to keep airports open for business as usual in the event of a strike. The Public Service Staff Relations Board (PSSRB) disagreed with the number designated by Treasury Board and designated the usual number. This action was overruled by the Federal Court of Appeal whose decision was subsequently upheld by the Supreme Court of Canada. I and others are very critical of the government for its action since it achieved a reversal of a major policy issue by using administrative tribunals rather than taking the matter to Parliament where it could have been debated and properly changed. (Findelman and Goldenberg 1983, 46; Subbaro, 1985). Hence as matters now stand, it is the employer (Treasury Board) which designates the number of employees in each class and the PSSBR lacks the power to do anything about it. Surely, this is a matter which must be addressed in a legislative way in order to clarify the policy and to clarify the role of the PSSRB in the designation process.

The negotiable issues vary depending on the procedure used. During bilateral negotiations between the two sides, anything may be negotiated except matters which would require a change in a statute. However, the merit principle is still upheld in appointments, promotions, etc., and this is administered by the Public Service Commission. A fairly large number of issues may be dealt with by a conciliation board. Arbitration, the alternative to the conciliation/strike route, however, is severely restricted in the items that may be dealt with by an arbitration board. Parties who choose this route and fail to reach agreement may submit only the issues of "rates of pay, hours of work, leave entitlements, standards of discipline, and other terms and conditions of employment directly related thereto" (PSSRA 1967, sec. 70(1)) to arbitration. The statute has been criticized for the limited number of issues that may be subject to arbitration. For example, if a union wishes to negotiate clauses to cushion the impact of technological change, and if the government does not wish to negotiate on this issue, the government negotiators may threaten to go to arbitration. However, this issue is not subject to an arbitration board's jurisdiction, hence, a bargaining agent using this route is put at a serious disadvantage.

While contract interpretation or rights disputes are usually dealt with in the union's name in the private sector, they are dealt with in the employee's name in the public sector. Also, the PSSRA makes provision for the adjudication (arbitration) of contract interpretation or rights disputes by its full-time or part-time members. One of the rather unique features of adjudication in the federal public sector is that an individual who is *not* part of a bargaining unit, but who has received disciplinary action resulting in suspended, discharged, or a financial penalty may take his/her case all the way to adjudication, usually with the assistance of a union. This is not found in the private sector.

Since the federal government granted bargaining rights to its employees, all provincial governments have also given their employees the right to collective bargaining, some with the right to strike and others with compulsory arbitration as the final dispute resolution process. Included in the latter category are the provinces of Alberta, Manitoba, Ontario, Nova Scotia, and Prince Edward Island. All the jurisdictions which give the right to strike also use the designation process for dealing with essential services. Some jurisdictions such as British Columbia and Quebec specify what essential services are in their statutes. Quebec established an Essential Services Council in 1982, and this council is given the power to designate the level of services to be maintained if the parties cannot agree on the number of employees required, or if the union does not designate a sufficient number of employees. The council plays a very critical role in the Quebec scheme, and its use should enable the legislators from using excessive special back-to-work legislation which has characterized the Quebec scene for years. In Newfoundland, where fifty percent of the employees in a bargaining unit are designated, the whole unit is considered as being designated.

Those jurisdictions in which arbitration is the final resort in contract negotiation disputes limit the number of issues that are subject to arbitration pretty much the same way as the federal government does. Most of the statutes set out fairly broad criteria for arbitrators to follow, the last of which in the federal regime is any other factor which to the board seems appropriate. Others add "the interests of the public"—whatever that is supposed to mean. Ontario and Alberta "require" that arbitrators or arbitration boards take the government's fiscal policies into account when rendering their awards. This has not gone over too well with arbitrators, for how are they to interpret what a province's fiscal policies are.

An interesting contrast exists among jurisdictions as far as the right to strike and arbitration are concerned. As mentioned previously, five jurisdictions require arbitration as the final step in the dispute resolution process. Quebec, however, refuses to have arbitration even when unions have requested it. That province's position is, regardless of which political party forms the government, that wages and salaries for public and parapublic workers represent about fifty percent of the government's budget, and that it does not wish an outside party deciding how its money should be spent. A feature which dramatizes the Quebec scene is that negotiations for public and parapublic sector workers take place about the same time, and they, therefore, have a very high profile. In addition, the negotiations in the Quebec public sector are very highly centralized, and politicians play a crucial role in the negotiations.

The Outputs of the Canadian Industrial Relations System

At the beginning of this chapter we defined the major purpose of an industrial relations system as that of determining the rewards employees receive for their services and the conditions under which workers offer their services. This is a very big topic and covers practically all the provisions contained in collective agreements, and most of these are very important from a personnel/human resource management point of view. The benefits to employees may be divided into three major categories (Craig 1983, Chapter 11). The first is the *wage and effort bargain* and includes the wages and other monetary benefits which workers receive for performing the tasks assigned to them by management. The second category is *job rights and due process* which includes the use of seniority and other factors such as ability in promotions, layoffs, and recall. Due process refers to access to the grievance procedure. The final category is *contingency benefits* which are conditional on something happening. For example, most collective agreements make provision for pension benefits which workers will receive *if* they live until retirement age. Other benefits included in this category are employer contributions to various medical and dental plans, but the proportion of employer contributions vary among employers.

Another output of the Canadian industrial relations system is that of work stoppages. Canada's record in this respect is a rather poor one in comparison with the United States and major European countries. The MacDonald Royal Commission Report (1985, 695–697) made some observations on Canada's poor record of industrial conflict and offered various explanations for it, including bad personal relations, union militancy or bargaining power, the imperfect information with which negotiators conduct negotiations, and various structural features of the Canadian economy. The commission suggested greater union, management, and worker cooperation and consultation as one of the major means of reducing the high incidence of such conflicts (MacDonald Royal Commission Report 1985, 698), as well as preventive mediation and quality of working-life programs (MacDonald Royal Commission Report 1985, 708–709). However, these themes are not new, and it is doubtful if the commission's recommendations will have any more impact than such exhortations in the past have had.

One topic which has been the subject of a good deal of controversy in literature in recent years has been the comparisons of wage increases in the private and public sectors. Some economists argue that there are no differences, while others argue that the settlements in the public sector exceed those in the private sector. Perhaps the best analysis on the subject so far concludes that public sector workers enjoyed a wage advantage during the early 1970s due to the increasing demand for labour in the public sector and the relative newness of unions in this sector. The greatest benefits have apparently gone to the lowest paid workers and to females. The latest conclusion is that the public sector advantage had largely dissipated towards the end of the 1970s, and that there may be further dissipation in the future due to fiscal restraints and as the union militancy, which is usually associated with the early stages of unions, begins to subside (Gunderson 1984, 32–33).

The Feedback Loop and the Outcomes of Canada's Industrial Relations System

I have argued elsewhere that industrial relations systems are open as opposed to closed systems, and that just as they are subject to influences from the environments in which they operate, so too may they influence other societal subsystems (Craig 1983, 12–13). For purposes of exposition, let me deal with wage settlements during recent periods in Canada's history and what has happened as a result.

There have been times when the wage outcomes of the Canadian system have been very high by almost any standard. This was true, for example, in 1974 and 1975 when negotiated wage increases for workers covered by collective agreements covering five hundred or more employees were 14.8 and 17.4 percent respectively (Craig 1983, 261). During 1975, Canada's wage settlements far outstripped American settlements, and labour costs per unit of output were greater in

Canada than they were in the United States. As a result of the high wage settlements in 1974, the federal government tried to work with unions and management to achieve a voluntary wage-and-price controls program. However, since there was no consensus on what a voluntary program should include, the federal government in October 1975, announced a wage-and-price controls program for the economy as a whole, and most of the provinces adopted similar programs for their public and parapublic sector workers. The program provided for maximum wage increases of eight, six, and four percent respectively during the three-year program, although exceptions were made for rectifying anomalies. It has been estimated that the controls program might have kept wage settlements about 4.5 percent below what they might otherwise have been (Reid 1982, 493). However, factors other than controls may have played a part in the lower than anticipated wage increases.

In 1981 wage increases for workers covered by collective agreements covering five hundred or more employees exceeded twelve percent. In response to these increases, the federal government, in 1982, enacted the Public Sector Compensation Restraint Act which limited wage increases for 1982 and 1983 to six and five percent respectfully for federal public servants. Also, the various provinces enacted their own restraint programs, perhaps the most severe being that in British Columbia where the provincial government curtailed what many perceived as necessary public services. Consequently, the province almost ended up with a province-wide strike of public and private sector unions. However, with the enactment of the public sector restraint programs, negotiated wages increases are now around 4.5 percent, a figure that has been realized only since the 1950s. What the previous discussion reveals is that if wage increases are perceived to be too high in terms of the public interest, the politicians will take action to bring settlements more into line with what what is perceived as acceptable limits. These examples show how the feedback loop may be useful for analytical purposes.

The previous discussion regarding wage outcomes applies equally as well to other outputs, such as strikes, in what are considered as essential services. Canada has experienced many an occasion, at both the federal and provincial levels, when politicians acted to end work stoppages in the interests of the public. Sometime this is done when public opinion pools show support for such action.

SUMMARY

What I have tried to show in this chapter is that the Canadian industrial relations system, like those of other countries, does not operate in a vacuum, but is conditioned by the various subsystems within which it operates. These subsystems impose constraints on the actors in the industrial relations system as they attempt to achieve their often conflicting goals. In addition, the legislatures have developed the rules of the game as far as bilateral negotiations are concerned. If the private parties are unable to achieve a settlement of their differences, various forms of third-party assistance are required and/or made available to help the parties achieve settlement without recourse to work stoppages. However, if work stoppages or the substantive outcomes of bilateral negotiations are perceived to be opposed to the public interest, then political action will usually be taken to protect the public interest, however that may be defined.

It is essential that personnel/human resource specialists be aware of how the Canadian industrial relations system works for many of them are working in unionized organizations, since about forty percent of nonagricultural workers in Canada are unionized. While it is crucial that personnel/human resource specialists be aware of the multiplicity of laws and regulations which affect their functions, it is equally as necessary to know how industrial relations systems affect that important function. It is hoped that this chapter will be of some help to both staff specialists and line managers, for both are involved in the management of their most important assets—their human resources.

References

Craig, Alton W. J. 1983. *The system of industrial relations in Canada.* Scarborough, Ontario: Prentice-Hall Canada Inc.

Dion, G. 1968. "Jurisdictional disputes." Chapter 8 in *Construction labour relations*, edited by H. C. Goldenberg and J. H. G. Crispo, 333–375. Ottawa: The Canadian Construction Association.

Findelman, J. and S. B. Goldenberg. 1983. *Collective bargaining in the public sector: The federal experience in Canada.* 2 Volumes. Montreal: The Institute for Research on Public Policy.

Gunderson, M. 1984. "The public/private sector compensation controversy." In *Conflict or compromise: The future of public sector industrial relations*, edited by M. Thompson and G. Swimmer, 1–44. Montreal: The Institute for Research on Public Policy.

Labour Canada. 1985. *Directory of labour organizations in Canada, 1985*, Ottawa: Supply and Services Canada.

MacDonald Royal Commission Report. 1985. Short title for Report of the Royal Commission on the Economic Union and the Development Prospects for Canada. 2 Volumes. Ottawa: Supply and Services Canada.

Matkin, J. 1986. The future of industrial relations in Canada. *Canadian Public Policy* xii Supplement, (February): 127–32.

Reid, F. 1982. "Wage-and-price controls in Canada." *Union-management relations in Canada*, edited by J. Anderson and M. Gunderson, 482–502. Don Mills, Ontario: Addison-Wesley Publishers.

Rose, J. B. 1980. *Public policy, bargaining structure and the construction industry.* Toronto: Butterworths.

Subbarao, A. V. 1985. Impasse choice in the Canadian federal service: An innovation and an intrigue. *Relations Industrielles/Industrial Relations* 40(3): 567–90.

Thompson, M. and A. A. Blum. 1983. International unionism in Canada: The move to local control. *Industrial Relations* 22(1) (Winter): 71–86.

Weiler, P. C. 1980. *Reconcilable differences.* Toronto: The Carswell Company Limited.

Woods, H. D. and S. Ostry. 1962. *Labour Policy and Labour Economics in Canada*, 24, footnote 21. Toronto: Macmillan of Canada.

26. The Shift in Labour-Management Relations as a Function of Changes in Social and Economic Conditions

Shimon L. Dolan, University of Montréal

INTRODUCTION

Traditionally, North American unions have been viewed as adversaries to management in the hostile business and legal environment of the 1800s and 1900s (Mills 1983a; Davis 1983). Lately, there is a growing recognition that relationships exist between labour and management which are not adversarial. It is convenient to classify labour/management groups as belonging to one of three types: (1) management/nonunionized labour with friendly, cooperative relations; (2) management/unionized labour with friendly, cooperative relations; or (3) management/unionized labour with adversarial relationships. These boundaries are fluid in that any one firm may exemplify each type of relationship at different periods of time. Yet, at any one point in time, these group distinctions are useful to reasonably classify the nature of their relations.

During union organizing campaigns in recent decades, employers have tended to force unions even more strongly into an overall antimanagement position (Mills 1983a; Raskin 1982). Collective bargaining in the United States and Canada involves "open conflict over the rights of employees, unions, and management in the workplace" (Mills 1983a). The prevalence of these adversarial union- or labour-management relationships in today's industries, characterized by little trust and open conflict, has encouraged the focus of the present paper to an adversarial labour/management relationship.

A variety of variables interact to influence the nature of labour/management relationships. These variables (including goal conflict, economic conditions, climate of the time, and internal industry variables) complicate the characterization of labour management relations in terms of the frequency of contact, the equality/inequality of the relationship, and the degree of friendly/unfriendly attitudes between them. In considering contact, inequality, and atti-

---

The author wishes to thank P. A. Petriello, a student at Northeastern University, whose excellent work on this subject inspired the completion of this paper.

This paper was written in 1986, while the author was visiting Professor at Boston University School of Management as well as Northeastern University.

tudes, it is important to realize that there are no clearly delineated variables attributable to each of these three relationship measures. That is, the variables which influence amount of contact, for example, are likely to be highly correlated with the variables which influence the other two measures.

Realistically, the topic of labour/management relations could not be dealt with in its entirety even in volumes of literature. There are many variables to consider which have potential influence on this relationship. Nonetheless, an attempt is made in this paper to narrow the scope of this issue by addressing the impact of a few salient variables, and by focusing on private sector unionized industries with traditionally adversarial relations.

The paper is organized into three major sections: the first section is an effort to paint the picture of change which is inherent in labour/management relations. In this section we will consider how changes in conflict and conflict resolution strategy, external changes in the economy, and how changes over time affect the nature of labour/management relations. Given this framework of change, the second section provides an analysis of three measures of group relations: frequency of contact, equality/inequality of relations, and attitudes of friendly/unfriendly relations. Finally, strategies for improving the relationship between labour and management are considered in the third section.

CHANGE AS A FRAMEWORK OF ANALYSIS

The nature of labour/management relations can best be characterized as dynamic; a constant interplay of a variety of variables influence these relationships. Issues of potential conflict between the two parties and strategies of conflict resolution change as a function of changes in the external economic conditions and as a function of time. A change in the economy provides a catalyst for other changes in issues of concern to both parties. Likewise, changes may occur as a function of a naturally occurring time cycle. Conflict, the economy, and time are three highly interdependent variables, but for the purpose of simplicity we can consider the impact of each on labour/management relations separately.

Conflict, Conflict Resolution Strategies, and Labour/Management Relations

It is realistic to propose that the type of relationships which exist between labour and management is inherent in the nature of the problem at hand. Labour negotiation's approaches, as strategies for conflict resolution, vary with the purpose of the negotiation.

Labour negotiations, as in instance of social negotiations, is comprised of four systems of activity, each with its own function for the interacting parties, its own internal logics, and its own identifiable set of instrumental acts or tactics. (Walton and McKersie 1965)

Three such systems of activity are: distributive bargaining, integrative bargaining, and attitudinal structuring.

"Distribution bargaining refers to the complex system of activities instrumental to the attainment of one party's goals when they are in basic conflict with those of the other party" (Walton and McKersie 1965). As Kreisberg (1982) points out, common goals within one party which are viewed as incompatible to the goals of another party are important as an impetus for conflict. The two parties can be viewed as in competition for resources (money, power, prestige). Competition leads to rivalry, which leads to conflict if the two parties are aware of their differences in goals, and can clearly attribute the incompatible goals as pertaining to their opponent, labour, or management. Walton and McKersie (1965) also state that goal conflict is assured to revolve around the allocation of economic power or status symbol resources. One party's gain is the other party's loss (i.e., zero sum game). Issues of negotiation refer to the area of common concern in which the objectives of the two parties are assumed to be in conflict. As such, the purpose of distributive bargaining is to resolve pure conflicts of interest.

Integrative bargaining refers to the system of activities which is instrumental to the attainment of objectives which are not in fundamental conflict with those of the other party and which therefore can be integrated to some degree. (Walton and McKersie 1965)

These objectives define a common concern or a problem. Integrative bargaining, like distributive bargaining, involves joint decision-making processes. Integrative potential exists when the nature of a problem permits solutions which can benefit both parties or at least when the gains of one party do not represent equal sacrifices by the other. Distributive bargaining and integrative bargaining both pertain to economic issues, and rights and obligations of the parties (Walton and McKersie 1965).

The third type of negotiation of importance here is attitudinal structuring. This is, according to Walton and McKersie (1965),

[the] system of activities instrumental to the attainment of desired relationship pattern knowledged to be influenced by many more enduring forces (such as the technical and economic context, the basic personality dispositions of the key participants, and the social belief systems which pervade the two parties), the negotiators can and do take advantage of the interaction system of negotiations to produce attitudinal change.

Attitudinal structuring will be considered further in the friendly/unfriendly part of the second section of this paper. Research has provided support for these three systems of activities in labour negotiations (Shilling, Stevens, Shackle, Follett, Sherif, Blake and Mouton and others as cited in Walton and McKersie 1965, 6-8).

Salient issues of concern or conflict change over time with changes in the external economic environment. Studies of collective bargaining cases indicate a shift from the traditional conflict issues of wage and benefit improvement to a greater emphasis on increased job security, greater participation in management decisions, and on company survival (Davis 1983; Ruben 1982; Kochan 1980; Kochan and Barocci 1985). These changes in conflict issues have been attributed to the recent economic recession. Next, we will review the impact of changes in the economy on labour/management relations, in particular the impact of increased concessions on these relations.

Economy, Concession Bargaining, and Labour/Management Relations

A consequence of 1980 economic difficulties in the steel, automobile, and even airline industry was an increase in the number of settlements calling for employee sacrifices, or wage and benefit reductions and deferrals (Ruben 1981). The quickened pace of wage and benefit concessions, and employment declines in major industries made labour and management aware of the imminent changes in their relationship, specifically the need for more cooperation, which is needed to survive and resolve mutual problems.

For the first time in years, during the recessionary period, management dominated wage negotiations. In the past, management would give in to demands to keep plants operating. Now management cannot afford to give in to union's demands, or doors will shut. Unions, realizing this during economically troubled times, have cut out talk of strikes and costly wage settlements. The concern shifted to job security.

Economically tough times placed financial difficulties in many industries. Motivated by the need for survival, management appealed to unions to accept wage and benefit concessions. These concessions affect the relationship between employees and management through major attitudinal changes. Employees lose faith in the competence of management because of the company's economic difficulties. They lose a sense of security in their jobs and wonder if they should look for better, alternative jobs. Consequently, company loyalty declined. However, to keep the company from folding, employees are usually willing to make personal sacrifices in terms of wages and work rule and to put forth greater effort (Mills 1983b).

Organized labour has taken an increasingly responsible position in regard to productivity and the competitiveness of American industry. Concession agreements presage less adversarial relations in some industries, yet lead to internal political squabbles as union leaders and members try to decide whether to give back hard won gains. Persuading union members to take deeper pay cuts when inflation is already cutting *real* wages often fails, even if the alternative is loss of jobs.

These attitudinal changes have implications for when the company regains its economic foothold. Since employees have made a personal investment in the firm, they expect a greater role in running the company and a greater share of profit. Management may have to accept the union in a much closer relationship to obtain concessions. Union leaders may become involved in more business meetings, and employees may have gained a greater share of the company's stocks through concessions. Concession-related changes in the relationship have implications for the relative power balance between the two parties (which will be considered in further detail in the equality/inequality part of the second section). Concessions may also encourage a more cooperative relationship in that newly formed common goals may contribute to the development of a collective identity. Mills (1983) has noted that increased participative management may stem from concessions because unions are more likely to support productivity improvements. Unions urge employees to be more cooperative with management so that they may obtain their common goals of improved productivity. In this way, concessions strengthen labour management relations through increased contacts, and through more friendly contact.

In a survey of ten companies and unions that had successfully completed concession bargaining, Mills (1983b) found that twenty percent of the companies that received concessions reported a change in the quality of union-management relations afterwards. Of these, four-fifths reported a move toward a more cooperative, less confrontational relationship, presumably leading to greater productivity. Ruben (1981) also finds that concession bargaining does have a benefit of leading to cooperation in countering mutual problems. He suggested that in some cases, this spirit of cooperation was known by the establishment of formal bipartite committees that would continue to exist after immediate difficulties were resolved. Thus, concession bargaining as a result of the recent economic recession, has created changes in labour/management relations.

Reduced business in many industries due to the recession has led to many changes in union contracts. In order to gain more job security for its members, unions are granting concessions to employers in order to skirt increasing layoffs and plants closings. Concessions improve the chances of affected employers to survive, yet make it more difficult for unions to win big wage and benefit gains in the future. Contract settlements are crucial in the long-term battle against inflation. Labor costs make up about two-thirds of the price of a company's product or service. It is really impossible to keep underlying rates of inflation below double digits if wages are increased at ten percent or more annually. Givebacks are a small but important step in the struggle against inflation.

Even though a recent leveling off of inflation has kept the economy stable, rising foreign competition, deregulation in the airline industry, and nonunion competition has led to little strike action, slim pay increases, and little wage freezing.

Speculation for the future is that bargaining has entered a period of moderation that should help sustain economic growth. Usually, economic expansion leads to unions winning large pay gains that top nonunion increases and inflation rates, and economists warn of impending spirals in prices. But, two years after recovery has begun, wage gains are lacking and no one is very worried about inflation. The gap between pay for nonunion and for union members is narrowing. According to Pollock (1984, 20), "Since 1982, union pay increases have trailed nonunion wage gains by 1.5%. First year increases in major contracts average 2.5 compared to 4.0% inflation this year." The trade-off for many unions has been job security for moderate pay increases (Kochan and Barocci 1985, 301). However, a lengthy recovery may eventually restore unions' bargaining leverage. Because of changes in economic and political circumstances, the feasibility of adversarial labour/management relations is in question. Declining American competitiveness and deregulation have signaled the United States as a time for finding more cooperative solutions to labour/management differences. In Canada, similarly, the MacDonald Royal Commission Report (1985) urged greater union-management cooperation as the major means to reduce conflicts.

Changes in Labour-Management Relations as a Function of Time

Implicit in the previous discussion of conflict change, and economic changes is that these events occur with the passing of time. Changes in relations may occur as a secondary result of these other changes. For instance, changes may occur as a conscious effort on the part of both parties to improve their relationship in the future, or changes may occur because of naturally occurring industrial climate shifts. In this section, we will consider change as a function of conscious effort and as a function of climate shifts.

Graham (1983) acknowledges a trend in some organizations towards a conscious effort to change the labour/management relationship from one of confrontation to one of problem-solving. Graham, formerly the chief executive officer of Jones and Laughlin Steel Corporation, recounts the details of their efforts to improve their relationship with the United Steelworkers Union:

> We have dropped adversarial posturing in favour of a serious and determined effort to solve operating problems. We have learned that when you make a suggestion to a local union official, you must be prepared to demonstrate that you really mean what you say, that you recognize the union's side of the issue, and that proposals are responsive to union concerns. (Graham 1983, 31)

This improved relationship arose from a number of strategies discussed in the third major section of this paper, but the point here is that conscious effort on the part of management and the union is one in which relationships can be improved over time. Improved relations serves the function of improving productivity and profitability.

Changes in the labour relations climate over time can be measured by assessing the changes that are processed by the National Labour Relations Board (NLRB), in the United States. In a study of unfair labour practice cases heard by the NLRB, it was noted that types of changes that occur in these cases can be broken down into five categories: (1) changes in regional distribution, (2) changes in the types of employers, (3) changes in the size of an employer, (4) changes in the types of cases, and (5) changes in election behaviour relative to cases (Karper 1982). Over time there has been an increase in the number of cases heard by the NLRB, but Karper (1982) concludes that this change is not due to the general movement of employment to the south and west. He also concludes that the increased incidence of cases is not because labour/management relations are becoming more hostile and lawless on the part of either party, since the relative mix of union and management legal violations has remained constant in recent years. Karper attributes an increase in the number of unfair labour cases partly to the increased jurisdiction of the NLRB to the services sector, such as health care institutions, private higher education institutions, and the United States Postal Service. This study provides example of the proposition that relationships between labour and management change because of naturally occurring industrial climate shifts due to national movement and changes in industry, along with changes in public policy.

This change in public policy is evident in Canada for example. Public opinion polls show declining support for organized labour (despite the fact that almost forty percent of Canadian workers are unionized). A Gallup poll, published in December of 1984 found that thirty-five percent of Canadians were hostile to the union movement (Miller 1985).

Given the dynamic nature of labour/management relations as a function of other changes, one can proceed with caution to generalize about other aspects of the nature of their relationships such as the amount and frequency of contact between the two groups, the equality/inequality of their relations, and the degree of friendliness apparent in their relations. As evident by the preceding discussion, there are many variables which impact upon contact, equality, and attitudes of the two groups as measures of intergroup relations.

MEASURES OF LABOUR/ MANAGEMENT RELATIONS: CONTACT, EQUALITY, ATTITUDES

The frequency of contact which occurs between two groups, the equality/inequality of their relations, and the degree of friendly/unfriendly attitudes which exist in the contact between two groups are not independently occurring phenomenon. For example, groups with the most contact are likely to be those who have similar socioeconomic status (i.e., opportunity for contact), and frequent interactions provide opportunity for attitude changes (Millen 1973; Bradburn 1971; Cook 1970). The following three subsections will present salient variables which impact on three measures of labour-management relations.

Frequency of Contact

There are a number of factors which influence the frequency of contact between labour and management. Contact may occur internal to the organization or external to the organization, with a number of factors influencing each. Internal organizational factors include the nature of the industry and management philosophy. External to the organization, factors include socioeconomic level as measured by income level, race, sex, and labour market forces such as the degree of unionization (Millen 1973; Bradburn 1971; Vanfossen 1979).

Internal to the work setting, the amount of contact between labour and management is a function of the type of work to be accomplished, and management philosophy. In some industries, the amount of contact may be high, and in some it may be low. For example, some jobs may require constant supervision and interaction, and other jobs may be more autonomous. The behaviour of contact may not be reflective of the attitudes of one group towards another (Bradburn 1971). Generally, attitudes and behaviour are consistent, yet the nature of the industry may encourage a lot of interaction in a climate of underlying hostility, or the industry may require little interaction at all in a peaceful cooperative climate. Management philosophy may foster participatory decision making, and/or quality circles (which may stem from concession bargaining). In this case, the frequency of contact between the two groups would be moderate to high. The type of communication modes used are also important in determining the amount of contact. For example, management philosophy which favours written communication over oral, face-to-face communication, would have less opportunity for contact and therefore, is likely to have less contact between management and labour. There are also varying degrees of information flow between organizations. Some organizations have an open communication flow, which leads to more contact, and some have a closed information flow, which leads to little contact. A final management philosophy variable considered here is the type and frequency of performance appraisal systems. Those organizations which do not have regular appraisals or rely on peer appraisals will have less contact than those organizations which support frequent supervisor-subordinate appraisals.

The actual amount of contact between labour and management within the work setting may not be the best indicator of attitudes towards contact. A measure of contact outside the work place may better indicate their attitudes toward contact. Work settings with high contact between labour and management may have low frequency of contact outside the work setting, and vice versa. A different set of variables predicts amount of contact outside the work place.

Opportunity for contact, such as the physical proximity of places of residence is an important variable. Labour and management are likely to live in the same neighborhoods if their economic and social status are similar. Economic and social status is best measured by income (Millen 1973; Bradburn 1971). In most industries, management has higher socioeconomic status (higher income) than labourers. There may be exceptions in industries that have highly skilled labour and/or highly unionized labour; in these industries labour may make comparable wages to management. In general, since most people look for housing which offers the best quality and value for the price (Millen 1973), labour cannot afford to live in the same neighborhoods as management, thus the amount of contact between these two groups *outside* the work setting is likely to be low.

Cultural and personal variables also play a role in the opportunity for contact. Bradburn discusses the role of cultural and personal variables on attitudes of racial integration, but these variables can be extended to attitudes towards desire for social contact between labour and management. If values, beliefs, and attitudes towards issues like getting ahead in life, and notions of entertainment activities are similar, then opportunity and desire for contact will increase. For example, if both labour and management enjoy and participate in the theatre and fine dining, then opportunity for contact is increased. Realistically, income constraints do not allow labour to have the opportunity for this kind of social interaction in most industries. Thus, if income discrepancies are large, and values, beliefs, and attitudes are dissimilar, then opportunity and desire for contact will be low.

Race and sex are correlated with the type of occupation employed in and the income level obtained. Minorities and women are more likely to be in the secondary labour market where little training or skill is required, where there is little job security, and low promotion opportunities. This secondary labour market occupies labour positions. White males are more likely to be in the primary labour market where there is job stability, good working conditions, higher education requirements, and mobility opportunities (Vanfossen 1979). The primary labour market occupies many management positions. Due to the differential composition of the labour and management work force and the associated income differences, it is safe to assume that contact between the two groups outside the work place is low.

There are other factors which have been shown to influence frequency of contact between two groups. These include attitudes of significant others and social norms, expectations of what contact with the other group is like, religious and ethnic differences, and proportions of one group to the other. These factors may have secondary importance when considering the nature of relationships between labour and management since the purpose of their interactions is for mutual benefit in economic goal attainment.

In summary, the frequency of contact which occurs between labour and management is a function of many variables. Contact inside the work place is dependent upon the nature of the work to be completed and management philosophies, where as contact outside the work place is likely to be low because of differences in socioeconomic status.

Equality/Inequality

Three dimensions of inequality between groups are economic resources, power, and prestige (Vanfossen 1979). Economic resources can best be measured by income. As mentioned in the previous section, income is likely to be higher for management than for labour. Labourers, typically young, minority, or female, are generally less educated than management. They are not as likely to have demonstrated motivation and abilities, through educational experience, and thus are not as highly rewarded by income and benefits. The role of external labour market conditions are also likely to affect economic resources available to labour and management. Since labour, generally less skilled, occupies "contested markets" and "free markets" (Vanfossen 1979), the supply of labour is generally greater than the demand for them. This structural explanation for income inequality, is based on the economic principle that low demand and high supply drives wages down. Blue-collar workers (labourers) tend to hit their earning peaks at a younger age than white-collar workers (management). Their earning power stabilizes or declines at a younger age, thus contributing to lower income (Vanfossen 1979). Thus, in terms of economic resources, management and labour are unequal, although studies (Lewis as cited in Vanfossen 1979) show that unions close this gap somewhat by raising labour income ten to fifteen percent higher than nonunionized labour income.

Relative power of labour and management depends on the strength of union bargaining power versus management bargaining power. A model of labour-management is a function of each party's ability to gain control of work rules and control of scarce resources needed by the other. The party with the most power has the most successful negotiation outcome, and thus has the most control of work rules and resources (Kochan and Barocci 1985, 298–300). Unions present a threat to management control and power. Paradoxically, they also represent a small loss of control to those they serve, labour. This is because employees must give up some of their power to this third party, who then bargains on behalf of the employees and on behalf of themselves for union survival. A recent study found that management resists unionization partly because of additional costs, but mostly because of their desire to maintain managerial control and flexibility. This same study found that workers view unions as a last resort rather than as a preferred means of improving job conditions (Boyce 1982).

As previously mentioned, concession bargaining in economic recessions may lead to the benefit of increased cooperation between labour and management, but it also may represent a new foothold of power to unions. By consenting to wage concessions, unions have been able to bargain their way into new areas. The most significant gain to unions is the entitlement to internal company information which they did not have in the past. Unions have been able to shrewdly trade off wages for an "erosion in managerial rights and entrepreneurial freedom" (Kassalow 1983). One consequence of widespread information sharing with unions is that management is losing power through the loss of ability to edit data provided to unions. Therefore, external economic conditions play a vital role in the relative power of unions and management, with the recent economic concessions potentially yielding far-reaching implications for increasing union power through its access to previously restricted information. The relative power between labour and management may favour either party of balance through equal effort to obtain their goals.

In summary, labour management relations are likely to be equal when considering its economic resources and prestige. Power depends on the relative bargaining strength of the two parties and may actually give the bargaining advantage. Power may be equal or even greater for labour.

Friendly/Unfriendly Attitudes

Attitudes can often be inferred from observed behaviour. Behaviour can also influence attitudes. Cook (1970) presents a model whereby the attitudes of one party are influenced by contact and exposure to another party, towards which the first party had previously negative attitudes. Cook also notes that research has shown that increasing the amount of contact one group has with another is not sufficient to produce friendly attitudes. The quality of the contact is more important. There are five characteristics of contact which favour friendly behaviour and positive attitudes. These are as follows: (1) the situation is such that both parties have equal status, (2) the situation encourages cooperation through common goals, (3) social norms favour positive attitudes, (4) attributes of the minority party are not stereotypical, and (5) the setting promotes getting to know the minority as an individual (Cook 1970).

In considering the extent of friendly interactions between labour and management, it is important to realize that work goals which are of cooperative interest (or work goals which are of competing interest) play an integral role. According to Mills and McCormick (1985, 85), adversarial labour-management relations are described as "conflict over the division of the economic pie, or of the company's profits for its members; the union seeks to gain a larger portion of profits for its members; the company seeks to retain profits for stockholders and managers." If one group perceives the other as an ally in the pursuit of common goals, then their attitudes are more likely to be friendly. In adversarial labour-management relations, the nature of the conflict is likely to influence the friendliness of their contacts; more conflict creates more hostility. If cooperation is encouraged, then friendly attitudes will result. If the company is involved in quality circles which are characterized by every participant carrying equal weight in decision making, then the equal status among members will lead to more friendly attitudes. Social norm can be taken to mean other similar companies in the industry. In summary, since the focus of this paper is on adversarial labour-management relations, the attitudes of one party towards the other are likely to be friendly. Collective bargaining negotiations tend to involve more conflict, competition, and opposition than problem solving.

STRATEGIES FOR RELATIONSHIP IMPROVEMENT

Unions exist as long as they serve the purpose of helping labour obtain their goals in the face of a management with differing goals. Inherent in a unionized setting is some type of conflict or problem between labour and management. The relationship between the two parties could be improved if conflict was removed, but this is not a realistic strategy, especially within a unionized setting. More realistic would be to use strategies for reducing conflict. The best and most realistic way to improve the relationship is to improve strategies for conflict resolution. Several strategies are presented here.

Stepp, Baker, and Barrett (1982) advocate the integration of effective preventative mediation with ongoing labour-management relations as a viable approach towards labour-management peace. Preventative mediation requires the mediator to be alert to symptoms of unhealthy labour-management relationships, to diagnose the problems accurately, and to prescribe effective remedies.

Further, the source, nature, and severity of the symptoms must be recognized and identified. The remedy must be suited to the location of the symptoms in the labour and/or management hierarchy. Finally, "the parties must be persuaded that the cure is preferable to the disease and is clearly in their self interests" (Stepp, Baker, and Barrett 1982). Before any labour-management relationship can be improved, both parties must be dissatisfied with the present relationship, and have some reasonable chance of succeeding. It is the role of the mediator to make the solutions apparent to both parties. The reasons for poor labour-management relationships are many. Examples cited by Stepp, Baker, and Barrett (1982) include: "One or both sides prefer it that way, they are not prepared to incur the political or economic costs they attach to improvement, they do not know how to gain the necessary credibility to move jointly forward, or they simply do not know what to do." The mediator, a trusted third party, can diplomatically allow the parties to focus on shortcomings in a relationship, by "minimizing political and economic costs of change, promoting trust and cooperation, and assisting both sides in developing a road map which, if followed, should lead to a positive, constructive relationship."

The key to improving labour-management relations seems to concentrate around one word, cooperation. It seems that the relationship would be at its best when power could be brought to an equal level along with trust and respect for both parties.

A means toward improving labour-management relations is through the use of labour-management committees (Leone and Eleey 1983). Committees act as a supplement to the traditional collective bargaining mechanisms to resolve problems not readily resolved through traditional means. The joint committees promote a problem-solving approach to issues. These autonomous work groups and committees deal with matters concerning productivity, increasing job security, making business more competitive, and improving the climate of labour relations through mutual understanding. These are some of the primary functions of joint committee's activities and not just the by-products. The major way committees improve labour-management relations is by improving communications between groups. Committees sponsor social events such as luncheons, dinners, annual conferences, workshops, and seminars. Dinners and luncheons serve to reduce tension and promote trust between the parties in the early stages of a committee's formation and throughout their existence. Annual conferences provide a forum where promoters of labour-management cooperation can exchange ideas about the concept of cooperation. Also, these conferences communicate to the people in the community where they are held, and to the national public, the fact that the leadership in the local area believe that with cooperation through participation in an area, labour-management committees can coexist with collective bargaining. Workshops and seminars supported by committees are designed to attract local foremen, shop stewards, managers, and employees who are able to assimilate themselves and communicate to their fellow coworkers the new ideas and approaches to worklife issues and problems. In general, dinners, conferences, and seminars promote trust, understanding, and mutual respect between the two parties. Area labour-management committees can promote worksite committee development by acting as a resource centre that provides information and assistance in quality of worklife techniques and labour-management cooperation. Labour-management committees serve as a network through which local unions and companies share ideas and experiences.

Committees also serve two additional functions. First, they facilitate collective bargaining by not dealing with traditional collective bargaining issues, and by having principle parties serve in an informal mediation role in contract negotiations or other labour disputes. Second, work site committees support the local economic development of a community to the extent that they are able to diffuse hostility in labour-management relations. In this way, local employers are encouraged to stay in the area, and other firms are attracted to the area. The fact that labour and management are interacting within the context of an area committee projects a more positive image for the local community.

A new and different strategy of achieving labour relations peace is called Relations by Objectives (RBO). RBO is basically a process which enables the parties to develop their own strategies for achieving labour peace. This special tool was developed to help correct a basically disruptive antagonistic labour relations relationship. The technical expertise of skilled mediators to guide the parties into a better relationship provided the framework for RBO. The actual process is only as good as the parties want to make it. It is not an end in itself and can only work with the full and continuing support and commitment of the parties. The RBO permits decisions to be made by the plant floor employees (which is where the decisions are to be implemented) and this is a major reason for RBO's apparent acceptance and success (Young 1982; Kochan 1980).

Strategies for relationship, improvement proposed by Mills (1983a) focuses on changes for the collective bargaining procedures and relationships between labour and management which would reflect less conflict and more cooperation in an effort to cope with increased international competition and changes in domestic needs. Raskin (1982) and Boyce (1982) point out that cooperation between labour and management, with or without unions, is best achieved through respect of the individual's ideas and dignity. That is, cooperative relations are fostered through careful consideration and utilization of human resources. Maintaining cooperative labour relations and nonunion status requires a deep commitment by management to involve employees in the company and to treat employees with respect and dignity. Preventative labor relations programs may prove to be costly, but they are a small price to pay for retaining managerial flexibility and control (Boyce 1982).

A number of conditions are usually present to facilitate labour-management cooperation. There are usually external pressures demanding company layoffs, or the like; losses to both sides, like a loss of markets to the company and a loss of jobs to the union, are usually because of noncooperation; where management resents union-organizing effects, cooperation is limited by distrust of each side; the fear that greater job efficiency will lead to a loss of jobs and job security must be dispelled; joint committees should be used to build cooperative relations; employees and management should be trained in problem solving, especially integrative problem solving where both sides can benefit from decisions; commitment and interest must be gathered from top management and union representatives; there should be a continuity of leadership to develop trustworthiness; efforts should be sustained, monitored, and maintained; information sharing must be present to inform employees of the company's financial and competition problems; there should be good communication with no surprises; management should be trained not to fear loss of control and to use participative management (not autocratic)—managers aren't relinquishing job duties and decision-making responsibility, but are still responsible for the performance of the business (advance notice, close communication, and union involvement is the key); there should be a balance of power for respect to be present; employees should participate in management decisions and not just be the endorsees of decisions; and lastly, unions should be made to recognize that cooperation is evidence of vitality and strength (not surrender) and that there will be respect and trust present (Mills and McCormick 1985).

These strategies are not all inclusive of potential means of influencing relationships between the two parties. Also, these strategies may not have a textbook effect in face of the many other forces which influence the relationship. Variables such as the technical and economic context, the basic personality dispositions of key participants, and the social belief systems which pervade the two parties may place constraints on the extent to which these and other strategies are able to improve the relationship between labour and management.

References

Boyce, M. T. 1982. Preventative labor relations. *Management World* (June): 16–18.

Bradburn, M. 1971. *Side by side: Integrated neighborhoods in America*, 87–117.

Cook, S. W. 1970. Motives in a Conceptual Analysis of Attitude Related Behavior. In *Nebraska symposium on motivation*, edited by W. J. Arnold and D. Levine. University of Nebraska Press, 1970.

Davis, W. M. 1983. Collective bargaining in 1983: A crowded agenda. *Labor Review* (January): 3–15.

English, C. W. 1985. A year of moderation for the nation's unions. *U.S. News and World Report*, December 31–January 1, 99–100.

Graham, T. C. 1983. Where every manager is responsible for Labor Relations. *Management-Review* (March): 31.

Karper, M. D. 1983. Can the NLRB caseload detect changes in labor relations climate? *Monthly Labor Review* (May).

Kassalow, E. M. 1983. Will union concessions expand areas for bargaining? *Monthly Labor Review* (March): 32–33.

Kochan, T. A. 1980. *Collective bargaining and industrial relations.* Homewood, Il.: Richard D. Irwin, Inc.

Kochan, T. A. and T. A. Barocci. 1985. *Human resource management and industrial relations, Ch. 8.* Boston: Little Brown and Co.

Kriesberg, L. 1982. *Social conflict*, 2d ed., 69–98. Englewood Cliffs, New Jersey: Prentice Hall.

Lacombe, J. J. and J. R. Connolly. 1985. Major agreements in 1984 provide record low wage increases. *Monthly Labor Review* (April): 39.

Leone, R. D. and Eleey, M. F. 1983. The origins and operations of area labor-management committees. *Monthly Labor Review* (May).

Lewin, D. 1983. Implications of concession bargaining: Lessons from the public sector. *Monthly Labor Review* (March): 33–35.

London, P. A. 1981. Inflationary secrets, *The New Republic*, March 28, 8–10.

MacDonald Royal Commission *Report*. 1985. Ottawa: Supply and Services Canada.

Millen, J. 1973. "Factors affecting racial mixing in residential areas." In *Segregation in residential areas*, edited by A. Hawley and V. Rock, 148–171.

Miller, R. 1985. Big labor's weakening grip. *MacLean's Magazine*, March 4, 38–40.

Mills, D. Q. 1983a. Reforming the U.S. system of collective bargaining. *Monthly Labor Review* (March): 18–22.

Mills, D. Q. 1983b. When employees make concessions. *Harvard Business Review* (May–June): 103–13.

Mills, D. Q. and J. McCormick. 1985. *Industrial relations in transition, cases and text.* New York: John Wiley & Sons.

Mitchell, D. B. 1983. Do 1982 Concessions by unions mark a turning point in bargaining? *Monthly Labor Review* (March): 31.

Pollock, M., Maralyn, E., and Arnold, B. 1984. Paycheck won't get much fatter. *Business Week*, December 24, 20.

Raskin, A. H. 1982. Can management and labor really become partners? *Across the Board* (July/August): 12–16.

Ruben, G. 1981. Industrial relation in 1980 influenced by inflation and recession. *Monthly Labor Review* (January): 15–20.

Ruben, G. 1982. Organized labor in 1981: A shifting of priorities. *Monthly Labor Review* (January): 21–28.

Ruben, G. 1983. Collective bargaining in 1982: Results dictated by economy. *Monthly Labor Review* (January): 18.

Stepp, J. R., R. P. Baker, and J. T. Barrett. 1982. Helping labor and management see and solve problems. *Monthly Labor Review* (September): 15–19.

Taylor, A. C. III. 1982. Hard times ahead for labor. *Time*, January 4, 68–69.

Vanfossen, B. 1979. *The structure of social inequality.* 118–135, 179–211. Boston: Little Brown.

Vroman, W. 1985. COL escalators and price wage linkages in the U.S. economy. *Monthly Labor Review.* (January): 225.

Walton, E. and R. B. McKersie. 1965. *A behavioral theory of labor negotiations.* New York: McGraw Hill Book Co.

Young, H. A. 1982. The causes of industrial peace re-visited: The case for RBO. *Human Resource Management* (Summer): 50–56.

27. Employee Rights versus Management Rights: Some Reflections Regarding Dismissal

Gilles Trudeau, Université de Montréal

INTRODUCTION

The power to dismiss an employee provides a striking illustration of the divergent interests that management and employees have to contend with in the scope of their working relationship. On the one hand, the prerogative of being able to fire an unsatisfactory employee is one of management's prime requisites in order for it to maintain the proper course of business. On the other hand, however, employees must be protected against any arbitrary abuse of this managerial right. Needless to say, the harm that a wrongful discharge may cause is a matter of concern for a large majority of the work force (Beatty 1980).

The aim of this paper is to discuss how these divergent interests have been dealt with by Canadian labour law. The traditional master and servant rules are examined first, since they still govern the employment contract of a majority of workers in Canada. Although the rules are relatively similar, it is necessary to distinguish the province of Quebec, where a civil law system prevails, from the other Canadian provinces whose legal system stems from English Common Law.

The management right to discipline and fire has long been an important bargaining matter between employers and certified unions. Thus, the second part of the paper will present the provisions generally settled upon in collective agreements regarding this delicate question.

Finally, the third section will summarily describe the statutory protection against wrongful dismissal for unorganized workers that has been enacted in the Canadian federal jurisdiction and in the provincial jurisdictions of Nova Scotia and Quebec. Special attention will be given to the dispositions set forth by these legislations in an attempt to reconcile the conflicting interests of both management and employees on the subject of job termination.

THE MASTER AND SERVANT RULES

If neither a collective agreement nor a specific statute governs an employment termination, the common law rules of the master and servant employment relations will then apply. Such is the case in a majority of dismissals or layoffs in Canada.[1] Each employment termination is disposed of according to the common law of each province. However, with the exception of the province of Quebec, the common law is to the same effect everywhere in Canada.

The Canadian Common Law

According to the common law the relationship, between an employer and an employee is established and regulated by an employment contract (Christie 1980). This agreement, as with any other contractual agreement, is subject to the assumption that the contracting parties are equal and consequently, that they can agree on whatever they wish, provided it is not unlawful (Beatty 1980). Thus, the parties are free to decide whether or not to consider the question of job termination and the subsequent definition of their respective rights. If they choose to do so, they are also free to elaborate the conditions most suited to their particular situation.

As an example, the contract may provide for a specific period of employment (Christie 1980). The relationship is then automatically terminated upon expiry of the term. No notice or other formality is required unless otherwise determined in the contract. Nevertheless, an employee cannot be dismissed without cause during the term of the contract. A prematurely dismissed employee will be entitled to recover the money he would have earned had the contract been duly fulfilled. Should the parties extend their relationship beyond the expiry of the term, the contract is then held as being one of an indefinite period of time (Harris 1984).

If no duration is specified in the contract, there is a strong presumption to the effect that the agreement was concluded for an indefinite period of time (Christie 1980). Such an employment contract can be terminated only upon notice by either party. Nevertheless, in such a case, no justification is required (Christie 1980; England 1978). This obligation to give a notice of the intention to terminate the relationship is an implied term found in each contract of employment for an indefinite period. It seems that the parties may contract out the benefit of the notice if it is done in sufficiently clear terms.[2] One may also think of a contract that explicitly provides for the length of the notice. Finally, an employer may terminate the employment of an employee hired for an indefinite period at any time, provided he gives him the wages the employee would have earned during the period of the notice.

The problem, therefore, is how much notice of the employer's intention to terminate the arrangement should be given to the employee. In every province, except New Brunswick, the minimal length of the requisite notice has been fixed legislatively.[3] At common law, the period of notice must be reasonable in all circumstances. The reasonableness of the notice must be determined with reference to the particular facts of the case such as the length of service of the employee, the employee's age and education, the nature and the hierarchical level of the employee's position, and the likelihood of the employee finding another equivalent job, among other things. Consequently, the length of the notice varies from one case to another. Indeed, a one month notice could be as reasonable as a twenty-one month notice depending on the circumstances (Christie 1980; Harris 1984). Christie, however, goes so far as to say:

It may as well be that at least in respect of managerial level employees of moderate seniority, there is now a working presumption in favour of one year's notice. (1980, 350, references omitted)

An employee, whether he has been hired for a fixed term or for an indefinite period, can always be dismissed "for cause". In such a case, the employee loses the benefit of the fixed term or the notice period depending upon his legal situation.

In Canada, the notion of cause for dismissal has significantly progressed over time. In the past, misconduct, neglect, and disobedience were considered as virtually automatic grounds for discharge. Nowadays, the employee's behaviour must constitute a serious breach of his contractual obligations. A mere mistake in the performance of the job, for instance, will not justify summary dismissal since the courts consider that employees are fallible human beings. The fault or misconduct must amount to the repudiation of the contract. According to England:

Modern cases have brought employee repudiation within general contract principles, so that the former "specific" rules relating to misconduct, neglect and disobedience are now subsumed under two general requirements that a repudiatory act must violate an "essential" condition of the contract and must be incompatible with the continuance of the employment relationship. This test enables the courts to consider the importance of the breach in the context of the relationship as a whole and to tailor their decisions more and more to prevailing standards of industrial "fairness". (1978, 482, references omitted)

These standards stem mainly from arbitrary decisions by virtue of collective agreements and have begun to be partially applied by the civil courts (England 1978; Christie 1980). Finally, it is also worthy to note that the economic difficulties of the employer are not a cause for summary dismissal (Harris 1984). The cause must rather be found in the employee's defect.

However, if no such defect is present, an employer wishing to rid himself summarily of an employee, might be tempted to place his employee in such straits that the latter would have no other choice but to resign from his position. This employer's behaviour may however be seen by the court as a repudiation of the employment contract and treated as the equivalent of a wrongful dismissal. This is what is known as constructive dismissal. The test generally applied by the Canadian courts to qualify the employer's behaviour as a constructive dismissal is described as follows by Professor Christie: "Whether there has been a unilateral change in the terms of employment by the employer sufficiently serious to justify the employee in treating the contract as repudiated" (Christie 1980).

Accordingly, Canadian common law certainly recognizes the right to dismiss for cause. In this respect, there is no infringement upon management's major prerogative. On the other hand, one could say that the protection offered to the employee against wrongful discharge remains somewhat limited. This is explained mainly by the three following reasons.

First, provided he gives lawful notice of his intent, an employer can dismiss his employee without cause. Even though some salaried workers have obtained notice periods of up to twelve or more months from the courts, the majority of the Canadian work force is more likely to receive only the statutory period of notice which is much shorter. How significant is a one to two month (which is usually the maximum) notice when the unemployment rate reaches ten percent?

The second major reason is the question of the remedy the common law provides for in cases of wrongful dismissals.

Generally speaking, the dismissed worker can only obtain damages that amount to the wages he would have earned during the notice period. Specific performance, that is reinstatement, is not available at common law, except in very special cases (Harris 1984).

The third reason shows that the notion of wrongful dismissal at common law, which is mainly based on the concept of repudiation of the contract, would not be able to ensure fair dismissal. Traditionally, the employer does not have to respect the requirements of "natural justice" (England 1978). For example, the employer would not be obliged to communicate to the employee the reasons for his discharge nor to listen to the employee's version.[4]

In Canadian jurisdictions, several statutes prohibit dismissal for certain specific grounds (Christie 1980). For instance, dismissal for union activity is unlawful in all the provinces as well as at federal level. Protection against discriminatory discharges is provided by the human rights legislation. Other specific grounds such as pregnancy and wage garnishment have been the object of a statutory ban in several provinces. These legislative interventions do not, however, provide a much higher degree of job security to nonunionized workers because of the limited scope of their grounds.

The Quebec Civil Law

The law of master and servant in Quebec is chiefly regulated by the Quebec Civil Code[5] which finds its origin in French law. Interestingly enough, the rules of the employment relationship in Quebec are surprisingly similar to those found in the other Canadian jurisdictions. This is mainly due to the fact that the broad principles of the Civil Code leave a great deal of room for interpretation. Consequently, an important body of case law has emerged from the application of these broad principles.

As stated in art. 1667 *C.c.*, the parties can contract for a definite period of time. Such contract of employment cannot be terminated by either party before the expiry of its term except for cause. An employee dismissed without cause before the term has expired is entitled to obtain judicial redress for the money he would have earned had he worked until the end of the period.[6] On the other hand, the employment relationship is automatically terminated by the expiry of the term unless the parties continue to perform their contractual obligations once the term is over. The contract is thus tacitly renewed for the same definite period.[7]

Most of the time, the parties do not specify the duration of employment at hiring, and therefore they become regulated by an employment contract for an indefinite period of time.[8] Since no person can be bound for an unlimited period of time by an employment contract, either party may terminate the arrangement at any time upon notice of his intent to the other party. No justification is required to do so. The employee in Quebec is thus placed in exactly the same situation as his Canadian counterpart with respect to his job security.

The employee hired for an indefinite period and whose employment is to be terminated without cause is entitled to a notice of the employer's intent or to wages in lieu thereof. The length of his notice is, therefore, crucial, especially for the employee who has to face a high unemployment rate. The Labour Standards Act of 1979 states the length of the notice for all employees except executive officers. It varies with the number of years of uninterrupted service with the same employer credited to the employee. The maximum is an eight week notice for the employee credited with ten years or more of uninterrupted service.[9]

The situation of employees performing a job at the management level is quite different. Since they are excluded from the scope of s.82 of the Labour Standards Act, the period of the notice they are entitled to has to be defined by the criteria developed at common law. This notice has to be reasonable according to the circumstances of the case. Such factors as the circumstances at the time of hiring of the employee, the nature and the importance of his job, the intent of the parties and the difficulties of finding another equivalent job, the employee's age and length of service with his employer influence the reasonableness of the notice.[10]

The notice period seems to have been shorter in Quebec than in other Canadian jurisdictions.[11] However, a new trend, recently emerged from the body of case law, has extended the length of the notice. In doing so, these decisions have referred to the Canadian case law concerning the question of job security. A twelve-month notice may soon become the rule rather than the exception for management officers in Quebec.

An employer may at any time discharge an employee for cause, whether the employment is for a definite or an indefinite period of time. The question is then what constitutes a cause for dismissal in civil law? The employee's negligence or misconduct has to be important enough to amount to a breach of contract. In a decision rendered in December, 1902, the Superior Court said the following:

The master, as we have stated at the outset of our remarks, has the right for just cause, to dismiss an employee, but not for trivial reasons which do not lead to any prejudice, or for the simple apprehension of a danger or prejudice.[12]

In the past, the notion of cause was certainly different from what it is today.

What may have been considered a grave misconduct at the turn of the century is somewhat less serious now (Blouin 1981). However, it is nearly impossible to define the concept with any degree of precision. Nevertheless, it can be said that a mere mistake or a minor misconduct does not justify a summary dismissal; the employee's misconduct must be of a serious nature.[13]

Specific statutes, as in other Canadian jurisdictions, prohibit dismissal on particular grounds in Quebec. An employee cannot be discharged, for instance, because he has become involved in union activities,[14] his wages have been garnished,[15] he speaks only French,[16] or because he has exercised a right under the Occupational Health and Safety Act [17] or under the Labour Standards Act.[18] Moreover, an employer cannot discriminate against an employee because of his race, colour, sex, sexual orientation, civil status, religion, political convictions, language, ethnic or national origin, social condition, or the fact that he is a handicapped person, or that he used any means to palliate his handicap.[19]

From a comprehensive point of view, the legal framework regulating the employer's power to dismiss in Quebec is similar to that prevailing in the other Canadian provinces. Not surprisingly, those rules have been modified through collective bargaining. The following section describes the limitations thereby imposed on management's prerogative to fire, as well as the nature of job security afforded to unionized employees.

DISCHARGE UNDER THE COLLECTIVE AGREEMENT

The greater achievement of collective bargaining concerning job security has been to deprive management of its prerogative to terminate any employee at any time upon giving a proper notice or wage in lieu thereof. More precisely, the collective agreement ensures a higher degree of job security by regulating the two different situations that can produce the employee's termination: a problem of job redundancy within the enterprise or the employee's failure to respect his obligations. The former situation may result in a layoff while the latter may justify a dismissal or discharge for cause.

A difficult economic situation, an administrative reorganization, or the advent of new technology may force the employer to reduce his work force. The collective agreement does not generally deny this right to the employer. The management rights clause found within most collective agreements acknowledges the employer's exclusive prerogative to decide whether or not his work force should be reduced. However, he cannot lay off whomever he chooses as is the case in common law. The employer must rather comply with the selection criteria laid down within the collective agreement. Those criteria generally are seniority, ability, and work performance. Each individual collective agreement determines the order of importance of the various factors of the selection process. Furthermore, the relationship between the employer and the employee is not automatically severed by a layoff. The latter, instead, maintains a right to be recalled before new employees can be hired. The names of laid off workers are placed on a list for a given period of time defined by the collective agreement and, as the work resumes or the employer's manpower needs increase, they are called back according to their position on the list.

The employer's power to dismiss a nonsatisfactory employee exists under the collective agreement, although it is not as wide as it is at common law. Nearly all collective agreements state that the employer can only dismiss or discipline an employee for just cause or just and reasonable cause.[20] This limitation has allowed the development of a real disciplinary law within the collective bargaining system.

The disputes arising from the application of the provisions of the collective agreement are referred to the grievance arbitrator for adjudication. In a dispute over a dismissal, the labour arbitrator must decide whether or not the employer has a just and reasonable cause for dismissal. If the employer fails to prove his case, the arbitrator will reinstate the grievor in his previous position. Furthermore, he may award damages to make up for the loss of earnings. The interpretation of the notion of just cause for dismissal by labour arbitrators has generated an impressive body of decisions that define broad principles which constitute the core of the disciplinary law now existing under a collective agreement. It is the application of these principles of due process combined with the existence of a wide range of remedies, including reinstatement, that permits a collective agreement to offer a significant degree of job security.

The expression just cause for discipline or dismissal is purposely vague and, therefore, highly flexible. For instance, the expression can be applied equally to cases involving mine workers and to cases involving hospital employees or public servants. The notion of just cause even allows the arbitrator to take into account the particular characteristics of each employee. Despite this flexibility, broad principles have emerged from the application of this standard which are all in keeping with the general rule that employees should be treated fairly at all times.

The just cause limitation ensures procedural fairness to the employee. Although the employer has the right to establish disciplinary rules, these rules must be fair and reasonable, and the employee must be made aware of them. Furthermore, they must be consistently enforced without unjustified discrimination between employees. The employer must perform a reasonable investigation before disciplining an employee and should give him an opportunity to be heard (Adams 1978). The rules evolved from the just cause concept do not allow an employee to be disciplined twice for a single act of wrongdoing. For instance, an employer could not impose a disciplinary suspension on an employee for a misconduct and then fire him upon his return to work. Once facing the arbitrator, the burden of proving the just cause for dismissal is upon the employer, who must not only establish the existence of the employee's misconduct, but also that this alleged misconduct is important enough to justify a summary dismissal.

The arbitrator examines the facts placed before him in order to decide whether or not the employee is guilty of any misconduct. Should the occurrence of the misconduct be established, he will then assess the severity of the sanction imposed upon the employee. If he reaches the conclusion that too severe a penalty has been imposed, he may replace it by a lesser one.[21] For instance, a dismissal can be modified to a disciplinary suspension or even to a simple warning. The prevailing principle is that the severity of the punishment must be in proportion to the seriousness of the misconduct.

Many broad principles are referred to in order to assess the penalty imposed. One of the most important is that industrial discipline must primarily be corrective. The employer must aim at improving the employee's behaviour rather than punishing him. In that perspective, arbitrators generally adhere to the notion of progressive discipline. An employer cannot resort to dismissal, the most repressive form of penalty, when disciplining the employee for the first time. Arbitrators require that the employee be made aware of his wrongdoing through lesser forms of discipline and that he have the opportunity to correct his behaviour before being dismissed. On the other hand, if the misconduct is so serious that the employment relationship cannot be maintained, the discharge will be upheld even though no lesser penalty has been previously imposed upon the employee.

Since discipline is essentially corrective, it cannot be properly used when the misconduct results from an involuntary shortcoming on the part of the employee. This does not mean that the employer cannot react in such a case. His reaction, however, will be perceived as a nondisciplinary measure by an arbitrator who will review it according to a slightly different set of rules (Weiler 1977; D'Aoust and Trudeau 1981).

The notion of just cause for discipline also requires that the penalty imposed be tailored to the wrongdoing committed and to the individual employee involved. Some offences are more serious than others and, therefore, generate more severe forms of discipline. For instance, a theft is a more important misconduct than lateness, and a more serious penalty would be expected. Moreover, the gravity of a specific misconduct may be mitigated by some particular circumstances related to the wrongdoing itself. Some arbitrators, for example, have gone so far as to decide that the lack of premeditation or the nominal value of the stolen object may lessen the seriousness of a theft (Brown and Beatty 1984; D'Aoust, Leclerc, and Trudeau 1982).

The degree of penalty imposed must also be adapted to the employee. In that perspective, arbitrators have resorted to the theory of mitigating and aggravating factors. This principle enables an arbitrator to take into account the personal factors of the employee in assessing the penalty imposed. Thus, factors like the employee's previous disciplinary record, length of service, age, educational background, as well as the nature of the position and the supervisor's attitude are weighed when determining the penalty. In certain circumstances, the previous disciplinary record of the employee may become crucial in the assessment of the punishment. This is the case when an employee does not commit any serious misconduct but rather several minor wrongdoings, none of them justifying dismissal in themselves. The employer may dismiss the employee upon proving that his final wrongdoing was the last straw. The culminating incident theory then allows the employer to refer to the previous incidents contained in the disciplinary record in order to justify the severity of the disciplinary measure. In other words, it is the failure of the previous discipline to improve the employee's behaviour that makes necessary the imposition of a stronger penalty. In such a case, the prohibition of a double sanction cannot be an objection since the dismissal follows the culminating incident which has to be a new incident. The previous wrongdoings only stress the need for a more severe penalty.

Just cause for discipline is thus a highly flexible notion that has permitted the development of an organized body of law ensuring fair treatment of disciplined employees. One of its most important features is that it allows the employer, and eventually the arbitrator, to take into account the particular circumstances of each case.

On the one hand, although subject to a tighter control, the employer keeps the power to dismiss an unsatisfactory employee. Before doing so, however, the employer must make sure that firing the employee is the only solution to the problem. On the other hand, collective bargaining has given an effective insurance to numerous workers against arbitrariness and abuse of the management prerogative to discipline and discharge.

In some Canadian jurisdictions, the legislature has recently granted unorganized workers a protection against unjust dismissal, which is similar to that found in the collective agreement. This statutory protection is discussed in the following section.

STATUTORY PROTECTION AGAINST UNJUST DISMISSAL FOR UNORGANIZED WORKERS

Three Canadian jurisdictions have so far enacted a general protection against unjust termination of employment. Nova Scotia was the first jurisdiction to resort to legislative action in an attempt to provide a remedy for all workers against unjust dismissal or suspension.[22] Under such legislation, an employee makes a complaint to the director of labour standards who first attempts to settle the case. If an agreement is not reached, the director will issue a decision which is binding, unless either party files an appeal with the Labour Standards Tribunal established by the same statute. The order issued by the director may require the reinstatement of the employee in the previous position. This protection, however, is only available to employees who have worked for a period of ten years or more with the same employer.

In 1978, the Canadian federal legislature enacted section 61.5 of the Canada Labour Code.[23] An employee who is not subject to a collective agreement, who having completed twelve months of continuous employment with the same employer, who believes that he or she has been unjustly dismissed is entitled to file a complaint with Labour Canada. If the inspector of Labour Canada fails in an attempt to bring the parties to an agreement, the Minister of Labour may appoint an adjudicator who will determine whether or not the complainant was unjustly dismissed. If so determined, the adjudicator is granted extensive remedial powers, reinstatement of the complainant in his or her job being one of them. The decision is final and binding upon the parties.

The province of Quebec, in 1979, enacted an Act Respecting Labour Standards a section of which provides for a recourse against dismissals which were without "good and sufficient cause".[24] This recourse, which has been in force since 16 April 1980, is open to all employees credited with five years of uninterrupted service with the same employer. The internal process of the complaint, as well as its adjudication by an arbitrator appointed by the *Commission des normes du travail*, follows approximately the same pattern as the one set up in s. 61.5 of the Canada Labour Code. The arbitrator acting under ss. 124 *et seq.* of the Quebec Labour Standards Act has large remedial powers, including the power to put the complainant back on the job with or without retroactive pay.

In order to assess the impact of this new statutory protection upon the rights of the parties to an employment contract, the following issues must be considered.

The Employees Covered by the Provision. Under each of the three statutes, an employee must have accumulated a certain amount of continuous service with the same employer in order to prevail him or herself of the right to recourse in the event of an unjust dismissal. This prerequisite period of time varies from ten years in Nova Scotia to five years in Quebec and one year in the federal jurisdiction. Needless to say, large segments of the work force are deprived of the statutory protection because of this condition. Their legal situation concerning employment termination is, therefore, determined exclusively by the common law principles as described in section I of this paper.

Aside from this constraint, the Quebec remedy applies to any category of employee, including managerial and professionnal employees. The Canada Labour Code excludes only higher level managers from the coverage of its section 61.5, whereas the Nova Scotia statute protects managerial workers while excluding large categories of professional employees.

The Employment Terminations Covered by the Provision. The remedy provided for by the three statutes is only available in case of unjust *dismissal*. This proviso effectively precludes all other types of employment termination, such as those stemming from abolition of jobs due to economic or administrative reasons, layoffs, voluntary resignations, or the expiry of a fixed term contract of employment. These diverse methods of extinction shall, therefore, remain within the exclusive ambit of the prevailing common law. It is within the power of the adjudicator or tribunal, acting pursuant to the statutory provisions, to conduct a hearing on the nature of the job termination in order to prevent an unjust dismissal from being alleged as another form of termination. Such would be the case of an employer selecting an employee to be laid off on arbitrary or discriminatory grounds.

The Definition of Unjust Dismissal. None of the statutes defines what amounts to an unjust dismissal. Not surprisingly, adjudicators and arbitrators have referred to the notion of just cause for discipline as defined by grievance arbitrators. This constitutes a major change in the rights of the parties to the employment contract. On the one hand, the employee is given the protection of fair treatment that traditional common law has been unable to work out. On the other hand, the employer must comply with the principles of corrective discipline as defined in arbitral case law. This is true even for categories of employees, such as managers, that are excluded from the scope of the collective agreement. Moreover, the statutory protection deprives the employer of the right to dismiss whomever he pleases upon reasonable notice. The fact that the employee is given such a notice does not provide the employer with a just cause for dismissal.

However, it must be remembered that the notion of just cause for dismissal acknowledges the management prerogative to terminate unsatisfactory employees. It does not deprive the employer of the necessary power to enforce the established personnel policies and the shop rules. Furthermore, adjudicators acting under these statutes have considered factors such as the type of employees protected by the legislation, their hierarchical levels, the nature of their jobs and, when pertinent, the size of the company in reaching their decisions.

The Type of Remedy Available. One of the major features of the considered statutes is the bestowal to the unjustly dismissed employee of the right to be reinstated in the job. This is an important breakthrough since reinstatement has never been ordered at common law. This remedy may however prove to be highly difficult to apply, especially when such categories of employees as managers and professionals are involved. This is why adjudicators and arbitrators have opted for a monetary compensation instead of specific performance in numerous cases. Complainants themselves often waive their right to be reinstated. It must also be said that adjudicators and arbitrators are given the power to substitute a less severe form of penalty for the discharge. Finally, the monetary compensations ordered pursuant to the statutory provisions vary largely from one case to another. Generally speaking, they are determined with reference to the common law notion of reasonable notice.

CONCLUSION

Traditionally, unionization and collective bargaining have been the only means for employees in obtaining a significant level of job security. Otherwise, they are left to the vicissitudes of the common law which recognizes for each party a unilateral prerogative to end the employment contract upon reasonable notice. Furthermore, an employer may fire an employee for cause at any time. The employee could challenge the dismissal only by filing an action before the regular courts of justice. A collective agreement generally deprives the employer of the right to terminate whomever he pleases upon reasonable notice and controls the employer's decision to fire an employee for just cause through the grievance procedure.

Some Canadian jurisdictions have recently enacted a provision for the protection against unjust dismissal, which gives unorganized employees a remedy similar to that found in collective agreements. Such a provision has a major impact on the administration of human resources of an enterprise. Discipline must be administered in accordance with the principles set out by grievance arbitrators. This is so, even in the case of managerial employees. Moreover, the employer is faced with the possibility of being obliged to reinstate an unjustly dismissed worker.

It is however submitted that from an overall point of view, this does not constitute an undue infringement upon management rights. The power to dismiss an unsatisfactory employee still exists although in a more restrained fashion. It forces the employer to set down a coherent system of disciplinary rules, which must be applied consistently, without discrimination or arbitrariness. On the other hand, employees are granted the right of fair treatment, which is a contribution to the enhancement of the quality of their work life. In the long run, one may even be witness to an increase in the levels of productivity to the benefit of the enterprise and all concerned.

Endnotes

1. This is mainly explained by the relatively low rate of unionization in Canada. In 1982, the union density reached thirty-nine percent in Canada (Kumar 1984).
2. Unless the length of the notice is fixed by a statute.
3. For a summary of the legislative provisions concerning notice of termination of employment throughout Canada, see: *Canadian Labour Law Reporter*, 1981 C.C.H. Canadian Limited, par. 1650, on p. 941. It seems that these statutory provisions set out only a minimum period of notice. An employee could therefore be entitled to a reasonable notice as defined by common law (Harris 1984).
4. A few decisions have somewhat tempered this position. See *Reilly* v. *Steel Case Canada Ltd.* (1979), 26 O.R. (2d) 725 on pp. 732–735; *Bell* v. *Cessna Aircraft*, 33 B.C.L.R. 181; *Pulsifier* v. *GTE Sylvania* (1982), 51 N.S.R. (2d) 298 (rejected on appeal, (1983), 56 N.S.R. (2d) 424); *Arnt* v. *Shuswap Okanagan Dairy Industries Co-operation Association*, (1983), 20 A.C.W.S. (2d) 81 (Harris 1984).
5. The specific rules applying to the employment contract are found at art. 1667 to 1671 of the *Civil Code*. The two most important provisions are the following:
Art. 1667: The contract of lease or hire of personal service can only be for a limited term, or for a determinate undertaking. It may be prolonged by tacit renewal.
Art. 1670: The rights and obligations arising from the lease or hire of personal service are subject to the rules common to contracts.
6. See e.g.: *Les commissaires d'école pour la corporation scolaire de Cap-de-la-Madeleine* v. *Dame Guillemette*, (1972) C.A. 453.
7. The duration of the renewed contract is limited to one year even when the period of the original contract was more than a year (D'Aoust 1970). It is to be remembered that at common law the prolongated contract is one of an indefinite duration.
8. Art. 1667 *C.c.* prohibits an employment contract for an unlimited period, that is for a life time, but it does not ban a contract that does not provide for a fixed term.
9. S.82, *An Act Respecting Labour Standards*, R.S.Q., c. N–1.1. Before 1979, art. 1668 *C.c.* fixed the length of the notice period for certain categories of workers. The notice period of the other categories, mainly salaried employees and management employees, was defined according to the courts' decisions on the question.
10. The leading case on this question appears to be: *Columbia Builders Supplies Co.* v. *Bartlett* (1967), B.R. 111. See also: *Jolicoeur* v. *Lithographie Montréal Limitée* (1982) C.S. 230, on pp. 234–235.
11. See: *Lecompte* v. *Steinberg's Limited* (1981) C.S. 211; *Jolicoeur* v. *Lithographie Montréal Limitée* (1982) C.S. 230, on p. 235.
12. *Millan* v. *Dominion Carpet Co.*, 22 C.S. 234 (1902), on p. 239.
13. For judicial examples, see: *Chalifour* v. *Hallmark Automotive Centers Ltd.*, (1976) R.D.T. 586 (Provincial Court); *Jolicoeur* v. *Lithographie Montréal Limitée*, (1982), C.S. 230.
14. Labour Code, R.S.Q., c. C–27, ss. 13–20.
15. Code of Judicial Procedure, R.S.Q., c. C–25, art. 650.
16. Charter of the French Language, R.S.Q., c. C–11, ss. 45–47.

17. R.S.Q., c. S–2.1, ss. 227–233.
18. R.S.Q., c. N–1.1, s. 122.
19. *Charter of Human Rights and Freedoms*, R.S.Q., c. C–12, s. 10 and s. 16.
20. If the just cause limitation is not expressly stated, an arbitrator may try to imply it from the other provisions of the collective agreement such as the seniority clause (Palmer 1983; D'Aoust, Leclerc, and Trudeau 1982).
21. A large controversy over the labour arbitrator's power to modify a penalty took place in Canada following the Canada Supreme Court decision in *Port Arthur Shipbuilding Co. Ltd.* v. *Arthur*, (1969), S.C.R. 1985. The Supreme Court has, however, reviewed its position in recent cases and has decided that the power to modify the penalty is inherent to the arbitrator unless a specific provision of the collective agreement states otherwise. See: *Heustis* v. *The New-Brunswick Electric Power Commission* (1979) 2 S.C.R. 768.
22. An *Act to amend chapter 10 of the Acts of 1972, The Labour Standards Code*, Statutes of Nova Scotia, 1975, s. 4. This legal recourse may be referred to as s. 67A of the *Labour Standards Code*. S.N.S. 1972, Chapter 10 (chap. L–1 of the consolidated statutes) as amended. This provision has recently been declared *ultra vires* (beyond the authority of) the Province of Nova Scotia by the Court of Appeal of that province. See: *Yeomans and al.* v. *Sobeys Stores Ltd.*, Nova Scotia Court of Appeal, October 28, 1985.
23. An *Act to amend the Canada Labour Code*, S.C., 1977–78, c. 27, s. 21. This legal recourse may be referred to as s. 61.5 of the *Canada Labour Code*, S.R.C. L–1, (as amended).
24. See ss. 124–135 of the *Act Respecting Labour Standards*, S.Q., 1979, c. 45. This statute may be referred to as R.S.Q., c. N–1. The Court of Appeal of the Province of Quebec has recognized the constitutional validity of that provision in *Asselin* v. *Industries Abex Ltée*, (1985) C.A. 72.

References

Adams, G. W. 1978. *Grievance arbitration of discharge cases.* Kingston, Ont.: Industrial Relations Center, Queen's University at Kingston.

Beatty, D. M. 1980. "Labour is not a commodity." In *Studies in Contract Law*, edited by B. J. Reiter & J. Swan. Toronto: Butterworths.

Blouin, R. 1981. Notion de cause juste et suffisante en contexte de congédiement. *Revue du Barreau, 41,* 807–832.

Brown, D.J.M. and D. M. Beatty. 1984. *Canadian labour arbitration*, 2d ed. Aurora, Ont.: Canada Law Book Ltd.

Christie, I. 1980. *Employment law in Canada.* Toronto: Butterworths.

D'Aoust, C. 1970. *Le contrat individuel de travail en droit québécois.* Montréal: Librairie des Presses de l'Université de Montréal.

D'Aoust, C., L. Leclerc, and G. Trudeau. 1982. *Les mesures disciplinaires: étude jurisprudentielle et doctrinale.* Montréal: École de relations industrielles, Université de Montréal.

D'Aoust, C. and G. Trudeau. 1981. La distinction entre les mesures disciplinaire et non disciplinaire (ou administrative). *Revue du Barreau* 41:514–564.

England, G. 1978. Recent developments in wrongful dismissal laws and some pointers for reform. *Alberta Law Review* 16: 470–520.

Harris, D. 1984. *Wrongful dismissal.* Toronto: Richard DeBoo Publishers.

Kumar, P. 1984. *Union growth in Canada: Retrospect and prospect.* Unpublished paper prepared for the Royal Commission on the Economic Union and Development Prospects for Canada.

Palmer, E. E. 1983. *Collective agreement arbitration in Canada*, 2d ed. Toronto: Butterworths.

Weiler, J. M. 1977. "Non Culpable Cause for Discharge: A New Perspective." In *Grievance arbitration: A review of current issues*, edited by M. A. Hickling. Vancouver: The Institute of Industrial Relations, the University of British Columbia.

28. New Structures and Techniques in Wage Determination: Final-Offer Selection—How Well Has it Worked?

Joseph M. Weiler, Asia Pacific Business Institute

THE PROBLEM WITH INTEREST ARBITRATION

How well is the mechanism of interest arbitration working? In attempting to answer this question we must decide on what useful criteria are available to assess the success or failure of interest arbitration in the resolution of collective bargaining disputes. Some possible criteria are the extent to which the parties implement or comply with interest arbitration awards, how many awards are appealed, how many post award work stoppages occurred and so forth. But these are crude yardsticks to judge how well this process is functioning. If a bargaining impasse is to be resolved by a method other than tests of economic strength through a strike or lockout, the success of this strike surrogate must be measured by how well it fits into our system of free collective bargaining. Professor Charles Morris has noted:

... interest arbitration or some other technique of impasse resolutions, will be meaningful only if

Professor Weiler is on leave from the Faculty of Law, University of British Columbia.

it is molded to fit within the system rather than designed to replace the system. Government machinery designed to break deadlocks, by substituting "reason" for force will surely fail unless such machinery also reinforces and strengthens the collective bargaining process.[1]

In other words, the best way of gauging the relative success of interest arbitration is to examine how this process impacts on the ability of the parties to engage in fruitful negotiations.[2] In the same vein, the best method of measuring the utility of a suggested improvement on the conventional interest arbitration process is to determine the extent to which the new process has caused the parties to reach voluntary settlements without the need for an arbitration award.

Critics of conventional interest arbitration cite several key pitfalls in its operation. It is alleged that conventional interest arbitration has had a narcotic or catnip effect on collective bargaining.[3] After repeated use of conventional arbitration, parties become arbitration addicts in the sense that they grow accustomed to having an arbitrator determine the outcome of their bargaining. The classic statement of this objection to interest arbitration was made by former Secretary of Labor Willard Wirtz in 1963:

> a statutory requirement that labor disputes be submitted to arbitration has a narcotic effect on private bargainers ... they will turn to it as an easy and habit-forming release from the ... obligation of hard, responsible bargaining.[4]

Surveys of various jurisdictions where compulsory interest arbitration exists suggest that once the parties have had their initial taste of conventional interest arbitration, they are much more prone to use arbitration to settle future bargaining impasses. For example, in my own province of British Columbia, where essential service employees have the option of striking or using conventional interest arbitration, labour pundits are hard pressed to remember voluntary settlements in the health care, police, firefighter, or public school sectors of our economy.[5]

Conventional interest arbitration is said to have a chilling effect upon the parties' incentive to negotiate their own agreements. It is alleged that the parties come to arbitration with long shopping lists of unresolved proposals or demands, which are then dumped into the lap of the arbitrator to resolve. Rather than make the difficult decisions themselves, the parties prefer to have the arbitrator decide these hard, politically charged issues. Why? It is sometimes easier to go back to one's constituents and use the arbitrator as a convenient scapegoat for not attaining a desired benefit than it is to take the personal responsibility of persuading one's principals to make a concession necessary for settlement.[6] But even where the unresolved issue is not a politically charged matter, the parties may be reluctant to reach agreement on a substantial number of issues or may be miles apart on key issues, such as wages, simply because of the manner in which these subjects are resolved in conventional arbitration. The parties anticipate that the conventional arbitrator, using the wisdom of Solomon, will issue an award which is a compromise or split of the difference between the positions taken by the parties at the hearing. Accordingly, each side is prone to maintain an extreme position, perhaps the same as posed at the outset of negotiations, in the hope of obtaining a more favourable split.[7] The dynamic at work here is that the parties avoid hard bargaining because there are no real significant costs of disagreement.

Not only will there be no strike costs, the uncertainties associated with continued disagreement are reduced because of the usual compromise outcome: the arbitrator gives less than the union has asked for and more than the employer has offered. In other words, since conventional arbitration imposes much smaller costs of disagreement than strikes, there is little incentive to avoid it.[8]

THE THEORY BEHIND THE FINAL-OFFER

Final-Offer Selection—Panacea or Pandora's Box?

In contrast to conventional arbitration which the parties anticipate will result in a compromise or saw-off award, under final-offer selection, the arbitrator must choose the entire package of either party as his award.[9] The rationale behind this model is that because of mutual fear that the arbitrator may select the other side's offer, both sides will be encouraged to develop more reasonable bargaining positions. The more reasonable the bargaining position adopted by each side, the narrower the contract zone and the greater the opportunity to reach a voluntary settlement. In other words, the possibility that either side might lose everything at arbitration will provide a potent incentive for them to seek security in their own agreement. The theory of final offer selection is to encourage fruitful bargaining by providing a considerable downside risk in going to arbitration. Final-offer arbitration thus serves an analogous function of a strike or lockout in motivating the parties to reach their own agreement, yet without the costs of a work stoppage. By forcing the parties to compromise rather than risk everything at arbitration, the result of this process is thought to be more acceptable than if an arbitrator had compromised the parties last positions in order to craft a reasonable award. Moreover, unlike in conventional arbitration, where the parties usually receive a saw-off or cut and paste award, under final-offer selection they retain greater control over the arbitration process. The result is literally dictated by one side.[10]

Critique of Final-Offer

While final-offer selection sounds good in theory, commentators have strong reservations about its actual operation. These criticisms include the following: (1) it is based on fear; (2) there is no room for any real intellectual exercise of independent judgement between competing rights and claims; consequently a palpable risk of bad spin-offs or side effects is created and; (3) there is no real evidence that final offer in fact encourages compromise in negotiations.[11] Let us examine these criticisms to see if they hold water.

The fear element enters final-offer selection since it is clear that the object of this process is to provide an incentive to each party to move toward a more reasonable negotiating position. It is suggested that to deliberately build into the process the sanction of fear of third-party intervention is bad public policy.[12] In my view, whether we call it pressure or fear or positive incentives, the fact that we provide a downside risk in going to arbitration should not be dismissed as bad public policy merely because the experience might be uncomfortable or somewhat irrational. If we are satisfied that the end result, i.e., a voluntary settlement can be achieved by placing the parties in a position where they assume more responsibility to bargain rather than send their contract to a third party to get them off the hook, then this result may justify the means.

The fact that the arbitrator under final-offer may not reconcile the parties' positions based on the data provided at the hearing, certainly produces some intellectual discomfort in the adjudicator. The arbitrator, faced with a multi-issue dispute, does not have the flexibility of fashioning an agreement which might be more rational, equitable, and desirable to the parties. There is always the potential problem of having to choose between two totally unacceptable offers, and thus producing an award that might be very difficult to administer. Furthermore, when final-offer selection takes place in the area of essential services, and when both parties' offers are unacceptable, the question which arises is: Will the arbitrator be forced into making a decision which is incompatible with the public interest?

It is difficult to refute these criticisms since they are based on the essential dynamic of final-offer, i.e., that it is a risky business, potentially unpleasant, thereby providing a positive incentive to avoid the use of this process. In some ways these criticisms can be downplayed as hypothetical horribles since the reported surveys of the actual experience with final-offer do not disclose totally unworkable awards, imposed agreements that had to be renegotiated, or the public interest being sold down the river by two irresponsible parties to a final-offer arbitration. The uncomfortable position in which the arbitrator is in when unable to choose items from each sides' proposals has not been the source of any complaints from the parties to these hearings. Only the adjudicators seem unhappy with this dilemma.[13] While it is suggested that the losing party, whose package has been rejected because of certain totally unacceptable demands, would be likely to cause trouble in order to save face, there is no reported experience of refusal to comply with these awards. In fact, the evidence is that the losing party need go through only one experience of losing its case in front of a final-offer arbitrator before they become convinced to moderate their demands in future. As we postulated earlier, pressuring for effect, while a valuable tactic in bargaining, is of little assistance in convincing an arbitrator that your offer is reasonable. Negotiators under final-offer report that their contract talks are significantly less political and emotional than under their previous experience with conventional arbitration.[14]

Some analysts cite the possibility that one side in final-offer arbitration will structure its offer by including a sleeper or zinger item that may, if awarded, damage the parties' long-term relationship. For example, one side may slip into its moderate economic package a major contract innovation such as a minimum two-man police patrol, or a reduced nurse-patient ratio. This innovation may be worded in innocuous language, but the arbitrator may be forced to accept this package, zinger included, because the other side has adamantly stuck to its guns on other issues that may be too expensive. The difficulty with an arbitration hearing is that in this setting it is hard for the parties to convey and register the relative intensity of their feelings about these issues or to illustrate the anticipated pitfalls in their implementation. The problem is aggravated if the arbitrator does not have close familiarity with the industry involved. It is feared that the unhappy fallout from this type of all-or-nothing decision will be experienced in due course.

While the inflexible nature of final-offer selection creates the potential for the sleeper item being awarded, the reported experience with this process to date does not cite any actual examples where this has occurred and the parties have been unable to adjust to this type of award. There is no doubt that the potential for this type of unacceptable spin-off of final offer selection has prompted some jurisdictions to modify the process to provide for final-offer by issue, final-offer rejection and a variety of other vehicles to increase the discretion of the adjudicator to avoid unacceptable awards. The problem with these adjustments in the final-offer selection model is that they may delete the risk of going to arbitration, thereby easing the pressure on the negotiators to reach a settlement.

Modified forms of final-offer will be examined in the following discussion, but at this point it is appropriate to respond to the criticism that the experience with final-offer selection does not show that the parties are more prone to reach voluntary agreements. The available evidence is clear that final-offer has produced more settlements than conventional interest arbitration. San Bernadino County and its employees perceived final-offer as having increased their willingness to negotiate as well as producing more innovations in their agreements. The monetary costs of settlement using this procedure were approximately equivalent of what would have occurred using normal bargaining. Both sides were satisfied with the procedure and were willing to recommend its use to others.[15] Reported instances of final-offer in public schools in Sault St. Marie and Wentworth County in Ontario support the view that final-offer selection made bargaining more civilized, less political, and less emotional than under conventional arbitration.[16]

A recent criticism of the final-offer concept is that it may lead to intertemporal compromise, i.e., in the purposive issuance of arbitration awards to achieve an even balance between arbitration winners and losers over time. It is suggested that arbitrators will attempt to satisfy both sides by alternating the winners and losers over time. The loser in the first round would become the winner in round two, the round two loser will be the winner in round three, and so forth. In other words, the negotiation incentives which are supposed to exist under final-offer may be illusory because of the possibility of longitudinal compromising behaviour by arbitrators and the parties' incorporation of such a possibility into their bargaining strategies. If this theory is accurate, then final-offer may do no more than conventional arbitration to promote true collective bargaining, because the process would merely replace the possibility of static or one-period compromise with the possibility of longitudinal or multi-period compromise.[17]

If this criticism of final-offer were accurate, surveys of the experience of final-offer would show the party which lost at arbitration would be encouraged to reuse arbitration during the next round of negotiations. Analysis of the bargaining history of major league baseball; the City of Eugene, Oregon; the States of Massachusetts and Wisconsin show no flip-flop awards or alternating winners, nor have parties who have used the process again been more likely to use this procedure than other parties who would be using it the first time, nor are the previous round's winners more likely to use the procedure again than the losers. The evidence has led analysts to conclude:

> ... there are a variety of criticisms which may be levied against final-offer arbitration, but intertemporal or longitudinal compromising does not appear to be one of the stronger ones. As a result, there is no reason to date for policy-makers to reject final-offer arbitration as an impasse resolution option because of the fear that arbitrators will attempt to keep the world in perfect balance.[18]

ARE BOUQUETS IN ORDER OR SHOULD WE CHANGE THE FLOWERS?

Having answered some of the worries about final-offer selection, it is time to cite some of the complimentary observations of this procedure. The evidence suggests that negotiations under final-offer are less emotional and less political than under conventional arbitration. The hearings tend to be shorter with more use of written briefs, rather than *viva voce* evidence. The decision-making process impasse to final award is much speedier since the number of items reaching arbitration appear to be drastically reduced.[19] In Wisconsin, for example, where local government employees, firefighters, and policemen bargain under a statute whereby the parties can opt for either conventional or final-offer arbitration, they rarely choose conventional arbitration. The number of issues arbitrated under conventional arbitration was approximately three times that settled under final-offer. Furthermore, the multi-noncompatible issue dilemma discussed earlier (under which the arbitrator is faced with offsetting reasonable and unreasonable demands on different issues which make it difficult to craft a balanced, workable contract) has not been a problem in Wisconsin. On the contrary, interviews and examinations of awards reveals that this defect with final-offer arbitration has powers to be more of an academician's dilemma than a practical problem.[20] Under final-offer, the parties tend to resolve the peripheral bargaining items leaving only the major monetary issues for arbitration. Apparently neither side wishes to chance a loss at arbitration because of their refusal to budge over relatively minor points.[21] The task of translating bargaining positions into written briefs to be scrutinized for their relative reasonableness has helped the parties to clarify their own thinking about how realistic and important their bargaining positions are, a mind set that is conducive to pre-arbitration settlement.

Despite these obvious net gains from the use of final-offer selection, and perhaps swayed by concerns about the need for more discretionary authority in the adjudicator, various jurisdictions have tinkered with the classic model of final-offer. The most popular variation on the final-offer procedure is to allow the arbitrator to select the more reasonable position of each party on individual items. As noted earlier, this modification may well decrease the incentive to settle voluntarily, yet these policymakers seem to be persuaded that the benefits of more acceptable awards (when they are actually made) outweigh the costs involved in the associated decrease in the downside risk of final-offer in its pristine form. However, while these jurisdictions have taken some of the potential sting out of the arbitration process in an effort to facilitate settlement short of arbitration, they have grafted mediation onto finality, multi-final-offer, and fact finding onto the final-offer by issue procedure. These hybrid versions of final-offer have proven quite successful in obtaining agreements without the need for final awards to be issued.

The Michigan public safety final-offer statute provides for issue-by-issue selection on economic issues and conventional arbitration on noneconomic issues. This model finesses the zinger clause problem noted earlier, since the sleeper management rights type issue cannot be buried in an otherwise conservative monetary package. The experience under the Michigan statute over the several years it has been in effect suggests that an increasing number of bargaining impasses are being reached. More cases are being submitted to arbitration, yet the number of awards has risen only slightly since in two-thirds of these cases settlements are being reached during the arbitration process. Apparently arbitrators are being pressed into service as mediators, and the arbitration process is serving as a vehicle for continued negotiation. The fact that arbitrators have the authority to remand the dispute back to the parties for additional bargaining, and that the deadline for final-offer submission comes during or even after the hearing, increases the potential for bargaining right up until the award is issued.

In Iowa, public service employees are permitted to negotiate their own impasse procedures from among mediation, fact-finding, final-offer issue selection or any combination of the above. Most have chosen to bypass fact finding and limit themselves to mediation leading to final-offer issue selection. Experience has shown that when fact finding was used, a filtering effect occurred wherein the number of issues going to arbitration was cut in half, from an average of 6.2 issues to 3.9 issues. One explanation for the success of fact finding in Iowa may be the fact that the arbitrator may select the fact-finder's report as a third final-offer. When the parties have already received one third-party neutral's view of what is reasonable, they are more apt to agree to these suggestions rather than risk loss at arbitration. Similarly, in Massachusetts, public safety employees using fact-finder before final-offer selection have reduced the number of issues to be arbitrated to an average of 4.8.[22] The Iowa multistep experience also shows that when the parties have gone through mediation, fact finding, and arbitration in one set of negotiations, they have yet to go to arbitration in the next round of negotiations. The complete absence of the narcotic effect of arbitration of the Iowa multistep procedure commends this process to policymakers elsewhere. When we compare the Iowa figures with statistics from similar employment sectors using conventional arbitration in British Columbia, it seems obvious that the multistep impasse resolution system in Iowa has also drastically reduced the chilling effect of interest arbitration. In the health care industry of British Columbia, which uses conventional interest arbitration under the Essential Services Disputes Act, an average of forty-five issues have gone to arbitration,[23] ten times the number under the Iowa procedure.

In summary, the evidence is clear that the parties come closer to negotiating a settlement under final-offer package than under final-offer by issue. Although when the latter is supplemented by mediation to finality or fact finding, the chilling effect of arbitration is drastically reduced. Both variations of final-offer have reduced both the narcotic and chilling effect that conventional arbitration has had on bargaining.[24] What is apparent is that when the deadline date for submission of the final-offer comes late in the procedure, when final offer is proceeded by fact finding, when the arbitrator acts as a mediator or has the authority to remand the case back to the parties for more bargaining, the parties are less apt to reach agreement at the earlier stages of this process. While a filtering effect takes place as the parties move along the multistep procedure, the process tends to drag on unnecessarily with impasses moving through several years.[25] In the absence of deadline pressures, the parties simply incorporate all phases of the multistep dispute resolution procedure into their bargaining strategies. With increased experience over years, parties are increasing their use of arbitration as a forum for continued negotiating since there is no risk involved if they use all the pre-arbitration impasse resolution steps.[26]

IMPROVING FINAL-OFFER ARBITRATION

The parties who are using final-offer in its many forms seem pleased with the process and favour its retention. The figures suggest that both the narcotic and chilling effect of arbitration on bargaining are reduced under the final-offer procedure. Yet there are several suggestions for reform of the process which deserve mention.

In order to avoid the dilemma of the final-offer arbitrator being faced with two totally unacceptable proposals, one writer has suggested three means of increasing the decision-making options of the adjudicator: (1) repeated-offer selections; (2) modified final-offer arbitration; and (3) multiple-offer selection.[27]

Repeated-Offer Selection

If the arbitrator is convinced either party's offer would be grossly unfair or unworkable, he or she simply rejects the offers and asks for a new final-offer. The parties are thus given a second opportunity to go back over their proposals to discover misjudgments or miscalculations. It is anticipated that both sides will be likely to make further concessions since the arbitrator has already indicated that their first offer does not provide a reasonable basis for an award.[28]

Modified Final-Offer Arbitration

If both offers are unacceptable, the arbitrator, under this procedure, could write a proposed settlement. If the parties agree with the arbitrator's proposal, then it becomes the award. If either side refuses to accept this proposed award, then the arbitrator must select one or the other party's original final-offer. Modified final-offer would work only where both original offers were of approximately equal unacceptability. As Professor Dunn points out, if the arbitrator's proposed settlement is closer to one side's offer than the other's, the former would always veto the arbitrator's proposal.[29]

Multiple-Offer Selection

Under this procedure each side can submit multiple offers. The arbitrator can then select the best from among the offers submitted. However, the arbitrator does not make this offer the award. He or she announces only which side has made the best offer. The other party then selects one of the three offers the chosen side has made and this becomes the award. Under this technique, each side has an incentive to make three genuinely different offers, because each additional offer increases that party's chance for one of its offers to be selected as the optional proposal.[30]

Med-Arb Final-Offer

These three variations of final-offer give the arbitrator more authority to send the impasse back to the parties for resolution. The other suggested strategy to reform the process of final-offer arbitration harks back to its original dynamic, i.e., to make arbitration a very risky business. These proposals would increase the costs of disagreement as the parties proceed beyond the impasse declaration point.

Peter Feuille proposes a unified mediation and final-offer procedure whereby the same person serves as mediator and arbitrator, and the final-offer submissions would occur as soon as the impasse is declared.[31] Under this system the third-party intervenor would initially attempt to mediate a settlement. If these efforts failed, he or she would then serve as a final-offer arbitrator and would select one entire package. The package selection would be between the two final offers originally submitted and would not be based on any movement that might have occurred during the mediation stage. The entire process would be limited by a strict timetable of not more than three months from impasse to final award. The rationale behind this process is to create a high degree of risk of remaining in disagreement at the moment of impasse declaration because the parties would not be able to modify or amend their final offers at a later date. The deadline pressures imposed by the strict bargaining timetable would be analogous with those commonly associated with strike deadlines. The suggestion is that deadline pressures increase the likelihood of agreement by reducing demands, aspirations, and bluffing.[32]

This process relies heavily on the skills and judgement of the mediator-arbitrator. The potential success of the mediation stage would appear to be enhanced by the fact that the mediator performs *more* than the roll of face-saver or messenger boy, as in the typical mediation setting. Under the med-arb process, the mediator has the authority to make a final-offer selection, a function which substantially increases his or her ability to reward concessions and punish intransigence. Since the mediator holds final decision-making power, he or she can make authoritative suggestions to the parties about unacceptable positions and possible areas of agreement. In addition, the parties would be well advised to take these suggestions to heart in fashioning their agreements. As you recall, the parties submit their final offers at the outset of mediation and these cannot be modified on a piecemeal basis if the med-arb neutral is forced to render an award.[33]

The Disputes Commission

The med-arb, final-offer process discussed above is designed to speed up the process while maintaining a high degree of risk of continued disagreement. This proposal responds to the experience in multistep impasse resolution in Iowa, Massachusetts, and Michigan which saw the parties incorporate all the avenues of third party intervention into their bargaining strategies. The last reform that I will commend to your consideration would add an additional imponderable choice into the process. While maintaining a pluralistic approach to dispute resolution, by making available mediation, fact finding, med-arb, final-offer by package or by issue, there would be no guarantee which one of these mechanisms would apply to which dispute. The choice of impasse-resolution devices would not be left to the parties. The parties would not be guaranteed the availability of any specific form of dispute resolution. Rather, an independent bipartisan commission of blue chip industrial relations experts would make this choice. This commission would monitor the course of bargaining until an impasse is declared and would select the form of dispute resolution mechanism it judged appropriate to settle the agreement, depending on the nature and cause of the deadlock. Under this arrangement, the parties would not be able to incorporate their choice of final-offer or fact finding, etc. into their bargaining strategies. The costs of disagreement would be augmented with the uncertainty of how their bargaining positions at impasse would be reflected in their next contract.[34]

CONCLUSION

The purpose of this paper is simply to outline some of the criticisms of final-offer selection and to provide you with some recent data about the experience of using this final-offer mechanism. What seems clear is that final-offer has proven to be relatively successful in inducing compromising behaviour. The hypothetical horrible of the zinger item emerged as a significant problem. There is almost unanimous praise for final-offer by both management and labour in the jurisdictions where final-offer has been implemented. This is not to say final-offer is the panacea or the final answer to impasse resolution. Additional research and analysis is necessary to determine what additional improvements can be made to this game of industrial Russian roulette.

Endnotes

1. Charles Morris, "The Role of Interest Arbitration in Collective Bargaining" in *The Future of Labour Arbitration in America* (New York: McGraw-Hill, 1976).
2. I should say that this view is premised only by the assumption that a voluntary settlement is as an exercise in self-govern-

ment, is more desirable for reasons of voluntary compliance and acceptability than an agreement imposed by a third party neutral. This view seems to be accepted without qualification by North American labour pundits yet has been challenged by a New Zealand scholar with reference to the virtues of interest arbitration awards in that country. (see A. J. Geare, "Final Offer Arbitration: A Critical Examination of the Theory", 20 *Journal of Industrial Relations* 373 (1978).)

3. Hoyt, N. Wheeler, "Compulsory Arbitration: A 'Narcotic Effect'?" *Industrial Relations* 14 (February, 1975): 117.
4. Robert Howlett, "Arbitration in the Public Sector" (*Proceedings*, Southwestern Legal Foundation, 15th Annual Institute on Labor Law, 1969): 234.
5. See generally, Joseph M. Weiler, "Interest Arbitration in Essential Services: The British Columbia Experience" (Paper delivered at the Continuing Legal Education Society of British Columbia Conference on *Interest Arbitration—A Matter of Public Policy*, April 15, 16, 1980, Vancouver B.C.) The papers delivered at this conference are to be published in book form by Carswell Company Ltd., in January, 1981.
6. B.C. Council of Public Sector Employers, "*Reference Report*" *No. 25*, April 27, 1979, 2.
7. Peter Feuille, "Final-Offer Arbitration and Negotiating Incentives" *Arbitration Journal* 32, (1978): 203.
8. Peter Feuille, "Final-Offer Arbitration and the Chilling Effect", *Industrial Relations* 14, (1975): 302.
9. Final-offer selection may have generated more names than applications. Final-offer selection has also been referred to as forced choice, either-or, last-best offer, sudden death, all-or-nothing, one-or-the-other, winner-take-all arbitration. Critics of this model dismiss it as an industrial relations form of Russian roulette.
10. S. A. Bellan, "Final Offer Selection: Two Canadian Case Studies and an American Digression" *Osgoode Hall Law Journal* 13, (1975): 851.
11. Dr. A. W. R. Carrothers, "Unresolved Issues in Public Sector Bargaining in the 1980's" (Address to Canadian Teachers' Federation, Toronto, June 9, 1980).
12. *Ibid.* 22.
13. See Fred Witney, "Final Offer Arbitration: The Indianapolis Experience" *Monthly Labor Review* 96 (May, 1973): 20–25.
14. *Ibid.* footnote 10, 876–77.
15. *Ibid.* footnote 6, 3.
16. *Ibid.* footnote 10, 877.
17. Peter Feuille and James Dworkin, "Final-Offer Arbitration and Intertemporal Compromise, or It's My Turn to Win", *I.R.R.A. Annual Proceedings* 87 (1978): 89.
18. *Ibid.* 95.
19. *Ibid.* footnote 12, 870.
20. *Ibid.* 871.
21. *Ibid.* 863.
22. Daniel Gallagher and Richard Pegnetter, "Impasse Resolution Under the Iowa Multi Step Procedure", *Industrial and Labor Relations Review* 32 (April 1979): 336.
23. *Ibid.* footnote 5, 32.
24. These figures are consistent with laboratory research which found a significant difference in the parties' concessionary behaviour between those negotiating under final-offer total package and final-offer by issue but no difference between total package final-offer and conventional arbitration. (see A. V. Subbarao, "The Impact of Binding Interest Arbitration on Negotiation and Process Outcome", *Journal of Conflict Resolution* 22 (March 1979): 88–99.
25. *Ibid.* footnote 7, 213.
26. *Ibid.* 216.
27. Clifford B. Donn, "Games Final-Offer Arbitrators Might Play", *The Industrial Relations* (October 1977): 311.
28. *Ibid.*
29. *Ibid.* 312.
30. *Ibid.* 313.
31. *Ibid.* footnote 7 at p. 216.
32. See Jeffrey Z. Rubin and Bert R. Brown, The Sociology of Social Psychology of Bargaining and Negotiation (New York: Academic Press, 1975): 120–24.
33. *Ibid.* footnote 7, 219.
34. P. C. Weiler, *Reconcilable Differences: New Directions in Canadian Labour Law*, (Toronto: Carswell, 1980), 235.

Section VII
Improving Health and Safety at Work

The three articles in this section illustrate ways PHRM can improve working conditions for the benefits of employees and their organizations. In the first article, Atherley provides an overview of health and safety acts, actors, and actions in Canada. Given the multiplicity of regulations, enforcement policies, and acts amongst Canadian federal, provincial, and territorial jurisdictions, Atherley's paper provides some clarity to this complex and varying mixture of responsibilities and rights. He then discusses the role of PHRM in improving health and safety through other personnel activities, such as: personnel selection, training, performance appraisal, management of absenteeism, worker's compensation, and even termination of employment.

Although employee health and safety is often related to only accidents and diseases generated by the physical work environment, a growing concern is being paid to the sociopsychological work environment. This concern arises from the association of individual stress with many aspects of the sociopsychological work environment. The two articles by Burke and by Van Ameringen, Leonard, Dolan, and Arsenault address themselves to this emerging PHRM concern. In his article, Burke explains first the notion of stress and burnout in organizations. This is followed by a review of common work stress research and models. Special emphasis in this review is given to personality traits which make some individuals to be more susceptible to develop stress-related illnesses (i.e., type A behavior). He then discusses the phases of burnout. Burke concludes his paper by summarizing a host of individual and organizational strategies to be used in reducing work stress.

Van Ameringen et al., attempts to demonstrate the link between stress and absenteeism. Following a presentation of different concepts of absenteeism the authors conclude that current models require more innovations in order to explain the complex phenomenon of being absent from work.

They, then present the results of their empirical work, whereby they suggest to link absenteeism to work stress. Their results suggest that intrinsic job stressors act as buffers to absenteeism while the extrinsic job stressors act to increase absenteeism. They also demonstrate how stress-absenteeism analysis at different levels of aggregation (i.e., personality, occupation and organization) can significantly contribute to our understanding of the causal linkages and may eventually lead to better programs of stress management.

29. Occupational Health and Safety: Acts, Actors, and Actions

Gordon Atherley, Canadian Centre for Occupational Health and Safety

ACTS

Occupational health and safety legislation lies in the federal, provincial, and territorial jurisdictions. Of Canada's employed work force, less than ten percent are covered by the federal jurisdiction, of which slightly over half are the federal government's own employees, directly or indirectly.

The thirteen principal acts, supporting regulations, enforcement policies, interpretations, and guidelines, present a complex and varying mixture of responsibilities and rights.

What sets off Canadian occupational health and safety legislation from that of most other countries is the emphasis it gives to the rights of workers to refuse dangerous work, to know about hazardous materials or dangerous conditions in the work place, and to participate in worksite occupational health and safety committees. These are often referred to as the three basic rights of occupational health and safety, and they are of special interest to personnel and human resource managers.

ACTORS

In theory, governments enforce occupational health and safety legislation, employers comply with it, and workers are protected by it.

In practice, things are much more complicated. Governments go beyond enforcing the legislation by becoming involved, directly or indirectly, with information, training and education, workers' compensation, and research. Employers may implement programs in the name of occupational health and safety which go well beyond actions required by the legislation. Workers and their trade union representatives, over the years, have shown less and less inclination to be passive recipients of the protection offered by the legislation. Instead, they have sought to influence employers' actions by bringing occupational health and safety issues to the bargaining table, and by putting various other pressures on employers and governments.

The chief actors are government officials, line managers, and workers and their trade union representatives. But numerous other people have parts to play, including specialists such as occupational physicians, industrial hygienists, safety professionals, occupational health nurses, researchers, and educators, as well as staff persons such as personnel and human resource managers. With so many actors, who is responsible for what actions becomes a complex problem.

ACTIONS

Starting with the ancient Greeks, if not earlier, socially-minded observers recognized that work can be dangerous to the life and limb of workers, and that actions are required to prevent the risks from materializing as injury, disease, or death. Towards the end of the eighteenth century, as industrialization developed in Europe, reformers saw that law was required to compel the factory-owning masters to take action to protect their worker-servants. The first legislation protected women and young people employed in factories because they were so obviously not in a position to protect themselves. Industrialization dramatized the power which the master could exercise over the servant. Law is one means whereby the power imbalance was redressed and trade unionism was another.

Industrialization showed that science and medicine often have to be invoked to understand the more subtle of the dangers and that research is needed if the problems are to be reacted to sooner rather than later.

Today's conditions in Canada's work places are improved substantially compared to those of the late 1800s. But it was clear by the early 1970s that occupational health and safety presented numerous unsolved problems. Starting with Saskatchewan, there began a series of reforms which by the mid 1980s had culminated in a substantial revision of virtually all Canada's occupational health and safety legislation. But the reforms were in some ways too late because workers' compensation costs—one measure of failure in occupational health and safety—had risen so steeply over the prior decade that several of the workers' compensation boards were technically bankrupt (see Exhibit 29–1).

Despite the spiralling costs, the boards were under pressure from trade unions to be more generous to injured workers. Alleged meanness of the Workers' Compensation Board even became an election issue in Ontario in the provincial election of 1985. Early actions by the new administration there led to the creation of a Workers' Compensation Appeals Tribunal through which an aggrieved worker could appeal the board's decisions, and to a ministerial statement aimed at considerably strengthening the Ministry of Labour's enforcement policy relative to the province's occupational health and safety legislation.

Throughout Canada, the mid 1980s saw the chief actors unhappy with the actions. Employers worried about spiralling workers' compensation costs; unions pressed for improved financial provisions for injured workers and stricter enforcement; the public believed that the legislation was ineffective or ineffectively enforced. The search for a new script had begun.

INFORMATION AS THE THEME

Most people instinctively obey the law; they need only to know what is required of them to comply. Even if there are special factors in occupational health and safety, information about the require-

Exhibit 29-1   WCB Costs—Canada

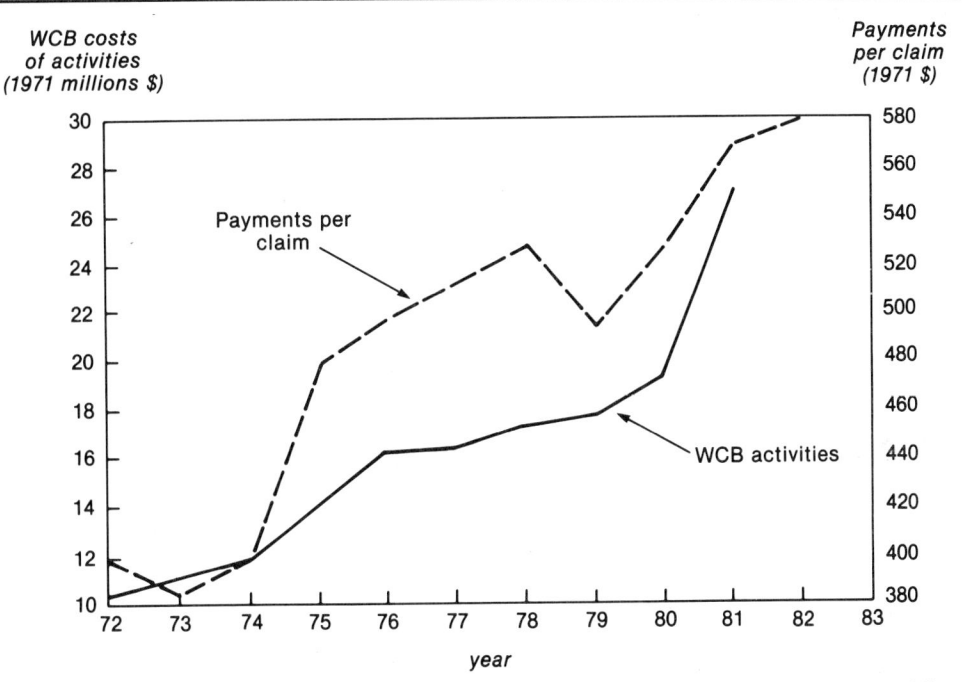

Activities include training information and research. Data from Labour Canada *Employment Injuries and Occupational Illnesses* March 1984—Table 1.22 and Table 1.28 (Adjusted for Inflation)

ments of the legislation appears to be the single most important factor in securing compliance from most employers, managers, and workers.

Information is the instructions for the actions for which the actors are responsible. Governments began to see in the 1980s just how important information is to occupational health and safety. They began to provide substantial information programs for many legislative developments, not only in occupational health and safety.

Line managers are responsible for organizing and securing production without jeopardizing the health and safety of workers. To fulfill this responsibility, they need information. Trade unions are responsible for safeguarding their members' interests by pressing for improvements in working conditions. To fulfill this responsibility, they need information. Government officials monitor compliance with legislation and enforce in response to noncompliance. To fulfill this responsibility, they need information. All of them need information which is trustworthy, understandable, relevant, and comprehensive in order to fulfill their responsibilities.

RESPONSIBILITY

In occupational health and safety, responsibility has a range of meanings and implications which need to be carefully distinguished.

Responsibility can have the meaning of *duty of care*, which refers to a legal relationship in which the employer owes a duty of care for the safety of the employee, to ensure that he or she is not injured by reason of the employer's personal negligence or that of persons for whom the employer is *responsible*. In the eighteenth century, the master-servant relationship, as it was then known in English laws, was defined so that the lion's share of the rights as well as the obligations (another meaning for *responsible*) lay with the master. The passage of time has seen the balance shift; parallels can be witnessed in the legal relationships of husband and wife, and parent and child.

Breach of the duty of care laid an employer open to legal action by an employee. Deficiencies in this common law legal remedy led Ontario to establish, in 1915, a statutory system for workers' compensation. Other provinces followed suit. In this new system, it was not necessary for an injured worker to prove the employer's negligence (another meaning for *responsible*) in order to substantiate a claim. This no-fault system, as it is sometimes called, removed most of the right of workers to sue employers for negligence.

Responsibility is used to mean blameworthiness. Within the rhetoric of industrial relations, one party blames unsafe conditions; the other, unsafe acts and the victim. In practice, the debate is often sterile, and is best avoided.

There is often talk of employers and employees having a joint *responsibility* for occupational health and safety. While both undoubtedly have duties (another meaning), there is a risk of such phrases being interpreted to mean that employers and employees share equally the burden (another meaning) for occupational health and safety, which can never be the case. As the English common law recognized long ago, much of the danger in a work place arises out of the things of the work place which, by definition, belong to the employer. To the extent that the individual worker by action or inaction can jeopardize the health or safety of himself, herself, or coworkers, the individual worker can be seen as responsible. But discussions about individual workers' obligations should always be tempered with the overriding sense that human beings are fallible, and that the employer has a *responsibility* to make allowances for this through fail-safe design of plant, equipment, and operating systems. In taking account of human fallibility, participants in the responsibility debate should not fall into the opposite error of discounting the skills, insights, and experience of workers.

Participation, for example through participant management, is a form of *responsibility* sharing which effectively harnesses the contribution of workers.

The internal *responsibility* system and its close relative, self-regulation, refer to attempts to create within industry the arrangements needed for management and workers to collaborate so that occupational health and safety is properly attended to, irrespective of the degree of regulatory activity by government. There is much to be said for such a system when it works effectively. But regulatory activity can never be dispensed with altogether because this provides the basic safety net which cannot be bargained away by ill-conceived agreements between management and workers.

The primary mechanism for the internal responsibility system is work-site occupational health and safety committees. Crucial to its success is information flow between the parties in such a way that all concerned trust the information and share readiness to respond to and act on it.

Responsibility means power and jurisdiction. The jurisdictions (governments) guard their sovereignty, and infringements are strongly resisted. Employers and trade unions guard their respected domains against intrusions, whether from each other or from governments.

THE PERSONNEL AND HUMAN RESOURCE MANAGER

The personnel and human resource manager approaching occupational health and safety should (a) understand the legal responsibilities, that is the duties, which the relevant acts lay upon employers, workers, and others; (b) be able to probe the understandings of the chief actors and others about the allocation of responsibilities and be able to perceive differing interpretations; and (c) be able to avoid confusion in uses and implications of responsibility as applied to occupational health and safety.

The personnel and human resource manager in the typical industrial or service organization is likely to be involved in management of information related to occupational health and safety, selection of personnel, instruction and training, performance appraisal, problems of absence and absenteeism, workers' compensation, and de-hiring and retirement. Each of these can involve occupational health and safety, each possesses a potential for tension, and each requires careful handling of information.

Management of Information

Information is essential to the success of the three basic rights of Canadian occupational health and safety legislation. *Knowing* involves information; a right to know is sterile unless there is access to the information one is supposed to have. *Refusing* involves knowing what is dangerous; a right to refuse is sterile unless there is access to information about the things one is supposed to perceive as dangerous. *Participating* involves sharing information; a right to participate is sterile unless there is access to the information about the policy or problem one is supposed to be sharing some responsibility for.

Participation is mostly through work-site occupational health and safety committees. By the mid 1980s, these were viewed as constructive, but underdeveloped instruments. While too little was known about their factors of success and failure, there was reason to believe that they were most likely to be successful when their members were well trained and, above all, well informed about occupational health and safety.

The personnel and human resource manager should be able to manage information so that the three rights of occupational health and safety function effectively and constructively.

Selection of Personnel

Through the selection process, candidates for employment are judged for their mental and physical capabilities for jobs or training. Medical assessments may seek to determine fitness for a job relative to its physical demands, to its risks for the applicant, and to the risks the applicant would bring to the coworkers, the public, and the organization. Risks to the organization include excessive sickness absence and a propensity to workers' compensation claims. Medical or other assessments may aim to detect and exclude risky individuals, or others unduly vulnerable to particular working conditions.

Recent years have seen the increasing use of pre-employment questionnaires and medical, biochemical, and psychological tests intended to predict the suitability of the individual for the particular employment. In the extreme, tests would be used to select only those individuals fit to join an ideal work-force. But such selection policies would raise serious legal and moral questions.

Recent years have also seen the development of human rights legislation which outlaws discrimination in employment on grounds of sex, age, racial background, or physical or mental disability. Under this legislation, rigorous selection procedures have been successfully challenged, to the point where employers have to reconsider carefully the use which they make of such testing. Increasingly challenged is blanket discrimination, the exclusion of complete categories of people, such as all diabetics, all epileptics, all women, all men aged over fifty, and so on. Instead, the employer has to establish *bona fide* job requirements for each job which show why a specific disability really is incompatible with a particular job.

The Canadian Human Rights Commission, particularly, has identified what is called the dignity of risk, a principle which holds that people should be given a fair chance to try at a job, even when there is some degree of risk to themselves. While managers and trade unionists have expressed misgivings about this principle, few critics deny its moral advantage of giving the benefit of the doubt to the individual.

There is always a doubt because all tests on human beings are to some degree unreliable, bringing the possibility of error. Human beings are versatile and adaptable. History abounds with instances of individuals overcoming the most appalling disabilities, against all predictions.[1] The lesson of history is that the best test is performance at the job itself. In evaluating selection tests, the personnel and human resource manager has to balance the risks of uncertain tests, unsuitable employees, and discriminatory employment practices.

How much information can an employer reasonably require a prospective employee to disclose? In the past, employers may well have required too much. Changing social values and revelations of abuses led to recognition of the need to apply information protection to employees (and others). Information protection is seen in privacy legislation, which institutionalizes the right to confidentiality of personal information, and in the various health disciplines acts, which safeguard confidentiality of medical data. In the mid 1980s, the situation was evolving in a direction which reduces the right of the employer to personal and medical information about a prospective or actual employee.

The personnel and human resource manager should be (a) familiar with protections afforded employees by human rights and health disciplines legislation, (b) able to define or get defined *bona fide* job requirements, and (c) establish who really needs what information, and why, relative to the mental and physical capabilities and health status of individual employees.

The personnel and human resource manager should be in a position to objectively evaluate an employer's information needs and the employee's rights to protection, and be able to advise a com-

---

1. Helen Keller is perhaps the most outstanding example of an individual's triumph over disability. She recognized how technology can be used to overcome disability. Her autobiography begins with these words to Alexander Graham Bell, the Canadian telephone pioneer, "who has taught the deaf to speak and enabled the listening ear to hear speech from the Atlantic to the Rockies, I dedicate this story of my life."

fortable middle course. Giving the benefit of the doubt to the individual, brings industrial relations benefits, which may well outweigh other risks that at times may be exaggerated by the proponents of rigorous pre-employment or preplacement testing.

Instruction and Training

Whether instruction and training in occupational heath and safety should be integrated into other work place training or be provided for separately by governments, compensation boards or their associations, trade unions, or health professionals is a question which has been much debated. Integration allows workers and managers to learn together in a way which directly relates to the work place what is taught. On the other hand, separate training may bring special insights necessary for complex problems.

Finding the best arrangement for instruction and training is not easy. Programs with a management orientation are criticized for playing down workers' rights to protections, the true extent of dangers, and for giving too much emphasis to business secrecy and too little to the worker's right to know. Programs with a trade union orientation are criticized for politicization and polarization. Programs by health professionals are criticized for excessive specialization. Personnel and human resource managers involved in instruction and training relative to occupational health and safety should be able to advise on balance, integration, and content.

Performance Appraisal

Appraisal of performance of individuals often brings out problems which appear to have their roots in ill-health, either mental or physical. But ill-health may be invoked as a convenient cover for other problems. If appropriate solutions are to be found, causes have to be carefully probed.

Appraisal of performance of an organization relative to occupational health and safety often relies on data pertaining to accidents, diseases, and work-related absences. Such data are also used for epidemiology, which is research into the health status of populations. Interpretation of such data is difficult scientifically, and concerns have been expressed about abuses.

In one company, a proposal for an extensive and continuing survey of the health of employees was closely questioned by trade unionists. They were alarmed when they were told that the company could give them no guarantee that any data collected would not be used against the interests of individual employees, for example in workers' compensation claims.

Health-related research is important, but the potential for controversy arising from an organization's collecting medical and personal data on their employees calls for considerable caution.

The personnel and human resource manager should have established sufficient confidence among workers and managers to be able to successfully probe seemingly health-related performance problems without infringing the individual's rights or protections. In practice, this means that the personnel and human resource manager must seek the individual's informed consent before asking any questions at all of a medical or personal nature. The individual should not be expected to give such consent unless the personnel and human resource manager is prepared to give a professional and binding undertaking about confidentiality. The personnel and human resource manager cannot expect to receive such consent unless he or she enjoys the confidence of the individual, on which the general attitude of the work force will be a powerful influence.

The personnel and human resource manager should be able to distinguish legitimate research from information-fishing expeditions and know what reassurances have to be given in exchange for the cooperation of the work force.

Absence and Absenteeism

Excessive absence, whether from sickness, occupational injury or disease, or other unscheduled reasons, is always a concern in any productivity-oriented organization. Absenteeism is used when patterns of absence have become a persistent problem.

For management beset with problems of absence and absenteeism, there is an understandable tendency to assign a policing role to personnel and human resource managers and health professionals. But this is not the solution to what can be a serious and apparently intractable problem. There is very little which any organization can do, whether through line management or staff persons, where an individual can produce valid medical certification about the reasons for absence. The causes of excess in absence or absenteeism must be sought within the organization itself, and eradicated in collaboration with the trade unions and the workers themselves. Absenteeism can not be successfully reversed where the underlying industrial relations climate is unsatisfactory. For this reason alone, policing by the personnel and human resource manager and, health professional could be doomed to a failure which serves only to impair their images as caring professionals. It must nevertheless be acknowledged that absenteeism presents senior management with a major resource problem.

Workers' Compensation

In the mid 1980s, employers faced an apparently interminable spiral of workers' compensation costs. There was argument whether the deteriorating situation was derived from unsatisfactory working conditions or from employment of workers who were bad health risks.

Back problems accounted for a major component of the problem. Predictive medical tests, such as spinal X-ray examinations, were shown to be not only useless, but also frankly dangerous, owing to the massive doses of X-rays which these entail. Redesign of work involving stresses on the spine appeared to be the only real promising strategy.

The personnel and human resource manager should be able to assist management and workers by maintaining a reliable and objective perspective on workers' compensation. Overestimating its impact is as harmful as neglecting it.

Termination of Employment

Aside from layoff and serious indiscipline, health and age are the major factors in termination. Ill-health presents the personnel and human resource manager with difficult problems, particularly where it has been caused or made worse by work. More difficult still is the situation where medical surveillance reveals persons whose health is presently reasonable, but who appear especially liable to deterioration as a result of working conditions, and for whom medical withdrawal is recommended. Medical opinion is often contradictory, and there remains a troublesome ethical question of whether an employer has a special responsibility to a worker whose health has deteriorated as a result of working conditions which are the responsibility of the employer.

The personnel and human resource manager should see termination on grounds of age or health as a particular challenge to humane human resource management, and always be on guard for any tendency for the system to be creating victims because of unnecessarily austere administrative criteria. Behind such criteria may well be the issue of how far procedures are intended to protect the organization rather than the individuals who work for it.

The personnel and human resource manager should be able to assemble the information required to fairly balance the organizational and individual interest. Giving the benefit of the doubt to the individual rather than the organization is often the safest position for the personnel and human resource manager striving to be a caring professional by facilitating humane and effective utilization of human resources, any organization's most vital asset.

30. Stress and Burnout in Organizations: Implications for Personnel and Human Resource Management

Ronald J. Burke, York University

The area of work stress and burnout has developed almost faddish aspects during the past five years. Many occupational groups (police officers, teachers, child care workers, air traffic controllers) seem eager to claim the higher stress label which they can then use to demand high pay from their employers. In addition, a stress industry has developed. There is a large service sector offering the latest work stress reduction techniques (TM, TA, relaxation, yoga, exercise) to members of the general public and organizations, to help them understand and manage work stress. *The Joy of Stress* (Hanson 1984) topped the nonfiction best-seller list as this chapter was being written. This heightened interest in work stress shown by lay individuals is matched by increasing research attention within the academic community. It is not an exaggeration to conclude that work stress has become a central variable in the field of organizational behavior (Staw 1984).

Preparation of this manuscript was supported in part by the Faculty of Administrative Studies, York University. Anita Citron assisted in the production of the manuscript. My colleagues Esther Greenglass and Jacob Wolpin provided useful guidance and feedback.

WHY AN INTEREST IN WORK STRESS?

There are several legitimate reasons why interest in the effects of work stress continues to remain high. Some of these reasons relate to *financial costs* borne by individuals, organizations, and the Canadian society as a whole. An individual who develops a physical or an emotional illness, either of short or long duration, usually requires some form of health care and is likely to be absent from work for some period of time. The direct and indirect costs borne by society as a whole as a consequence of work-related illness are staggering (Lalonde 1974). In addition, organizations endure a cost since individuals experiencing greater work stress are likely to be less productive, to have more work-related accidents, to be absent or late for work more often, and to more frequently quit their organization and have to be replaced (Quick and Quick 1984). Thus work stress is likely to be related to lowered individual and organizational performance. Ivancevich and Matteson (1980) estimate the societal costs of stress to be approximately ten percent of gross national production.

There has also been a trend in North America to increasingly place legal responsibility on the organization for the emotional and physical well-being of its employees (Ivancevich, Matteson, and Richards 1985). And there is considerable evidence that work stress and burnout are associated with adverse health and well-being (Maslach and Jackson 1981; Golembiewski 1984; Burke, Shearer, and Deszca 1984; Cooper and Payne 1978, 1980). Finally, there has developed an increasingly widespread belief among senior management in organizations that employees indeed represent assets which must be supported and developed if their organization is to be effective. Organizations that search for excellence care about the health and well-being of their personnel (Peters and Waterman 1982).

UNDERSTANDING STRESS AND BURNOUT

Exhibit 30–1 presents a simple framework for understanding stress and burnout in organizations. This model suggests that to understand stress and burnout in organizations one must consider the environment (both organizational and extraorganizational) in which individuals' function and the individuals' themselves (what individuals bring with them as they interact with events in their environment). The environment is the source of stressors or demands on the individual. Individuals differ (e.g., past experience, personality, behavioural repetoire, social support) in what they bring to the challenges, opportunities and demands in their environments. The concept of stress, then, is an interactional or transactional one. Individuals with particular characteristics interact with work and home environments with certain characteristics, which results in varying amounts of experienced stress. Exhibit 30–1 also makes a distinction between short-term stress reaction or symptoms (acute stress) and long-term stress (chronic stress) resulting in disease, illness, or death. The model proposes that the experience of stressors results in stress reactions (or strain) which in turn leads to disease.

Let us now flesh out the model by providing concrete examples within each of the panels starting with *stress reactions or symptoms*. Individuals react to stressors with responses of various kinds. Stress reactions can be *physiological* (rapid heart rate, heavy breathing, elevated blood pressure), *emotional* (depression, resentment, dissatisfaction, anger near the surface, resignation) and *behavioural* (smoking, drinking or eating more, reduced appetite, light sleep, inability to sleep, apathy, listlessness, aches and pains, headaches, taking medication). These responses, then, describe an individual's immediate (short-term) responses to experienced stress. These responses are typically exhibited by all individuals and are in some senses involuntary (Cannon 1929).

The panel labelled *disease* includes instances of morbidity and mortality (coronary heart disease, stroke, ulcers, mental illness, hypertension). The model in Exhibit 30–1 proposes that the experience of long-term or chronic stress is likely to result in the individual developing emotional and/or physical health problems.

The panel labelled *individual difference characteristics* includes: constitutional predispositions to illness or health, health practices, coping responses, personal ambition, perfectionism, impatience, inability to say no, fear of failure, liking of tension, lack of confidence, chronic anxiety, shyness and timidity.

The final panel in Exhibit 30-1, *sources of stress in the environment*, includes diverse work and life stressors. Work stressors might include: job complexity, quantitum overload, rate and pace of change, role conflict and role ambiguity, job future ambiguity, time pressures, poor physical working conditions, poor relations with one's superiors, peers or subordinates, lack of participation in decision making, and boredom. Life stresses might include: financial difficulties, life crises, family problems, as well as daily hassles (car difficulties, broken shoelaces, rush hour traffic). Most models of stress and burnout pay only fleeting attention to extra work demands and satisfactions. However, the research that is available (Burke and Bradshaw 1981; Bhagat 1983) shows clearly that work experiences influence off-work experiences and vice versa.

MODELS OF STRESS AND BURNOUT

There has been considerable convergence on the nature of stress and burnout experiences in organization. Exhibit 30-2 presents a common work stress research paradigm. Individuals perceive stress in response to certain objective social conditions. These conditions are usually perceived as stressful when the demands on individuals exceed their abilities, or when individuals are unable to fulfill strong needs or values. In other words, the individual's needs or abilities do not match or fit with their environment. No objective work situation will produce the same perceptions of stress or resultant physiological, psychological, or behavioural responses, or health outcomes in all individuals exposed to these conditions. Thus, how individuals perceive a given condition will depend on other personal and situational factors.

A comprehensive model of burnout has been proposed by Cherniss (1980). Cherniss and his associates interviewed twenty-eight beginning professionals in four fields (mental health, poverty law, public health nursing, and high school teachers). All individuals were interviewed several times over a one to two year period of time. The process model he proposed is shown in Exhibit 30-3. The variables in the model were distilled from interviews with and observations of these new professionals.

This model proposes that particular work setting characteristics interact with individuals who enter the job with certain career orientations. These individuals also bring with them their own unique extra work demands and supports. These factors, in concern, result in

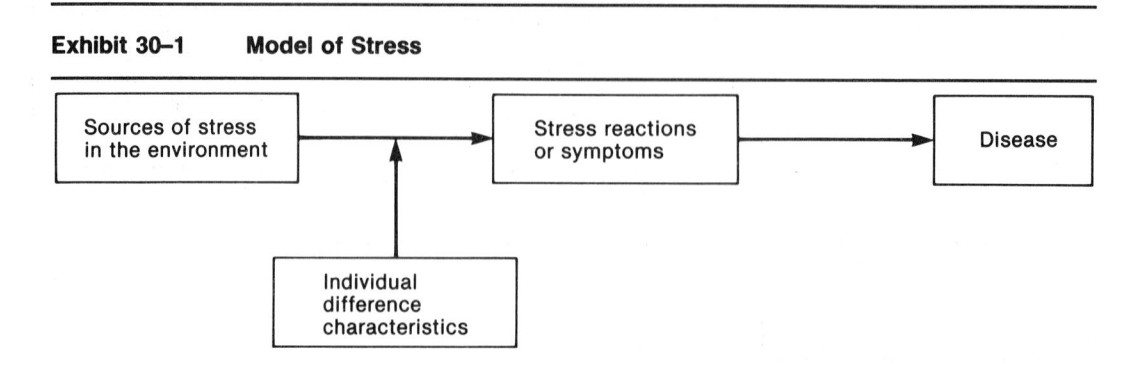

Exhibit 30-1   Model of Stress

STRESS IN ORGANIZATIONS **403**

particular sources of stress being experienced to varying degrees by job incumbents. Individuals cope with these stresses in different ways. Some employ

Exhibit 30–2   A Paradigm of Stress Research

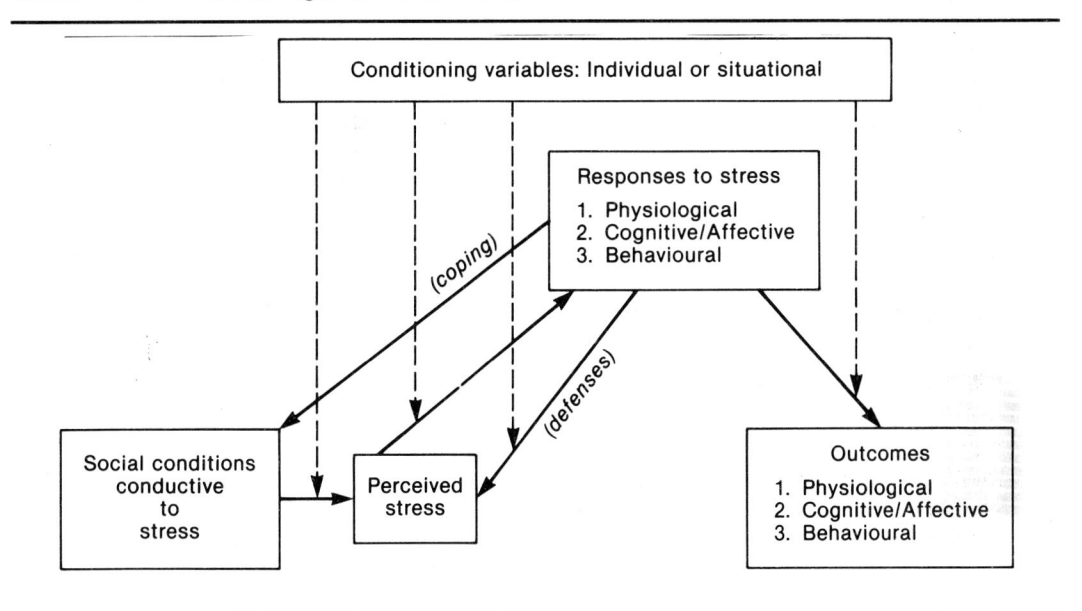

```
                    ┌─────────────────────────────────────────────┐
                    │ Conditioning variables: Individual or situational │
                    └─────────────────────────────────────────────┘
                               │        │        │        │
                               ▼        │        ▼        ▼
                                    Responses to stress
                                    1. Physiological
                                    2. Cognitive/Affective
                                    3. Behavioural
                 (coping)
                                    (defenses)
   Social conditions         Perceived                    Outcomes
      conductive      →       stress                      1. Physiological
         to                                               2. Cognitive/Affective
       stress                                             3. Behavioural
```

Exhibit 30–3   Cherniss Process Model of Burnout

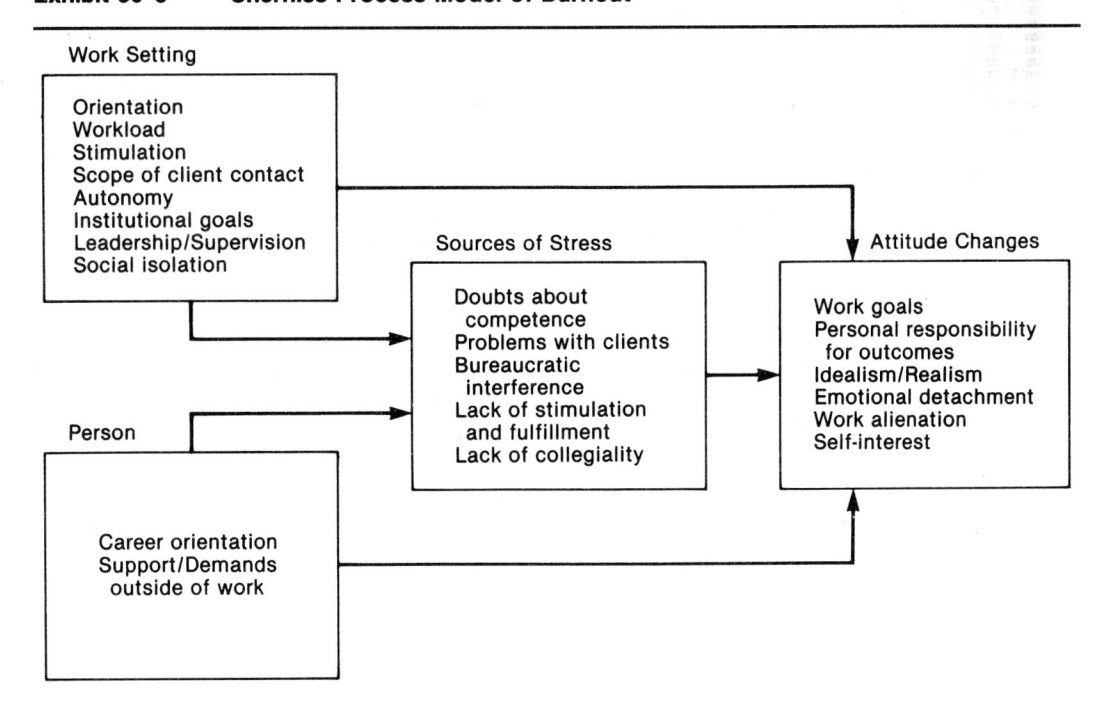

Work Setting

Orientation
Workload
Stimulation
Scope of client contact
Autonomy
Institutional goals
Leadership/Supervision
Social isolation

Sources of Stress

Doubts about
  competence
Problems with clients
Bureaucratic
  interference
Lack of stimulation
  and fulfillment
Lack of collegiality

Attitude Changes

Work goals
Personal responsibility
  for outcomes
Idealism/Realism
Emotional detachment
Work alienation
Self-interest

Person

Career orientation
Support/Demands
  outside of work

techniques and strategies which might be termed active problem solving while others cope by exhibiting the negative attitude changes Cherniss identified in his definition of burnout. Burnout, for Cherniss, occurs over time—it is a process—and represents one way of adapting to, or coping with, particular sources of stress.

WORK STRESS RESEARCH

There are at least five important bodies of research findings, or research thrusts, that can be identified in Canadian work stress research. These include: (1) replications and extensions of the work environment and well-being framework developed by the Institute of Social Research at the University of Michigan, (2) studies of coronary-prone or Type A behaviour, (3) investigations of burnout in work settings, (4) examinations of various effects of social support on work stress and well-being, and (5) studies of work stress among working women.

Work Stress and Individual Well-Being

Several studies have been conducted to establish links between work stresses of various kinds and several different aspects of individual well-being. Most of these studies have used the person environment fit model developed by the Institute for Social Research and many of ISR's measures (Caplan, Cobb, French, and Harrison 1975). These investigations have included samples such as male and female administrators of correctional institutions (Burke and Weir 1980a), female managers (Greenglass 1984a), female nurses (Jamal 1984), males and females employed in a variety of jobs in hospitals (Arsenault and Dolan 1982), male air traffic controllers (MacBride 1978) and male and female managers (Nicholson and Goh 1983). They have examined a range of work stresses such as role ambiguity (Howard, Cunningham, and Rechnitzer, in press; Nicholson and Goh 1983) role conflict (Greenglass 1984a), shiftwork (Jamal 1981; Jamal and Jamal 1982) and responsibility for people and things (Burke and Weir 1980a). In addition, they have included several different measures of emotional and physical well-being. These included: psychosomatic symptoms (Burke and Weir 1980a; Greenglass 1984a, b) job satisfaction (Arsenault and Dolan 1982; Greenglass 1984a, b) and biochemical and cardiovascular responses (Howard, Cunningham, and Rechnitzer, in press).

These studies have generally shown modest statistically significant associations between measures of work stress and individual well-being. They have served to keep the work stress-health relationship in the mainstream of Canadian organizational psychological research. They have also replicated and extended several findings reported previously (Caplan et al. 1975). Greenglass (1984a) has extended the P-E fit model to include work stresses of particular relevances to women such as discrimination, token status and role conflict between work and home.

Coronary-Prone or Type A Behaviour

Type A behaviour or coronary-prone behaviour is an individual difference characteristic about which much is known. It was identified in the late 1950s by two cardiologists, Friedman and Rosenman (1974) as a factor in the incidence of coronary heart disease exhibited by men. Early descriptions of Type A behaviour included as characteristics unbridled ambition, competitiveness, free-floating hostility, time urgency, aggressiveness, and impatience. Data from large scale prospective research studies indicated that Type *A*'s were at least two times as likely to exhibit coronary heart disease as were Type *B*'s (defined by the opposite characteristics of Type *A*'s), controlling for other known coronary risk factors. In fact, Type *A* behaviour constituted about the same degree of risk as other known coronary factors.

The research findings that have accumulated during the past two decades have also provided a clearer picture of Type *A* behaviours that seem to be particularly implicated in the development of coronary heart disease. There is considerable support for the central role played by anger, hostility, and cynicism (Friedman and Ulmer 1984; Barefoot, Dahlstrom, and Williams 1983; Chesney and Rosenman 1985) in this regard.

Type *A* behaviour, then, is a characteristic way some individuals respond to challenges in their environment. Although women exhibit different degrees of particular Type *A* characteristics than men as a result of different socialization experiences (Price 1982), Type *A* working women were four times as likely to exhibit coronary heart disease as were Type *B* working women (Haynes 1984).

Work Correlates of Type *A* Behaviour. Empirical research on Type *A* behaviour has been ongoing in Canada for almost a decade. The first programmatic effort was undertaken by John Howard and his colleagues (Howard, Cunningham, and Rechnitzer 1976, 1977). Their work examined work and health patterns associated with Type *A* behaviour. They found that Type *A*'s worked more hours per week, and travelled more days per year, but were not necessarily more job satisfied than their Type *B* counterparts. Another important conclusion they noted was that some organizations in their sample of twelve had a greater proportion of Type *A*'s than others. This raised the intriguing question of whether phenomena such as Type *A* organizations, Type *A* professions, or Type *A* work exist. That is, might Type *A*'s be more attracted to particular professions and organizations than are Type *B*'s.

Type *A* Behaviour as an Interpersonal Style. Burke and his associates (Burke and Weir 1980a; Burke, Weir, and DuWors 1979, 1980) examined the influence of Type *A* behaviour of job incumbents on their nonwork or family lives, and on the experiences of their spouses. They found, consistent with anecdotal reports of Friedman and Rosenman (1974), that Type *A*'s were less satisfied in their marriages and reported that their jobs had a greater negative impact on their family, home, and personal lives than did Type *B*'s. This pattern was also present among the Type *A*'s wives. Thus spouses of Type *A*'s also reported less marital satisfaction and a more negative impact of their spouses job on home, family, and personal lives. In addition, these women reported less emotional and psychological support (social support) from others, fewer friendships, and less social participation. Thus, not only did these women experience greater stress in their lives, they had fewer resources to deal with this situation.

Acquiring and Maintaining Type *A* Behaviour. Another line of Type *A* research has attempted to sharpen our understanding of the psychodynamics of the Type *A* behaviour pattern. One aspect of this (Burke 1985) examined beliefs and fears or anxieties thought to underlie Type *A* behaviour (Price 1982). They found that individuals scoring more Type *A* on the Jenkins Activity Survey (JAS) also reported greater fears, anxieties, and beliefs consistent with having to prove themselves through acquiring material possessions.

Working Women and Type A Behaviour. Greenglass (1984b, 1985a) has replicated some of the previous studies of career and organizational experiences of Type A men using female professionals and managers. This focus, though relatively neglected to date, will become increasingly important as more women enter the work world and nontraditional occupations in particular. Greenglass (1985c) has also recently investigated the role of anger in Type A behaviour and specifically how anger is evoked in the female manager.

Changing Type A Behaviour. The final area of Canadian research dealing with Type A behaviour that will be discussed involves attempts to reduce Type A behaviour. Roskies and her colleagues (1978, 1979, 1983, 1985a, b, c) have devoted the last ten years to developing and evaluating various treatment approaches. She has shown that both behaviour modification and traditional psychotherapy can produce alterations in Type A behaviour among individuals who have already had coronary heart disease. She has attempted to reduce Type A behaviour among healthy males with less success however.

Burnout in Work Settings

Another area of work stress interest evident in Canada deals with the concept of burnout. Burnout has been defined in various ways by different researchers. The broadest definitions (Freudenberger 1980) equate burnout with stress, connect burnout with an endless list of adverse health and well-being variables, and suggest it is caused by the relentless pursuit of success. Other definitions are narrower, relating burnout to human service professions with interpersonal stress as its cause (Maslach and Jackson 1981); that is, emotional burnout is related to feelings experienced by people whose jobs require repeated exposure to emotionally charged interpersonal situations (Maslach 1978).

Three recent Canadian contributions to our understanding of burnout are noteworthy. These include: (1) the creation of a measure of burnout, (2) attempts to validate the Cherniss (1980) process model of burnout, and (3) an examination of the existence of progressive phases of burnout.

Measuring Burnout. The most widely used measure is the Maslach Burnout Inventory (MBI) created by Maslach and Jackson (1981). This measure taps three aspects of burnout: emotional exhaustion, depersonalization, and lack of personal accomplishment. Cherniss (1980) proposed a different set of components of burnout. These included: reduced work goals, lowered personal responsibility for outcomes, less idealism, emotional detachment, work alienation and greater self-interest. This measure was found to correlate .60 with the MBI in studies of 828 police officers (Burke, Shearer, and Deszca 1984b) and 833 teachers (Burke and Greenglass 1985a).

The Cherniss based measure of burnout has some conceptual overlap with the MBI, but also examines some unique work attitudes. Both measures were found to correlate in similar ways with various work setting antecedents and health and well-being consequences in published (Burke, Shearer, and Deszca 1984b) and unpublished (Burke and Greenglass 1985a) reports.

Validating the Cherniss Burnout Model. Several investigations were designed to validate the Cherniss model in a study of burnout among men and women in police work, and in teaching. Measures of this concept had to be created for the research since none existed. The data (Burke, Shearer, and Deszca 1984b; Burke and Greenglass 1985a) provided considerable support for the model.

Examining Progressive Phases of Burnout. A third contribution examines the notion of progressive stages or phases of burnout. Golembiewski and his colleagues, (Golembiewski 1984; Golembiewski and Munzenrider 1981) proposed the existence of eight progressive phases of burnout. They operationalized these phases using the three scales of the MBI. They hypothesized that depersonalization was the least potent contributor to burnout, that lack of personal accomplishment was more potent and that emotional exhaustion was the most potent contributor to burnout. Eight progressive phases of burnout could then be created by dichotomizing scores on the three MBI scales. Individuals in the least advanced phase of burnout would score low (bottom half) on the three MBI subscales. Individuals in the most advanced phase of burnout would score high (top half) on the three MBI subscales. Individuals with other combinations of low and high subscale scores would represent phases of burnout somewhere between the two extremes.

Recent research (Golembiewski, Munzenrider, and Carter 1983; Golembiewski and Munzenrider 1984) has validated the notion of progressive phases of burnout by comparing individuals in the various phases of burnout on other measures. In general, these studies provide support for the preparation that individuals at different phases of burnout also differ on antecedents and consequences of burnout. This is particularly important since individuals may have the same *total* MBI score, but fall into different phases of burnout.

It is also possible to compare the distributions of individuals falling into various phases of burnout from different occupational and organizational groups. Thus, there is evidence showing significant organizational and occupational differences. It is also possible to compare individuals over time. That is, individuals may move from one phase to another. This raises important questions about the stability of the burnout experience and consequence of moving into or out of more advanced phases of burnout.

Work Stress of Women

Studies of work stress have mainly focused on men. However, with the dramatic rise in women's employment in recent years, and their increasing visibility in nontraditional areas such as management, there is a growing need for the systematic investigation of factors related to women's work stress. Moreover, evidence suggests that even in the same employment situation, men and women may experience different stressors (Greenglass 1982).

In a study of female managers, Greenglass (1985a) observed a relationship between stressors in female managers such as perceived sex discrimination, inequity of pay, underutilization of skills and depression, anxiety, and psychosomatic symptoms. Further research by Greenglass (1985b) has demonstrated the psychological consequences of token status associated with the female managerial role. Data collected from a sample of managerial women indicated that female managers tended to perceive their jobs as primarily socially evaluative. These women's reactions to their job may be a reflection of their token status, one which leads to greater scrutiny and evaluation of their work. Thus, this data points to another source of stress in female managers, a subtle source whose psychological implications have only begun to be studied.

Additional research by Greenglass (1985a) has investigated the antecedents and consequences of role conflict in female workers. Role conflict was conceptualized as simultaneous demands for action and emotional involvement from various spheres such as home and work. Rigid work schedules and work overload were significantly related to role conflict, which in turn was associated with depression, irritation, and anxiety. The research by Greenglass (1985a) has demonstrated the deleterious effects of role conflict on women's health—both physical and psychological.

In a study of female managers, Greenglass (1984a) found that the Type A behaviour pattern plays a moderating role in these women's stress reactions to challenges in the work environment. This research extended the Type A theory to women by showing that Type A women, like their male counterparts, responded with more distress to challenges in the work environment than did Type B women. In response to stress, Type A women were significantly more likely than their Type B counterparts to want to quit their jobs—an action-oriented type of coping. Moreover, intention to turnover was significantly associated with stressful consequences to a greater extent in Type A's than in Type B's.

Research by Greenglass (1984b, 1984a) with women who occupy faculty and managerial roles has reported greater role conflict for Type A women than for Type B's. Type A women, as expected, had greater difficulty meeting all of their self-imposed demands both in the home and at work. This data suggests that in women, the Type A behaviour pattern is reflected in both family and work roles as Burke and Weir (1980) reported for men. This data also indicates an even greater health risk associated with Type A behaviour in women—a health risk which is considerably heightened given it is significantly and positively associated with role conflict between home and work roles.

The relationship between anger and Type A behaviour among female managers was the subject of another study conducted by Greenglass (1985a). Increasingly, anger and hostility have been identified as critical components of Type A behaviour in contributing to the etiology of CHD. Results showed a positive relationship between state and trait anger (Spielberger 1983) in Type A's but not in Type B's. This suggests that trait anger is a mediator of state anger in Type A's—the higher the trait anger in Type A's, the more easily they are provoked to anger in situations. Contrary to the assumption that anger and hostility always characterize Type A's, this data suggests that Type A's vary in their predisposition to anger provocation according to their level of trait anger. While all respondents reacted with anger to high role conflict and underutilization of skills, only Type A's showed a positive association between perceived sex discrimination on the job and state anger.

REDUCING AND PREVENTING STRESS AND BURNOUT

Exhibit 30–1 proposed that in order to understand work stress and burnout in organizations, one must consider both individual difference characteristics and the environment in which individuals are functioning. That is, stress and burnout result from the interaction of people and environments. It follows from this framework, then, that there are at least two ways to reduce work stress and burnout in organizations. The first is to strengthen or augment individual resources. If individuals can be strengthened, they will experience less stress in their work settings. The second is to reduce the demands or stressors that individuals experience in their environment. If organizations can reduce the demands or stressors they place on their employees, individuals will experience less stress. The former involve personal coping strategies; the latter, organizational strategies to reduce and prevent stress and burnout (Newman and Beehr 1979).

Personal Coping Strategies

Table 30-1 indicates a variety of activities individuals can undertake to reduce their levels of experienced stress. Let us consider each of these briefly.

The first two, aimed at an individuals psychological state, involve better use of one's time (time management), priority setting and planning, and the pursuit of more realistic but still challenging aspirations. The former would include saying no in order to avoid beng overloaded, scheduling demands in a way that allows some slack and delegating some of your work to your staff (Lakein 1973). The latter would include knowing your strengths and weaknesses, knowing the kind of work you like and dislike, and making job and career choices accordingly. Some individuals create inordinate stress for themselves while pursuing unrealistic goals. Maslach (1982) offers ways of using these individual coping responses to reduce burnout.

The next set of activities are designed to improve the level of one's physical fitness. There is evidence that suggests that individuals who are physically fit are both better able to deal with the stress they encounter and report experiencing less stress (Burke and Weir 1980b).

The next set of personal coping strategies involve change in one's behaviour. The first deals with reducing the level of one's Type A behaviour (Friedman and Rosenman 1974; Friedman and Ulmer 1984). Individuals who are able to reduce the level of their Type A behaviour will simultaneously reduce the level of their experienced stress and lower their risk of coronary heart disease. The second involves the practising of the relaxation response (Benson 1975). Benson observed a common element in several Far East meditation and yoga techniques which involved aspects of relaxation. He distilled the core of these techniques into an easy-to-learn relaxation technique. Benson and his colleagues (1974a, 1974b) have shown that individuals who practise his relaxation response twice daily for a period of one month or more will significantly alter the levels of their physiological functioning. The last two activities in this set involve becoming both less work-oriented and more involved in the lives of other individuals. There is an increasing body of research evidence indicating that social support from others has both a direct effect on stress response and a buf-

---

Table 30-1   Personal Coping Strategies

1. Aimed at Psychological Conditions
   Plan ahead—Manage one's life
   Realistic assessment of self, aspirations
2. Aimed at Physical/Physiological Conditions
   Diet
   Exercise
   Sleep
3. Changing One's Behaviour
   Becoming less Type A
   Using the Relaxation Response
   Taking time off for fun (holiday)
   Develop close friendships (social support)
4. Changing One's Work Environment
   Change jobs
   Change organizations

fering effect on the stress-strain relationship (House 1981).

The final personal coping strategy encourages individuals to find an improved person-environment fit, if all else fails, by changing jobs or changing employers. Some individuals, for a variety of reasons, find themselves to be square pegs in round holes. These individuals are often able to improve their functioning and reduce their levels of experienced stress after moving to another job or organization.

Organizational Strategies

Let us now consider some ways in which organizations can act to reduce or prevent work stress and burnout. Table 30–2 lists some possible organization-level interventions aimed at organizational, role, and task characteristics.

The first cluster of strategies are aimed at the structure of an organization. Employees may, for example, experience less stress if the structure is changed to introduce more participation (Jackson 1984) and autonomy through decentralization or through improving information flow and communication speed and accuracy by reducing the number of levels or channels in the organizational hierarchy channels through which information must pass. Also, if the reward system is changed to be more equitable in the eyes of employees, less stress will be experienced. Similarly, if the selection, training, and development system is changed to reduce reality shock (Cherniss 1980; Kramer 1974), newcomers will experience less stress. The last cluster of actions are aimed directly at the emotional and physical health of employees. These involve the provision of health services, exercise facilities that support employee physical fitness, and employee assistance programs to both help employees with personal and organizational problems and prevent such problems from escalating into major difficulties (Quick and Quick 1984).

Table 30–2 also outlines organizational actions aimed at the roles individuals fulfill in organizations. There is research evidence that role conflict, role ambiguity, and role overloads are common organizational problems (Kahn et al. 1964). These actions suggest that redefining roles that are found to be ambiguous, reducing role overload by providing additional support, and reducing role conflict by permitting the individual in conflict to discuss the conflict with relevant role senders will reduce role conflict.

Finally, changing aspects of the jobs or tasks that individuals are performing is another way to reduce levels of experienced stress. This might involve improving the lighting, improving the ventilation system if fumes or chemicals are involved, or improving the lack of chairs if individuals are working with VDT's, training individuals so they can be as successful and skillful on their jobs as they possibly can, and enriching some jobs to reduce boredom—a widespread source of stress among blue-collar and clerical workers.

INTERVENTIONS TO REDUCE WORK STRESS

Canadian organizations have taken four approaches in assisting their employees to deal with work stress. The first involves the area of *physical fitness*. Many Canadian organizations will pay for their employees (mostly professional and managerial) to join fitness clubs. The widely held belief is that an individual who is fit and healthy will both experience less stress (prevention) and be able to cope

Table 30–2	**Organizational Strategies**

1. **Changing Organizational Characteristics or Conditions**
   (Processes, structures, programs)
   — Structure—decentralize, integrate, reduce levels of hierarchy or number of channels
   — Change reward system, change selection, training and development system, change socialization processes, change transfer and job rotation policies, more employee-oriented supervision
   — Develop health services

2. **Changing Role Characteristics or Conditions**
   — Redefine roles
   — Reduce role overload—redistribution—more support
   — Increase participation in decision making
   — Contact role senders — conflicting messages
       — too much/too little
       — delegate sharing

3. **Changing Task/Job Characteristics or Conditions**
   — Design jobs in light of workers' abilities and preferences
   — Workers' preferences in selection placement
   — Training programs so worker can be skillful
   — Individualized treatment of workers

better with whatever stress he or she encounters. A few organizations have built first rate facilities on their premises, complete with qualified staff. Although great claims are often made about the benefits of these programs, the basis for such evaluations are often weak (Burke and Weir 1980b).

Cox and his colleagues have conducted an excellent evaluation of the benefit of a fitness programme introduced into an organization (Cox, Shephard and Corey 1981; Shephard, Cox, and Corey 1981). The head offices of two large Canadian assurance companies located in Toronto participated in the research. One, with 1281 employees, served as the test company, while the other, with 579 employees, served as the control. Baseline data on fitness and worker satisfaction were obtained in both companies in September 1977 and January 1978. A professionally directed employee fitness program was initiated at the test company for a six-month period commencing in January 1978. Repeat measures of fitness and worker satisfaction were undertaken in June 1978. Quarterly departmental records of productivity were provided by both companies from September 1976 to June 1978. Absenteeism was noted on a bimonthly basis from October 1977 to June 1978. Employee turnover at the test company only was reported retrospectively for the period from September 1988 to June 1978.

About twenty percent of the test company employees participated in the exercise class. Gains of maximum oxygen intake and flexibility, with a loss of body fat were seen in the group of subjects as a whole, changes being largest among those who participated more frequently. The general attitudes of employees toward their work improved, but this finding was not present on the JDI (Smith,

Kendall and Hulin 1969). Employee turnover over a ten-month period was substantially lower in the adherents than in the remainder of company employees. Productivity showed small gains in both test and control companies. Absenteeism of high adherents was reduced by twenty-two percent relative to other employees.

The researchers (Shephard, Corey, Renzland, and Cox 1983) also examined the effects of this program on health care costs. At the test company, health care cost data were collected for one year before and one year after implementation of the employee fitness program. Health care costs were obtained from the government controlled Ontario Health Insurance Plan (OHIP). Initially, *hospital utilization* was somewhat greater for employees at the test company. This trend underwent a dramatic reversal with the institution of the employee fitness program. The total cost of *medical care* was initially very similar for test and control companies. At the control company, costs showed a substantial jump from 1977 to 1978, but there was little change at the test company.

This data thus suggest that the institution of an employee fitness program helped contain health care costs. The one disturbing feature of the findings was that the advantage of the experimental group depended largely on an increase of costs of the control group. Reduced health care costs at the test company were shown equally by participants and nonparticipants. Thus, the savings in health care costs arose, not from participation in the fitness program, but from an overall increment in health awareness, or a health halo. The overall health care savings amounted to 0.57 hospital days per employee per year, plus $28.50 in medical fees, an overall sum of about $85.00 per person.

The second intervention is an *educational* one. It involves exposing employees in organizations to material on work stress and coping. Some of these also involve the spouses of job incumbents (Burke 1980c), either together with, or separate from their partners. Although the participants are almost uniformly positive about these experiences, there is little other evidence that these offerings make any difference.

A third type of organizational intervention involves changes in policies, work design, and organizational roles and structure. The Children's Aid Society (CAS) of Metropolitan Toronto developed an interesting intervention to reduce burnout among entering frontline social workers in child welfare (Falconer and Hronick 1983). This program radically different in many ways from their emotional and orientation practices involved (1) hiring frontline workers in batches, (2) keeping these newly hired workers in small group numbers equalling five or six for their first six months of employment, (3) gradually increasing their caseload so that it eventually reached sixty percent of the normal caseload by the six month point, (4) an enhanced supervisors role emphasizing education (accompanied by a reduction of other supervisory duties), (5) an improved training program (one to two days of training every two weeks), (6) increased social support for the group, and (7) attempts to deal with stressors found to be associated with burnout in previous research (e.g., promoting clear, consistent, and specific feedback; clarifying rules, policies, and roles; allowing for autonomy and innovation).

The research employed a pretest extended post-test design with a nonequivalent camparison group. The project, designed to run for two and one-half years, was cut short because of budget cutbacks resulting from the general economic recession. The resulting sample sizes rendered the quantitative data of little use. Qualitative data indicated general satisfaction with the program and beliefs that the goals of the program were realized. Supervisors felt that frontline workers in the program achieved a level of skill during the six months comparable to that achieved in one year under the traditional program.

The fourth organizational intervention which appears to offer much potential in reducing work stress are *Employee Assistance Programs* (Santa Barbara 1984). EAP's were developed in the 1960s to assist alcoholic employees. They then broadened their focus to assist employees with a wider range of personal problems. Anything that interfered with the capacity of the employee to perform his or her job became a legitimate problem for discussion. Organizations made appropriate referrals to external agencies or hired qualified professionals as internal counselors. Some EAP's now include the family of job incumbents under their umbrella. In addition, some encourage employees to deal with sources of work stress, as well as sources of nonwork stress. EAP's appear to be able to offer assistance to those in need and to offer help in preventing work stress from leading to negative outcomes (Hasek 1984).

IMPLICATIONS FOR PERSONAL AND HUMAN RESOURCES MANAGEMENT

The research evidence indicates that there are considerable individual, organizational, and societal costs from mismanaged stress (Cooper and Marshall 1976; Brief, Schuler, and Van Sell 1980). As organizations place increased value on their human resources (Peters and Austin 1985), the role of stress and burnout in human resource management will be heightened. It seems likely, then, that efforts aimed at treating or preventing stress and burnout in organizations will continue to increase. The emphasis will likely be placed on the stress of managers and executives, since organizations believe that the performance of executives has a strong effect on their effectiveness.

There has been a much greater reliance to date on individual coping strategies than organizational coping strategies. This results from a perception that stress and burnout are experienced by individuals and, therefore, must be addressed by individuals and the presence of vast resources available to individuals (self-help books, counselors, and therapists). It is important to use more strategies in which the organization is the target of intervention, since these deal with the *causes* of stress and burnout.

There are three initiatives that managers and human resource specialists might undertake to reduce or prevent work stress and burnout. First, a *diagnosis of stress levels* should be undertaken. This involves periodic monitoring of stress and its consequences. In order to treat stress, it is necessary to determine whether it exists in the organization, where it exists in the organization, and what stressors and stress symptoms exist. Ivancevich and Matteson (1980) and Quick and Quick (1984) discuss a variety of diagnostic tools. Second, some attempts should be made to *attack costs* to individual and organizational stress consequences. This will be useful in determining potential cost savings resulting from any interventions that are undertaken. Thus *treatment or remedial actions need to be identified*. Some of the traditional human resource management functions have a useful role to play in reducing work stress and burnout. Thus, the diagnosis may emphasize a selection and placement intervention (keep stress-prone individuals out of a particular job), a training intervention (training to help employees deal with their own stress), an employee orientation intervention (to provide anticipatory socialization experience), a career planning intervention (individual's ability to handle specific kinds of stress), a job redesign intervention (provide complete responsibility for a smaller number of clients), or a performance feedback intervention (providing more feedback, more frequently). Thus several human resource management practices have a bearing on a pressing individual and organizational problem—work stress and burnout.

References

Arsenault, A. and S. Dolan. 1982. Organizational and individual consequence of work stress. Final Report to Quebec Institute for Research on Health and Safety.

Barefoot, J. C., W. G. Dahlstrom, and R. B. Williams. 1983. Hostility, CHD incidence, and total mortality: A 25-year follow-up study of 255 physicians. *Psychological Medicine* 45:59–63.

Benson, H. 1975. *The relaxation response.* New York: Avon Books.

Benson, H., B. A. Rosner, B. R. Marzetta, and H. P. Klemchuk. 1974a. Decreased bloodpressure in borderline hypertensive subjects who practiced medication. *Journal of Chronic Disease* 26:163–69.

Benson, H., B. A. Rosner, B. R. Marzetta, and H. P. Klemchuk. 1974b. Decreased bloodpressure in pharmacologically treated hypertensive patients who regularly elicited the relaxation response. *The Lancet*, February 23, 289–91.

Bhagat, R. S. 1983. Effects of stressful life events upon individual performance, effectiveness and work adjustment process within in organizational settings: A research model. *Academy of Management Review* 8:660–71.

Brief, A. P., R. S. Schuler, and M. Van Sell. 1980. *Managing stress.* Boston: Little, Brown.

Burke, R. J. 1980. Examining the work-family interface: An idea of whose time has come. *Canadian Training Methods* 11:12–14.

Burke, R. J. 1985. Beliefs and fears underlying Type *A* behavior: What makes Sammy run so fast and aggressively? *Journal of Human Stress* 11:174–82.

Burke, R. J. and P. Bradshaw. 1981. Occupational and life stress and the family. *Small Group Behavior* 1980a. 12:329–75.

Burke, R. J. and E. R. Greenglass. 1985. Burnout among men and women in teaching: An examination of the Cherniss model. Unpublished manuscript.

Burke, R. J., J. Shearer, and G. Deszca. 1984a. Burnout among men and women in police work: An examination of the Cherniss model. *Journal of Health and Human Resources Administration* 7:162–88.

Burke, R. J., J. Shearer, and G. Deszca. 1984b. Correlates of burnout phases among police officers. *Group and Organization Studies* 9:451–66.

Burke, R. J. and T. Weir. Work demands on administrators and spouse well-being. *Human Relations* 33a:253–78.

Burke, R. J. and T. Weir. 1980b. "Coping with the stress of managerial occupations." In *Current concerns in occupational stress*, edited by C. L. Cooper & R. L. Payne. New York: John Wiley.

Burke, R. J. and T. Weir. 1980c. The Type *A* experience: Occupational and life demands, satisfaction and well-being. *Journal of Human Stress*, 28–38.

Burke, R. J., T. Weir, and R. E. DuWors. 1979. Type *A* behavior of administrators and wives' reports of marital satisfaction and well-being. *Journal of Applied Psychology* 64:57–65.

Burke, R. J., T. Weir, and R. E. DuWors. 1980. Perceived Type *A* behavior of husbands' and wives' satisfaction and well-being. *Journal of Occupational Behavior* 1: 139–50.

Cannon, W. B. 1929. Organization for physiological homeostesis. *Physiological Review* 9: 339–430.

Caplan, R. D., S. Cobb, J. R. P. French, R. V. Harrison, and S. R. Pinneau. 1975. *Job demands and worker health.* HEW Publication No. (NIOSH), 75–160.

Cherniss, C. 1980. *Professional burnout in human service organizations,* New York: Praeger.

Chesney, M. A. and R. H. Rosenman. 1985. *Anger and hostility in cardiovascular and behavioral disorders.* New York: Hemisphere Publishing Corp.

Cooper, C. L. and J. Marshall. 1976. Occupational sources of stress: A review of the literature relating to coronary heart disease and mental ill health. *Journal of Occupational Psychology* 49:11–28.

Cooper, C. L. and R. Payne. 1978. *Stress at work.* New York: John Wiley.

Cooper, C. L. and R. Payne. 1980. *Current concerns in occupational stress.* New York: John Wiley.

Cox, M., R. J. Shephard, and P. Corey. 1981. Influence of an employee fitness program upon fitness, productivity, and absenteeism. *Ergonomics* 24:795–806.

Falconer, N. E. and J. P. Hornick. 1983. *Attack on burnout: The importance of early training.* Toronto, Children's Aid Society of Metropolitan Toronto.

Freudenberger, H. J. 1980. *Burnout: The high cost of human achievement.* Garden City, N.Y.: Anchor Press.

Friedman, M. and D. Ulmer. 1984. *Treating Type A behavior and your heart.* New York: Knopf.

Friedman, M. and R. H. Rosenman. 1974. *Type A behavior and your heart.* New York: Knopf.

Golembiewski, R. T. 1984. An orientation to psychological burnout: Probably something old, definitely something new. *Journal of Health and Human Resources Administration* 7:153–61.

Golembiewski, R. T. and R. Munzenrider. 1981. Efficacy of three versions of one burnout measure. *Journal of Health and Human Resources Administration* 4:208–244.

Golembiewski, R. T. and R. Munzenrider. 1984. Active and passive reactions to psychological burnout? Toward greater specificity in a phase model. *Journal of Health and Human Resources Administration* 7:264–89.

Golembiewski, R. T., R. Munzenrider, and D. Carter. 1983. Phases of progressive burnout and their work-site covariants. *Journal of Applied Behavioral Science* 19:461–82.

Greenglass, E. R. 1982. *A world of difference: Gender roles in perspective.* Toronto: John Wiley.

Greenglass, E. R. 1984a. Type *A* behavior and job-related stress in managerial women. Paper presented at the annual meeting of the Academy of Management, Boston. August.

Greenglass, E. R. 1984b. Type *A* behavior and role conflict in employed women. Paper presented at the third annual conference on Women and Organizations, Boston.

Greenglass, E. R. 1985a. Psychological implications of sex bias in the workplace. *Academic Psychology Bulletin* 7:227–40.

Greenglass, E. R. 1985b. An interactional perspective on job-related stress in managerial women. *The Souther Psychologist* 2:42–48.

Greenglass, E. R. 1985c. Type *A* behavior and anger: Implications for coronary heart disease. Paper presented at the annual meeting of the Canadian Psychological Association, Halifax.

Hanson, P. 1985. *The Joy of Stress.*

Hasek, J. 1984. Stress in the Halton Regional Police Force. *Ontario Police Commission Newsletter* (December).

Haynes, S. G. 1984. Type A behavior, employment status, and coronary heart disease in women. *Behavioral Medicine Update* 6:11–15.

House, J. S. 1981. *Work stress and social support*, Reading, Mass.: Addison-Wesley.

Howard, J. H., D. A. Cunningham, and P. A. Rechnitzer. In press Role ambiguity, Type *A* behavior and job satisfaction: The moderating effects on cardiovascular and biochemical responses associated with coronary risk. *Journal of Applied Psychology*.

Howard, J. H. 1984. "Sociocultural patterns of stress in a Canadian organization." In *Current issues in occupational stress: Research and intervention*, edited by R. J. Burke. Toronto: York University.

Howard, J. H., D. A. Cunningham, and P. A. Rechnitzer. 1977. Work patterns associated with Type *A* behavior: A managerial population. *Human Relations* 30:825–36.

Howard, J. H., D. A. Cunningham, and P. A. Rechnitzer. 1976. Health patterns associated with Type *A* behavior: A managerial population. *Journal of Human Stress* 2:24–31.

Ivancevich, J. M., M. T. Matteson, and E. P. Richards. 1985. Who's liable for stress on the job? *Harvard Business Review* 63:60–68.

Ivancevich, J. M. and M. T. Matteson. 1980. *Stress and work*. Glenview, Ill: Scott, Foresman.

Jackson, S. E. 1984. "Organization practices for preventing burnout." In *Handbook of organizational stress coping strategies*. Cambridge, MASS: Ballinger, 1984, pp. 89–111.

Jamal, M. 1981. Shift work related to job attitudes, social participation, and withdrawal behavior: A study of nurses and industrial workers. *Personnel Psychology* 34:535–47.

Jamal, M. and S. M. Jamal. 1982. Work and nonwork experiences of employees on fixed and rotating shifts: An empirical assessment. *Journal of Vocational Behavior* 20:282–93.

Jamal, M. 1984. "Job stress and outcome relationship: Employees' cultural background as a moderator?" In *Current issues in occupational stress: research and intervention*, edited by R. J. Burke. Toronto: York University.

Kahn, R. L., D. M. Wolfe, R. P. Quinn, J. D. Snoek, and R. A. Rosenthal. 1981. *Organizational stress: Studies in role conflict and ambiguity*. New York: John Wiley.

Kramer, M. 1974. *Reality shock: Why nurses leave nursing*. St. Louis: Mosby.

Lakein, A. 1973. *How to get control of your time and your life*. New York: Peter Wyden.

Lalonde, M. 1974. *A new perspective on the health of Canadian*. Cat. No. 1131–1374, Government of Canada, Ottawa.

MacBride, A. 1978. Psychosocial stress among Ontario Air Traffic Controllers. Report to Transport Canada and the Canadian Air Traffic Control Association.

Maslach, C. 1982. *Burnout: The Cost of Caring*. Englewood Cliffs, N.J.: Prentice-Hall.

Maslach, C. 1978. The client role in staff burnout. *Journal of Social Issues*. 34:111–24.

Maslach, C. and S. E. Jackson. 1981. Measurement of experienced burnout. *Journal of Occupational Behavior* 2:99–113.

Newman, J. E. and T. A. Beehr. 1979. Personal and organizational strategies for handling job stress: A review of research and opinion. *Personnel Psychology* 32:1–41.

Nicholson, P. J. and S. C. Goh. 1983. The relationship of organization structure and interpersonal attitudes to role conflict and ambiguity in different work environments. *Academy of Management Journal* 26:148–55.

Peters, T. J. and N. Austin. 1985. *A passion for excellence*. New York: Random House.

Peters, T. J. and R. Waterman. 1982. *In search of excellence*. New York: Harper & Row.

Price, V. A. 1982. *Type A behavior pattern: A model for research and practice*. New York: Academic Press.

Price, V. A. 1982. What is Type A? A cognitive social learning model. *Journal of Occupational Behavior* 3:109–30.

Quick, J. C. and J. D. Quick. 1984. *Organizational stress and preventative management*. New York: McGraw-Hill.

Roskies, E., P. Seraganian, R. Oseasohn, J. A. Hanley, R. Collu, N. Martin, C. Smilga, and B. Hollander. 1985a. The Montreal Type A intervention project: I. Design and rationale. Unpublished manuscript.

Roskies, E., P. Seraganian, R. Oseasohn, J. A. Hanley, R. Collu, N. Martin, and C. Smilga. 1985b. The Montreal Type A intervention project: II. Major findings. Unpublished manuscript.

Roskies, E., P. Seraganian, R. Oseasohn, C. Smilga, N. Martin, and J. A. Hanley. 1985c, in press. "Treatment of psychological stress responses in healthy Type A men." In *Advances in the Investigation of Psychological Stress*, edited by R.W.J. Neufeld, New York: John Wiley.

Roskies, E. 1983. "Stress management for Type A individuals." In *Stress reduction and prevention*, edited by D. Meichenbaum and M. Jaremko. New York: Plenum.

Roskies, E., H. Kearney, M. Spevack, A. Surkis, C. Cohen, and S. Gilman. 1979. Generalizability and durability of treatment effects in an intervention program for coronary-prone Type A managers. *Journal of Behavioral Medicine* 2:195–207.

Roskies, E., M. Spevack, A. Surkis, C. Cohen, and S. Gilman. 1978. Changing the coronary-prone Type A behavior pattern in a nonclinical population. *Journal of Behavioral Medicine* 1:201–16.

Santa Barbara, J. 1984. Employee assistance programs: An alternative resource for mental health service delivery. *Canada's Mental Health* 32:35–38.

Shephard, R. J., P. Corey, P. Renzland, and M. Cox. 1983. The impact of changes in fitness and lifestyle upon health care utilization. *Canadian Journal of Public Health* 74:51–54.

Shephard, R. J., M. Cox, and P. Corey. 1981. Fitness program participation: Its effect on worker performances. *Journal of Occupational Medicine* 23:359–63.

Smith, P. C., L. M. Kendall, and C. L. Hulin. 1969. *The measurement of satisfaction in work and retirement*. Chicago: Rand McNally.

Spielberger, C. D. 1983. *Manual for the State-Trait Anxiety Inventory* (STAI form Y), Palo Alto, CA: Consulting Psychologists Press.

Staw, B. M. 1984. "Organizational behavior: A review and reformulation of the field's outcome variables." In *Annual Review of Psychology*, edited by J. Rosenzweig and L. W. Porter, Vol. 35, 627–66. Palo Alto, Calif: Annual Reviews Inc.

31. Stress and Absenteeism at Work: Old Questions and New Research Avenues

Marie Reine van Ameringen

Christine Léonard

Shimon L. Dolan

André Arsenault

Employee absenteeism is a costly personal and organizational problem and has been a major concern for managers and researchers alike. Yet, in the last decade only limited progress has been made in identifying its primary causes and in developing effective intervention programs. On the other hand, the interest in organizational stress has grown remarkably in recent years, and performance, turnover, and absenteeism have often been included as organizational consequences in stress models (McGrath 1976; Ivancevitch and Matteson 1980; Davidson and Cooper 1981; Arsenault and Dolan 1983a). In this paper, an attempt will be made first, to describe how the problem has so far been examined and second to discuss some of the conceptual gaps and inconsistencies emerging from many studies, and finally to present recent evidence which may suggest new avenues for future research, as well as purposeful intervention strategies for human resource administration.

The authors are members of the Groupe de Recherche Stress et Saûté au Travail at the University of Montréal.

ABSENTEEISM: ITS CONCEPTUALIZATION

On a practical level, absenteeism may be viewed quite differently by the administration and by the employee; the former view it as a menace to organizational performance and productivity, while the latter may use it as a relief from occupational tensions.

Despite the impressive volume of data accumulated on absenteeism determinants, no consensus seems to exist as to a viable conceptual definition. Lyons (1972) described absenteeism research as a "hodgepodge of conceptually and operationally differing definitions" (p. 279). Examples of terminology used include: hidden conflicts of organizational tensions (Weiss 1975), adaptive processes (Nicholson 1977), stress reactions (Parkes 1983), individual or group resistance or flight (Chadwick-Jones, Nicholson, and Brown 1982). Thus absence from work, "a social fact in need of theory," (As 1962) remains an ill-defined and ambiguous concept (Muchinsky 1977; Nicholson 1977).

Although most theoretical models concern general organizational behaviour and remain speculative concerning the role of absenteeism, a brief examination of the various approaches proposed so far is presented.

Nicholson (1977) has attempted a synthesis of these different models and proposed an interesting typology: (1) *pain-avoidance models*, where absenteeism is defined as an evasion, or flight from an intolerable situation; (2) *adjustment-maladjustment models*, which conceive absence as an adaptive consequence to work demands, and (3) *decision models*, where the decision to be absent becomes a rational decision or choice process, following a definite goal.

Pain-Avoidance Models

The concept of absenteeism proposed by these models originates principally from the studies on job satisfaction. The hypothesis is that if individuals are happy and satisfied with their work, they will be motivated to remain on the job (Argyle 1972). Although a large number of studies have reported a significant negative relationship between job satisfaction and absenteeism (Muchinsky 1977; Steers and Rhodes 1978, 1984), others disagree and rather support the idea that satisfaction may play only a very minor role. For these authors, this approach seems to be somewhat restrictive (Nicholson, Brown, and Chadwick-Jones 1976; Terborg, Lee, Smith, Davis, and Tubin 1982; Clegg 1983; Hackett and Guion 1985). Multidimensional models which study the interactions between a number of attitudinal, individual, and organizational variables may be more appropriate.

Steers and Rhodes (1978) in particular have attempted a more articulate model. Attendance at work would depend on a number of factors. The worker's satisfaction with the job, pressures put upon him or her by the organization, as well as extraorganizational (social) pressures would tend to influence his or her motivation. Moreover, his or her ability (more or less physical capacity) to come to work would become an additional factor. Yet, all these studies have failed to explain why absenteeism is such a prominent situation.

Adjustment-Maladjustment Models

A number of researchers have viewed absence as an outcome of organizational socialization and other adaptive processes to job demands. Some models of absence culture have been described where the motivation, manners, and differing forms of withdrawal behaviour are a function of the many explicit organizational rules and regulations, as well as of all the implicit, accepted, social norms particular to the working group concerned (Chadwick-Jones et al. 1982; Nicholson and Johns 1985). Argyris (1960) has portrayed absence behaviour as one of the possible reactions in what he describes as a positive feedback loop, where management pressures provoke greater withdrawal behaviour. Another type of readjustment model has been proposed by Gibson (1966) where absence is a function of the contractual relationship between the individual and the organization. The problem with most of those models is their relatively high level of abstraction, where the original conceptualizations remain quite far from the methodological applications and the empirical findings which are reported (Nicholson 1977).

Decision Models

Two schools of thought have developed decision models: rationalists and motivational theorists. Both define absenteeism as a rational choice resulting from the subjective perception which the individual has of the cost-benefit action of staying on the job. Decision models have not been proposed to explain organizational behaviour in general and are not specifically related to absenteeism.

Gowler (1969), a rationalist, has described absenteeism as a means of establishing the equilibrium between the work effort and the benefits after the relationship has been interrupted by overtime.

On the other hand, Vroom (1964), a motivational theorist, has attempted to explain work behaviour as a function of how an individual perceives that his or her work effort will yield results, as well as of the emphasis on the instrumentality he or she applies to the anticipated rewards and the value of these rewards. He suggested a decision path matrix and a rational evaluation of the pros and cons of increasing one's efforts.

Fishbein (1967) proposed that organizational behaviour results from the addition of two factors: (1) *attitudes*, they depend on the expected consequences which an individual associates to a particular behavior; (2) *normative social beliefs*, which depend on an individual's attitudes as well as on his or her motivation to conform to the perception of social norms. However, empirical analysis has not yielded the expected results (Newman 1974).

The models described so far, however, do overlook a various number of points. Their level of abstraction is too high in order to render them operationally feasible; they may not present a specific orientation to the variable under study, named by absenteeism; and many are not empirically supported.

Another criticism found in the literature is that absenteeism has been viewed as a unique concept. Nicholson et al. (1976) and Nicholson (1977) suggest that diverse conceptions be integrated in order to better analyse this complex phenomenon. They propose that absence is an adaptive and proactive behaviour resulting from diverse individual needs, goals and habits, and from situational constraints, norms, and rules. Moreover, they suggest a study of the dynamics of attendance motivation, whereby the concept is influenced by four groups of factors, namely: personality traits, professional orientation, job involvement and work relations. Each of which is related to personal and organizational situational factors (Nicholson 1977). Youngblood (1984) has proposed absenteeism to be a function of motivation processes involved in the attachment to both work and nonwork domains.

In summary, many studies do imply and support the notion that absenteeism is a complex phenomenon which must be viewed as a multidimensional concept involving interactions between the individual and both work and nonwork environments. Thus, theoretical innovations and improvements are greatly needed.

EMPIRICAL RESULTS

We have already mentioned some of the problems associated with the conceptualization of absenteeism. Empirical weaknesses exist as well, one being that most of the research reported concern bivariate analysis between absence and a limited number of variables which differ from one study to the next. Moreover, methodological inadequacies further render interpretations difficult.

Attitudinal, Organizational and Individual Variables

Job satisfaction is the one attitudinal variable most often looked at in relation to absenteeism, yet the results are quite divergent and lead to a deadlock. (Nicholson et al. 1976; Clegg 1983). When significant correlations are established between absence and job satisfaction, they are low (Nicholson et al. 1976; Steers and Rhodes 1978; Hackett and Guion 1985) and many studies fail to document significant relationships. Moreover, multivariate studies indicate that job satisfaction is not a good predictor of absenteeism (Steers and Rhodes 1984). Conflicting opinions may be explained by three main reasons: (1) weakness of the methodological approach, both in the measures and in the statistical analysis (Clegg 1983); (2) the pertinence of the job satisfaction measure as a significant predictor (Nicholson et al. 1976; Hackett and Guion 1985); and (3) the important contribution of additional individual and situational moderator variables which must be taken into account (Waters and Roach 1973; Newman 1974; Muchinsky 1977; Steers and Rhodes 1978; Cheloha and Farr 1980; Fitzgibbons and Moch 1980). Among the attitudinal variables, job involvement would seem to be a better predictor of absence behaviour (Steers and Rhodes 1984).

Many organizational variables have also been studied in relation to absenteeism. Significant correlations have been reported between job characteristics such as autonomy, responsibility, variety of tasks, unit and/or organizational size (Muchinsky 1977), role conflict, ambiguity and overload, skill underutilization and resource inadequacies (Gupta and Beehr 1979; Arsenault and Dolan 1983a), and absence behaviour.

Personal characteristics and values and personality variables have received little attention, but they appear worthy of study. Many sociodemographic variables have been studied (Keller 1983), yet among them, only age and sex have been significantly related to absenteeism (Muchinsky 1977; Chadwick-Jones et al. 1982). Significant relationships have been established between absence and personality and value variables, but the exact nature of these relationships remain obscure, be they direct (Bernardin 1977; Keller 1983) or indirect (Mowday and Spencer 1981). Moreover, some authors measure personality traits such as rigidity, ambition, and anxiety (Bernardin 1977), whereas others use personality construct such as Type A and Locus of control (Arsenault and Dolan 1983b; Jamal and Ahmed 1985).

ABSENCE MEASURES

Absenteeism has been conceived and measured in different manners, not all of which tend to agree. Opinions vary concerning psychometric properties, typologies, and which absence measure is most appropriate (Muchinsky 1977; Hammer and Landau 1981; Johns and Nicholson 1982).

Before looking at the problems concerning absence measures, one needs to stress the fact that absenteeism is a nonunitary variable, and that certain operational definitions are completely independent from others (Burke and Wilcox 1972; Nicholson and Goodge 1976; Hackett and Guion 1985). The multidimensional nature of absenteeism has led to a classification which is most often dichotomous yielding a number of typologies, namely; voluntary, nonvoluntary; certified, noncertified; justified, nonjustified; with or without pay; short- or long-term; and sometimes simply using the absence motivation inscribed on the presence registers (Nicholson 1977).

Voluntary and involuntary absence is the typology most frequently found in the literature (Chadwick-Jones, Brown, and Nicholson 1973; Steers and Rhodes 1978; Hammer and Landau 1981; Hackett and Guion 1985). Voluntary absence has been defined as being under the direct control of the worker, thus, a direct function of his or her motivational presence at work and thereby under organizational influence. On the other hand, involuntary absence has been thought of as resulting from the worker's impossibility to attend because of sickness, accident, death in the family, transportation problems, etc. The organization considers this form of absence difficult to compress.

The problem with this dichotomy is that voluntary absences are in a sense associated with an individual's will to be present or not at work. Moreover, in that context will and motivation seem to be equated. Yet, certain motivational forces are not necessarily conscious and may even be obscure and uncontrollable. The psychological implications of health are no longer doubtful (Johns and Nicholson 1982). Moreover, the working environment may well be conducive to sickness and accidents (Smulders 1980) and it therefore becomes difficult to separate voluntary from involuntary absences only on the basis of willingness.

Most other typologies of absence behaviour, as mentioned earlier, are more or less closely associated with the idea underlying the voluntary-involuntary dichotomy and as such not one can satisfy all researchers. A search for a better understanding of the factors associated with absenteeism must continue in order to yield some acceptable procedure for discriminating its various forms and functions (Johns and Nicholson 1982). On the other hand, absenteeism might be better conceptualized on a "continuum of justifiability" (Hackett and Guion 1985).

The types of measures referred to principally in the literature consists of frequency indicators and time lost indicators. The first refers to the number of absence periods within a given time, whereas the second indicates the total number of days spent away from work. Frequency indicators have been most often associated with voluntary absences. On the other hand, time lost or duration indicators which give a more precise measure of long-term absenteeism (usually related to sickness or work accidents) have most often been used to measure involuntary absence behaviour (Chadwick-Jones et al. 1982). Usually weekends and holidays are excluded. Furthermore a number of factors (example: basic mathematical count, motives of absence, consideration of days or hours lost and of the length of the absence period, aggregation level) which may or may not be included from study to study makes comparisons difficult. Avery and Hotz (1984) have recently reviewed statistical models for analysing absentee behaviour. They insist on the importance of controlling for sources of heterogeneity such as different industries and occupations, as well as seasonal variations.

ABSENTEEISM AND OCCUPATIONAL STRESS

In recent years stress research has taken over the interest of numerous authors. Among the various occupational stress models proposed, some have been enlarged to include organizational consequences such as performance, turnover, and absenteeism (Beehr and Newman 1978; Ivancevitch and Matteson 1980, 1984; Davidson and Cooper 1981; Arsenault and Dolan 1983a). These are complex multidimensional models which attempt to describe the dynamic reactions between the individual and his or her environment. The main justification for taking absenteeism as an important outcome variable comes from the many studies which have looked at the relationships of absenteeism as part of either motivational, anxiety-avoidance or adjustment-maladjustment models (as described above). Moreover, absenteeism represents an objective and independent measurement that has minimal chances of interacting with the experimental intervention (Payne et al. 1982; Huse and Cummings 1985). Finally, the indirect outcome of occupational stress in terms of the financial impact and worker's compensation, is suggested to be a factor in the increased importance of stress for students of organizations (Beehr and Schuler 1980). Absenteeism becomes an organizational consequence generated by a misfit between the individual, his or her personal characteristics, and work-demands environment. Many recent reviews of the literature conclude that this definition of occupational stress is among the most readily adopted by social science researchers (Blau 1981).

Arsenault and Dolan have been working on an ongoing study of occupational stress in the hospital environment for a number of years. The conceptual model which guided the authors is detailed elsewhere (Dolan and Arsenault 1980; Arsenault and Dolan 1983a). However, the principal elements in this model are: major working conditions peculiar to each occupation and organization are cognitively identified. These become stressors only if they are perceived by the individual as representing a threat so that both perception of overstimulation or understimulation could become stressful. Tolerance of stressors depends also on several individual-personal characteristics such as personality (Type A, locus of control), cultural background, and social support. The interaction between stressors and individual characteristics results in either fit or misfit, which can be measured by the presence or absence of various signs and symptoms of strain, be they physiological (blood pressure, obesity, cholesterol, etc.); psychological (depression, anxiety, job dissatisfaction, etc.); or behavioural (performance, absenteeism, excessive smoking, drinking, etc.). In the long run, recurrent appearances of such signs and symptoms might be conducive to the development of more chronic forms of physical and/or mental illnesses.

Among the numerous psychosocial work stressors cited in the literature (Caplan et al. 1975; Beehr and Newman 1978; Ivancevitch and Matteson 1980), the model suggested by Arsenault and Dolan (1983a) retains seven dimensions of stress related to job content, and eight dimensions related to job context, all pertinent to the hospital work environment in Québec. These sources have been classified into two global work dimensions respectively, the intrinsic stress index and the extrinsic stress index. A detailed rationale for the psychometric properties of these measures, as well as their discriminant validity, has already been documented (Arsenault and Dolan 1983b; Dolan and Arsenault 1984).

Results support the idea that intrinsic stressors have a positive feedback effect and predict a significant decrease in absenteeism, while extrinsic stressors appear to act through opposite negative motivational feedback and predict a significant increase in absenteeism (Arsenault and Dolan 1983b). The fact that job content stress tends to decrease absenteeism could be explained by some general tendency for all individuals to stay on the job when confronted with increased challenge. This is in opposition with the increased avoidance behaviour generated by job context stressors.

Aggregating for personality types, for different occupations and, for different organizations highlights several interesting structural effects, particularly in response to job context (extrinsic) stress. Two opposite personality types respond to job context stress by increasing their absence behaviour patterns. Individuals who are high striver-achiever's and who also possess an internal locus of control were labelled in the study as *HOT–CATS*, and those who are low striver-achievers with an external locus of control were labelled as *COOL–DOGS*. These two diametrically opposed individuals exhibit a significant tendency for engaging in a fight-flight reaction to an excessive, extrinsic stress environment. In this study population, executives and professionnals were overrepresented in the internal high striver-achiever personality group (HOT–CATS), while blue-collar workers tended to be external low striver-achievers (COOL–DOGS). Registered nurses and laboratory technicians were closer to the general mean, yet nurses tended to be slightly more internal and higher striver-achievers than technicians and clerks (Arsenault and Dolan 1983a). Moreover, in the particular multicultural environment of the province of Québec, a structural effect is revealed where metropolitan English-speaking hospitals respond significantly to higher job context stress with an increase in absenteeism. There is no significant effect for the French-speaking hospitals. This is strongly contrasted to the differences in mean values which are lowest for the English cultural organization as compared to the metropolitan French-speaking hospitals which have the highest mean values for absenteeism (about 2.5 times more than the other group), but whose absence behaviour pattern is not related to occupational stress (Arsenault and Dolan 1983b). Other factors, not measured in the study, probably affect the absence patterns in the French-speaking hospitals.

Consequently, the study illustrates that a more comprehensive approach may be more useful in developing models and theories in the domain of occupational stress. It is suggested that a great deal of information is revealed when multiple outcomes are studied simultaneously, when the moderators are treated at three (or more) levels of aggregation, and when the sources of stress are classified using summary indices such as intrinsic and extrinsic stressors. Notwithstanding, these results have some limitations. The study was cross-sectional and based on a nonrandom sample.

However, results are forthcoming on a longitudinal aspect of a sample of the same population and should provide further interesting insights. Preliminary results confirm the diametrically opposed predictor effect of both sources of stress (i.e., decrease for intrinsic stress and increase for extrinsic stress) on absenteeism. Moreover, time-series analysis of absence patterns over a five-year period for a subsample of 177 hospital employees has clearly shown the prominence of a long-term decreasing trend in the frequency of absences from year to year. There is also a significant seasonal fluctuation with peak levels corresponding to the first and last quarter every year (Léonard, Arsenault, and Dolan 1986). This may lead to the conclusion that the winter peak correlates with environmental factors, while the autumn peak could correspond to the seasonal behaviour of employees dealing with opportunity costs of getting rid of accumulated days in the absence bank (Avery and Hotz 1984).

References

Argyle, M. 1972. *The social psychology of work.* Harmondworth: Penguin.

Argyris, C. 1960. *Understanding organizational behavior.* Homewood, Ill: Dorsey.

Arsenault, A. and S. Dolan. 1983a. *Le stress au travail et ses effets sur l'individu et l'organisation.* Rapport du recherche. Notes et rapports scientifiques et techniques. Montréal: IRSST.

Arsenault, A. and S. Dolan. 1983b. The role of personality, occupation and organization in understanding the relationship between job stress, performance and absenteeism. *Journal of Occupational Psychology* 56: 227–40.

As, D. 1962. Absenteeism—A social fact in need of a theory. *Acta Sociologica* 6(4): 278–85.

Avery, R. B. and V. J. Hotz. 1984. "Statistical models for analysing absentee behavior." In *Absenteeism. New approaches to understanding, measuring and managing employee absence*, edited by P. S. Goodman, R. S. Atkin & Associates, 159–193. London: Jossey-Bass Publishers.

Beehr, T. A. and J. E. Newman. 1978. Job stress, employee health and organizational effectiveness: A facet analysis model and literature review. *Personnel Psychology* 31: 665–69.

Beehr, T. A. and R. S. Schuler. 1980. *Current and future perspectives on stress in organizations.* Working Paper #WPS80-35, Ohio State University, College of Administrative Studies.

Bernardin, H. J. 1977. The relationship of personality variables to organizational withdrawal. *Personnel Psychology* 30:17–27.

Blau, G. 1981. An empirical investigation of job-stress, social support, service length, and job strain. *Organizational Behavior and Human Performance* 27:279–302.

Burke, R. J. and D. S. Wilcox. 1972. Absenteeism and turnover among female telephone operators. *Personnel Psychology* 25: 639–48.

Caplan, R. D., S. Cobb, J. R. P. French, Jr., R. D. Van Harrison, and S. R. Pinneau, Jr. 1975. *Job demands and workers health.* Washington, D.C.: NIOSH Government Printing Office.

Chadwick-Jones, J. K., C. A. Brown, and N. Nicholson. 1973. Absence from work: Its meaning, measurement and control. *International Review of Applied Psychology* 22(2): 137–55.

Chadwick-Jones, J. K., N. Nicholson, and C. Brown. 1982. *Social psychology of absenteeism.* New York: Preager.

Cheloha, R. S. and J. L. Farr. 1980. Absenteeism, job involvement, and job satisfaction in an organizational setting. *Journal of Applied Psychology* 65(4): 467–73.

Clegg, C. W. 1983. Psychology of employee lateness, absence, and turnover: A methodological critique and an empirical study. *Journal of Applied Psychology* 68(1): 88–101.

Cooper, C. L. and R. Payne, eds. 1980. *Current concerns in occupational stress.* John Wiley & Sons.

Davidson, M. J. and C. L. Cooper. 1981. A model of occupational stress. *Journal of Occupational Medicine* 23(8): 564–74.

Dolan, S. and A. Arsenault. 1980. *Stress, santé et rendement au travail.* Monographie #5, Université de Montréal, Ecole de relations industrielles.

Dolan, S. and A. Arsenault. 1984. "Job demands related cognitions and psychosomatic ailments." In *The self in anxiety, stress and depression*, edited by R. Schwarzer, 265–82. Amsterdam: Elsevier Science Publ., North-Holland.

Fishbein, M. 1967. Attitude and the prediction of behavior. In *Readings in attitude theory and measurement*, edited by M. Fishbein. New York: Wiley.

Fitzgibbons, D. and M. Moch. 1980. Employee absenteeism: A multivariate analysis with replication. *Organizational Behavior and Human Performance* 26:349–72.

Gibson, J. O. 1966. Toward a conceptualization of absence behavior of personnel in organizations. *Administrative Science Quaterly* 11(1): 107–33.

Gowler, D. 1969. Determinants of the supply of labour to the firm. *The Journal of Management Studies* 6(1): 73–95.

Gupta, N. and T. A. Beehr. 1979. Job stress and employee behaviors. *Organizational Behavior and Human Performance* 23(3): 373–87.

Hackett, R. D. and R. M. Guion. 1985. A reevaluation of the absenteeism-job satisfaction relationship. *Organizational Behavior and Human Decision Processes* 35:340–81.

Hammer, T. H. and J. Landau. 1981. Methodological issues in the use of absence data. *Journal of Applied Psychology* 66:574–81.

Huse, E. F. and T. G. Cummings, eds. 1985. *Organizational development and change.* St. Paul: West Publishing Co.

Ivancevitch, J. M. and M. T. Matteson. 1980. *Stress at work.* Glenview, Ill.: Scott, Foresman.

Ivancevitch, J. M. and M. T. Matteson. 1984. A type A–B person-work environment interaction model for examining occupational stress and consequences. *Human Relations* 37:491–513.

Jamal, M. and S. W. Ahmed. 1985. Job stress, stress-prone type A behavior, and personal and organizational consequences. *Canadian Journal of Administrative Sciences* 2:360–74.

Johns, G., and N. Nicholson. 1982. The meanings of absence: New strategies for theory and research. *Research in Organizational Behavior,* (JAI Press) 4:127–72.

Keller, R. T. 1983. Predicting absenteeism from prior absenteeism, attitudinal factors, and nonattitudinal factors. *Journal of Applied Psychology* 68(3): 536–40.

Léonard, C., A. Arsenault, and S. L. Dolan. 1986. Analyse de la stabilité des mesures de fréquence et durée des absences au travail. Paper presented at the 4e Congrès international de psychologie du travail de langue française, May, Montréal, Québec.

Lyons, T. F. 1972. Turnover and absenteeism: A review of relationships and shared correlates. *Personnel Psychology* 25:271–81.

Mcgrath, J. E. 1976. "Stress and behavior in organizations." In *Handbook of industrial and organizational psychology,* edited by M. Dunnette. Chicago: Rand McNally.

Mowday, R. T. and D. G. Spencer. 1981. The influence of task and personality characteristics on employee turnover and absenteeism incidents. *Academy of Management Journal* 24(3): 634–42.

Muchinsky, P. M. 1977. Employee absenteeism: A review of the literature. *Journal of Vocational Behavior* 10:316–40.

Newman, J. E. 1974. Predicting absenteeism and turnover: A field comparison of Fishbein's model and traditional job attitudes measures. *Journal of Applied Psychology* 59(5): 610–15.

Nicholson, N. 1977. Absence behaviour and attendance motivation: A conceptual synthesis. *The Journal of Management Studies* 14(3): 231–51.

Nicholson, N., C. A. Brown, and J. K. Chadwick-Jones. 1976. Absence from work and job satisfaction. *Journal of Applied Psychology* 61(6): 728–37.

Nicholson, N. and P. M. Goodge. 1976. The influence of social, organizational, and biographical factors on female absence. *Journal of Management Studies* 13:234–54.

Nicholson, N. and G. Johns. 1985. The absence culture and the psychological contract: Who's in control of absence? *Academy of Management Review* 10(3): 397–407.

Parkes, K. R. 1983. Smoking as a moderator of the relationship between affective state and absence from work. *Journal of Applied Psychology* 68(4): 698–708.

Payne R., T. D. Jick, and R. J. Burke. 1982. Whitter Stress Research: An Agenda for the 1980's. *Journal of Occupational Behavior* 3: 131–45.

Smulders, P. G. W. 1980. Comments on employee absence/attendance as a dependent variable in organizational research. *Journal of Applied Psychology* 65(3): 368–73.

Steers, R. M. and S. R. Rhodes. 1978. Major influences on employee attendance: A process model. *Journal of Applied Psychology* 63(4): 391–407.

Steers, R. M. and S. R. Rhodes. 1984. "Knowledge and speculation about absenteeism." In *Absenteeism. New approaches to understanding, measuring and managing employee absence*, edited by P. S. Goodman, R. S. Atkin & Associates, 229–75. London: Jossey-Bass Publishers.

Terborg, J. R., T. W. Lee, F. J. Smith, G. A. Davis, and M. S. Turbin. 1982. Extension of the Schmidt and Hunter validity generalization procedure to the prediction of absenteeism behavior from knowledge of job satisfaction and organizational commitment. *Journal of Applied Psychology* 67(4): 440–49.

Vroom, V. H. 1964. *Work and motivation.* New York: Wiley.

Waters, L. K. and D. Roach. 1973. Job attitudes as predictors of termination and absenteeism: Consistency over time and across organizational units. *Journal of Applied Psychology* 57(3): 341–42.

Weiss D. 1975. Notes *sur l'absenteeism. Production et Gestion* No. 276.

Youngblood, S. A. 1984. Work, Nonwork and Withdrawal. *Journal of Applied Psychology* 69(1): 106–17.

Section VIII
Integrating, Trends, and Comparisons

The four articles in this last section provide an overview of some of the more contemporary and future trends in personnel and human resource management. The first emerging PHRM function is career planning and relocation counselling. In their article, Axmith and Mozes depict the evolution of this emerging concern in Canada. They then describe current trends in relocation counselling and in career planning. The message in their concluding arguments is very clear: while relocation counselling has matured as a legitimate function for many PHRM practitioners in Canada, career planning as an area of concern is only now evolving. They predict that both functions will be integrated into the PHRM practices in the future.

During the 1908's PHRM managers searched for new concepts and techniques to be used effectively in Canada. Japanese and other European practices were looked upon as possible examples for effective management of human resources. Jaeger, in the second article examines the possibilities of importing and applying the theory Z approach in Canadian firms. He first introduces the underlying principles of theory Z, and then evaluates the appropriateness of this model for Canada. Jaeger concludes his analysis by stressing that although many benefits could be associated with the application of the Z model in Canadian firms, PHRM practitioners should be sensitive to the many constraints which prevent the adaption of the pure form of theory Z. Thus, he calls for a home grown type Z application.

In a period of technological innovations and growing professionalism in the field of PHRM, Harvey and Blakeley discuss in the third paper the ways to maximize the use of the company's human resource information system (HRIS). First, they introduce some basic data system requirements. This is followed by illustration of policy/planning uses of the HRIS in four areas: organizational demographics, planning and analysis, employment equity planning and monitoring, scenario building (i.e., projecting the effects of alternative policy options) and productivity analysis, and program evaluation. Next, they discuss the use of external data source. They conclude their article by offering six major guidelines for maximizing the use of HRIS in human resource administration.

One of the greatest challenges for PHRM today is the use of proper tools to assess its overall effectiveness. The literature in this area, keeps on repeating the needs for proper evaluation. The final article in this book, by Biles, addresses this issue. Biles presents the components of an integrated PHRM audit. Following a definition of what an audit is all about, he suggests three levels of analysis for its conduct: strategic, managerial and operational. To illustrate these analytical frameworks, Biles suggests a model for auditing PHRM functional areas. The various steps in this model are described in a sequential order.

32. Career Planning and Relocation Counselling: An Emerging Personnel Function

Murray Axmith

Barbara Moses

Introduction

Organizational support for career planning—whether to assist employees in their successful relocation to a new job after termination, or to help in managing their careers within the organization—is a relatively new development on the Canadian corporate scene. Relocation counselling for terminated employees is hardly a decade old in Canada. Internal employee career planning programs, in most organizations, are an even newer phenomenon. Both reflect similar trends in our society.

Traditionally, rather than supporting employees in planning out their own careers, organizations have imposed plans for the individual's development from above. As long as a job was regarded as a life-long career, and as long as advancement came rapidly, employees were prepared to acquiesce to this situation.

Murray Axmith is president of Murray Axmith and Associates, a Canadian management consulting group specializing in providing career transition services on behalf of corporate clients.

Barbara Moses is president of BBM Human Resource Consultants Inc., a firm specializing in career development in organizations.

Economic and technological change, however, have spelled the end of the life-long career. Slow economic growth, demographic change, and frequent organizational restructuring exercises have led to an escalating rate of white-collar terminations. The same trends have reduced opportunities for advancement for those who remain employed, making them restless at their lack of progress, and insecure about the future.

The development of the relocation counselling function over the past decade has assisted organizations in handling terminations more effectively. Similarly, employee career planning programs are now being utilized to help organizations to improve morale and productivity. In this article, we explore the major issues and trends in these emerging personnel functions.

Relocation Counselling

The development of relocation counselling (or outplacement) can be traced to the founding of THinc. in New York City in 1968. While there had been companies which offered career planning and job search assistance before this, they provided these services almost exclusively to individuals at the individual's own expense. THinc. dealt only with organizations, who would retain its services on behalf of terminated employees. Moreover, THinc. also consulted extensively to the organization on the handling of the termination.

The same concept arrived in Canada in the early 1970s. The nonprofit 40+ group was one pioneer, building up a small corporate clientele while also offering services directly to individuals. Similarly, a number of general management consulting firms began to offer limited relocation or dehiring services. Typically this would involve an executive recruiter switching hats to spend one or two sessions, billed for at an hourly rate, "helping X put his resume together" and "giving some tips on job interviews." There was rarely any career planning, consultation on handling the termination, or follow-up on the individual's success in finding new employment.

Soon afterwards, the first full-fledged services in the field emerged. Murray Axmith & Associates, a firm specializing in relocation counselling was established in 1975, while Thorne Stevenson Kellogg, a large general management consulting firm, set up its relocation unit in 1976. Others would soon follow.

Like THinc., these firms offered extensive consulting with the client organization prior to the termination, as well as in-depth career planning assistance and job search support for the individual. Counselling was on a one-to-one basis, continuing until the individual relocated successfully. The service was billed to the organization on a flat-fee basis, based upon the individual's salary prior to termination.

Organizations made use of these services for both idealistic and pragmatic reasons. There was a recognition that money alone was not enough to ease the trauma of termination, and that individuals would also benefit from help in re-establishing their careers. There would also be a positive impact on the organization's image, internally as well as externally—since the way in which a termination is handled can have a powerful impact on the morale of the survivors.

At the same time, there was growing concern about the increase in wrongful dismissal suits, tying up managers in court and undermining the public image. These suits were often sparked as much by the individual's anger at how he or she had been treated as by dissatisfaction with the monetary settlement. Offering relocation counselling helped to defuse that anger and to reduce the danger of litigation. Moreover, if there was conflict over the severance pay, the individual with counselling assistance would usually relocate more rapidly—reducing the company's liability in the eventual court case.

Providing unlimited assistance to the individual was a Cadillac service model. Typically companies reserved it for long-serving employees to whom they felt most responsibility, and for those likely to have most difficulty in relocating. Prior to the recession of 1981–82, it was usually the older, more senior and most highly paid ($40,000–100,000) individuals who were thought to most need assistance, since there were fewer openings at the upper end of the job market.

Less expensive services aimed at more junior employees did begin to emerge in the late 1970s, including limited-time individual counselling, group relocation, and the training of corporate human resources staff to provide internal counselling assistance in the case of large-scale layoffs. However, these services were not of major significance until the recession of 1981–82, which proved in many ways to be a watershed in the relocation counselling field.

In the worst recession since the Depression, there was a tremendous increase in the level of terminations, including major downsizing exercises affecting employees at all levels. At the same time, of course, hiring freezes were almost universal. For individuals receiving full-service relocation counselling at Murray Axmith & Associates the amount of time required to find a new position climbed from an average of 4.8 months to as high as 8 months. (It has since declined to 6.5 months, still above the prerecessionary low.) Similarly, where seventy-five percent had once found a job paying as well or better than the one they had lost this fell sharply to sixty percent. (It has since risen to sixty-five percent.) Obviously the situation was more difficult still for those without relocation assistance.

Individual counselling services for senior employees grew during the recession to the point where some sixty percent of the largest five hundred companies now use them on at least an occasional basis. At the same time, as organizations recognized that more junior staff were also facing a very difficult job market, there was a great expansion in group programs and the setting up of internal relocation services.

The recession also saw widespread voluntary attrition programs, aiming to cut manpower through financial inducements to older employees to take early retirement. In some cases, organizations offered preretirement counselling assistance to individuals to help them make the decision on whether or not to retire. Counselling continued for those who did go, assisting either in finding new full- or part-time employment or in making the transition to retirement.

Retirement counselling, on an individual or group basis, has since become a rapidly developing career transition service and part of an overall broadening of services in the relocation counselling field. The forthcoming end of mandatory retirement will no doubt stimulate further development in this area.

Although the 1981–82 recession is now behind us, there has been no return to the former status quo in the Canadian managerial/professional job market. Determined to remain lean and competitive, corporations have become very selective about hiring. Preoccupied with cost controls, many are continuing to reorganize and to downsize, making further manpower cuts where necessary. Even those companies expanding, or growing in new directions, are now much quicker to replace individuals whose skills no longer match their requirements. Moreover, growing concern about deficits has led public sector organizations to make cuts of unprecedented scope, helping to legitimize existing private sector practices.

There is also a new determination to weed out marginal performers as soon as possible. This trend will gain additional momentum with the end of mandatory retirement. Corporations will terminate marginal performers well before normal retirement age to avoid being seen as discriminating on the basis of age.

Current Trends in Relocation Counselling

Most forecasts suggest that jobs will continue to be eliminated in both the private and public sectors as organizations become less labor intensive, turning to new technology to remain competitive. Many are also striving to become more responsive to market conditions by flattening out hierarchies, reducing the number of middle management positions between senior management and line personnel.

As always, some new jobs will be created as old ones are being eliminated, but they are likely to require different skills then those possessed by the individuals being displaced. According to some predictions, unemployment levels will reach forty percent by the year 2000.

Obviously, all this will add up to an extremely difficult job market. Relocation specialists as well as job seekers will have to adjust to some major challenges, including the following.

Growing Importance of the Small Business Sector. In the past decade, seventy-five to eighty percent of all new jobs in Canada have been created by companies employing less than twenty people. As larger companies continue to downsize and reorganize, many more job seekers will have to adjust their expectations downwards to seek employment in smaller companies at a lower base salary (although possibly with profit sharing and equity incentives) and without the support of a large corporate bureaucracy in doing their work.

Shift to Contract Work. In a rapidly changing economic environment, many companies will prefer to employ individuals on short-term employment contracts. This trend will gain further momentum with the lifting of mandatory retirement, which will make companies even more cautious about employing more senior employees on a full-time basis.

Growing Interest in Entrepreneurship. With corporate opportunities diminishing, more terminated individuals will be drawn to the idea of starting their own business.

For Some It Will Be "Mission Impossible". Some individuals will find opportunities to further their career completely closed off and will have to find satisfaction and purpose through other activities.

To meet these challenges, relocation counselling firms will have to develop entirely new programs to help individuals:

—Identify their potential for retraining for other career paths

—Prepare for seeking employment in smaller companies, or for working on a short-term contract basis

—Assess their ability to work in their own business, and prepare themselves to make that transition

—Develop meaningful alternatives to work, where necessary

—Become more flexible and adaptable, developing attitudes and expectations which increase their employability in a rapidly changing job market.

Until now, relocation counsellors have typically had either applied behavioural science training or substantial business experience. It has always been preferable, of course, for the same person to have both those qualities. In meeting these future challenges, such a combination is likely to become almost mandatory.

Career Planning in Organizations

Career planning is the process through which individuals frame and set out to achieve meaningful realistic career goals. Traditionally, organizations have done little to encourage employees in such planning. Those in obvious career distress might be referred to someone in personnel to have a talk, or sent for testing by an industrial psychologist. Otherwise, the subject might come up in passing during the performance appraisal process, where the manager might ask, "Where do you see yourself in five years?" and note down the answer.

For the most part, where companies did talk about career planning they were talking about succession or human resources planning, through which management estimated individual potential to fill future slots. As long as they were able to motivate employees through the prospect of promotion, few organizations felt a need to do more than this.

Today, however, many managers and professionals are experiencing restricted opportunities for advancement. The maturing of the post-war Baby Boom generation is creating too many qualified contenders for too few jobs at a time when many organizations are restructuring to reflect slower economic growth. As a result, employees are plateauing—reaching the level in their organizations from which further progress becomes unlikely—at an earlier age and stage in their careers.

Employee opinion surveys consistently show widespread concern about careers. Employees want their organizations to provide support for their individual career planning activities, information about other jobs in the organization, and the training and development experiences they require to achieve their goals.

At the same time, organizations have begun to recognize that providing career planning assistance to their employees can assist in keeping employees motivated and productive in a situation of restricted opportunities for advancement.

Career planning brings employees' aspirations and concerns into the open, and helps them deal with them in a constructive way. It assists individuals in matching up their skills, interests, and goals with the opportunities that are *realistically* available to them, in terms of both their skills and potential, and the needs and requirements of the organization. This helps employees in understanding better the new realities of organizational life, focusing on both the opportunities and the potential restraints.

At the same time, a career planning program can help improve employee morale in the face of limited career opportunities by emphasizing that *up is not the only direction*, and that career goals can take many forms (e.g., lateral moves, skill acquisition, job enrichment, etc.). Stressing these alternatives to upward mobility is similarly valuable in renewing or improving the plateaued mid-career employee's enthusiasm and motivation to perform effectively.

Career planning also supports performance management programs. The employee gains a new appreciation of the links between performance, skills, jobs and organizational requirements, and advancement. The manager gains the opportunity to offer feedback on areas of strength and weakness in a clearly supportive way, outside the emotionally loaded atmosphere of the performance review process.

Moreover, when employees are encouraged to identify and carefully articulate their interests, skills, goals, and developmental requirements to their managers, the organization gains an important new vehicle for capturing information. This information can be used in a broad range of human resource planning and development activities, including succession planning, to achieve better utilization of human resources now and in the future and to ensure a continuing supply of qualified candidates for future job positions.

A career planning program also assists an organization in demonstrating its commitment to equity initiatives and helps in meeting that commitment by assisting in better mobilizing all its human resources. Organizations with a large female work force, such as those in the financial services sector, have been among the leaders in introducing career planning programs.

Current Trends in Organizational Career Planning

As organizational career planning programs have grown in both size and sophistication, a number of trends have emerged.

Changing Methods of Implementation. Individual career counselling, although valuable in special situations, is rarely a viable option for a broad-based career development program due both to cost and the limited availability of professional resources. Instead organizations are using such tools as *career planning workshops* and *self-study career planning workbooks*.

Workshops have the built-in advantage of bringing together individuals from different parts of the organization, providing the opportunity for them to learn about jobs and work climates outside their own department. There are also some employees, particularly at more junior levels, who prefer the high degree of structure imposed by a workshop format.

However, although less costly than counselling, a workshop is still quite expensive in terms of taking employees away from their work. Moreover, it is a slow and inefficient method for spreading career planning, particularly through a large and geographically dispersed organization.

There are other difficulties with a workshop approach. It can be ineffective for individuals reluctant to discuss their personal career interests in a large group—especially with individuals who may be competing with them for the same jobs in the future. It is also inflexible, to the extent that it requires all participants to work on the same issues for the same amount of time. People can have different career interests, depending on their age, the stage of career development they have reached, and other factors. Allowing them to pursue their own needs and interests from a larger menu of offerings may be more effective.

Self-study career planning workbooks, permitting a self-guided and self-paced approach, are becoming an increasingly popular alternative to workshops. More cost effective than workshops, this approach can also be more effective overall by allowing individuals to choose the exercises most appropriate to their own concerns—whether in assessing strengths and weaknesses, defining ideal work setting, clarifying values, or whatever else—and work through them at their own speed.

Where employees do require a higher degree of structure, as may be the case with more junior employees, elements of the two approaches can be combined by having employees meet regularly in leaderless groups to discuss their progress in completing the self-study exercises.

Supporting the Manager. As well as providing tools to assist individuals, organizations are also giving increased support to managers in carrying out their role in the career planning process.

Typically, it is the manager's responsibility to hold regular career discussions with employees to assist them in defining their strengths, weaknesses, developmental requirements, and potential opportunities within the organization. This need not be a difficult assignment if employees have the tools to do the preliminary work of self-assessment and research for themselves, and are therefore able to clearly articulate their interests, skills, and developmental requirements. With the onus on the employee to move the discussion forward, the manager's role is primarily reactive, responding to the employee's well-framed questions rather than working to draw them out.

To prepare managers for this role, organizations typically provide written guidelines on achieving open and effective communication in the career discussion—listening effectively, giving constructive feedback, and so on—as well as some questions that employees are likely to ask.

These guidelines may be supplemented with coaching and counselling skills workshops, which also offer managers the opportunity to work on planning their own careers. This helps them to understand the process employees are going through, and increases their own interest in and commitment to the process.

Broadening in Target Population. Rather than reserving career planning assistance for managerial/professional staff, a growing number of organizations are extending it to more junior white-collar staff, and in some cases to blue-collar staff as well.

Customization of Materials to Different Employee Groups. In spreading career planning through an organization, materials are now increasingly customized to the requirements of different employee groups (e.g., secretarial/administrative staff) in terms of language used and job examples, although the overall architecture may be quite similar.

Use of Career Planning to Encourage Voluntary Attrition. Just as preretirement counselling can help older employees in making the decision to retire early, career planning assistance for younger employees can help organizations in meeting downsizing goals. Once they have completed a thorough assessment of themselves and of the opportunities available to them, employees who are dissatisfied with their career prospects may decide to move on.

Conclusion

Although a relatively recent development on the Canadian corporate scene, the provision of relocation counselling to terminated employees has already entered the realm of best practices for personnel practitioners. The provision of career planning assistance to current employees is now following a similar evolutionary path. Both represent creative responses on the part of organizations to economic, social, and technological change. Both are personnel practices which clearly benefit the organization as well as the individual employee.

33. The Applicability of Theory Z in Canada: Implications for the Human Resource Function

Alfred M. Jaeger, McGill University

Management books which provided approaches for meeting the competitive challenge of Japanese firms gained immense popularity in North America and around the world in the early 1980s. One of the most popular and widely discussed was a book which directly compared American and Japanese organizational models and introduced an alternative American model of organization whose characteristics resembled those of Japanese firms, but which was nevertheless decidedly home grown. This model was dubbed the Type Z organization and was popularized in the best selling book by William G. Ouchi, *Theory Z: How American Business Can Meet the Japanese Challenge* (1981).

This article will examine the Theory Z approach, keeping two objectives in mind which directly address the subject of this text: evaluating the appropriateness of this model for Canada, and drawing out any general lessons for the management of human resources. To do this, the analysis will proceed as follows. First we will review the characteristics of the Type Z organization and examine the factors which contribute to its success in certain situations in its country of origin, the United States. Then we will look at how these factors differ, if at all, in Canada. Third, we will review the evidence of the success of Type Z or Type Z-like firms in Canada. Finally, we will discuss the general implications of the Type Z model for the management of human resources.

WHAT IS THEORY Z?

Theory Z is not really a theory in the true sense (nor are Theory X and Theory Y theories in the true sense either), but rather it is an approach to the management of the large organization. It is based on an organizational ideal type (ideal in the Weberian sense): the Type Z organization. The Type Z organization is described in terms of seven dimensions which are used to differentiate it from the Japanese organization and the traditional American organization (Ouchi and Jaeger 1978). Most of these dimensions are human resource related. The seven dimensions are length of employment, type of decision making, locus of responsibility, speed of evaluation and promotion, type of control, specialization of career path and type of concern for employee.

The specific characterisitics of the Type Z organization are as follows:

—— Long-term employment
—— Consensual decision making
—— Individual responsibility
—— Slow evaluation and promotion
—— Implicit informal control, with explicit formalized measures
—— Moderately specialized career paths
—— Holistic concern, including family

These factors are not independent of one another, but rather form a configuration (Miller and Mintzberg 1983) which is a logical whole of self-reinforcing characteristics. The Type Z organization is founded on long-term employment, i.e., a no layoff policy, which means that in general the average tenure of individuals in Type Z firms is relatively high. The prospect of long-term employment allows the firm to take its time in evaluation and promotion of employees leading to better promotions, and to employees with greater company experience being in more responsible positions. Moving employees through the firm in moderately specialized career paths creates information networks within the organization which become useful for coordination and integration of organizational activities.

All of the aforementioned factors are related to a strong organization-wide culture which is the basis for control in a Type Z organization (Ouchi 1981; Jaeger 1983). This culture is made possible by the prospect of long-term employment, is reinforced through consensual decision making and moderately specialized career paths, and is manifested in implicit informal control, which can at times be likened to social pressure.

It is the fact that Type Z organizations have an integrated culture, care for their employees, and involve them in organizational life which results in a high degree of commitment and motivation in the carrying out of the organization's activities. This, in turn, is seen as being responsible for the success of well-known Type Z organizations such as IBM, Hewlett-Packard, and Eastman Kodak.

The Type Z organization is not without certain characteristics which in some situations can be potentially serious faults. The most important of these are all related to the fact that the organization has a strong organizational culture. A culture implies or requires a certain homogeneity of values. For organizations in the main stream of economic activity, these values can be expected to generally reflect the culture surrounding the organization. Thus, there may be a problem of integrating ethnic minorities or outgroups into the organization. They may therefore be left out, not deliberately, but by default. (A preliminary study has shown a much greater ethnic mix at the managerial level in a traditional American organization which was compared with a well-known Type Z firm [Jaeger 1984]). Another potential problem is the relationship of Type Z firms to unions (Jaeger 1982). The Type Z firms resemble very closely the nonunion firms described by Foulkes (1981). This is not surprising as a union would be competing for the loyalty of the organization's employees as well as most likely providing a competing set of values which could undermine the organization's culture. Of those Type Z organizations with which the author is familiar, few have unions. Of those which do, they generally are company unions which are more likely to reflect and actually be a part of the organization's culture. A final potential problem with Type Z organizations is that in a traditional context they will be actively transmitting a culture of foreign origin into a third country (Jaeger 1983). This culture does carry with it many management orientations which may be particularly useful in developing countries. Nevertheless, the accompanying value orientation may be undesirable from a nationalistic point of view. This effect is more obvious in developing countries, but more subtle and difficult to evaluate in the case of United States Type Z firms operating in Canada.

SITUATIONS WHERE TYPE Z ORGANIZATIONS ARE SUCCESSFUL

Although well known Type Z organizations such as Hewlett-Packard, IBM, and Eastman Kodak are successful in the United States and around the world, one would suspect that this form of inclusive organization would not necessarily be popular in the United States, a nation where individualism is valued very highly (Hofstede 1980). In fact, this was one of the major questions which this author had when the typology was developed, based on knowledge of actual organizations. The dilemma was resolved by looking at the needs which a Type Z organization filled in the lives of its members, and thus making it more attractive than the traditional type of formal organization. The main potential attraction of the Type Z organization is that it provides its members with a source of affiliation through its more integrated culture and concern for the individual as a whole. This, however, may not be a positive aspect for all and probably only for a minority. Ouchi and Jaeger (1978) hypothesized that the Type Z organization would be appropriate for individuals who had a low level of affiliation outside of the organization and thus whose needs for affiliation would not be met in their off-work activities. Examples of such people would be ones whose family ties had weakened, either through geographical separation or family break-up, or persons who were not affiliated with outside organizations, such as the traditional church or service club. This type of environment seemed to describe California and could probably describe other locales as well, due to the relatively high rate of mobility in the United States.

An important internal factor which contributes to the success of a Type Z organization is the presence of a relatively continuous and stable leadership. Often, as in the case of IBM or Hewlett-Packard for example, the founder or founders remain with the organization and have instilled their values in the firms, as well as having provided the necessary sense of continuity for these values to survive over time.

A final outside factor, probably due to choices made by the leadership, but necessary for the maintenance of a Type Z culture, is that Type Z organizations generally operate in relatively noncyclical markets so that employment stability can be maintained. Where the market is not so stable, but where the firm should logically operate, differentiation strategies such as IBM's reputation for service or Hewlett-Packard's reputation for quality generally protect the firm in the part of the market it serves.

Several internal factors and practices also contribute to the maintenance of a Type Z organization in the United States. In contrast to a more traditional western organization and based more on the bureaucratic model, a Type Z organization generally must place more emphasis on two aspects of human resource management: selection and training of employees. Selection is very important in the Type Z organization as it must find organization members who are receptive to the particular values of the organization as well as the particular type of environment which a Type Z firm provides. As membership in the Type Z organization requires acceptance of specific organizational values, the selection process must pay attention to these as well as the specific technical requirements of a position (Jaeger 1983).

Training also becomes more important in the Type Z organization. Given the strong culture of the organization, the need for socialization is great. Although the values of the organization are often reflected in statements of company philosophy (Ouchi 1981), and socialization occurs naturally as employees move through the organization, explicit socialization also takes place as part of the human resource function. This can range from new employee orientation meetings and the circulation of company newsletters to regular meetings of all international employees for the purposes of reinforcing values and establishing and maintaining interpersonal contacts (Jaeger 1983).

In addition, a Type Z organization can transfer its culture overseas into what might be considered a relatively hostile cultural environment. In a study comparing the operations of an American Type Z firm and a more traditional American firm in Brazil, Jaeger (1983) confirmed a greater cultural similarity between the headquarters and subsidiary of the Type Z firm and documented the process by which this occurs. The Type Z firm invested a substantial amount of resources in maintaining personal contact with the subsidiary and socializing employees both at the subsidiary and headquarters levels. Thus visits of employees to the headquarters and the subsidiary were frequent. Subsidiary employees regularly spent time at the headquarters, to the point of even living and working at the headquarters with their families for periods of up to nine months. All of this was reinforced at the subsidiary level by the adoption of many of the rites and rituals practised at the headquarters.

IMPLICATIONS FOR HUMAN RESOURCE MANAGEMENT IN CANADA

What does all of this mean for human resource management in Canada? First, we can look at the Canadian situation and see whether it seems to be appropriate for Type Z firms. Then we can examine the implications for human resource management in this context.

In the earlier section which discussed the factors that facilitated the Type Z firms in the United States and elsewhere (there has been little, if any, systematic research on Type Z firms in Canada), two main themes emerged:

——The Type Z firm is more appropriate for certain demographic groups as well as certain industries.

——With an investment of resources, a Type Z culture can be transmitted to and maintained in a foreign culture.

Looking at the situational factors which favour a Type Z firm and comparing them to the Canadian situation, a mixed picture emerges. In comparison to the United States, one might even say that overall the conditions are less favourable. For example, Canada has been characterized as a cultural mosaic, meaning that the various ethnic groups tend to maintain their original cultural identities, a force which would work against the trend toward the homogenization of values in Type Z firms. Futhermore, Canadians seem generally to be less geographically mobile than Americans and thus would be more likely to have maintained family and social ties. Therefore, the need for affiliation and belonging which a Type Z firm could fulfill would be less salient. In fact, in such a situation, membership in a Type Z firm could cause what Ouchi and Jaeger (1978) have termed "affiliation overload." One could speculate, all other things being equal, that a Type Z firm would be more welcome to Canadians who had moved west and had no local social ties and thus would be needing the type of affiliation provided by a Type Z environment.

Another potential factor which would inhibit a Type Z firm would be the relatively high degree of unionization of the Canadian labour force (I. R. Centre, Queen's University 1985). As was pointed out earlier, a union is a competing factor for employees loyalty. In fact, most Japanese firms locating in the United States have chosen geographical areas where union activity is minimal, principally in the South and Southwest. No such comparable region exists in Canada.

In spite of the foregoing somewhat negative assessment of the overall appropriateness of the Type Z organizational form in Canada, there are other indications that there are numerous examples of Type Z-like firms operating successfully in Canada. The most obvious ones, of course, are the subsidiaries of American Type Z firms which are well established in Canada. In comparison to these firms' subsidiaries outside North America, one would expect the transplanting of a Z culture to Canada to be much simpler, akin often to the establishment of a domestic United States operation.

Another indication of successful Type Z-like firms in Canada emerges from a study of excellent firms by McKinsey & Company (Financial Post 1981). This was a companion study to the one which was the basis for the world wide best seller, *In Search of Excellence* (Peters and Waterman 1983). This study describes the characteristics and histories of thirty Canadian firms which are considered exemplary, such as Canadian Tire and Northern Telecom. The characteristics of such firms are very similar to those of the Type Z firm, including a strong organizational culture, employment stability, continuity of leadership, as well as promotion from within and a generally high concern for employees. Thus one can see that a home grown Type Z concept has also taken hold in some firms in Canada.

What are the lessons for human resource management which arise out of the preceding discussion? The main ones are related to the policy of long-term employment and the presence of a strong organizational culture in a Type Z firm. These are seen as the bases of the competitive strength of the Type Z firm which is founded in greater commitment of employees, a more integrated organizational system and a greater shared base of knowledge and experience. In such an organization, the human resource function becomes very important as the firm can and does pay more attention to the selection and training of its human resources. Furthermore, the firm can invest more in its human resources through more extensive training with less fear that this investment will move on to another firm.

One potential danger which a Type Z organization faces is that due to its strong internal culture it may become isolated from the outside world which in turn would affect its competitiveness (Jaeger and Baliga 1985). Therefore, another role for the human resource function to play would be to help maintain a balance in all forms of socialization between the propogation of internal values and an openness to ideas from outside.

Overall, one can say that in a Type Z firm the human resource function becomes very important because around it revolves the maintenance of the glue which holds the organization together, the organizational culture. In the Canadian context, the human resource manager in a Type Z firm may face a greater challenge than a United States counterpart in helping the organization to find the type of employees who will fit in, and in providing to these employees an environment which meets their needs.

References

Foulkes, F. M. 1981. How top non-union companies manage their employees. *Harvard Business Review* (Sept.–Oct.): 90–96.

Hofstede, G. 1980. *Culture's consequences.* Beverly Hills, CA: Sage Publications.

Industrial Relations Centre, Queen's University. 1985. *The current industrial relations scene, 1985.* Kingston, ON.

Jaeger, A. M. 1982. Contrasting control modes in the multinational corporation theory, practice, and implications. *International Studies of Management and Organization* 12(1): 59–82.

Jaeger, A. M. 1983. The transfer of organizational culture overseas: An approach to control in the multinational corporation. *Journal of International Business Studies* 14(2): 91–114.

Jaeger, A. M. 1984. Organizational culture and control: An empirical investigation. Working Paper, Montreal: McGill University Faculty of Management.

Jaeger, A. M. and B. R. Baliga. 1985. Control systems and strategic adaptation: Lessons from the Japanese experience. *Strategic Management Journal* 6(2): 115–34.

Miller, D. and H. Mintzberg. 1983. "The case for configuration." In *Beyond Method: Strategies for Social Research*, edited by G. Morgan, 57–73. Beverly Hills, CA: Sage Publications.

Ouchi, W. G. 1981. *Theory Z: How American business can meet the Japanese challenge.* Reading, MA: Addison Wesley.

Ouchi, W. G. and A. M. Jaeger. 1978. Type Z organization: Stability in the midst of mobility. *Academy of Management Review* 3(2): 305–14.

Peters, T. J. and R. H. Waterman, Jr. 1983. *In search of excellence: Lessons from America's best run companies.* New York: Harper and Row.

Visions help focus companies. 1981. The Financial Post, June 6. Toronto, ON.

34. Maximizing Use of Human Resource Information Systems (HRIS)

Edward B. Harvey, University of Toronto

John H. Blakely, Cornell University

INTRODUCTION

While popular management strategy books encourage a "bias for action" in managerial decision making, the underlying—and often neglected—assumption is that the best possible information is readily available and applied to the decisions at hand. This is no less true for critical programming and policy decisions that concern human resources. Yet, information gathering and processing has traditionally been costly and sporadic and intended to address narrowly defined, decision-making problems. Indeed, human resource information systems (HRIS) have greatly expanded the delivery of routine personnel activities, but their mandates still are often narrowly defined and inflexible in terms of their application to critical human resource programming and policy decisions.

This paper discusses ways of maximizing the use of a company's HRIS by presenting several applications to human resource programming and policy decisions and evaluation. First a discussion of some basic data system requirements is presented. While these requirements are applicable to most HRIS's, they are discussed in terms of their specific uses for program and policy decision making. This is followed by policy/planning uses of the HRIS in four areas: organizational demographics, planning and analysis, employment equity planning and monitoring, scenario building (projecting the effects of alternative policy options), productivity analysis, and program evaluation. The next section discusses the use of external data sources. The final section offers some concluding observations.

DATA SYSTEM REQUIREMENTS

There is a growing literature on how to set up an HRIS, the recommended major data categories and elements, and the nature and format of the data outputs (Walker 1982a, 1982b; Bassett 1976; Heneman, Schwab, Fossum, and Dyer 1983). A basic structure for an HRIS is presented in Exhibit 34-1. Moreover, these sources provide useful guidelines on which data elements are likely to appear in an HRIS.[1] In general, these deci-

Exhibit 34-1 Elements of an HRIS

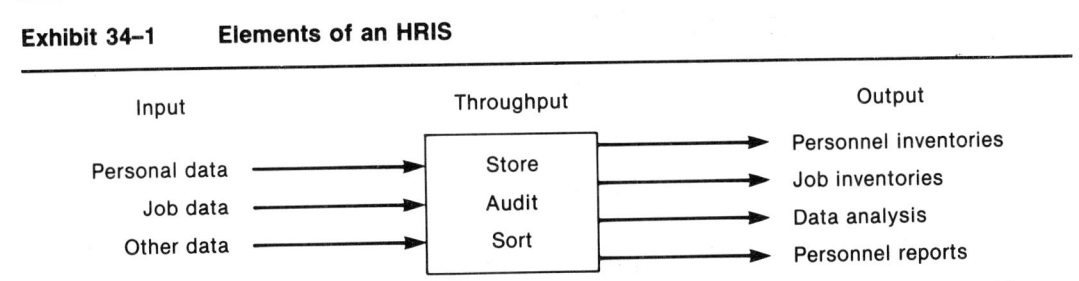

Input	Throughput	Output
Personal data →	Store	→ Personnel inventories
Job data →	Audit	→ Job inventories
Other data →	Sort	→ Data analysis
		→ Personnel reports

Source: H. G. Heneman, D. P. Schwab, J. A. Fossum and L. D. Dyer "*Personnel and Human Resource Management*" 3rd ed. © 1986 p. 212. Reprinted with Permission of Richard D. Irwin Inc.

sions are centered on information which managers and outside agencies must have and additional useful information that may be included if space and data collection costs permit. However, the distinction between essential and desirable capabilities is partly determined by the employer's commitment to programming and policy analysis. Assuming that this commitment exists, the following data system requirements appear to be especially important.

Assured Historical Continuity of Data Elements. An important policy/programming use of an HRIS is the ability to evaluate changes in relevant measures over time. However, over time, such data elements as performance rating, job or salary classification, or even health/safety/accident data are subject to change due to changes in definition of the data elements. For example, a job classification system may be altered by technological changes or job redesign or certain types of grievances or minor accidents may be more or less likely to be recorded due to changes in reporting procedures. While these structural and procedural changes will always occur in dynamic organizations, it is equally important that what is measured remains comparable over time. They can be achieved by ensuring that changes in structures or reporting procedures are defined in terms of what they replace so that equivalent states can be defined for the pre-and post-change periods.

Open Space So New Data Elements Can Be Added Later. The realities of changing organization in changing product and regulatory environments demonstrate the need for open space so that unanticipated needs can be accommodated. The expected passage of Bill C–62, which requires employers that come under the Canada Labour Code and federal contractors to develop employment equity plans and report to a public monitoring body, is an example of a regulatory change that has created new data needs for visible minority status and disability. Some evidence reported by the Abella Commission (1984) suggests that even some sophisticated employers were unable to add new data elements in light of the proposed employment equity changes. Instead, they were faced with the need to extensively overhaul their HRIS's.

Ability to Track Over Time Specific Combinations of Individuals (e.g., all female clerical workers in a given department). This is critical for analysis for human resource and employment equity planning (Milkovich 1978; Niehaus 1979). The implications are that key data elements on individuals should not necessarily be purged when they move into a different state. This requirement implies that employers are able to cross tabulate information on groups of individuals in one time period with information on the same individuals in a future or past time period so that questions about how shares of promotion opportunities, pay increases, layoffs, and turnovers are allocated across groups can be answered.

Ability to Compare Data System Outputs with Other Data Sources, Such as Census Information on the External Availability of Workers, Information on Applicants, or Other Internal Data Bases. In terms of other internal data bases, there is often a tendency for other departments (e.g., finance) to make their own information system investments without explicit consideration of the implications of the decisions on other HRIS activities. This can seriously impair the HRIS's capabilities for policy analysis on critical pay or job classification variables, or on evaluating changes over time. In terms of external data bases, external availability analysis and employment equity reporting are proceeding on the basis of a job classification system that has been defined in terms of the *Canadian Classification and Dictionary of Occupations* (see following discussion). This facilitates—and to some extent requires—the development of HRIS's that permit comparisons with external data sources.

Rules Need to Be Developed About Which Data Will Be Kept Forever. These rules may be partially mandated by external regulation (e.g., on pensions) policy and programming needs (e.g., the ability to do long-term historical time series analyses), or even by custom and habit. The basic point is that while information storage is expensive, it is almost impossible to retrieve old information that is removed from the system. This merely emphasizes that the (potential) relevance of old information must be carefully assessed by decision makers.

Interactive Access to the Data System. Experience shows that access to data (subject to necessary access and confidentiality rules) facilitates usage of the data in a wider range of applications than would otherwise be the case. This positive access can be encouraged by the use of relatively nontechnical software that operates in an interactive (as opposed to a batch) mode. A related point is that disaggregated access to the data base through departmental terminals or microcomputers should be possible. Again, this is subject to appropriate access and confidentiality rules. This disaggregated access facilitates programming and policy analysis on matters of departmental concern—for example, the setting of departmental employment equity goals, timetables and plans.

Rules Need to Be Developed With Regard to Data Access and Confidentiality. Some of the most important information for program and policy development (e.g., information on physical disabilities) can also be some of the most sensitive. Employee confidence in the HRIS is a function of the integrity of the designers and of the individuals given the responsibility to work with and interpret the data. A basic guideline is that data be unmistakably job related and controlled on a need to know basis. (Heneman et al. 1983). Unfortunately, in policy-related analysis, the need to know criterion can vary considerably from decision to decision, which in turn can complicate the policy analysis user. Partially in response to these concerns, Walker (1982b) has recommended the creation, in large organizations, of a human resources data administrator position that can reconcile competing demands on the HRIS, and ensure the integrity of security and privacy maintenance.

POLICY/PLANNING USES OF HRIS

Policy analysis is defined in an organizational context as the information gathering and processing that is undertaken in support of basic human resource decisions that set the pattern for current and future operational decisions. Examples of policy decisions could include decisions to implement employment equity programs or training programs, decisions to implement hiring freezes, early retirement programs or layoffs, decisions to recruit qualifiable people to fill anticipated employment requirements or to recruit fully qualified people to fill urgent needs, and decisions to alter salary and benefit structures. Analytical issues that may be pursued in support of these decisions include assessments of internal and external availability to establish employment equity goals and timetables, evaluation of the implications of staffing reductions on future requirements, evaluation of the training and orientation times of qualified and qualifiable recruits, and evaluation of future wage and benefit commitments in terms of current and projected work force composition.

The following sections present some specific issues and HRIS applications to policy analysis.

Organizational Demography, Planning and Analysis

Demography in an organizational context refers to the composition, in terms of basic attributes such as age, sex, educational level, length of service, race, and so forth of the organization under study (Pfeffer 1983). Even in stable organizations, these basic attributes change over time, as existing work force age experience differential turnover and/or promotion rates or increase their vocational and general educational competencies on or off the job. The ability to track these basic attributes over time will facilitate decisions in all personnel-related areas, particularly in succession planning, benefits/utilization analysis, and wage/productivity analysis.

Exhibits 34–2a and 2b illustrate some of these analytical issues in terms of a projection of the age distribution of an existing work force. This projection assumes the organization's three percent historical attrition rate and a policy decision to implement an across the board hiring freeze. The policy-related questions are: how many people (men, women, and total) would be employed after five years given historical attrition rates and a hiring freeze, and what would be the age distribution of this work force? These questions could be viewed as relevant to the evaluation of the availability of funds for future benefits payouts (in a case where net payouts were a function of seniority), to the future wage structure (in a case where wages were partly determined by seniority), and to planning to meet future skill requirements. The policy-related decisions that could be addressed by the analysis include: whether or not the proposed hiring freeze is an appropriate course of action given these expected (cost and staffing levels) outcomes and whether the proposed policy should be implemented in conjunction with policies to accelerate or decelerate the historic attrition rate, to augment or weaken the seniority basis of pay and benefit determination, or to encourage early retirement. In this case, the costs of a proposed hiring freeze might be viewed as high relative to the expected benefits, given the expected increase in the number of older workers (see Exhibit 34–2b) and its implications for future benefits and wage payments. The analysis, for example, could lead to the decision to imple-

448 INTEGRATING, TRENDS, AND COMPARISONS

Exhibit 34–2a   Age Projection of the Salaried Workforce

Years of age	1984 M	1984 F	1984 T	1985 M	1985 F	1985 T	1986 M	1986 F	1986 T	1987 M	1987 F	1987 T	1988 M	1988 F	1988 T	1989 M	1989 F	1989 T
18	0	4	4	0	0	0	0	0	0	0	0	0	0	0	0	0	0	0
19	0	3	3	0	4	4	0	0	0	0	0	0	0	0	0	0	0	0
20	5	13	18	0	3	3	0	4	4	0	0	0	0	0	0	0	0	0
21	8	21	29	5	13	18	0	3	3	0	4	4	0	0	0	0	0	0
22	10	47	57	8	20	28	5	12	17	0	4	4	0	4	4	0	0	0
23	40	51	91	10	46	56	8	20	28	5	12	17	0	3	3	0	3	3
24	73	109	182	39	49	88	9	44	53	7	19	26	4	12	16	0	3	3
25	94	80	174	71	106	177	38	48	86	9	43	52	7	19	26	4	11	15
26	111	97	208	91	78	169	69	103	172	37	47	84	9	42	51	7	18	25
27	128	79	207	108	94	202	88	75	163	67	99	166	35	45	80	8	40	48
28	120	81	207	124	77	201	105	91	196	86	73	159	65	96	161	34	44	78
29	116	72	188	122	79	201	120	74	194	102	89	191	83	71	154	63	94	157
30	141	67	208	113	70	183	118	76	194	117	72	189	99	86	185	81	69	150
31	119	46	165	137	65	202	109	68	177	115	74	189	113	70	183	96	83	179
32	105	53	158	116	45	161	133	63	196	106	66	172	111	72	183	110	68	178
33	132	52	184	102	51	153	112	43	165	129	61	190	103	64	167	108	70	178
34	103	37	140	128	50	178	99	50	149	109	42	151	125	59	184	100	62	162
35	97	29	126	100	36	136	124	49	173	96	48	146	106	41	147	121	58	179
36	110	38	148	94	28	122	97	35	132	120	47	167	93	47	136	103	40	143
37	111	34	145	107	37	144	91	27	118	94	34	128	117	46	163	90	46	136
38	65	29	94	108	33	141	103	36	139	89	26	115	91	33	124	113	45	158
39	79	26	105	63	28	91	105	32	137	100	35	135	86	26	102	88	32	120
40	73	26	99	77	25	102	61	27	88	102	31	133	97	34	131	83	25	108
41	76	14	90	71	25	96	74	24	98	59	26	85	99	30	129	94	33	127
42	69	20	89	74	14	88	69	24	93	72	24	96	58	26	84	96	29	125
43	61	21	82	67	19	86	72	13	85	67	24	91	70	23	93	56	25	81
44	74	12	86	59	20	79	65	19	84	69	13	82	65	23	88	68	22	90
45	53	18	71	72	12	84	57	20	77	63	18	81	67	13	80	63	22	85

Continued on next page

Exhibit 34-2a—Continued

Years of age	1984 M	1984 F	1984 T	1985 M	1985 F	1985 T	1986 M	1986 F	1986 T	1987 M	1987 F	1987 T	1988 M	1988 F	1988 T	1989 M	1989 F	1989 T
46	66	14	80	51	17	68	70	11	81	56	19	75	61	18	79	65	12	77
47	60	24	84	64	14	78	50	17	67	68	11	79	54	19	73	59	17	76
48	74	13	87	58	23	81	62	13	75	48	16	64	66	11	77	52	18	70
49	72	12	84	72	13	85	56	23	79	60	13	73	47	16	63	64	10	74
50	86	14	100	70	12	82	70	12	82	55	22	77	58	13	71	46	15	61
51	89	17	106	83	14	97	68	11	79	68	12	80	53	21	74	57	12	69
52	100	16	116	86	16	102	81	13	94	66	11	77	66	12	78	52	21	73
53	101	15	116	97	16	113	84	16	100	78	13	91	64	11	75	64	11	75
54	71	13	84	98	15	113	94	15	109	81	15	96	76	13	89	62	10	72
55	82	12	94	69	13	82	95	14	109	91	15	106	79	15	94	74	12	86
56	59	20	79	80	12	92	67	12	79	92	14	106	89	14	103	76	14	90
57	71	6	77	57	19	76	77	11	88	65	12	77	90	13	103	86	14	100
58	41	12	53	69	6	75	56	19	75	75	11	85	63	12	75	88	13	101
59	38	8	46	40	12	52	67	6	73	54	18	72	73	11	84	61	11	72
60	26	9	35	37	8	45	39	11	50	65	5	70	52	18	70	70	10	80
61	21	6	27	25	9	34	36	8	44	37	11	48	63	5	68	51	17	68
62	10	5	15	20	6	26	24	9	33	35	7	42	36	11	47	61	5	66
63	13	2	15	10	5	15	20	6	26	24	8	32	34	7	41	35	7	46
64	6	1	7	13	2	15	9	5	14	19	5	24	23	8	31	33	7	40
Total	3265	1398	4663	3165	1359	4524	3056	1312	4368	2957	1268	4225	2850	1233	4083	2742	1182	3924

EXHIBIT 34-2b   Age Projection of the Salaried Work Force

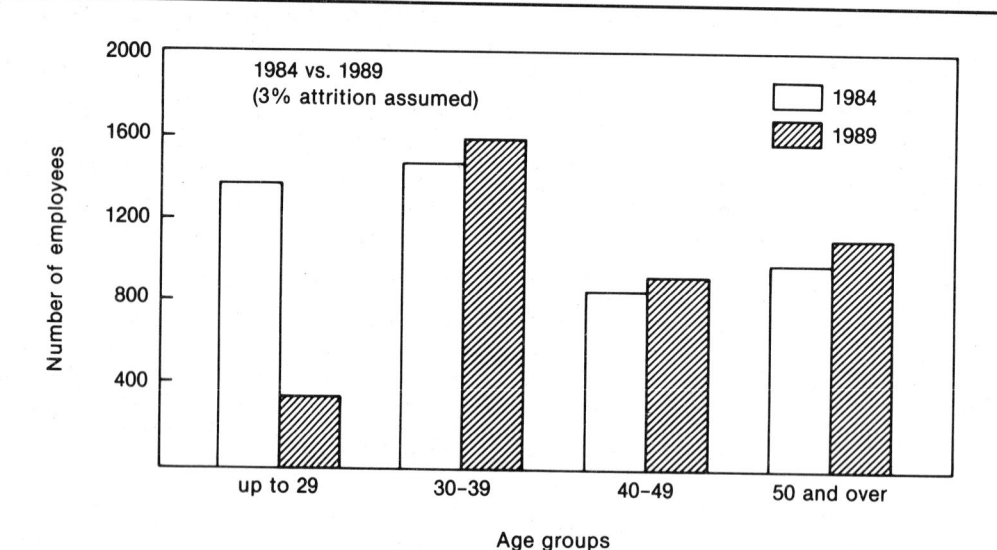

ment a shorter-term hiring freeze in conjunction with an early retirement policy.

The exhibits present the analysis in two forms. Exhibit 34-2a shows the current (1984) and projected work force broken down by year, single years of age, and sex. In turn, these results are presented in a visual format in Exhibit 34-2b. More complicated and realistic procedures could have permitted different attrition assumptions for men and for women, for different age groups, or for different years. Also, separate analyses could have been conducted for employees in different occupations, in different seniority or experience groups, or in different educational background groups.

To summarize, the primary objective of using demographic characteristics in planning and analysis is to evaluate the effects of existing or proposed programs on the basic demographic composition of the organization. We illustrated a policy analysis application in terms of an age projection, however, any basic attribute (or combination of attributes) could have been the focus of attention. The HRIS requirements for this type of analysis are that these basic attributes can be identified (as in the single-year age breakdowns in Exhibit 34-2a), and that the necessary basic computations can be performed.

Employment Equity Planning and Monitoring

Although employment equity programming for women, visible minorities, and people with disabilities can be viewed as an organizational demography problem, the array of relevant analytical techniques warrant special attention. These techniques apply both to analysis of the external labour market and to internal analysis. Moreover, they are motivated partly by proposed reporting requirements under Bill C-62, and partly by the implicit responsibility under the proposed legislation to develop employment equity plans to eliminate systemic bias.

The HRIS implications of the reporting requirements should be noted. First, information on new hires, promotions, transfers, and exits will be required for disabled people and visible minorities as well as for women (Canada Employment and Immigration Commission 1986). This raises the question of whether sensitive information on current employees should be gathered using supervisor identification or a survey of the current work force (Pearn and Ungerson 1979; Crofts 1984). Also, procedures for collecting data on new employees will often undergo evaluation and revision in light of the proposed regulations. Second, as Exhibit 34–3 (a sample reporting form) shows, the reporting requirements are based on a twelve-fold category typology of occupations. The regulations require organizations to

Exhibit 34–3   Distribution of Designated Group Employees Hired During Reporting Year

Name of Business:	Employer's Industrial Sector:	Employees' Employment Status: Permanent full-time ☐ Permanent part-time ☐ Seasonal ☐ (use separate sheet for each)						Report for Calendar Year:		
Occupational Categories	All Employees Hired			Persons with Disabilities Hired			Aboriginal Peoples Hired			Visible Minorities Hired		
	TOTAL #	M	F	TOTAL #	M	F	TOTAL #	M	F	TOTAL #	M	F
Upper level managers												
Middle and other managers												
Professionals												
Semiprofessionals & technicians												
Supervisors												
Foremen/women												
Clerical workers												
Sales workers												
Services workers												
Skilled crafts and trades workers												
Semiskilled manual workers												
Other manual workers												
TOTALS												

report promotions, transfers, and exits within and between these occupational groups. This, in turn, requires organizations to define (or redefine) their occupational classification system in terms that can be aggregated to the level of the typology. Third, the typology itself consists of aggregations of occupations defined in terms of the four digit *Canadian Classification and Dictionary of Occupations* (CCDO). The ability to disaggregate the typology in terms of the four-digit CCDO facilitates external availability analysis, since the most important external data sources report in terms of this standardized classification system.

To summarize, employment equity reporting, planning, and analysis can be supported by the HRIS: (1) if the organization's occupational classification system can be collapsed into the standardized employment equity reporting categories, and (2) if these reporting categories can then be disaggregated and re-expressed in terms of CCDO definitions. This implies that three pieces of occupational information are collected for each individual: (1) the organization's usual occupational code, (2) the employment equity code, and (3) the CCDO. Moreover, this implies that these three pieces of information can be linked to each other. Finally, new data on visible minority status and disability status will have to be collected on new and existing employees so that analysis can proceed.

In addition to the reporting requirements, Bill C-62 states that it is an organization's responsibility to develop employment equity plans to eliminate systemic bias. Readers should consult recent employment equity research in order to familiarize themselves with stocks, flows, availability, and utilization analyses (Phillips 1985; Harvey and Blakely 1985; Milkovich 1978). Here, it is asserted that the HRIS should be able to track the movements of individuals over time, and to present these movements into compact, readable reports.

Exhibits 34-4 (a and b) and 34-5 present the principal outputs for employment equity and planning. Exhibit 34-4a shows the numerical movements of a total work force and for males and females only. The movements that can be identified are promotions, demotions (although none are shown in this exhibit), exits (turnover), and new recruits (from outside). For example, twenty-four people were employed in job level five in period T-1; eighteen of these people are still in job level five at period T, three were promoted to level six, and three left the organization; five people were promoted into level five from level four, one person was promoted in from level three, and two people were recruited from the outside. Therefore, at period T, twenty-six people were employed in job level five.

These numerical movements are translated into transition probabilities in Exhibit 34-4b. These transition probabilities provide basic measures of the relative success of an organization's staffing policies. In this example, nine percent of women who were at level one at period T-1 moved to level two, compared with thirty-three percent of men. This diagnostic statistic would warrant further investigation to see if it reveals systemic bias in the employer's promotion policies.

Exhibit 34-5 extracts from Exhibit 34-4a useful summaries of staffing transactions that can be used to pinpoint specific problem areas. In short, while Exhibits 34-4a and 34-4b provide a framework for evaluating the organization's overall progress towards an employment equity condition, Exhibit 34-5 presents summary information for recruiters (#2), internal staffing specialists (#3), and turnover analysts (#4).

Exhibit 34-4a   Transition Matrices for a Department

Males and Females Combined
To (Period T)

Level	8	7	6	5	4	3	2	1	Exit	Total
8	3								1	4
7	1	8							2	11
6			15						1	16
5			3	18					3	28
4				5	20				5	30
3				1	2	15			5	23
2						5	35		10	50
1							10	40	20	70
From outside	0	4	0	2	8	0	5	35	—	—
Total	4	12	18	26	30	20	50	75	—	235/228

From (Period T−1)

Males Only

Level	8	7	6	5	4	3	2	1	Exit	Total
8	3								1	4
7	0	8							2	10
6			12						1	13
5			2	15					3	20
4				4	15				4	23
3				1	2	6			3	12
2						5	10		0	15
1							5	8	2	15
From outside	0	4	0	2	5	0	1	5	—	—
Total	3	12	14	22	22	11	16	13	—	113/112

Females Only

Level	8	7	6	5	4	3	2	1	Exit	Total
8	0								0	0
7	1	0							0	1
6			3						0	3
5			1	3					0	4
4				1	5				1	7
3					0	9			2	11
2						0	25		10	35
1							5	32	18	55
From outside	0	0	0	0	3	0	4	30	—	—
Total	1	0	4	4	8	9	34	62	—	122/116

Exhibit 34-4b   **Transition Probability Matrices for a Department**

Males and Females Combined
To (Period T)

	Level	8	7	6	5	4	3	2	1	Exit	Total	(N)
From (Period T−1)	8	.75								.25	1.00	(4)
	7	.09	.73							.18	1.00	(11)
	6			.94						.06	1.00	(16)
	5			.13	.75					.13	1.00	(24)
	4				.17	.67				.17	1.00	(30)
	3				.04	.09	.65			.22	1.00	(23)
	2						.10	.70		.20	1.00	(50)
	1							.14	.57	.29	1.00	(70)
	From outside		.07		.04	.15		.09	.65	—	1.00	(54)
	Total	—	—	—	—	—	—	—	—	—	—	—

Males

	Level	8	7	6	5	4	3	2	1	Exit	Total	(N)
From (Period T−1)	8	.75								.25	1.00	(4)
	7		.80							.20	1.00	(10)
	6			.92						.08	1.00	(13)
	5			.10	.75					.15	1.00	(20)
	4				.17	.65				.17	1.00	(23)
	3				.08	.17	.50			.25	1.00	(12)
	2						.33	.67		.00	1.00	(15)
	1							.33	.53	.13	1.00	(15)
	From outside		.24		.12	.29		.06	.29	—	1.00	(17)
	Total									—	—	—

Females

	Level	8	7	6	5	4	3	2	1	Exit	Total	(N)
From (Period T−1)	8	.00								.00	.00	(0)
	7	1.00	.00							.00	1.00	(1)
	6			1.00						.00	1.00	(3)
	5				.25	.75				.00	1.00	(8)
	4				.14	.71				.16	1.00	(7)
	3						.82			.18	1.00	(11)
	2							.71		.29	1.00	(35)
	1							.09	.58	.33	1.00	(55)
	From outside					.08		.11	.81	—		(37)
	Total									—	—	—

Exhibit 34–5 Stock Figures Taken from Exhibit 34–4a

1. Employment at T–1 and at T was as follows:

	Male		Female		Total	
	T–1	T	T–1	T	T–1	T
8	4	3	0	1	4	8
7	10	12	1	0	11	12
6	13	14	3	4	16	18
5	20	22	4	4	24	26
4	23	22	7	8	30	30
3	12	11	11	9	23	20
2	15	16	35	34	50	50
1	15	13	55	62	70	75
Total	112	113	116	122	228	235

2. New entrants over the period between T–1 and T are as follows:

	Male	Female	Total
8	0	0	0
7	4	0	4
6	0	0	0
5	2	0	2
4	5	3	8
3	0	0	0
2	1	4	5
1	5	30	35
Total	17	37	54

3. Number of promotions over the period between T–1 and T are as follows:

		Male	Female	Total
(TO)	8	0	1	1
	7	0	0	0
	6	2	1	3
	5	5	1	6
	4	2	0	2
	3	5	0	5
	2	5	5	10
	Total	19	8	27

4. Turnover (exits) over the period between T–1 and T are as follows:

	Male	Female	Total
8	1	0	1
7	2	0	2
6	1	0	1
5	3	0	3
4	4	1	5
3	3	2	5
2	0	10	10
1	2	18	20
Total	16	31	47

The policy analysis of the transition matrices will be made apparent by careful inspection of the exhibits. One may note the following specific sources of concern that might warrant further investigation, and possible remedies: (1) men were recruited from outside into jobs seven and five, but not women; (2) at present, there is no evidence of availability of any women to fill any future vacancies in job seven; (3) men and women flow through jobs four, five and six in roughly equal proportions, but the staffing levels for women are much lower than for men; (4) men are promoted from job three to job four or five, but not women—i.e., job three appears to be a terminal point for women, even though it is part of a longer career path for men; (5) turnover is higher for men in higher level positions and lower in lower level positions—the reverse is true for women; (6) over half of all women at time T are employed in job one compared with ten percent of all men. On the other hand, forty-five percent of men are employed in jobs five to eight, compared with seven percent of women; and (7) even though employment of women went up more than it did for men, all of this employment growth is in job one. In the good jobs (five to eight), there was very little improvement in the number of women employed.

Scenario-Building and Forecasting

The next application involves using the HRIS outputs as a basis for forecasting the effects of alternative scenarios. Exhibit 34-6, for example, shows a projection of the female share of employment by job level under two scenarios. Scenario A (projection of past trend plus three percent attrition) estimates the expected size of the female work force based upon a transition probability matrix of the share of female recruits, promotions, and turnover that occurred in the two years prior to the forecast period. Scenario B (no sex differential plus three percent attrition) estimated the expected size of the female work force based upon the assumption that men and women have equal recruitment, promotion, and turnover probabilities. While this example extends the discussion of employment equity analysis, it should be noted that forecasting the effects of alternative scenarios has a wide range of human resource planning applications in identifying future skills shortages or surpluses, career pathing, or succession planning. Policy analysis questions could include: comparing past and projected recruitment, promotion, and turnover patterns for high and low performing employees under proposed alternative incentive payment schemes; forecasting the number of fully trained employees under alternative training and recruitment programs; and projecting the distribution of the work force under alternative growth or contraction scenarios.

The analysis assumes a matrix multiplication capability, where the transition probability matrix is either derived from past trends or from assumptions about what the employer wants the transition probabilities to be. Beyond these basic forecasting capabilities there are stochastic process models in the manpow-

Exhibit 34-6   Female Share of Employment by Job Level

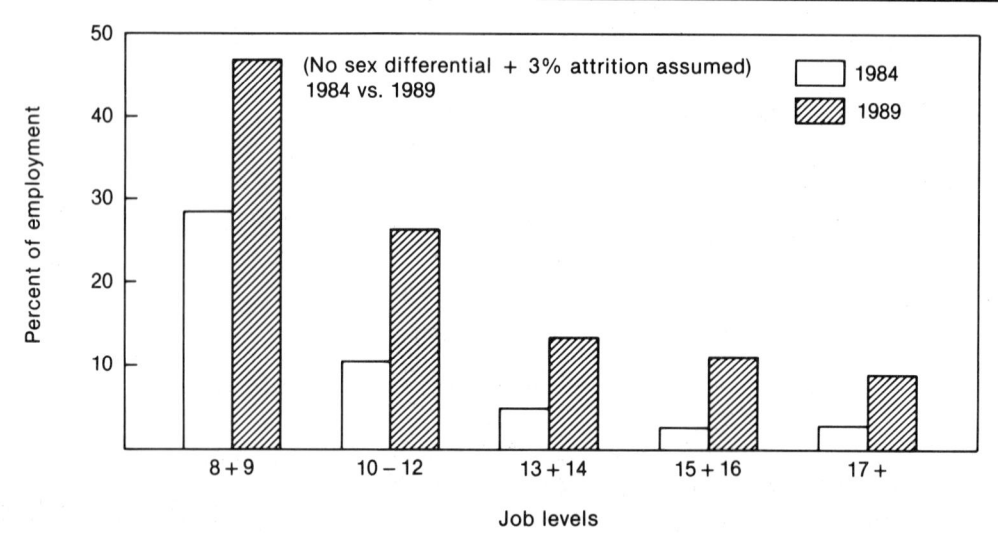

er modelling research in large organizations (Grinold and Marshall 1977) which can capture more realistic assumptions about stayers and movers in dynamic organizational settings.

Productivity Analysis and Programme Evaluation

The final application discussed in this paper involves using the HRIS for productivity analysis and program evaluation. The productivity analysis may have a strict planning application. This may be the case when changes in a valid measure of total output of a good or service are compared with changes in total employment. Given budget estimates of the costs of facilities, equipment and energy, a human resource planner may face decisions on allocating employment and compensation in ways that meet output (and profit) objectives. On the other extreme, daily output measures may be available for individual employees, and linked directly to the HRIS. This form of monitoring individual performance may be attacked on a number of grounds, not least of which is the difficulty in finding a valid output measure. Some unit effectiveness measures are presented in Exhibit 34–7 to show the range of potentially valid measures in specific organizational settings.

Exhibit 34–7   Some Measures to Assess Unit Effectiveness

ENGINEERING, RESEARCH, AND DEVELOPMENT UNIT

$$\frac{\text{Employees}}{\text{Managers}} \quad \frac{\text{Dept. Hay Points}}{\text{Secretaries}} \quad \frac{\text{Technical Staff}}{\text{Clerical Staff}}$$

$$\frac{\text{Total Unit Hours}}{\text{Routined Work Hours}}$$

$$\frac{\text{Project Hours}}{\text{Total Unit Hours}} = \text{Effectiveness}$$

$$\frac{\text{Project Hours Less Lost Time}^*}{\text{Project Hours}} = \text{Efficiency}$$

*errors, sidetracks, learning time

MATERIALS MANAGEMENT AND PRODUCTION UNIT

$$\frac{\text{Net Sales}}{\text{Dollar Purchases}} \quad \frac{\text{Dollar Purchases}}{\text{Buying Costs}} \quad \frac{\text{Buying Costs}}{\text{\# of Purchase Orders}}$$

$$\frac{\text{Total \$ Purchases}}{\text{\$ Rejected}} \quad \frac{\text{Total \$ Purchases}}{\text{\$ Value of Overdue Orders}} \quad \frac{\text{Dollar Purchases}}{\text{\# of Vendors}}$$

$$\frac{\text{Dollar Purchases}}{\text{Purchase Price Variances}} \quad \frac{\text{Cost of Goods Manufactured}}{\text{Avg. Inventory}}$$

$$\frac{\text{Costs of Goods Manufactured}}{\text{Direct Labor}} \quad \frac{\text{Cost of Goods Manufactured}}{\text{Energy}}$$

$$\frac{\text{Costs of Goods Manufactured}}{\text{Overhead Costs}} \quad \frac{\text{Direct Labor}}{\text{Total Payroll \& Benefits}}$$

Continued on next page

Exhibit 34-7—Continued

$$\frac{\text{Forklift Time}}{\text{Total Time Available}} \quad \frac{\text{Total Carload Lots}}{\text{Less Than Carload Lots}}$$

$$\frac{\text{Total Truckload Lots}}{\text{Less Than Truckload Lots}} \quad \frac{\text{Total Shipment Value}}{\text{Demurrage}}$$

$$\frac{\text{Warehouse Space Utilized}}{\text{Total Warehouse Space}} \quad \frac{\text{Costs of Goods Manufactured}}{\text{Quality Control Costs}}$$

$$\frac{\text{Direct Labor Employees}}{\text{Quality Control Employees}} \quad \frac{\text{Direct Labor Employees}}{\text{Indirect Employees}}$$

MARKETING UNIT

$$\frac{\text{Net Sales}}{\text{Base Year Net Sales}} \quad \frac{\text{Net Sales}}{\text{Marketing Costs}} \quad \frac{\text{Net Sales}}{\text{Warehouse \& Shipping}}$$

$$\frac{\text{Net Sales}}{\text{Advertising Costs}} \quad \frac{\text{Net Sales}}{\text{Selling Costs}} \quad \frac{\text{Net Sales}}{\text{Avg. Accounts Receivable}}$$

$$\frac{\text{Net Sales}}{\text{Number of Orders}} \quad \frac{\text{Net Sales}}{\text{Sales Admin. Costs}} \quad \frac{\text{Net Sales}}{\text{Direct Sales Reps.}}$$

DIRECT SELLING UNIT

$$\frac{\text{Net Sales}}{\text{Direct Selling Expenses}} \quad \frac{\text{Net Sales}}{\text{Salesman's Calls}} \quad \frac{\text{Physician Calls}}{\text{Days of Territory}}$$

ADMINISTRATIVE UNIT

$$\frac{\text{Serviced Areas Payroll \& Benefits \$'s}}{\text{Servicing Area Payroll \& Benefits \$'s}} \quad \frac{\text{Employees}}{\text{Managers}}$$

$$\frac{\text{Dept. Hay Points}}{\text{Secretaries}} \quad \frac{\text{Total Unit Hours}}{\text{Routined Work Hours}} \quad \frac{\text{Project Hours}}{\text{Total Unit Hours}}$$

$$\frac{\text{Operating Division Costs}}{\text{Administration Area Costs}} \quad \frac{\text{Recruiting Costs}}{\text{\# of New Employees}} \quad \frac{\text{Training Costs}}{\text{Avg. \# of Employees}}$$

$$\frac{\text{Employees Trained}}{\text{Training Costs}} \quad \frac{\text{Payroll Checks}}{\text{Payroll Dept. Exp.}} \quad \frac{\text{Suppliers Checks}}{\text{Payable Dept. Exp.}}$$

PERSONNEL UNIT

$$\frac{\text{Total Employees}}{\text{Personnel Employees}}$$

$$\frac{\text{Total Pay}}{\text{Personnel Dept. Pay}}$$

Source: Milkovich, Dyer and Mahoney, in H. G. Heneman III, D. P. Schwab, J. A. Fossum and L. D. Dyer *Personnel/Human Resource Management,* Third ed. (Homewood, Ill.: Richard D. Irwin Inc.), © 1986, p. 212. Used with permission.

A middle ground (between simply averaging output across a group of employees and attempting to monitor individual performance) involves using the HRIS to monitor the effects of training programs and of other productivity improvement programs on various performance measures. These performance measures might include supervisors' performance ratings (if available), direct productivity performance, or effectiveness measures. In this case, the objective is not to evaluate individual performance. Rather, it is to evaluate a program's effect on the performance trend of a group of employees so that evidence of the cost effectiveness of the program can be presented to senior management, who allocates funding across competing human resource and nonhuman resource requirements.

THE USE OF EXTERNAL DATA

While very few organizations develop formal planning models that link data from the labour market with organization-specific data, there are numerous cases where informal linking processes occur. First, employment equity planning requires assessments of availability in relevant external labour markets. This involves evaluating census and labour force survey data as well as assessments of the number of qualifiable people in vocational and educational institutions and in other occupations (Harvey and Blakely 1985). Second, an important part of human resource planning involves quantitative assessments of labour market trends so that future labour, recruitment, and training costs can be reliably predicted. Private economic forecasting agencies as well as government labour force forecasting models are available for these purposes (see R. J. Clifford and Associates 1982, for a review of these sources and their use in Canadian firms). Third, an equally important part of human resource planning involves gathering together difficult to quantify labour and product market information that suggests what the future is going to look like. This environmental scanning process can be regarded as an early warning system for identifying changes that can upset a company's best laid plans (Frantzreb 1980). In the context of the later 1980s, this includes planning for widespread skills shortages, which seem almost unthinkable in terms of current high unemployment rates—although highly probable in the near future due to demographic changes.

CONCLUSIONS

The principal conclusions of this paper are as follows: First, while company HRIS's are becoming increasingly important for routine personnel activities, they are often underutilized for policy and planning analysis. Second, seven data system requirements with particular relevance for policy and planning analysis were identified. Third, the specific policy applications are weighted toward demographic analysis, which can be relevant for employment equity planning or general human resource planning. With respect to employment equity planning, there are new data needs for visible minorities and the disabled. Moreover, new reporting regulations will require some standardization across employers in terms of occupational classification systems, and recruitment, promotion, and turnover measurement. Fourth, the other critical policy applications are in forecasting and in productivity analysis and program evaluation. Fifth, while external data are seldom formally linked to an organization's HRIS, they are critical in a number of policy analysis and planning applications and are very much a part of the policy analyst's mandate. Finally, it is reiterated that investment in the HRIS for policy analysis is not a dreaded symptom of bureaucratization in a modern, flexible organization. It is a critical tool for making the best possible decisions as quickly as possible and is, therefore, of strategic importance to the success of the organization.

Endnotes

1. See for example, the list in Heneman et al.: (1) personal data; (2) recruitment/selection data; (3) work experience data; (4) compensation data; (5) performance appraisal/promotability data; (6) attitude/morale data; (7) benefit plan data; (8) health/safety/accident data.

References

Abella, Judge R. S. 1984. *Equality in Employment: A Royal Commission Report.* Ottawa, Minister of Supply and Services Canada.

Bassett, G. A. 1976. "PAIR records and information systems." In *Planning and Auditing PAIR*, edited by D. Yoder and H. G. Heneman, 58–90. Washington: Bureau of National Affairs.

Clifford, R. J. and Associates 1982. Survey of manpower planning practices in Canada. Technical Study #7, Task Force on Labour Market Development. Ottawa: Canada Employment and Immigration Commission.

Canada. Canada Employment and Immigration Commission 1986. "Draft Regulations in Respect of Employment Equity (Bill C-62)", mimeo.

Crofts, P. 1984. Counting on monitoring for racial equality. *Personnel Management* (March): 26–30.

Frantzreb, R. B., ed. 1980. *Manpower planning* Vol. 3, #11.

Grinold, R. C. and K. T. Marshall. 1977. *Manpower Planning Models.* New York: North-Holland Publishers.

Harvey, E. B. and J. H. Blakely. 1985. "Strategies for establishing affirmative action goals and timetables." In *Equality in Employment: Research Studies*, 113–30. Ottawa: Minister of Supply and Services Canada.

Heneman, H. G., D. P. Schwab, J. A. Fossum, and L. D. Dyer, 1983. *Personnel/human resource management.* Homewood, Ill.: Irwin.

Milkovich, G. T. et al. 1983. "HRM Planning." In *Human resources management in the 1980's*, edited by S. J. Carroll and R. S. Schuler. Washington, Bureau of National Affairs.

Milkovich, G. T. 1978. "An analysis of issues related to availability." In *Perspectives on availability: A symposium on determining protected group representation in internal and external labor markets.* Washington, D.C.: Equal Employment Advisory Council.

Niehaus, R. J. 1979. *Computer assisted human resource planning.* New York: John Wiley and Sons.

Pearn, M. and B. Ungerson. 1979. Ethnic recording for racial equality. *Personnel Management* (March): 28–45.

Pfeffer, J. 1983. Organizational Demography. *Research in organizational behavior* 5:229–357.

Phillips, R. 1985. "Equity in the Labour Market: The Potential of Affirmative Action." In *Equality in Employment: Research Studies*, edited by R. S. Abella, 49–112. Ottawa: Minister of Supply and Services.

Walker, A. J. 1982a. *HRIS development.* New York: Van Nostrand Reinhold.

Walker, A. J. 1982b. The newest job in personnel: Human resources data administrator. *Personnel Journal* (December): 924–28.

35. Auditing the Effectiveness of Human Resources Management Functions

G. Biles, American University

Auditing is "... an independent appraisal activity within an organization [to] review ... operations ...."[1] A human resource management audit is a systematic, formal, and comprehensive review of the functional areas of a human resources department. These functional areas include:[2]

— Employment practices
    Human resources planning
    Job design
    Job analysis
    Recruitment
    Selection
    Placement
    Employee orientation
    Employee rights
    Communications
    Performance appraisal
— Equal employment opportunity
— Training and development
— Career development
— Organizational development
— Compensation and benefits
    Direct compensation
    Incentive pay program
    Benefits
— Employee and labour relations
    Employer-employee relations
    Negotiations
    Contract administration and grievance
— Health, safety and security
— Plant and office security
— Personnel research
— International human resources management

In order to assess whether these functional areas contribute to organizational success, human resource management effectiveness data need to be captured and analysed. Such an analysis can be made through the auditing process. A human resource management audit:

1. Assesses the current state of an organization's human resources management policies and practices
2. Defines what the state of an organization's human resource management practices should be based on a

Based on materials taken from the *Audit Handbook for Human Resource Management Practices* (Alexandria, VA: ASPA, 1986).

careful assessment of predetermined performance standards

3. Develops necessary action plans for moving from state 1. to state 2., i.e., specifies how to improve the organization's human resource management policies and practices.

A human resource management audit should respond to critical questions concerning management effectiveness:

1. Is the human resources department responsive to its external environment? That is, does top management consider that its production, marketing, servicing, financial, product, and facilities functions are being properly served by the human resource department? Do line managers perceive the human resource department as being responsive, alert, and competent in accomplishing its service-oriented mission? Does the organization's labour force perceive the employer as being fair?
2. Is the human resource department organized to accomplish its service-oriented mission effectively? Are the human resource department policies and practices integrated into strategic business planning?
3. Is the human resource department staffed by people who are competent, knowledgeable, and sensitive to collaborating with other elements of the organization to achieve strategic goals? [3]

A human resource department audit should be conducted from three analytical levels:

Strategic. The strategic level of analysis focuses on human resources practices from top management's perspective. This includes (1) auditing what is the extent human resources management practices are incorporated into an organization's strategic planning, and (2) the extent one human resources practice is linked with other human resources functional areas.

Managerial. The managerial level of analysis should focus on the human resource department's impact upon line managers. The extent line managers correctly implement human resources department practices should be analysed.

Operational. The operational level of analysis focuses on detailed human resource department functional area practices.[4]

A human resource department audit should satisfy the broadly defined, long-term, and general interests of top executives. It should also satisfy the narrower, shorter-term and specific interests of line managers and human resource practitioners. Accordingly, such an audit must appeal to several entities. A human resource audit should be designed:

1. To provide the framework for *top line executives* to analyse their organization's human resources function
2. To provide an analytical basis for *top human resources executives* to identify the strengths and weaknesses of their human resources departments
3. To provide data for *top human resources executives* to demonstrate to other parts of the organization what the benefits of effective human resources management practises and procedures are
4. To provide a checklist for *human resource specialists* to accomplish human resources practices and procedures effectively
5. To pinpoint where organizational resistance may be encountered

when human resource practices are improved

6. To compare human resources functional area practices against commonly accepted performance standards

This chapter suggests a model that can be used for auditing human resource management functional areas. One example for auditing a functional area is provided.

A HUMAN RESOURCE MANAGEMENT AUDITING MODEL

The audit model follows a series of steps:

Step 1 is to analyze if the human resources functions are managed effectively. An organization may routinely audit its human resource practices. More often, it waits until a warning signal or trigger for action indicates that something is wrong. A trigger for action is a signal that indicates an audit is necessary.

Step 2 in the human resource management auditing process is to determine how badly changes are needed. This is done by comparing current human resource management practices with predetermined standards of acceptable performance. This means that human resource management performance standards must be developed and disseminated.[5] By comparing performance standards against current practices, information can be obtained on which human resource practices, if any, have to be changed.

Step 3 in the auditing process details action plans that improve human resource management effectiveness.

A Sample Human Resource Management Department Audit for the Functional Area of Performance Appraisal

One human resource management functional area is analysed below to demonstrate how an audit is conducted and action plans are developed. This example shows each auditing step.

Step 1: Triggers for Action. Good employee performance is a characteristic of organizational success. Performance appraisal systems measure employee performance. An organization should create a performance appraisal system that describes who the effective performers are.

If one or more of the warning signals in the following list are observed, they should be construed as signals to audit the performance appraisal system.

—Profits are beginning to decline

—Productivity levels are beginning to decline

—Effective employees are beginning to quit in increasing numbers

—Charges have been filed that the organization's performance appraisal data are subjective

—Performance levels of employees do not seem to improve over time

Step 2: Determining How Badly Changes Are Needed in the Performance Appraisal System. A crucial part of Step 2 is knowing what are acceptable standards of performance. What actually occurs in the organization can then be compared to performance standards.

Performance standards should be reviewed on the basis of how true they are and how desirable it is to meet them. If, for example, a performance standard is being met and it is considered to be very desirable to meet it, the organization would need to take no remedial action. If, on the other hand, a standard is not being met and it is undesirable to meet it, again, no action needs to be taken to improve that particular human resource activity. A third condition would exist if a performance standard was not being met, but it was considered very desirable to meet it. Action would have to be taken to improve that functional activity. A final contingency is that if the standard was being met, but it was not considered desirable to meet it, then no action would need to be taken to change that human resource practice other than, perhaps, eliminating it altogether.

Examples of performance standards for a performance appraisal system are:

Strategic Level Performance Standards:
1. Our performance appraisal system is closely tied to the requirements of specific jobs
2. Performance appraisal data are used in validating selection tests and practices

Managerial Level Performance Standards:
3. Employees are able to appraise the performance of their supervisors
4. Line managers are trained in giving feedback
5. Line managers are involved in changes made in the performance appraisal system

Operational Level Performance Standards:
6. Performance standards exist for all jobs so employees can judge how they are doing
7. The appraisal system we use is helpful in clearly communicating to employees how they will be evaluated
8. Past performance records are helpful in making effective decisions regarding pay, promotion, and transfers
9. Performance appraisal is helpful in guiding the career development progress of employees
10. Employees have a right to appeal performance appraisal decisions
11. Procedures exist for employees to self-appraise their own performance
12. Performance appraisal results are quickly, regularly, and accurately provided to employees
13. Employees always know what their promotion opportunities are
14. Employees are aided in correcting poor performance
15. Our organization has a clearly stated absenteeism policy

Step 3: Writing Action Plans. The third step in a performance appraisal audit is to develop specific action plans. The action plans are best written as prescriptive statements that can improve a performance appraisal system.

Strategic Level Action Plans:
1. Top management should ensure that line managers and the human resource department directly link performance expectations written in job descriptions to the performance appraisal system
2. Top management should ensure organizational policies and procedures are designed to minimize employee absenteeism.
3. Top management should state that performance appraisals are crucial to employee career development. Top management should make line managers and the human resource department

aware that upward mobility along lines of progression should be a direct long-term result of the performance appraisal process.
4. Top management should ensure that the organization's performance appraisal system offers every employee a formal performance appraisal, at the minimum, annually.

Managerial Level Action Plans:
5. Line managers should be given training in the organization's performance appraisal system
6. Line managers should use performance appraisals as tools to communicate performance expectations to employees; attainment of previously set goals should be discussed; performance goals and targets for the next reporting period should be set
7. Line managers should ensure performance appraisals are provided often; informal appraisals should be provided as often as possible and after completion of any significant task
8. Line managers should ensure employees are aware that absenteeism causes adverse impacts upon organizational productivity.
9. Line managers should advise employees who have personal problems that adversely affect job-related work performance (such as substance abuse, excessive stress-related problems, alcoholism, etc.) to seek counselling at an employee assistance referral program.

Operational Level Action Plans:
10. The human resource department should directly link performance expectations written in job descriptions to the performance appraisal system
11. The human resource department should train line managers to appraise performance objectively
12. The human resource department should ensure performance appraisals are used as a key criterion in validating selection tests
13. The human resource department should ensure effective job analyses are conducted that lead to accurate job descriptions; job descriptions should list duties, tasks, responsibilities, and performance expectations for the job
14. The human resource department should train line managers to communicate performance expectations and set future performance goals and targets to employees
15. Performance appraisals should be used as a key decision-making input for personnel actions such as pay, promotion, training, and transfer.
16. The performance appraisal system should permit employees to appeal their appraisals if they are perceived to be unfair, inequitable, inaccurate, or overly subjective.
17. Employees should self-assess their performance and discuss their results with their supervisors during a performance appraisal interview. The human resource department should design a form that provides an opportunity for employees to self-assess their performance.

18. The human resource department should permit employees to evaluate supervisors' performance. Research shows subordinate-superior appraisals are effective in improving communications and productivity in some organizational settings.
19. The human resource department should train line managers to provide appraisals of employee performance often. This training should emphasize that appraisals should be offered often and after completion of any significant task. It should emphasize the importance of receiving periodic feedback about job-related performance.
20. The human resource department should advise managers and employees about the organization's absenteeism policy. The policy should emphasize that absenteeism adversely impacts human resource planning, organizational profitability, work scheduling, and productivity.
21. The human resource department should refer employees experiencing personal problems that adversely affect their job-related work performance (such as substance abuse, excessive stress-related problems, alcoholism, etc.) to counselling.
22. The human resource department should ensure each employee has a current job description that clearly defines duties, tasks, responsibilities, and accountabilities of his or her job.
23. The human resource department should develop a performance appraisal system that is linked to employee career development.
24. If the human resource department wants to change the performance appraisal system, input from line managers should be sought and incorporated in the redesign.

SUMMARY

Organizations should seek information on how well their resources are contributing to the organization's mission, goals, and objectives. One useful way to obtain this data is to conduct an audit. A human resource audit examines human resource management functional areas from strategic, managerial, and operational perspectives. The human resource functions range from planning how to use people, maintaining them in the organization, utilizing them effectively, and developing them into better performing individuals. If these functions are being managed ineffectively, competitiveness, profitability, organizational growth, and even the ultimate survival of the organization are at risk.

A human resource audit consists of three stages:

1. Taking stock of where the organization's human resource management practices are now
2. Determining what the human resource management practises should be in the future and how much internal resistance may be encountered if changes are made to these practices
3. Developing prescriptive action plans to take the organization from state 1 to state 2.

By following this model, an organization can achieve seven outcomes. They are:

1. Top line executives can assess the effectiveness of the human resource management functions. This assessment provides data on whether and to what extent the functions are being performed.
2. Top human resource management executives can assess the strengths and weaknesses of their own departments.
3. Top human resource management executives can demonstrate the benefit effective human resource management has to the rest of the organization.
4. Human resource management specialists can develop a checklist of what human resource management practices they should be performing.
5. An organization can improve its human resource utilization.
6. Relevant and timely feedback can be given to top management, human resource managers, line managers, and human resource specialists.
7. An indication of internal resistance to improving the organization's human resource management practices can be determined.

Achieving these seven outcomes can result in improved organizational productivity, more effective compliance with legal constraints, and a better quality of work life for employees.

Endnotes

1. Kuraitis, V. P., "The Personnel Audit," *Personnel Administrator* (November 1981): 30. See also Mathis, R. L. and G. Cameron, "Auditing Personnel Practices in Smaller-Sized Organizations: A Realistic Approach," *Personnel Administrator* (April 1981): 45–49.
2. These functional areas are discussed at length in Schuler, R. S. and S. A. Youngblood, *Effective Personnel Management*, 2nd ed. (St. Paul: West Publishing, 1986). See also Biles, G. E. and Schuler, R. S., *Auditing Human Resource Management Effectiveness* (Alexandria, VA: American Society for Personnel Management, 1986) for discussions concerning the auditing of each of these functional human resource management areas.
3. Devanna, M. A., C. Fombrun and N. Tichy, "Human Resources Management: A Strategic Perspective," in *Human Resources Management: Issues for the 1980s*, Devanna, M. A., C. Fombrun, N. Tichy, L. Warren and E. K. Warren, eds. (New York: Columbia Business School Center for Research in Career Development, 1983), 9–12. See also Devanna, M. A., D. Fombrun and N. Tichy, "Human Resources Management: A Strategic Perspective," *Organizational Dynamics* (Winter 1981): 51–67; Devanna, M. A., D. Fombrun and N. Tichy, "Increasing HR Departments' Effectiveness," *Management Review* (June 1984): 32; and Fombrun, D., N. Tichy and M. A. Devanna, eds. *Strategic Human Resource Management* (New York: John Wiley & Sons, 1984).
4. Biles and Schuler, *Management Effectiveness*, Chapter 1.
5. Biles and Schuler, *Management Effectiveness*. This book compiles survey results from various human resource departments, inputs from the American Society for Personnel Administration functional area committees and surveys of recent human resource management literature into audit statements that serve as human resource department performance standards.